StarPU 1.3 Reference Manual

A catalogue record for this book is available from the Hong Kong Public Libraries.

Published in Hong Kong by Samurai Media Limited.

Email: info@samuraimedia.org

ISBN 978-988-8407-14-9

Background Cover Image by https://www.flickr.com/people/webtreatsetc/

This manual documents the usage of StarPU version 1.3.0. Its contents was last updated on 01 June 2017.

Contents

Chapter 1

Introduction

1.1 Motivation

The use of specialized hardware such as accelerators or coprocessors offers an interesting approach to overcome the physical limits encountered by processor architects. As a result, many machines are now equipped with one or several accelerators (e.g. a GPU), in addition to the usual processor(s). While a lot of efforts have been devoted to offload computation onto such accelerators, very little attention as been paid to portability concerns on the one hand, and to the possibility of having heterogeneous accelerators and processors to interact on the other hand.

StarPU is a runtime system that offers support for heterogeneous multicore architectures, it not only offers a unified view of the computational resources (i.e. CPUs and accelerators at the same time), but it also takes care of efficiently mapping and executing tasks onto an heterogeneous machine while transparently handling low-level issues such as data transfers in a portable fashion.

1.2 StarPU in a Nutshell

StarPU is a software tool aiming to allow programmers to exploit the computing power of the available CPUs and GPUs, while relieving them from the need to specially adapt their programs to the target machine and processing units.

At the core of StarPU is its run-time support library, which is responsible for scheduling application-provided tasks on heterogeneous CPU/GPU machines. In addition, StarPU comes with programming language support, in the form of extensions to languages of the C family (C Extensions), as well as an OpenCL front-end (SOCL OpenCL Extensions).

StarPU's run-time and programming language extensions support a task-based programming model. Applications submit computational tasks, with CPU and/or GPU implementations, and StarPU schedules these tasks and associated data transfers on available CPUs and GPUs. The data that a task manipulates are automatically transferred among accelerators and the main memory, so that programmers are freed from the scheduling issues and technical details associated with these transfers.

StarPU takes particular care of scheduling tasks efficiently, using well-known algorithms from the literature (Task Scheduling Policies). In addition, it allows scheduling experts, such as compiler or computational library developers, to implement custom scheduling policies in a portable fashion (Defining A New Scheduling Policy).

The remainder of this section describes the main concepts used in StarPU.

1.2.1 Codelet and Tasks

One of the StarPU primary data structures is the **codelet**. A codelet describes a computational kernel that can possibly be implemented on multiple architectures such as a CPU, a CUDA device or an OpenCL device.

Another important data structure is the **task**. Executing a StarPU task consists in applying a codelet on a data set, on one of the architectures on which the codelet is implemented. A task thus describes the codelet that it uses, but also which data are accessed, and how they are accessed during the computation (read and/or write). StarPU tasks are asynchronous: submitting a task to StarPU is a non-blocking operation. The task structure can also specify a **callback** function that is called once StarPU has properly executed the task. It also contains optional fields that the application may use to give hints to the scheduler (such as priority levels).

By default, task dependencies are inferred from data dependency (sequential coherency) by StarPU. The application can however disable sequential coherency for some data, and dependencies can be specifically expressed. A task may be identified by a unique 64-bit number chosen by the application which we refer as a **tag**. Task dependencies can be enforced either by the means of callback functions, by submitting other tasks, or by expressing dependencies between tags (which can thus correspond to tasks that have not yet been submitted).

1.2.2　StarPU Data Management Library

Because StarPU schedules tasks at runtime, data transfers have to be done automatically and "just-in-time" between processing units, relieving application programmers from explicit data transfers. Moreover, to avoid unnecessary transfers, StarPU keeps data where it was last needed, even if was modified there, and it allows multiple copies of the same data to reside at the same time on several processing units as long as it is not modified.

1.3　Application Taskification

TODO

1.4　Glossary

A **codelet** records pointers to various implementations of the same theoretical function.

A **memory node** can be either the main RAM, GPU-embedded memory or a disk memory.

A **bus** is a link between memory nodes.

A **data handle** keeps track of replicates of the same data (**registered** by the application) over various memory nodes. The data management library manages to keep them coherent.

The **home** memory node of a data handle is the memory node from which the data was registered (usually the main memory node).

A **task** represents a scheduled execution of a codelet on some data handles.

A **tag** is a rendez-vous point. Tasks typically have their own tag, and can depend on other tags. The value is chosen by the application.

A **worker** execute tasks. There is typically one per CPU computation core and one per accelerator (for which a whole CPU core is dedicated).

A **driver** drives a given kind of workers. There are currently CPU, CUDA, and OpenCL drivers. They usually start several workers to actually drive them.

A **performance model** is a (dynamic or static) model of the performance of a given codelet. Codelets can have execution time performance model as well as energy consumption performance models.

A data **interface** describes the layout of the data: for a vector, a pointer for the start, the number of elements and the size of elements ; for a matrix, a pointer for the start, the number of elements per row, the offset between rows, and the size of each element ; etc. To access their data, codelet functions are given interfaces for the local memory node replicates of the data handles of the scheduled task.

Partitioning data means dividing the data of a given data handle (called **father**) into a series of **children** data handles which designate various portions of the former.

A **filter** is the function which computes children data handles from a father data handle, and thus describes how the partitioning should be done (horizontal, vertical, etc.)

Acquiring a data handle can be done from the main application, to safely access the data of a data handle from its home node, without having to unregister it.

1.5 Research Papers

Research papers about StarPU can be found at http://starpu.gforge.inria.fr/publications/.

A good overview is available in the research report at http://hal.archives-ouvertes.fr/inria-00467677.

1.6 StarPU Applications

You can first have a look at the chapters Basic Examples and Advanced Examples. A tutorial is also installed in the directory share/doc/starpu/tutorial/.

Many examples are also available in the StarPU sources in the directory examples/. Simple examples include:

incrementer/ Trivial incrementation test.

basic_examples/ Simple documented Hello world and vector/scalar product (as shown in Basic Examples), matrix product examples (as shown in Performance Model Example), an example using the blocked matrix data interface, an example using the variable data interface, and an example using different formats on CPUs and GPUs.

matvecmult/ OpenCL example from NVidia, adapted to StarPU.

axpy/ AXPY CUBLAS operation adapted to StarPU.

native_fortran/ Example of using StarPU's native Fortran support.

fortran90/ Example of Fortran 90 bindings, using C marshalling wrappers.

fortran/ Example of Fortran 77 bindings, using C marshalling wrappers.

More advanced examples include:

filters/ Examples using filters, as shown in Partitioning Data.

lu/ LU matrix factorization, see for instance xlu_implicit.c

cholesky/ Cholesky matrix factorization, see for instance cholesky_implicit.c.

1.7 Further Reading

The documentation chapters include

- Part 1: StarPU Basics
    - Building and Installing StarPU
    - Basic Examples
- Part 2: StarPU Quick Programming Guide
    - Advanced Examples
    - Check List When Performance Are Not There
- Part 3: StarPU Inside

- – Tasks In StarPU
- – Data Management
- – Scheduling
- – Scheduling Contexts
- – Scheduling Context Hypervisor
- – Modularized Schedulers
- – Debugging Tools
- – Online Performance Tools
- – Offline Performance Tools
- – Frequently Asked Questions

- Part 4: StarPU Extensions

  - – Out Of Core
  - – MPI Support
  - – FFT Support
  - – MIC Xeon Phi / SCC Support
  - – C Extensions
  - – The StarPU Native Fortran Support
  - – SOCL OpenCL Extensions
  - – SimGrid Support
  - – The StarPU OpenMP Runtime Support (SORS)
  - – Clustering A Machine

- Part 5: StarPU Reference API

  - – Execution Configuration Through Environment Variables
  - – Compilation Configuration
  - – Module Documentation
  - – File Documentation
  - – Deprecated List

- Part: Appendix

  - – Full source code for the 'Scaling a Vector' example
  - – The GNU Free Documentation License

Make sure to have had a look at those too!

Part I

StarPU Basics

Chapter 2

Building and Installing StarPU

2.1 Installing a Binary Package

One of the StarPU developers being a Debian Developer, the packages are well integrated and very uptodate. To see which packages are available, simply type:

```
$ apt-cache search starpu
```

To install what you need, type for example:

```
$ sudo apt-get install libstarpu-1.3 libstarpu-dev
```

2.2 Installing from Source

StarPU can be built and installed by the standard means of the GNU autotools. The following chapter is intended to briefly remind how these tools can be used to install StarPU.

2.2.1 Optional Dependencies

The hwloc (http://www.open-mpi.org/software/hwloc) topology discovery library is not mandatory to use StarPU but strongly recommended. It allows for topology aware scheduling, which improves performance. libhwloc is available in major free operating system distributions, and for most operating systems.

If libhwloc is not available on your system, the option --without-hwloc should be explicitly given when calling the configure script. If libhwloc is installed in a standard location, no option is required, it will be detected automatically, otherwise --with-hwloc=<directory> should be used to specify its location.

2.2.2 Getting Sources

StarPU's sources can be obtained from the download page of the StarPU website (http://starpu.gforge.-inria.fr/files/).

All releases and the development tree of StarPU are freely available on INRIA's gforge under the LGPL license. Some releases are available under the BSD license.

The latest release can be downloaded from the INRIA's gforge (http://gforge.inria.fr/frs/?group-_id=1570) or directly from the StarPU download page (http://starpu.gforge.inria.fr/files/).

The latest nightly snapshot can be downloaded from the StarPU gforge website (http://starpu.gforge.-inria.fr/testing/).

```
$ wget http://starpu.gforge.inria.fr/testing/starpu-nightly-latest.tar.gz
```

And finally, current development version is also accessible via svn. It should be used only if you need the very latest changes (i.e. less than a day!). Note that the client side of the software Subversion can be obtained from http-://subversion.tigris.org. If you are running on Windows, you will probably prefer to use TortoiseSVN (http://tortoisesvn.tigris.org/).

```
$ svn checkout svn://scm.gforge.inria.fr/svn/starpu/trunk StarPU
```

2.2.3 Configuring StarPU

Running `autogen.sh` is not necessary when using the tarball releases of StarPU. If you are using the source code from the svn repository, you first need to generate the configure scripts and the Makefiles. This requires the availability of `autoconf` and `automake` >= 2.60.

```
$ ./autogen.sh
```

You then need to configure StarPU. Details about options that are useful to give to `./configure` are given in Compilation Configuration.

```
$ ./configure
```

If `configure` does not detect some software or produces errors, please make sure to post the contents of the file `config.log` when reporting the issue.

By default, the files produced during the compilation are placed in the source directory. As the compilation generates a lot of files, it is advised to put them all in a separate directory. It is then easier to cleanup, and this allows to compile several configurations out of the same source tree. For that, simply enter the directory where you want the compilation to produce its files, and invoke the `configure` script located in the StarPU source directory.

```
$ mkdir build
$ cd build
$ ../configure
```

By default, StarPU will be installed in `/usr/local/bin`, `/usr/local/lib`, etc. You can specify an installation prefix other than `/usr/local` using the option `-prefix`, for instance:

```
$ ../configure --prefix=$HOME/starpu
```

2.2.4 Building StarPU

```
$ make
```

Once everything is built, you may want to test the result. An extensive set of regression tests is provided with StarPU. Running the tests is done by calling `make check`. These tests are run every night and the result from the main profile is publicly available (http://starpu.gforge.inria.fr/testing/).

```
$ make check
```

2.2.5 Installing StarPU

In order to install StarPU at the location that was specified during configuration:

```
$ make install
```

Libtool interface versioning information are included in libraries names (`libstarpu-1.3.so`, `libstarpumpi-1.-3.so` and `libstarpufft-1.3.so`).

2.3   Setting up Your Own Code

2.3.1   Setting Flags for Compiling, Linking and Running Applications

StarPU provides a `pkg-config` executable to obtain relevant compiler and linker flags. As compiling and linking an application against StarPU may require to use specific flags or libraries (for instance `CUDA` or `libspe2`).

If StarPU was not installed at some standard location, the path of StarPU's library must be specified in the environment variable `PKG_CONFIG_PATH` so that `pkg-config` can find it. For example if StarPU was installed in `$STARPU_PATH`:

```
$ PKG_CONFIG_PATH=$PKG_CONFIG_PATH:$STARPU_PATH/lib/pkgconfig
```

The flags required to compile or link against StarPU are then accessible with the following commands:

```
$ pkg-config --cflags starpu-1.3   # options for the compiler
$ pkg-config --libs starpu-1.3     # options for the linker
```

Note that it is still possible to use the API provided in the version 1.0 of StarPU by calling `pkg-config` with the `starpu-1.0` package. Similar packages are provided for `starpumpi-1.0` and `starpufft-1.0`. It is also possible to use the API provided in the version 0.9 of StarPU by calling `pkg-config` with the `libstarpu` package. Similar packages are provided for `libstarpumpi` and `libstarpufft`.

Make sure that `pkg-config -libs starpu-1.3` actually produces some output before going further: `PKG_CONFIG_PATH` has to point to the place where `starpu-1.3.pc` was installed during `make install`.

Also pass the option `-static` if the application is to be linked statically.

It is also necessary to set the environment variable `LD_LIBRARY_PATH` to locate dynamic libraries at runtime.

```
$ LD_LIBRARY_PATH=$STARPU_PATH/lib:$LD_LIBRARY_PATH
```

When using a Makefile, the following lines can be added to set the options for the compiler and the linker:

```
CFLAGS          +=      $$(pkg-config --cflags starpu-1.3)
LDFLAGS         +=      $$(pkg-config --libs starpu-1.3)
```

2.3.2   Running a Basic StarPU Application

Basic examples using StarPU are built in the directory `examples/basic_examples/` (and installed in `$STARPU_PATH/lib/starpu/examples/`). You can for example run the example `vector_scal`.

```
$ ./examples/basic_examples/vector_scal
BEFORE: First element was 1.000000
AFTER: First element is 3.140000
```

When StarPU is used for the first time, the directory `$STARPU_HOME/.starpu/` is created, performance models will be stored in that directory (STARPU_HOME).

Please note that buses are benchmarked when StarPU is launched for the first time. This may take a few minutes, or less if `libhwloc` is installed. This step is done only once per user and per machine.

2.3.3   Running a Basic StarPU Application on Microsoft Visual C

Batch files are provided to run StarPU applications under Microsoft Visual C. They are installed in `$STARPU_PATH/bin/msvc`.

To execute a StarPU application, you first need to set the environment variable STARPU_PATH.

```
c:\....> cd c:\cygwin\home\ci\starpu\
c:\....> set STARPU_PATH=c:\cygwin\home\ci\starpu\
c:\....> cd bin\msvc
c:\....> starpu_open.bat starpu_simple.c
```

The batch script will run Microsoft Visual C with a basic project file to run the given application.

The batch script `starpu_clean.bat` can be used to delete all compilation generated files.

The batch script `starpu_exec.bat` can be used to compile and execute a StarPU application from the command prompt.

```
c:\....> cd c:\cygwin\home\ci\starpu\
c:\....> set STARPU_PATH=c:\cygwin\home\ci\starpu\
c:\....> cd bin\msvc
c:\....> starpu_exec.bat ..\..\..\..\examples\basic_examples\hello_world.c

MSVC StarPU Execution
...
/out:hello_world.exe
...
Hello world (params = {1, 2.00000})
Callback function got argument 0000042
c:\....>
```

2.3.4 Kernel Threads Started by StarPU

StarPU automatically binds one thread per CPU core. It does not use SMT/hyperthreading because kernels are usually already optimized for using a full core, and using hyperthreading would make kernel calibration rather random.

Since driving GPUs is a CPU-consuming task, StarPU dedicates one core per GPU.

While StarPU tasks are executing, the application is not supposed to do computations in the threads it starts itself, tasks should be used instead.

TODO: add a StarPU function to bind an application thread (e.g. the main thread) to a dedicated core (and thus disable the corresponding StarPU CPU worker).

2.3.5 Enabling OpenCL

When both CUDA and OpenCL drivers are enabled, StarPU will launch an OpenCL worker for NVIDIA GPUs only if CUDA is not already running on them. This design choice was necessary as OpenCL and CUDA can not run at the same time on the same NVIDIA GPU, as there is currently no interoperability between them.

To enable OpenCL, you need either to disable CUDA when configuring StarPU:

```
$ ./configure --disable-cuda
```

or when running applications:

```
$ STARPU_NCUDA=0 ./application
```

OpenCL will automatically be started on any device not yet used by CUDA. So on a machine running 4 GPUS, it is therefore possible to enable CUDA on 2 devices, and OpenCL on the 2 other devices by doing so:

```
$ STARPU_NCUDA=2 ./application
```

2.4 Benchmarking StarPU

Some interesting benchmarks are installed among examples in `$STARPU_PATH/lib/starpu/examples/`. Make sure to try various schedulers, for instance `STARPU_SCHED=dmda`.

2.4.1 Task Size Overhead

This benchmark gives a glimpse into how long a task should be (in µs) for StarPU overhead to be low enough to keep efficiency. Running `tasks_size_overhead.sh` generates a plot of the speedup of tasks of various sizes, depending on the number of CPUs being used.

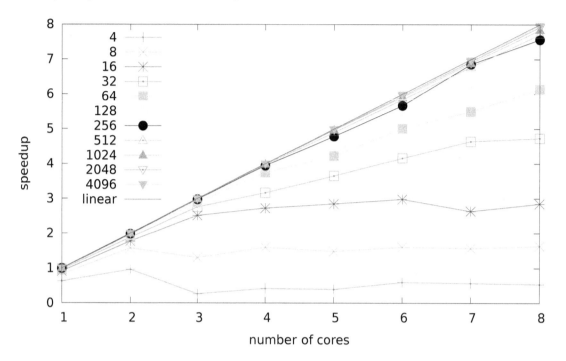

2.4.2 Data Transfer Latency

`local_pingpong` performs a ping-pong between the first two CUDA nodes, and prints the measured latency.

2.4.3 Matrix-Matrix Multiplication

`sgemm` and `dgemm` perform a blocked matrix-matrix multiplication using BLAS and cuBLAS. They output the obtained GFlops.

2.4.4 Cholesky Factorization

`cholesky_*` perform a Cholesky factorization (single precision). They use different dependency primitives.

2.4.5 LU Factorization

`lu_*` perform an LU factorization. They use different dependency primitives.

2.4.6 Simulated benchmarks

It can also be convenient to try simulated benchmarks, if you want to give a try at CPU-GPU scheduling without actually having a GPU at hand. This can be done by using the simgrid version of StarPU: first install the simgrid simulator from `http://simgrid.gforge.inria.fr/` (we tested with simgrid 3.11, 3.12 and 3.13, other versions may have compatibility issues), then configure StarPU with --enable-simgrid and rebuild and install it, and then you can simulate the performance for a few virtualized systems shipped along StarPU: attila, mirage, idgraf, and sirocco.

For instance:

```
$ export STARPU_PERF_MODEL_DIR=$STARPU_PATH/share/starpu/perfmodels/sampling
$ export STARPU_HOSTNAME=attila
$ $STARPU_PATH/lib/starpu/examples/cholesky_implicit -size $((960*20)) -nblocks 20
```

Will show the performance of the cholesky factorization with the attila system. It will be interesting to try with different matrix sizes and schedulers.

Performance models are available for cholesky_*, lu_*, *gemm, with block sizes 320, 640, or 960 (plus 1440 for sirocco), and for stencil with block size 128x128x128, 192x192x192, and 256x256x256.

Chapter 3

Basic Examples

3.1 Hello World Using The C Extension

This section shows how to implement a simple program that submits a task to StarPU using the StarPU C extension (C Extensions). The complete example, and additional examples, is available in the directory `gcc-plugin/examples` of the StarPU distribution. A similar example showing how to directly use the Star-PU's API is shown in Hello World Using StarPU's API.

GCC from version 4.5 permit to use the StarPU GCC plug-in (C Extensions). This makes writing a task both simpler and less error-prone. In a nutshell, all it takes is to declare a task, declare and define its implementations (for CPU, OpenCL, and/or CUDA), and invoke the task like a regular C function. The example below defines `my_task` which has a single implementation for CPU:

```
#include <stdio.h>

/* Task declaration.  */
static void my_task (int x) __attribute__ ((task));

/* Definition of the CPU implementation of 'my_task'.  */
static void my_task (int x)
{
  printf ("Hello, world!  With x = %d\n", x);
}

int main ()
{
  /* Initialize StarPU. */
#pragma starpu initialize

  /* Do an asynchronous call to 'my_task'. */
  my_task (42);

  /* Wait for the call to complete.  */
#pragma starpu wait

  /* Terminate. */
#pragma starpu shutdown

  return 0;
}
```

The code can then be compiled and linked with GCC and the flag `-fplugin`:

```
$ gcc `pkg-config starpu-1.3 --cflags` hello-starpu.c \
    -fplugin=`pkg-config starpu-1.3 --variable=gccplugin` \
    `pkg-config starpu-1.3 --libs`
```

The code can also be compiled without the StarPU C extension and will behave as a normal sequential code.

```
$ gcc hello-starpu.c
hello-starpu.c:33:1: warning: 'task' attribute directive ignored [-Wattributes]
$ ./a.out
Hello, world! With x = 42
```

As can be seen above, the C extensions allows programmers to use StarPU tasks by essentially annotating "regular" C code.

3.2   Hello World Using StarPU's API

This section shows how to achieve the same result as in the previous section using StarPU's standard C API.

3.2.1   Required Headers

The header starpu.h should be included in any code using StarPU.

```
#include <starpu.h>
```

3.2.2   Defining A Codelet

A codelet is a structure that represents a computational kernel. Such a codelet may contain an implementation of the same kernel on different architectures (e.g. CUDA, x86, ...). For compatibility, make sure that the whole structure is properly initialized to zero, either by using the function starpu_codelet_init(), or by letting the compiler implicitly do it as examplified below.

The field starpu_codelet::nbuffers specifies the number of data buffers that are manipulated by the codelet: here the codelet does not access or modify any data that is controlled by our data management library.

We create a codelet which may only be executed on CPUs. When a CPU core will execute a codelet, it will call the function cpu_func, which *must* have the following prototype:

```
void (*cpu_func)(void *buffers[], void *cl_arg);
```

In this example, we can ignore the first argument of this function which gives a description of the input and output buffers (e.g. the size and the location of the matrices) since there is none. We also ignore the second argument which is a pointer to optional arguments for the codelet.

```
void cpu_func(void *buffers[], void *cl_arg)
{
    printf("Hello world\n");
}

struct starpu_codelet cl =
{
    .cpu_funcs = { cpu_func },
    .nbuffers = 0
};
```

3.2.3   Submitting A Task

Before submitting any tasks to StarPU, starpu_init() must be called. The NULL argument specifies that we use the default configuration. Tasks can then be submitted until the termination of StarPU – done by a call to starpu_-shutdown().

In the example below, a task structure is allocated by a call to starpu_task_create(). This function allocates and fills the task structure with its default settings, it does not submit the task to StarPU.

The field starpu_task::cl is a pointer to the codelet which the task will execute: in other words, the codelet structure describes which computational kernel should be offloaded on the different architectures, and the task structure is a wrapper containing a codelet and the piece of data on which the codelet should operate.

If the field starpu_task::synchronous is non-zero, task submission will be synchronous: the function starpu_task-_submit() will not return until the task has been executed. Note that the function starpu_shutdown() does not guarantee that asynchronous tasks have been executed before it returns, starpu_task_wait_for_all() can be used to that effect, or data can be unregistered (starpu_data_unregister()), which will implicitly wait for all the tasks scheduled to work on it, unless explicitly disabled thanks to starpu_data_set_default_sequential_consistency_flag() or starpu_data_set_sequential_consistency_flag().

```
int main(int argc, char **argv)
{
    /* initialize StarPU */
    starpu_init(NULL);

    struct starpu_task *task = starpu_task_create(
      );

    task->cl = &cl; /* Pointer to the codelet defined above */

    /* starpu_task_submit will be a blocking call. If unset,
    starpu_task_wait() needs to be called after submitting the task. */
    task->synchronous = 1;

    /* submit the task to StarPU */
    starpu_task_submit(task);

    /* terminate StarPU */
    starpu_shutdown();

    return 0;
}
```

3.2.4 Execution Of Hello World

```
$ make hello_world
cc $(pkg-config --cflags starpu-1.3) hello_world.c -o hello_world $(pkg-config --libs starpu-1.3)
$ ./hello_world
Hello world
```

3.2.5 Passing Arguments To The Codelet

The optional field starpu_task::cl_arg field is a pointer to a buffer (of size starpu_task::cl_arg_size) with some parameters for the kernel described by the codelet. For instance, if a codelet implements a computational kernel that multiplies its input vector by a constant, the constant could be specified by the means of this buffer, instead of registering it as a StarPU data. It must however be noted that StarPU avoids making copy whenever possible and rather passes the pointer as such, so the buffer which is pointed at must be kept allocated until the task terminates, and if several tasks are submitted with various parameters, each of them must be given a pointer to their own buffer.

```
struct params
{
    int i;
    float f;
};
void cpu_func(void *buffers[], void *cl_arg)
{
    struct params *params = cl_arg;

    printf("Hello world (params = {%i, %f} )\n", params->i, params->f);
}
```

As said before, the field starpu_codelet::nbuffers specifies the number of data buffers that are manipulated by the codelet. It does not count the argument — the parameter `cl_arg` of the function `cpu_func` — since it is not managed by our data management library, but just contains trivial parameters.

Be aware that this may be a pointer to a *copy* of the actual buffer, and not the pointer given by the programmer: if the codelet modifies this buffer, there is no guarantee that the initial buffer will be modified as well: this for instance implies that the buffer cannot be used as a synchronization medium. If synchronization is needed, data has to be registered to StarPU, see Vector Scaling Using StarPU's API.

```
int main(int argc, char **argv)
{
    /* initialize StarPU */
    starpu_init(NULL);
```

```
struct starpu_task *task = starpu_task_create(
    );

task->cl = &cl; /* Pointer to the codelet defined above */

struct params params = { 1, 2.0f };
task->cl_arg = &params;
task->cl_arg_size = sizeof(params);

/* starpu_task_submit will be a blocking call */
task->synchronous = 1;

/* submit the task to StarPU */
starpu_task_submit(task);

/* terminate StarPU */
starpu_shutdown();

    return 0;
}
```

```
$ make hello_world
cc $(pkg-config --cflags starpu-1.3) hello_world.c -o hello_world $(pkg-config --libs starpu-1.3)
$ ./hello_world
Hello world (params = {1, 2.000000} )
```

3.2.6 Defining A Callback

Once a task has been executed, an optional callback function starpu_task::callback_func is called when defined. While the computational kernel could be offloaded on various architectures, the callback function is always executed on a CPU. The pointer starpu_task::callback_arg is passed as an argument of the callback function. The prototype of a callback function must be:

```
void (*callback_function)(void *);
```

```
void callback_func(void *callback_arg)
{
    printf("Callback function (arg %x)\n", callback_arg);
}

int main(int argc, char **argv)
{
    /* initialize StarPU */
    starpu_init(NULL);

    struct starpu_task *task = starpu_task_create(
        );

    task->cl = &cl; /* Pointer to the codelet defined above */

    task->callback_func = callback_func;
    task->callback_arg = 0x42;

    /* starpu_task_submit will be a blocking call */
    task->synchronous = 1;

    /* submit the task to StarPU */
    starpu_task_submit(task);

    /* terminate StarPU */
    starpu_shutdown();

        return 0;
}
```

```
$ make hello_world
cc $(pkg-config --cflags starpu-1.3) hello_world.c -o hello_world $(pkg-config --libs starpu-1.3)
$ ./hello_world
Hello world
Callback function (arg 42)
```

3.2.7 Where To Execute A Codelet

```
struct starpu_codelet cl =
```

```
{
    .where = STARPU_CPU,
    .cpu_funcs = { cpu_func },
    .cpu_funcs_name = { "cpu_func" },
    .nbuffers = 0
};
```

We create a codelet which may only be executed on the CPUs. The optional field starpu_codelet::where is a bitmask that defines where the codelet may be executed. Here, the value STARPU_CPU means that only CPUs can execute this codelet. When the optional field starpu_codelet::where is unset, its value is automatically set based on the availability of the different fields XXX_funcs.

TODO: explain starpu_codelet::cpu_funcs_name

3.3 Vector Scaling Using the C Extension

The previous example has shown how to submit tasks. In this section, we show how StarPU tasks can manipulate data.

We will first show how to use the C language extensions provided by the GCC plug-in (C Extensions). The complete example, and additional examples, is available in the directory gcc-plugin/examples of the StarPU distribution. These extensions map directly to StarPU's main concepts: tasks, task implementations for CPU, OpenCL, or CUDA, and registered data buffers. The standard C version that uses StarPU's standard C programming interface is given in Vector Scaling Using StarPU's API.

First of all, the vector-scaling task and its simple CPU implementation has to be defined:

```
/* Declare the 'vector_scal' task. */
static void vector_scal (unsigned size, float vector[size],
                         float factor)
  __attribute__ ((task));

/* Define the standard CPU implementation. */
static void
vector_scal (unsigned size, float vector[size], float factor)
{
  unsigned i;
  for (i = 0; i < size; i++)
    vector[i] *= factor;
}
```

Next, the body of the program, which uses the task defined above, can be implemented:

```
int main (void)
{
#pragma starpu initialize

#define NX     0x100000
#define FACTOR 3.14

  {
    float vector[NX]
      __attribute__ ((heap_allocated, registered));

    size_t i;
    for (i = 0; i < NX; i++)
      vector[i] = (float) i;

    vector_scal (NX, vector, FACTOR);

#pragma starpu wait
  } /* VECTOR is automatically freed here. */

#pragma starpu shutdown

  return valid ? EXIT_SUCCESS : EXIT_FAILURE;
}
```

The function main above does several things:

- It initializes StarPU.

- It allocates `vector` in the heap; it will automatically be freed when its scope is left. Alternatively, good old `malloc` and `free` could have been used, but they are more error-prone and require more typing.

- It registers the memory pointed to by `vector`. Eventually, when OpenCL or CUDA task implementations are added, this will allow StarPU to transfer that memory region between GPUs and the main memory. Removing this `pragma` is an error.

- It invokes the task `vector_scal`. The invocation looks the same as a standard C function call. However, it is an asynchronous invocation, meaning that the actual call is performed in parallel with the caller's continuation.

- It waits for the termination of the asynchronous call `vector_scal`.

- Finally, StarPU is shut down.

The program can be compiled and linked with GCC and the flag `-fplugin`:

```
$ gcc `pkg-config starpu-1.3 --cflags` vector_scal.c
    -fplugin=`pkg-config starpu-1.3 --variable=gccplugin`
    `pkg-config starpu-1.3 --libs`
```

And voilà!

3.3.1 Adding an OpenCL Task Implementation

Now, this is all fine and great, but you certainly want to take advantage of these newfangled GPUs that your lab just bought, don't you?

So, let's add an OpenCL implementation of the task `vector_scal`. We assume that the OpenCL kernel is available in a file, `vector_scal_opencl_kernel.cl`, not shown here. The OpenCL task implementation is similar to that used with the standard C API (Definition of the OpenCL Kernel). It is declared and defined in our C file like this:

```
/* The OpenCL programs, loaded from 'main' (see below). */
static struct starpu_opencl_program cl_programs;

static void vector_scal_opencl (unsigned size, float vector[size],
                                float factor)
  __attribute__ ((task_implementation ("opencl", vector_scal)));

static void
vector_scal_opencl (unsigned size, float vector[size], float factor)
{
  int id, devid, err;
  cl_kernel kernel;
  cl_command_queue queue;
  cl_event event;

  /* VECTOR is GPU memory pointer, not a main memory pointer. */
  cl_mem val = (cl_mem) vector;

  id = starpu_worker_get_id ();
  devid = starpu_worker_get_devid (id);

  /* Prepare to invoke the kernel.  In the future, this will be largely
       automated.  */
  err = starpu_opencl_load_kernel (&kernel, &queue, &
     cl_programs,
                              "vector_mult_opencl", devid);
    (err != CL_SUCCESS)
    STARPU_OPENCL_REPORT_ERROR (err);

  err = clSetKernelArg (kernel, 0, sizeof (size), &size);
  err |= clSetKernelArg (kernel, 1, sizeof (val), &val);
  err |= clSetKernelArg (kernel, 2, sizeof (factor), &factor);
    (err)
    STARPU_OPENCL_REPORT_ERROR (err);

  size_t global = 1, local = 1;
  err = clEnqueueNDRangeKernel (queue, kernel, 1, NULL, &global,
                              &local, 0, NULL, &event);
    (err != CL_SUCCESS)
```

```
    STARPU_OPENCL_REPORT_ERROR (err);

  clFinish (queue);
  starpu_opencl_collect_stats (event);
  clReleaseEvent (event);

  /* Done with KERNEL. */
  starpu_opencl_release_kernel (kernel);
}
```

The OpenCL kernel itself must be loaded from `main`, sometime after the pragma `initialize`:

```
starpu_opencl_load_opencl_from_file ("
    vector_scal_opencl_kernel.cl",
                                &cl_programs, "");
```

And that's it. The task `vector_scal` now has an additional implementation, for OpenCL, which StarPU's sched-uler may choose to use at run-time. Unfortunately, the `vector_scal_opencl` above still has to go through the common OpenCL boilerplate; in the future, additional extensions will automate most of it.

3.3.2 Adding a CUDA Task Implementation

Adding a CUDA implementation of the task is very similar, except that the implementation itself is typically written in CUDA, and compiled with `nvcc`. Thus, the C file only needs to contain an external declaration for the task implementation:

```
extern void vector_scal_cuda (unsigned size, float vector[size],
                              float factor)
  __attribute__ ((task_implementation ("cuda", vector_scal)));
```

The actual implementation of the CUDA task goes into a separate compilation unit, in a `.cu` file. It is very close to the implementation when using StarPU's standard C API (Definition of the CUDA Kernel).

```
/* CUDA implementation of the `vector_scal` task, to be compiled with `nvcc`.
     */

#include <starpu.h>
#include <stdlib.h>

static __global__ void
vector_mult_cuda (unsigned n, float *val, float factor)
{
  unsigned i = blockIdx.x * blockDim.x + threadIdx.x;

  if (i < n)
    val[i] *= factor;
}

/* Definition of the task implementation declared in the C file. */
extern "C" void vector_scal_cuda (size_t size, float vector[], float factor)
{
  unsigned threads_per_block = 64;
  unsigned nblocks = (size + threads_per_block - 1) / threads_per_block;

  vector_mult_cuda <<< nblocks, threads_per_block, 0,
    starpu_cuda_get_local_stream () >>> (size,
      vector, factor);

  cudaStreamSynchronize (starpu_cuda_get_local_stream
      ());
}
```

The complete source code, in the directory `gcc-plugin/examples/vector_scal` of the StarPU distribu-tion, also shows how an SSE-specialized CPU task implementation can be added.

For more details on the C extensions provided by StarPU's GCC plug-in, see C Extensions.

3.4 Vector Scaling Using StarPU's API

This section shows how to achieve the same result as explained in the previous section using StarPU's standard C API.

The full source code for this example is given in Full source code for the 'Scaling a Vector' example.

3.4.1   Source Code of Vector Scaling

Programmers can describe the data layout of their application so that StarPU is responsible for enforcing data coherency and availability across the machine. Instead of handling complex (and non-portable) mechanisms to perform data movements, programmers only declare which piece of data is accessed and/or modified by a task, and StarPU makes sure that when a computational kernel starts somewhere (e.g. on a GPU), its data are available locally.

Before submitting those tasks, the programmer first needs to declare the different pieces of data to StarPU using the functions `starpu_*_data_register`. To ease the development of applications for StarPU, it is possible to describe multiple types of data layout. A type of data layout is called an **interface**. There are different predefined interfaces available in StarPU: here we will consider the **vector interface**.

The following lines show how to declare an array of NX elements of type `float` using the vector interface:

```
float vector[NX];

starpu_data_handle_t vector_handle;
starpu_vector_data_register(&vector_handle,
    STARPU_MAIN_RAM, (uintptr_t)vector, NX,
                        sizeof(vector[0]));
```

The first argument, called the **data handle**, is an opaque pointer which designates the array within StarPU. This is also the structure which is used to describe which data is used by a task. The second argument is the node number where the data originally resides. Here it is STARPU_MAIN_RAM since the array `vector` is in the main memory. Then comes the pointer `vector` where the data can be found in main memory, the number of elements in the vector and the size of each element. The following shows how to construct a StarPU task that will manipulate the vector and a constant factor.

```
float factor = 3.14;
struct starpu_task *task = starpu_task_create();

task->cl = &cl;                          /* Pointer to the codelet defined
      below */
task->handles[0] = vector_handle;       /* First parameter of the codelet
      */
task->cl_arg = &factor;
task->cl_arg_size = sizeof(factor);
task->synchronous = 1;

starpu_task_submit(task);
```

Since the factor is a mere constant float value parameter, it does not need a preliminary registration, and can just be passed through the pointer starpu_task::cl_arg like in the previous example. The vector parameter is described by its handle. starpu_task::handles should be set with the handles of the data, the access modes for the data are defined in the field starpu_codelet::modes (STARPU_R for read-only, STARPU_W for write-only and STARPU_RW for read and write access).

The definition of the codelet can be written as follows:

```
void scal_cpu_func(void *buffers[], void *cl_arg)
{
    unsigned i;
    float *factor = cl_arg;

    /* length of the vector */
    unsigned n = STARPU_VECTOR_GET_NX(buffers[0]);
    /* CPU copy of the vector pointer */
    float *val = (float *)STARPU_VECTOR_GET_PTR(buffers[0]
      );

    for (i = 0; i < n; i++)
        val[i] *= *factor;
}

struct starpu_codelet cl =
{
    .cpu_funcs = { scal_cpu_func },
```

```
        .cpu_funcs_name = { "scal_cpu_func" },
        .nbuffers = 1,
        .modes = { STARPU_RW }
};
```

The first argument is an array that gives a description of all the buffers passed in the array starpu_task::handles. The size of this array is given by the field starpu_codelet::nbuffers. For the sake of genericity, this array contains pointers to the different interfaces describing each buffer. In the case of the **vector interface**, the location of the vector (resp. its length) is accessible in the starpu_vector_interface::ptr (resp. starpu_vector_interface::nx) of this interface. Since the vector is accessed in a read-write fashion, any modification will automatically affect future accesses to this vector made by other tasks.

The second argument of the function `scal_cpu_func` contains a pointer to the parameters of the codelet (given in starpu_task::cl_arg), so that we read the constant factor from this pointer.

3.4.2 Execution of Vector Scaling

```
$ make vector_scal
cc $(pkg-config --cflags starpu-1.3) vector_scal.c -o vector_scal $(pkg-config --libs starpu-1.3)
$ ./vector_scal
0.000000 3.000000 6.000000 9.000000 12.000000
```

3.5 Vector Scaling on an Hybrid CPU/GPU Machine

Contrary to the previous examples, the task submitted in this example may not only be executed by the CPUs, but also by a CUDA device.

3.5.1 Definition of the CUDA Kernel

The CUDA implementation can be written as follows. It needs to be compiled with a CUDA compiler such as nvcc, the NVIDIA CUDA compiler driver. It must be noted that the vector pointer returned by STARPU_VECTOR_GET_-PTR is here a pointer in GPU memory, so that it can be passed as such to the kernel call `vector_mult_cuda`.

```
#include <starpu.h>

static __global__ void vector_mult_cuda(unsigned n, float *val,
                                        float factor)
{
        unsigned i = blockIdx.x*blockDim.x + threadIdx.x;
        if (i < n)
                val[i] *= factor;
}

extern "C" void scal_cuda_func(void *buffers[], void *_args)
{
        float *factor = (float *)_args;

        /* length of the vector */
        unsigned n = STARPU_VECTOR_GET_NX(buffers[0]);
        /* local copy of the vector pointer */
        float *val = (float *)STARPU_VECTOR_GET_PTR(
buffers[0]);
        unsigned threads_per_block = 64;
        unsigned nblocks = (n + threads_per_block-1) / threads_per_block;

        vector_mult_cuda<<<nblocks,threads_per_block, 0,
        starpu_cuda_get_local_stream()>>>
                        (n, val, *factor);

        cudaStreamSynchronize(starpu_cuda_get_local_stream
        ());
}
```

3.5.2 Definition of the OpenCL Kernel

The OpenCL implementation can be written as follows. StarPU provides tools to compile a OpenCL kernel stored in a file.

```
__kernel void vector_mult_opencl(int nx, __global float* val, float factor)
{
        const int i = get_global_id(0);
        if (i < nx)
        {
                val[i] *= factor;
        }
}
```

Contrary to CUDA and CPU, STARPU_VECTOR_GET_DEV_HANDLE has to be used, which returns a `cl_mem` (which is not a device pointer, but an OpenCL handle), which can be passed as such to the OpenCL kernel. The difference is important when using partitioning, see Partitioning Data.

```
#include <starpu.h>

extern struct starpu_opencl_program programs;

void scal_opencl_func(void *buffers[], void *_args)
{
    float *factor = _args;
    int id, devid, err;                     /* OpenCL specific code */
    cl_kernel kernel;                       /* OpenCL specific code */
    cl_command_queue queue;                 /* OpenCL specific code */
    cl_event event;                         /* OpenCL specific code */

    /* length of the vector */
    unsigned n = STARPU_VECTOR_GET_NX(buffers[0]);
    /* OpenCL copy of the vector pointer */
    cl_mem val = (cl_mem)STARPU_VECTOR_GET_DEV_HANDLE
      (buffers[0]);

    {  /* OpenCL specific code */
        id = starpu_worker_get_id();
        devid = starpu_worker_get_devid(id);

        err = starpu_opencl_load_kernel(&kernel, &
      queue,
                                    &programs,
                                    "vector_mult_opencl", /* Name of the
       codelet */
                                    devid);
        if (err != CL_SUCCESS) STARPU_OPENCL_REPORT_ERROR
      (err);

        err = clSetKernelArg(kernel, 0, sizeof(n), &n);
        err |= clSetKernelArg(kernel, 1, sizeof(val), &val);
        err |= clSetKernelArg(kernel, 2, sizeof(*factor), factor);
        if (err) STARPU_OPENCL_REPORT_ERROR(err);
    }

    {  /* OpenCL specific code */
        size_t global=n;
        size_t local;
        size_t s;
        cl_device_id device;

        starpu_opencl_get_device(devid, &device);
        err = clGetKernelWorkGroupInfo (kernel, device,
      CL_KERNEL_WORK_GROUP_SIZE,
                                    sizeof(local), &local, &s);
        if (err != CL_SUCCESS) STARPU_OPENCL_REPORT_ERROR
      (err);
        if (local > global) local=global;

        err = clEnqueueNDRangeKernel(queue, kernel, 1, NULL, &global, &local, 0
      ,
                                    NULL, &event);
        if (err != CL_SUCCESS) STARPU_OPENCL_REPORT_ERROR
      (err);
    }

    {  /* OpenCL specific code */
        clFinish(queue);
        starpu_opencl_collect_stats(event);
        clReleaseEvent(event);

        starpu_opencl_release_kernel(kernel);
```

```
        }
}
```

3.5.3 Definition of the Main Code

The CPU implementation is the same as in the previous section.

Here is the source of the main application. You can notice that the fields starpu_codelet::cuda_funcs and starpu_-codelet::opencl_funcs are set to define the pointers to the CUDA and OpenCL implementations of the task.

```c
/*
 * This example demonstrates how to use StarPU to scale an array by a factor.
 * It shows how to manipulate data with StarPU's data management library.
 *  1- how to declare a piece of data to StarPU (starpu_vector_data_register)
 *  2- how to describe which data are accessed by a task (task->handles[0])
 *  3- how a kernel can manipulate the data (buffers[0].vector.ptr)
 */
#include <starpu.h>

#define   NX    2048

extern void scal_cpu_func(void *buffers[], void *_args);
extern void scal_sse_func(void *buffers[], void *_args);
extern void scal_cuda_func(void *buffers[], void *_args);
extern void scal_opencl_func(void *buffers[], void *_args);

static struct starpu_codelet cl =
{
    .where = STARPU_CPU | STARPU_CUDA | STARPU_OPENCL
    ,
    /* CPU implementation of the codelet */
    .cpu_funcs = { scal_cpu_func, scal_sse_func },
    .cpu_funcs_name = { "scal_cpu_func", "scal_sse_func" },
#ifdef STARPU_USE_CUDA
    /* CUDA implementation of the codelet */
    .cuda_funcs = { scal_cuda_func },
#endif
#ifdef STARPU_USE_OPENCL
    /* OpenCL implementation of the codelet */
    .opencl_funcs = { scal_opencl_func },
#endif
    .nbuffers = 1,
    .modes = { STARPU_RW }
};

#ifdef STARPU_USE_OPENCL
struct starpu_opencl_program programs;
#endif

int main(int argc, char **argv)
{
    /* We consider a vector of float that is initialized just as any of C
     * data */
    float vector[NX];
    unsigned i;
    for (i = 0; i < NX; i++)
        vector[i] = 1.0f;

    fprintf(stderr, "BEFORE: First element was %f\n", vector[0]);

    /* Initialize StarPU with default configuration */
    starpu_init(NULL);

#ifdef STARPU_USE_OPENCL
    starpu_opencl_load_opencl_from_file(
            "examples/basic_examples/vector_scal_opencl_kernel.cl", &
    programs, NULL);
#endif

    /* Tell StaPU to associate the "vector" vector with the "vector_handle"
     * identifier. When a task needs to access a piece of data, it should
     * refer to the handle that is associated to it.
     * In the case of the "vector" data interface:
     *  - the first argument of the registration method is a pointer to the
     *    handle that should describe the data
     *  - the second argument is the memory node where the data (ie. "vector")
     *    resides initially: STARPU_MAIN_RAM stands for an address in main
     *  memory, as
     *    opposed to an adress on a GPU for instance.
     *  - the third argument is the adress of the vector in RAM
     *  - the fourth argument is the number of elements in the vector
     *  - the fifth argument is the size of each element.
```

```
  */
  starpu_data_handle_t vector_handle;
  starpu_vector_data_register(&vector_handle,
    STARPU_MAIN_RAM, (uintptr_t)vector,
                          NX, sizeof(vector[0]));

  float factor = 3.14;

  /* create a synchronous task: any call to starpu_task_submit will block
   * until it is terminated */
  struct starpu_task *task = starpu_task_create(
    );
  task->synchronous = 1;

  task->cl = &cl;

  /* the codelet manipulates one buffer in RW mode */
  task->handles[0] = vector_handle;

  /* an argument is passed to the codelet, beware that this is a
   * READ-ONLY buffer and that the codelet may be given a pointer to a
   * COPY of the argument */
  task->cl_arg = &factor;
  task->cl_arg_size = sizeof(factor);

  /* execute the task on any eligible computational ressource */
  starpu_task_submit(task);

  /* StarPU does not need to manipulate the array anymore so we can stop
   * monitoring it */
  starpu_data_unregister(vector_handle);

#ifdef STARPU_USE_OPENCL
  starpu_opencl_unload_opencl(&programs);
#endif

  /* terminate StarPU, no task can be submitted after */
  starpu_shutdown();

  fprintf(stderr, "AFTER First element is %f\n", vector[0]);

      0;
}
```

3.5.4 Execution of Hybrid Vector Scaling

The Makefile given at the beginning of the section must be extended to give the rules to compile the CUDA source code. Note that the source file of the OpenCL kernel does not need to be compiled now, it will be compiled at run-time when calling the function starpu_opencl_load_opencl_from_file().

```
CFLAGS  += $(shell pkg-config --cflags starpu-1.3)
LDFLAGS += $(shell pkg-config --libs starpu-1.3)
CC      = gcc

vector_scal: vector_scal.o vector_scal_cpu.o vector_scal_cuda.o vector_scal_opencl.o

%.o: %.cu
      nvcc $(CFLAGS) $< -c $@

clean:
      rm -f vector_scal *.o
```

```
$ make
```

and to execute it, with the default configuration:

```
$ ./vector_scal
0.000000 3.000000 6.000000 9.000000 12.000000
```

or for example, by disabling CPU devices:

```
$ STARPU_NCPU=0 ./vector_scal
0.000000 3.000000 6.000000 9.000000 12.000000
```

or by disabling CUDA devices (which may permit to enable the use of OpenCL, see Enabling OpenCL) :

```
$ STARPU_NCUDA=0 ./vector_scal
0.000000 3.000000 6.000000 9.000000 12.000000
```

Part II

StarPU Quick Programming Guide

Chapter 4

Advanced Examples

TODO

Chapter 5

Check List When Performance Are Not There

TODO: improve!

To achieve good performance, we give below a list of features which should be checked.

5.1 Configuration That May Improve Performance

The --enable-fast configuration option disables all assertions. This makes StarPU more performant for really small tasks by disabling all sanity checks. Only use this for measurements and production, not for development, since this will drop all basic checks.

5.2 Data Related Features That May Improve Performance

link to Data Management

link to Data Prefetch

5.3 Task Related Features That May Improve Performance

link to Task Granularity

link to Task Submission

link to Task Priorities

5.4 Scheduling Related Features That May Improve Performance

link to Task Scheduling Policies

link to Task Distribution Vs Data Transfer

link to Energy-based Scheduling

link to Static Scheduling

5.5 CUDA-specific Optimizations

Due to CUDA limitations, StarPU will have a hard time overlapping its own communications and the codelet computations if the application does not use a dedicated CUDA stream for its computations instead of the default stream,

which synchronizes all operations of the GPU. StarPU provides one by the use of starpu_cuda_get_local_stream()
which can be used by all CUDA codelet operations to avoid this issue. For instance:

```
func <<<grid,block,0,starpu_cuda_get_local_stream()>>> (foo, bar);
cudaStreamSynchronize(starpu_cuda_get_local_stream(
      ));
```

Unfortunately, some CUDA libraries do not have stream variants of kernels. That will lower the potential for overlapping.

Calling starpu_cublas_init() makes StarPU already do appropriate calls for the CUBLAS library. Some libraries
like Magma may however change the current stream of CUBLAS v1, one then has to call `cublasSetKernel-`
`Stream(starpu_cuda_get_local_stream())` at the beginning of the codelet to make sure that CUBL-
AS is really using the proper stream. When using CUBLAS v2, starpu_cublas_get_local_handle() can be called to
queue CUBLAS kernels with the proper configuration.

Similarly, calling starpu_cusparse_init() makes StarPU create CUSPARSE handles on each CUDA device, starpu-
_cusparse_get_local_handle() can then be used to queue CUSPARSE kernels with the proper configuration.

If the kernel can be made to only use this local stream or other self-allocated streams, i.e. the whole kernel
submission can be made asynchronous, then one should enable asynchronous execution of the kernel. That means
setting the flag STARPU_CUDA_ASYNC in the corresponding field starpu_codelet::cuda_flags, and dropping the
`cudaStreamSynchronize()` call at the end of the `cuda_func` function, so that it returns immediately after
having queued the kernel to the local stream. That way, StarPU will be able to submit and complete data transfers
while kernels are executing, instead of only at each kernel submission. The kernel just has to make sure that StarPU
can use the local stream to synchronize with the kernel startup and completion.

If the kernel uses its own non-default stream, one can synchronize that stream with the StarPU-provided stream this
way:

```
cudaEvent_t event;
call_kernel_with_its_own_stream()
cudaEventCreateWithFlags(&event, cudaEventDisableTiming);
cudaEventRecord(event, get_kernel_stream());
cudaStreamWaitEvent(starpu_cuda_get_local_stream(), event, 0);
cudaEventDestroy(event);
```

That code makes the StarPU-provided stream wait for a new event, which will be triggered by the completion of the
kernel.

Using the flag STARPU_CUDA_ASYNC also permits to enable concurrent kernel execution, on cards which support
it (Kepler and later, notably). This is enabled by setting the environment variable STARPU_NWORKER_PER_C-
UDA to the number of kernels to execute concurrently. This is useful when kernels are small and do not feed the
whole GPU with threads to run.

5.6   OpenCL-specific Optimizations

If the kernel can be made to only use the StarPU-provided command queue or other self-allocated queues, i.e.
the whole kernel submission can be made asynchronous, then one should enable asynchronous execution of the
kernel. This means setting the flag STARPU_OPENCL_ASYNC in the corresponding field starpu_codelet::opencl-
_flags and dropping the `clFinish()` and starpu_opencl_collect_stats() calls at the end of the kernel, so that it
returns immediately after having queued the kernel to the provided queue. That way, StarPU will be able to submit
and complete data transfers while kernels are executing, instead of only at each kernel submission. The kernel just
has to make sure that StarPU can use the command queue it has provided to synchronize with the kernel startup
and completion.

5.7   Detecting Stuck Conditions

It may happen that for some reason, StarPU does not make progress for a long period of time. Reason are sometimes due to contention inside StarPU, but sometimes this is due to external reasons, such as stuck MPI driver, or
CUDA driver, etc.

```
export STARPU_WATCHDOG_TIMEOUT=10000 (STARPU_WATCHDOG_TIMEOUT)
```

allows to make StarPU print an error message whenever StarPU does not terminate any task for 10ms, but lets the application continue normally. In addition to that,

```
export STARPU_WATCHDOG_CRASH=1 (STARPU_WATCHDOG_CRASH)
```

raises `SIGABRT` in that condition, thus allowing to catch the situation in gdb. It can also be useful to type `handle SIGABRT nopass` in `gdb` to be able to let the process continue, after inspecting the state of the process.

5.8   How to Limit Memory Used By StarPU And Cache Buffer Allocations

By default, StarPU makes sure to use at most 90% of the memory of GPU devices, moving data in and out of the device as appropriate and with prefetch and writeback optimizations. Concerning the main memory, by default it will not limit its consumption, since by default it has nowhere to push the data to when memory gets tight. This also means that by default StarPU will not cache buffer allocations in main memory, since it does not know how much of the system memory it can afford.

In the case of GPUs, the STARPU_LIMIT_CUDA_MEM, STARPU_LIMIT_CUDA_devid_MEM, STARPU_LIMIT_-OPENCL_MEM, and STARPU_LIMIT_OPENCL_devid_MEM environment variables can be used to control how much (in MiB) of the GPU device memory should be used at most by StarPU (their default values are 90% of the available memory).

In the case of the main memory, the STARPU_LIMIT_CPU_MEM environment variable can be used to specify how much (in MiB) of the main memory should be used at most by StarPU for buffer allocations. This way, StarPU will be able to cache buffer allocations (which can be a real benefit if a lot of bufferes are involved, or if allocation fragmentation can become a problem), and when using Out Of Core, StarPU will know when it should evict data out to the disk.

It should be noted that by default only buffer allocations automatically done by StarPU are accounted here, i.e. allocations performed through starpu_malloc_on_node() which are used by the data interfaces (matrix, vector, etc.). This does not include allocations performed by the application through e.g. malloc(). It does not include allocations performed through starpu_malloc() either, only allocations performed explicitly with the STARPU_MALLOC_COU-NT flag, i.e. by calling

```
starpu_malloc_flags(STARPU_MALLOC_COUNT)
```

are taken into account. If the application wants to make StarPU aware of its own allocations, so that StarPU knows precisely how much data is allocated, and thus when to evict allocation caches or data out to the disk, starpu_-memory_allocate() can be used to specify an amount of memory to be accounted for. starpu_memory_deallocate() can be used to account freed memory back. Those can for instance be used by data interfaces with dynamic data buffers: instead of using starpu_malloc_on_node(), they would dynamically allocate data with malloc/realloc, and notify starpu of the delta thanks to starpu_memory_allocate() and starpu_memory_deallocate() calls.

starpu_memory_get_total() and starpu_memory_get_available() can be used to get an estimation of how much memory is available. starpu_memory_wait_available() can also be used to block until an amount of memory becomes available, but it may be preferrable to call

```
starpu_memory_allocate(STARPU_MEMORY_WAIT
    )
```

to reserve that amount immediately.

5.9   How To Reduce The Memory Footprint Of Internal Data Structures

It is possible to reduce the memory footprint of the task and data internal structures of StarPU by describing the shape of your machine and/or your application at the configure step.

To reduce the memory footprint of the data internal structures of StarPU, one can set the --enable-maxcpus, --enable-maxcudadev, --enable-maxopencldev and --enable-maxnodes configure parameters to give StarPU the architecture of the machine it will run on, thus tuning the size of the structures to the machine.

To reduce the memory footprint of the task internal structures of StarPU, one can set the --enable-maxbuffers configure parameter to give StarPU the maximum number of buffers that a task can use during an execution. For example, in the Cholesky factorization (dense linear algebra application), the GEMM task uses up to 3 buffers, so it is possible to set the maximum number of task buffers to 3 to run a Cholesky factorization on StarPU.

The size of the various structures of StarPU can be printed by `tests/microbenchs/display_-structures_size`.

It is also often useless to submit *all* the tasks at the same time. One can make the starpu_task_submit() function block when a reasonable given number of tasks have been submitted, by setting the STARPU_LIMIT_MIN_SUBMITTED_TASKS and STARPU_LIMIT_MAX_SUBMITTED_TASKS environment variables, for instance:

`export STARPU_LIMIT_MAX_SUBMITTED_TASKS=10000`

`export STARPU_LIMIT_MIN_SUBMITTED_TASKS=9000`

To make StarPU block submission when 10000 tasks are submitted, and unblock submission when only 9000 tasks are still submitted, i.e. 1000 tasks have completed among the 10000 that were submitted when submission was blocked. Of course this may reduce parallelism if the threshold is set too low. The precise balance depends on the application task graph.

An idea of how much memory is used for tasks and data handles can be obtained by setting the STARPU_MAX_MEMORY_USE environment variable to 1.

5.10   How To Reuse Memory

When your application needs to allocate more data than the available amount of memory usable by StarPU (given by starpu_memory_get_available()), the allocation cache system can reuse data buffers used by previously executed tasks. For that system to work with MPI tasks, you need to submit tasks progressively instead of as soon as possible, because in the case of MPI receives, the allocation cache check for reusing data buffers will be done at submission time, not at execution time.

You have two options to control the task submission flow. The first one is by controlling the number of submitted tasks during the whole execution. This can be done whether by setting the environment variables STARPU_LIMIT_MAX_SUBMITTED_TASKS and STARPU_LIMIT_MIN_SUBMITTED_TASKS to tell StarPU when to stop submitting tasks and when to wake up and submit tasks again, or by explicitly calling starpu_task_wait_for_n_submitted() in your application code for finest grain control (for example, between two iterations of a submission loop).

The second option is to control the memory size of the allocation cache. This can be done in the application by using jointly starpu_memory_get_available() and starpu_memory_wait_available() to submit tasks only when there is enough memory space to allocate the data needed by the task, i.e when enough data are available for reuse in the allocation cache.

5.11   Performance Model Calibration

Most schedulers are based on an estimation of codelet duration on each kind of processing unit. For this to be possible, the application programmer needs to configure a performance model for the codelets of the application (see Performance Model Example for instance). History-based performance models use on-line calibration. StarPU will automatically calibrate codelets which have never been calibrated yet, and save the result in $STARPU_HOME/.starpu/sampling/codelets. The models are indexed by machine name.

By default, StarPU stores separate performance models according to the hostname of the system. To avoid having to calibrate performance models for each node of a homogeneous cluster for instance, the model can be shared by using `export STARPU_HOSTNAME=some_global_name` (STARPU_HOSTNAME), where `some_global_name` is the name of the cluster for instance, which thus overrides the hostname of the system.

By default, StarPU stores separate performance models for each GPU. To avoid having to calibrate performance

models for each GPU of a homogeneous set of GPU devices for instance, the model can be shared by set-
ting `export STARPU_PERF_MODEL_HOMOGENEOUS_CUDA=1` , `export STARPU_PERF_MODEL_HO-
MOGENEOUS_OPENCL=1` , `export STARPU_PERF_MODEL_HOMOGENEOUS_MIC=1` , `export STARP-
U_PERF_MODEL_HOMOGENEOUS_MPI_MS=1` , or `export STARPU_PERF_MODEL_HOMOGENEOUS_SC-
C=1` (depending on your GPU device type).

To force continuing calibration, use `export STARPU_CALIBRATE=1` (STARPU_CALIBRATE). This may be
necessary if your application has not-so-stable performance. StarPU will force calibration (and thus ignore the
current result) until 10 (`_STARPU_CALIBRATION_MINIMUM`) measurements have been made on each architecture, to avoid badly scheduling tasks just because the first measurements were not so good. Details on the
current performance model status can be obtained from the tool `starpu_perfmodel_display`: the `-l` option lists the available performance models, and the `-s` option permits to choose the performance model to be
displayed. The result looks like:

```
$ starpu_perfmodel_display -s starpu_slu_lu_model_11
performance model for cpu_impl_0
# hash    size     flops         mean         dev          n
914f3bef  1048576  0.000000e+00  2.503577e+04  1.982465e+02  8
3e921964  65536    0.000000e+00  5.527003e+02  1.848114e+01  7
e5a07e31  4096     0.000000e+00  1.717457e+01  5.190038e+00  14
...
```

Which shows that for the LU 11 kernel with a 1MiB matrix, the average execution time on CPUs was about 25ms,
with a 0.2ms standard deviation, over 8 samples. It is a good idea to check this before doing actual performance
measurements.

A graph can be drawn by using the tool `starpu_perfmodel_plot`:

```
$ starpu_perfmodel_plot -s starpu_slu_lu_model_11
4096 16384 65536 262144 1048576 4194304
$ gnuplot starpu_starpu_slu_lu_model_11.gp
$ gv starpu_starpu_slu_lu_model_11.eps
```

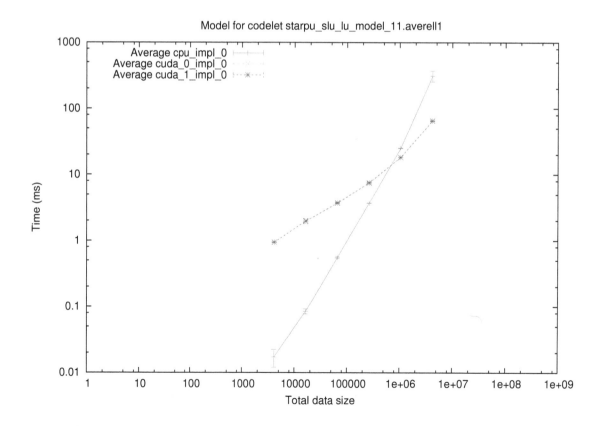

If a kernel source code was modified (e.g. performance improvement), the calibration information is stale and should be dropped, to re-calibrate from start. This can be done by using `export STARPU_CALIBRATE=2` (STARPU_CALIBRATE).

Note: history-based performance models get calibrated only if a performance-model-based scheduler is chosen.

The history-based performance models can also be explicitly filled by the application without execution, if e.g. the application already has a series of measurements. This can be done by using starpu_perfmodel_update_history(), for instance:

```
static struct starpu_perfmodel perf_model =
{
    .type = STARPU_HISTORY_BASED,
    .symbol = "my_perfmodel",
};

struct starpu_codelet cl =
{
    .cuda_funcs = { cuda_func1, cuda_func2 },
    .nbuffers = 1,
    .modes = {STARPU_W},
    .model = &perf_model
};

void feed(void)
{
    struct my_measure *measure;
    struct starpu_task task;
    starpu_task_init(&task);

    task.cl = &cl;

    (measure = &measures[0]; measure < measures[last]; measure++)
    {
        starpu_data_handle_t handle;
        starpu_vector_data_register(&handle, -1, 0,
    measure->size, sizeof(float));
        task.handles[0] = handle;
        starpu_perfmodel_update_history(&
    perf_model, &task,
                                 STARPU_CUDA_DEFAULT + measure->cudadev,
     0,
                                 measure->implementation, measure->time)
    ;
        starpu_task_clean(&task);
        starpu_data_unregister(handle);
    }
}
```

Measurement has to be provided in milliseconds for the completion time models, and in Joules for the energy consumption models.

5.12 Profiling

A quick view of how many tasks each worker has executed can be obtained by setting `export STARPU_WO‐RKER_STATS=1` (STARPU_WORKER_STATS). This is a convenient way to check that execution did happen on accelerators, without penalizing performance with the profiling overhead.

A quick view of how much data transfers have been issued can be obtained by setting `export STARPU_BUS_‐STATS=1` (STARPU_BUS_STATS).

More detailed profiling information can be enabled by using `export STARPU_PROFILING=1` (STARPU_PR‐OFILING) or by calling starpu_profiling_status_set() from the source code. Statistics on the execution can then be obtained by using `export STARPU_BUS_STATS=1` and `export STARPU_WORKER_STATS=1` . More details on performance feedback are provided in the next chapter.

5.13 Overhead Profiling

Offline Performance Tools can already provide an idea of to what extent and which part of StarPU bring overhead on the execution time. To get a more precise analysis of the parts of StarPU which bring most overhead, `gprof` can be used.

First, recompile and reinstall StarPU with `gprof` support:

```
./configure --enable-perf-debug --disable-shared --disable-build-tests --
    disable-build-examples
```

Make sure not to leave a dynamic version of StarPU in the target path: remove any remaining `libstarpu-*.so`

Then relink your application with the static StarPU library, make sure that running `ldd` on your application does not mention any libstarpu (i.e. it's really statically-linked).

```
gcc test.c -o test $(pkg-config --cflags starpu-1.3) $(pkg-config --libs starpu
    -1.3)
```

Now you can run your application, and a `gmon.out` file should appear in the current directory, you can process it by running `gprof` on your application:

```
gprof ./test
```

That will dump an analysis of the time spent in StarPU functions.

Part III

StarPU Inside

Chapter 6

Tasks In StarPU

6.1 Task Granularity

Like any other runtime, StarPU has some overhead to manage tasks. Since it does smart scheduling and data management, that overhead is not always neglectable. The order of magnitude of the overhead is typically a couple of microseconds, which is actually quite smaller than the CUDA overhead itself. The amount of work that a task should do should thus be somewhat bigger, to make sure that the overhead becomes neglectible. The offline performance feedback can provide a measure of task length, which should thus be checked if bad performance are observed. To get a grasp at the scalability possibility according to task size, one can run `tests/microbenchs/tasks-_size_overhead.sh` which draws curves of the speedup of independent tasks of very small sizes.

The choice of scheduler also has impact over the overhead: for instance, the scheduler `dmda` takes time to make a decision, while `eager` does not. `tasks_size_overhead.sh` can again be used to get a grasp at how much impact that has on the target machine.

6.2 Task Submission

To let StarPU make online optimizations, tasks should be submitted asynchronously as much as possible. Ideally, all the tasks should be submitted, and mere calls to starpu_task_wait_for_all() or starpu_data_unregister() be done to wait for termination. StarPU will then be able to rework the whole schedule, overlap computation with communication, manage accelerator local memory usage, etc.

6.3 Task Priorities

By default, StarPU will consider the tasks in the order they are submitted by the application. If the application programmer knows that some tasks should be performed in priority (for instance because their output is needed by many other tasks and may thus be a bottleneck if not executed early enough), the field starpu_task::priority should be set to transmit the priority information to StarPU.

6.4 Setting Many Data Handles For a Task

The maximum number of data a task can manage is fixed by the environment variable STARPU_NMAXBUFS which has a default value which can be changed through the configure option --enable-maxbuffers.

However, it is possible to define tasks managing more data by using the field starpu_task::dyn_handles when defining a task and the field starpu_codelet::dyn_modes when defining the corresponding codelet.

```
enum starpu_data_access_mode modes[STARPU_NMAXBUFS
    +1] =
```

```
{
        STARPU_R, STARPU_R, ...
};

struct starpu_codelet dummy_big_cl =
{
        .cuda_funcs = { dummy_big_kernel },
        .opencl_funcs = { dummy_big_kernel },
        .cpu_funcs = { dummy_big_kernel },
        .cpu_funcs_name = { "dummy_big_kernel" },
        .nbuffers = STARPU_NMAXBUFS+1,
        .dyn_modes = modes
};

task = starpu_task_create();
task->cl = &dummy_big_cl;
task->dyn_handles = malloc(task->cl->nbuffers * sizeof(
        starpu_data_handle_t));
    (i=0 ; i<task->cl->nbuffers ; i++)
{
        task->dyn_handles[i] = handle;
}
starpu_task_submit(task);


starpu_data_handle_t *handles = malloc(dummy_big_cl.
        nbuffers * sizeof(starpu_data_handle_t));
    (i=0 ; i<dummy_big_cl.nbuffers ; i++)
{
        handles[i] = handle;
}
starpu_task_insert(&dummy_big_cl,
                STARPU_VALUE, &dummy_big_cl.nbuffers,
        sizeof(dummy_big_cl.nbuffers),
                STARPU_DATA_ARRAY, handles, dummy_big_cl.
        nbuffers,
                0);
```

The whole code for this complex data interface is available in the directory `examples/basic_-examples/dynamic_handles.c`.

6.5   Setting a Variable Number Of Data Handles For a Task

Normally, the number of data handles given to a task is fixed in the starpu_codelet::nbuffers codelet field. This field can however be set to STARPU_VARIABLE_NBUFFERS, in which case the starpu_task::nbuffers task field must be set, and the starpu_task::modes field (or starpu_task::dyn_modes field, see Setting Many Data Handles For a Task) should be used to specify the modes for the handles.

6.6   Using Multiple Implementations Of A Codelet

One may want to write multiple implementations of a codelet for a single type of device and let StarPU choose which one to run. As an example, we will show how to use SSE to scale a vector. The codelet can be written as follows:

```
#include <xmmintrin.h>

void scal_sse_func(void *buffers[], void *cl_arg)
{
    float *vector = (float *) STARPU_VECTOR_GET_PTR(
        buffers[0]);
    unsigned int n = STARPU_VECTOR_GET_NX(buffers[0]);
    unsigned int n_iterations = n/4;
    (n % 4 != 0)
        n_iterations++;

    __m128 *VECTOR = (__m128*) vector;
    __m128 factor __attribute__((aligned(16)));
    factor = _mm_set1_ps(*(float *) cl_arg);

    unsigned int i;
    (i = 0; i < n_iterations; i++)
        VECTOR[i] = _mm_mul_ps(factor, VECTOR[i]);
}
```

```
struct starpu_codelet cl =
{
    .cpu_funcs = { scal_cpu_func, scal_sse_func },
    .cpu_funcs_name = { "scal_cpu_func", "scal_sse_func" },
    .nbuffers = 1,
    .modes = { STARPU_RW }
};
```

Schedulers which are multi-implementation aware (only `dmda` and `pheft` for now) will use the performance models of all the implementations it was given, and pick the one that seems to be the fastest.

6.7 Enabling Implementation According To Capabilities

Some implementations may not run on some devices. For instance, some CUDA devices do not support double floating point precision, and thus the kernel execution would just fail; or the device may not have enough shared memory for the implementation being used. The field starpu_codelet::can_execute permits to express this. For instance:

```
static int can_execute(unsigned workerid, struct starpu_task
        *task, unsigned nimpl)
{
  const struct cudaDeviceProp *props;
  if (starpu_worker_get_type(workerid) ==
      STARPU_CPU_WORKER)
    return 1;
  /* Cuda device */
  props = starpu_cuda_get_device_properties(
      workerid);
  if (props->major >= 2 || props->minor >= 3)
    /* At least compute capability 1.3, supports doubles */
    return 1;
  /* Old card, does not support doubles */
  return 0;
}

struct starpu_codelet cl =
{
    .can_execute = can_execute,
    .cpu_funcs = { cpu_func },
    .cpu_funcs_name = { "cpu_func" },
    .cuda_funcs = { gpu_func }
    .nbuffers = 1,
    .modes = { STARPU_RW }
};
```

This can be essential e.g. when running on a machine which mixes various models of CUDA devices, to take benefit from the new models without crashing on old models.

Note: the function starpu_codelet::can_execute is called by the scheduler each time it tries to match a task with a worker, and should thus be very fast. The function starpu_cuda_get_device_properties() provides a quick access to CUDA properties of CUDA devices to achieve such efficiency.

Another example is to compile CUDA code for various compute capabilities, resulting with two CUDA functions, e.g. `scal_gpu_13` for compute capability 1.3, and `scal_gpu_20` for compute capability 2.0. Both functions can be provided to StarPU by using starpu_codelet::cuda_funcs, and starpu_codelet::can_execute can then be used to rule out the `scal_gpu_20` variant on a CUDA device which will not be able to execute it:

```
static int can_execute(unsigned workerid, struct starpu_task
        *task, unsigned nimpl)
{
  const struct cudaDeviceProp *props;
  if (starpu_worker_get_type(workerid) ==
      STARPU_CPU_WORKER)
    return 1;
  /* Cuda device */
  if (nimpl == 0)
    /* Trying to execute the 1.3 capability variant, we assume it is ok in all
        cases. */
    return 1;
  /* Trying to execute the 2.0 capability variant, check that the card can do
      it. */
  props = starpu_cuda_get_device_properties(
      workerid);
```

```
   (props->major >= 2 || props->minor >= 0)
    /* At least compute capability 2.0, can run it */
        1;
   /* Old card, does not support 2.0, will not be able to execute the 2.0
       variant. */
       0;
}

struct starpu_codelet cl =
{
    .can_execute = can_execute,
    .cpu_funcs = { cpu_func },
    .cpu_funcs_name = { "cpu_func" },
    .cuda_funcs = { scal_gpu_13, scal_gpu_20 },
    .nbuffers = 1,
    .modes = { STARPU_RW }
};
```

Another example is having specialized implementations for some given common sizes, for instance here we have a specialized implementation for 1024x1024 matrices:

```
static int can_execute(unsigned workerid, struct starpu_task
        *task, unsigned nimpl)
{
  const struct cudaDeviceProp *props;
    if (starpu_worker_get_type(workerid) ==
      STARPU_CPU_WORKER)
        1;
   /* Cuda device */
        (nimpl)
    {
        0:
      /* Trying to execute the generic capability variant. */
        1;
        1:
     {
      /* Trying to execute the size == 1024 specific variant. */
      struct starpu_matrix_interface *interface =
      starpu_data_get_interface_on_node(task->
      handles[0]);
        STARPU_MATRIX_GET_NX(interface) == 1024 &&
      STARPU_MATRIX_GET_NY(interface == 1024);
     }
   }
}

struct starpu_codelet cl =
{
    .can_execute = can_execute,
    .cpu_funcs = { cpu_func },
    .cpu_funcs_name = { "cpu_func" },
    .cuda_funcs = { potrf_gpu_generic, potrf_gpu_1024 },
    .nbuffers = 1,
    .modes = { STARPU_RW }
};
```

Note: the most generic variant should be provided first, as some schedulers are not able to try the different variants.

6.8 Insert Task Utility

StarPU provides the wrapper function starpu_task_insert() to ease the creation and submission of tasks.

Here the implementation of the codelet:

```
void func_cpu(void *descr[], void *_args)
{
        int *x0 = (int *)STARPU_VARIABLE_GET_PTR(descr[0
    ]);
        float *x1 = (float *)STARPU_VARIABLE_GET_PTR(
    descr[1]);
        int ifactor;
        float ffactor;

        starpu_codelet_unpack_args(_args, &ifactor, &
    ffactor);
        *x0 = *x0 * ifactor;
        *x1 = *x1 * ffactor;
}
```

```
struct starpu_codelet mycodelet =
{
        .cpu_funcs = { func_cpu },
        .cpu_funcs_name = { "func_cpu" },
        .nbuffers = 2,
        .modes = { STARPU_RW, STARPU_RW }
};
```

And the call to the function starpu_task_insert():

```
starpu_task_insert(&mycodelet,
                   STARPU_VALUE, &ifactor, sizeof(ifactor),
                   STARPU_VALUE, &ffactor, sizeof(ffactor),
                   STARPU_RW, data_handles[0],
                   STARPU_RW, data_handles[1],
                   0);
```

The call to starpu_task_insert() is equivalent to the following code:

```
struct starpu_task *task = starpu_task_create();
task->cl = &mycodelet;
task->handles[0] = data_handles[0];
task->handles[1] = data_handles[1];
char *arg_buffer;
size_t arg_buffer_size;
starpu_codelet_pack_args(&arg_buffer, &arg_buffer_size,
                   STARPU_VALUE, &ifactor, sizeof(ifactor),
                   STARPU_VALUE, &ffactor, sizeof(ffactor),
                   0);
task->cl_arg = arg_buffer;
task->cl_arg_size = arg_buffer_size;
int ret = starpu_task_submit(task);
```

Here a similar call using STARPU_DATA_ARRAY.

```
starpu_task_insert(&mycodelet,
                   STARPU_DATA_ARRAY, data_handles, 2,
                   STARPU_VALUE, &ifactor, sizeof(ifactor),
                   STARPU_VALUE, &ffactor, sizeof(ffactor),
                   0);
```

If some part of the task insertion depends on the value of some computation, the macro STARPU_DATA_AC-QUIRE_CB can be very convenient. For instance, assuming that the index variable i was registered as handle A_handle[i]:

```
/* Compute which portion we will work on, e.g. pivot */
starpu_task_insert(&which_index, STARPU_W, i_handle,
     0);

/* And submit the corresponding task */
STARPU_DATA_ACQUIRE_CB(i_handle, STARPU_R,
                   starpu_task_insert(&work,
                                      STARPU_RW, A_handle[i],
                                      0));
```

The macro STARPU_DATA_ACQUIRE_CB submits an asynchronous request for acquiring data i for the main application, and will execute the code given as third parameter when it is acquired. In other words, as soon as the value of i computed by the codelet which_index can be read, the portion of code passed as third parameter of STARPU_DATA_ACQUIRE_CB will be executed, and is allowed to read from i to use it e.g. as an index. Note that this macro is only avaible when compiling StarPU with the compiler gcc.

There is several ways of calling the function starpu_codelet_unpack_args().

```
void func_cpu(void *descr[], void *_args)
{
        int ifactor;
        float ffactor;

        starpu_codelet_unpack_args(_args, &ifactor, &
     ffactor);
}
```

```
void func_cpu(void *descr[], void *_args)
{
        int ifactor;
        float ffactor;

        starpu_codelet_unpack_args(_args, &ifactor, 0
    );
        starpu_codelet_unpack_args(_args, &ifactor, &
    ffactor);
}


void func_cpu(void *descr[], void *_args)
{
        int ifactor;
        float ffactor;
        char buffer[100];

        starpu_codelet_unpack_args_and_copyleft
    (_args, buffer, 100, &ifactor, 0);
        starpu_codelet_unpack_args(buffer, &ffactor);
}
```

6.9   Getting Task Children

It may be interesting to get the list of tasks which depend on a given task, notably when using implicit dependencies, since this list is computed by StarPU. starpu_task_get_task_succs() provides it. For instance:

```
struct starpu_task *tasks[4];
ret = starpu_task_get_task_succs(task, sizeof(tasks)/
    sizeof(*tasks), tasks);
```

6.10   Parallel Tasks

StarPU can leverage existing parallel computation libraries by the means of parallel tasks. A parallel task is a task which gets worked on by a set of CPUs (called a parallel or combined worker) at the same time, by using an existing parallel CPU implementation of the computation to be achieved. This can also be useful to improve the load balance between slow CPUs and fast GPUs: since CPUs work collectively on a single task, the completion time of tasks on CPUs become comparable to the completion time on GPUs, thus relieving from granularity discrepancy concerns. hwloc support needs to be enabled to get good performance, otherwise StarPU will not know how to better group cores.

Two modes of execution exist to accomodate with existing usages.

6.10.1   Fork-mode Parallel Tasks

In the Fork mode, StarPU will call the codelet function on one of the CPUs of the combined worker. The codelet function can use starpu_combined_worker_get_size() to get the number of threads it is allowed to start to achieve the computation. The CPU binding mask for the whole set of CPUs is already enforced, so that threads created by the function will inherit the mask, and thus execute where StarPU expected, the OS being in charge of choosing how to schedule threads on the corresponding CPUs. The application can also choose to bind threads by hand, using e.g. sched_getaffinity to know the CPU binding mask that StarPU chose.

For instance, using OpenMP (full source is available in examples/openmp/vector_scal.c):

```
void scal_cpu_func(void *buffers[], void *_args)
{
    unsigned i;
    float *factor = _args;
    struct starpu_vector_interface *vector = buffers[0];
    unsigned n = STARPU_VECTOR_GET_NX(vector);
    float *val = (float *)STARPU_VECTOR_GET_PTR(vector);

#pragma omp parallel for num_threads(starpu_combined_worker_get_size())
    for (i = 0; i < n; i++)
        val[i] *= *factor;
}
```

```
static struct starpu_codelet cl =
{
    .modes = { STARPU_RW },
    .where = STARPU_CPU,
    .type = STARPU_FORKJOIN,
    .max_parallelism = INT_MAX,
    .cpu_funcs = {scal_cpu_func},
    .cpu_funcs_name = {"scal_cpu_func"},
    .nbuffers = 1,
};
```

Other examples include for instance calling a BLAS parallel CPU implementation (see `examples/mult/xgemm.-c`).

6.10.2 SPMD-mode Parallel Tasks

In the SPMD mode, StarPU will call the codelet function on each CPU of the combined worker. The codelet function can use starpu_combined_worker_get_size() to get the total number of CPUs involved in the combined worker, and thus the number of calls that are made in parallel to the function, and starpu_combined_worker_get_rank() to get the rank of the current CPU within the combined worker. For instance:

```
static void func(void *buffers[], void *args)
{
    unsigned i;
    float *factor = _args;
    struct starpu_vector_interface *vector = buffers[0];
    unsigned n = STARPU_VECTOR_GET_NX(vector);
    float *val = (float *)STARPU_VECTOR_GET_PTR(vector);

    /* Compute slice to compute */
    unsigned m = starpu_combined_worker_get_size
        ();
    unsigned j = starpu_combined_worker_get_rank
        ();
    unsigned slice = (n+m-1)/m;

    for (i = j * slice; i < (j+1) * slice && i < n; i++)
        val[i] *= *factor;
}
static struct starpu_codelet cl =
{
    .modes = { STARPU_RW },
    .type = STARPU_SPMD,
    .max_parallelism = INT_MAX,
    .cpu_funcs = { func },
    .cpu_funcs_name = { "func" },
    .nbuffers = 1,
}
```

Of course, this trivial example will not really benefit from parallel task execution, and was only meant to be simple to understand. The benefit comes when the computation to be done is so that threads have to e.g. exchange intermediate results, or write to the data in a complex but safe way in the same buffer.

6.10.3 Parallel Tasks Performance

To benefit from parallel tasks, a parallel-task-aware StarPU scheduler has to be used. When exposed to codelets with a flag STARPU_FORKJOIN or STARPU_SPMD, the schedulers `pheft` (parallel-heft) and `peager` (parallel eager) will indeed also try to execute tasks with several CPUs. It will automatically try the various available combined worker sizes (making several measurements for each worker size) and thus be able to avoid choosing a large combined worker if the codelet does not actually scale so much.

6.10.4 Combined Workers

By default, StarPU creates combined workers according to the architecture structure as detected by `hwloc`. It means that for each object of the `hwloc` topology (NUMA node, socket, cache, ...) a combined worker will be created. If some nodes of the hierarchy have a big arity (e.g. many cores in a socket without a hierarchy of shared caches), StarPU will create combined workers of intermediate sizes. The variable STARPU_SYNTHESIZE_ARIT-Y_COMBINED_WORKER permits to tune the maximum arity between levels of combined workers.

The combined workers actually produced can be seen in the output of the tool `starpu_machine_display` (the environment variable STARPU_SCHED has to be set to a combined worker-aware scheduler such as `pheft` or `peager`).

6.10.5 Concurrent Parallel Tasks

Unfortunately, many environments and librairies do not support concurrent calls.

For instance, most OpenMP implementations (including the main ones) do not support concurrent `pragma omp parallel` statements without nesting them in another `pragma omp parallel` statement, but StarPU does not yet support creating its CPU workers by using such pragma.

Other parallel libraries are also not safe when being invoked concurrently from different threads, due to the use of global variables in their sequential sections for instance.

The solution is then to use only one combined worker at a time. This can be done by setting the field starpu_conf-::single_combined_worker to 1, or setting the environment variable STARPU_SINGLE_COMBINED_WORKER to 1. StarPU will then run only one parallel task at a time (but other CPU and GPU tasks are not affected and can be run concurrently). The parallel task scheduler will however still however still try varying combined worker sizes to look for the most efficient ones.

6.10.6 Synchronization Tasks

For the application conveniency, it may be useful to define tasks which do not actually make any computation, but wear for instance dependencies between other tasks or tags, or to be submitted in callbacks, etc.

The obvious way is of course to make kernel functions empty, but such task will thus have to wait for a worker to become ready, transfer data, etc.

A much lighter way to define a synchronization task is to set its starpu_task::cl field to NULL. The task will thus be a mere synchronization point, without any data access or execution content: as soon as its dependencies become available, it will terminate, call the callbacks, and release dependencies.

An intermediate solution is to define a codelet with its starpu_codelet::where field set to STARPU_NOWHERE, for instance:

```
struct starpu_codelet cl =
{
        .where = STARPU_NOWHERE,
        .nbuffers = 1,
        .modes = { STARPU_R },
}

task = starpu_task_create();
task->cl = &cl;
task->handles[0] = handle;
starpu_task_submit(task);
```

will create a task which simply waits for the value of `handle` to be available for read. This task can then be depended on, etc.

Chapter 7

Data Management

TODO: intro qui parle de coherency entre autres

7.1 Data Interface

StarPU provides several data interfaces for programmers to describe the data layout of their application. There are predefined interfaces already available in StarPU. Users can define new data interfaces as explained in Defining A New Data Interface. All functions provided by StarPU are documented in Data Interfaces. You will find a short list below.

7.1.1 Variable Data Interface

A variable is a given size byte element, typically a scalar. Here an example of how to register a variable data to StarPU by using starpu_variable_data_register().

```
float var = 42.0;
starpu_data_handle_t var_handle;
starpu_variable_data_register(&var_handle,
    STARPU_MAIN_RAM, (uintptr_t)&var, sizeof(var));
```

7.1.2 Vector Data Interface

A vector is a fixed number of elements of a given size. Here an example of how to register a vector data to StarPU by using starpu_vector_data_register().

```
float vector[NX];
starpu_data_handle_t vector_handle;
starpu_vector_data_register(&vector_handle,
    STARPU_MAIN_RAM, (uintptr_t)vector, NX, sizeof(vector[0]));
```

7.1.3 Matrix Data Interface

To register 2-D matrices with a potential padding, one can use the matrix data interface. Here an example of how to register a matrix data to StarPU by using starpu_matrix_data_register().

```
float *matrix;
starpu_data_handle_t matrix_handle;
matrix = (float*)malloc(width * height * sizeof(float));
starpu_matrix_data_register(&matrix_handle,
    STARPU_MAIN_RAM, (uintptr_t)matrix, width, width, height, sizeof
    (float));
```

7.1.4 Block Data Interface

To register 3-D blocks with potential paddings on Y and Z dimensions, one can use the block data interface. Here an example of how to register a block data to StarPU by using starpu_block_data_register().

```
float *block;
starpu_data_handle_t block_handle;
block = (float*)malloc(nx*ny*nz*sizeof(float));
starpu_block_data_register(&block_handle,
      STARPU_MAIN_RAM, (uintptr_t)block, nx, nx*ny, nx, ny, nz, sizeof
      (float));
```

7.1.5 BCSR Data Interface

BCSR (Blocked Compressed Sparse Row Representation) sparse matrix data can be registered to StarPU using the bcsr data interface. Here an example on how to do so by using starpu_bcsr_data_register().

```
/*
   We use the following matrix:

   +----------------+
   |  0    1    0    0  |
   |  2    3    0    0  |
   |  4    5    8    9  |
   |  6    7   10   11  |
   +----------------+

   nzval  = [0, 1, 2, 3] ++ [4, 5, 6, 7] ++ [8, 9, 10, 11]
   colind = [0, 0, 1]
   rowptr = [0, 1 ]
   r = c = 2
*/

/* Size of the blocks */
int R = 2;
int C = 2;

int NROW = 2;
int NNZ_BLOCKS = 3;      /* out of 4 */
int NZVAL_SIZE = (R*C*NNZ_BLOCKS);

int nzval[NZVAL_SIZE]  =
{
      0, 1, 2, 3,      /* First block  */
      4, 5, 6, 7,      /* Second block */
      8, 9, 10, 11     /* Third block  */
};
uint32_t colind[NNZ_BLOCKS] =
{
      0, /* block-column index for first block in nzval */
      0, /* block-column index for second block in nzval */
      1  /* block-column index for third block in nzval */
};
uint32_t rowptr[NROW] =
{
      0, / * block-index in nzval of the first block of the first row. */
      1  / * block-index in nzval of the first block of the second row. */
};

starpu_data_handle_t bcsr_handle;
starpu_bcsr_data_register(&bcsr_handle,
                          STARPU_MAIN_RAM,
                          NNZ_BLOCKS,
                          NROW,
                          (uintptr_t) nzval,
                          colind,
                          rowptr,
                          0, /* firstentry */
                          R,
                          C,
                          sizeof(nzval[0]));
```

StarPU provides an example on how to deal with such matrices in examples/spmv.

7.1.6 CSR Data Interface

TODO

7.2 Data Management

When the application allocates data, whenever possible it should use the starpu_malloc() function, which will ask CUDA or OpenCL to make the allocation itself and pin the corresponding allocated memory, or to use the starpu_memory_pin() function to pin memory allocated by other ways, such as local arrays. This is needed to permit asynchronous data transfer, i.e. permit data transfer to overlap with computations. Otherwise, the trace will show that the `DriverCopyAsync` state takes a lot of time, this is because CUDA or OpenCL then reverts to synchronous transfers.

By default, StarPU leaves replicates of data wherever they were used, in case they will be re-used by other tasks, thus saving the data transfer time. When some task modifies some data, all the other replicates are invalidated, and only the processing unit which ran that task will have a valid replicate of the data. If the application knows that this data will not be re-used by further tasks, it should advise StarPU to immediately replicate it to a desired list of memory nodes (given through a bitmask). This can be understood like the write-through mode of CPU caches.

```
starpu_data_set_wt_mask(img_handle, 1<<0);
```

will for instance request to always automatically transfer a replicate into the main memory (node 0), as bit 0 of the write-through bitmask is being set.

```
starpu_data_set_wt_mask(img_handle, ~0U);
```

will request to always automatically broadcast the updated data to all memory nodes.

Setting the write-through mask to ~0U can also be useful to make sure all memory nodes always have a copy of the data, so that it is never evicted when memory gets scarse.

Implicit data dependency computation can become expensive if a lot of tasks access the same piece of data. If no dependency is required on some piece of data (e.g. because it is only accessed in read-only mode, or because write accesses are actually commutative), use the function starpu_data_set_sequential_consistency_flag() to disable implicit dependencies on that data.

In the same vein, accumulation of results in the same data can become a bottleneck. The use of the mode STARPU_REDUX permits to optimize such accumulation (see Data Reduction). To a lesser extent, the use of the flag STARPU_COMMUTE keeps the bottleneck (see Commute Data Access), but at least permits the accumulation to happen in any order.

Applications often need a data just for temporary results. In such a case, registration can be made without an initial value, for instance this produces a vector data:

```
starpu_vector_data_register(&handle, -1, 0, n,
    sizeof(float));
```

StarPU will then allocate the actual buffer only when it is actually needed, e.g. directly on the GPU without allocating in main memory.

In the same vein, once the temporary results are not useful any more, the data should be thrown away. If the handle is not to be reused, it can be unregistered:

```
starpu_data_unregister_submit(handle);
```

actual unregistration will be done after all tasks working on the handle terminate.

If the handle is to be reused, instead of unregistering it, it can simply be invalidated:

```
starpu_data_invalidate_submit(handle);
```

the buffers containing the current value will then be freed, and reallocated only when another task writes some value to the handle.

7.3   Data Prefetch

The scheduling policies `heft`, `dmda` and `pheft` perform data prefetch (see STARPU_PREFETCH): as soon as a scheduling decision is taken for a task, requests are issued to transfer its required data to the target processing unit, if needed, so that when the processing unit actually starts the task, its data will hopefully be already available and it will not have to wait for the transfer to finish.

The application may want to perform some manual prefetching, for several reasons such as excluding initial data transfers from performance measurements, or setting up an initial statically-computed data distribution on the machine before submitting tasks, which will thus guide StarPU toward an initial task distribution (since StarPU will try to avoid further transfers).

This can be achieved by giving the function starpu_data_prefetch_on_node() the handle and the desired target memory node. The starpu_data_idle_prefetch_on_node() variant can be used to issue the transfer only when the bus is idle.

Conversely, one can advise StarPU that some data will not be useful in the close future by calling starpu_data_-wont_use(). StarPU will then write its value back to its home node, and evict it from GPUs when room is needed.

7.4   Partitioning Data

An existing piece of data can be partitioned in sub parts to be used by different tasks, for instance:

```
int vector[NX];
starpu_data_handle_t handle;

/* Declare data to StarPU */
starpu_vector_data_register(&handle, STARPU_MAIN_RAM
    , (uintptr_t)vector,
                        NX, sizeof(vector[0]));
/* Partition the vector in PARTS sub-vectors */
struct starpu_data_filter f =
{
    .filter_func = starpu_vector_filter_block
    ,
    .nchildren = PARTS
};
starpu_data_partition(handle, &f);
```

The task submission then uses the function starpu_data_get_sub_data() to retrieve the sub-handles to be passed as tasks parameters.

```
/* Submit a task on each sub-vector */
for (i=0; i<starpu_data_get_nb_children(handle); i++
    )
{
    /* Get subdata number i (there is only 1 dimension) */
    starpu_data_handle_t sub_handle =
      starpu_data_get_sub_data(handle, 1, i);
    struct starpu_task *task = starpu_task_create(
      );

    task->handles[0] = sub_handle;
    task->cl = &cl;
    task->synchronous = 1;
    task->cl_arg = &factor;
    task->cl_arg_size = sizeof(factor);

    starpu_task_submit(task);
}
```

Partitioning can be applied several times, see `examples/basic_examples/mult.c` and `examples/filters/`.

Wherever the whole piece of data is already available, the partitioning will be done in-place, i.e. without allocating new buffers but just using pointers inside the existing copy. This is particularly important to be aware of when using OpenCL, where the kernel parameters are not pointers, but handles. The kernel thus needs to be also passed the offset within the OpenCL buffer:

```
void opencl_func(void *buffers[], void *cl_arg)
{
    cl_mem vector = (cl_mem) STARPU_VECTOR_GET_DEV_HANDLE
      (buffers[0]);
    unsigned offset = STARPU_BLOCK_GET_OFFSET(buffers[0]
      );

    ...
    clSetKernelArg(kernel, 0, sizeof(vector), &vector);
    clSetKernelArg(kernel, 1, sizeof(offset), &offset);
    ...
}
```

And the kernel has to shift from the pointer passed by the OpenCL driver:

```
__kernel void opencl_kernel(__global int *vector, unsigned offset)
{
    block = (__global void *)block + offset;
    ...
}
```

StarPU provides various interfaces and filters for matrices, vectors, etc., but applications can also write their own data interfaces and filters, see `examples/interface` and `examples/filters/custom_mf` for an example.

7.5 Asynchronous Partitioning

The partitioning functions described in the previous section are synchronous: starpu_data_partition() and starpu_data_unpartition() both wait for all the tasks currently working on the data. This can be a bottleneck for the application.

An asynchronous API also exists, it works only on handles with sequential consistency. The principle is to first plan the partitioning, which returns data handles of the partition, which are not functional yet. Along other task submission, one can submit the actual partitioning, and then use the handles of the partition. Before using the handle of the whole data, one has to submit the unpartitioning. `fmultiple_submit` is a complete example using this technique.

In short, we first register a matrix and plan the partitioning:

```
starpu_matrix_data_register(&handle, STARPU_MAIN_RAM
    , (uintptr_t)matrix, NX, NX, NY, sizeof(matrix[0]));
struct starpu_data_filter f_vert =
{
    .filter_func = starpu_matrix_filter_block
    ,
    .nchildren = PARTS
};
starpu_data_partition_plan(handle, &f_vert,
    vert_handle);
```

starpu_data_partition_plan() returns the handles for the partition in `vert_handle`.

One can submit tasks working on the main handle, but not yet on the `vert_handle` handles. Now we submit the partitioning:

```
starpu_data_partition_submit(handle, PARTS,
    vert_handle);
```

And now we can submit tasks working on `vert_handle` handles (and not on the main handle any more). Eventually we want to work on the main handle again, so we submit the unpartitioning:

```
starpu_data_unpartition_submit(handle, PARTS,
    vert_handle, -1);
```

And now we can submit tasks working on the main handle again.

All this code is asynchronous, just submitting which tasks, partitioning and unpartitioning should be done at runtime.

Planning several partitioning of the same data is also possible, one just has to submit unpartitioning (to get back to the initial handle) before submitting another partitioning.

It is also possible to activate several partitioning at the same time, in read-only mode, by using starpu_data_-partition_readonly_submit(). A complete example is available in `examples/filters/fmultiple_submit-_readonly.c`.

7.6   Manual Partitioning

One can also handle partitioning by hand, by registering several views on the same piece of data. The idea is then to manage the coherency of the various views through the common buffer in the main memory. `fmultiple_-manual` is a complete example using this technique.

In short, we first register the same matrix several times:

```
starpu_matrix_data_register(&handle, STARPU_MAIN_RAM
    , (uintptr_t)matrix, NX, NX, NY, sizeof(matrix[0]));

    (i = 0; i < PARTS; i++)
        starpu_matrix_data_register(&vert_handle[i],
        STARPU_MAIN_RAM, (uintptr_t)&matrix[0][i*(NX/PARTS)], NX, NX/
        PARTS, NY, sizeof(matrix[0][0]));
```

Since StarPU is not aware that the two handles are actually pointing to the same data, we have a danger of inadvertently submitting tasks to both views, which will bring a mess since StarPU will not guarantee any coherency between the two views. To make sure we don't do this, we invalidate the view that we will not use:

```
    (i = 0; i < PARTS; i++)
        starpu_data_invalidate(vert_handle[i]);
```

Then we can safely work on `handle`.

When we want to switch to the vertical slice view, all we need to do is bring coherency between them by running an empty task on the home node of the data:

```
void empty(void *buffers[] STARPU_ATTRIBUTE_UNUSED, void
        *cl_arg STARPU_ATTRIBUTE_UNUSED)
{ }
struct starpu_codelet cl_switch =
{
        .cpu_funcs = {empty},
        .nbuffers = STARPU_VARIABLE_NBUFFERS,
};

ret = starpu_task_insert(&cl_switch, STARPU_RW,
    handle,
                    STARPU_W, vert_handle[0],
                    STARPU_W, vert_handle[1],
                    0);
```

The execution of the `switch` task will get back the matrix data into the main memory, and thus the vertical slices will get the updated value there.

Again, we prefer to make sure that we don't accidentally access the matrix through the whole-matrix handle:

```
starpu_data_invalidate_submit(handle);
```

And now we can start using vertical slices, etc.

7.7   Data Reduction

In various cases, some piece of data is used to accumulate intermediate results. For instances, the dot product of a vector, maximum/minimum finding, the histogram of a photograph, etc. When these results are produced along the whole machine, it would not be efficient to accumulate them in only one place, incurring data transmission each and access concurrency.

StarPU provides a mode STARPU_REDUX, which permits to optimize that case: it will allocate a buffer on each memory node, and accumulate intermediate results there. When the data is eventually accessed in the normal mode STARPU_R, StarPU will collect the intermediate results in just one buffer.

For this to work, the user has to use the function starpu_data_set_reduction_methods() to declare how to initialize these buffers, and how to assemble partial results.

For instance, cg uses that to optimize its dot product: it first defines the codelets for initialization and reduction:

```
struct starpu_codelet bzero_variable_cl =
{
        .cpu_funcs = { bzero_variable_cpu },
        .cpu_funcs_name = { "bzero_variable_cpu" },
        .cuda_funcs = { bzero_variable_cuda },
        .nbuffers = 1,
}

static void accumulate_variable_cpu(void *descr[], void *cl_arg)
{
        double *v_dst = (double *)STARPU_VARIABLE_GET_PTR
(descr[0]);
        double *v_src = (double *)STARPU_VARIABLE_GET_PTR
(descr[1]);
        *v_dst = *v_dst + *v_src;
}

static void accumulate_variable_cuda(void *descr[], void *cl_arg)
{
        double *v_dst = (double *)STARPU_VARIABLE_GET_PTR
(descr[0]);
        double *v_src = (double *)STARPU_VARIABLE_GET_PTR
(descr[1]);
        cublasaxpy(1, (double)1.0, v_src, 1, v_dst, 1);
        cudaStreamSynchronize(starpu_cuda_get_local_stream
());
}

struct starpu_codelet accumulate_variable_cl =
{
        .cpu_funcs = { accumulate_variable_cpu },
        .cpu_funcs_name = { "accumulate_variable_cpu" },
        .cuda_funcs = { accumulate_variable_cuda },
        .nbuffers = 1,
}
```

and attaches them as reduction methods for its handle dtq:

```
starpu_variable_data_register(&dtq_handle, -1,
    NULL, sizeof(type));
starpu_data_set_reduction_methods(dtq_handle,
        &accumulate_variable_cl, &bzero_variable_cl);
```

and dtq_handle can now be used in mode STARPU_REDUX for the dot products with partitioned vectors:

```
for (b = 0; b < nblocks; b++)
   starpu_task_insert(&dot_kernel_cl,
      STARPU_REDUX, dtq_handle,
      STARPU_R, starpu_data_get_sub_data(v1,
   1, b),
      STARPU_R, starpu_data_get_sub_data(v2,
   1, b),
      0);
```

During registration, we have here provided NULL, i.e. there is no initial value to be taken into account during reduction. StarPU will thus only take into account the contributions from the tasks dot_kernel_cl. Also, it will not allocate any memory for dtq_handle before tasks dot_kernel_cl are ready to run.

If another dot product has to be performed, one could unregister dtq_handle, and re-register it. But one can also call starpu_data_invalidate_submit() with the parameter dtq_handle, which will clear all data from the handle, thus resetting it back to the initial status register(NULL).

The example cg also uses reduction for the blocked gemv kernel, leading to yet more relaxed dependencies and more parallelism.

STARPU_REDUX can also be passed to starpu_mpi_task_insert() in the MPI case. That will however not produce any MPI communication, but just pass STARPU_REDUX to the underlying starpu_task_insert(). It is up to the application to call starpu_mpi_redux_data(), which posts tasks that will reduce the partial results among MPI nodes into the MPI node which owns the data. For instance, some hypothetical application which collects partial results into data `res`, then uses it for other computation, before looping again with a new reduction:

```
    (i = 0; i < 100; i++)
{

    starpu_mpi_task_insert(MPI_COMM_WORLD, &init_res,
        STARPU_W, res, 0);
    starpu_mpi_task_insert(MPI_COMM_WORLD, &work,
        STARPU_RW, A,
            STARPU_R, B, STARPU_REDUX, res, 0);
    starpu_mpi_redux_data(MPI_COMM_WORLD, res);
    starpu_mpi_task_insert(MPI_COMM_WORLD, &work2,
        STARPU_RW, B, STARPU_R, res, 0);
}
```

7.8 Commute Data Access

By default, the implicit dependencies computed from data access use the sequential semantic. Notably, write accesses are always serialized in the order of submission. In some applicative cases, the write contributions can actually be performed in any order without affecting the eventual result. In that case it is useful to drop the strictly sequential semantic, to improve parallelism by allowing StarPU to reorder the write accesses. This can be done by using the STARPU_COMMUTE data access flag. Accesses without this flag will however properly be serialized against accesses with this flag. For instance:

```
starpu_task_insert(&cl1,
    STARPU_R, h,
    STARPU_RW, handle,
    0);
starpu_task_insert(&cl2,
    STARPU_R, handle1,
    STARPU_RW|STARPU_COMMUTE, handle,
    0);
starpu_task_insert(&cl2,
    STARPU_R, handle2,
    STARPU_RW|STARPU_COMMUTE, handle,
    0);
starpu_task_insert(&cl3,
    STARPU_R, g,
    STARPU_RW, handle,
    0);
```

The two tasks running `cl2` will be able to commute: depending on whether the value of `handle1` or `handle2` becomes available first, the corresponding task running `cl2` will start first. The task running `cl1` will however always be run before them, and the task running `cl3` will always be run after them.

If a lot of tasks use the commute access on the same set of data and a lot of them are ready at the same time, it may become interesting to use an arbiter, see Concurrent Data Accesses.

7.9 Concurrent Data Accesses

When several tasks are ready and will work on several data, StarPU is faced with the classical Dining Philosophers problem, and has to determine the order in which it will run the tasks.

Data accesses usually use sequential ordering, so data accesses are usually already serialized, and thus by default StarPU uses the Dijkstra solution which scales very well in terms of overhead: tasks will just acquire data one by one by data handle pointer value order.

When sequential ordering is disabled or the STARPU_COMMUTE flag is used, there may be a lot of concurrent accesses to the same data, and the Dijkstra solution gets only poor parallelism, typically in some pathological cases which do happen in various applications. In that case, one can use a data access arbiter, which implements the classical centralized solution for the Dining Philosophers problem. This is more expensive in terms of overhead since it is centralized, but it opportunistically gets a lot of parallelism. The centralization can also be avoided by using several arbiters, thus separating sets of data for which arbitration will be done. If a task accesses data from different arbiters, it will acquire them arbiter by arbiter, in arbiter pointer value order.

See the `tests/datawizard/test_arbiter.cpp` example.

Arbiters however do not support the STARPU_REDUX flag yet.

7.10 Temporary Buffers

There are two kinds of temporary buffers: temporary data which just pass results from a task to another, and scratch data which are needed only internally by tasks.

7.10.1 Temporary Data

Data can sometimes be entirely produced by a task, and entirely consumed by another task, without the need for other parts of the application to access it. In such case, registration can be done without prior allocation, by using the special memory node number -1, and passing a zero pointer. StarPU will actually allocate memory only when the task creating the content gets scheduled, and destroy it on unregistration.

In addition to that, it can be tedious for the application to have to unregister the data, since it will not use its content anyway. The unregistration can be done lazily by using the function starpu_data_unregister_submit(), which will record that no more tasks accessing the handle will be submitted, so that it can be freed as soon as the last task accessing it is over.

The following code examplifies both points: it registers the temporary data, submits three tasks accessing it, and records the data for automatic unregistration.

```
starpu_vector_data_register(&handle, -1, 0, n,
    sizeof(float));
starpu_task_insert(&produce_data, STARPU_W, handle, 0
    );
starpu_task_insert(&compute_data, STARPU_RW, handle,
    0);
starpu_task_insert(&summarize_data, STARPU_R, handle,
    STARPU_W, result_handle, 0);
starpu_data_unregister_submit(handle);
```

The application may also want to see the temporary data initialized on the fly before being used by the task. This can be done by using starpu_data_set_reduction_methods() to set an initialization codelet (no redux codelet is needed).

7.10.2 Scratch Data

Some kernels sometimes need temporary data to achieve the computations, i.e. a workspace. The application could allocate it at the start of the codelet function, and free it at the end, but that would be costly. It could also allocate one buffer per worker (similarly to How To Initialize A Computation Library Once For Each Worker?), but that would make them systematic and permanent. A more optimized way is to use the data access mode STARPU_SCRATCH, as examplified below, which provides per-worker buffers without content consistency. The buffer is registered only once, using memory node -1, i.e. the application didn't allocate memory for it, and StarPU will allocate it on demand at task execution.

```
starpu_vector_data_register(&workspace, -1, 0,
    sizeof(float));
for (i = 0; i < N; i++)
    starpu_task_insert(&compute, STARPU_R, input[i],
                STARPU_SCRATCH, workspace, STARPU_W
    , output[i], 0);
```

StarPU will make sure that the buffer is allocated before executing the task, and make this allocation per-worker: for CPU workers, notably, each worker has its own buffer. This means that each task submitted above will actually have its own workspace, which will actually be the same for all tasks running one after the other on the same worker.

Also, if for instance memory becomes scarce, StarPU will notice that it can free such buffers easily, since the content does not matter.

The example `examples/pi` uses scratches for some temporary buffer.

7.11 The Multiformat Interface

It may be interesting to represent the same piece of data using two different data structures: one that would only be used on CPUs, and one that would only be used on GPUs. This can be done by using the multiformat interface. StarPU will be able to convert data from one data structure to the other when needed. Note that the scheduler dmda is the only one optimized for this interface. The user must provide StarPU with conversion codelets:

```
#define NX 1024
struct point array_of_structs[NX];
starpu_data_handle_t handle;

/*
 * The conversion of a piece of data is itself a task, though it is created,
 * submitted and destroyed by StarPU internals and not by the user. Therefore,
 * we have to define two codelets.
 * Note that for now the conversion from the CPU format to the GPU format has
        to
 * be executed on the GPU, and the conversion from the GPU to the CPU has to be
 * executed on the CPU.
 */
#ifdef STARPU_USE_OPENCL
void cpu_to_opencl_opencl_func(void *buffers[], void *args);
struct starpu_codelet cpu_to_opencl_cl =
{
    .where = STARPU_OPENCL,
    .opencl_funcs = { cpu_to_opencl_opencl_func },
    .nbuffers = 1,
    .modes = { STARPU_RW }
};

void opencl_to_cpu_func(void *buffers[], void *args);
struct starpu_codelet opencl_to_cpu_cl =
{
    .where = STARPU_CPU,
    .cpu_funcs = { opencl_to_cpu_func },
    .cpu_funcs_name = { "opencl_to_cpu_func" },
    .nbuffers = 1,
    .modes = { STARPU_RW }
};
#endif

struct starpu_multiformat_data_interface_ops
        format_ops =
{
#ifdef STARPU_USE_OPENCL
    .opencl_elemsize = 2 * sizeof(float),
    .cpu_to_opencl_cl = &cpu_to_opencl_cl,
    .opencl_to_cpu_cl = &opencl_to_cpu_cl,
#endif
    .cpu_elemsize = 2 * sizeof(float),
    ...
};

starpu_multiformat_data_register(handle,
        STARPU_MAIN_RAM, &array_of_structs, NX, &format_ops);
```

Kernels can be written almost as for any other interface. Note that STARPU_MULTIFORMAT_GET_CPU_PTR shall only be used for CPU kernels. CUDA kernels must use STARPU_MULTIFORMAT_GET_CUDA_PTR, and OpenCL kernels must use STARPU_MULTIFORMAT_GET_OPENCL_PTR. STARPU_MULTIFORMAT_GET_NX may be used in any kind of kernel.

```
static void
multiformat_scal_cpu_func(void *buffers[], void *args)
{
    struct point *aos;
    unsigned int n;

    aos = STARPU_MULTIFORMAT_GET_CPU_PTR(buffers[
    0]);
    n = STARPU_MULTIFORMAT_GET_NX(buffers[0]);
    ...
```

```
}

extern "C" void multiformat_scal_cuda_func(void *buffers[], void *_args)
{
    unsigned int n;
    struct struct_of_arrays *soa;

    soa = (struct struct_of_arrays *) STARPU_MULTIFORMAT_GET_CUDA_PTR
      (buffers[0]);
    n = STARPU_MULTIFORMAT_GET_NX(buffers[0]);

    ...
}
```

A full example may be found in `examples/basic_examples/multiformat.c`.

7.12 Defining A New Data Interface

Let's define a new data interface to manage complex numbers.

```
/* interface for complex numbers */
struct starpu_complex_interface
{
        double *real;
        double *imaginary;
        int nx;
};
```

Registering such a data to StarPU is easily done using the function starpu_data_register(). The last parameter of the function, `interface_complex_ops`, will be described below.

```
void starpu_complex_data_register(starpu_data_handle_t *
    handle,
    unsigned home_node, double *real, double *imaginary, int nx)
{
        struct starpu_complex_interface complex =
        {
                .real = real,
                .imaginary = imaginary,
                .nx = nx
        };

        if (interface_complex_ops.interfaceid ==
    STARPU_UNKNOWN_INTERFACE_ID)
        {
                interface_complex_ops.interfaceid =
        starpu_data_interface_get_next_id();
        }

        starpu_data_register(handleptr, home_node, &complex
    , &interface_complex_ops);
}
```

Different operations need to be defined for a data interface through the type starpu_data_interface_ops. We only define here the basic operations needed to run simple applications. The source code for the different functions can be found in the file `examples/interface/complex_interface.c`.

```
static struct starpu_data_interface_ops
    interface_complex_ops =
{
        .register_data_handle =
    complex_register_data_handle,
        .allocate_data_on_node = complex_allocate_data_on_node,
        .copy_methods = &complex_copy_methods,
        .get_size = complex_get_size,
        .footprint = complex_footprint,
        .interfaceid = STARPU_UNKNOWN_INTERFACE_ID,
        .interface_size = sizeof(struct starpu_complex_interface),
};
```

Functions need to be defined to access the different fields of the complex interface from a StarPU data handle.

```
double *starpu_complex_get_real(starpu_data_handle_t handle
      )
{
        struct starpu_complex_interface *complex_interface =
          (struct starpu_complex_interface *) starpu_data_get_interface_on_node
      (handle, STARPU_MAIN_RAM);
              complex_interface->real;
}

double *starpu_complex_get_imaginary(starpu_data_handle_t
      handle);
int starpu_complex_get_nx(starpu_data_handle_t handle);
```

Similar functions need to be defined to access the different fields of the complex interface from a `void *` pointer to be used within codelet implementations.

```
#define STARPU_COMPLEX_GET_REAL(interface)        \
        (((struct starpu_complex_interface *)(interface))->real)
#define STARPU_COMPLEX_GET_IMAGINARY(interface) \
        (((struct starpu_complex_interface *)(interface))->imaginary)
#define STARPU_COMPLEX_GET_NX(interface)       \
        (((struct starpu_complex_interface *)(interface))->nx)
```

Complex data interfaces can then be registered to StarPU.

```
double real = 45.0;
double imaginary = 12.0;
starpu_complex_data_register(&handle1, STARPU_MAIN_RAM, &real, &
      imaginary, 1);
starpu_task_insert(&cl_display, STARPU_R, handle1, 0)
      ;
```

and used by codelets.

```
void display_complex_codelet(void *descr[], __attribute__ ((unused)) void *
      _args)
{
        int nx = STARPU_COMPLEX_GET_NX(descr[0]);
        double *real = STARPU_COMPLEX_GET_REAL(descr[0]);
        double *imaginary = STARPU_COMPLEX_GET_IMAGINARY(descr[0]);
        int i;

        (i=0 ; i<nx ; i++)
        {
                fprintf(stderr, "Complex[%d] = %3.2f + %3.2f i\n", i, real[i],
      imaginary[i]);
        }
}
```

The whole code for this complex data interface is available in the directory `examples/interface/`.

7.13 Specifying A Target Node For Task Data

When executing a task on a GPU for instance, StarPU would normally copy all the needed data for the tasks on the embedded memory of the GPU. It may however happen that the task kernel would rather have some of the datas kept in the main memory instead of copied in the GPU, a pivoting vector for instance. This can be achieved by setting the starpu_codelet::specific_nodes flag to 1, and then fill the starpu_codelet::nodes array (or starpu_-codelet::dyn_nodes when starpu_codelet::nbuffers is greater than STARPU_NMAXBUFS) with the node numbers where data should be copied to, or −1 to let StarPU copy it to the memory node where the task will be executed. For instance, with the following codelet:

```
struct starpu_codelet cl =
{
        .cuda_funcs = { kernel },
        .nbuffers = 2,
        .modes = {STARPU_RW, STARPU_RW},
        .specific_nodes = 1,
        .nodes = {STARPU_MAIN_RAM, -1},
};
```

the first data of the task will be kept in the main memory, while the second data will be copied to the CUDA GPU as usual.

Chapter 8

Scheduling

8.1 Task Scheduling Policies

The basics of the scheduling policy are that:

- The scheduler gets to schedule tasks (`push` operation) when they become ready to be executed, i.e. they are not waiting for some tags, data dependencies or task dependencies.

- Workers pull tasks (`pop` operation) one by one from the scheduler.

This means scheduling policies usually contain at least one queue of tasks to store them between the time when they become available, and the time when a worker gets to grab them.

By default, StarPU uses the simple greedy scheduler `eager`. This is because it provides correct load balance even if the application codelets do not have performance models. Other non-modelling scheduling policies can be selected among the list below, thanks to the environment variable STARPU_SCHED. For instance `export STARPU_SCHED=dmda`. Use `help` to get the list of available schedulers.

Non Performance Modelling Policies:

The **eager** scheduler uses a central task queue, from which all workers draw tasks to work on concurrently. This however does not permit to prefetch data since the scheduling decision is taken late. If a task has a non-0 priority, it is put at the front of the queue.

The **random** scheduler uses a queue per worker, and distributes tasks randomly according to assumed worker overall performance.

The **ws** (work stealing) scheduler uses a queue per worker, and schedules a task on the worker which released it by default. When a worker becomes idle, it steals a task from the most loaded worker.

The **lws** (locality work stealing) scheduler uses a queue per worker, and schedules a task on the worker which released it by default. When a worker becomes idle, it steals a task from neighbour workers. It also takes into account priorities.

The **prio** scheduler also uses a central task queue, but sorts tasks by priority specified by the programmer (between -5 and 5).

8.2 Performance Model-Based Task Scheduling Policies

If (**and only if**) your application **codelets have performance models** (Performance Model Example), you should change the scheduler thanks to the environment variable STARPU_SCHED, to select one of the policies below, in order to take advantage of StarPU's performance modelling. For instance `export STARPU_SCHED=dmda`. Use `help` to get the list of available schedulers.

Note: Depending on the performance model type chosen, some preliminary calibration runs may be needed for the model to converge. If the calibration has not been done, or is insufficient yet, or if no performance model is specified for a codelet, every task built from this codelet will be scheduled using an **eager** fallback policy.

Troubleshooting: Configuring and recompiling StarPU using the `-enable-verbose` configure flag displays some statistics at the end of execution about the percentage of tasks that have been scheduled by a DM* family policy using performance model hints. A low or zero percentage may be the sign that performance models are not converging or that codelets do not have performance models enabled.

Performance Modelling Policies:

The **dm** (deque model) scheduler takes task execution performance models into account to perform a HEFT-similar scheduling strategy: it schedules tasks where their termination time will be minimal. The difference with HEFT is that **dm** schedules tasks as soon as they become available, and thus in the order they become available, without taking priorities into account.

The **dmda** (deque model data aware) scheduler is similar to dm, but it also takes into account data transfer time.

The **dmdar** (deque model data aware ready) scheduler is similar to dmda, but it also sorts tasks on per-worker queues by number of already-available data buffers on the target device.

The **dmdas** (deque model data aware sorted) scheduler is similar to dmdar, except that it sorts tasks by priority order, which allows to become even closer to HEFT by respecting priorities after having made the scheduling decision (but it still schedules tasks in the order they become available).

The **dmdasd** (deque model data aware sorted decision) scheduler is similar to dmdas, except that when scheduling a task, it takes into account its priority when computing the minimum completion time, since this task may get executed before others, and thus the latter should be ignored.

The **heft** (heterogeneous earliest finish time) scheduler is a deprecated alias for **dmda**.

The **pheft** (parallel HEFT) scheduler is similar to dmda, it also supports parallel tasks (still experimental). Should not be used when several contexts using it are being executed simultaneously.

The **peager** (parallel eager) scheduler is similar to eager, it also supports parallel tasks (still experimental). Should not be used when several contexts using it are being executed simultaneously.

TODO: describe modular schedulers

8.3 Task Distribution Vs Data Transfer

Distributing tasks to balance the load induces data transfer penalty. StarPU thus needs to find a balance between both. The target function that the scheduler `dmda` of StarPU tries to minimize is `alpha * T_execution + beta * T_data_transfer`, where `T_execution` is the estimated execution time of the codelet (usually accurate), and `T_data_transfer` is the estimated data transfer time. The latter is estimated based on bus calibration before execution start, i.e. with an idle machine, thus without contention. You can force bus re-calibration by running the tool `starpu_calibrate_bus`. The beta parameter defaults to 1, but it can be worth trying to tweak it by using `export STARPU_SCHED_BETA=2` (STARPU_SCHED_BETA) for instance, since during real application execution, contention makes transfer times bigger. This is of course imprecise, but in practice, a rough estimation already gives the good results that a precise estimation would give.

8.4 Energy-based Scheduling

If the application can provide some energy consumption performance model (through the field starpu_codelet-::energy_model), StarPU will take it into account when distributing tasks. The target function that the scheduler `dmda` minimizes becomes `alpha * T_execution + beta * T_data_transfer + gamma * Consumption`, where `Consumption` is the estimated task consumption in Joules. To tune this parameter, use `export STARPU_SCHED_GAMMA=3000` (STARPU_SCHED_GAMMA) for instance, to express that each Joule (i.e kW during 1000us) is worth 3000us execution time penalty. Setting `alpha` and `beta` to zero permits to only take into account energy consumption.

This is however not sufficient to correctly optimize energy: the scheduler would simply tend to run all computations on the most energy-conservative processing unit. To account for the consumption of the whole machine (including idle processing units), the idle power of the machine should be given by setting `export STARPU_IDLE_PO-WER=200` (STARPU_IDLE_POWER) for 200W, for instance. This value can often be obtained from the machine power supplier.

The energy actually consumed by the total execution can be displayed by setting `export STARPU_PROFILI-NG=1 STARPU_WORKER_STATS=1`.

On-line task consumption measurement is currently only supported through the `CL_PROFILING_POWER_C-ONSUMED` OpenCL extension, implemented in the MoviSim simulator. Applications can however provide explicit measurements by using the function starpu_perfmodel_update_history() (examplified in Performance Model Example with the `energy_model` performance model). Fine-grain measurement is often not feasible with the feedback provided by the hardware, so the user can for instance run a given task a thousand times, measure the global consumption for that series of tasks, divide it by a thousand, repeat for varying kinds of tasks and task sizes, and eventually feed StarPU with these manual measurements through starpu_perfmodel_update_history(). For instance, for CUDA devices, `nvidia-smi -q -d POWER` can be used to get the current consumption in Watt. Multiplying that value by the average duration of a single task gives the consumption of the task in Joules, which can be given to starpu_perfmodel_update_history().

8.5 Static Scheduling

In some cases, one may want to force some scheduling, for instance force a given set of tasks to GPU0, another set to GPU1, etc. while letting some other tasks be scheduled on any other device. This can indeed be useful to guide StarPU into some work distribution, while still letting some degree of dynamism. For instance, to force execution of a task on CUDA0:

```
task->execute_on_a_specific_worker = 1;
task->workerid = starpu_worker_get_by_type(
    STARPU_CUDA_WORKER, 0);
```

One can also specify the order in which tasks must be executed by setting the starpu_task::workerorder field. If this field is set to a non-zero value, it provides the per-worker consecutive order in which tasks will be executed, starting from 1. For a given of such task, the worker will thus not execute it before all the tasks with smaller order value have been executed, notably in case those tasks are not available yet due to some dependencies. This eventually gives total control of task scheduling, and StarPU will only serve as a "self-timed" task runtime. Of course, the provided order has to be runnable, i.e. a task should should not depend on another task bound to the same worker with a bigger order.

Note however that using scheduling contexts while statically scheduling tasks on workers could be tricky. Be careful to schedule the tasks exactly on the workers of the corresponding contexts, otherwise the workers' corresponding scheduling structures may not be allocated or the execution of the application may deadlock. Moreover, the hypervisor should not be used when statically scheduling tasks.

8.6 Defining A New Scheduling Policy

A full example showing how to define a new scheduling policy is available in the StarPU sources in the directory `examples/scheduler/`.

The scheduler has to provide methods:

```
static struct starpu_sched_policy dummy_sched_policy =
{
    .init_sched = init_dummy_sched,
    .deinit_sched = deinit_dummy_sched,
    .add_workers = dummy_sched_add_workers,
    .remove_workers = dummy_sched_remove_workers,
    .push_task = push_task_dummy,
    .pop_task = pop_task_dummy,
    .policy_name = "dummy",
    .policy_description = "dummy scheduling strategy"
};
```

The idea is that when a task becomes ready for execution, the starpu_sched_policy::push_task method is called. When a worker is idle, the starpu_sched_policy::pop_task method is called to get a task. It is up to the scheduler to implement what is between. A simple eager scheduler is for instance to make starpu_sched_policy::push_task push the task to a global list, and make starpu_sched_policy::pop_task pop from that list.

The starpu_sched_policy section provides the exact rules that govern the methods of the policy.

Make sure to have a look at the Scheduling Policy section, which provides a list of the available functions for writing advanced schedulers, such as starpu_task_expected_length(), starpu_task_expected_data_transfer_time(), starpu_task_expected_energy(), etc. Other useful functions include starpu_transfer_bandwidth(), starpu_transfer_-latency(), starpu_transfer_predict(), ...

Usual functions can also be used on tasks, for instance one can do

```
size = 0;
write = 0;
   (task->cl)
       (i = 0; i < STARPU_TASK_GET_NBUFFERS(task); i++
   )
   {
       starpu_data_handle_t data = STARPU_TASK_GET_HANDLE
   (task, i)
       size_t datasize = starpu_data_get_size(data);
       size += datasize;
       if (STARPU_TASK_GET_MODE(task, i) & STARPU_W
   )
           write += datasize;
   }
```

And various queues can be used in schedulers. A variety of examples of schedulers can be read in `src/sched-_policies`, for instance `random_policy.c`, `eager_central_policy.c`, `work_stealing_-policy.c`

8.7   Graph-based Scheduling

For performance reasons, most of the schedulers shipped with StarPU use simple list-scheduling heuristics, assuming that the application has already set priorities. That is why they do their scheduling between when tasks become available for execution and when a worker becomes idle, without looking at the task graph.

Other heuristics can however look at the task graph. Recording the task graph is expensive, so it is not available by default, the scheduling heuristic has to set _starpu_graph_record to 1 from the initialization function, to make it available. Then the `_starpu_graph*` functions can be used.

`src/sched_policies/graph_test_policy.c` is an example of simple greedy policy which automatically computes priorities by bottom-up rank.

The idea is that while the application submits tasks, they are only pushed to a bag of tasks. When the application is finished with submitting tasks, it calls starpu_do_schedule() (or starpu_task_wait_for_all(), which calls starpu_-do_schedule()), and the starpu_sched_policy::do_schedule method of the scheduler is called. This method calls _starpu_graph_compute_depths to compute the bottom-up ranks, and then uses these rank to set priorities over tasks.

It then has two priority queues, one for CPUs, and one for GPUs, and uses a dumb heuristic based on the duration of the task over CPUs and GPUs to decide between the two queues. CPU workers can then pop from the CPU priority queue, and GPU workers from the GPU priority queue.

8.8   Debugging Scheduling

All the Online Performance Tools and Offline Performance Tools can be used to get information about how well the execution proceeded, and thus the overall quality of the execution.

Precise debugging can also be performed by using the STARPU_TASK_BREAK_ON_PUSH, STARPU_TASK_B-REAK_ON_SCHED, STARPU_TASK_BREAK_ON_POP, and STARPU_TASK_BREAK_ON_EXEC environment variables. By setting the job_id of a task in these environment variables, StarPU will raise `SIGTRAP` when the task is being scheduled, pushed, or popped by the scheduler. That means that when one notices that a task is being scheduled in a seemingly odd way, one can just reexecute the application in a debugger, with some of those variables set, and the execution will stop exactly at the scheduling points of that task, thus allowing to inspect the scheduler state, etc.

Chapter 9

Scheduling Contexts

TODO: improve!

9.1 General Ideas

Scheduling contexts represent abstracts sets of workers that allow the programmers to control the distribution of computational resources (i.e. CPUs and GPUs) to concurrent kernels. The main goal is to minimize interferences between the execution of multiple parallel kernels, by partitioning the underlying pool of workers using contexts. Scheduling contexts additionally allow a user to make use of a different scheduling policy depending on the target resource set.

9.2 Creating A Context To Partition a GPU

By default, the application submits tasks to an initial context, which disposes of all the computation resources available to StarPU (all the workers). If the application programmer plans to launch several kernels simultaneously, by default these kernels will be executed within this initial context, using a single scheduler policy(see Task Scheduling Policies). Meanwhile, if the application programmer is aware of the demands of these kernels and of the specificity of the machine used to execute them, the workers can be divided between several contexts. These scheduling contexts will isolate the execution of each kernel and they will permit the use of a scheduling policy proper to each one of them.

Scheduling Contexts may be created in two ways: either the programmers indicates the set of workers corresponding to each context (providing he knows the identifiers of the workers running within StarPU), or the programmer does not provide any worker list and leaves the Hypervisor assign workers to each context according to their needs (Scheduling Context Hypervisor).

Both cases require a call to the function starpu_sched_ctx_create(), which requires as input the worker list (the exact list or a NULL pointer), the amount of workers (or −1 to designate all workers on the platform) and a list of optional parameters such as the scheduling policy, terminated by a 0. The scheduling policy can be a character list corresponding to the name of a StarPU predefined policy or the pointer to a custom policy. The function returns an identifier of the context created which you will use to indicate the context you want to submit the tasks to.

```
/* the list of resources the context will manage */
int workerids[3] = {1, 3, 10};

/* indicate the list of workers assigned to it, the number of workers,
the name of the context and the scheduling policy to be used within
the context */
int id_ctx = starpu_sched_ctx_create(workerids, 3, "
    my_ctx", STARPU_SCHED_CTX_POLICY_NAME, "dmda", 0);

/* let StarPU know that the following tasks will be submitted to this context
    */
starpu_sched_ctx_set_task_context(id);
```

```
/* submit the task to StarPU */
starpu_task_submit(task);
```

Note: Parallel greedy and parallel heft scheduling policies do not support the existence of several disjoint contexts on the machine. Combined workers are constructed depending on the entire topology of the machine, not only the one belonging to a context.

9.2.1 Creating A Context With The Default Behavior

If **no scheduling policy** is specified when creating the context, it will be used as **another type of resource**: a cluster. A cluster is a context without scheduler (eventually delegated to another runtime). For more information see Clustering A Machine. It is therefore **mandatory** to stipulate a scheduler to use the contexts in this traditional way.

To create a **context** with the default scheduler, that is either controlled through the environment variable STARPU-_SCHED or the StarPU default scheduler, one can explicitly use the option STARPU_SCHED_CTX_POLICY_N-AME, "" as in the following example:

```
/* the list of resources the context will manage */
int workerids[3] = {1, 3, 10};

/* indicate the list of workers assigned to it, the number of workers,
and use the default scheduling policy. */
int id_ctx = starpu_sched_ctx_create(workerids, 3, "
    my_ctx", STARPU_SCHED_CTX_POLICY_NAME, "", 0);

/* .... */
```

9.3 Creating A Context To Partition a GPU

The contexts can also be used to group set of SMs of an NVIDIA GPU in order to isolate the parallel kernels and allow them to coexecution on a specified partiton of the GPU.

Each context will be mapped to a stream and the user can indicate the number of SMs. The context can be added to a larger context already grouping CPU cores. This larger context can use a scheduling policy that assigns tasks to both CPUs and contexts (partitions of the GPU) based on performance models adjusted to the number of SMs.

The GPU implementation of the task has to be modified accordingly and receive as a parameter the number of SMs.

```
/* get the available streams (suppose we have nstreams = 2 by specifying them
    with STARPU_NWORKER_PER_CUDA=2 */
int nstreams = starpu_worker_get_stream_workerids(gpu_devid, stream_workerids,
    STARPU_CUDA_WORKER);

int sched_ctx[nstreams];
sched_ctx[0] = starpu_sched_ctx_create(&stream_workerids
    [0], 1, "subctx", STARPU_SCHED_CTX_CUDA_NSMS, 6, 0);
sched_ctx[1] = starpu_sched_ctx_create(&stream_workerids
    [1], 1, "subctx", STARPU_SCHED_CTX_CUDA_NSMS, 7, 0);

int ncpus = 4;
int workers[ncpus+nstreams];
workers[ncpus+0] = stream_workerids[0];
workers[ncpus+1] = stream_workerids[1];

big_sched_ctx = starpu_sched_ctx_create(workers, ncpus+
    nstreams, "ctx1", STARPU_SCHED_CTX_SUB_CTXS, sched_ctxs,
    nstreams, STARPU_SCHED_CTX_POLICY_NAME, "dmdas", 0)
    ;

starpu_task_submit_to_ctx(task, big_sched_ctx);
```

9.4 Modifying A Context

A scheduling context can be modified dynamically. The application may change its requirements during the execution and the programmer can add additional workers to a context or remove those no longer needed. In the following example we have two scheduling contexts `sched_ctx1` and `sched_ctx2`. After executing a part of the tasks some of the workers of `sched_ctx1` will be moved to context `sched_ctx2`.

```
/* the list of ressources that context 1 will give away */
int workerids[3] = {1, 3, 10};

/* add the workers to context 1 */
starpu_sched_ctx_add_workers(workerids, 3,
    sched_ctx2);

/* remove the workers from context 2 */
starpu_sched_ctx_remove_workers(workerids, 3,
    sched_ctx1);
```

9.5   Submitting Tasks To A Context

The application may submit tasks to several contexts either simultaneously or sequnetially. If several threads of submission are used the function starpu_sched_ctx_set_context() may be called just before starpu_task_submit(). Thus StarPU considers that the current thread will submit tasks to the coresponding context.

When the application may not assign a thread of submission to each context, the id of the context must be indicated by using the function starpu_task_submit_to_ctx() or the field STARPU_SCHED_CTX for starpu_task_insert().

9.6   Deleting A Context

When a context is no longer needed it must be deleted. The application can indicate which context should keep the resources of a deleted one. All the tasks of the context should be executed before doing this. Thus, the programmer may use either a barrier and then delete the context directly, or just indicate that other tasks will not be submitted later on to the context (such that when the last task is executed its workers will be moved to the inheritor) and delete the context at the end of the execution (when a barrier will be used eventually).

```
/* when the context 2 is deleted context 1 inherits its resources */
starpu_sched_ctx_set_inheritor(sched_ctx2,
    sched_ctx1);

/* submit tasks to context 2 */
for (i = 0; i < ntasks; i++)
    starpu_task_submit_to_ctx(task[i],sched_ctx2);

/* indicate that context 2 finished submitting and that */
/* as soon as the last task of context 2 finished executing */
/* its workers can be moved to the inheritor context */
starpu_sched_ctx_finished_submit(sched_ctx1);

/* wait for the tasks of both contexts to finish */
starpu_task_wait_for_all();

/* delete context 2 */
starpu_sched_ctx_delete(sched_ctx2);

/* delete context 1 */
starpu_sched_ctx_delete(sched_ctx1);
```

9.7   Emptying A Context

A context may have no resources at the begining or at a certain moment of the execution. Task can still be submitted to these contexts and they will be executed as soon as the contexts will have resources. A list of tasks pending to be executed is kept and when workers are added to the contexts these tasks start being submitted. However, if resources are never allocated to the context the program will not terminate. If these tasks have low priority the programmer can forbid the application to submit them by calling the function starpu_sched_ctx_stop_task_-submission().

Chapter 10

Scheduling Context Hypervisor

10.1   What Is The Hypervisor

StarPU proposes a platform to construct Scheduling Contexts, to delete and modify them dynamically. A parallel kernel, can thus be isolated into a scheduling context and interferences between several parallel kernels are avoided. If users know exactly how many workers each scheduling context needs, they can assign them to the contexts at their creation time or modify them during the execution of the program.

The Scheduling Context Hypervisor Plugin is available for users who do not dispose of a regular parallelism, who cannot know in advance the exact size of the context and need to resize the contexts according to the behavior of the parallel kernels.

The Hypervisor receives information from StarPU concerning the execution of the tasks, the efficiency of the resources, etc. and it decides accordingly when and how the contexts can be resized. Basic strategies of resizing scheduling contexts already exist but a platform for implementing additional custom ones is available.

10.2   Start the Hypervisor

The Hypervisor must be initialized once at the beginning of the application. At this point a resizing policy should be indicated. This strategy depends on the information the application is able to provide to the hypervisor as well as on the accuracy needed for the resizing procedure. For example, the application may be able to provide an estimation of the workload of the contexts. In this situation the hypervisor may decide what resources the contexts need. However, if no information is provided the hypervisor evaluates the behavior of the resources and of the application and makes a guess about the future. The hypervisor resizes only the registered contexts.

10.3   Interrogate The Runtime

The runtime provides the hypervisor with information concerning the behavior of the resources and the application. This is done by using the `performance_counters` which represent callbacks indicating when the resources are idle or not efficient, when the application submits tasks or when it becomes to slow.

10.4   Trigger the Hypervisor

The resizing is triggered either when the application requires it (sc_hypervisor_resize_ctxs()) or when the initials distribution of resources alters the performance of the application (the application is to slow or the resource are idle for too long time). If the environment variable SC_HYPERVISOR_TRIGGER_RESIZE is set to `speed` the monitored speed of the contexts is compared to a theoretical value computed with a linear program, and the resizing is triggered whenever the two values do not correspond. Otherwise, if the environment variable is set to `idle` the hypervisor triggers the resizing algorithm whenever the workers are idle for a period longer than the threshold indicated by the programmer. When this happens different resizing strategy are applied that target minimizing the total execution of the application, the instant speed or the idle time of the resources.

10.5 Resizing Strategies

The plugin proposes several strategies for resizing the scheduling context.

The **Application driven** strategy uses users's input concerning the moment when they want to resize the contexts. Thus, users tag the task that should trigger the resizing process. One can set directly the field starpu_task::hypervisor_tag or use the macro STARPU_HYPERVISOR_TAG in the function starpu_task_insert().

```
task.hypervisor_tag = 2;
```

or

```
starpu_task_insert(&codelet,
                ...,
                STARPU_HYPERVISOR_TAG, 2,
                0);
```

Then users have to indicate that when a task with the specified tag is executed the contexts should resize.

```
sc_hypervisor_resize(sched_ctx, 2);
```

Users can use the same tag to change the resizing configuration of the contexts if they consider it necessary.

```
sc_hypervisor_ctl(sched_ctx,
                SC_HYPERVISOR_MIN_WORKERS, 6,
                SC_HYPERVISOR_MAX_WORKERS, 12,
                SC_HYPERVISOR_TIME_TO_APPLY, 2,
                NULL);
```

The **Idleness** based strategy moves workers unused in a certain context to another one needing them. (see Scheduling Context Hypervisor - Regular usage)

```
int workerids[3] = {1, 3, 10};
int workerids2[9] = {0, 2, 4, 5, 6, 7, 8, 9, 11};
sc_hypervisor_ctl(sched_ctx_id,
        SC_HYPERVISOR_MAX_IDLE, workerids, 3, 10000.0
    ,
        SC_HYPERVISOR_MAX_IDLE, workerids2, 9, 50000.
    0,
        NULL);
```

The **Gflops rate** based strategy resizes the scheduling contexts such that they all finish at the same time. The speed of each of them is computed and once one of them is significantly slower the resizing process is triggered. In order to do these computations users have to input the total number of instructions needed to be executed by the parallel kernels and the number of instruction to be executed by each task.

The number of flops to be executed by a context are passed as parameter when they are registered to the hypervisor,

```
sc_hypervisor_register_ctx(sched_ctx_id, flops)
```

and the one to be executed by each task are passed when the task is submitted. The corresponding field is starpu_task::flops and the corresponding macro in the function starpu_task_insert() is STARPU_FLOPS (**Caution**: but take care of passing a double, not an integer, otherwise parameter passing will be bogus). When the task is executed the resizing process is triggered.

```
task.flops = 100;
```

or

```
starpu_task_insert(&codelet,
                   ...,
                   STARPU_FLOPS, (double) 100,
                   0);
```

The **Feft** strategy uses a linear program to predict the best distribution of resources such that the application finishes in a minimum amount of time. As for the **Gflops rate** strategy the programmers has to indicate the total number of flops to be executed when registering the context. This number of flops may be updated dynamically during the execution of the application whenever this information is not very accurate from the beginning. The function sc_hypervisor_update_diff_total_flops() is called in order to add or to remove a difference to the flops left to be executed. Tasks are provided also the number of flops corresponding to each one of them. During the execution of the application the hypervisor monitors the consumed flops and recomputes the time left and the number of resources to use. The speed of each type of resource is (re)evaluated and inserter in the linear program in order to better adapt to the needs of the application.

The **Teft** strategy uses a linear program too, that considers all the types of tasks and the number of each of them and it tries to allocates resources such that the application finishes in a minimum amount of time. A previous calibration of StarPU would be useful in order to have good predictions of the execution time of each type of task.

The types of tasks may be determines directly by the hypervisor when they are submitted. However there are applications that do not expose all the graph of tasks from the beginning. In this case in order to let the hypervisor know about all the tasks the function sc_hypervisor_set_type_of_task() will just inform the hypervisor about future tasks without submitting them right away.

The **Ispeed** strategy divides the execution of the application in several frames. For each frame the hypervisor computes the speed of the contexts and tries making them run at the same speed. The strategy requires less contribution from users as the hypervisor requires only the size of the frame in terms of flops.

```
int workerids[3] = {1, 3, 10};
int workerids2[9] = {0, 2, 4, 5, 6, 7, 8, 9, 11};
sc_hypervisor_ctl(sched_ctx_id,
                  SC_HYPERVISOR_ISPEED_W_SAMPLE,
     workerids, 3, 2000000000.0,
                  SC_HYPERVISOR_ISPEED_W_SAMPLE,
     workerids2, 9, 200000000000.0,
                  SC_HYPERVISOR_ISPEED_CTX_SAMPLE
     , 60000000000.0,
         NULL);
```

The **Throughput** strategy focuses on maximizing the throughput of the resources and resizes the contexts such that the machine is running at its maximum efficiency (maximum instant speed of the workers).

10.6 Defining A New Hypervisor Policy

While Scheduling Context Hypervisor Plugin comes with a variety of resizing policies (see Resizing Strategies), it may sometimes be desirable to implement custom policies to address specific problems. The API described below allows users to write their own resizing policy.

Here an example of how to define a new policy

```
struct sc_hypervisor_policy dummy_policy =
{
     .handle_poped_task = dummy_handle_poped_task,
     .handle_pushed_task = dummy_handle_pushed_task,
     .handle_idle_cycle = dummy_handle_idle_cycle,
     .handle_idle_end = dummy_handle_idle_end,
     .handle_post_exec_hook = dummy_handle_post_exec_hook,
     .custom = 1,
     .name = "dummy"
};
```

Chapter 11

Modularized Scheduler

11.1 Introduction

StarPU's Modularized Schedulers are made of individual Scheduling Components Modularizedly assembled as a Scheduling Tree. Each Scheduling Component has an unique purpose, such as prioritizing tasks or mapping tasks over resources. A typical Scheduling Tree is shown below.

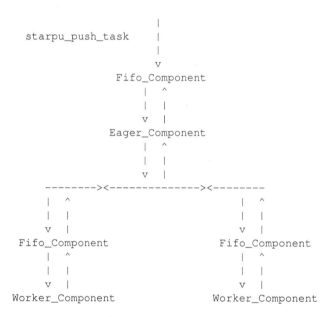

When a task is pushed by StarPU in a Modularized Scheduler, the task moves from a Scheduling Component to an other, following the hierarchy of the Scheduling Tree, and is stored in one of the Scheduling Components of the strategy. When a worker wants to pop a task from the Modularized Scheduler, the corresponding Worker Component of the Scheduling Tree tries to pull a task from its parents, following the hierarchy, and gives it to the worker if it succeded to get one.

11.2 Using Modularized Schedulers

11.2.1 Existing Modularized Schedulers

StarPU is currently shipped with the following pre-defined Modularized Schedulers :

- Eager-based Schedulers (with/without prefetching) :

Naive scheduler, which tries to map a task on the first available resource it finds.

- Prio-based Schedulers (with/without prefetching) :

  Similar to Eager-Based Schedulers. Can handle tasks which have a defined priority and schedule them accordingly.

- Random-based Schedulers (with/without prefetching) :

  Selects randomly a resource to be mapped on for each task.

- HEFT Scheduler :

  Heterogeneous Earliest Finish Time Scheduler. This scheduler needs that every task submitted to StarPU have a defined performance model (Performance Model Calibration) to work efficiently, but can handle tasks without a performance model.

To use one of these schedulers, one can set the environment variable STARPU_SCHED. All modularized schedulers are named following the RE tree-*

11.2.2 An Example : The Tree-Eager-Prefetching Strategy

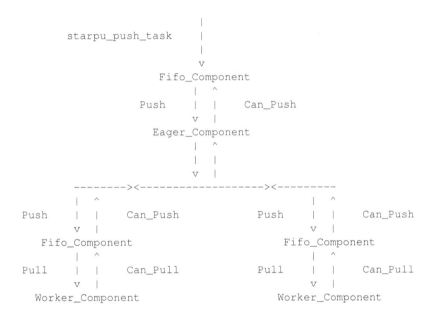

11.2.3 Interface

Each Scheduling Component must follow the following pre-defined Interface to be able to interact with other Scheduling Components.

- Push (Caller_Component, Child_Component, Task)

  The calling Scheduling Component transfers a task to its Child Component. When the Push function returns, the task no longer belongs to the calling Component. The Modularized Schedulers' model relies on this function to perform prefetching. See starpu_sched_component::push_task for more details

- Pull (Caller_Component, Parent_Component) -> Task

  The calling Scheduling Component requests a task from its Parent Component. When the Pull function ends, the returned task belongs to the calling Component. See starpu_sched_component::pull_task for more details

- Can_Push (Caller_Component, Parent_Component)

  The calling Scheduling Component notifies its Parent Component that it is ready to accept new tasks. See starpu_sched_component::can_push for more details

- Can_Pull (Caller_Component, Child_Component)

  The calling Scheduling Component notifies its Child Component that it is ready to give new tasks. See starpu_sched_component::can_pull for more details

11.3 Building a Modularized Scheduler

11.3.1 Pre-implemented Components

StarPU is currently shipped with the following four Scheduling Components :

- Flow-control Components : Fifo, Prio

  Components which store tasks. They can also prioritize them if they have a defined priority. It is possible to define a threshold for those Components following two criterias : the number of tasks stored in the Component, or the sum of the expected length of all tasks stored in the Component.

- Resource-Mapping Components : Mct, Heft, Eager, Random, Work-Stealing

  "Core" of the Scheduling Strategy, those Components are the ones who make scheduling choices.

- Worker Components : Worker

  Each Worker Component modelize a concrete worker.

- Special-Purpose Components : Perfmodel_Select, Best_Implementation

  Components dedicated to original purposes. The Perfmodel_Select Component decides which Resource-- Mapping Component should be used to schedule a task. The Best_Implementation Component chooses which implementation of a task should be used on the choosen resource.

11.3.2 Progression And Validation Rules

Some rules must be followed to ensure the correctness of a Modularized Scheduler :

- At least one Flow-control Component without threshold per Worker Component is needed in a Modularized Scheduler, to store incoming tasks from StarPU and to give tasks to Worker Components who asks for it. It is possible to use one Flow-control Component per Worker Component, or one for all Worker Components, depending on how the Scheduling Tree is defined.

- At least one Resource-Mapping Component is needed in a Modularized Scheduler. Resource-Mapping Components are the only ones who can make scheduling choices, and so the only ones who can have several child.

11.3.3 Implementing a Modularized Scheduler

The following code shows how the Tree-Eager-Prefetching Scheduler shown in Section An Example : The Tree-- Eager-Prefetching Strategy is implemented :

```
#define _STARPU_SCHED_NTASKS_THRESHOLD_DEFAULT 2
#define _STARPU_SCHED_EXP_LEN_THRESHOLD_DEFAULT 1000000000.0

static void initialize_eager_prefetching_center_policy(unsigned sched_ctx_id)
```

```
{
  unsigned ntasks_threshold = _STARPU_SCHED_NTASKS_THRESHOLD_DEFAULT;
  double exp_len_threshold = _STARPU_SCHED_EXP_LEN_THRESHOLD_DEFAULT;

  [...]

  starpu_sched_ctx_create_worker_collection
    (sched_ctx_id, STARPU_WORKER_LIST);

  /* Create the Scheduling Tree */
  struct starpu_sched_tree * t =
    starpu_sched_tree_create(sched_ctx_id);

  /* The Root Component is a Flow-control Fifo Component */
  t->root = starpu_sched_component_fifo_create
      (NULL);

  /* The Resource-mapping Component of the strategy is an Eager Component
   */
  struct starpu_sched_component * eager_component =
    starpu_sched_component_eager_create(NULL);

  /* Create links between Components : the Eager Component is the child
     of the Root Component */
  t->root->add_child
    (t->root, eager_component);
  eager_component->add_father
    (eager_component, t->root);

  /* A task threshold is set for the Flow-control Components which will
     be connected to Worker Components. By doing so, this Modularized
     Scheduler will be able to perform some prefetching on the resources
   */
  struct starpu_sched_component_fifo_data
      fifo_data =
  {
    .ntasks_threshold = ntasks_threshold,
    .exp_len_threshold = exp_len_threshold,
  };

  unsigned i;
    (i = 0;
    i < starpu_worker_get_count() +
    starpu_combined_worker_get_count();
    i++)
  {
    /* Each Worker Component has a Flow-control Fifo Component as
       father */
    struct starpu_sched_component * worker_component =
        starpu_sched_component_worker_new(i);
    struct starpu_sched_component * fifo_component =
        starpu_sched_component_fifo_create(
      &fifo_data);
    fifo_component->add_child
      (fifo_component, worker_component);
    worker_component->add_father
      (worker_component, fifo_component);

    /* Each Flow-control Fifo Component associated to a Worker
       Component is linked to the Eager Component as one of its
       children */
    eager_component->add_child
      (eager_component, fifo_component);
    fifo_component->add_father
      (fifo_component, eager_component);
  }

  starpu_sched_tree_update_workers(t);
  starpu_sched_ctx_set_policy_data
    (sched_ctx_id, (void*)t);
}

/* Properly destroy the Scheduling Tree and all its Components */
static void deinitialize_eager_prefetching_center_policy(unsigned sched_ctx_id)
{
  struct starpu_sched_tree * tree =
      (struct starpu_sched_tree*)
      starpu_sched_ctx_get_policy_data(sched_ctx_id);
  starpu_sched_tree_destroy(tree);
  starpu_sched_ctx_delete_worker_collection
    (sched_ctx_id);
}

/* Initializing the starpu_sched_policy struct associated to the Modularized
   Scheduler : only the init_sched and deinit_sched needs to be defined to
   implement a Modularized Scheduler */
struct starpu_sched_policy
```

```
      _starpu_sched_tree_eager_prefetching_policy =
{
  .init_sched = initialize_eager_prefetching_center_policy,
  .deinit_sched = deinitialize_eager_prefetching_center_policy,
  .add_workers = starpu_sched_tree_add_workers,
  .remove_workers = starpu_sched_tree_remove_workers
            ,
  .push_task = starpu_sched_tree_push_task,
  .pop_task = starpu_sched_tree_pop_task,
  .pre_exec_hook = starpu_sched_component_worker_pre_exec_hook
            ,
  .post_exec_hook = starpu_sched_component_worker_post_exec_hook
            ,
  .pop_every_task = NULL,
  .policy_name = "tree-eager-prefetching",
  .policy_description = "eager with prefetching tree policy"
};
```

11.4 Writing a Scheduling Component

11.4.1 Generic Scheduling Component

Each Scheduling Component is instantiated from a Generic Scheduling Component, which implements a generic version of the Interface. The generic implementation of Pull, Can_Pull and Can_Push functions are recursive calls to their parents (respectively to their children). However, as a Generic Scheduling Component do not know how much children it will have when it will be instantiated, it does not implement the Push function.

11.4.2 Instantiation : Redefining the Interface

A Scheduling Component must implement all the functions of the Interface. It is so necessary to implement a Push function to instantiate a Scheduling Component. The implemented Push function is the "fingerprint" of a Scheduling Component. Depending on how functionalities or properties the programmer wants to give to the Scheduling Component he is implementing, it is possible to reimplement all the functions of the Interface. For example, a Flow-control Component reimplements the Pull and the Can_Push functions of the Interface, allowing him to catch the generic recursive calls of these functions. The Pull function of a Flow-control Component can, for example, pop a task from the local storage queue of the Component, and give it to the calling Component which asks for it.

11.4.3 Detailed Progression and Validation Rules

- A Reservoir is a Scheduling Component which redefines a Push and a Pull function, in order to store tasks into it. A Reservoir delimit Scheduling Areas in the Scheduling Tree.

- A Pump is the engine source of the Scheduler : it pushes/pulls tasks to/from a Scheduling Component to an other. Native Pumps of a Scheduling Tree are located at the root of the Tree (incoming Push calls from StarPU), and at the leafs of the Tree (Pop calls coming from StarPU Workers). Pre-implemented Scheduling Components currently shipped with Pumps are Flow-Control Components and the Resource-Mapping Component Heft, within their defined Can_Push functions.

- A correct Scheduling Tree requires a Pump per Scheduling Area and per Execution Flow.

The Tree-Eager-Prefetching Scheduler shown in Section An Example : The Tree-Eager-Prefetching Strategy follows the previous assumptions :

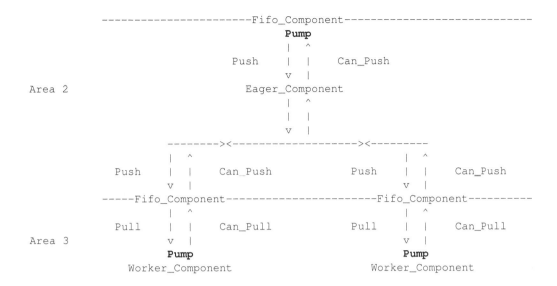

Chapter 12

Debugging Tools

StarPU provides several tools to help debugging applications. Execution traces can be generated and displayed graphically, see Generating Traces With FxT.

12.1 TroubleShooting In General

Generally-speaking, if you have troubles, pass --enable-debug to `./configure` to enable some checks which impact performance, but will catch common issues, possibly earlier than the actual problem you are observing, which may just be a consequence of a bug that happened earlier. Also, make sure not to have the --enable-fast option which drops very useful catchup assertions. If your program is valgrind-safe, you can use it, see Using Other Debugging Tools.

Depending on your toolchain, it might happen that you get `undefined reference to '__stack_chk_-guard'` errors. In that case, use the `-disable-fstack-protector-all` option to avoid the issue.

Then, if your program crashes with an assertion error, a segfault, etc. you can send us the result of

```
thread apply all bt
```

run in `gdb` at the point of the crash.

In case your program just hangs, but it may also be useful in case of a crash too, it helps to source `gdbinit` as described in the next section to be able to run and send us the output of the following commands:

```
starpu-workers
starpu-tasks
starpu-print-requests
starpu-print-prequests
starpu-print-frrequests
starpu-print-irrequests
```

To give us an idea of what is happening within StarPU. If the outputs are not too long, you can even run

```
starpu-all-tasks
starpu-print-all-tasks
starpu-print-datas-summary
starpu-print-datas
```

12.2 Using The Gdb Debugger

Some `gdb` helpers are provided to show the whole StarPU state:

```
(gdb) source tools/gdbinit
(gdb) help starpu
```

For instance,

- one can print all tasks with `starpu-print-all-tasks`,

- print all datas with `starpu-print-datas`,

- print all pending data transfers with `starpu-print-prequests`, `starpu-print-requests`, `starpu-print-frequests`, `starpu-print-irequests`,

- print pending MPI requests with `starpu-mpi-print-detached-requests`

Some functions can only work if --enable-debug was passed to `./configure` (because they impact performance)

12.3   Using Other Debugging Tools

Valgrind can be used on StarPU: valgrind.h just needs to be found at `./configure` time, to tell valgrind about some known false positives and disable host memory pinning. Other known false positives can be suppressed by giving the suppression files in `tools/valgrind/*.suppr` to valgrind's `-suppressions` option.

The environment variable STARPU_DISABLE_KERNELS can also be set to `1` to make StarPU does everything (schedule tasks, transfer memory, etc.) except actually calling the application-provided kernel functions, i.e. the computation will not happen. This permits to quickly check that the task scheme is working properly.

12.4   Using The Temanejo Task Debugger

StarPU can connect to Temanejo >= 1.0rc2 (see http://www.hlrs.de/temanejo), to permit nice visual task debugging. To do so, build Temanejo's `libayudame.so`, install `Ayudame.h` to e.g. `/usr/local/include`, apply the `tools/patch-ayudame` to it to fix C build, re-`./configure`, make sure that it found it, rebuild StarPU. Run the Temanejo GUI, give it the path to your application, any options you want to pass it, the path to `libayudame.so`.

It permits to visualize the task graph, add breakpoints, continue execution task-by-task, and run `gdb` on a given task, etc.

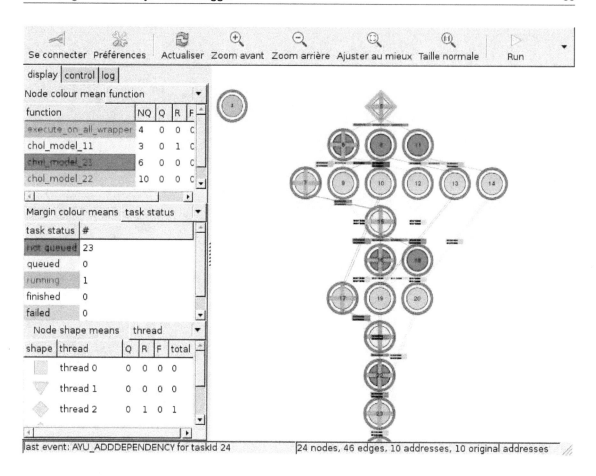

Make sure to specify at least the same number of CPUs in the dialog box as your machine has, otherwise an error will happen during execution. Future versions of Temanejo should be able to tell StarPU the number of CPUs to use.

Tag numbers have to be below `4000000000000000000ULL` to be usable for Temanejo (so as to distinguish them from tasks).

Chapter 13

Online Performance Tools

13.1 On-line Performance Feedback

13.1.1 Enabling On-line Performance Monitoring

In order to enable online performance monitoring, the application can call starpu_profiling_status_set() with the parameter STARPU_PROFILING_ENABLE. It is possible to detect whether monitoring is already enabled or not by calling starpu_profiling_status_get(). Enabling monitoring also reinitialize all previously collected feedback. The environment variable STARPU_PROFILING can also be set to 1 to achieve the same effect. The function starpu_-profiling_init() can also be called during the execution to reinitialize performance counters and to start the profiling if the environment variable STARPU_PROFILING is set to 1.

Likewise, performance monitoring is stopped by calling starpu_profiling_status_set() with the parameter STARPU_-PROFILING_DISABLE. Note that this does not reset the performance counters so that the application may consult them later on.

More details about the performance monitoring API are available in Profiling.

13.1.2 Per-task Feedback

If profiling is enabled, a pointer to a structure starpu_profiling_task_info is put in the field starpu_task::profiling_-info when a task terminates. This structure is automatically destroyed when the task structure is destroyed, either automatically or by calling starpu_task_destroy().

The structure starpu_profiling_task_info indicates the date when the task was submitted (starpu_profiling_task_-info::submit_time), started (starpu_profiling_task_info::start_time), and terminated (starpu_profiling_task_info::end-_time), relative to the initialization of StarPU with starpu_init(). It also specifies the identifier of the worker that has executed the task (starpu_profiling_task_info::workerid). These date are stored as timespec structures which the user may convert into micro-seconds using the helper function starpu_timing_timespec_to_us().

It it worth noting that the application may directly access this structure from the callback executed at the end of the task. The structure starpu_task associated to the callback currently being executed is indeed accessible with the function starpu_task_get_current().

13.1.3 Per-codelet Feedback

The field starpu_codelet::per_worker_stats is an array of counters. The i-th entry of the array is incremented every time a task implementing the codelet is executed on the i-th worker. This array is not reinitialized when profiling is enabled or disabled.

13.1.4 Per-worker Feedback

The second argument returned by the function starpu_profiling_worker_get_info() is a structure starpu_profiling_worker_info that gives statistics about the specified worker. This structure specifies when StarPU started collecting profiling information for that worker (starpu_profiling_worker_info::start_time), the duration of the profiling measurement interval (starpu_profiling_worker_info::total_time), the time spent executing kernels (starpu_profiling_worker_info::executing_time), the time spent sleeping because there is no task to execute at all (starpu_profiling_worker_info::sleeping_time), and the number of tasks that were executed while profiling was enabled. These values give an estimation of the proportion of time spent do real work, and the time spent either sleeping because there are not enough executable tasks or simply wasted in pure StarPU overhead.

Calling starpu_profiling_worker_get_info() resets the profiling information associated to a worker.

To easily display all this information, the environment variable STARPU_WORKER_STATS can be set to 1 (in addition to setting STARPU_PROFILING to 1). A summary will then be displayed at program termination:

```
Worker stats:
CUDA 0.0 (4.7 GiB)
480 task(s)
total: 1574.82 ms executing: 1510.72 ms sleeping: 0.00 ms overhead 64.10 ms
325.217970 GFlop/s

CPU 0
22 task(s)
total: 1574.82 ms executing: 1364.81 ms sleeping: 0.00 ms overhead 210.01 ms
7.512057 GFlop/s

CPU 1
14 task(s)
total: 1574.82 ms executing: 1500.13 ms sleeping: 0.00 ms overhead 74.69 ms
6.675853 GFlop/s

CPU 2
14 task(s)
total: 1574.82 ms executing: 1553.12 ms sleeping: 0.00 ms overhead 21.70 ms
7.152886 GFlop/s
```

The number of GFlops is available because the starpu_task::flops field of the tasks were filled (or STARPU_FLOPS used in starpu_task_insert()).

When an FxT trace is generated (see Generating Traces With FxT), it is also possible to use the tool starpu_workers_activity (see Monitoring Activity) to generate a graphic showing the evolution of these values during the time, for the different workers.

13.1.5 Bus-related Feedback

The bus speed measured by StarPU can be displayed by using the tool starpu_machine_display, for instance:

```
StarPU has found:
        3 CUDA devices
                CUDA 0 (Tesla C2050 02:00.0)
                CUDA 1 (Tesla C2050 03:00.0)
                CUDA 2 (Tesla C2050 84:00.0)
from    to RAM          to CUDA 0       to CUDA 1       to CUDA 2
RAM     0.000000        5176.530428     5176.492994     5191.710722
CUDA 0  4523.732446     0.000000        2414.074751     2417.379201
CUDA 1  4523.718152     2414.078822     0.000000        2417.375119
CUDA 2  4534.229519     2417.069025     2417.060863     0.000000
```

Statistics about the data transfers which were performed and temporal average of bandwidth usage can be obtained by setting the environment variable STARPU_BUS_STATS to 1; a summary will then be displayed at program termination:

```
Data transfer stats:
```

```
RAM 0 -> CUDA 0 319.92 MB 213.10 MB/s (transfers : 91 - avg 3.52 MB)
CUDA 0 -> RAM 0 214.45 MB 142.85 MB/s (transfers : 61 - avg 3.52 MB)
RAM 0 -> CUDA 1 302.34 MB 201.39 MB/s (transfers : 86 - avg 3.52 MB)
CUDA 1 -> RAM 0 133.59 MB 88.99 MB/s (transfers : 38 - avg 3.52 MB)
CUDA 0 -> CUDA 1 144.14 MB 96.01 MB/s (transfers : 41 - avg 3.52 MB)
CUDA 1 -> CUDA 0 130.08 MB 86.64 MB/s (transfers : 37 - avg 3.52 MB)
RAM 0 -> CUDA 2 312.89 MB 208.42 MB/s (transfers : 89 - avg 3.52 MB)
CUDA 2 -> RAM 0 133.59 MB 88.99 MB/s (transfers : 38 - avg 3.52 MB)
CUDA 0 -> CUDA 2 151.17 MB 100.69 MB/s (transfers : 43 - avg 3.52 MB)
CUDA 2 -> CUDA 0 105.47 MB 70.25 MB/s (transfers : 30 - avg 3.52 MB)
CUDA 1 -> CUDA 2 175.78 MB 117.09 MB/s (transfers : 50 - avg 3.52 MB)
CUDA 2 -> CUDA 1 203.91 MB 135.82 MB/s (transfers : 58 - avg 3.52 MB)
Total transfers: 2.27 GB
```

13.1.6 StarPU-Top Interface

StarPU-Top is an interface which remotely displays the on-line state of a StarPU application and permits the user to change parameters on the fly.

Variables to be monitored can be registered by calling the functions starpu_top_add_data_boolean(), starpu_top_add_data_integer(), starpu_top_add_data_float(), e.g.:

```
starpu_top_data *data = starpu_top_add_data_integer
    ("mynum", 0, 100, 1);
```

The application should then call starpu_top_init_and_wait() to give its name and wait for StarPU-Top to get a start request from the user. The name is used by StarPU-Top to quickly reload a previously-saved layout of parameter display.

```
starpu_top_init_and_wait("the application");
```

The new values can then be provided thanks to starpu_top_update_data_boolean(), starpu_top_update_data_integer(), starpu_top_update_data_float(), e.g.:

```
starpu_top_update_data_integer(data, mynum);
```

Updateable parameters can be registered thanks to starpu_top_register_parameter_boolean(), starpu_top_register_parameter_integer(), starpu_top_register_parameter_float(), e.g.:

```
float alpha;
starpu_top_register_parameter_float("alpha",
    &alpha, 0, 10, modif_hook);
```

modif_hook is a function which will be called when the parameter is being modified, it can for instance print the new value:

```
void modif_hook(struct starpu_top_param *d)
{
    fprintf(stderr,"%s has been modified: %f\n", d->name, alpha);
}
```

Task schedulers should notify StarPU-Top when it has decided when a task will be scheduled, so that it can show it in its Gantt chart, for instance:

```
starpu_top_task_prevision(task, workerid, begin, end);
```

Starting StarPU-Top (StarPU-Top is started via the binary starpu_top) and the application can be done in two ways:

- The application is started by hand on some machine (and thus already waiting for the start event). In the Preference dialog of StarPU-Top, the SSH checkbox should be unchecked, and the hostname and port (default is 2011) on which the application is already running should be specified. Clicking on the connection button will thus connect to the already-running application.

- StarPU-Top is started first, and clicking on the connection button will start the application itself (possibly on a remote machine). The SSH checkbox should be checked, and a command line provided, e.g.:

```
$ ssh myserver STARPU_SCHED=dmda ./application
```

If port 2011 of the remote machine can not be accessed directly, an ssh port bridge should be added:

```
$ ssh -L 2011:localhost:2011 myserver STARPU_SCHED=dmda ./application
```

and "localhost" should be used as IP Address to connect to.

13.2 Task And Worker Profiling

A full example showing how to use the profiling API is available in the StarPU sources in the directory `examples/profiling/`.

```
struct starpu_task *task = starpu_task_create();
task->cl = &cl;
task->synchronous = 1;
/* We will destroy the task structure by hand so that we can
   query the profiling info before the task is destroyed. */
task->destroy = 0;

/* Submit and wait for completion (since synchronous was set to 1) */
starpu_task_submit(task);

/* The task is finished, get profiling information */
struct starpu_profiling_task_info *info = task->
    profiling_info;

/* How much time did it take before the task started ? */
double delay += starpu_timing_timespec_delay_us(
    &info->submit_time, &info->start_time);

/* How long was the task execution ? */
double length += starpu_timing_timespec_delay_us
    (&info->start_time, &info->end_time);

/* We no longer need the task structure */
starpu_task_destroy(task);


/* Display the occupancy of all workers during the test */
int worker;
    (worker = 0; worker < starpu_worker_get_count();
    worker++)
{
        struct starpu_profiling_worker_info
    worker_info;
        int ret = starpu_profiling_worker_get_info
    (worker, &worker_info);
        STARPU_ASSERT(!ret);

        double total_time = starpu_timing_timespec_to_us
    (&worker_info.total_time);
        double executing_time = starpu_timing_timespec_to_us
    (&worker_info.executing_time);
        double sleeping_time = starpu_timing_timespec_to_us
    (&worker_info.sleeping_time);
        double overhead_time = total_time - executing_time - sleeping_time
    ;

        float executing_ratio = 100.0*executing_time/total_time;
        float sleeping_ratio = 100.0*sleeping_time/total_time;
        float overhead_ratio = 100.0 - executing_ratio - sleeping_ratio;

        char workername[128];
        starpu_worker_get_name(worker, workername, 128);
        fprintf(stderr, "Worker %s:\n", workername);
        fprintf(stderr, "\ttotal time: %.2lf ms\n", total_time*1e-3);
        fprintf(stderr, "\texec time: %.2lf ms (%.2f %%)\n",
            executing_time*1e-3, executing_ratio);
        fprintf(stderr, "\tblocked time: %.2lf ms (%.2f %%)\n",
            sleeping_time*1e-3, sleeping_ratio);
        fprintf(stderr, "\toverhead time: %.2lf ms (%.2f %%)\n",
            overhead_time*1e-3, overhead_ratio);
}
```

13.3   Performance Model Example

To achieve good scheduling, StarPU scheduling policies need to be able to estimate in advance the duration of a task. This is done by giving to codelets a performance model, by defining a structure starpu_perfmodel and providing its address in the field starpu_codelet::model. The fields starpu_perfmodel::symbol and starpu_perfmodel::type are mandatory, to give a name to the model, and the type of the model, since there are several kinds of performance models. For compatibility, make sure to initialize the whole structure to zero, either by using explicit memset(), or by letting the compiler implicitly do it as examplified below.

- Measured at runtime (model type STARPU_HISTORY_BASED). This assumes that for a given set of data input/output sizes, the performance will always be about the same. This is very true for regular kernels on GPUs for instance (<0.1% error), and just a bit less true on CPUs (~=1% error). This also assumes that there are few different sets of data input/output sizes. StarPU will then keep record of the average time of previous executions on the various processing units, and use it as an estimation. History is done per task size, by using a hash of the input and ouput sizes as an index. It will also save it in $STARPU_HOME/.starpu/sampling/codelets for further executions, and can be observed by using the tool starpu_perfmodel_display, or drawn by using the tool starpu_perfmodel_plot (Performance Model Calibration). The models are indexed by machine name. To share the models between machines (e.g. for a homogeneous cluster), use export STARPU_HOSTNAME=some_global_name. Measurements are only done when using a task scheduler which makes use of it, such as dmda. Measurements can also be provided explicitly by the application, by using the function starpu_perfmodel_update_history().

  The following is a small code example.

  If e.g. the code is recompiled with other compilation options, or several variants of the code are used, the symbol string should be changed to reflect that, in order to recalibrate a new model from zero. The symbol string can even be constructed dynamically at execution time, as long as this is done before submitting any task using it.

```
static struct starpu_perfmodel mult_perf_model =
{
    .type = STARPU_HISTORY_BASED,
    .symbol = "mult_perf_model"
};

struct starpu_codelet cl =
{
    .cpu_funcs = { cpu_mult },
    .cpu_funcs_name = { "cpu_mult" },
    .nbuffers = 3,
    .modes = { STARPU_R, STARPU_R, STARPU_W },
    /* for the scheduling policy to be able to use performance models */
    .model = &mult_perf_model
};
```

- Measured at runtime and refined by regression (model types STARPU_REGRESSION_BASED and STARPU_NL_REGRESSION_BASED). This still assumes performance regularity, but works with various data input sizes, by applying regression over observed execution times. STARPU_REGRESSION_BASED uses an $a*n^b$ regression form, STARPU_NL_REGRESSION_BASED uses an $a*n^b+c$ (more precise than STARPU_REGRESSION_BASED, but costs a lot more to compute).

  For instance, tests/perfmodels/regression_based.c uses a regression-based performance model for the function memset().

  Of course, the application has to issue tasks with varying size so that the regression can be computed. StarPU will not trust the regression unless there is at least 10% difference between the minimum and maximum observed input size. It can be useful to set the environment variable STARPU_CALIBRATE to 1 and run the application on varying input sizes with STARPU_SCHED set to dmda scheduler, so as to feed the performance model for a variety of inputs. The application can also provide the measurements explictly by using the function starpu_perfmodel_update_history(). The tools starpu_perfmodel_display and starpu_perfmodel_plot can be used to observe how much the performance model is calibrated (Performance Model Calibration); when their output look good, STARPU_CALIBRATE can be reset to 0 to let StarPU use the resulting performance model without recording new measures, and STARPU_SCHED can be set to dmda to benefit from the performance models. If the data input sizes vary a lot, it is really important to set STARPU_CALIBRATE to 0, otherwise StarPU will continue adding the measures, and result with a very big performance model, which will take time a lot of time to load and save.

For non-linear regression, since computing it is quite expensive, it is only done at termination of the application. This means that the first execution of the application will use only history-based performance model to perform scheduling, without using regression.

- Another type of model is STARPU_MULTIPLE_REGRESSION_BASED, which is based on multiple linear regression. In this model, the user defines both the relevant parameters and the equation for computing the task duration.

$$T_{kernel} = a + b(M^{\alpha_1} * N^{\beta_1} * K^{\gamma_1}) + c(M^{\alpha_2} * N^{\beta_2} * K^{\gamma_2}) + ...$$

M, N, K are the parameters of the task, added at the task creation. These need to be extracted by the cl_-perf_func function, which should be defined by the user. α, β, γ are the exponents defined by the user in model->combinations table. Finally, coefficients a, b, c are computed automatically by the StarPU at the end of the execution, using least squares method of the dgels_ LAPACK function.

examples/mlr/mlr.c example provides more details on the usage of STARPU_MULTIPLE_REGRESSION_BASED models.

Coefficients computation is done at the end of the execution, and the results are stored in standard codelet perfmodel files. Additional files containing the duration of task together with the value of each parameter are stored in .starpu/sampling/codelets/tmp/ directory. These files are reused when STARPU_C-ALIBRATE environment variable is set to 1, to recompute coefficients based on the current, but also on the previous executions. Additionally, when multiple linear regression models are disabled (using "--disable-mlr" configuration option) or when the model->combinations are not defined, StarPU will still write output files into .starpu/sampling/codelets/tmp/ to allow performing an analysis. This analysis typically aims at finding the most appropriate equation for the codelet and tools/starpu_mlr_analysis script provides an example of how to perform such study.

- Provided as an estimation from the application itself (model type STARPU_COMMON and field starpu_perfmodel::cost_function), see for instance examples/common/blas_model.h and examples/common/blas_model.c.

- Provided explicitly by the application (model type STARPU_PER_ARCH): either field starpu_perfmodel::arch_cost_function, or the fields .per_arch[arch][nimpl].cost_function have to be filled with pointers to functions which return the expected duration of the task in micro-seconds, one per architecture, see for instance tests/datawizard/locality.c

For STARPU_HISTORY_BASED, STARPU_REGRESSION_BASED, and STARPU_NL_REGRESSION_BASED, the dimensions of task data (both input and output) are used as an index by default. STARPU_HISTORY_BASED uses a CRC hash of the dimensions as an index to distinguish histories, and STARPU_REGRESSION_BASED and STARPU_NL_REGRESSION_BASED use the total size as an index for the regression.

The starpu_perfmodel::size_base and starpu_perfmodel::footprint fields however permit the application to override that, when for instance some of the data do not matter for task cost (e.g. mere reference table), or when using sparse structures (in which case it is the number of non-zeros which matter), or when there is some hidden parameter such as the number of iterations, or when the application actually has a very good idea of the complexity of the algorithm, and just not the speed of the processor, etc. The example in the directory examples/pi uses this to include the number of iterations in the base size. starpu_perfmodel::size_base should be used when the variance of the actual performance is known (i.e. bigger returned value is longer execution time), and thus particularly useful for STARPU-_REGRESSION_BASED or STARPU_NL_REGRESSION_BASED. starpu_perfmodel::footprint can be used when the variance of the actual performance is unknown (irregular performance behavior, etc.), and thus only useful for STARPU_HISTORY_BASED. starpu_task_data_footprint() can be used as a base and combined with other parameters through starpu_hash_crc32c_be() for instance.

StarPU will automatically determine when the performance model is calibrated, or rather, it will assume the performance model is calibrated until the application submits a task for which the performance can not be predicted. For STARPU_HISTORY_BASED, StarPU will require 10 (STARPU_CALIBRATE_MINIMUM) measurements for a given size before estimating that an average can be taken as estimation for further executions with the same size. For STARPU_REGRESSION_BASED and STARPU_NL_REGRESSION_BASED, StarPU will require 10 (STARP-U_CALIBRATE_MINIMUM) measurements, and that the minimum measured data size is smaller than 90% of the maximum measured data size (i.e. the measurement interval is large enough for a regression to have a meaning). Calibration can also be forced by setting the STARPU_CALIBRATE environment variable to 1, or even reset by setting it to 2.

How to use schedulers which can benefit from such performance model is explained in Task Scheduling Policies.

The same can be done for task energy consumption estimation, by setting the field starpu_codelet::energy_model the same way as the field starpu_codelet::model. Note: for now, the application has to give to the energy consumption performance model a name which is different from the execution time performance model.

The application can request time estimations from the StarPU performance models by filling a task structure as usual without actually submitting it. The data handles can be created by calling any of the functions starpu_*_-data_register with a NULL pointer and -1 node and the desired data sizes, and need to be unregistered as usual. The functions starpu_task_expected_length() and starpu_task_expected_energy() can then be called to get an estimation of the task cost on a given arch. starpu_task_footprint() can also be used to get the footprint used for indexing history-based performance models. starpu_task_destroy() needs to be called to destroy the dummy task afterwards. See tests/perfmodels/regression_based.c for an example.

13.4 Data trace and tasks length

It is possible to get statistics about tasks length and data size by using :

```
$ starpu_fxt_data_trace filename [codelet1 codelet2 ... codeletn]
```

Where filename is the FxT trace file and codeletX the names of the codelets you want to profile (if no names are specified, starpu_fxt_data_trace will profile them all). This will create a file, data_trace.gp which can be executed to get a .eps image of these results. On the image, each point represents a task, and each color corresponds to a codelet.

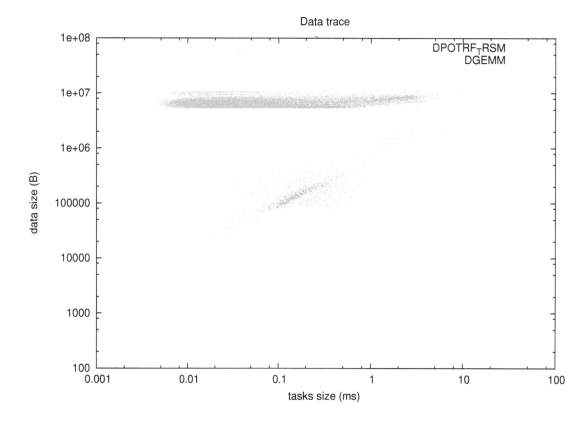

Chapter 14

Offline Performance Tools

To get an idea of what is happening, a lot of performance feedback is available, detailed in this chapter. The various informations should be checked for.

- What does the Gantt diagram look like? (see Creating a Gantt Diagram)

  - If it's mostly green (tasks running in the initial context) or context specific color prevailing, then the machine is properly utilized, and perhaps the codelets are just slow. Check their performance, see Performance Of Codelets.

  - If it's mostly purple (FetchingInput), tasks keep waiting for data transfers, do you perhaps have far more communication than computation? Did you properly use CUDA streams to make sure communication can be overlapped? Did you use data-locality aware schedulers to avoid transfers as much as possible?

  - If it's mostly red (Blocked), tasks keep waiting for dependencies, do you have enough parallelism? It might be a good idea to check what the DAG looks like (see Creating a DAG With Graphviz).

  - If only some workers are completely red (Blocked), for some reason the scheduler didn't assign tasks to them. Perhaps the performance model is bogus, check it (see Performance Of Codelets). Do all your codelets have a performance model? When some of them don't, the schedulers switches to a greedy algorithm which thus performs badly.

You can also use the Temanejo task debugger (see Using The Temanejo Task Debugger) to visualize the task graph more easily.

14.1 Off-line Performance Feedback

14.1.1 Generating Traces With FxT

StarPU can use the FxT library (see https://savannah.nongnu.org/projects/fkt/) to generate traces with a limited runtime overhead.

You can either get a tarball:

```
$ wget http://download.savannah.gnu.org/releases/fkt/fxt-0.2.11.tar.gz
```

or use the FxT library from CVS (autotools are required):

```
$ cvs -d :pserver:anonymous\@cvs.sv.gnu.org:/sources/fkt co FxT
$ ./bootstrap
```

Compiling and installing the FxT library in the $FXTDIR path is done following the standard procedure:

```
$ ./configure --prefix=$FXTDIR
$ make
$ make install
```

In order to have StarPU to generate traces, StarPU should be configured with the option --with-fxt :

```
$ ./configure --with-fxt=$FXTDIR
```

Or you can simply point the `PKG_CONFIG_PATH` to `$FXTDIR/lib/pkgconfig` and pass --with-fxt to `./configure`

When FxT is enabled, a trace is generated when StarPU is terminated by calling starpu_shutdown(). The trace is a binary file whose name has the form `prof_file_XXX_YYY` where `XXX` is the user name, and `YYY` is the pid of the process that used StarPU. This file is saved in the `/tmp/` directory by default, or by the directory specified by the environment variable STARPU_FXT_PREFIX.

The additional configure option --enable-fxt-lock can be used to generate trace events which describes the locks behaviour during the execution. It is however very heavy and should not be used unless debugging StarPU's internal locking.

The environment variable STARPU_FXT_TRACE can be set to 0 to disable the generation of the `prof_file_-XXX_YYY` file.

14.1.2   Creating a Gantt Diagram

When the FxT trace file `prof_file_something` has been generated, it is possible to generate a trace in the Paje format by calling:

```
$ starpu_fxt_tool -i /tmp/prof_file_something
```

Or alternatively, setting the environment variable STARPU_GENERATE_TRACE to 1 before application execution will make StarPU do it automatically at application shutdown.

This will create a file `paje.trace` in the current directory that can be inspected with the ViTE (http://vite.-gforge.inria.fr/) trace visualizing open-source tool. It is possible to open the file `paje.trace` with ViTE by using the following command:

```
$ vite paje.trace
```

To get names of tasks instead of "unknown", fill the optional starpu_codelet::name, or use a performance model for them.

In the MPI execution case, STARPU_GENERATE_TRACE will not work as expected (each node will try to generate paje.trace, thus mixing outputs...), you have to collect the trace files from the MPI nodes, and specify them all on the command `starpu_fxt_tool`, for instance:

```
$ starpu_fxt_tool -i /tmp/prof_file_something*
```

By default, all tasks are displayed using a green color. To display tasks with varying colors, pass option -c to `starpu_fxt_tool`.

By default, the trace contains all informations. To reduce the trace size, various -no-foo options can be passed to `starpu_fxt_tool`, see `starpu_fxt_tool -help`.

To identify tasks precisely, the application can set the starpu_task::tag_id field of the task (or use STARPU_TAG_-ONLY when using starpu_task_insert()), and the value of the tag will show up in the trace.

It can also set the starpu_task::name field of the task (or use STARPU_NAME) when using starpu_task_insert()), to replace in traces the name of the codelet with an arbitrarily chosen name.

It can also set the iteration number, by just calling starpu_iteration_push() at the beginning of submission loops and starpu_iteration_pop() at the end of submission loops. These iteration numbers will show up in traces for all tasks submitted from there.

Coordinates can also be given to data with the starpu_data_set_coordinates() or starpu_data_set_coordinates_array() function. In the trace, tasks will then be assigned the coordinates of the first data they write to.

Traces can also be inspected by hand by using the tool `fxt_print`, for instance:

```
$ fxt_print -o -f /tmp/prof_file_something
```

Timings are in nanoseconds (while timings as seen in ViTE are in milliseconds).

14.1.3   Creating a DAG With Graphviz

When the FxT trace file `prof_file_something` has been generated, it is possible to generate a task graph in the DOT format by calling:

```
$ starpu_fxt_tool -i /tmp/prof_file_something
```

This will create a `dag.dot` file in the current directory. This file is a task graph described using the DOT language. It is possible to get a graphical output of the graph by using the graphviz library:

```
$ dot -Tpdf dag.dot -o output.pdf
```

14.1.4   Getting Task Details

When the FxT trace file `prof_file_something` has been generated, details on the executed tasks can be retrieved by calling:

```
$ starpu_fxt_tool -i /tmp/prof_file_something
```

This will create a `tasks.rec` file in the current directory. This file is in the recutils format, i.e. `Field:   value` lines, and empty lines to separate each task. This can be used as a convenient input for various ad-hoc analysis tools. By default it only contains information about the actual execution. Performance models can be obtained by running `starpu_tasks_rec_complete` on it:

```
$ starpu_tasks_rec_complete tasks.rec tasks2.rec
```

which will add `EstimatedTime` lines which contain the performance model-estimated time (in µs) for each worker starting from 0. Since it needs the performance models, it needs to be run the same way as the application execution, or at least with `STARPU_HOSTNAME` set to the hostname of the machine used for execution, to get the performance models of that machine.

14.1.5   Monitoring Activity

When the FxT trace file `prof_file_something` has been generated, it is possible to generate an activity trace by calling:

```
$ starpu_fxt_tool -i /tmp/prof_file_something
```

This will create a file `activity.data` in the current directory. A profile of the application showing the activity of StarPU during the execution of the program can be generated:

```
$ starpu_workers_activity activity.data
```

This will create a file named `activity.eps` in the current directory. This picture is composed of two parts. The first part shows the activity of the different workers. The green sections indicate which proportion of the time was spent executed kernels on the processing unit. The red sections indicate the proportion of time spent in StartPU: an important overhead may indicate that the granularity may be too low, and that bigger tasks may be appropriate to use the processing unit more efficiently. The black sections indicate that the processing unit was blocked because there was no task to process: this may indicate a lack of parallelism which may be alleviated by creating more tasks when it is possible.

The second part of the picture `activity.eps` is a graph showing the evolution of the number of tasks available in the system during the execution. Ready tasks are shown in black, and tasks that are submitted but not schedulable yet are shown in grey.

14.1.6 Getting Modular Scheduler Animation

When using modular schedulers (i.e. schedulers which use a modular architecture, and whose name start with "modular-"), the command

```
$ starpu_fxt_tool -i /tmp/prof_file_something
```

will also produce a `trace.html` file which can be viewed in a javascript-enabled web browser. It shows the flow of tasks between the components of the modular scheduler.

14.1.7 Limiting The Scope Of The Trace

For computing statistics, it is useful to limit the trace to a given portion of the time of the whole execution. This can be achieved by calling

```
starpu_fxt_autostart_profiling(0)
```

before calling starpu_init(), to prevent tracing from starting immediately. Then

```
starpu_fxt_start_profiling();
```

and

```
starpu_fxt_stop_profiling();
```

can be used around the portion of code to be traced. This will show up as marks in the trace, and states of workers will only show up for that portion.

14.2 Performance Of Codelets

The performance model of codelets (see Performance Model Example) can be examined by using the tool `starpu_perfmodel_display`:

```
$ starpu_perfmodel_display -l
file: <malloc_pinned.hannibal>
file: <starpu_slu_lu_model_21.hannibal>
file: <starpu_slu_lu_model_11.hannibal>
file: <starpu_slu_lu_model_22.hannibal>
file: <starpu_slu_lu_model_12.hannibal>
```

Here, the codelets of the example `lu` are available. We can examine the performance of the kernel `22` (in microseconds), which is history-based:

```
$ starpu_perfmodel_display -s starpu_slu_lu_model_22
performance model for cpu
# hash       size        mean         dev          n
57618ab0     19660800    2.851069e+05 1.829369e+04 109
performance model for cuda_0
# hash       size        mean         dev          n
57618ab0     19660800    1.164144e+04 1.556094e+01 315
performance model for cuda_1
# hash       size        mean         dev          n
57618ab0     19660800    1.164271e+04 1.330628e+01 360
performance model for cuda_2
# hash       size        mean         dev          n
57618ab0     19660800    1.166730e+04 3.390395e+02 456
```

We can see that for the given size, over a sample of a few hundreds of execution, the GPUs are about 20 times faster than the CPUs (numbers are in us). The standard deviation is extremely low for the GPUs, and less than 10% for CPUs.

This tool can also be used for regression-based performance models. It will then display the regression formula, and in the case of non-linear regression, the same performance log as for history-based performance models:

```
$ starpu_perfmodel_display -s non_linear_memset_regression_based
performance model for cpu_impl_0
Regression : #sample = 1400
Linear: y = alpha size ^ beta
alpha = 1.335973e-03
beta = 8.024020e-01
Non-Linear: y = a size ^b + c
a = 5.429195e-04
b = 8.654899e-01
c = 9.009313e-01
# hash size mean stddev n
a3d3725e 4096          4.763200e+00    7.650928e-01    100
870a30aa 8192          1.827970e+00    2.037181e-01    100
48e988e9 16384         2.652800e+00    1.876459e-01    100
961e65d2 32768         4.255530e+00    3.518025e-01    100
...
```

The same can also be achieved by using StarPU's library API, see Performance Model and notably the function starpu_perfmodel_load_symbol(). The source code of the tool starpu_perfmodel_display can be a useful example.

The tool starpu_perfmodel_plot can be used to draw performance models. It writes a .gp file in the current directory, to be run with the tool gnuplot, which shows the corresponding curve.

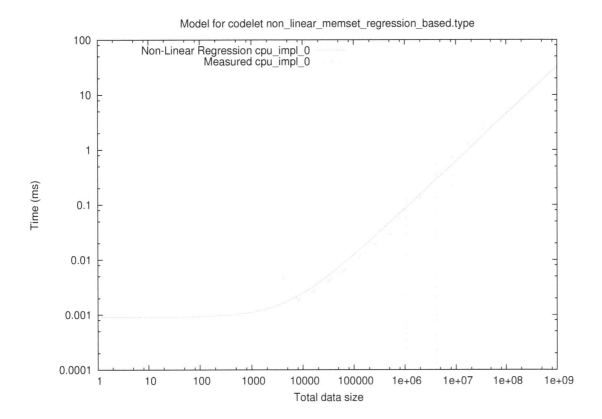

When the field starpu_task::flops is set (or STARPU_FLOPS is passed to starpu_task_insert()), `starpu_-perfmodel_plot` can directly draw a GFlops curve, by simply adding the `-f` option:

```
$ starpu_perfmodel_plot -f -s chol_model_11
```

This will however disable displaying the regression model, for which we can not compute GFlops.

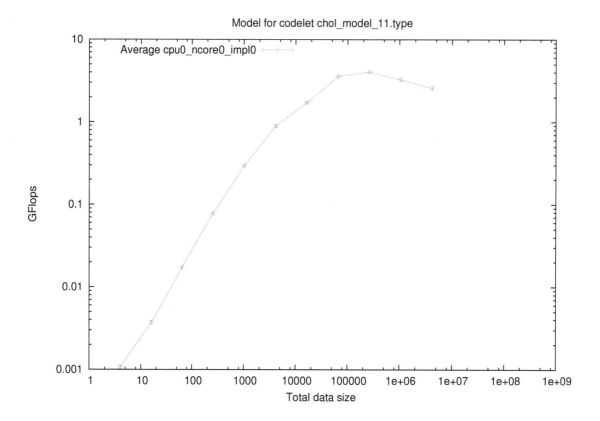

When the FxT trace file `prof_file_something` has been generated, it is possible to get a profiling of each codelet by calling:

```
$ starpu_fxt_tool -i /tmp/prof_file_something
$ starpu_codelet_profile distrib.data codelet_name
```

This will create profiling data files, and a `distrib.data.gp` file in the current directory, which draws the distribution of codelet time over the application execution, according to data input size.

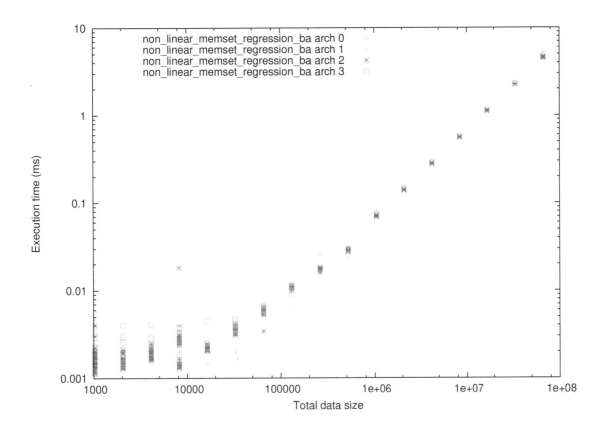

This is also available in the tool `starpu_perfmodel_plot`, by passing it the fxt trace:

```
$ starpu_perfmodel_plot -s non_linear_memset_regression_based -i /tmp/prof_file_foo_0
```

It will produce a `.gp` file which contains both the performance model curves, and the profiling measurements.

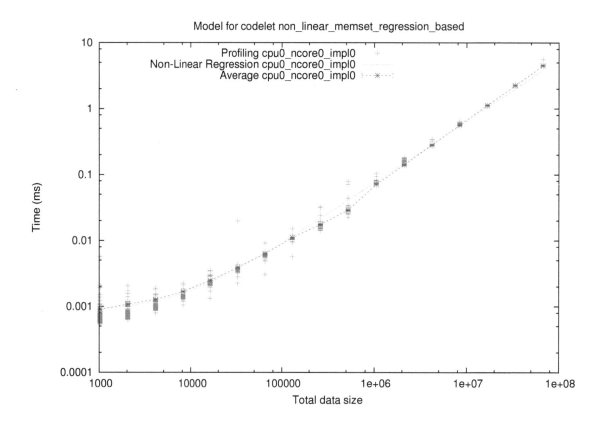

If you have the statistical tool R installed, you can additionally use

```
$ starpu_codelet_histo_profile distrib.data
```

Which will create one `.pdf` file per codelet and per input size, showing a histogram of the codelet execution time distribution.

Histogram of val[val > quantile(val, 0.01) & val < quantile(val, 0.99)]

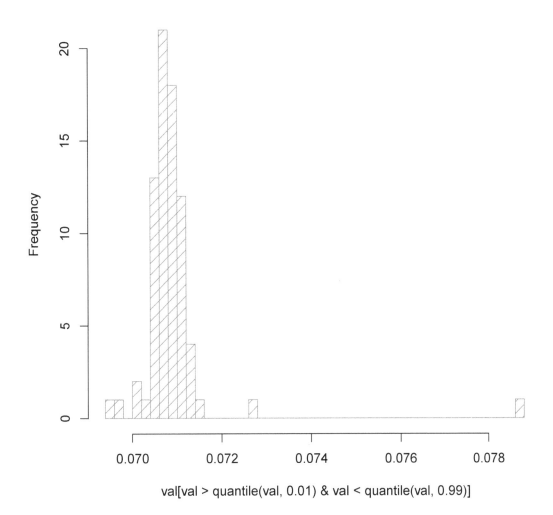

val[val > quantile(val, 0.01) & val < quantile(val, 0.99)]

14.3 Trace Statistics

More than just codelet performance, it is interesting to get statistics over all kinds of StarPU states (allocations, data transfers, etc.). This is particularly useful to check what may have gone wrong in the accurracy of the simgrid simulation.

This requires the `R` statistical tool, with the `plyr`, `ggplot2` and `data.table` packages. If your system distribution does not have packages for these, one can fetch them from `CRAN`:

```
$ R
> install.packages("plyr")
> install.packages("ggplot2")
> install.packages("data.table")
> install.packages("knitr")
```

The `pj_dump` tool from `pajeng` is also needed (see https://github.com/schnorr/pajeng)

One can then get textual or `.csv` statistics over the trace states:

```
$ starpu_paje_state_stats -v native.trace simgrid.trace
"Value"          "Events_native.csv" "Duration_native.csv" "Events_simgrid.csv" "Duration_simgrid.csv"
"Callback"       220                 0.075978              220                  0
"chol_model_11"  10                  565.176               10                   572.8695
"chol_model_21"  45                  9184.828              45                   9170.719
"chol_model_22"  165                 64712.07              165                  64299.203
$ starpu_paje_state_stats native.trace simgrid.trace
```

An other way to get statistics of StarPU states (without installing `R` and `pj_dump`) is to use the `starpu_trace_state_stats.py` script which parses the generated `trace.rec` file instead of the `paje.trace` file. The output is similar to the previous script but it doesn't need any dependencies.

The different prefixes used in `trace.rec` are:

```
E: Event type
N: Event name
C: Event category
W: Worker ID
T: Thread ID
S: Start time
```

Here's an example on how to use it:

```
$ python starpu_trace_state_stats.py trace.rec | column -t -s ","
"Name" "Count" "Type" "Duration"
"Callback"       220 Runtime 0.075978
"chol_model_11"  10 Task 565.176
"chol_model_21"  45 Task 9184.828
"chol_model_22"  165 Task 64712.07
```

`starpu_trace_state_stats.py` can also be used to compute the different efficiencies. Refer to the usage description to show some examples.

And one can plot histograms of execution times, of several states for instance:

```
$ starpu_paje_draw_histogram -n chol_model_11,chol_model_21,chol_model_22 native.trace simgrid.trace
```

and see the resulting pdf file:

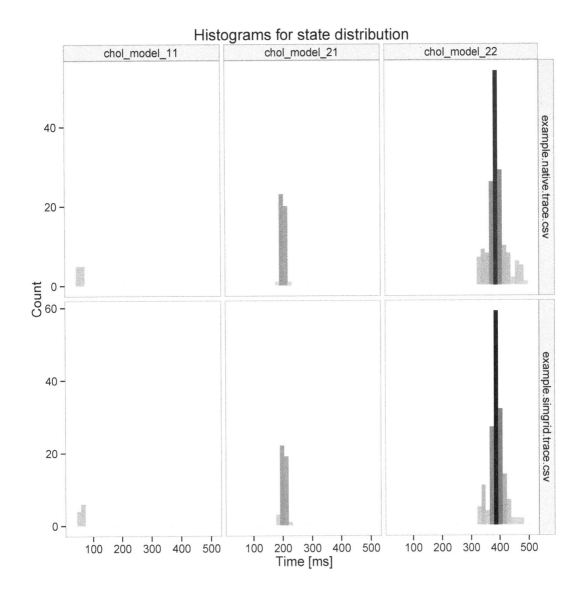

A quick statistical report can be generated by using:

```
$ starpu_paje_summary native.trace simgrid.trace
```

it includes gantt charts, execution summaries, as well as state duration charts and time distribution histograms.

Other external Paje analysis tools can be used on these traces, one just needs to sort the traces by timestamp order (which not guaranteed to make recording more efficient):

```
$ starpu_paje_sort paje.trace
```

14.4 Theoretical Lower Bound On Execution Time

StarPU can record a trace of what tasks are needed to complete the application, and then, by using a linear system, provide a theoretical lower bound of the execution time (i.e. with an ideal scheduling).

The computed bound is not really correct when not taking into account dependencies, but for an application which have enough parallelism, it is very near to the bound computed with dependencies enabled (which takes a huge lot more time to compute), and thus provides a good-enough estimation of the ideal execution time.

Theoretical Lower Bound On Execution Time Example provides an example on how to use this.

14.5   Theoretical Lower Bound On Execution Time Example

For kernels with history-based performance models (and provided that they are completely calibrated), StarPU can very easily provide a theoretical lower bound for the execution time of a whole set of tasks. See for instance `examples/lu/lu_example.c`: before submitting tasks, call the function starpu_bound_start(), and after complete execution, call starpu_bound_stop(). starpu_bound_print_lp() or starpu_bound_print_mps() can then be used to output a Linear Programming problem corresponding to the schedule of your tasks. Run it through `lp_solve` or any other linear programming solver, and that will give you a lower bound for the total execution time of your tasks. If StarPU was compiled with the library `glpk` installed, starpu_bound_compute() can be used to solve it immediately and get the optimized minimum, in ms. Its parameter `integer` allows to decide whether integer resolution should be computed and returned

The `deps` parameter tells StarPU whether to take tasks, implicit data, and tag dependencies into account. Tags released in a callback or similar are not taken into account, only tags associated with a task are. It must be understood that the linear programming problem size is quadratic with the number of tasks and thus the time to solve it will be very long, it could be minutes for just a few dozen tasks. You should probably use `lp_solve -timeout 1 test.pl -wmps test.mps` to convert the problem to MPS format and then use a better solver, `glpsol` might be better than `lp_solve` for instance (the `-pcost` option may be useful), but sometimes doesn't manage to converge. `cbc` might look slower, but it is parallel. For `lp_solve`, be sure to try at least all the `-B` options. For instance, we often just use `lp_solve -cc -B1 -Bb -Bg -Bp -Bf -Br -BG -Bd -Bs -BB -Bo -Bc -Bi`, and the `-gr` option can also be quite useful. The resulting schedule can be observed by using the tool `starpu_lp2paje`, which converts it into the Paje format.

Data transfer time can only be taken into account when `deps` is set. Only data transfers inferred from implicit data dependencies between tasks are taken into account. Other data transfers are assumed to be completely overlapped.

Setting `deps` to 0 will only take into account the actual computations on processing units. It however still properly takes into account the varying performances of kernels and processing units, which is quite more accurate than just comparing StarPU performances with the fastest of the kernels being used.

The `prio` parameter tells StarPU whether to simulate taking into account the priorities as the StarPU scheduler would, i.e. schedule prioritized tasks before less prioritized tasks, to check to which extend this results to a less optimal solution. This increases even more computation time.

14.6   Memory Feedback

It is possible to enable memory statistics. To do so, you need to pass the option --enable-memory-stats when running `configure`. It is then possible to call the function starpu_data_display_memory_stats() to display statistics about the current data handles registered within StarPU.

Moreover, statistics will be displayed at the end of the execution on data handles which have not been cleared out. This can be disabled by setting the environment variable STARPU_MEMORY_STATS to 0.

For example, if you do not unregister data at the end of the complex example, you will get something similar to:

```
$ STARPU_MEMORY_STATS=0 ./examples/interface/complex
Complex[0] = 45.00 + 12.00 i
Complex[0] = 78.00 + 78.00 i
Complex[0] = 45.00 + 12.00 i
Complex[0] = 45.00 + 12.00 i


$ STARPU_MEMORY_STATS=1 ./examples/interface/complex
Complex[0] = 45.00 + 12.00 i
Complex[0] = 78.00 + 78.00 i
Complex[0] = 45.00 + 12.00 i
Complex[0] = 45.00 + 12.00 i
```

```
#--------------------
Memory stats:
#-------
Data on Node #3
#-----
Data : 0x553ff40
Size : 16

#--
Data access stats
/!\ Work Underway
Node #0
Direct access : 4
Loaded (Owner) : 0
Loaded (Shared) : 0
Invalidated (was Owner) : 0

Node #3
Direct access : 0
Loaded (Owner) : 0
Loaded (Shared) : 1
Invalidated (was Owner) : 0

#-----
Data : 0x5544710
Size : 16

#--
Data access stats
/!\ Work Underway
Node #0
Direct access : 2
Loaded (Owner) : 0
Loaded (Shared) : 1
Invalidated (was Owner) : 1

Node #3
Direct access : 0
Loaded (Owner) : 1
Loaded (Shared) : 0
Invalidated (was Owner) : 0
```

14.7 Data Statistics

Different data statistics can be displayed at the end of the execution of the application. To enable them, you need to define the environment variable STARPU_ENABLE_STATS. When calling starpu_shutdown() various statistics will be displayed, execution, MSI cache statistics, allocation cache statistics, and data transfer statistics. The display can be disabled by setting the environment variable STARPU_STATS to 0.

```
$ ./examples/cholesky/cholesky_tag
Computation took (in ms)
518.16
Synthetic GFlops : 44.21
#--------------------
MSI cache stats :
TOTAL MSI stats hit 1622 (66.23 %) miss 827 (33.77 %)
...

$ STARPU_STATS=0 ./examples/cholesky/cholesky_tag
Computation took (in ms)
518.16
Synthetic GFlops : 44.21
```

Chapter 15

Frequently Asked Questions

15.1 How To Initialize A Computation Library Once For Each Worker?

Some libraries need to be initialized once for each concurrent instance that may run on the machine. For instance, a C++ computation class which is not thread-safe by itself, but for which several instanciated objects of that class can be used concurrently. This can be used in StarPU by initializing one such object per worker. For instance, the libstarpufft example does the following to be able to use FFTW on CPUs.

Some global array stores the instanciated objects:

```
fftw_plan plan_cpu[STARPU_NMAXWORKERS];
```

At initialisation time of libstarpu, the objects are initialized:

```
int workerid;
for (workerid = 0; workerid < starpu_worker_get_count();
     workerid++)
{
    switch (starpu_worker_get_type(workerid))
    {
        case STARPU_CPU_WORKER:
            plan_cpu[workerid] = fftw_plan(...);
            break;
    }
}
```

And in the codelet body, they are used:

```
static void fft(void *descr[], void *_args)
{
    int workerid = starpu_worker_get_id();
    fftw_plan plan = plan_cpu[workerid];
    ...

    fftw_execute(plan, ...);
}
```

This however is not sufficient for FFT on CUDA: initialization has to be done from the workers themselves. This can be done thanks to starpu_execute_on_each_worker(). For instance libstarpufft does the following.

```
static void fft_plan_gpu(void *args)
{
    plan plan = args;
    int n2 = plan->n2[0];
    int workerid = starpu_worker_get_id();

    cufftPlan1d(&plan->plans[workerid].plan_cuda, n, _CUFFT_C2C, 1);
    cufftSetStream(plan->plans[workerid].plan_cuda,
        starpu_cuda_get_local_stream());
}
void starpufft_plan(void)
{
    starpu_execute_on_each_worker(fft_plan_gpu,
        plan, STARPU_CUDA);
}
```

15.2   Using The Driver API

Running Drivers

```
int ret;
struct starpu_driver =
{
    .type = STARPU_CUDA_WORKER,
    .id.cuda_id = 0
};
ret = starpu_driver_init(&d);
    (ret != 0)
    error();
        (some_condition)
{
    ret = starpu_driver_run_once(&d);
        (ret != 0)
        error();
}
ret = starpu_driver_deinit(&d);
    (ret != 0)
    error();
```

To add a new kind of device to the structure starpu_driver, one needs to:

1. Add a member to the union starpu_driver::id

2. Modify the internal function `_starpu_launch_drivers()` to make sure the driver is not always launched.

3. Modify the function starpu_driver_run() so that it can handle another kind of architecture.

4. Write the new function `_starpu_run_foobar()` in the corresponding driver.

15.3   On-GPU Rendering

Graphical-oriented applications need to draw the result of their computations, typically on the very GPU where these happened. Technologies such as OpenGL/CUDA interoperability permit to let CUDA directly work on the OpenGL buffers, making them thus immediately ready for drawing, by mapping OpenGL buffer, textures or renderbuffer objects into CUDA. CUDA however imposes some technical constraints: peer memcpy has to be disabled, and the thread that runs OpenGL has to be the one that runs CUDA computations for that GPU.

To achieve this with StarPU, pass the option --disable-cuda-memcpy-peer to `./configure` (TODO: make it dynamic), OpenGL/GLUT has to be initialized first, and the interoperability mode has to be enabled by using the field starpu_conf::cuda_opengl_interoperability, and the driver loop has to be run by the application, by using the field starpu_conf::not_launched_drivers to prevent StarPU from running it in a separate thread, and by using starpu_driver_run() to run the loop. The examples `gl_interop` and `gl_interop_idle` show how it articulates in a simple case, where rendering is done in task callbacks. The former uses `glutMainLoopEvent` to make GLUT progress from the StarPU driver loop, while the latter uses `glutIdleFunc` to make StarPU progress from the GLUT main loop.

Then, to use an OpenGL buffer as a CUDA data, StarPU simply needs to be given the CUDA pointer at registration, for instance:

```
/* Get the CUDA worker id */
    (workerid = 0; workerid < starpu_worker_get_count();
        workerid++)
            (starpu_worker_get_type(workerid) ==
        STARPU_CUDA_WORKER)
                        ;

/* Build a CUDA pointer pointing at the OpenGL buffer */
cudaGraphicsResourceGetMappedPointer((void**)&output, &num_bytes, resource);

/* And register it to StarPU */
starpu_vector_data_register(&handle,
    starpu_worker_get_memory_node(workerid),
                        output, num_bytes / sizeof(float4), sizeof(float4))
```

```
    ;

/* The handle can now be used as usual */
starpu_task_insert(&cl, STARPU_RW, handle, 0);

/* ... */

/* This gets back data into the OpenGL buffer */
starpu_data_unregister(handle);
```

and display it e.g. in the callback function.

15.4 Using StarPU With MKL 11 (Intel Composer XE 2013)

Some users had issues with MKL 11 and StarPU (versions 1.1rc1 and 1.0.5) on Linux with MKL, using 1 thread for MKL and doing all the parallelism using StarPU (no multithreaded tasks), setting the environment variable MKL_- NUM_THREADS to 1, and using the threaded MKL library, with iomp5.

Using this configuration, StarPU only uses 1 core, no matter the value of STARPU_NCPU. The problem is actually a thread pinning issue with MKL.

The solution is to set the environment variable KMP_AFFINITY to disabled (http://software.intel.- com/sites/products/documentation/studio/composer/en-us/2011Update/compiler- _c/optaps/common/optaps_openmp_thread_affinity.htm).

15.5 Thread Binding on NetBSD

When using StarPU on a NetBSD machine, if the topology discovery library hwloc is used, thread binding will fail. To prevent the problem, you should at least use the version 1.7 of hwloc, and also issue the following call:

```
$ sysctl -w security.models.extensions.user_set_cpu_affinity=1
```

Or add the following line in the file /etc/sysctl.conf

```
security.models.extensions.user_set_cpu_affinity=1
```

15.6 Interleaving StarPU and non-StarPU code

If your application only partially uses StarPU, and you do not want to call starpu_init() / starpu_shutdown() at the beginning/end of each section, StarPU workers will poll for work between the sections. To avoid this behavior, you can "pause" StarPU with the starpu_pause() function. This will prevent the StarPU workers from accepting new work (tasks that are already in progress will not be frozen), and stop them from polling for more work.

Note that this does not prevent you from submitting new tasks, but they won't execute until starpu_resume() is called. Also note that StarPU must not be paused when you call starpu_shutdown(), and that this function pair works in a push/pull manner, i.e you need to match the number of calls to these functions to clear their effect.

One way to use these functions could be:

```
starpu_init(NULL);
starpu_pause(); // To submit all the tasks without a single one
        executing
submit_some_tasks();
starpu_resume(); // The tasks start executing


starpu_task_wait_for_all();
starpu_pause(); // Stop the workers from polling


starpu_resume();

starpu_shutdown();
```

15.7 When running with CUDA or OpenCL devices, I am seeing less CPU cores

Yes, this is on purpose.

Since GPU devices are way faster than CPUs, StarPU needs to react quickly when a task is finished, to feed the GPU with another task (StarPU actually submits a couple of tasks in advance so as to pipeline this, but filling the pipeline still has to be happening often enough), and thus it has to dedicate threads for this, and this is a very CPU-consuming duty. StarPU thus dedicates one CPU core for driving each GPU by default.

Such dedication is also useful when a codelet is hybrid, i.e. while kernels are running on the GPU, the codelet can run some computation, which thus be run by the CPU core instead of driving the GPU.

One can choose to dedicate only one thread for all the CUDA devices by setting the STARPU_CUDA_THREAD_-PER_DEV environment variable to 1. The application however should use STARPU_CUDA_ASYNC on its CUDA codelets (asynchronous execution), otherwise the execution of a synchronous CUDA codelet will monopolize the thread, and other CUDA devices will thus starve while it is executing.

15.8 StarPU does not see my CUDA device

First make sure that CUDA is properly running outside StarPU: build and run the following program with -lcudart:

```
int main(void)
{
        int n, i, version;
        cudaError_t err;

        err = cudaGetDeviceCount(&n);
        if (err)
        {
                fprintf(stderr,"cuda error %d\n", err);
                exit(1);
        }
        cudaDriverGetVersion(&version);
        printf("driver version %d\n", version);
        cudaRuntimeGetVersion(&version);
        printf("runtime version %d\n", version);
        printf("\n");

        for (i = 0; i < n; i++)
        {
                struct cudaDeviceProp props;
                printf("CUDA%d\n", i);
                err = cudaGetDeviceProperties(&props, i);
                if (err)
                {
                        fprintf(stderr,"cuda error %d\n", err);
                        continue;
                }
                printf("%s\n", props.name);
                printf("%0.3f GB\n", (float) props.totalGlobalMem / (1<<30));
                printf("%u MP\n", props.multiProcessorCount);
                printf("\n");
        }
        return 0;
}
```

If that program does not find your device, the problem is not at the StarPU level, but the CUDA drivers, check the documentation of your CUDA setup.

15.9 StarPU does not see my OpenCL device

First make sure that OpenCL is properly running outside StarPU: build and run the following program with -lOpenCL:

```
int main(void)
{
    cl_device_id did[16];
    cl_int err;
    cl_platform_id pid, pids[16];
    cl_uint nbplat, nb;
```

```
char buf[128];
size_t size;
int i, j;

err = clGetPlatformIDs(sizeof(pids)/sizeof(pids[0]), pids, &nbplat);
assert(err == CL_SUCCESS);
printf("%u platforms\n", nbplat);
for (j = 0; j < nbplat; j++)
{
    pid = pids[j];
    printf("    platform %d\n", j);
    err = clGetPlatformInfo(pid, CL_PLATFORM_VERSION, sizeof(buf)-1, buf, &
size);
    assert(err == CL_SUCCESS);
    buf[size] = 0;
    printf("        platform version %s\n", buf);

    err = clGetDeviceIDs(pid, CL_DEVICE_TYPE_ALL, sizeof(did)/sizeof(did[0]
), did, &nb);
    assert(err == CL_SUCCESS);
    printf("%d devices\n", nb);
    for (i = 0; i < nb; i++)
    {
        err = clGetDeviceInfo(did[i], CL_DEVICE_VERSION, sizeof(buf)-1, buf
, &size);
        buf[size] = 0;
        printf("    device %d version %s\n", i, buf);
    }
}

return 0;
}
```

If that program does not find your device, the problem is not at the StarPU level, but the OpenCL drivers, check the documentation of your OpenCL implementation.

15.10 I keep getting a "Incorrect performance model file" error

The performance model file, used by StarPU to record the performance of codelets, seem to have been corrupted. Perhaps a previous run of StarPU stopped abruptly, and thus could not save it properly. You can have a look at the file if you can fix it, but the simplest way is to just remove the file and run again, StarPU will just have to re-perform calibration for the corresponding codelet.

Part IV

StarPU Extensions

Chapter 16

Out Of Core

16.1 Introduction

When using StarPU, one may need to store more data than what the main memory (RAM) can store. This part describes the method to add a new memory node on a disk and to use it.

The principle is that one first registers a disk location, seen by StarPU as a `void*`, which can be for instance a Unix path for the stdio or unistd case, or a database file path for a leveldb case, etc. The disk backend opens this place with the plug method.

If the disk backend provides an alloc method, StarPU can then start using it to allocate room and store data there with the write method, without user intervention.

The user can also use starpu_disk_open() to explicitly open an object within the disk, e.g. a file name in the stdio or unistd cases, or a database key in the leveldb case, and then use `starpu_*_register` functions to turn it into a StarPU data handle. StarPU will then automatically read and write data as appropriate.

16.2 Use a new disk memory

To use a disk memory node, you have to register it with this function:

```
int new_dd = starpu_disk_register(&starpu_disk_unistd_ops
    , (void *) "/tmp/", 1024*1024*200);
```

Here, we use the unistd library to realize the read/write operations, i.e. fread/fwrite. This structure must have a path where to store files, as well as the maximum size the software can afford storing on the disk.

Don't forget to check if the result is correct!

This can also be achieved by just setting environment variables:

```
export STARPU_DISK_SWAP=/tmp
export STARPU_DISK_SWAP_BACKEND=unistd
export STARPU_DISK_SWAP_SIZE=200
```

When the register function is called, StarPU will benchmark the disk. This can take some time.

Warning: the size thus has to be at least STARPU_DISK_SIZE_MIN bytes !

StarPU will automatically try to evict unused data to this new disk. One can also use the standard StarPU memory node API, see the Standard Memory Library and the Data Interfaces .

The disk is unregistered during the starpu_shutdown().

16.3   Disk functions

There are various ways to operate a disk memory node, described by the structure starpu_disk_ops. For instance, the variable starpu_disk_unistd_ops uses read/write functions.

All structures are in Out Of Core.

16.4   Examples: disk_copy

```
/* Try to write into disk memory
 * Use mechanism to push datas from main ram to disk ram
 */

#include <starpu.h>
#include <stdlib.h>
#include <stdio.h>
#include <math.h>

/* size of one vector */
#define NX      (30*1000000/sizeof(double))
#define FPRINTF(ofile, fmt, ...) do { if (!getenv("STARPU_SSILENT"))
    {fprintf(ofile, fmt, ## __VA_ARGS__); }} while(0)


int main(int argc, char **argv)
{
        double * A,*B,*C,*D,*E,*F;

        /* limit main ram to force to push in disk */
        setenv("STARPU_LIMIT_CPU_MEM", "160", 1);

        /* Initialize StarPU with default configuration */
        int ret = starpu_init(NULL);

        if (ret == -ENODEV) goto enodev;

        /* register a disk */
        int new_dd = starpu_disk_register(&
    starpu_disk_unistd_ops, (void *) "/tmp/", 1024*1024*200);
        /* can't write on /tmp/ */
        if (new_dd == -ENOENT) goto enoent;

        /* allocate two memory spaces */
        starpu_malloc_flags((void **)&A, NX*sizeof(double),
    STARPU_MALLOC_COUNT);
        starpu_malloc_flags((void **)&F, NX*sizeof(double),
    STARPU_MALLOC_COUNT);

        FPRINTF(stderr, "TEST DISK MEMORY \n");

        unsigned int j;
        /* initialization with bad values */
        for (j = 0; j < NX; ++j)
        {
                A[j] = j;
                F[j] = -j;
        }

        starpu_data_handle_t vector_handleA, vector_handleB
    , vector_handleC, vector_handleD, vector_handleE, vector_handleF;

        /* register vector in starpu */
        starpu_vector_data_register(&vector_handleA,
    STARPU_MAIN_RAM, (uintptr_t)A, NX, sizeof(double));
        starpu_vector_data_register(&vector_handleB,
    -1, (uintptr_t) NULL, NX, sizeof(double));
        starpu_vector_data_register(&vector_handleC,
    -1, (uintptr_t) NULL, NX, sizeof(double));
        starpu_vector_data_register(&vector_handleD,
    -1, (uintptr_t) NULL, NX, sizeof(double));
        starpu_vector_data_register(&vector_handleE,
    -1, (uintptr_t) NULL, NX, sizeof(double));
        starpu_vector_data_register(&vector_handleF,
    STARPU_MAIN_RAM, (uintptr_t)F, NX, sizeof(double));

        /* copy vector A->B, B->C... */
        starpu_data_cpy(vector_handleB, vector_handleA, 0, NULL,
    NULL);
        starpu_data_cpy(vector_handleC, vector_handleB, 0, NULL,
    NULL);
```

```
        starpu_data_cpy(vector_handleD, vector_handleC, 0, NULL,
NULL);
        starpu_data_cpy(vector_handleE, vector_handleD, 0, NULL,
NULL);
        starpu_data_cpy(vector_handleF, vector_handleE, 0, NULL,
NULL);

        /* StarPU does not need to manipulate the array anymore so we can stop
         * monitoring it */

        /* free them */
        starpu_data_unregister(vector_handleA);
        starpu_data_unregister(vector_handleB);
        starpu_data_unregister(vector_handleC);
        starpu_data_unregister(vector_handleD);
        starpu_data_unregister(vector_handleE);
        starpu_data_unregister(vector_handleF);

        /* check if computation is correct */
        int try = 1;
        for (j = 0; j < NX; ++j)
                if (A[j] != F[j])
                {
                        printf("Fail A %f != F %f \n", A[j], F[j]);
                        try = 0;
                }

        /* free last vectors */
        starpu_free_flags(A, NX*sizeof(double),
STARPU_MALLOC_COUNT);
        starpu_free_flags(F, NX*sizeof(double),
STARPU_MALLOC_COUNT);

        /* terminate StarPU, no task can be submitted after */
        starpu_shutdown();

        if(try)
                FPRINTF(stderr, "TEST SUCCESS\n");
        else
                FPRINTF(stderr, "TEST FAIL\n");
        return (try ? EXIT_SUCCESS : EXIT_FAILURE);

enodev:
        return 77;
enoent:
        return 77;
}
```

16.5   Examples: disk_compute

```
/* Try to write into disk memory
 * Use mechanism to push datas from main ram to disk ram
 */

#include <starpu.h>
#include <stdlib.h>
#include <stdio.h>
#include <sys/types.h>
#include <unistd.h>
#include <math.h>

#define NX (1024)

int main(int argc, char **argv)
{
        /* Initialize StarPU with default configuration */
        int ret = starpu_init(NULL);

        if (ret == -ENODEV) goto enodev;

        /* Initialize path and name */
        char pid_str[16];
        int pid = getpid();
        snprintf(pid_str, 16, "%d", pid);

        const char *name_file_start = "STARPU_DISK_COMPUTE_DATA_";
        const char *name_file_end = "STARPU_DISK_COMPUTE_DATA_RESULT_";

        char * path_file_start = malloc(strlen(base) + 1 + strlen(
    name_file_start) + 1);
        strcpy(path_file_start, base);
        strcat(path_file_start, "/");
```

```
    strcat(path_file_start, name_file_start);

    char * path_file_end = malloc(strlen(base) + 1 + strlen(name_file_end)
+ 1);
    strcpy(path_file_end, base);
    strcat(path_file_end, "/");
    strcat(path_file_end, name_file_end);

    /* register a disk */
    int new_dd = starpu_disk_register(&
starpu_disk_unistd_ops, (void *) base, 1024*1024*1);
    /* can't write on /tmp/ */
    if (new_dd == -ENOENT) goto enoent;

    unsigned dd = (unsigned) new_dd;

    printf("TEST DISK MEMORY \n");

    /* Imagine, you want to compute datas */
    int *A;
    int *C;

    starpu_malloc_flags((void **)&A, NX*sizeof(int),
STARPU_MALLOC_COUNT);
    starpu_malloc_flags((void **)&C, NX*sizeof(int),
STARPU_MALLOC_COUNT);

    unsigned int j;
    /* you register them in a vector */
    for (j = 0; j < NX; ++j)
    {
            A[j] = j;
            C[j] = 0;
    }




    /* you create a file to store the vector ON the disk */
    FILE * f = fopen(path_file_start, "wb+");
    if (f == NULL)
            goto enoent2;

    /* store it in the file */
    fwrite(A, sizeof(int), NX, f);

    /* close the file */
    fclose(f);


    /* create a file to store result */
    f = fopen(path_file_end, "wb+");
    if (f == NULL)
                goto enoent2;

    /* replace all datas by 0 */
    fwrite(C, sizeof(int), NX, f);

    /* close the file */
    fclose(f);

    /* And now, you want to use your datas in StarPU */
    /* Open the file ON the disk */
    void * data = starpu_disk_open(dd, (void *)
name_file_start, NX*sizeof(int));
    void * data_result = starpu_disk_open(dd, (void *)
name_file_end, NX*sizeof(int));

    starpu_data_handle_t vector_handleA, vector_handleC
;

    /* register vector in starpu */
    starpu_vector_data_register(&vector_handleA,
dd, (uintptr_t) data, NX, sizeof(int));

    /* and do what you want with it, here we copy it into an other vector
*/
    starpu_vector_data_register(&vector_handleC,
dd, (uintptr_t) data_result, NX, sizeof(int));

    starpu_data_cpy(vector_handleC, vector_handleA, 0, NULL,
NULL);

    /* free them */
    starpu_data_unregister(vector_handleA);
    starpu_data_unregister(vector_handleC);
```

```
        /* close them in StarPU */
        starpu_disk_close(dd, data, NX*sizeof(int));
        starpu_disk_close(dd, data_result, NX*sizeof(int));

        /* check results */
        f = fopen(path_file_end, "rb+");
        if (f == NULL)
                goto enoent;
        /* take datas */
        int size = fread(C, sizeof(int), NX, f);

        /* close the file */
        fclose(f);

        int try = 1;
        for (j = 0; j < NX; ++j)
                if (A[j] != C[j])
                {
                        printf("Fail A %d != C %d \n", A[j], C[j]);
                        try = 0;
                }

        starpu_free_flags(A, NX*sizeof(int),
    STARPU_MALLOC_COUNT);
        starpu_free_flags(C, NX*sizeof(int),
    STARPU_MALLOC_COUNT);

        unlink(path_file_start);
        unlink(path_file_end);

        free(path_file_start);
        free(path_file_end);

        /* terminate StarPU, no task can be submitted after */
        starpu_shutdown();

        if(try)
                printf("TEST SUCCESS\n");
        else
                printf("TEST FAIL\n");
        return (try ? EXIT_SUCCESS : EXIT_FAILURE);

enodev:
        return 77;
enoent2:
        starpu_free_flags(A, NX*sizeof(int),
    STARPU_MALLOC_COUNT);
        starpu_free_flags(C, NX*sizeof(int),
    STARPU_MALLOC_COUNT);
enoent:
        unlink(path_file_start);
        unlink(path_file_end);

        free(path_file_start);
        free(path_file_end);

        starpu_shutdown();
        return 77;
}
```

Chapter 17

MPI Support

The integration of MPI transfers within task parallelism is done in a very natural way by the means of asynchronous interactions between the application and StarPU. This is implemented in a separate `libstarpumpi` library which basically provides "StarPU" equivalents of `MPI_*` functions, where `void *` buffers are replaced with starpu_data-_handle_t, and all GPU-RAM-NIC transfers are handled efficiently by StarPU-MPI. The user has to use the usual `mpirun` command of the MPI implementation to start StarPU on the different MPI nodes.

An MPI Insert Task function provides an even more seamless transition to a distributed application, by automatically issuing all required data transfers according to the task graph and an application-provided distribution.

17.1 Example used in this documentation

The example below will be used as the base for this documentation. It initializes a token on node 0, and the token is passed from node to node, incremented by one on each step. The code is not using StarPU yet.

```
for (loop = 0; loop < nloops; loop++)
{
    int tag = loop*size + rank;

    if (loop == 0 && rank == 0)
    {
        token = 0;
        fprintf(stdout, "Start with token value %d\n", token);
    }
    else
    {
        MPI_Recv(&token, 1, MPI_INT, (rank+size-1)%size, tag, MPI_COMM_WORLD);
    }

    token++;

    if (loop == last_loop && rank == last_rank)
    {
        fprintf(stdout, "Finished: token value %d\n", token);
    }
    else
    {
        MPI_Send(&token, 1, MPI_INT, (rank+1)%size, tag+1, MPI_COMM_WORLD);
    }
}
```

17.2 About not using the MPI support

Although StarPU provides MPI support, the application programmer may want to keep his MPI communications as they are for a start, and only delegate task execution to StarPU. This is possible by just using starpu_data_acquire(), for instance:

```
for (loop = 0; loop < nloops; loop++)
{
```

```
    int tag = loop*size + rank;

    /* Acquire the data to be able to write to it */
    starpu_data_acquire(token_handle, STARPU_W);
    if (loop == 0 && rank == 0)
    {
        token = 0;
        fprintf(stdout, "Start with token value %d\n", token);
    }
    else
    {
        MPI_Recv(&token, 1, MPI_INT, (rank+size-1)%size, tag, MPI_COMM_WORLD);
    }
    starpu_data_release(token_handle);

    /* Task delegation to StarPU to increment the token. The execution might
       be performed on a CPU, a GPU, etc. */
    increment_token();

    /* Acquire the update data to be able to read from it */
    starpu_data_acquire(token_handle, STARPU_R);
    if (loop == last_loop && rank == last_rank)
    {
        fprintf(stdout, "Finished: token value %d\n", token);
    }
    else
    {
        MPI_Send(&token, 1, MPI_INT, (rank+1)%size, tag+1, MPI_COMM_WORLD);
    }
    starpu_data_release(token_handle);
}
```

In that case, `libstarpumpi` is not needed. One can also use `MPI_Isend()` and `MPI_Irecv()`, by calling starpu_data_release() after `MPI_Wait()` or `MPI_Test()` have notified completion.

It is however better to use `libstarpumpi`, to save the application from having to synchronize with starpu_data_-acquire(), and instead just submit all tasks and communications asynchronously, and wait for the overall completion.

17.3 Simple Example

The flags required to compile or link against the MPI layer are accessible with the following commands:

```
$ pkg-config --cflags starpumpi-1.3   # options for the compiler
$ pkg-config --libs starpumpi-1.3     # options for the linker
```

```
void increment_token(void)
{
    struct starpu_task *task = starpu_task_create(
        );

    task->cl = &increment_cl;
    task->handles[0] = token_handle;

    starpu_task_submit(task);
}

int main(int argc, char **argv)
{
    int rank, size;

    starpu_init(NULL);
    starpu_mpi_init(&argc, &argv, 1);
    starpu_mpi_comm_rank(MPI_COMM_WORLD, &rank);
    starpu_mpi_comm_size(MPI_COMM_WORLD, &size);

    starpu_vector_data_register(&token_handle,
        STARPU_MAIN_RAM, (uintptr_t)&token, 1, sizeof(unsigned));

    unsigned nloops = NITER;
    unsigned loop;

    unsigned last_loop = nloops - 1;
    unsigned last_rank = size - 1;

    for (loop = 0; loop < nloops; loop++)
    {
        int tag = loop*size + rank;
```

```
if (loop == 0 && rank == 0)
{
    starpu_data_acquire(token_handle, STARPU_W
);
    token = 0;
    fprintf(stdout, "Start with token value %d\n", token);
    starpu_data_release(token_handle);
}
else
{
    starpu_mpi_irecv_detached(token_handle, (
rank+size-1)%size, tag,
            MPI_COMM_WORLD, NULL, NULL);
}

increment_token();

if (loop == last_loop && rank == last_rank)
{
    starpu_data_acquire(token_handle, STARPU_R
);
    fprintf(stdout, "Finished: token value %d\n", token);
    starpu_data_release(token_handle);
}
else
{
    starpu_mpi_isend_detached(token_handle, (
rank+1)%size, tag+1,
            MPI_COMM_WORLD, NULL, NULL);
}
}

starpu_task_wait_for_all();

starpu_mpi_shutdown();
starpu_shutdown();

if (rank == last_rank)
{
    fprintf(stderr, "[%d] token = %d == %d * %d ?\n", rank, token, nloops,
size);
    STARPU_ASSERT(token == nloops*size);
}
```

We have here replaced MPI_Recv() and MPI_Send() with starpu_mpi_irecv_detached() and starpu_mpi_-
isend_detached(), which just submit the communication to be performed. The only remaining synchronization with
starpu_data_acquire() is at the beginning and the end.

17.4 How to Initialize StarPU-MPI

As seen in the previous example, one has to call starpu_mpi_init() to initialize StarPU-MPI. The third parameter of
the function indicates if MPI should be initialized by StarPU or if the application will do it itself. If the application
initializes MPI itself, it must call MPI_Init_thread() with MPI_THREAD_SERIALIZED or MPI_THREAD-
_MULTIPLE, since StarPU-MPI uses a separate thread to perform the communications. MPI_THREAD_MULT-
IPLE is necessary if the application also performs some MPI communications.

17.5 Point To Point Communication

The standard point to point communications of MPI have been implemented. The semantic is similar to the MPI
one, but adapted to the DSM provided by StarPU. A MPI request will only be submitted when the data is available
in the main memory of the node submitting the request.

There are two types of asynchronous communications: the classic asynchronous communications and the detached
communications. The classic asynchronous communications (starpu_mpi_isend() and starpu_mpi_irecv()) need
to be followed by a call to starpu_mpi_wait() or to starpu_mpi_test() to wait for or to test the completion of the
communication. Waiting for or testing the completion of detached communications is not possible, this is done
internally by StarPU-MPI, on completion, the resources are automatically released. This mechanism is similar to
the pthread detach state attribute which determines whether a thread will be created in a joinable or a detached
state.

For send communications, data is acquired with the mode STARPU_R. When using the configure option --enable-mpi-pedantic-isend, the mode STARPU_RW is used to make sure there is no more than 1 concurrent MPI_Isend call accessing a data.

Internally, all communication are divided in 2 communications, a first message is used to exchange an envelope describing the data (i.e its tag and its size), the data itself is sent in a second message. All MPI communications submitted by StarPU uses a unique tag which has a default value, and can be accessed with the functions starpu_mpi_get_communication_tag() and starpu_mpi_set_communication_tag(). The matching of tags with corresponding requests is done within StarPU-MPI.

For any userland communication, the call of the corresponding function (e.g starpu_mpi_isend()) will result in the creation of a StarPU-MPI request, the function starpu_data_acquire_cb() is then called to asynchronously request StarPU to fetch the data in main memory; when the data is ready and the corresponding buffer has already been received by MPI, it will be copied in the memory of the data, otherwise the request is stored in the *early requests list*. Sending requests are stored in the *ready requests list*.

While requests need to be processed, the StarPU-MPI progression thread does the following:

1. it polls the *ready requests list*. For all the ready requests, the appropriate function is called to post the corresponding MPI call. For example, an initial call to starpu_mpi_isend() will result in a call to MPI_-Isend(). If the request is marked as detached, the request will then be added in the *detached requests list*.

2. it posts a MPI_Irecv() to retrieve a data envelope.

3. it polls the *detached requests list*. For all the detached requests, it tests its completion of the MPI request by calling MPI_Test(). On completion, the data handle is released, and if a callback was defined, it is called.

4. finally, it checks if a data envelope has been received. If so, if the data envelope matches a request in the *early requests list* (i.e the request has already been posted by the application), the corresponding MPI call is posted (similarly to the first step above).

   If the data envelope does not match any application request, a temporary handle is created to receive the data, a StarPU-MPI request is created and added into the *ready requests list*, and thus will be processed in the first step of the next loop.

MPIPtpCommunication gives the list of all the point to point communications defined in StarPU-MPI.

17.6 Exchanging User Defined Data Interface

New data interfaces defined as explained in Defining A New Data Interface can also be used within StarPU-MPI and exchanged between nodes. Two functions needs to be defined through the type starpu_data_interface_ops. The function starpu_data_interface_ops::pack_data takes a handle and returns a contiguous memory buffer allocated with

```
starpu_malloc_flags(ptr, size, 0)
```

along with its size where data to be conveyed to another node should be copied. The reversed operation is implemented in the function starpu_data_interface_ops::unpack_data which takes a contiguous memory buffer and recreates the data handle.

```
static int complex_pack_data(starpu_data_handle_t handle,
    unsigned node, void **ptr, ssize_t *count)
{
  STARPU_ASSERT(starpu_data_test_if_allocated_on_node(handle, node
    ));

  struct starpu_complex_interface *complex_interface =
    (struct starpu_complex_interface *) starpu_data_get_interface_on_node
    (handle, node);

  *count = complex_get_size(handle);
  starpu_malloc_flags(ptr, *count, 0);
```

```
    memcpy(*ptr, complex_interface->real, complex_interface->nx*sizeof(double));
    memcpy(*ptr+complex_interface->nx*sizeof(double), complex_interface->
        imaginary,
            complex_interface->nx*sizeof(double));

    return 0;
}

static int complex_unpack_data(starpu_data_handle_t handle,
        unsigned node, void *ptr, size_t count)
{
    STARPU_ASSERT(starpu_data_test_if_allocated_on_node(handle, node
        ));

    struct starpu_complex_interface *complex_interface =
        (struct starpu_complex_interface *) starpu_data_get_interface_on_node
        (handle, node);

    memcpy(complex_interface->real, ptr, complex_interface->nx*sizeof(double));
    memcpy(complex_interface->imaginary, ptr+complex_interface->nx*sizeof(double)
        ,
            complex_interface->nx*sizeof(double));

    return 0;
}

static struct starpu_data_interface_ops
        interface_complex_ops =
{
    ...
    .pack_data = complex_pack_data,
    .unpack_data = complex_unpack_data
};
```

Instead of defining pack and unpack operations, users may want to attach a MPI type to their user defined data interface. The function starpu_mpi_datatype_register() allows to do so. This function takes 3 parameters: the data handle for which the MPI datatype is going to be defined, a function's pointer that will create the MPI datatype, and a function's pointer that will free the MPI datatype.

```
starpu_data_interface handle;
starpu_complex_data_register(&handle, STARPU_MAIN_RAM, real,
        imaginary, 2);
starpu_mpi_datatype_register(handle,
        starpu_complex_interface_datatype_allocate, starpu_complex_interface_datatype_free);
```

The functions to create and free the MPI datatype are defined as follows.

```
void starpu_complex_interface_datatype_allocate(starpu_data_handle_t
        handle, MPI_Datatype *mpi_datatype)
{
        int ret;

        int blocklengths[2];
        MPI_Aint displacements[2];
        MPI_Datatype types[2] = {MPI_DOUBLE, MPI_DOUBLE};

        struct starpu_complex_interface *complex_interface =
            (struct starpu_complex_interface *) starpu_data_get_interface_on_node
        (handle, STARPU_MAIN_RAM);

        MPI_Address(complex_interface, displacements);
        MPI_Address(&complex_interface->imaginary, displacements+1);
        displacements[1] -= displacements[0];
        displacements[0] = 0;

        blocklengths[0] = complex_interface->nx;
        blocklengths[1] = complex_interface->nx;

        ret = MPI_Type_create_struct(2, blocklengths, displacements, types,
        mpi_datatype);
        STARPU_ASSERT_MSG(ret == MPI_SUCCESS, "
        MPI_Type_contiguous failed");

        ret = MPI_Type_commit(mpi_datatype);
        STARPU_ASSERT_MSG(ret == MPI_SUCCESS, "MPI_Type_commit
        failed");
}

void starpu_complex_interface_datatype_free(MPI_Datatype *mpi_datatype)
{
        MPI_Type_free(mpi_datatype);
}
```

Note that it is important to make sure no communication is going to occur before the function starpu_mpi_datatype-_register() is called. That would produce an undefined result as the data may be received before the function is called, and so the MPI datatype would not be known by the StarPU-MPI communication engine, and the data would be processed with the pack and unpack operations.

```
starpu_data_interface handle;
starpu_complex_data_register(&handle, STARPU_MAIN_RAM, real,
        imaginary, 2);
starpu_mpi_datatype_register(handle,
        starpu_complex_interface_datatype_allocate, starpu_complex_interface_datatype_free);

starpu_mpi_barrier(MPI_COMM_WORLD);
```

17.7 MPI Insert Task Utility

To save the programmer from having to explicit all communications, StarPU provides an "MPI Insert Task Utility". The principe is that the application decides a distribution of the data over the MPI nodes by allocating it and notifying StarPU of that decision, i.e. tell StarPU which MPI node "owns" which data. It also decides, for each handle, an MPI tag which will be used to exchange the content of the handle. All MPI nodes then process the whole task graph, and StarPU automatically determines which node actually execute which task, and trigger the required MPI transfers.

The list of functions is described in MPIInsertTask.

Here an stencil example showing how to use starpu_mpi_task_insert(). One first needs to define a distribution function which specifies the locality of the data. Note that the data needs to be registered to MPI by calling starpu_mpi_data_register(). This function allows to set the distribution information and the MPI tag which should be used when communicating the data. It also allows to automatically clear the MPI communication cache when unregistering the data.

```
/* Returns the MPI node number where data is */
int my_distrib(int x, int y, int nb_nodes)
{
  /* Block distrib */
  return ((int)(x / sqrt(nb_nodes) + (y / sqrt(nb_nodes)) * sqrt(nb_nodes))) %
    nb_nodes;

  // /* Other examples useful for other kinds of computations */
  // /* / distrib */
  // return (x+y) % nb_nodes;

  // /* Block cyclic distrib */
  // unsigned side = sqrt(nb_nodes);
  // return x % side + (y % side) * size;
}
```

Now the data can be registered within StarPU. Data which are not owned but will be needed for computations can be registered through the lazy allocation mechanism, i.e. with a home_node set to -1. StarPU will automatically allocate the memory when it is used for the first time.

One can note an optimization here (the else if test): we only register data which will be needed by the tasks that we will execute.

```
unsigned matrix[X][Y];
starpu_data_handle_t data_handles[X][Y];

for (x = 0; x < X; x++)
{
    for (y = 0; y < Y; y++)
    {
        int mpi_rank = my_distrib(x, y, size);
        if (mpi_rank == my_rank)
            /* Owning data */
            starpu_variable_data_register(&
    data_handles[x][y], STARPU_MAIN_RAM,
                                (uintptr_t)&(matrix[x][y]), sizeof(
    unsigned));
        else if (my_rank == my_distrib(x+1, y, size) || my_rank == my_distrib(x
    -1, y, size)
            || my_rank == my_distrib(x, y+1, size) || my_rank == my_distrib(x
    , y-1, size))
            /* I don't own that index, but will need it for my computations */
```

```
        starpu_variable_data_register(&
data_handles[x][y], -1,
                                        (uintptr_t)NULL, sizeof(unsigned));
    else
        /* I know it's useless to allocate anything for this */
        data_handles[x][y] = NULL;
    if (data_handles[x][y])
    {
        starpu_mpi_data_register(data_handles[x][y]
, x*X+y, mpi_rank);
    }
    }
}
}
```

Now starpu_mpi_task_insert() can be called for the different steps of the application.

```
for(loop=0 ; loop<niter; loop++)
    for (x = 1; x < X-1; x++)
        for (y = 1; y < Y-1; y++)
            starpu_mpi_task_insert(MPI_COMM_WORLD, &
stencil5_cl,
                                    STARPU_RW, data_handles[x][y],
                                    STARPU_R, data_handles[x-1][y],
                                    STARPU_R, data_handles[x+1][y],
                                    STARPU_R, data_handles[x][y-1],
                                    STARPU_R, data_handles[x][y+1],
                                    0);
starpu_task_wait_for_all();
```

I.e. all MPI nodes process the whole task graph, but as mentioned above, for each task, only the MPI node which owns the data being written to (here, `data_handles[x][y]`) will actually run the task. The other MPI nodes will automatically send the required data.

This can be a concern with a growing number of nodes. To avoid this, the application can prune the task for loops according to the data distribution, so as to only submit tasks on nodes which have to care about them (either to execute them, or to send the required data).

A way to do some of this quite easily can be to just add an `if` like this:

```
for(loop=0 ; loop<niter; loop++)
    for (x = 1; x < X-1; x++)
        for (y = 1; y < Y-1; y++)
            if (my_distrib(x,y,size) == my_rank
            || my_distrib(x-1,y,size) == my_rank
            || my_distrib(x+1,y,size) == my_rank
            || my_distrib(x,y-1,size) == my_rank
            || my_distrib(x,y+1,size) == my_rank)
                starpu_mpi_task_insert(MPI_COMM_WORLD, &
stencil5_cl,
                                        STARPU_RW, data_handles[x][y],
                                        STARPU_R, data_handles[x-1][y],
                                        STARPU_R, data_handles[x+1][y],
                                        STARPU_R, data_handles[x][y-1],
                                        STARPU_R, data_handles[x][y+1],
                                        0);
starpu_task_wait_for_all();
```

This permits to drop the cost of function call argument passing and parsing.

If the `my_distrib` function can be inlined by the compiler, the latter can improve the test.

If the `size` can be made a compile-time constant, the compiler can considerably improve the test further.

If the distribution function is not too complex and the compiler is very good, the latter can even optimize the `for` loops, thus dramatically reducing the cost of task submission.

To estimate quickly how long task submission takes, and notably how much pruning saves, a quick and easy way is to measure the submission time of just one of the MPI nodes. This can be achieved by running the application on just one MPI node with the following environment variables:

```
export STARPU_DISABLE_KERNELS=1
export STARPU_MPI_FAKE_RANK=2
export STARPU_MPI_FAKE_SIZE=1024
```

Here we have disabled the kernel function call to skip the actual computation time and only keep submission time, and we have asked StarPU to fake running on MPI node 2 out of 1024 nodes.

A function starpu_mpi_task_build() is also provided with the aim to only construct the task structure. All MPI nodes need to call the function, only the node which is to execute the task will return a valid task structure, others will return NULL. That node must submit that task. All nodes then need to call the function starpu_mpi_task_post_build() – with the same list of arguments as starpu_mpi_task_build() – to post all the necessary data communications.

```
struct starpu_task *task;
task = starpu_mpi_task_build(MPI_COMM_WORLD, &cl,
                        STARPU_RW, data_handles[0],
                        STARPU_R, data_handles[1],
                        0);
if (task) starpu_task_submit(task);
starpu_mpi_task_post_build(MPI_COMM_WORLD, &cl,
                        STARPU_RW, data_handles[0],
                        STARPU_R, data_handles[1],
                        0);
```

17.8 MPI cache support

StarPU-MPI automatically optimizes duplicate data transmissions: if an MPI node B needs a piece of data D from MPI node A for several tasks, only one transmission of D will take place from A to B, and the value of D will be kept on B as long as no task modifies D.

If a task modifies D, B will wait for all tasks which need the previous value of D, before invalidating the value of D. As a consequence, it releases the memory occupied by D. Whenever a task running on B needs the new value of D, allocation will take place again to receive it.

Since tasks can be submitted dynamically, StarPU-MPI can not know whether the current value of data D will again be used by a newly-submitted task before being modified by another newly-submitted task, so until a task is submitted to modify the current value, it can not decide by itself whether to flush the cache or not. The application can however explicitly tell StarPU-MPI to flush the cache by calling starpu_mpi_cache_flush() or starpu_mpi_cache_flush_all_data(), for instance in case the data will not be used at all any more (see for instance the cholesky example in mpi/examples/matrix_decomposition), or at least not in the close future. If a newly-submitted task actually needs the value again, another transmission of D will be initiated from A to B. A mere starpu_mpi_cache_flush_all_data() can for instance be added at the end of the whole algorithm, to express that no data will be reused after that (or at least that it is not interesting to keep them in cache). It may however be interesting to add fine-graph starpu_mpi_cache_flush() calls during the algorithm; the effect for the data deallocation will be the same, but it will additionally release some pressure from the StarPU-MPI cache hash table during task submission.

One can determine whether a piece of is cached with starpu_mpi_cached_receive() and starpu_mpi_cached_send().

The whole caching behavior can be disabled thanks to the STARPU_MPI_CACHE environment variable. The variable STARPU_MPI_CACHE_STATS can be set to 1 to enable the runtime to display messages when data are added or removed from the cache holding the received data.

17.9 MPI Data migration

The application can dynamically change its mind about the data distribution, to balance the load over MPI nodes for instance. This can be done very simply by requesting an explicit move and then change the registered rank. For instance, we here switch to a new distribution function my_distrib2: we first register any data that wasn't registered already and will be needed, then migrate the data, and register the new location.

```
for (x = 0; x < X; x++)
{
    for (y = 0; y < Y; y++)
    {
        int mpi_rank = my_distrib2(x, y, size);
        if (!data_handles[x][y] && (mpi_rank == my_rank
            || my_rank == my_distrib(x+1, y, size) || my_rank == my_distrib(x
        -1, y, size)
            || my_rank == my_distrib(x, y+1, size) || my_rank == my_distrib(x
        , y-1, size)))
            /* Register newly-needed data */
            starpu_variable_data_register(&
```

```
            data_handles[x][y], -1,
                                        (uintptr_t)NULL, sizeof(unsigned));
            if (data_handles[x][y])
          {
               /* Migrate the data */
               starpu_mpi_data_migrate(MPI_COMM_WORLD,
        data_handles[x][y], mpi_rank);
          }
      }
  }
```

From then on, further tasks submissions will use the new data distribution, which will thus change both MPI communications and task assignments.

Very importantly, since all nodes have to agree on which node owns which data so as to determine MPI communications and task assignments the same way, all nodes have to perform the same data migration, and at the same point among task submissions. It thus does not require a strict synchronization, just a clear separation of task submissions before and after the data redistribution.

Before data unregistration, it has to be migrated back to its original home node (the value, at least), since that is where the user-provided buffer resides. Otherwise the unregistration will complain that it does not have the latest value on the original home node.

```
for (x = 0; x < X; x++)
{
    for (y = 0; y < Y; y++)
    {
        if (data_handles[x][y])
        {
            int mpi_rank = my_distrib(x, y, size);
            /* Get back data to original place where the user-provided buffer
        is. */
            starpu_mpi_get_data_on_node_detached
        (MPI_COMM_WORLD, data_handles[x][y], mpi_rank, NULL, NULL);
            /* And unregister it */
            starpu_data_unregister(data_handles[x][y]);
        }
    }
}
```

17.10 MPI Collective Operations

The functions are described in MPICollectiveOperations.

```
if (rank == root)
{
    /* Allocate the vector */
    vector = malloc(nblocks * sizeof(float *));
    for(x=0 ; x<nblocks ; x++)
    {
        starpu_malloc((void **)&vector[x], block_size*sizeof(float
    ));
    }
}

/* Allocate data handles and register data to StarPU */
data_handles = malloc(nblocks*sizeof(starpu_data_handle_t
    *));
for (x = 0; x < nblocks ;  x++)
{
    int mpi_rank = my_distrib(x, nodes);
    if (rank == root)
    {
        starpu_vector_data_register(&data_handles[x]
    , STARPU_MAIN_RAM, (uintptr_t)vector[x],
                            blocks_size, sizeof(float));
    }
    else if ((mpi_rank == rank) || ((rank == mpi_rank+1 || rank == mpi_rank-1))
    )
    {
        /* I own that index, or i will need it for my computations */
        starpu_vector_data_register(&data_handles[x]
    , -1, (uintptr_t)NULL,
                            block_size, sizeof(float));
    }
    else
```

```
    {
        /* I know it's useless to allocate anything for this */
        data_handles[x] = NULL;
    }
      (data_handles[x])
    {
        starpu_mpi_data_register(data_handles[x], x*
    nblocks+y, mpi_rank);
    }
}

/* Scatter the matrix among the nodes */
starpu_mpi_scatter_detached(data_handles, nblocks,
    root, MPI_COMM_WORLD);

/* Calculation */
  (x = 0; x < nblocks ;  x++)
{
      (data_handles[x])
    {
        int owner = starpu_data_get_rank(data_handles[x]);
          (owner == rank)
        {
            starpu_task_insert(&cl, STARPU_RW,
    data_handles[x], 0);
        }
    }
}

/* Gather the matrix on main node */
starpu_mpi_gather_detached(data_handles, nblocks, 0,
    MPI_COMM_WORLD);
```

Other collective operations would be easy to define, just ask starpu-devel for them!

17.11 Debugging MPI

Communication trace will be enabled when the environment variable STARPU_MPI_COMM is set to 1, and StarPU has been configured with the option --enable-verbose.

Statistics will be enabled for the communication cache when the environment variable STARPU_MPI_CACHE_S-TATS is set to 1. It prints messages on the standard output when data are added or removed from the received communication cache.

17.12 More MPI examples

MPI examples are available in the StarPU source code in mpi/examples:

- comm shows how to use communicators with StarPU-MPI

- complex is a simple example using a user-define data interface over MPI (complex numbers),

- stencil5 is a simple stencil example using starpu_mpi_task_insert(),

- matrix_decomposition is a cholesky decomposition example using starpu_mpi_task_insert(). The non-distributed version can check for <algorithm correctness in 1-node configuration, the distributed version uses exactly the same source code, to be used over MPI,

- mpi_lu is an LU decomposition example, provided in three versions: plu_example uses explicit MPI data transfers, plu_implicit_example uses implicit MPI data transfers, plu_outofcore_example uses implicit MPI data transfers and supports data matrices which do not fit in memory (out-of-core).

17.13 MPI Master Slave Support

StarPU includes an other way to execute the application across many nodes. The Master Slave support permits to use remote cores without thinking about data distribution. This support can be activated with the --enable-mpi-master-slave. However, you should not activate both MPI support and MPI Master-Slave support.

If a codelet contains a kernel for CPU devices, it is automatically eligible to be executed on a MPI Slave device. However, you can decide to execute the codelet on a MPI Slave by filling the starpu_codelet::mpi_ms_funcs variable. The functions have to be globally-visible (i.e. not static) for StarPU to be able to look them up, and -rdynamic must be passed to gcc (or -export-dynamic to ld) so that symbols of the main program are visible.

By default, one core is dedicated on the master to manage the entire set of slaves. If MPI has a good multiple threads support, you can use --with-mpi-master-slave-multiple-thread to dedicate one core per slave.

If you want to chose the number of cores on the slave device, use the STARPU_NMPIMSTHREADS=<number> with <number> is the number of cores wanted. The default value is all the slave's cores. To select the number of slaves nodes, change the -n parameter when executing the application with mpirun or mpiexec.

The node chosen by default is the with the MPI rank 0. To modify this, use the environment variable STARPU_MP-I_MASTER_NODE=<number> with <number> is the MPI rank wanted.

Chapter 18

FFT Support

StarPU provides `libstarpufft`, a library whose design is very similar to both `fftw` and `cufft`, the difference being that it takes benefit from both CPUs and GPUs. It should however be noted that GPUs do not have the same precision as CPUs, so the results may different by a negligible amount.

Different precisions are available, namely float, double and long double precisions, with the following fftw naming conventions:

- double precision structures and functions are named e.g. starpufft_execute()

- float precision structures and functions are named e.g. starpufftf_execute()

- long double precision structures and functions are named e.g. starpufftl_execute()

The documentation below is given with names for double precision, replace `starpufft_` with `starpufftf_` or `starpufftl_` as appropriate.

Only complex numbers are supported at the moment.

The application has to call starpu_init() before calling `starpufft` functions.

Either main memory pointers or data handles can be provided.

- To provide main memory pointers, use starpufft_start() or starpufft_execute(). Only one FFT can be performed at a time, because StarPU will have to register the data on the fly. In the starpufft_start() case, starpufft_-cleanup() needs to be called to unregister the data.

- To provide data handles (which is preferrable), use starpufft_start_handle() (preferred) or starpufft_execute-_handle(). Several FFTs tasks can be submitted for a given plan, which permits e.g. to start a series of FFT with just one plan. starpufft_start_handle() is preferrable since it does not wait for the task completion, and thus permits to enqueue a series of tasks.

All functions are defined in FFT Support.

18.1 Compilation

The flags required to compile or link against the FFT library are accessible with the following commands:

```
$ pkg-config --cflags starpufft-1.3   # options for the compiler
$ pkg-config --libs starpufft-1.3    # options for the linker
```

Also pass the option `-static` if the application is to be linked statically.

Chapter 19

MIC/SCC Support

19.1 Compilation

SCC support just needs the presence of the RCCE library.

MIC Xeon Phi support actually needs two compilations of StarPU, one for the host and one for the device. The `PATH` environment variable has to include the path to the cross-compilation toolchain, for instance `/usr/linux-k1om-4.7/bin` . The `SINK_PKG_CONFIG_PATH` environment variable should include the path to the cross-compiled `hwloc.pc`. The script `mic-configure` can then be used to achieve the two compilations: it basically calls `configure` as appropriate from two new directories: `build_mic` and `build-_host`. `make` and `make install` can then be used as usual and will recurse into both directories. If different configuration options are needed for the host and for the mic, one can use `-with-host-param=-with-fxt` for instance to specify the `-with-fxt` option for the host only, or `-with-mic-param=-with-fxt` for the mic only.

One can also run StarPU just natively on the Xeon Phi, i.e. it will only run directly on the Phi without any exchange with the host CPU. The binaries in `build_mic` can be run that way.

For MPI support, you will probably have to specify different MPI compiler path or option for the host and the device builds, for instance:

```
./mic-configure --with-mic-param=--with-mpicc="/.../mpiicc -mmic" \
    --with-host-param=--with-mpicc=/.../mpiicc
```

In case you have troubles with the coi or scif libraries (the Intel paths are really not standard, it seems...), you can still make a build in native mode only, by using `mic-configure -enable-native-mic` (and notably without `-enable-mic` since in that case we don't need mic offloading support).

19.2 Porting Applications To MIC Xeon Phi / SCC

The simplest way to port an application to MIC Xeon Phi or SCC is to set the field starpu_codelet::cpu_funcs_name, to provide StarPU with the function name of the CPU implementation, so for instance:

```
struct starpu_codelet cl =
{
    .cpu_funcs = {myfunc},
    .cpu_funcs_name = {"myfunc"},
    .nbuffers = 1,
}
```

StarPU will thus simply use the existing CPU implementation (cross-rebuilt in the MIC Xeon Phi case). The functions have to be globally-visible (i.e. not `static`) for StarPU to be able to look them up, and -rdynamic must be passed to gcc (or -export-dynamic to ld) so that symbols of the main program are visible.

If you have used the `.where` field, you additionally need to add in it `STARPU_MIC` for the Xeon Phi, and/or `STARPU_SCC` for the SCC.

For non-native MIC Xeon Phi execution, the 'main' function of the application, on the sink, should call starpu_init() immediately upon start-up; the starpu_init() function never returns. On the host, the 'main' function may freely perform application related initialization calls as usual, before calling starpu_init().

For MIC Xeon Phi, the application may programmatically detect whether executing on the sink or on the host, by checking whether the STARPU_SINK environment variable is defined (on the sink) or not (on the host).

For SCC execution, the function starpu_initialize() also has to be used instead of starpu_init(), so as to pass `argc` and `argv`.

19.3 Launching Programs

SCC programs are started through RCCE.

MIC programs are started from the host. StarPU automatically starts the same program on MIC devices. It however needs to get the MIC-cross-built binary. It will look for the file given by the environment variable STARPU_MIC_SIN-K_PROGRAM_NAME or in the directory given by the environment variable STARPU_MIC_SINK_PROGRAM_PA-TH, or in the field starpu_conf::mic_sink_program_path. It will also look in the current directory for the same binary name plus the suffix `-mic` or `_mic`.

The testsuite can be started by simply running `make check` from the top directory. It will recurse into both `build_host` to run tests with only the host, and into `build_mic` to run tests with both the host and the MIC devices. Single tests with the host and the MIC can be run by starting `./loader-cross.sh ./the_test` from `build_mic/tests`.

Chapter 20

C Extensions

When GCC plug-in support is available, StarPU builds a plug-in for the GNU Compiler Collection (GCC), which defines extensions to languages of the C family (C, C++, Objective-C) that make it easier to write StarPU code. This feature is only available for GCC 4.5 and later; it is known to work with GCC 4.5, 4.6, and 4.7. You may need to install a specific -dev package of your distro, such as gcc-4.6-plugin-dev on Debian and derivatives. In addition, the plug-in's test suite is only run when GNU Guile (http://www.gnu.org/software/guile/) is found at configure-time. Building the GCC plug-in can be disabled by configuring with --disable-gcc-extensions.

Those extensions include syntactic sugar for defining tasks and their implementations, invoking a task, and manipulating data buffers. Use of these extensions can be made conditional on the availability of the plug-in, leading to valid C sequential code when the plug-in is not used (Using C Extensions Conditionally).

When StarPU has been installed with its GCC plug-in, programs that use these extensions can be compiled this way:

```
$ gcc -c -fplugin=`pkg-config starpu-1.3 --variable=gccplugin` foo.c
```

When the plug-in is not available, the above pkg-config command returns the empty string.

In addition, the -fplugin-arg-starpu-verbose flag can be used to obtain feedback from the compiler as it analyzes the C extensions used in source files.

This section describes the C extensions implemented by StarPU's GCC plug-in. It does not require detailed knowledge of the StarPU library.

Note: this is still an area under development and subject to change.

20.1 Defining Tasks

The StarPU GCC plug-in views tasks as "extended" C functions:

- tasks may have several implementations—e.g., one for CPUs, one written in OpenCL, one written in CUDA;

- tasks may have several implementations of the same target—e.g., several CPU implementations;

- when a task is invoked, it may run in parallel, and StarPU is free to choose any of its implementations.

Tasks and their implementations must be *declared*. These declarations are annotated with attributes (http://gcc.gnu.org/onlinedocs/gcc/Attribute-Syntax.html#Attribute-Syntax): the declaration of a task is a regular C function declaration with an additional task attribute, and task implementations are declared with a task_implementation attribute.

The following function attributes are provided:

task Declare the given function as a StarPU task. Its return type must be `void`. When a function declared as `task` has a user-defined body, that body is interpreted as the implicit definition of the task's CPU implementation (see example below). In all cases, the actual definition of a task's body is automatically generated by the compiler.

Under the hood, declaring a task leads to the declaration of the corresponding `codelet` (Codelet and Tasks). If one or more task implementations are declared in the same compilation unit, then the codelet and the function itself are also defined; they inherit the scope of the task.

Scalar arguments to the task are passed by value and copied to the target device if need be—technically, they are passed as the buffer starpu_task::cl_arg (Codelet and Tasks).

Pointer arguments are assumed to be registered data buffers—the handles argument of a task (starpu_-task::handles) ; `const`-qualified pointer arguments are viewed as read-only buffers (STARPU_R), and non-`const`-qualified buffers are assumed to be used read-write (STARPU_RW). In addition, the `output` type attribute can be as a type qualifier for output pointer or array parameters (STARPU_W).

task_implementation (target, task) Declare the given function as an implementation of `task` to run on `target`. `target` must be a string, currently one of `"cpu"`, `"opencl"`, or `"cuda"`.

Here is an example:

```
#define __output  __attribute__ ((output))

static void matmul (const float *A, const float *B,
                    __output float *C,
                    unsigned nx, unsigned ny, unsigned nz)
  __attribute__ ((task));

static void matmul_cpu (const float *A, const float *B,
                        __output float *C,
                        unsigned nx, unsigned ny, unsigned nz)
  __attribute__ ((task_implementation ("cpu", matmul)));


static void
matmul_cpu (const float *A, const float *B, __output float *C,
            unsigned nx, unsigned ny, unsigned nz)
{
  unsigned i, j, k;

    for (j = 0; j < ny; j++)
      for (i = 0; i < nx; i++)
      {
          for (k = 0; k < nz; k++)
            C[j * nx + i] += A[j * nz + k] * B[k * nx + i];
      }
}
```

A `matmult` task is defined; it has only one implementation, `matmult_cpu`, which runs on the CPU. Variables `A` and `B` are input buffers, whereas `C` is considered an input/output buffer.

For convenience, when a function declared with the `task` attribute has a user-defined body, that body is assumed to be that of the CPU implementation of a task, which we call an implicit task CPU implementation. Thus, the above snippet can be simplified like this:

```
#define __output  __attribute__ ((output))

static void matmul (const float *A, const float *B,
                    __output float *C,
                    unsigned nx, unsigned ny, unsigned nz)
  __attribute__ ((task));

/* Implicit definition of the CPU implementation of the
   'matmul' task.  */
static void
matmul (const float *A, const float *B, __output float *C,
        unsigned nx, unsigned ny, unsigned nz)
{
  unsigned i, j, k;

    for (j = 0; j < ny; j++)
      for (i = 0; i < nx; i++)
      {
          for (k = 0; k < nz; k++)
            C[j * nx + i] += A[j * nz + k] * B[k * nx + i];
      }
}
```

Use of implicit CPU task implementations as above has the advantage that the code is valid sequential code when StarPU's GCC plug-in is not used (Using C Extensions Conditionally).

CUDA and OpenCL implementations can be declared in a similar way:

```
static void matmul_cuda (const float *A, const float *B, float *C,
                         unsigned nx, unsigned ny, unsigned nz)
  __attribute__ ((task_implementation ("cuda", matmul)));

static void matmul_opencl (const float *A, const float *B, float *C,
                           unsigned nx, unsigned ny, unsigned nz)
  __attribute__ ((task_implementation ("opencl", matmul)));
```

The CUDA and OpenCL implementations typically either invoke a kernel written in CUDA or OpenCL (for similar code, CUDA Kernel, and OpenCL Kernel), or call a library function that uses CUDA or OpenCL under the hood, such as CUBLAS functions:

```
static void
matmul_cuda (const float *A, const float *B, float *C,
             unsigned nx, unsigned ny, unsigned nz)
{
  cublasSgemm ('n', 'n', nx, ny, nz,
               1.0f, A, 0, B, 0,
               0.0f, C, 0);
  cudaStreamSynchronize (starpu_cuda_get_local_stream ());
}
```

A task can be invoked like a regular C function:

```
matmul (&A[i * zdim * bydim + k * bzdim * bydim],
        &B[k * xdim * bzdim + j * bxdim * bzdim],
        &C[i * xdim * bydim + j * bxdim * bydim],
        bxdim, bydim, bzdim);
```

This leads to an asynchronous invocation, whereby `matmult`'s implementation may run in parallel with the continuation of the caller.

The next section describes how memory buffers must be handled in StarPU-GCC code. For a complete example, see the `gcc-plugin/examples` directory of the source distribution, and Vector Scaling Using the C Extension.

20.2 Initialization, Termination, and Synchronization

The following pragmas allow user code to control StarPU's life time and to synchronize with tasks.

#pragma starpu initialize Initialize StarPU. This call is compulsory and is *never* added implicitly. One of the reasons this has to be done explicitly is that it provides greater control to user code over its resource usage.

#pragma starpu shutdown Shut down StarPU, giving it an opportunity to write profiling info to a file on disk, for instance (Off-line Performance Feedback).

#pragma starpu wait Wait for all task invocations to complete, as with starpu_task_wait_for_all().

20.3 Registered Data Buffers

Data buffers such as matrices and vectors that are to be passed to tasks must be registered. Registration allows StarPU to handle data transfers among devices—e.g., transferring an input buffer from the CPU's main memory to a task scheduled to run a GPU (StarPU Data Management Library).

The following pragmas are provided:

#pragma starpu register ptr [size] Register `ptr` as a `size`-element buffer. When `ptr` has an array type whose size is known, `size` may be omitted. Alternatively, the `registered` attribute can be used (see below.)

#pragma starpu unregister ptr Unregister the previously-registered memory area pointed to by `ptr`. As a side-effect, `ptr` points to a valid copy in main memory.

#pragma starpu acquire ptr Acquire in main memory an up-to-date copy of the previously-registered memory area pointed to by `ptr`, for read-write access.

#pragma starpu release ptr Release the previously-register memory area pointed to by `ptr`, making it available to the tasks.

Additionally, the following attributes offer a simple way to allocate and register storage for arrays:

registered This attributes applies to local variables with an array type. Its effect is to automatically register the array's storage, as per `#pragma starpu register`. The array is automatically unregistered when the variable's scope is left. This attribute is typically used in conjunction with the `heap_allocated` attribute, described below.

heap_allocated This attributes applies to local variables with an array type. Its effect is to automatically allocate the array's storage on the heap, using starpu_malloc() under the hood. The heap-allocated array is automatically freed when the variable's scope is left, as with automatic variables.

The following example illustrates use of the `heap_allocated` attribute:

```
extern void cholesky(unsigned nblocks, unsigned size,
                     float mat[nblocks][nblocks][size])
  __attribute__ ((task));

int
main (int argc, char *argv[])
{
#pragma starpu initialize

  /* ... */

  int nblocks, size;
  parse_args (&nblocks, &size);

  /* Allocate an array of the required size on the heap,
     and register it.  */

  {
    float matrix[nblocks][nblocks][size]
      __attribute__ ((heap_allocated, registered));

    cholesky (nblocks, size, matrix);

#pragma starpu wait

  }    /* MATRIX is automatically unregistered & freed here.  */

#pragma starpu shutdown

       EXIT_SUCCESS;
}
```

20.4 Using C Extensions Conditionally

The C extensions described in this chapter are only available when GCC and its StarPU plug-in are in use. Yet, it is possible to make use of these extensions when they are available—leading to hybrid CPU/GPU code—and discard them when they are not available—leading to valid sequential code.

To that end, the GCC plug-in defines the C preprocessor macro — `STARPU_GCC_PLUGIN` — when it is being used. When defined, this macro expands to an integer denoting the version of the supported C extensions.

The code below illustrates how to define a task and its implementations in a way that allows it to be compiled without the GCC plug-in:

```
/* This program is valid, whether or not StarPU's GCC plug-in
   is being used.  */
```

```
#include <stdlib.h>

/* The attribute below is ignored when GCC is not used.  */
static void matmul (const float *A, const float *B, float * C,
                    unsigned nx, unsigned ny, unsigned nz)
  __attribute__ ((task));

static void
matmul (const float *A, const float *B, float * C,
        unsigned nx, unsigned ny, unsigned nz)
{
  /* Code of the CPU kernel here...  */
}

#ifdef STARPU_GCC_PLUGIN
/* Optional OpenCL task implementation.  */

static void matmul_opencl (const float *A, const float *B, float * C,
                           unsigned nx, unsigned ny, unsigned nz)
  __attribute__ ((task_implementation ("opencl", matmul)));

static void
matmul_opencl (const float *A, const float *B, float * C,
               unsigned nx, unsigned ny, unsigned nz)
{
  /* Code that invokes the OpenCL kernel here...  */
}
#endif

int
main (int argc, char *argv[])
{
  /* The pragmas below are simply ignored when StarPU-GCC
     is not used.  */
#pragma starpu initialize

  float A[123][42][7], B[123][42][7], C[123][42][7];

#pragma starpu register A
#pragma starpu register B
#pragma starpu register C

  /* When StarPU-GCC is used, the call below is asynchronous;
     otherwise, it is synchronous.  */
  matmul ((float *) A, (float *) B, (float *) C, 123, 42, 7);

#pragma starpu wait
#pragma starpu shutdown

  return EXIT_SUCCESS;
}
```

The above program is a valid StarPU program when StarPU's GCC plug-in is used; it is also a valid sequential program when the plug-in is not used.

Note that attributes such as `task` as well as `starpu` pragmas are simply ignored by GCC when the StarPU plug-in is not loaded. However, `gcc -Wall` emits a warning for unknown attributes and pragmas, which can be inconvenient. In addition, other compilers may be unable to parse the attribute syntax (In practice, Clang and several proprietary compilers implement attributes.), so you may want to wrap attributes in macros like this:

```
/* Use the 'task' attribute only when StarPU's GCC plug-in
   is available.  */
#ifdef STARPU_GCC_PLUGIN
# define __task  __attribute__ ((task))
#else
# define __task
#endif

static void matmul (const float *A, const float *B, float *C,
                    unsigned nx, unsigned ny, unsigned nz) __task;
```

Chapter 21

Native Fortran Support

StarPU provides the necessary routines and support to natively access most of its functionalities from Fortran 2008+ codes.

All symbols (functions, constants) are defined in `fstarpu_mod.f90`. Every symbol of the Native Fortran support API is prefixed by `fstarpu_`.

Note: Mixing uses of `fstarpu_` and `starpu_` symbols in the same Fortran code has unspecified behaviour. See Valid API Mixes and Language Mixes for a discussion about valid and unspecified combinations.

21.1 Implementation Details and Specificities

21.1.1 Prerequisites

The Native Fortran support relies on Fortran 2008 specific constructs, as well as on the support of interoperability of assumed-shape arrays introduced as part of Fortran's Technical Specification ISO/IEC TS 29113:2012, for which no equivalent are available in previous versions of the standard. It has currently been tested successfully with GNU GFortran 4.9, GFortran 5.x, GFortran 6.x and the Intel Fortran Compiler >= 2016. It is known not to work with GNU GFortran < 4.9, Intel Fortran Compiler < 2016.

See Section Using StarPU with Older Fortran Compilers on information on how to write StarPU Fortran code with older compilers.

21.1.2 Configuration

The Native Fortran API is enabled and its companion `fstarpu_mod.f90` Fortran module source file is installed by default when a Fortran compiler is found, unless the detected Fortran compiler is known not to support the requirements for the Native Fortran API. The support can be disabled through the configure option --disable-fortran. Conditional compiled source codes may check for the availability of the Native Fortran Support by testing whether the preprocessor macro `STARPU_HAVE_FC` is defined or not.

21.1.3 Examples

Several examples using the Native Fortran API are provided in StarPU's `examples/native_fortran/` examples directory, to showcase the Fortran flavor of various basic and more advanced StarPU features.

21.1.4 Compiling a Native Fortran Application

The Fortran module `fstarpu_mod.f90` installed in StarPU's `include/` directory provides all the necessary API definitions. It must be compiled with the same compiler (same vendor, same version) as the application itself, and the resulting `fstarpu_mod.o` object file must linked with the application executable.

Each example provided in StarPU's `examples/native_fortran/` examples directory comes with its own dedicated Makefile for out-of-tree build. Such example Makefiles may be used as starting points for building application codes with StarPU.

21.2 Fortran Translation for Common StarPU API Idioms

All these examples assume that the standard Fortran module `iso_c_binding` is in use.

- Specifying a `NULL` pointer

```
type(c_ptr) :: my_ptr   ! variable to store the pointer
! [...]
my_ptr = c_null_ptr     ! assign standard constant for null ptr
```

- Obtaining a pointer to some object:

```
real(8), dimension(:), allocatable, target :: va
type(c_ptr) :: p_va   ! variable to store a pointer to array va
! [...]
p_va = c_loc(va)
```

- Obtaining a pointer to some subroutine:

```
! pointed routine definition
recursive subroutine myfunc () bind(C)
! [...]
type(c_funptr) :: p_fun   ! variable to store the routine pointer
! [...]
p_fun = c_funloc(my_func)
```

- Obtaining the size of some object:

```
real(8) :: a
integer(c_size_t) :: sz_a   ! variable to store the size of a
! [...]
sz_a = c_sizeof(a)
```

- Obtaining the length of an array dimension:

```
real(8), dimension(:,:), allocatable, target :: vb
intger(c_int) :: ln_vb_1   ! variable to store the length of vb's dimension 1
intger(c_int) :: ln_vb_2   ! variable to store the length of vb's dimension 2
! [...]
ln_vb_1 = 1+ubound(vb,1)-lbound(vb,1)   ! get length of dimension 1 of vb
ln_vb_2 = 1+ubound(vb,2)-lbound(vb,2)   ! get length of dimension 2 of vb
```

- Specifying a string constant:

```
type(c_ptr) :: my_cl   ! a StarPU codelet
! [...]

! set the name of a codelet to string 'my_codele't:
call fstarpu_codelet_set_name(my_cl, c_char_"my_codelet"//c_null_char)

! note: using the C_CHAR_ prefix and the //C_NULL_CHAR concatenation at the end
        ensures
! that the string constant is properly '\0' terminated, and compatible with
        StarPU's
! internal C routines
!
! note: plain Fortran string constants are not '\0' terminated, and as such,
        must not be
! passed to starpu routines.
```

- Combining multiple flag constants with a bitwise 'or':

```
type(c_ptr) :: my_cl   ! a pointer for the codelet structure
! [...]

! add a managed buffer to a codelet, specifying both the Read/Write access mode
        and the Locality hint
call fstarpu_codelet_add_buffer(my_cl, fstarpu_rw.ior.fstarpu_locality)
```

21.3 Initialization and Shutdown

The snippet below show an example of minimal StarPU code using the Native Fortran support. The program should use the standard module `iso_c_binding` as well as StarPU's `fstarpu_mod`. The StarPU runtime engine is initialized with a call to function `fstarpu_init`, which returns an integer status of 0 if successful or non-0 otherwise. Eventually, a call to `fstarpu_shutdown` ends the runtime engine and frees all internal StarPU data structures.

```
program nf_initexit
        use iso_c_binding      ! C interfacing module
        use fstarpu_mod        ! StarPU interfacing module
        implicit none          ! Fortran recommended best practice

        integer(c_int) :: err   ! return status for fstarpu_init

        ! initialize StarPU with default settings
        err = fstarpu_init(c_null_ptr)
        if (err /= 0) then
                stop 1             ! StarPU initialization failure
        end if

        ! - add StarPU Native Fortran API calls here

        ! shut StarPU down
        call fstarpu_shutdown()
end program nf_initexit
```

21.4 Fortran Flavor of StarPU's Variadic Insert_task

Fortran does not have a construction similar to C variadic functions on which `starpu_insert_task` relies at the time of this writing. However, Fortran's variable length arrays of `c_ptr` elements enable to emulate much of the convenience of C's variadic functions. This is the approach retained for implementing `fstarpu_insert_task`.

The general syntax for using `fstarpu_insert_task` is as follows:

```
call fstarpu_insert_task((/ <codelet ptr>         &
    [, <access mode flags>, <data handle>]*        &
    [, <argument type constant>, <argument>]*      &
    , c_null_ptr /))
```

There is thus a unique array argument (/ ... /) passed to `fstarpu_insert_task` which itself contains the task settings. Each element of the array must be of type `type(c_ptr)`. The last element of the array must be `C_NULL_PTR`.

Example extracted from nf_vector.f90:

```
call fstarpu_insert_task((/ cl_vec,               &   ! codelet
    fstarpu_r, dh_va,                             &   ! a first data handle
    fstarpu_rw.ior.fstarpu_locality, dh_vb,       &   ! a second data handle
    c_null_ptr /))                                    ! no more args
```

21.5 Functions and Subroutines Expecting Data Structures Arguments

Several StarPU structures that are expected to be passed to the C API, are replaced by function/subroutine wrapper sets to allocate, set fields and free such structure. This strategy has been prefered over defining native Fortran equivalent of such structures using Fortran's derived types, to avoid potential layout mismatch between C and Fortran StarPU data structures. Examples of such data structures wrappers include `fstarpu_conf_allocate` and alike, `fstarpu_codelet_allocate` and alike, `fstarpu_data_filter_allocate` and alike.

Here is an example of allocating, filling and deallocating a codelet structure:

```
! a pointer for the codelet structure
type(c_ptr) :: cl_vec
! [...]
! allocate an empty codelet structure
```

```
cl_vec = fstarpu_codelet_allocate()
! add a CPU implementation function to the codelet
call fstarpu_codelet_add_cpu_func(cl_vec, c_funloc(cl_cpu_func_vec))
! set the codelet name
call fstarpu_codelet_set_name(cl_vec, c_char_"my_vec_codelet"//c_null_char)
! add a Read-only mode data buffer to the codelet
call fstarpu_codelet_add_buffer(cl_vec, fstarpu_r)
! add a Read-Write mode data buffer to the codelet
call fstarpu_codelet_add_buffer(cl_vec, fstarpu_rw.ior.fstarpu_locality)
! [...]
! free codelet structure
call fstarpu_codelet_free(cl_vec)
```

21.6   Additional Notes about the Native Fortran Support

21.6.1   Using StarPU with Older Fortran Compilers

When using older compilers, Fortran applications may still interoperate with StarPU using C marshalling functions as exemplified in StarPU's `examples/fortran/` and `examples/fortran90/` example directories, though the process will be less convenient.

Basically, the main FORTRAN code calls some C wrapper functions to submit tasks to StarPU. Then, when StarPU starts a task, another C wrapper function calls the FORTRAN routine for the task.

Note that this marshalled FORTRAN support remains available even when specifying configure option --disable-fortran (which only disables StarPU's native Fortran layer).

21.6.2   Valid API Mixes and Language Mixes

Mixing uses of `fstarpu_` and `starpu_` symbols in the same Fortran code has unspecified behaviour. Using `fstarpu_` symbols in C code has unspecified behaviour.

For multi-language applications using both C and Fortran source files:

- C source files must use `starpu_` symbols exclusively

- Fortran sources must uniformly use either `fstarpu_` symbols exclusively, or `starpu_` symbols exclusively. Every other combination has unspecified behaviour.

Chapter 22

SOCL OpenCL Extensions

SOCL is an OpenCL implementation based on StarPU. It gives a unified access to every available OpenCL device-: applications can now share entities such as Events, Contexts or Command Queues between several OpenCL implementations.

In addition, command queues that are created without specifying a device provide automatic scheduling of the submitted commands on OpenCL devices contained in the context to which the command queue is attached.

Setting the CL_QUEUE_OUT_OF_ORDER_EXEC_MODE_ENABLE flag on a command queue also allows StarPU to reorder kernels queued on the queue, otherwise they would be serialized and several command queues would be necessary to see kernels dispatched on the various OpenCL devices.

Note: this is still an area under development and subject to change.

When compiling StarPU, SOCL will be enabled if a valid OpenCL implementation is found on your system. To be able to run the SOCL test suite, the environment variable SOCL_OCL_LIB_OPENCL needs to be defined to the location of the file libOpenCL.so of the OCL ICD implementation. You should for example add the following line in your file .bashrc

```
export SOCL_OCL_LIB_OPENCL=/usr/lib/x86_64-linux-gnu/libOpenCL.so
```

You can then run the test suite in the directory socl/examples.

```
$ make check
...
PASS: basic/basic
PASS: testmap/testmap
PASS: clinfo/clinfo
PASS: matmul/matmul
PASS: mansched/mansched
==================
All 5 tests passed
==================
```

The environment variable OCL_ICD_VENDORS has to point to the directory where the socl.icd ICD file is installed. When compiling StarPU, the files are in the directory socl/vendors. With an installed version of StarPU, the files are installed in the directory $prefix/share/starpu/opencl/vendors.

To run the tests by hand, you have to call for example,

```
$ LD_PRELOAD=$SOCL_OCL_LIB_OPENCL OCL_ICD_VENDORS=socl/vendors/ socl/examples/clinfo/clinfo
Number of platforms: 2
  Plaform Profile: FULL_PROFILE
  Plaform Version: OpenCL 1.1 CUDA 4.2.1
  Plaform Name: NVIDIA CUDA
  Plaform Vendor: NVIDIA Corporation
  Plaform Extensions: cl_khr_byte_addressable_store cl_khr_icd cl_khr_gl_sharing cl_nv_compiler_options cl_n

  Plaform Profile: FULL_PROFILE
```

```
Plaform Version: OpenCL 1.0 SOCL Edition (0.1.0)
Plaform Name: SOCL Platform
Plaform Vendor: INRIA
Plaform Extensions: cl_khr_icd
....
$
```

To enable the use of CPU cores via OpenCL, one can set the STARPU_OPENCL_ON_CPUS environment variable to 1 and STARPU_NCPUS to 0 (to avoid using CPUs both via the OpenCL driver and the normal CPU driver).

Chapter 23

SimGrid Support

StarPU can use Simgrid in order to simulate execution on an arbitrary platform. This was tested with simgrid from 3.11 to 3.15, other versions may have compatibility issues.

23.1 Preparing Your Application For Simulation

There are a few technical details which need to be handled for an application to be simulated through Simgrid.

If the application uses gettimeofday to make its performance measurements, the real time will be used, which will be bogus. To get the simulated time, it has to use starpu_timing_now() which returns the virtual timestamp in us.

For some technical reason, the application's .c file which contains main() has to be recompiled with starpu_simgrid-_wrap.h, which in the simgrid case will # define main() into starpu_main(), and it is libstarpu which will provide the real main() and will call the application's main().

To be able to test with crazy data sizes, one may want to only allocate application data if STARPU_SIMGRID is not defined. Passing a NULL pointer to starpu_data_register functions is fine, data will never be read/written to by StarPU in Simgrid mode anyway.

To be able to run the application with e.g. CUDA simulation on a system which does not have CUDA installed, one can fill the cuda_funcs with (void*)1, to express that there is a CUDA implementation, even if one does not actually provide it. StarPU will not actually run it in Simgrid mode anyway by default (unless the STARPU_CODELET_SIM-GRID_EXECUTE or STARPU_CODELET_SIMGRID_EXECUTE_AND_INJECT flags are set in the codelet)

```
static struct starpu_codelet cl11 =
{
        .cpu_funcs = {chol_cpu_codelet_update_u11},
        .cpu_funcs_name = {"chol_cpu_codelet_update_u11"},
#ifdef STARPU_USE_CUDA
        .cuda_funcs = {chol_cublas_codelet_update_u11},
#elif defined(STARPU_SIMGRID)
        .cuda_funcs = {(void*)1},
#endif
        .nbuffers = 1,
        .modes = {STARPU_RW},
        .model = &chol_model_11
};
```

23.2 Calibration

The idea is to first compile StarPU normally, and run the application, so as to automatically benchmark the bus and the codelets.

```
$ ./configure && make
$ STARPU_SCHED=dmda ./examples/matvecmult/matvecmult
```

```
[starpu][_starpu_load_history_based_model] Warning: model matvecmult
    is not calibrated, forcing calibration for this run. Use the
    STARPU_CALIBRATE environment variable to control this.
$ ...
$ STARPU_SCHED=dmda ./examples/matvecmult/matvecmult
TEST PASSED
```

Note that we force to use the scheduler `dmda` to generate performance models for the application. The application may need to be run several times before the model is calibrated.

23.3   Simulation

Then, recompile StarPU, passing --enable-simgrid to `./configure`. Make sure to keep all other `./configure` options the same, and notably options such as `-enable-maxcudadev`.

```
$ ./configure --enable-simgrid
```

To specify the location of SimGrid, you can either set the environment variables SIMGRID_CFLAGS and SIMG-RID_LIBS, or use the configure options --with-simgrid-dir, --with-simgrid-include-dir and --with-simgrid-lib-dir, for example

```
$ ./configure --with-simgrid-dir=/opt/local/simgrid
```

You can then re-run the application.

```
$ make
$ STARPU_SCHED=dmda ./examples/matvecmult/matvecmult
TEST FAILED !!!
```

It is normal that the test fails: since the computation are not actually done (that is the whole point of simgrid), the result is wrong, of course.

If the performance model is not calibrated enough, the following error message will be displayed

```
$ STARPU_SCHED=dmda ./examples/matvecmult/matvecmult
[starpu][_starpu_load_history_based_model] Warning: model matvecmult
    is not calibrated, forcing calibration for this run. Use the
    STARPU_CALIBRATE environment variable to control this.
[starpu][_starpu_simgrid_execute_job][assert failure] Codelet
    matvecmult does not have a perfmodel, or is not calibrated enough
```

The number of devices can be chosen as usual with STARPU_NCPU, STARPU_NCUDA, and STARPU_NOPE-NCL, and the amount of GPU memory with STARPU_LIMIT_CUDA_MEM, STARPU_LIMIT_CUDA_devid_MEM, STARPU_LIMIT_OPENCL_MEM, and STARPU_LIMIT_OPENCL_devid_MEM.

23.4   Simulation On Another Machine

The simgrid support even permits to perform simulations on another machine, your desktop, typically. To achieve this, one still needs to perform the Calibration step on the actual machine to be simulated, then copy them to your desktop machine (the `$STARPU_HOME/.starpu` directory). One can then perform the Simulation step on the desktop machine, by setting the environment variable STARPU_HOSTNAME to the name of the actual machine, to make StarPU use the performance models of the simulated machine even on the desktop machine.

If the desktop machine does not have CUDA or OpenCL, StarPU is still able to use simgrid to simulate execution with CUDA/OpenCL devices, but the application source code will probably disable the CUDA and OpenCL codelets in thatcd sc case. Since during simgrid execution, the functions of the codelet are actually not called by default, one can use dummy functions such as the following to still permit CUDA or OpenCL execution.

23.5 Simulation Examples

StarPU ships a few performance models for a couple of systems: attila, mirage, idgraf, and sirocco. See section Simulated benchmarks for the details.

23.6 Simulations On Fake Machines

It is possible to build fake machines which do not exist, by modifying the platform file in `$STARPU_HOME/.starpu/sampling/bus/machine.platform.xml` by hand: one can add more CPUs, add GPUs (but the performance model file has to be extended as well), change the available GPU memory size, PCI memory bandwidth, etc.

23.7 Tweaking Simulation

The simulation can be tweaked, to be able to tune it between a very accurate simulation and a very simple simulation (which is thus close to scheduling theory results), see the STARPU_SIMGRID_CUDA_MALLOC_COST, STARPU_SIMGRID_CUDA_QUEUE_COST, STARPU_SIMGRID_TASK_SUBMIT_COST, STARPU_SIMGRID_FETCHING_INPUT_COST and STARPU_SIMGRID_SCHED_COST environment variables.

23.8 MPI Applications

StarPU-MPI applications can also be run in simgrid mode. It needs to be compiled with smpicc, and run using the `starpu_smpirun` script, for instance:

```
$ STARPU_SCHED=dmda starpu_smpirun -platform cluster.xml -hostfile hostfile ./mpi/tests/pingpong
```

Where cluster.xml is a Simgrid-MPI platform description, and hostfile the list of MPI nodes to be used. StarPU currently only supports homogeneous MPI clusters: for each MPI node it will just replicate the architecture referred by STARPU_HOSTNAME.

23.9 Debugging Applications

By default, simgrid uses its own implementation of threads, which prevents gdb from being able to inspect stacks of all threads. To be able to fully debug an application running with simgrid, pass the `-cfg=contexts/factory:thread` option to the application, to make simgrid use system threads, which gdb will be able to manipulate as usual.

23.10 Memory Usage

Since kernels are not actually run and data transfers are not actually performed, the data memory does not actually need to be allocated. This allows for instance to simulate the execution of applications processing very big data on a small laptop.

The application can for instance pass 1 (or whatever bogus pointer) to starpu data registration functions, instead of allocating data. This will however require the application to take care of not trying to access the data, and will not work in MPI mode, which performs transfers.

Another way is to pass the STARPU_MALLOC_SIMULATION_FOLDED flag to the starpu_malloc_flags() function. This will make it allocate a memory area which one can read/write, but optimized so that this does not actually consume memory. Of course, the values read from such area will be bogus, but this allows the application to keep e.g. data load, store, initialization as it is, and also work in MPI mode.

Note however that notably Linux kernels refuse obvious memory overcommitting by default, so a single allocation can typically not be bigger than the amount of physical memory, see `https://www.kernel.org/doc/-Documentation/vm/overcommit-accounting` This prevents for instance from allocating a single huge matrix. Allocating a huge matrix in several tiles is not a problem, however. `sysctl vm.overcommit_-memory=1` can also be used to allow such overcommit.

Note however that this folding is done by remapping the same file several times, and Linux kernels will also refuse to create too many memory areas. `sysctl vm.max_map_count` can be used to check and change the default (65535). By default, StarPU uses a 1MiB file, so it hopefully fits in the CPU cache. This however limits the amount of such folded memory to a bit below 64GiB. The STARPU_MALLOC_SIMULATION_FOLD environment variable can be used to increase the size of the file.

Chapter 24

OpenMP Runtime Support

StarPU provides the necessary routines and support to implement an OpenMP (http://www.openmp.org/) runtime compliant with the revision 3.1 of the language specification, and compliant with the task-related data dependency functionalities introduced in the revision 4.0 of the language. This StarPU OpenMP Runtime Support (SORS) has been designed to be targetted by OpenMP compilers such as the Klang-OMP compiler. Most supported OpenMP directives can both be implemented inline or as outlined functions.

All functions are defined in OpenMP Runtime Support.

24.1 Implementation Details and Specificities

24.1.1 Main Thread

When using the SORS, the main thread gets involved in executing OpenMP tasks just like every other threads, in order to be compliant with the specification execution model. This contrasts with StarPU's usual execution model where the main thread submit tasks but does not take part in executing them.

24.1.2 Extended Task Semantics

The semantics of tasks generated by the SORS are extended with respect to regular StarPU tasks in that SORS' tasks may block and be preempted by SORS call, whereas regular StarPU tasks cannot. SORS tasks may coexist with regular StarPU tasks. However, only the tasks created using SORS API functions inherit from extended semantics.

24.2 Configuration

The SORS can be compiled into libstarpu through the configure option --enable-openmp. Conditional compiled source codes may check for the availability of the OpenMP Runtime Support by testing whether the C preprocessor macro STARPU_OPENMP is defined or not.

24.3 Initialization and Shutdown

The SORS needs to be executed/terminated by the starpu_omp_init() / starpu_omp_shutdown() instead of starpu_init() / starpu_shutdown(). This requirement is necessary to make sure that the main thread gets the proper execution environment to run OpenMP tasks. These calls will usually be performed by a compiler runtime. Thus, they can be executed from a constructor/destructor such as this:

```
__attribute__((constructor))
```

```
static void omp_constructor(void)
{
        int ret = starpu_omp_init();
        STARPU_CHECK_RETURN_VALUE(ret, "
    starpu_omp_init");
}

__attribute__((destructor))
static void omp_destructor(void)
{
        starpu_omp_shutdown();
}
```

See Also

    starpu_omp_init()

    starpu_omp_shutdown()

24.4 Parallel Regions and Worksharing

The SORS provides functions to create OpenMP parallel regions as well as mapping work on participating workers. The current implementation does not provide nested active parallel regions: Parallel regions may be created recursively, however only the first level parallel region may have more than one worker. From an internal point-of-view, the SORS' parallel regions are implemented as a set of implicit, extended semantics StarPU tasks, following the execution model of the OpenMP specification. Thus the SORS' parallel region tasks may block and be preempted, by SORS calls, enabling constructs such as barriers.

24.4.1 Parallel Regions

Parallel regions can be created with the function starpu_omp_parallel_region() which accepts a set of attributes as parameter. The execution of the calling task is suspended until the parallel region completes. The field starpu_omp_parallel_region_attr::cl is a regular StarPU codelet. However only CPU codelets are supported for parallel regions. Here is an example of use:

```
void parallel_region_f(void *buffers[], void *args)
{
        (void) buffers;
        (void) args;
        pthread_t tid = pthread_self();
        int worker_id = starpu_worker_get_id();
        printf("[tid %p] task thread = %d\n", (void *)tid, worker_id);
}

void f(void)
{
        struct starpu_omp_parallel_region_attr
    attr;
        memset(&attr, 0, sizeof(attr));
        attr.cl.cpu_funcs[0] = parallel_region_f;
        attr.cl.where        = STARPU_CPU;
        attr.if_clause       = 1;
        starpu_omp_parallel_region(&attr);
                0;
}
```

See Also

    struct starpu_omp_parallel_region_attr

    starpu_omp_parallel_region()

24.4.2 Parallel For

OpenMP `for` loops are provided by the starpu_omp_for() group of functions. Variants are available for inline or outlined implementations. The SORS supports `static`, `dynamic`, and `guided` loop scheduling clauses. The `auto` scheduling clause is implemented as `static`. The `runtime` scheduling clause honors the scheduling mode selected through the environment variable OMP_SCHEDULE or the starpu_omp_set_schedule() function. For loops with the `ordered` clause are also supported. An implicit barrier can be enforced or skipped at the end of the worksharing construct, according to the value of the `nowait` parameter.

The canonical family of starpu_omp_for() functions provide each instance with the first iteration number and the number of iterations (possibly zero) to perform. The alternate family of starpu_omp_for_alt() functions provide each instance with the (possibly empty) range of iterations to perform, including the first and excluding the last.

The family of starpu_omp_ordered() functions enable to implement OpenMP's ordered construct, a region with a parallel for loop that is guaranteed to be executed in the sequential order of the loop iterations.

```
void for_g(unsigned long long i, unsigned long long nb_i, void *arg)
{
        (void) arg;
        for (; nb_i > 0; i++, nb_i--)
        {
                array[i] = 1;
        }
}

void parallel_region_f(void *buffers[], void *args)
{
        (void) buffers;
        (void) args;
        starpu_omp_for(for_g, NULL, NB_ITERS, CHUNK,
        starpu_omp_sched_static, 0, 0);
}
```

See Also

starpu_omp_for()
starpu_omp_for_inline_first()
starpu_omp_for_inline_next()
starpu_omp_for_alt()
starpu_omp_for_inline_first_alt()
starpu_omp_for_inline_next_alt()
starpu_omp_ordered()
starpu_omp_ordered_inline_begin()
starpu_omp_ordered_inline_end()

24.4.3 Sections

OpenMP `sections` worksharing constructs are supported using the set of starpu_omp_sections() variants. The general principle is either to provide an array of per-section functions or a single function that will redirect to execution to the suitable per-section functions. An implicit barrier can be enforced or skipped at the end of the worksharing construct, according to the value of the `nowait` parameter.

```
void parallel_region_f(void *buffers[], void *args)
{
        (void) buffers;
        (void) args;

        section_funcs[0] = f;
        section_funcs[1] = g;
        section_funcs[2] = h;
        section_funcs[3] = i;

        section_args[0] = arg_f;
        section_args[1] = arg_g;
        section_args[2] = arg_h;
        section_args[3] = arg_i;

        starpu_omp_sections(4, section_f, section_args, 0);
}
```

See Also

starpu_omp_sections()
starpu_omp_sections_combined()

24.4.4 Single

OpenMP `single` workharing constructs are supported using the set of starpu_omp_single() variants. An implicit barrier can be enforced or skipped at the end of the worksharing construct, according to the value of the `nowait` parameter.

```
void single_f(void *arg)
{
        (void) arg;
        pthread_t tid = pthread_self();
        int worker_id = starpu_worker_get_id();
        printf("[tid %p] task thread = %d -- single\n", (void *)tid, worker_id)
      ;
}

void parallel_region_f(void *buffers[], void *args)
{
        (void) buffers;
        (void) args;
        starpu_omp_single(single_f, NULL, 0);
}
```

The SORS also provides dedicated support for `single` sections with `copyprivate` clauses through the starpu-_omp_single_copyprivate() function variants. The OpenMP `master` directive is supported as well using the starpu-_omp_master() function variants.

See Also

    starpu_omp_master()

    starpu_omp_master_inline()

    starpu_omp_single()

    starpu_omp_single_inline()

    starpu_omp_single_copyprivate()

    starpu_omp_single_copyprivate_inline_begin()

    starpu_omp_single_copyprivate_inline_end()

24.5 Tasks

The SORS implements the necessary support of OpenMP 3.1 and OpenMP 4.0's so-called explicit tasks, together with OpenMP 4.0's data dependency management.

24.5.1 Explicit Tasks

Explicit OpenMP tasks are created with the SORS using the starpu_omp_task_region() function. The implementation supports `if`, `final`, `untied` and `mergeable` clauses as defined in the OpenMP specification. Unless specified otherwise by the appropriate clause(s), the created task may be executed by any participating worker of the current parallel region.

The current SORS implementation requires explicit tasks to be created within the context of an active parallel region. In particular, an explicit task cannot be created by the main thread outside of a parallel region. Explicit OpenMP tasks created using starpu_omp_task_region() are implemented as StarPU tasks with extended semantics, and may as such be blocked and preempted by SORS routines.

The current SORS implementation supports recursive explicit tasks creation, to ensure compliance with the OpenMP specification. However, it should be noted that StarPU is not designed nor optimized for efficiently scheduling of recursive task applications.

The code below shows how to create 4 explicit tasks within a parallel region.

```
void task_region_g(void *buffers[], void *args)
{
        (void) buffers;
        (void) args;
```

```
        pthread tid = pthread_self();
        int worker_id = starpu_worker_get_id();
        printf("[tid %p] task thread = %d: explicit task \"g\"\n", (void *)tid,
    worker_id);
}

void parallel_region_f(void *buffers[], void *args)
{
        (void) buffers;
        (void) args;
        struct starpu_omp_task_region_attr attr;

        memset(&attr, 0, sizeof(attr));
        attr.cl.cpu_funcs[0]  = task_region_g;
        attr.cl.where         = STARPU_CPU;
        attr.if_clause        = 1;
        attr.final_clause     = 0;
        attr.untied_clause    = 1;
        attr.mergeable_clause = 0;
        starpu_omp_task_region(&attr);
        starpu_omp_task_region(&attr);
        starpu_omp_task_region(&attr);
        starpu_omp_task_region(&attr);
}
```

See Also

> struct starpu_omp_task_region_attr
> starpu_omp_task_region()

24.5.2 Data Dependencies

The SORS implements inter-tasks data dependencies as specified in OpenMP 4.0. Data dependencies are expressed using regular StarPU data handles (starpu_data_handle_t) plugged into the task's `attr.cl` codelet. The family of starpu_vector_data_register() -like functions and the starpu_data_lookup() function may be used to register a memory area and to retrieve the current data handle associated with a pointer respectively. The testcase `./tests/openmp/task_02.c` gives a detailed example of using OpenMP 4.0 tasks dependencies with the SORS implementation.

Note: the OpenMP 4.0 specification only supports data dependencies between sibling tasks, that is tasks created by the same implicit or explicit parent task. The current SORS implementation also only supports data dependencies between sibling tasks. Consequently the behaviour is unspecified if dependencies are expressed beween tasks that have not been created by the same parent task.

24.5.3 TaskWait and TaskGroup

The SORS implements both the `taskwait` and `taskgroup` OpenMP task synchronization constructs specified in OpenMP 4.0, with the starpu_omp_taskwait() and starpu_omp_taskgroup() functions respectively.

An example of starpu_omp_taskwait() use, creating two explicit tasks and waiting for their completion:

```
void task_region_g(void *buffers[], void *args)
{
        (void) buffers;
        (void) args;
        printf("Hello, World!\n");
}

void parallel_region_f(void *buffers[], void *args)
{
        (void) buffers;
        (void) args;
        struct starpu_omp_task_region_attr attr;
        memset(&attr, 0, sizeof(attr));
        attr.cl.cpu_funcs[0]  = task_region_g;
        attr.cl.where         = STARPU_CPU;
        attr.if_clause        = 1;
        attr.final_clause     = 0;
        attr.untied_clause    = 1;
        attr.mergeable_clause = 0;
        starpu_omp_task_region(&attr);
        starpu_omp_task_region(&attr);
        starpu_omp_taskwait();
```

An example of starpu_omp_taskgroup() use, creating a task group of two explicit tasks:

```
void task_region_g(void *buffers[], void *args)
{
        (void) buffers;
        (void) args;
        printf("Hello, World!\n");
}

void taskgroup_f(void *arg)
{
        (void)arg;
        struct starpu_omp_task_region_attr attr;
        memset(&attr, 0, sizeof(attr));
        attr.cl.cpu_funcs[0]  = task_region_g;
        attr.cl.where         = STARPU_CPU;
        attr.if_clause        = 1;
        attr.final_clause     = 0;
        attr.untied_clause    = 1;
        attr.mergeable_clause = 0;
        starpu_omp_task_region(&attr);
        starpu_omp_task_region(&attr);
}

void parallel_region_f(void *buffers[], void *args)
{
        (void) buffers;
        (void) args;
        starpu_omp_taskgroup(taskgroup_f, (void *)NULL);
}
```

See Also

> starpu_omp_task_region()
> starpu_omp_taskwait()
> starpu_omp_taskgroup()
> starpu_omp_taskgroup_inline_begin()
> starpu_omp_taskgroup_inline_end()

24.6   Synchronization Support

The SORS implements objects and method to build common OpenMP synchronization constructs.

24.6.1   Simple Locks

The SORS Simple Locks are opaque starpu_omp_lock_t objects enabling multiple tasks to synchronize with each others, following the Simple Lock constructs defined by the OpenMP specification. In accordance with such specification, simple locks may not by acquired multiple times by the same task, without being released in-between; otherwise, deadlocks may result. Codes requiring the possibility to lock multiple times recursively should use Nestable Locks (Nestable Locks). Codes NOT requiring the possibility to lock multiple times recursively should use Simple Locks as they incur less processing overhead than Nestable Locks.

See Also

> starpu_omp_lock_t
> starpu_omp_init_lock()
> starpu_omp_destroy_lock()
> starpu_omp_set_lock()
> starpu_omp_unset_lock()
> starpu_omp_test_lock()

24.6.2   Nestable Locks

The SORS Nestable Locks are opaque starpu_omp_nest_lock_t objects enabling multiple tasks to synchronize with each others, following the Nestable Lock constructs defined by the OpenMP specification. In accordance with such specification, nestable locks may by acquired multiple times recursively by the same task without deadlocking. Nested locking and unlocking operations must be well parenthesized at any time, otherwise deadlock and/or undefined behaviour may occur. Codes requiring the possibility to lock multiple times recursively should use Nestable Locks. Codes NOT requiring the possibility to lock multiple times recursively should use Simple Locks (Simple Locks) instead, as they incur less processing overhead than Nestable Locks.

See Also

starpu_omp_nest_lock_t
starpu_omp_init_nest_lock()
starpu_omp_destroy_nest_lock()
starpu_omp_set_nest_lock()
starpu_omp_unset_nest_lock()
starpu_omp_test_nest_lock()

24.6.3 Critical Sections

The SORS implements support for OpenMP critical sections through the family of starpu_omp_critical functions. Critical sections may optionally be named. There is a single, common anonymous critical section. Mutual exclusion only occur within the scope of single critical section, either a named one or the anonymous one.

See Also

starpu_omp_critical()
starpu_omp_critical_inline_begin()
starpu_omp_critical_inline_end()

24.6.4 Barriers

The SORS provides the starpu_omp_barrier() function to implement barriers over parallel region teams. In accordance with the OpenMP specification, the starpu_omp_barrier() function waits for every implicit task of the parallel region to reach the barrier and every explicit task launched by the parallel region to complete, before returning.

See Also

starpu_omp_barrier()

Chapter 25

Clustering a Machine

TODO: clarify and put more explanations, express how to create clusters using the context API.

25.1 General Ideas

Clusters are a concept introduced in this paper. This comes from a basic idea, making use of two level of parallelism in a DAG. We keep the DAG parallelism but consider on top of it that a task can contain internal parallelism. A good example is if each task in the DAG is OpenMP enabled.

The particularity of such tasks is that we will combine the power of two runtime systems: StarPU will manage the DAG parallelism and another runtime (e.g. OpenMP) will manage the internal parallelism. The challenge is in creating an interface between the two runtime systems so that StarPU can regroup cores inside a machine (creating what we call a "cluster") on top of which the parallel tasks (e.g. OpenMP tasks) will be ran in a contained fashion.

The aim of the cluster API is to facilitate this process in an automatic fashion. For this purpose, we depend on the hwloc tool to detect the machine configuration and then partition it into usable clusters.

An example of code running on clusters is available in `examples/sched_ctx/parallel_tasks_with_-cluster_api.c`.

Let's first look at how to create one in practice, then we will detail their internals.

25.2 Creating Clusters

Partitioning a machine into clusters with the cluster API is fairly straightforward. The simplest way is to state under which machine topology level we wish to regroup all resources. This level is an HwLoc object, of the type `hwloc-_obj_type_t`. More can be found in the hwloc documentation.

Once a cluster is created, the full machine is represented with an opaque structure starpu_cluster_machine. This can be printed to show the current machine state.

```
struct starpu_cluster_machine *clusters;
clusters = starpu_cluster_machine(HWLOC_OBJ_SOCKET, 0);
starpu_cluster_print(clusters);


starpu_uncluster_machine(clusters);
```

The following graphic is an example of what a particular machine can look like once clusterized. The main difference is that we have less worker queues and tasks which will be executed on several resources at once. The execution of these tasks will be left to the internal runtime system, represented with a dashed box around the resources.

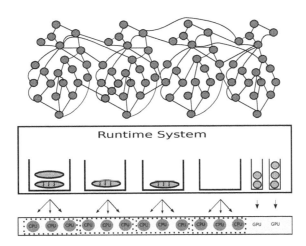

Figure 25.1: StarPU using parallel tasks

Creating clusters as shown in the example above will create workers able to execute OpenMP code by default. The cluster API aims in allowing to parametrize the cluster creation and can take a `va_list` of arguments as input after the HwLoc object (always terminated by a 0 value). These can help creating clusters of a type different from OpenMP, or create a more precise partition of the machine.

25.3 Example Of Constraining OpenMP

Clusters require being able to constrain the runtime managing the internal task parallelism (internal runtime) to the resources set by StarPU. The purpose of this is to express how StarPU must communicate with the internal runtime to achieve the required cooperation. In the case of OpenMP, StarPU will provide an awake thread from the cluster to execute this liaison. It will then provide on demand the process ids of the other resources supposed to be in the region. Finally, thanks to an OpenMP region we can create the required number of threads and bind each of them on the correct region. These will then be reused each time we encounter a `#pragma omp parallel` in the following computations of our program.

The following graphic is an example of what an OpenMP-type cluster looks like and how it represented in StarPU. We can see that one StarPU (black) thread is awake, and we need to create on the other resources the OpenMP threads (in pink).

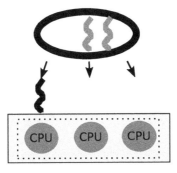

Figure 25.2: StarPU with an OpenMP cluster

Finally, the following code shows how to force OpenMP to cooperate with StarPU and create the aforementioned OpenMP threads constrained in the cluster's resources set:

```
void starpu_openmp_prologue(void * sched_ctx_id)
  int sched_ctx = *(int*)sched_ctx_id;
```

```
    int *cpuids = NULL;
    int ncpuids = 0;
    int workerid = starpu_worker_get_id();

    //we can target only CPU workers
    if (starpu_worker_get_type(workerid) ==
        STARPU_CPU_WORKER)
    {
        //grab all the ids inside the cluster
        starpu_sched_ctx_get_available_cpuids(sched_ctx, &cpuids, &ncpuids);
        //set the number of threads
        omp_set_num_threads(ncpuids);
#pragma omp parallel
        {
            //bind each threads to its respective resource
            starpu_sched_ctx_bind_current_thread_to_cpuid(cpuids[omp_get_thread_num()
            ]);
        }
        free(cpuids);
    }
    return;
}
```

This is in fact exactly the default function used when we don't specify anything. As can be seen, we based the clusters on several tools and models present in the StarPU contexts, and merely extended them to allow to represent and carry clusters. More on contexts can be read here Scheduling Contexts.

25.4 Creating Custom Clusters

As was previously said it is possible to create clusters using another cluster type, in order to bind another internal runtime inside StarPU. This can be done with in several ways:

- By using the currently available functions

- By passing as argument a user defined function

Here are two examples:

```
struct starpu_cluster_machine *clusters;
clusters = starpu_cluster_machine(HWLOC_OBJ_SOCKET,
                                  STARPU_CLUSTER_TYPE, GNU_OPENMP_MKL,
                                  0);
```

This type of clusters is available by default only if StarPU is compiled with MKL. It uses MKL functions to set the number of threads which is more reliable when using an OpenMP implementation different from the Intel one.

```
void foo_func(void* foo_arg);

\\...
int foo_arg = 0;
struct starpu_cluster_machine *clusters;
clusters = starpu_cluster_machine(HWLOC_OBJ_SOCKET,
                                  STARPU_CLUSTER_CREATE_FUNC, &foo_func,
                                  STARPU_CLUSTER_CREATE_FUNC_ARG, &foo_arg,
                                  0);
```

25.5 Clusters With Scheduling

Contexts API As previously mentioned, the cluster API is implemented on top of Scheduling Contexts. Its main addition is to ease the creation of a machine CPU partition with no overlapping by using HwLoc, whereas scheduling contexts can use any number of any resources.

It is therefore possible, but not recommended, to create clusters using the scheduling contexts API. This can be useful mostly in the most complex machine configurations where the user has to dimension precisely clusters by hand using his own algorithm.

```
/* the list of resources the context will manage */
int workerids[3] = {1, 3, 10};

/* indicate the list of workers assigned to it, the number of workers,
the name of the context and the scheduling policy to be used within
the context */
int id_ctx = starpu_sched_ctx_create(workerids, 3, "
      my_ctx", 0);

/* let StarPU know that the following tasks will be submitted to this context
      */
starpu_sched_ctx_set_task_context(id);

task->prologue_callback_pop_func=
      runtime_interface_function_here;

/* submit the task to StarPU */
starpu_task_submit(task);
```

As this example illustrates, creating a context without scheduling policy will create a cluster. The important change is that the user will have to specify an interface function between the two runtimes he plans to use. This can be done in the `prologue_callback_pop_func` field of the task. Such a function can be similar to the OpenMP thread team creation one.

Note that the OpenMP mode is the default one both for clusters and contexts. The result of a cluster creation is a woken up master worker and sleeping "slaves" which allow the master to run tasks on their resources. To create a cluster with woken up workers one can use the flag STARPU_SCHED_CTX_AWAKE_WORKERS with the scheduling context API and STARPU_CLUSTER_AWAKE_WORKERS with the cluster API as parameter to the creation function.

Part V

StarPU Reference API

Chapter 26

Execution Configuration Through Environment Variables

The behavior of the StarPU library and tools may be tuned thanks to the following environment variables.

26.1 Configuring Workers

STARPU_NCPU Specify the number of CPU workers (thus not including workers dedicated to control accelerators). Note that by default, StarPU will not allocate more CPU workers than there are physical CPUs, and that some CPUs are used to control the accelerators.

STARPU_NCPUS This variable is deprecated. You should use STARPU_NCPU.

STARPU_NCUDA Specify the number of CUDA devices that StarPU can use. If STARPU_NCUDA is lower than the number of physical devices, it is possible to select which CUDA devices should be used by the means of the environment variable STARPU_WORKERS_CUDAID. By default, StarPU will create as many CUDA workers as there are CUDA devices.

STARPU_NWORKER_PER_CUDA Specify the number of workers per CUDA device, and thus the number of kernels which will be concurrently running on the devices. The default value is 1.

STARPU_CUDA_THREAD_PER_WORKER Specify if the cuda driver should provide a thread per stream or a single thread dealing with all the streams. 0 if one thread per stream, 1 otherwise. The default value is 0. Setting it to 1 is contradictory with setting STARPU_CUDA_THREAD_PER_DEV to 1.

STARPU_CUDA_THREAD_PER_DEV Specify if the cuda driver should provide a thread per device or a single thread dealing with all the devices. 0 if one thread per device, 1 otherwise. The default value is 1, unless STARPU_CUDA_THREAD_PER_WORKER is set to 1. Setting it to 1 is contradictory with setting STARPU_CUDA_THREAD_PER_WORKER to 1.

STARPU_CUDA_PIPELINE Specify how many asynchronous tasks are submitted in advance on CUDA devices. This for instance permits to overlap task management with the execution of previous tasks, but it also allows concurrent execution on Fermi cards, which otherwise bring spurious synchronizations. The default is 2. Setting the value to 0 forces a synchronous execution of all tasks.

STARPU_NOPENCL OpenCL equivalent of the environment variable STARPU_NCUDA.

STARPU_OPENCL_PIPELINE Specify how many asynchronous tasks are submitted in advance on OpenCL devices. This for instance permits to overlap task management with the execution of previous tasks, but it also allows concurrent execution on Fermi cards, which otherwise bring spurious synchronizations. The default is 2. Setting the value to 0 forces a synchronous execution of all tasks.

STARPU_OPENCL_ON_CPUS By default, the OpenCL driver only enables GPU and accelerator devices. By setting the environment variable STARPU_OPENCL_ON_CPUS to 1, the OpenCL driver will also enable CPU devices.

STARPU_OPENCL_ONLY_ON_CPUS   By default, the OpenCL driver enables GPU and accelerator devices. By setting the environment variable STARPU_OPENCL_ONLY_ON_CPUS to 1, the OpenCL driver will ONLY enable CPU devices.

STARPU_NMIC   MIC equivalent of the environment variable STARPU_NCUDA, i.e. the number of MIC devices to use.

STARPU_NMICTHREADS   Number of threads to use on the MIC devices.

STARPU_NMPI_MS   MPI Master Slave equivalent of the environment variable STARPU_NCUDA, i.e. the number of MPI Master Slave devices to use.

STARPU_NMPIMSTHREADS   Number of threads to use on the MPI Slave devices.

STARPU_MPI_MASTER_NODE   This variable allows to chose which MPI node (with the MPI ID) will be the master.

STARPU_NSCC   SCC equivalent of the environment variable STARPU_NCUDA.

STARPU_WORKERS_NOBIND   Setting it to non-zero will prevent StarPU from binding its threads to CPUs. This is for instance useful when running the testsuite in parallel.

STARPU_WORKERS_CPUID   Passing an array of integers in STARPU_WORKERS_CPUID specifies on which logical CPU the different workers should be bound. For instance, if STARPU_WORKERS_CPUID = "0 1 4 5", the first worker will be bound to logical CPU #0, the second CPU worker will be bound to logical CPU #1 and so on. Note that the logical ordering of the CPUs is either determined by the OS, or provided by the library hwloc in case it is available. Ranges can be provided: for instance, STARPU_WORKERS_CPUID = "1-3 5" will bind the first three workers on logical CPUs #1, #2, and #3, and the fourth worker on logical C-PU #5. Unbound ranges can also be provided: STARPU_WORKERS_CPUID = "1-" will bind the workers starting from logical CPU #1 up to last CPU.

Note that the first workers correspond to the CUDA workers, then come the OpenCL workers, and finally the CPU workers. For example if we have STARPU_NCUDA=1, STARPU_NOPENCL=1, STARPU_NCPU=2 and STARPU_WORKERS_CPUID = "0 2 1 3", the CUDA device will be controlled by logical CPU #0, the OpenCL device will be controlled by logical CPU #2, and the logical CPUs #1 and #3 will be used by the CPU workers.

If the number of workers is larger than the array given in STARPU_WORKERS_CPUID, the workers are bound to the logical CPUs in a round-robin fashion: if STARPU_WORKERS_CPUID = "0 1", the first and the third (resp. second and fourth) workers will be put on CPU #0 (resp. CPU #1).

This variable is ignored if the field starpu_conf::use_explicit_workers_bindid passed to starpu_init() is set.

STARPU_WORKERS_CUDAID   Similarly to the STARPU_WORKERS_CPUID environment variable, it is possible to select which CUDA devices should be used by StarPU. On a machine equipped with 4 GPUs, setting S-TARPU_WORKERS_CUDAID = "1 3" and STARPU_NCUDA=2 specifies that 2 CUDA workers should be created, and that they should use CUDA devices #1 and #3 (the logical ordering of the devices is the one reported by CUDA).

This variable is ignored if the field starpu_conf::use_explicit_workers_cuda_gpuid passed to starpu_init() is set.

STARPU_WORKERS_OPENCLID   OpenCL equivalent of the STARPU_WORKERS_CUDAID environment variable.

This variable is ignored if the field starpu_conf::use_explicit_workers_opencl_gpuid passed to starpu_init() is set.

STARPU_WORKERS_MICID   MIC equivalent of the STARPU_WORKERS_CUDAID environment variable.

This variable is ignored if the field starpu_conf::use_explicit_workers_mic_deviceid passed to starpu_init() is set.

STARPU_WORKERS_SCCID   SCC equivalent of the STARPU_WORKERS_CUDAID environment variable.

This variable is ignored if the field starpu_conf::use_explicit_workers_scc_deviceid passed to starpu_init() is set.

STARPU_WORKER_TREE Define to 1 to enable the tree iterator in schedulers.

STARPU_SINGLE_COMBINED_WORKER If set, StarPU will create several workers which won't be able to work concurrently. It will by default create combined workers which size goes from 1 to the total number of CPU workers in the system. STARPU_MIN_WORKERSIZE and STARPU_MAX_WORKERSIZE can be used to change this default.

STARPU_MIN_WORKERSIZE STARPU_MIN_WORKERSIZE permits to specify the minimum size of the combined workers (instead of the default 2)

STARPU_MAX_WORKERSIZE STARPU_MAX_WORKERSIZE permits to specify the minimum size of the combined workers (instead of the number of CPU workers in the system)

STARPU_SYNTHESIZE_ARITY_COMBINED_WORKER Let the user decide how many elements are allowed between combined workers created from hwloc information. For instance, in the case of sockets with 6 cores without shared L2 caches, if STARPU_SYNTHESIZE_ARITY_COMBINED_WORKER is set to 6, no combined worker will be synthesized beyond one for the socket and one per core. If it is set to 3, 3 intermediate combined workers will be synthesized, to divide the socket cores into 3 chunks of 2 cores. If it set to 2, 2 intermediate combined workers will be synthesized, to divide the the socket cores into 2 chunks of 3 cores, and then 3 additional combined workers will be synthesized, to divide the former synthesized workers into a bunch of 2 cores, and the remaining core (for which no combined worker is synthesized since there is already a normal worker for it).

The default, 2, thus makes StarPU tend to building a binary trees of combined workers.

STARPU_DISABLE_ASYNCHRONOUS_COPY Disable asynchronous copies between CPU and GPU devices. The AMD implementation of OpenCL is known to fail when copying data asynchronously. When using this implementation, it is therefore necessary to disable asynchronous data transfers.

STARPU_DISABLE_ASYNCHRONOUS_CUDA_COPY Disable asynchronous copies between CPU and CUDA devices.

STARPU_DISABLE_ASYNCHRONOUS_OPENCL_COPY Disable asynchronous copies between CPU and OpenCL devices. The AMD implementation of OpenCL is known to fail when copying data asynchronously. When using this implementation, it is therefore necessary to disable asynchronous data transfers.

STARPU_DISABLE_ASYNCHRONOUS_MIC_COPY Disable asynchronous copies between CPU and MIC devices.

STARPU_DISABLE_ASYNCHRONOUS_MPI_MS_COPY Disable asynchronous copies between CPU and MPI Slave devices.

STARPU_ENABLE_CUDA_GPU_GPU_DIRECT Enable (1) or Disable (0) direct CUDA transfers from GPU to GPU, without copying through RAM. The default is Enabled. This permits to test the performance effect of GPU-Direct.

STARPU_DISABLE_PINNING Disable (1) or Enable (0) pinning host memory allocated through starpu_malloc, starpu_memory_pin and friends. The default is Enabled. This permits to test the performance effect of memory pinning.

STARPU_MIC_SINK_PROGRAM_NAME todo

STARPU_MIC_SINK_PROGRAM_PATH todo

STARPU_MIC_PROGRAM_PATH todo

26.2 Configuring The Scheduling Engine

STARPU_SCHED Choose between the different scheduling policies proposed by StarPU: work random, stealing, greedy, with performance models, etc.

Use STARPU_SCHED=help to get the list of available schedulers.

STARPU_MIN_PRIO Set the mininum priority used by priorities-aware schedulers.

STARPU_MAX_PRIO   Set the maximum priority used by priorities-aware schedulers.

STARPU_CALIBRATE   If this variable is set to 1, the performance models are calibrated during the execution. If it is set to 2, the previous values are dropped to restart calibration from scratch. Setting this variable to 0 disable calibration, this is the default behaviour.

Note: this currently only applies to `dm` and `dmda` scheduling policies.

STARPU_CALIBRATE_MINIMUM   This defines the minimum number of calibration measurements that will be made before considering that the performance model is calibrated. The default value is 10.

STARPU_BUS_CALIBRATE   If this variable is set to 1, the bus is recalibrated during intialization.

STARPU_PREFETCH   This variable indicates whether data prefetching should be enabled (0 means that it is disabled). If prefetching is enabled, when a task is scheduled to be executed e.g. on a GPU, StarPU will request an asynchronous transfer in advance, so that data is already present on the GPU when the task starts. As a result, computation and data transfers are overlapped. Note that prefetching is enabled by default in StarPU.

STARPU_SCHED_ALPHA   To estimate the cost of a task StarPU takes into account the estimated computation time (obtained thanks to performance models). The alpha factor is the coefficient to be applied to it before adding it to the communication part.

STARPU_SCHED_BETA   To estimate the cost of a task StarPU takes into account the estimated data transfer time (obtained thanks to performance models). The beta factor is the coefficient to be applied to it before adding it to the computation part.

STARPU_SCHED_GAMMA   Define the execution time penalty of a joule (Energy-based Scheduling).

STARPU_IDLE_POWER   Define the idle power of the machine (Energy-based Scheduling).

STARPU_PROFILING   Enable on-line performance monitoring (Enabling On-line Performance Monitoring).

26.3   Extensions

SOCL_OCL_LIB_OPENCL   THE SOCL test suite is only run when the environment variable SOCL_OCL_LIB_O-PENCL is defined. It should contain the location of the file `libOpenCL.so` of the OCL ICD implementation.

OCL_ICD_VENDORS   When using SOCL with OpenCL ICD (`https://forge.imag.fr/projects/ocl-icd/`), this variable may be used to point to the directory where ICD files are installed. The default directory is `/etc/OpenCL/vendors`. StarPU installs ICD files in the directory `$prefix/share/starpu/opencl/vendors`.

STARPU_COMM_STATS   Communication statistics for starpumpi (MPI Support) will be enabled when the environment variable STARPU_COMM_STATS is defined to an value other than 0.

STARPU_MPI_CACHE   Communication cache for starpumpi (MPI Support) will be disabled when the environment variable STARPU_MPI_CACHE is set to 0. It is enabled by default or for any other values of the variable ST-ARPU_MPI_CACHE.

STARPU_MPI_COMM   Communication trace for starpumpi (MPI Support) will be enabled when the environment variable STARPU_MPI_COMM is set to 1, and StarPU has been configured with the option --enable-verbose.

STARPU_MPI_CACHE_STATS   When set to 1, statistics are enabled for the communication cache (MPI Support). For now, it prints messages on the standard output when data are added or removed from the received communication cache.

STARPU_MPI_FAKE_SIZE   Setting to a number makes StarPU believe that there are as many MPI nodes, even if it was run on only one MPI node. This allows e.g. to simulate the execution of one of the nodes of a big cluster without actually running the rest. It of course does not provide computation results and timing.

STARPU_MPI_FAKE_RANK   Setting to a number makes StarPU believe that it runs the given MPI node, even if it was run on only one MPI node. This allows e.g. to simulate the execution of one of the nodes of a big cluster without actually running the rest. It of course does not provide computation results and timing.

STARPU_SIMGRID_CUDA_MALLOC_COST When set to 1 (which is the default), CUDA malloc costs are taken into account in simgrid mode.

STARPU_SIMGRID_CUDA_QUEUE_COST When set to 1 (which is the default), CUDA task and transfer queueing costs are taken into account in simgrid mode.

STARPU_PCI_FLAT When unset or set to 0, the platform file created for simgrid will contain PCI bandwidths and routes.

STARPU_SIMGRID_QUEUE_MALLOC_COST When unset or set to 1, simulate within simgrid the GPU transfer queueing.

STARPU_MALLOC_SIMULATION_FOLD This defines the size of the file used for folding virtual allocation, in MiB. The default is 1, thus allowing 64GiB virtual memory when Linux's `sysctl vm.max_map_count` value is the default 65535.

STARPU_SIMGRID_TASK_SUBMIT_COST When set to 1 (which is the default), task submission costs are taken into account in simgrid mode. This provides more accurate simgrid predictions, especially for the beginning of the execution.

STARPU_SIMGRID_FETCHING_INPUT_COST When set to 1 (which is the default), fetching input costs are taken into account in simgrid mode. This provides more accurate simgrid predictions, especially regarding data transfers.

STARPU_SIMGRID_SCHED_COST When set to 1 (0 is the default), scheduling costs are taken into account in simgrid mode. This provides more accurate simgrid predictions, and allows studying scheduling overhead of the runtime system. However, it also makes simulation non-deterministic.

26.4 Miscellaneous And Debug

STARPU_HOME This specifies the main directory in which StarPU stores its configuration files. The default is `$HOME` on Unix environments, and `$USERPROFILE` on Windows environments.

STARPU_PATH Only used on Windows environments. This specifies the main directory in which StarPU is installed (Running a Basic StarPU Application on Microsoft Visual C)

STARPU_PERF_MODEL_DIR This specifies the main directory in which StarPU stores its performance model files. The default is `$STARPU_HOME/.starpu/sampling`.

STARPU_PERF_MODEL_HOMOGENEOUS_CPU When this is set to 0, StarPU will assume that CPU devices do not have the same performance, and thus use different performance models for them, thus making kernel calibration much longer, since measurements have to be made for each CPU core.

STARPU_PERF_MODEL_HOMOGENEOUS_CUDA When this is set to 1, StarPU will assume that all CUDA devices have the same performance, and thus share performance models for them, thus allowing kernel calibration to be much faster, since measurements only have to be once for all CUDA GPUs.

STARPU_PERF_MODEL_HOMOGENEOUS_OPENCL When this is set to 1, StarPU will assume that all OPEN-CL devices have the same performance, and thus share performance models for them, thus allowing kernel calibration to be much faster, since measurements only have to be once for all OPENCL GPUs.

STARPU_PERF_MODEL_HOMOGENEOUS_MIC When this is set to 1, StarPU will assume that all MIC devices have the same performance, and thus share performance models for them, thus allowing kernel calibration to be much faster, since measurements only have to be once for all MIC GPUs.

STARPU_PERF_MODEL_HOMOGENEOUS_MPI_MS When this is set to 1, StarPU will assume that all MPI Slave devices have the same performance, and thus share performance models for them, thus allowing kernel calibration to be much faster, since measurements only have to be once for all MPI Slaves.

STARPU_PERF_MODEL_HOMOGENEOUS_SCC When this is set to 1, StarPU will assume that all SCC devices have the same performance, and thus share performance models for them, thus allowing kernel calibration to be much faster, since measurements only have to be once for all SCC GPUs.

STARPU_HOSTNAME   When set, force the hostname to be used when dealing performance model files. Models are indexed by machine name. When running for example on a homogenenous cluster, it is possible to share the models between machines by setting `export STARPU_HOSTNAME=some_global_name`.

STARPU_OPENCL_PROGRAM_DIR   This specifies the directory where the OpenCL codelet source files are located. The function starpu_opencl_load_program_source() looks for the codelet in the current directory, in the directory specified by the environment variable STARPU_OPENCL_PROGRAM_DIR, in the directory `share/starpu/opencl` of the installation directory of StarPU, and finally in the source directory of StarPU.

STARPU_SILENT   This variable allows to disable verbose mode at runtime when StarPU has been configured with the option --enable-verbose. It also disables the display of StarPU information and warning messages.

STARPU_LOGFILENAME   This variable specifies in which file the debugging output should be saved to.

STARPU_FXT_PREFIX   This variable specifies in which directory to save the trace generated if FxT is enabled. It needs to have a trailing '/' character.

STARPU_FXT_TRACE   This variable specifies whether to generate (1) or not (0) the FxT trace in /tmp/prof_file_-XXX_YYY . The default is 1 (generate it)

STARPU_LIMIT_CUDA_devid_MEM   This variable specifies the maximum number of megabytes that should be available to the application on the CUDA device with the identifier `devid`. This variable is intended to be used for experimental purposes as it emulates devices that have a limited amount of memory. When defined, the variable overwrites the value of the variable STARPU_LIMIT_CUDA_MEM.

STARPU_LIMIT_CUDA_MEM   This variable specifies the maximum number of megabytes that should be available to the application on each CUDA devices. This variable is intended to be used for experimental purposes as it emulates devices that have a limited amount of memory.

STARPU_LIMIT_OPENCL_devid_MEM   This variable specifies the maximum number of megabytes that should be available to the application on the OpenCL device with the identifier `devid`. This variable is intended to be used for experimental purposes as it emulates devices that have a limited amount of memory. When defined, the variable overwrites the value of the variable STARPU_LIMIT_OPENCL_MEM.

STARPU_LIMIT_OPENCL_MEM   This variable specifies the maximum number of megabytes that should be available to the application on each OpenCL devices. This variable is intended to be used for experimental purposes as it emulates devices that have a limited amount of memory.

STARPU_LIMIT_CPU_MEM   This variable specifies the maximum number of megabytes that should be available to the application in the main CPU memory. Setting it enables allocation cache in main memory

STARPU_MINIMUM_AVAILABLE_MEM   This specifies the minimum percentage of memory that should be available in GPUs (or in main memory, when using out of core), below which a reclaiming pass is performed. The default is 0%.

STARPU_TARGET_AVAILABLE_MEM   This specifies the target percentage of memory that should be reached in GPUs (or in main memory, when using out of core), when performing a periodic reclaiming pass. The default is 0%.

STARPU_MINIMUM_CLEAN_BUFFERS   This specifies the minimum percentage of number of buffers that should be clean in GPUs (or in main memory, when using out of core), below which asynchronous writebacks will be issued. The default is 5%.

STARPU_TARGET_CLEAN_BUFFERS   This specifies the target percentage of number of buffers that should be reached in GPUs (or in main memory, when using out of core), when performing an asynchronous writeback pass. The default is 10%.

STARPU_DIDUSE_BARRIER   When set to 1, StarPU will never evict a piece of data if it has not been used by at least one task. This avoids odd behaviors under high memory pressure, but can lead to deadlocks, so is to be considered experimental only.

STARPU_DISK_SWAP   This specifies a path where StarPU can push data when the main memory is getting full.

STARPU_DISK_SWAP_BACKEND This specifies then backend to be used by StarPU to push data when the main memory is getting full. The default is unistd (i.e. using read/write functions), other values are stdio (i.e. using fread/fwrite), unistd_o_direct (i.e. using read/write with O_DIRECT), and leveldb (i.e. using a leveldb database).

STARPU_DISK_SWAP_SIZE This specifies then maximum size in MiB to be used by StarPU to push data when the main memory is getting full. The default is unlimited.

STARPU_LIMIT_MAX_SUBMITTED_TASKS This variable allows the user to control the task submission flow by specifying to StarPU a maximum number of submitted tasks allowed at a given time, i.e. when this limit is reached task submission becomes blocking until enough tasks have completed, specified by STARPU_LIMIT_MIN_SUBMITTED_TASKS. Setting it enables allocation cache buffer reuse in main memory.

STARPU_LIMIT_MIN_SUBMITTED_TASKS This variable allows the user to control the task submission flow by specifying to StarPU a submitted task threshold to wait before unblocking task submission. This variable has to be used in conjunction with STARPU_LIMIT_MAX_SUBMITTED_TASKS which puts the task submission thread to sleep. Setting it enables allocation cache buffer reuse in main memory.

STARPU_TRACE_BUFFER_SIZE This sets the buffer size for recording trace events in MiB. Setting it to a big size allows to avoid pauses in the trace while it is recorded on the disk. This however also consumes memory, of course. The default value is 64.

STARPU_GENERATE_TRACE When set to 1, this variable indicates that StarPU should automatically generate a Paje trace when starpu_shutdown() is called.

STARPU_ENABLE_STATS When defined, enable gathering various data statistics (Data Statistics).

STARPU_MEMORY_STATS When set to 0, disable the display of memory statistics on data which have not been unregistered at the end of the execution (Memory Feedback).

STARPU_MAX_MEMORY_USE When set to 1, display at the end of the execution the maximum memory used by StarPU for internal data structures during execution.

STARPU_BUS_STATS When defined, statistics about data transfers will be displayed when calling starpu_shutdown() (Profiling).

STARPU_WORKER_STATS When defined, statistics about the workers will be displayed when calling starpu_shutdown() (Profiling). When combined with the environment variable STARPU_PROFILING, it displays the energy consumption (Energy-based Scheduling).

STARPU_STATS When set to 0, data statistics will not be displayed at the end of the execution of an application (Data Statistics).

STARPU_WATCHDOG_TIMEOUT When set to a value other than 0, allows to make StarPU print an error message whenever StarPU does not terminate any task for the given time (in µs), but lets the application continue normally. Should be used in combination with STARPU_WATCHDOG_CRASH (see Detecting Stuck Conditions).

STARPU_WATCHDOG_CRASH When set to a value other than 0, it triggers a crash when the watch dog is reached, thus allowing to catch the situation in gdb, etc (see Detecting Stuck Conditions)

STARPU_TASK_BREAK_ON_PUSH When this variable contains a job id, StarPU will raise SIGTRAP when the task with that job id is being pushed to the scheduler, which will be nicely caught by debuggers (see Debugging Scheduling)

STARPU_TASK_BREAK_ON_SCHED When this variable contains a job id, StarPU will raise SIGTRAP when the task with that job id is being scheduled by the scheduler (at a scheduler-specific point), which will be nicely caught by debuggers. This only works for schedulers which have such a scheduling point defined (see Debugging Scheduling)

STARPU_TASK_BREAK_ON_POP When this variable contains a job id, StarPU will raise SIGTRAP when the task with that job id is being popped from the scheduler, which will be nicely caught by debuggers (see Debugging Scheduling)

STARPU_TASK_BREAK_ON_EXEC When this variable contains a job id, StarPU will raise SIGTRAP when the task with that job id is being executed, which will be nicely caught by debuggers (see Debugging Scheduling)

STARPU_DISABLE_KERNELS When set to a value other than 1, it disables actually calling the kernel functions, thus allowing to quickly check that the task scheme is working properly, without performing the actual application-provided computation.

STARPU_HISTORY_MAX_ERROR History-based performance models will drop measurements which are really far froom the measured average. This specifies the allowed variation. The default is 50 (%), i.e. the measurement is allowed to be x1.5 faster or /1.5 slower than the average.

STARPU_RAND_SEED The random scheduler and some examples use random numbers for their own working. Depending on the examples, the seed is by default juste always 0 or the current time() (unless simgrid mode is enabled, in which case it is always 0). STARPU_RAND_SEED allows to set the seed to a specific value.

STARPU_IDLE_TIME When set to a value being a valid filename, a corresponding file will be created when shutting down StarPU. The file will contain the sum of all the workers' idle time.

STARPU_GLOBAL_ARBITER When set to a positive value, StarPU will create a arbiter, which implements an advanced but centralized management of concurrent data accesses (see Concurrent Data Accesses).

26.5 Configuring The Hypervisor

SC_HYPERVISOR_POLICY Choose between the different resizing policies proposed by StarPU for the hypervisor: idle, app_driven, feft_lp, teft_lp; ispeed_lp, throughput_lp etc.

Use SC_HYPERVISOR_POLICY=help to get the list of available policies for the hypervisor

SC_HYPERVISOR_TRIGGER_RESIZE Choose how should the hypervisor be triggered: speed if the resizing algorithm should be called whenever the speed of the context does not correspond to an optimal precomputed value, idle it the resizing algorithm should be called whenever the workers are idle for a period longer than the value indicated when configuring the hypervisor.

SC_HYPERVISOR_START_RESIZE Indicate the moment when the resizing should be available. The value correspond to the percentage of the total time of execution of the application. The default value is the resizing frame.

SC_HYPERVISOR_MAX_SPEED_GAP Indicate the ratio of speed difference between contexts that should trigger the hypervisor. This situation may occur only when a theoretical speed could not be computed and the hypervisor has no value to compare the speed to. Otherwise the resizing of a context is not influenced by the the speed of the other contexts, but only by the the value that a context should have.

SC_HYPERVISOR_STOP_PRINT By default the values of the speed of the workers is printed during the execution of the application. If the value 1 is given to this environment variable this printing is not done.

SC_HYPERVISOR_LAZY_RESIZE By default the hypervisor resizes the contexts in a lazy way, that is workers are firstly added to a new context before removing them from the previous one. Once this workers are clearly taken into account into the new context (a task was poped there) we remove them from the previous one. However if the application would like that the change in the distribution of workers should change right away this variable should be set to 0

SC_HYPERVISOR_SAMPLE_CRITERIA By default the hypervisor uses a sample of flops when computing the speed of the contexts and of the workers. If this variable is set to time the hypervisor uses a sample of time (10% of an aproximation of the total execution time of the application)

Chapter 27

Compilation Configuration

The behavior of the StarPU library and tools may be tuned thanks to the following configure options.

27.1 Common Configuration

–enable-debug   Enable debugging messages.

–enable-spinlock-check   Enable checking that spinlocks are taken and released properly.

–enable-fast   Disable assertion checks, which saves computation time.

–enable-verbose   Increase the verbosity of the debugging messages. This can be disabled at runtime by setting the environment variable STARPU_SILENT to any value. `-enable-verbose=extra` increase even more the verbosity.

```
$ STARPU_SILENT=1 ./vector_scal
```

–enable-coverage   Enable flags for the coverage tool `gcov`.

–enable-quick-check   Specify tests and examples should be run on a smaller data set, i.e allowing a faster execution time

–enable-long-check   Enable some exhaustive checks which take a really long time.

–enable-new-check   Enable new testcases which are known to fail.

–with-hwloc   Specify `hwloc` should be used by StarPU. `hwloc` should be found by the means of the tool `pkg-config`.

–with-hwloc=`prefix`   Specify `hwloc` should be used by StarPU. `hwloc` should be found in the directory specified by `prefix`

–without-hwloc   Specify `hwloc` should not be used by StarPU.

–disable-build-doc   Disable the creation of the documentation.   This should be done on a machine which does not have the tools `doxygen` and `latex` (plus the packages `latex-xcolor` and `texlive-latex-extra`).

Additionally, the script `configure` recognize many variables, which can be listed by typing `./configure -help`. For example, `./configure NVCCFLAGS="-arch sm_20"` adds a flag for the compilation of CUDA kernels, and `NVCC_CC=gcc-5` allows to change the C++ compiler used by nvcc.

27.2 Configuring Workers

--enable-maxcpus=`count` Use at most `count` CPU cores. This information is then available as the macro STARPU_MAXCPUS.

--disable-cpu Disable the use of CPUs of the machine. Only GPUs etc. will be used.

--enable-maxcudadev=`count` Use at most `count` CUDA devices. This information is then available as the macro STARPU_MAXCUDADEVS.

--disable-cuda Disable the use of CUDA, even if a valid CUDA installation was detected.

--with-cuda-dir=`prefix` Search for CUDA under `prefix`, which should notably contain the file `include/cuda.-h`.

--with-cuda-include-dir=`dir` Search for CUDA headers under `dir`, which should notably contain the file `cuda.h`. This defaults to `/include` appended to the value given to --with-cuda-dir.

--with-cuda-lib-dir=`dir` Search for CUDA libraries under `dir`, which should notably contain the CUDA shared libraries—e.g., `libcuda.so`. This defaults to `/lib` appended to the value given to --with-cuda-dir.

--disable-cuda-memcpy-peer Explicitly disable peer transfers when using CUDA 4.0.

--enable-maxopencldev=`count` Use at most `count` OpenCL devices. This information is then available as the macro STARPU_MAXOPENCLDEVS.

--disable-opencl Disable the use of OpenCL, even if the SDK is detected.

--with-opencl-dir=`prefix` Search for an OpenCL implementation under `prefix`, which should notably contain `include/CL/cl.h` (or `include/OpenCL/cl.h` on Mac OS).

--with-opencl-include-dir=`dir` Search for OpenCL headers under `dir`, which should notably contain `CL/cl.h` (or `OpenCL/cl.h` on Mac OS). This defaults to `/include` appended to the value given to --with-opencl-dir.

--with-opencl-lib-dir=`dir` Search for an OpenCL library under `dir`, which should notably contain the OpenCL shared libraries—e.g. `libOpenCL.so`. This defaults to `/lib` appended to the value given to --with-opencl-dir.

--enable-opencl-simulator Enable considering the provided OpenCL implementation as a simulator, i.e. use the kernel duration returned by OpenCL profiling information as wallclock time instead of the actual measured real time. This requires simgrid support.

--enable-maximplementations=`count` Allow for at most `count` codelet implementations for the same target device. This information is then available as the macro STARPU_MAXIMPLEMENTATIONS macro.

--enable-max-sched-ctxs=`count` Allow for at most `count` scheduling contexts This information is then available as the macro STARPU_NMAX_SCHED_CTXS.

--disable-asynchronous-copy Disable asynchronous copies between CPU and GPU devices. The AMD implementation of OpenCL is known to fail when copying data asynchronously. When using this implementation, it is therefore necessary to disable asynchronous data transfers.

--disable-asynchronous-cuda-copy Disable asynchronous copies between CPU and CUDA devices.

--disable-asynchronous-opencl-copy Disable asynchronous copies between CPU and OpenCL devices. The AMD implementation of OpenCL is known to fail when copying data asynchronously. When using this implementation, it is therefore necessary to disable asynchronous data transfers.

--enable-maxmicthreads Specify the maximum number of MIC threads

--disable-asynchronous-mic-copy Disable asynchronous copies between CPU and MIC devices.

--disable-asynchronous-mpi-master-slave-copy Disable asynchronous copies between CPU and MPI Slave devices.

--enable-maxnodes=`count` Use at most `count` memory nodes. This information is then available as the macro STARPU_MAXNODES. Reducing it allows to considerably reduce memory used by StarPU data structures.

27.3 Extension Configuration

–disable-mpi Disable the build of libstarpumpi. By default, it is enabled when MPI is found.

–with-mpicc=path Use the compiler `mpicc` at `path`, for StarPU-MPI. (MPI Support).

–enable-mpi-pedantic-isend Before performing any MPI communication, StarPU-MPI waits for the data to be available in the main memory of the node submitting the request. For send communications, data is acquired with the mode STARPU_R. When enabling the pedantic mode, data are instead acquired with the STARPU-_RW which thus ensures that there is not more than 1 concurrent MPI_Isend calls accessing the data.

–enable-mpi-master-slave Enable the MPI Master-Slave support. By default, it is disabled.

–with-mpi-master-slave-multiple-thread Create one thread per MPI Slave on the MPI master to manage communications.

–disable-fortran Disable the fortran extension. By default, it is enabled when a fortran compiler is found.

–disable-socl Disable the SOCL extension (SOCL OpenCL Extensions). By default, it is enabled when an OpenCL implementation is found.

–disable-starpu-top Disable the StarPU-Top interface (StarPU-Top Interface). By default, it is enabled when the required dependencies are found.

–disable-gcc-extensions Disable the GCC plug-in (C Extensions). By default, it is enabled when the GCC compiler provides a plug-in support.

–with-coi-dir Specify the directory to the COI library for MIC support. The default value is `/opt/intel/mic/coi`

–mic-host Specify the precise MIC architecture host identifier. The default value is `x86_64-k1om-linux`

–enable-openmp Enable OpenMP Support (The StarPU OpenMP Runtime Support (SORS))

27.4 Advanced Configuration

–enable-perf-debug Enable performance debugging through gprof.

–enable-model-debug Enable performance model debugging.

–enable-fxt-lock Enable additional trace events which describes locks behaviour.

–enable-maxbuffers Define the maximum number of buffers that tasks will be able to take as parameters, then available as the macro STARPU_NMAXBUFS.

–enable-allocation-cache Enable the use of a data allocation cache to avoid the cost of it with CUDA. Still experimental.

–enable-opengl-render Enable the use of OpenGL for the rendering of some examples.

–enable-blas-lib=prefix Specify the blas library to be used by some of the examples. Librairies available :

- none [default] : no BLAS library is used
- atlas: use ATLAS library
- goto: use GotoBLAS library
- mkl: use MKL library (you may need to set specific CFLAGS and LDFLAGS with –with-mkl-cflags and –with-mkl-ldflags)

–enable-leveldb Enable linking with LevelDB if available

–disable-starpufft Disable the build of libstarpufft, even if `fftw` or `cuFFT` is available.

–enable-starpufft-examples Enable the compilation and the execution of the libstarpufft examples. By default, they are neither compiled nor checked.

–with-fxt=`prefix`   Search for FxT under `prefix`. FxT (`http://savannah.nongnu.org/projects/fkt`) is used to generate traces of scheduling events, which can then be rendered them using ViTE (Off-line Performance Feedback). `prefix` should notably contain `include/fxt/fxt.h`.

–with-perf-model-dir=`dir`   Store performance models under `dir`, instead of the current user's home.

–with-goto-dir=`prefix`   Search for GotoBLAS under `prefix`, which should notably contain `libgoto.so` or `libgoto2.so`.

–with-atlas-dir=`prefix`   Search for ATLAS under `prefix`, which should notably contain `include/cblas.-h`.

–with-mkl-cflags=`cflags`   Use `cflags` to compile code that uses the MKL library.

–with-mkl-ldflags=`ldflags`   Use `ldflags` when linking code that uses the MKL library. Note that the MKL website (`http://software.intel.com/en-us/articles/intel-mkl-link-line-advisor/`) provides a script to determine the linking flags.

–disable-glpk   Disable the use of libglpk for computing area bounds.

–disable-build-tests   Disable the build of tests.

–disable-build-examples   Disable the build of examples.

–disable-build-tests   Disable the build of tests.

–enable-sc-hypervisor   Enable the Scheduling Context Hypervisor plugin (Scheduling Context Hypervisor). By default, it is disabled.

–enable-memory-stats   Enable memory statistics (Memory Feedback).

–enable-simgrid   Enable simulation of execution in simgrid, to allow easy experimentation with various numbers of cores and GPUs, or amount of memory, etc. Experimental.

   The path to simgrid can be specified through the `SIMGRID_CFLAGS` and `SIMGRID_LIBS` environment variables, for instance:

```
export SIMGRID_CFLAGS="-I/usr/local/simgrid/include"
export SIMGRID_LIBS="-L/usr/local/simgrid/lib -lsimgrid"
```

–with-simgrid-dir   Similar to the option --enable-simgrid but also allows to specify the location to the SimGrid library.

–with-simgrid-include-dir   Similar to the option --enable-simgrid but also allows to specify the location to the SimGrid include directory.

–with-simgrid-lib-dir   Similar to the option --enable-simgrid but also allows to specify the location to the SimGrid lib directory.

–with-smpirun=`path`   Use the smpirun at `path`

–enable-simgrid-mc   Enable the Model Checker in simulation of execution in simgrid, to allow exploring various execution paths.

–enable-calibration-heuristic   Allows to set the maximum authorized percentage of deviation for the history-based calibrator of StarPU. A correct value of this parameter must be in [0..100]. The default value of this parameter is 10. Experimental.

Chapter 28

Module Index

28.1 Modules

Here is a list of all modules:

Chapter 29

Module Documentation a.k.a StarPU's API

29.1 Versioning

Macros

- #define STARPU_MAJOR_VERSION
- #define STARPU_MINOR_VERSION
- #define STARPU_RELEASE_VERSION

Functions

- void starpu_get_version (int ∗major, int ∗minor, int ∗release)

29.1.1 Detailed Description

29.1.2 Macro Definition Documentation

29.1.2.1 #define STARPU_MAJOR_VERSION

Define the major version of StarPU. This is the version used when compiling the application.

29.1.2.2 #define STARPU_MINOR_VERSION

Define the minor version of StarPU. This is the version used when compiling the application.

29.1.2.3 #define STARPU_RELEASE_VERSION

Define the release version of StarPU. This is the version used when compiling the application.

29.1.3 Function Documentation

29.1.3.1 void starpu_get_version (int ∗ *major,* int ∗ *minor,* int ∗ *release*)

Return as 3 integers the version of StarPU used when running the application.

29.2   Initialization and Termination

Data Structures

- struct starpu_conf

Functions

- int starpu_init (struct starpu_conf *conf) STARPU_WARN_UNUSED_RESULT
- int starpu_initialize (struct starpu_conf *user_conf, int *argc, char ***argv)
- int starpu_conf_init (struct starpu_conf *conf)
- void starpu_shutdown (void)
- void starpu_pause (void)
- void starpu_resume (void)
- int starpu_asynchronous_copy_disabled (void)
- int starpu_asynchronous_cuda_copy_disabled (void)
- int starpu_asynchronous_opencl_copy_disabled (void)
- int starpu_asynchronous_mic_copy_disabled (void)
- int starpu_asynchronous_mpi_ms_copy_disabled (void)
- void starpu_topology_print (FILE *f)

29.2.1   Detailed Description

29.2.2   Data Structure Documentation

29.2.2.1   struct starpu_conf

This structure is passed to the starpu_init() function in order to configure StarPU. It has to be initialized with starpu_conf_init(). When the default value is used, StarPU automatically selects the number of processing units and takes the default scheduling policy. The environment variables overwrite the equivalent parameters.

Data Fields

- int magic
- const char * sched_policy_name
- struct starpu_sched_policy * sched_policy
- void(* sched_policy_init)(unsigned)
- int ncpus
- int ncuda
- int nopencl
- int nmic
- int nscc
- int nmpi_ms
- unsigned use_explicit_workers_bindid
- unsigned workers_bindid [STARPU_NMAXWORKERS]
- unsigned use_explicit_workers_cuda_gpuid
- unsigned workers_cuda_gpuid [STARPU_NMAXWORKERS]
- unsigned use_explicit_workers_opencl_gpuid
- unsigned workers_opencl_gpuid [STARPU_NMAXWORKERS]
- unsigned use_explicit_workers_mic_deviceid
- unsigned workers_mic_deviceid [STARPU_NMAXWORKERS]
- unsigned use_explicit_workers_scc_deviceid
- unsigned workers_scc_deviceid [STARPU_NMAXWORKERS]

- unsigned use_explicit_workers_mpi_ms_deviceid
- unsigned workers_mpi_ms_deviceid [STARPU_NMAXWORKERS]
- int bus_calibrate
- int calibrate
- int single_combined_worker
- char * mic_sink_program_path
- int disable_asynchronous_copy
- int disable_asynchronous_cuda_copy
- int disable_asynchronous_opencl_copy
- int disable_asynchronous_mic_copy
- int disable_asynchronous_mpi_ms_copy
- unsigned * cuda_opengl_interoperability
- unsigned n_cuda_opengl_interoperability
- struct starpu_driver * not_launched_drivers
- unsigned n_not_launched_drivers
- unsigned trace_buffer_size
- int global_sched_ctx_min_priority
- int global_sched_ctx_max_priority

29.2.2.1.1 Field Documentation

29.2.2.1.1.1 int starpu_conf::magic

Will be initialized by starpu_conf_init(). Should not be set by hand.

29.2.2.1.1.2 const char * starpu_conf::sched_policy_name

Name of the scheduling policy. This can also be specified with the environment variable STARPU_SCHED. (default = NULL).

29.2.2.1.1.3 struct **starpu_sched_policy** * starpu_conf::sched_policy

Definition of the scheduling policy. This field is ignored if starpu_conf::sched_policy_name is set. (default = NULL)

29.2.2.1.1.4 void(* **starpu_conf::sched_policy_init**)(unsigned)

todo

29.2.2.1.1.5 int starpu_conf::ncpus

Number of CPU cores that StarPU can use. This can also be specified with the environment variable STARPU_N-CPU . (default = -1)

29.2.2.1.1.6 int starpu_conf::ncuda

Number of CUDA devices that StarPU can use. This can also be specified with the environment variable STARPU-_NCUDA. (default = -1)

29.2.2.1.1.7 int starpu_conf::nopencl

Number of OpenCL devices that StarPU can use. This can also be specified with the environment variable STAR-PU_NOPENCL. (default = -1)

29.2.2.1.1.8 int starpu_conf::nmic

Number of MIC devices that StarPU can use. This can also be specified with the environment variable STARPU_-NMIC. (default = -1)

29.2.2.1.1.9   int starpu_conf::nscc

Number of SCC devices that StarPU can use. This can also be specified with the environment variable STARPU_-NSCC. (default = -1)

29.2.2.1.1.10   int starpu_conf::nmpi_ms

Number of MPI Master Slave devices that StarPU can use. This can also be specified with the environment variable STARPU_NMPI_MS. (default = -1)

29.2.2.1.1.11   unsigned starpu_conf::use_explicit_workers_bindid

If this flag is set, the starpu_conf::workers_bindid array indicates where the different workers are bound, otherwise StarPU automatically selects where to bind the different workers. This can also be specified with the environment variable STARPU_WORKERS_CPUID. (default = 0)

29.2.2.1.1.12   unsigned starpu_conf::workers_bindid[**STARPU_NMAXWORKERS**]

If the starpu_conf::use_explicit_workers_bindid flag is set, this array indicates where to bind the different workers. The i-th entry of the starpu_conf::workers_bindid indicates the logical identifier of the processor which should execute the i-th worker. Note that the logical ordering of the CPUs is either determined by the OS, or provided by the hwloc library in case it is available.

29.2.2.1.1.13   unsigned starpu_conf::use_explicit_workers_cuda_gpuid

If this flag is set, the CUDA workers will be attached to the CUDA devices specified in the starpu_conf::workers_-cuda_gpuid array. Otherwise, StarPU affects the CUDA devices in a round-robin fashion. This can also be specified with the environment variable STARPU_WORKERS_CUDAID. (default = 0)

29.2.2.1.1.14   unsigned starpu_conf::workers_cuda_gpuid[**STARPU_NMAXWORKERS**]

If the starpu_conf::use_explicit_workers_cuda_gpuid flag is set, this array contains the logical identifiers of the CUDA devices (as used by `cudaGetDevice()`).

29.2.2.1.1.15   unsigned starpu_conf::use_explicit_workers_opencl_gpuid

If this flag is set, the OpenCL workers will be attached to the OpenCL devices specified in the starpu_conf::workers_opencl_gpuid array. Otherwise, StarPU affects the OpenCL devices in a round-robin fashion. This can also be specified with the environment variable STARPU_WORKERS_OPENCLID. (default = 0)

29.2.2.1.1.16   unsigned starpu_conf::workers_opencl_gpuid[**STARPU_NMAXWORKERS**]

If the starpu_conf::use_explicit_workers_opencl_gpuid flag is set, this array contains the logical identifiers of the OpenCL devices to be used.

29.2.2.1.1.17   unsigned starpu_conf::use_explicit_workers_mic_deviceid

If this flag is set, the MIC workers will be attached to the MIC devices specified in the array starpu_conf::workers_-mic_deviceid. Otherwise, StarPU affects the MIC devices in a round-robin fashion. This can also be specified with the environment variable STARPU_WORKERS_MICID. (default = 0)

29.2.2.1.1.18   unsigned starpu_conf::workers_mic_deviceid[**STARPU_NMAXWORKERS**]

If the flag starpu_conf::use_explicit_workers_mic_deviceid is set, the array contains the logical identifiers of the MIC devices to be used.

29.2.2.1.1.19   unsigned starpu_conf::use_explicit_workers_scc_deviceid

If this flag is set, the SCC workers will be attached to the SCC devices specified in the array starpu_conf::workers-_scc_deviceid. (default = 0)

29.2.2.1.1.20 unsigned starpu_conf::workers_scc_deviceid[STARPU_NMAXWORKERS]

If the flag starpu_conf::use_explicit_workers_scc_deviceid is set, the array contains the logical identifiers of the SCC devices to be used. Otherwise, StarPU affects the SCC devices in a round-robin fashion. This can also be specified with the environment variable STARPU_WORKERS_SCCID.

29.2.2.1.1.21 unsigned starpu_conf::use_explicit_workers_mpi_ms_deviceid

If this flag is set, the MPI Master Slave workers will be attached to the MPI Master Slave devices specified in the array starpu_conf::workers_mpi_ms_deviceid. Otherwise, StarPU affects the MPI Master Slave devices in a round-robin fashion. (default = 0)

29.2.2.1.1.22 unsigned starpu_conf::workers_mpi_ms_deviceid[STARPU_NMAXWORKERS]

If the flag starpu_conf::use_explicit_workers_mpi_ms_deviceid is set, the array contains the logical identifiers of the MPI Master Slave devices to be used.

29.2.2.1.1.23 int starpu_conf::bus_calibrate

If this flag is set, StarPU will recalibrate the bus. If this value is equal to -1, the default value is used. This can also be specified with the environment variable STARPU_BUS_CALIBRATE. (default = 0)

29.2.2.1.1.24 int starpu_conf::calibrate

If this flag is set, StarPU will calibrate the performance models when executing tasks. If this value is equal to -1, the default value is used. If the value is equal to 1, it will force continuing calibration. If the value is equal to 2, the existing performance models will be overwritten. This can also be specified with the environment variable STARPU_CALIBRATE. (default = 0)

29.2.2.1.1.25 int starpu_conf::single_combined_worker

By default, StarPU executes parallel tasks concurrently. Some parallel libraries (e.g. most OpenMP implementations) however do not support concurrent calls to parallel code. In such case, setting this flag makes StarPU only start one parallel task at a time (but other CPU and GPU tasks are not affected and can be run concurrently). The parallel task scheduler will however still try varying combined worker sizes to look for the most efficient ones. This can also be specified with the environment variable STARPU_SINGLE_COMBINED_WORKER. (default = 0)

29.2.2.1.1.26 char * starpu_conf::mic_sink_program_path

Path to the kernel to execute on the MIC device, compiled for MIC architecture. When set to NULL, StarPU automatically looks next to the host program location. (default = NULL)

29.2.2.1.1.27 int starpu_conf::disable_asynchronous_copy

This flag should be set to 1 to disable asynchronous copies between CPUs and all accelerators. This can also be specified with the environment variable STARPU_DISABLE_ASYNCHRONOUS_COPY. The AMD implementation of OpenCL is known to fail when copying data asynchronously. When using this implementation, it is therefore necessary to disable asynchronous data transfers. This can also be specified at compilation time by giving to the configure script the option --disable-asynchronous-copy. (default = 0)

29.2.2.1.1.28 int starpu_conf::disable_asynchronous_cuda_copy

This flag should be set to 1 to disable asynchronous copies between CPUs and CUDA accelerators. This can also be specified with the environment variable STARPU_DISABLE_ASYNCHRONOUS_CUDA_COPY. This can also be specified at compilation time by giving to the configure script the option --disable-asynchronous-cuda-copy. (default = 0)

29.2.2.1.1.29 int starpu_conf::disable_asynchronous_opencl_copy

This flag should be set to 1 to disable asynchronous copies between CPUs and OpenCL accelerators. This can also be specified with the environment variable STARPU_DISABLE_ASYNCHRONOUS_OPENCL_COPY. The A-

MD implementation of OpenCL is known to fail when copying data asynchronously. When using this implementation, it is therefore necessary to disable asynchronous data transfers. This can also be specified at compilation time by giving to the configure script the option --disable-asynchronous-opencl-copy. (default = 0)

29.2.2.1.1.30 int starpu_conf::disable_asynchronous_mic_copy

This flag should be set to 1 to disable asynchronous copies between CPUs and MIC accelerators. This can also be specified with the environment variable STARPU_DISABLE_ASYNCHRONOUS_MIC_COPY. This can also be specified at compilation time by giving to the configure script the option --disable-asynchronous-mic-copy. (default = 0).

29.2.2.1.1.31 int starpu_conf::disable_asynchronous_mpi_ms_copy

This flag should be set to 1 to disable asynchronous copies between CPUs and MPI Master Slave devices. This can also be specified with the environment variable STARPU_DISABLE_ASYNCHRONOUS_MPI_MS_COPY. This can also be specified at compilation time by giving to the configure script the option --disable-asynchronous-mpi-master-slave-copy. (default = 0).

29.2.2.1.1.32 unsigned ∗ starpu_conf::cuda_opengl_interoperability

Enable CUDA/OpenGL interoperation on these CUDA devices. This can be set to an array of CUDA device identifiers for which `cudaGLSetGLDevice()` should be called instead of `cudaSetDevice()`. Its size is specified by the starpu_conf::n_cuda_opengl_interoperability field below (default = NULL)

29.2.2.1.1.33 unsigned starpu_conf::n_cuda_opengl_interoperability

todo

29.2.2.1.1.34 struct **starpu_driver** ∗ starpu_conf::not_launched_drivers

Array of drivers that should not be launched by StarPU. The application will run in one of its own threads. (default = NULL)

29.2.2.1.1.35 unsigned starpu_conf::n_not_launched_drivers

The number of StarPU drivers that should not be launched by StarPU. (default = 0)

29.2.2.1.1.36 starpu_conf::trace_buffer_size

Specify the buffer size used for FxT tracing. Starting from FxT version 0.2.12, the buffer will automatically be flushed when it fills in, but it may still be interesting to specify a bigger value to avoid any flushing (which would disturb the trace).

29.2.2.1.1.37 starpu_conf::global_sched_ctx_min_priority

todo

29.2.2.1.1.38 starpu_conf::global_sched_ctx_max_priority

todo

29.2.3 Function Documentation

29.2.3.1 int starpu_init (struct **starpu_conf** ∗ conf)

This is StarPU initialization method, which must be called prior to any other StarPU call. It is possible to specify StarPU's configuration (e.g. scheduling policy, number of cores, ...) by passing a non-NULL conf. Default configuration is used if conf is NULL. Upon successful completion, this function returns 0. Otherwise, -ENODEV indicates that no worker was available (and thus StarPU was not initialized).

29.2.3.2 int starpu_initialize (struct starpu_conf * user_conf, int * argc, char * argv)**

This is the same as starpu_init(), but also takes the `argc` and `argv` as defined by the application. This is needed for SCC execution to initialize the communication library. Do not call starpu_init() and starpu_initialize() in the same program.

29.2.3.3 int starpu_conf_init (struct starpu_conf * conf)

Initialize the `conf` structure with the default values. In case some configuration parameters are already specified through environment variables, starpu_conf_init() initializes the fields of `conf` according to the environment variables. For instance if STARPU_CALIBRATE is set, its value is put in the field starpu_conf::calibrate of `conf`. Upon successful completion, this function returns 0. Otherwise, `-EINVAL` indicates that the argument was `NULL`.

29.2.3.4 void starpu_shutdown (void)

This is StarPU termination method. It must be called at the end of the application: statistics and other post-mortem debugging information are not guaranteed to be available until this method has been called.

29.2.3.5 void starpu_pause (void)

Suspend the processing of new tasks by workers. It can be used in a program where StarPU is used during only a part of the execution. Without this call, the workers continue to poll for new tasks in a tight loop, wasting CPU time. The symmetric call to starpu_resume() should be used to unfreeze the workers.

29.2.3.6 void starpu_resume (void)

This is the symmetrical call to starpu_pause(), used to resume the workers polling for new tasks.

29.2.3.7 int starpu_asynchronous_copy_disabled (void)

Return 1 if asynchronous data transfers between CPU and accelerators are disabled.

29.2.3.8 int starpu_asynchronous_cuda_copy_disabled (void)

Return 1 if asynchronous data transfers between CPU and CUDA accelerators are disabled.

29.2.3.9 int starpu_asynchronous_opencl_copy_disabled (void)

Return 1 if asynchronous data transfers between CPU and OpenCL accelerators are disabled.

29.2.3.10 int starpu_asynchronous_mic_copy_disabled (void)

Return 1 if asynchronous data transfers between CPU and MIC devices are disabled.

29.2.3.11 int starpu_asynchronous_mpi_ms_copy_disabled (void)

Return 1 if asynchronous data transfers between CPU and MPI Slave devices are disabled.

29.2.3.12 void starpu_topology_print (FILE * f)

Print a description of the topology on `f`.

29.3   Standard Memory Library

Macros

- #define starpu_data_malloc_pinned_if_possible
- #define starpu_data_free_pinned_if_possible
- #define STARPU_MALLOC_PINNED
- #define STARPU_MALLOC_COUNT
- #define STARPU_MALLOC_NORECLAIM
- #define STARPU_MALLOC_SIMULATION_FOLDED
- #define STARPU_MEMORY_WAIT
- #define STARPU_MEMORY_OVERFLOW

Functions

- int starpu_malloc_flags (void **A, size_t dim, int flags) STARPU_ATTRIBUTE_ALLOC_SIZE(2)
- void starpu_malloc_set_align (size_t align)
- int starpu_malloc (void **A, size_t dim) STARPU_ATTRIBUTE_ALLOC_SIZE(2)
- int starpu_free (void *A)
- int starpu_free_flags (void *A, size_t dim, int flags)
- int starpu_memory_pin (void *addr, size_t size)
- int starpu_memory_unpin (void *addr, size_t size)
- starpu_ssize_t starpu_memory_get_total (unsigned node)
- starpu_ssize_t starpu_memory_get_total_all_nodes ()
- starpu_ssize_t starpu_memory_get_available (unsigned node)
- starpu_ssize_t starpu_memory_get_available_all_nodes ()
- int starpu_memory_allocate (unsigned node, size_t size, int flags)
- void starpu_memory_deallocate (unsigned node, size_t size)
- void starpu_memory_wait_available (unsigned node, size_t size)

29.3.1   Detailed Description

29.3.2   Macro Definition Documentation

29.3.2.1   #define starpu_data_malloc_pinned_if_possible

Deprecated Equivalent to starpu_malloc(). This macro is provided to avoid breaking old codes.

29.3.2.2   #define starpu_data_free_pinned_if_possible

Deprecated Equivalent to starpu_free(). This macro is provided to avoid breaking old codes.

29.3.2.3   #define STARPU_MALLOC_PINNED

Value passed to the function starpu_malloc_flags() to indicate the memory allocation should be pinned.

29.3.2.4 #define STARPU_MALLOC_COUNT

Value passed to the function starpu_malloc_flags() to indicate the memory allocation should be in the limit defined by the environment variables STARPU_LIMIT_CUDA_devid_MEM, STARPU_LIMIT_CUDA_MEM, STARPU_LIMIT_OPENCL_devid_MEM, STARPU_LIMIT_OPENCL_MEM and STARPU_LIMIT_CPU_MEM (see Section How to Limit Memory Used By StarPU And Cache Buffer Allocations). If no memory is available, it tries to reclaim memory from StarPU. Memory allocated this way needs to be freed by calling the function starpu_free_flags() with the same flag.

29.3.2.5 #define STARPU_MALLOC_NORECLAIM

Value passed to the function starpu_malloc_flags() along STARPU_MALLOC_COUNT to indicate that while the memory allocation should be kept in the limits defined for STARPU_MALLOC_COUNT, no reclaiming should be performed by starpu_malloc_flags() itself, thus potentially overflowing the memory node a bit. StarPU will reclaim memory after next task termination, according to the STARPU_MINIMUM_AVAILABLE_MEM, STARPU_TARGET_AVAILABLE_MEM, STARPU_MINIMUM_CLEAN_BUFFERS, and STARPU_TARGET_CLEAN_BUFFERS environment variables. If STARPU_MEMORY_WAIT is set, no overflowing will happen, starpu_malloc_flags() will wait for other eviction mechanisms to release enough memory.

29.3.2.6 #define STARPU_MALLOC_SIMULATION_FOLDED

Value passed to the function starpu_malloc_flags() to indicate that when StarPU is using simgrid, the allocation can be "folded", i.e. a memory area is allocated, but its content is actually a replicate of the same memory area, to avoid having to actually allocate that much memory . This thus allows to have a memory area that does not actually consumes memory, to which one can read from and write to normally, but get bogus values.

29.3.2.7 #define STARPU_MEMORY_WAIT

Value passed to starpu_memory_allocate() to specify that the function should wait for the requested amount of memory to become available, and atomically allocate it.

29.3.2.8 #define STARPU_MEMORY_OVERFLOW

Value passed to starpu_memory_allocate() to specify that the function should allocate the amount of memory, even if that means overflowing the total size of the memory node.

29.3.3 Function Documentation

29.3.3.1 int starpu_malloc_flags (void ∗∗ A, size_t dim, int flags)

Perform a memory allocation based on the constraints defined by the given flag.

29.3.3.2 void starpu_malloc_set_align (size_t align)

Set an alignment constraints for starpu_malloc() allocations. align must be a power of two. This is for instance called automatically by the OpenCL driver to specify its own alignment constraints.

29.3.3.3 int starpu_malloc (void ∗∗ A, size_t dim)

Allocate data of the given size dim in main memory, and return the pointer to the allocated data through A. It will also try to pin it in CUDA or OpenCL, so that data transfers from this buffer can be asynchronous, and thus permit data transfer and computation overlapping. The allocated buffer must be freed thanks to the starpu_free() function.

29.3.3.4   int starpu_free (void * A)

Free memory which has previously been allocated with starpu_malloc().

29.3.3.5   int starpu_free_flags (void * A, size_t dim, int flags)

Free memory by specifying its size. The given flags should be consistent with the ones given to starpu_malloc_-flags() when allocating the memory.

29.3.3.6   int starpu_memory_pin (void * addr, size_t size)

Pin the given memory area, so that CPU-GPU transfers can be done asynchronously with DMAs. The memory must be unpinned with starpu_memory_unpin() before being freed. Returns 0 on success, -1 on error.

29.3.3.7   int starpu_memory_unpin (void * addr, size_t size)

Unpin the given memory area previously pinned with starpu_memory_pin(). Returns 0 on success, -1 on error.

29.3.3.8   ssize_t starpu_memory_get_total (unsigned node)

If a memory limit is defined on the given node (see Section How to Limit Memory Used By StarPU And Cache Buffer Allocations), return the amount of total memory on the node. Otherwise return -1.

29.3.3.9   ssize_t starpu_memory_get_total_all_nodes ( )

Return the amount of total memory on all memory nodes for whose a memory limit is defined (see Section How to Limit Memory Used By StarPU And Cache Buffer Allocations).

29.3.3.10   ssize_t starpu_memory_get_available (unsigned node)

If a memory limit is defined on the given node (see Section How to Limit Memory Used By StarPU And Cache Buffer Allocations), return the amount of available memory on the node. Otherwise return -1.

29.3.3.11   ssize_t starpu_memory_get_available_all_nodes ( )

Return the amount of available memory on all memory nodes for whose a memory limit is defined (see Section How to Limit Memory Used By StarPU And Cache Buffer Allocations).

29.3.3.12   int starpu_memory_allocate (unsigned node, size_t size, int flags)

If a memory limit is defined on the given node (see Section How to Limit Memory Used By StarPU And Cache Buffer Allocations), try to allocate some of it. This does not actually allocate memory, but only accounts for it. This can be useful when the application allocates data another way, but want StarPU to be aware of the allocation size e.g. for memory reclaiming. By default, the function returns -ENOMEM if there is not enough room on the given node. flags can be either STARPU_MEMORY_WAIT or STARPU_MEMORY_OVERFLOW to change this.

29.3.3.13   void starpu_memory_deallocate (unsigned node, size_t size)

If a memory limit is defined on the given node (see Section How to Limit Memory Used By StarPU And Cache Buffer Allocations), free some of it. This does not actually free memory, but only accounts for it, like starpu_memory_-allocate(). The amount does not have to be exactly the same as what was passed to starpu_memory_allocate(), only the eventual amount needs to be the same, i.e. one call to starpu_memory_allocate() can be followed by several calls to starpu_memory_deallocate() to declare the deallocation piece by piece.

29.3.3.14 void starpu_memory_wait_available (unsigned *node*, size_t *size*)

If a memory limit is defined on the given node (see Section How to Limit Memory Used By StarPU And Cache Buffer Allocations), this will wait for `size` bytes to become available on `node`. Of course, since another thread may be allocating memory concurrently, this does not necessarily mean that this amount will be actually available, just that it was reached. To atomically wait for some amount of memory and reserve it, starpu_memory_allocate() should be used with the STARPU_MEMORY_WAIT flag.

29.4 Toolbox

The following macros allow to make GCC extensions portable, and to have a code which can be compiled with any C compiler.

Macros

- #define STARPU_GNUC_PREREQ(maj, min)
- #define STARPU_UNLIKELY(expr)
- #define STARPU_LIKELY(expr)
- #define STARPU_ATTRIBUTE_UNUSED
- #define STARPU_ATTRIBUTE_INTERNAL
- #define STARPU_ATTRIBUTE_MALLOC
- #define STARPU_ATTRIBUTE_WARN_UNUSED_RESULT
- #define STARPU_ATTRIBUTE_PURE
- #define STARPU_ATTRIBUTE_ALIGNED(size)
- #define STARPU_WARN_UNUSED_RESULT
- #define STARPU_POISON_PTR
- #define STARPU_MIN(a, b)
- #define STARPU_MAX(a, b)
- #define STARPU_ASSERT(x)
- #define STARPU_ASSERT_MSG(x, msg,...)
- #define STARPU_ABORT()
- #define STARPU_ABORT_MSG(msg,...)
- #define STARPU_CHECK_RETURN_VALUE(err, message,...)
- #define STARPU_CHECK_RETURN_VALUE_IS(err, value, message,...)
- #define STARPU_RMB()
- #define STARPU_WMB()

Functions

- static __starpu_inline int starpu_get_env_number (const char ∗str)

29.4.1 Detailed Description

The following macros allow to make GCC extensions portable, and to have a code which can be compiled with any C compiler.

29.4.2 Macro Definition Documentation

29.4.2.1 #define STARPU_GNUC_PREREQ(*maj, min*)

Return true (non-zero) if GCC version `maj.min` or later is being used (macro taken from glibc.)

29.4.2.2 #define STARPU_UNLIKELY(*expr*)

When building with a GNU C Compiler, allow programmers to mark an expression as unlikely.

29.4.2.3 #define STARPU_LIKELY(*expr*)

When building with a GNU C Compiler, allow programmers to mark an expression as likely.

29.4.2.4 #define STARPU_ATTRIBUTE_UNUSED

When building with a GNU C Compiler, defined to __attribute__((unused))

29.4.2.5 #define STARPU_ATTRIBUTE_INTERNAL

When building with a GNU C Compiler, defined to __attribute__((visibility ("internal")))

29.4.2.6 #define STARPU_ATTRIBUTE_MALLOC

When building with a GNU C Compiler, defined to __attribute__((malloc))

29.4.2.7 #define STARPU_ATTRIBUTE_WARN_UNUSED_RESULT

When building with a GNU C Compiler, defined to __attribute__((warn_unused_result))

29.4.2.8 #define STARPU_ATTRIBUTE_PURE

When building with a GNU C Compiler, defined to __attribute__((pure))

29.4.2.9 #define STARPU_ATTRIBUTE_ALIGNED(*size*)

When building with a GNU C Compiler, defined to__attribute__((aligned(size)))

29.4.2.10 #define STARPU_WARN_UNUSED_RESULT

When building with a GNU C Compiler, defined to__attribute__((__warn_unused_result__))

29.4.2.11 #define STARPU_POISON_PTR

Define a value which can be used to mark pointers as invalid values.

29.4.2.12 #define STARPU_MIN(*a, b*)

Return the min of the two parameters.

29.4.2.13   #define STARPU_MAX(*a, b*)

Return the max of the two parameters.

29.4.2.14   #define STARPU_ASSERT(*x*)

Unless StarPU has been configured with the option --enable-fast, this macro will abort if the expression is false.

29.4.2.15   #define STARPU_ASSERT_MSG(*x, msg, ...*)

Unless StarPU has been configured with the option --enable-fast, this macro will abort if the expression is false. The given message will be displayed.

29.4.2.16   #define STARPU_ABORT( )

Abort the program.

29.4.2.17   #define STARPU_ABORT_MSG(*msg, ...*)

Abort the program, and display the given message.

29.4.2.18   #define STARPU_CHECK_RETURN_VALUE(*err, message, ...*)

Abort the program (after displaying `message`) if `err` has a value which is not 0.

29.4.2.19   #define STARPU_CHECK_RETURN_VALUE_IS(*err, value, message, ...*)

Abort the program (after displaying `message`) if `err` is different from `value`.

29.4.2.20   #define STARPU_RMB( )

This macro can be used to do a synchronization.

29.4.2.21   #define STARPU_WMB( )

This macro can be used to do a synchronization.

29.4.3   Function Documentation

29.4.3.1   int starpu_get_env_number (const char $*$ *str*)   `[static]`

Return the integer value of the environment variable named `str`. Return 0 otherwise (the variable does not exist or has a non-integer value).

29.5   Threads

This section describes the thread facilities provided by StarPU. The thread function are either implemented on top of the pthread library or the Simgrid library when the simulated performance mode is enabled (SimGrid Support).

Macros

- #define STARPU_PTHREAD_CREATE_ON(name, thread, attr, routine, arg, where)
- #define STARPU_PTHREAD_CREATE(thread, attr, routine, arg)
- #define STARPU_PTHREAD_MUTEX_INIT(mutex, attr)
- #define STARPU_PTHREAD_MUTEX_DESTROY(mutex)
- #define STARPU_PTHREAD_MUTEX_LOCK(mutex)
- #define STARPU_PTHREAD_MUTEX_UNLOCK(mutex)
- #define STARPU_PTHREAD_KEY_CREATE(key, destr)
- #define STARPU_PTHREAD_KEY_DELETE(key)
- #define STARPU_PTHREAD_SETSPECIFIC(key, ptr)
- #define STARPU_PTHREAD_GETSPECIFIC(key)
- #define STARPU_PTHREAD_RWLOCK_INIT(rwlock, attr)
- #define STARPU_PTHREAD_RWLOCK_RDLOCK(rwlock)
- #define STARPU_PTHREAD_RWLOCK_WRLOCK(rwlock)
- #define STARPU_PTHREAD_RWLOCK_UNLOCK(rwlock)
- #define STARPU_PTHREAD_RWLOCK_DESTROY(rwlock)
- #define STARPU_PTHREAD_COND_INIT(cond, attr)
- #define STARPU_PTHREAD_COND_DESTROY(cond)
- #define STARPU_PTHREAD_COND_SIGNAL(cond)
- #define STARPU_PTHREAD_COND_BROADCAST(cond)
- #define STARPU_PTHREAD_COND_WAIT(cond, mutex)
- #define STARPU_PTHREAD_BARRIER_INIT(barrier, attr, count)
- #define STARPU_PTHREAD_BARRIER_DESTROY(barrier)
- #define STARPU_PTHREAD_BARRIER_WAIT(barrier)
- #define STARPU_PTHREAD_MUTEX_INITIALIZER
- #define STARPU_PTHREAD_COND_INITIALIZER

Functions

- int starpu_pthread_create (starpu_pthread_t *thread, const starpu_pthread_attr_t *attr, void *(*start_-routine)(void *), void *arg)
- int starpu_pthread_join (starpu_pthread_t thread, void **retval)
- int starpu_pthread_exit (void *retval) STARPU_ATTRIBUTE_NORETURN
- int starpu_pthread_attr_init (starpu_pthread_attr_t *attr)
- int starpu_pthread_attr_destroy (starpu_pthread_attr_t *attr)
- int starpu_pthread_attr_setdetachstate (starpu_pthread_attr_t *attr, int detachstate)
- int starpu_pthread_mutex_init (starpu_pthread_mutex_t *mutex, const starpu_pthread_mutexattr_-t *mutexattr)
- int starpu_pthread_mutex_destroy (starpu_pthread_mutex_t *mutex)
- int starpu_pthread_mutex_lock (starpu_pthread_mutex_t *mutex)
- int starpu_pthread_mutex_unlock (starpu_pthread_mutex_t *mutex)
- int starpu_pthread_mutex_trylock (starpu_pthread_mutex_t *mutex)
- int starpu_pthread_mutexattr_gettype (const starpu_pthread_mutexattr_t *attr, int *type)
- int starpu_pthread_mutexattr_settype (starpu_pthread_mutexattr_t *attr, int type)
- int starpu_pthread_mutexattr_destroy (starpu_pthread_mutexattr_t *attr)
- int starpu_pthread_mutexattr_init (starpu_pthread_mutexattr_t *attr)
- int starpu_pthread_key_create (starpu_pthread_key_t *key, void(*destr_function)(void *))
- int starpu_pthread_key_delete (starpu_pthread_key_t key)
- int starpu_pthread_setspecific (starpu_pthread_key_t key, const void *pointer)
- void * starpu_pthread_getspecific (starpu_pthread_key_t key)
- int starpu_pthread_cond_init (starpu_pthread_cond_t *cond, starpu_pthread_condattr_t *cond_attr)
- int starpu_pthread_cond_signal (starpu_pthread_cond_t *cond)
- int starpu_pthread_cond_broadcast (starpu_pthread_cond_t *cond)

- int starpu_pthread_cond_wait (starpu_pthread_cond_t *cond, starpu_pthread_mutex_t *mutex)
- int starpu_pthread_cond_timedwait (starpu_pthread_cond_t *cond, starpu_pthread_mutex_t *mutex, const struct timespec *abstime)
- int starpu_pthread_cond_destroy (starpu_pthread_cond_t *cond)
- int starpu_pthread_rwlock_init (starpu_pthread_rwlock_t *rwlock, const starpu_pthread_rwlockattr_t *attr)
- int starpu_pthread_rwlock_destroy (starpu_pthread_rwlock_t *rwlock)
- int starpu_pthread_rwlock_rdlock (starpu_pthread_rwlock_t *rwlock)
- int starpu_pthread_rwlock_tryrdlock (starpu_pthread_rwlock_t *rwlock)
- int starpu_pthread_rwlock_wrlock (starpu_pthread_rwlock_t *rwlock)
- int starpu_pthread_rwlock_trywrlock (starpu_pthread_rwlock_t *rwlock)
- int starpu_pthread_rwlock_unlock (starpu_pthread_rwlock_t *rwlock)
- int starpu_pthread_barrier_init (starpu_pthread_barrier_t *barrier, const starpu_pthread_barrierattr_t *attr, unsigned count)
- int starpu_pthread_barrier_destroy (starpu_pthread_barrier_t *barrier)
- int starpu_pthread_barrier_wait (starpu_pthread_barrier_t *barrier)
- int starpu_pthread_spin_init (starpu_pthread_spinlock_t *lock, int pshared)
- int starpu_pthread_spin_destroy (starpu_pthread_spinlock_t *lock)
- int starpu_pthread_spin_lock (starpu_pthread_spinlock_t *lock)
- int starpu_pthread_spin_trylock (starpu_pthread_spinlock_t *lock)
- int starpu_pthread_spin_unlock (starpu_pthread_spinlock_t *lock)
- void starpu_sleep (float nb_sec)

29.5.1 Detailed Description

This section describes the thread facilities provided by StarPU. The thread function are either implemented on top of the pthread library or the Simgrid library when the simulated performance mode is enabled (SimGrid Support).

29.5.2 Macro Definition Documentation

29.5.2.1 #define STARPU_PTHREAD_CREATE_ON(name, thread, attr, routine, arg, where)

Call starpu_pthread_create_on() and abort on error.

29.5.2.2 #define STARPU_PTHREAD_CREATE(thread, attr, routine, arg)

Call starpu_pthread_create() and abort on error.

29.5.2.3 #define STARPU_PTHREAD_MUTEX_INIT(mutex, attr)

Call starpu_pthread_mutex_init() and abort on error.

29.5.2.4 #define STARPU_PTHREAD_MUTEX_DESTROY(mutex)

Call starpu_pthread_mutex_destroy() and abort on error.

29.5.2.5 #define STARPU_PTHREAD_MUTEX_LOCK(mutex)

Call starpu_pthread_mutex_lock() and abort on error.

29.5.2.6 #define STARPU_PTHREAD_MUTEX_UNLOCK(mutex)

Call starpu_pthread_mutex_unlock() and abort on error.

29.5.2.7   #define STARPU_PTHREAD_KEY_CREATE(*key, destr*)

Call starpu_pthread_key_create() and abort on error.

29.5.2.8   #define STARPU_PTHREAD_KEY_DELETE(*key*)

Call starpu_pthread_key_delete() and abort on error.

29.5.2.9   #define STARPU_PTHREAD_SETSPECIFIC(*key, ptr*)

Call starpu_pthread_setspecific() and abort on error.

29.5.2.10   #define STARPU_PTHREAD_GETSPECIFIC(*key*)

Call starpu_pthread_getspecific() and abort on error.

29.5.2.11   #define STARPU_PTHREAD_RWLOCK_INIT(*rwlock, attr*)

Call starpu_pthread_rwlock_init() and abort on error.

29.5.2.12   #define STARPU_PTHREAD_RWLOCK_RDLOCK(*rwlock*)

Call starpu_pthread_rwlock_rdlock() and abort on error.

29.5.2.13   #define STARPU_PTHREAD_RWLOCK_WRLOCK(*rwlock*)

Call starpu_pthread_rwlock_wrlock() and abort on error.

29.5.2.14   #define STARPU_PTHREAD_RWLOCK_UNLOCK(*rwlock*)

Call starpu_pthread_rwlock_unlock() and abort on error.

29.5.2.15   #define STARPU_PTHREAD_RWLOCK_DESTROY(*rwlock*)

Call starpu_pthread_rwlock_destroy() and abort on error.

29.5.2.16   #define STARPU_PTHREAD_COND_INIT(*cond, attr*)

Call starpu_pthread_cond_init() and abort on error.

29.5.2.17   #define STARPU_PTHREAD_COND_DESTROY(*cond*)

Call starpu_pthread_cond_destroy() and abort on error.

29.5.2.18   #define STARPU_PTHREAD_COND_SIGNAL(*cond*)

Call starpu_pthread_cond_signal() and abort on error.

29.5.2.19 #define STARPU_PTHREAD_COND_BROADCAST(*cond*)

Call starpu_pthread_cond_broadcast() and abort on error.

29.5.2.20 #define STARPU_PTHREAD_COND_WAIT(*cond, mutex*)

Call starpu_pthread_cond_wait() and abort on error.

29.5.2.21 #define STARPU_PTHREAD_BARRIER_INIT(*barrier, attr, count*)

Call starpu_pthread_barrier_init() and abort on error.

29.5.2.22 #define STARPU_PTHREAD_BARRIER_DESTROY(*barrier*)

Call starpu_pthread_barrier_destroy() and abort on error.

29.5.2.23 #define STARPU_PTHREAD_BARRIER_WAIT(*barrier*)

Call starpu_pthread_barrier_wait() and abort on error.

29.5.2.24 STARPU_PTHREAD_MUTEX_INITIALIZER

Initialize the mutex given in parameter.

29.5.2.25 STARPU_PTHREAD_COND_INITIALIZER

Initialize the condition variable given in parameter.

29.5.3 Function Documentation

29.5.3.1 int starpu_pthread_create (starpu_pthread_t ∗ *thread,* const starpu_pthread_attr_t ∗ *attr,* void ∗(∗)(void ∗) *start_routine,* void ∗ *arg*)

Start a new thread in the calling process. The new thread starts execution by invoking `start_routine`; `arg` is passed as the sole argument of `start_routine`.

29.5.3.2 int starpu_pthread_join (starpu_pthread_t *thread,* void ∗∗ *retval*)

Wait for the thread specified by `thread` to terminate. If that thread has already terminated, then the function returns immediately. The thread specified by `thread` must be joinable.

29.5.3.3 int starpu_pthread_exit (void ∗ *retval*)

Terminate the calling thread and return a value via `retval` that (if the thread is joinable) is available to another thread in the same process that calls starpu_pthread_join().

29.5.3.4 int starpu_pthread_attr_init (starpu_pthread_attr_t ∗ *attr*)

Initialize the thread attributes object pointed to by `attr` with default attribute values.

Do not do anything when the simulated performance mode is enabled (SimGrid Support).

29.5.3.5   int starpu_pthread_attr_destroy (starpu_pthread_attr_t * *attr*)

Destroy a thread attributes object which is no longer required. Destroying a thread attributes object has no effect on threads that were created using that object.

Do not do anything when the simulated performance mode is enabled (SimGrid Support).

29.5.3.6   int starpu_pthread_attr_setdetachstate (starpu_pthread_attr_t * *attr,* int *detachstate*)

Set the detach state attribute of the thread attributes object referred to by `attr` to the value specified in `detachstate`. The detach state attribute determines whether a thread created using the thread attributes object `attr` will be created in a joinable or a detached state.

Do not do anything when the simulated performance mode is enabled (SimGrid Support).

29.5.3.7   int starpu_pthread_mutex_init (starpu_pthread_mutex_t * *mutex,* const starpu_pthread_mutexattr_t * *mutexattr*)

Initialize the mutex object pointed to by `mutex` according to the mutex attributes specified in `mutexattr`. If `mutexattr` is `NULL`, default attributes are used instead.

29.5.3.8   int starpu_pthread_mutex_destroy (starpu_pthread_mutex_t * *mutex*)

Destroy a mutex object, and free the resources it might hold. The mutex must be unlocked on entrance.

29.5.3.9   int starpu_pthread_mutex_lock (starpu_pthread_mutex_t * *mutex*)

Lock the given `mutex`. If `mutex` is currently unlocked, it becomes locked and owned by the calling thread, and the function returns immediately. If `mutex` is already locked by another thread, the function suspends the calling thread until `mutex` is unlocked.

This function also produces trace when the configure option --enable-fxt-lock is enabled.

29.5.3.10   int starpu_pthread_mutex_unlock (starpu_pthread_mutex_t * *mutex*)

Unlock the given `mutex`. The mutex is assumed to be locked and owned by the calling thread on entrance to starpu_pthread_mutex_unlock().

This function also produces trace when the configure option --enable-fxt-lock is enabled.

29.5.3.11   int starpu_pthread_mutex_trylock (starpu_pthread_mutex_t * *mutex*)

Behave identically to starpu_pthread_mutex_lock(), except that it does not block the calling thread if the mutex is already locked by another thread (or by the calling thread in the case of a "fast" mutex). Instead, the function returns immediately with the error code `EBUSY`.

This function also produces trace when the configure option --enable-fxt-lock is enabled.

29.5.3.12   int starpu_pthread_mutexattr_gettype (const starpu_pthread_mutexattr_t * *attr,* int * *type*)

todo

29.5.3.13   int starpu_pthread_mutexattr_settype (starpu_pthread_mutexattr_t * *attr,* int *type*)

todo

29.5.3.14   int starpu_pthread_mutexattr_destroy (starpu_pthread_mutexattr_t ∗ *attr*)

todo

29.5.3.15   int starpu_pthread_mutexattr_init (starpu_pthread_mutexattr_t ∗ *attr*)

todo

29.5.3.16   int starpu_pthread_key_create (starpu_pthread_key_t ∗ *key,* void(∗)(void ∗) *destr_function*)

Allocate a new TSD key. The key is stored in the location pointed to by `key`.

29.5.3.17   int starpu_pthread_key_delete (starpu_pthread_key_t *key*)

Deallocate a TSD key. Do not check whether non-`NULL` values are associated with that key in the currently executing threads, nor call the destructor function associated with the key.

29.5.3.18   int starpu_pthread_setspecific (starpu_pthread_key_t *key,* const void ∗ *pointer*)

Change the value associated with `key` in the calling thread, storing the given `pointer` instead.

29.5.3.19   void ∗ starpu_pthread_getspecific (starpu_pthread_key_t *key*)

Return the value associated with `key` on success, and `NULL` on error.

29.5.3.20   int starpu_pthread_cond_init (starpu_pthread_cond_t ∗ *cond,* starpu_pthread_condattr_t ∗ *cond_attr*)

Initialize the condition variable `cond`, using the condition attributes specified in `cond_attr`, or default attributes if `cond_attr` is `NULL`.

29.5.3.21   int starpu_pthread_cond_signal (starpu_pthread_cond_t ∗ *cond*)

Restart one of the threads that are waiting on the condition variable `cond`. If no threads are waiting on `cond`, nothing happens. If several threads are waiting on `cond`, exactly one is restarted, but it is not specified which.

29.5.3.22   int starpu_pthread_cond_broadcast (starpu_pthread_cond_t ∗ *cond*)

Restart all the threads that are waiting on the condition variable `cond`. Nothing happens if no threads are waiting on `cond`.

29.5.3.23   int starpu_pthread_cond_wait (starpu_pthread_cond_t ∗ *cond,* starpu_pthread_mutex_t ∗ *mutex*)

Atomically unlock `mutex` (as per starpu_pthread_mutex_unlock()) and wait for the condition variable `cond` to be signaled. The thread execution is suspended and does not consume any CPU time until the condition variable is signaled. The mutex must be locked by the calling thread on entrance to starpu_pthread_cond_wait(). Before returning to the calling thread, the function re-acquires mutex (as per starpu_pthread_mutex_lock()).

This function also produces trace when the configure option --enable-fxt-lock is enabled.

29.5.3.24 int starpu_pthread_cond_timedwait (starpu_pthread_cond_t * *cond*, starpu_pthread_mutex_t * *mutex*, const struct timespec * *abstime*)

Atomicall unlocks `mutex` and wait on `cond`, as starpu_pthread_cond_wait() does, but also bound the duration of the wait with `abstime`.

29.5.3.25 int starpu_pthread_cond_destroy (starpu_pthread_cond_t * *cond*)

Destroy a condition variable, freeing the resources it might hold. No threads must be waiting on the condition variable on entrance to the function.

29.5.3.26 int starpu_pthread_rwlock_init (starpu_pthread_rwlock_t * *rwlock*, const starpu_pthread_rwlockattr_t * *attr*)

Similar to starpu_pthread_mutex_init().

29.5.3.27 int starpu_pthread_rwlock_destroy (starpu_pthread_rwlock_t * *rwlock*)

Similar to starpu_pthread_mutex_destroy().

29.5.3.28 int starpu_pthread_rwlock_rdlock (starpu_pthread_rwlock_t * *rwlock*)

Similar to starpu_pthread_mutex_lock().

29.5.3.29 int starpu_pthread_rwlock_tryrdlock (starpu_pthread_rwlock_t * *rwlock*)

todo

29.5.3.30 int starpu_pthread_rwlock_wrlock (starpu_pthread_rwlock_t * *rwlock*)

Similar to starpu_pthread_mutex_lock().

29.5.3.31 int starpu_pthread_rwlock_trywrlock (starpu_pthread_rwlock_t * *rwlock*)

todo

29.5.3.32 int starpu_pthread_rwlock_unlock (starpu_pthread_rwlock_t * *rwlock*)

Similar to starpu_pthread_mutex_unlock().

29.5.3.33 int starpu_pthread_barrier_init (**starpu_pthread_barrier_t** * *barrier*, const starpu_pthread_barrierattr_t * *attr*, unsigned *count*)

todo

29.5.3.34 int starpu_pthread_barrier_destroy (**starpu_pthread_barrier_t** * *barrier*)

todo

29.5.3.35 int starpu_pthread_barrier_wait (**starpu_pthread_barrier_t** ∗ *barrier*)

todo

29.5.3.36 int starpu_pthread_spin_init (**starpu_pthread_spinlock_t** ∗ *lock*, int *pshared*)

todo

29.5.3.37 int starpu_pthread_spin_destroy (**starpu_pthread_spinlock_t** ∗ *lock*)

todo

29.5.3.38 int starpu_pthread_spin_lock (**starpu_pthread_spinlock_t** ∗ *lock*)

todo

29.5.3.39 int starpu_pthread_spin_trylock (**starpu_pthread_spinlock_t** ∗ *lock*)

todo

29.5.3.40 int starpu_pthread_spin_unlock (**starpu_pthread_spinlock_t** ∗ *lock*)

todo

29.5.3.41 void starpu_sleep (float *nb_sec*)

Similar to calling Unix' `sleep` function, except that it takes a float to allow sub-second sleeping, and when StarPU is compiled in simgrid mode it does not really sleep but just makes simgrid record that the thread has taken some time to sleep.

29.6 Bitmap

This section describes the bitmap facilities provided by StarPU.

Data Structures

- struct starpu_bitmap

Functions

- struct starpu_bitmap ∗ starpu_bitmap_create (void) STARPU_ATTRIBUTE_MALLOC
- void starpu_bitmap_destroy (struct starpu_bitmap ∗b)
- void starpu_bitmap_set (struct starpu_bitmap ∗b, int e)
- void starpu_bitmap_unset (struct starpu_bitmap ∗b, int e)
- void starpu_bitmap_unset_all (struct starpu_bitmap ∗b)
- int starpu_bitmap_get (struct starpu_bitmap ∗b, int e)
- void starpu_bitmap_unset_and (struct starpu_bitmap ∗a, struct starpu_bitmap ∗b, struct starpu_bitmap ∗c)
- void starpu_bitmap_or (struct starpu_bitmap ∗a, struct starpu_bitmap ∗b)
- int starpu_bitmap_and_get (struct starpu_bitmap ∗b1, struct starpu_bitmap ∗b2, int e)

- int starpu_bitmap_cardinal (struct starpu_bitmap *b)
- int starpu_bitmap_first (struct starpu_bitmap *b)
- int starpu_bitmap_last (struct starpu_bitmap *b)
- int starpu_bitmap_next (struct starpu_bitmap *b, int e)
- int starpu_bitmap_has_next (struct starpu_bitmap *b, int e)

29.6.1 Detailed Description

This section describes the bitmap facilities provided by StarPU.

29.6.2 Data Structure Documentation

29.6.2.1 struct starpu_bitmap

todo

29.6.3 Function Documentation

29.6.3.1 struct **starpu_bitmap** * starpu_bitmap_create (void) `[read]`

create a empty starpu_bitmap

29.6.3.2 void starpu_bitmap_destroy (struct **starpu_bitmap** * *b*)

free

29.6.3.3 void starpu_bitmap_set (struct **starpu_bitmap** * *b,* int *e*)

set bit e in b

29.6.3.4 void starpu_bitmap_unset (struct **starpu_bitmap** * *b,* int *e*)

unset bit e in b

29.6.3.5 void starpu_bitmap_unset_all (struct **starpu_bitmap** * *b*)

unset all bits in b

29.6.3.6 int starpu_bitmap_get (struct **starpu_bitmap** * *b,* int *e*)

return true iff bit e is set in b

29.6.3.7 void starpu_bitmap_unset_and (struct **starpu_bitmap** * *a,* struct **starpu_bitmap** * *b,* struct **starpu_bitmap** * *c*)

Basically compute `starpu_bitmap_unset_all(a)`; a = b & c;

29.6.3.8 void starpu_bitmap_or (struct **starpu_bitmap** * *a,* struct **starpu_bitmap** * *b*)

Basically compute a |= b

29.6.3.9 int starpu_bitmap_and_get (struct **starpu_bitmap** * *b1,* struct **starpu_bitmap** * *b2,* int *e*)

return 1 iff e is set in b1 AND e is set in b2

29.6.3.10 int starpu_bitmap_cardinal (struct **starpu_bitmap** * *b*)

return the number of set bits in b

29.6.3.11 int starpu_bitmap_first (struct **starpu_bitmap** * *b*)

return the index of the first set bit of b, -1 if none

29.6.3.12 int starpu_bitmap_last (struct **starpu_bitmap** * *b*)

return the position of the last set bit of b, -1 if none

29.6.3.13 int starpu_bitmap_next (struct **starpu_bitmap** * *b,* int *e*)

return the position of set bit right after e in b, -1 if none

29.6.3.14 int starpu_bitmap_has_next (struct **starpu_bitmap** * *b,* int *e*)

todo

29.7 Workers' Properties

Data Structures

- struct starpu_worker_collection
- struct starpu_sched_ctx_iterator

Macros

- #define STARPU_NMAXWORKERS
- #define STARPU_MAXCPUS
- #define STARPU_MAXNODES
- #define starpu_worker_get_id_check()

Enumerations

- enum starpu_node_kind {
  STARPU_UNUSED, STARPU_CPU_RAM, STARPU_CUDA_RAM, STARPU_OPENCL_RAM,
  STARPU_DISK_RAM, STARPU_MIC_RAM, STARPU_SCC_RAM, STARPU_SCC_SHM,
  STARPU_MPI_MS_RAM }
- enum starpu_worker_archtype {
  STARPU_CPU_WORKER, STARPU_CUDA_WORKER, STARPU_OPENCL_WORKER, STARPU_MIC_-
  WORKER,
  STARPU_SCC_WORKER, STARPU_MPI_MS_WORKER, STARPU_ANY_WORKER }
- enum starpu_worker_collection_type { STARPU_WORKER_TREE, STARPU_WORKER_LIST }

Functions

- unsigned starpu_worker_get_count (void)
- int starpu_worker_get_count_by_type (enum starpu_worker_archtype type)
- unsigned starpu_cpu_worker_get_count (void)
- unsigned starpu_cuda_worker_get_count (void)
- unsigned starpu_mic_worker_get_count (void)
- unsigned starpu_mic_device_get_count (void)
- unsigned starpu_mpi_ms_worker_get_count (void)
- unsigned starpu_scc_worker_get_count (void)
- unsigned starpu_opencl_worker_get_count (void)
- int starpu_worker_get_id (void)
- unsigned starpu_worker_get_ids_by_type (enum starpu_worker_archtype type, int *workerids, unsigned maxsize)
- int starpu_worker_get_by_type (enum starpu_worker_archtype type, int num)
- int starpu_worker_get_by_devid (enum starpu_worker_archtype type, int devid)
- int starpu_worker_get_devid (int id)
- enum starpu_worker_archtype starpu_worker_get_type (int id)
- void starpu_worker_get_name (int id, char *dst, size_t maxlen)
- void starpu_worker_display_names (FILE *output, enum starpu_worker_archtype type)
- unsigned starpu_worker_get_memory_node (unsigned workerid)
- enum starpu_node_kind starpu_node_get_kind (unsigned node)
- char * starpu_worker_get_type_as_string (enum starpu_worker_archtype type)
- int starpu_worker_sched_op_pending (void)
- void starpu_worker_relax_on (void)
- void starpu_worker_relax_off (void)
- int starpu_worker_get_relax_state (void)
- void starpu_worker_lock (int workerid)
- int starpu_worker_trylock (int workerid)
- void starpu_worker_unlock (int workerid)
- void starpu_worker_lock_self (void)
- void starpu_worker_unlock_self (void)
- int starpu_wake_worker_relax (int workerid)

29.7.1 Detailed Description

29.7.2 Data Structure Documentation

29.7.2.1 struct starpu_worker_collection

A scheduling context manages a collection of workers that can be memorized using different data structures. Thus, a generic structure is available in order to simplify the choice of its type. Only the list data structure is available but further data structures(like tree) implementations are foreseen.

Data Fields

- int * workerids
- void * collection_private
- unsigned nworkers
- void * unblocked_workers
- unsigned nunblocked_workers
- void * masters
- unsigned nmasters
- char present [STARPU_NMAXWORKERS]

- char is_unblocked [STARPU_NMAXWORKERS]
- char is_master [STARPU_NMAXWORKERS]
- enum starpu_worker_collection_type type
- unsigned(∗ has_next)(struct starpu_worker_collection ∗workers, struct starpu_sched_ctx_iterator ∗it)
- int(∗ get_next)(struct starpu_worker_collection ∗workers, struct starpu_sched_ctx_iterator ∗it)
- int(∗ add)(struct starpu_worker_collection ∗workers, int worker)
- int(∗ remove)(struct starpu_worker_collection ∗workers, int worker)
- void(∗ init)(struct starpu_worker_collection ∗workers)
- void(∗ deinit)(struct starpu_worker_collection ∗workers)
- void(∗ init_iterator)(struct starpu_worker_collection ∗workers, struct starpu_sched_ctx_iterator ∗it)
- void(∗ init_iterator_for_parallel_tasks)(struct starpu_worker_collection ∗workers, struct starpu_sched_ctx_-iterator ∗it, struct starpu_task ∗task)

29.7.2.1.1 Field Documentation

29.7.2.1.1.1 void ∗ starpu_worker_collection::workerids

The workerids managed by the collection

29.7.2.1.1.2 void ∗ starpu_worker_collection::collection_private

todo

29.7.2.1.1.3 unsigned starpu_worker_collection::nworkers

The number of workers in the collection

29.7.2.1.1.4 void ∗ starpu_worker_collection::unblocked_workers

todo

29.7.2.1.1.5 unsigned starpu_worker_collection::nunblocked_workers

todo

29.7.2.1.1.6 void ∗ starpu_worker_collection::masters

todo

29.7.2.1.1.7 unsigned starpu_worker_collection::nmasters

todo

29.7.2.1.1.8 char starpu_worker_collection::present[STARPU_NMAXWORKERS]

todo

29.7.2.1.1.9 char starpu_worker_collection::is_unblocked[STARPU_NMAXWORKERS]

todo

29.7.2.1.1.10 char starpu_worker_collection::is_master[STARPU_NMAXWORKERS]

todo

29.7.2.1.1.11 enum starpu_worker_collection_type starpu_worker_collection::type

The type of structure

29.7.2.1.1.12 unsigned(∗ starpu_worker_collection::has_next)(struct **starpu_worker_collection** ∗workers, struct **starpu_sched_ctx_iterator** ∗it)

Check if there is another element in collection

29.7.2.1.1.13 int(∗ starpu_worker_collection::get_next)(struct **starpu_worker_collection** ∗workers, struct **starpu_sched_ctx_iterator** ∗it)

Return the next element in the collection

29.7.2.1.1.14 int(∗ starpu_worker_collection::add)(struct **starpu_worker_collection** ∗workers, int worker)

Add a new element in the collection

29.7.2.1.1.15 int(∗ starpu_worker_collection::remove)(struct **starpu_worker_collection** ∗workers, int worker)

Remove an element from the collection

29.7.2.1.1.16 void(∗ starpu_worker_collection::init)(struct **starpu_worker_collection** ∗workers)

Initialize the collection

29.7.2.1.1.17 void(∗ starpu_worker_collection::deinit)(struct **starpu_worker_collection** ∗workers)

Deinitialize the colection

29.7.2.1.1.18 void(∗ starpu_worker_collection::init_iterator)(struct **starpu_worker_collection** ∗workers, struct **starpu_sched_ctx_iterator** ∗it)

Initialize the cursor if there is one

29.7.2.1.1.19 void(∗ starpu_worker_collection::init_iterator_for_parallel_tasks)(struct **starpu_worker_collection** ∗workers, struct **starpu_sched_ctx_iterator** ∗it, struct **starpu_task** ∗task)

todo

29.7.2.2 struct starpu_sched_ctx_iterator

Structure needed to iterate on the collection

Data Fields

int	cursor	The index of the current worker in the collection, needed when iterating on the collection.
void ∗	value	
void ∗	possible_value	
char	visited	
int	possibly_parallel	

29.7.3 Macro Definition Documentation

29.7.3.1 #define STARPU_NMAXWORKERS

Define the maximum number of workers managed by StarPU.

29.7.3.2 #define STARPU_MAXCPUS

Define the maximum number of CPU workers managed by StarPU. The default value can be modified at configure by using the option --enable-maxcpus.

29.7.3.3 #define STARPU_MAXNODES

Define the maximum number of memory nodes managed by StarPU. The default value can be modified at configure by using the option --enable-maxnodes. Reducing it allows to considerably reduce memory used by StarPU data structures.

29.7.3.4 unsigned starpu_worker_get_id_check( )

Similar to starpu_worker_get_id(), but abort when called from outside a worker (i.e. when starpu_worker_get_id() would return -1).

29.7.4 Enumeration Type Documentation

29.7.4.1 enum **starpu_node_kind**

TODO

Enumerator:

> ***STARPU_UNUSED*** TODO
>
> ***STARPU_CPU_RAM*** TODO
>
> ***STARPU_CUDA_RAM*** TODO
>
> ***STARPU_OPENCL_RAM*** TODO
>
> ***STARPU_DISK_RAM*** TODO
>
> ***STARPU_MIC_RAM*** TODO
>
> ***STARPU_SCC_RAM*** This node kind is not used anymore, but implementations in interfaces will be useful for MPI.
>
> ***STARPU_SCC_SHM*** TODO
>
> ***STARPU_MPI_MS_RAM*** TODO

29.7.4.2 enum **starpu_worker_archtype**

Worker Architecture Type

Enumerator:

> ***STARPU_CPU_WORKER*** CPU core
>
> ***STARPU_CUDA_WORKER*** NVIDIA CUDA device
>
> ***STARPU_OPENCL_WORKER*** OpenCL device
>
> ***STARPU_MIC_WORKER*** Intel MIC device
>
> ***STARPU_SCC_WORKER*** Intel SCC device
>
> ***STARPU_MPI_MS_WORKER*** MPI Slave device
>
> ***STARPU_ANY_WORKER*** any worker, used in the hypervisor

29.7.4.3   enum starpu_worker_collection_type

Types of structures the worker collection can implement

Enumerator:

STARPU_WORKER_TREE   The collection is a tree
STARPU_WORKER_LIST   The collection is an array

29.7.5   Function Documentation

29.7.5.1   unsigned starpu_worker_get_count (void)

Return the number of workers (i.e. processing units executing StarPU tasks). The returned value should be at most STARPU_NMAXWORKERS.

29.7.5.2   int starpu_worker_get_count_by_type (enum **starpu_worker_archtype** *type*)

Return the number of workers of type. A positive (or NULL) value is returned in case of success, -EINVAL indicates that type is not valid otherwise.

29.7.5.3   unsigned starpu_cpu_worker_get_count (void)

Return the number of CPUs controlled by StarPU. The returned value should be at most STARPU_MAXCPUS.

29.7.5.4   unsigned starpu_cuda_worker_get_count (void)

Return the number of CUDA devices controlled by StarPU. The returned value should be at most STARPU_MAXC-UDADEVS.

29.7.5.5   unsigned starpu_mic_worker_get_count (void)

Return the number of MIC workers controlled by StarPU.

29.7.5.6   unsigned starpu_mic_device_get_count (void)

Return the number of MIC devices controlled by StarPU. The returned value should be at most STARPU_MAXMI-CDEVS.

29.7.5.7   unsigned starpu_mpi_ms_worker_get_count (void)

Return the number of MPI Master Slave workers controlled by StarPU.

29.7.5.8   unsigned starpu_scc_worker_get_count (void)

Return the number of SCC devices controlled by StarPU. The returned value should be at most STARPU_MAXSC-CDEVS.

29.7.5.9   unsigned starpu_opencl_worker_get_count (void)

Return the number of OpenCL devices controlled by StarPU. The returned value should be at most STARPU_MA-XOPENCLDEVS.

29.7.5.10 int starpu_worker_get_id (void)

Return the identifier of the current worker, i.e the one associated to the calling thread. The returned value is either -1 if the current context is not a StarPU worker (i.e. when called from the application outside a task or a callback), or an integer between 0 and starpu_worker_get_count() - 1.

29.7.5.11 unsigned starpu_worker_get_ids_by_type (enum starpu_worker_archtype *type,* int * *workerids,* unsigned *maxsize*)

Get the list of identifiers of workers of `type`. Fill the array `workerids` with the identifiers of the `workers`. The argument `maxsize` indicates the size of the array `workerids`. The returned value gives the number of identifiers that were put in the array. `-ERANGE` is returned is `maxsize` is lower than the number of workers with the appropriate type: in that case, the array is filled with the `maxsize` first elements. To avoid such overflows, the value of maxsize can be chosen by the means of the function starpu_worker_get_count_by_type(), or by passing a value greater or equal to STARPU_NMAXWORKERS.

29.7.5.12 int starpu_worker_get_by_type (enum starpu_worker_archtype *type,* int *num*)

Return the identifier of the `num` -th worker that has the specified `type`. If there is no such worker, -1 is returned.

29.7.5.13 int starpu_worker_get_by_devid (enum starpu_worker_archtype *type,* int *devid*)

Return the identifier of the worker that has the specified `type` and device id `devid` (which may not be the n-th, if some devices are skipped for instance). If there is no such worker, -1 is returned.

29.7.5.14 int starpu_worker_get_devid (int *id*)

Return the device id of the worker `id`. The worker should be identified with the value returned by the starpu_-worker_get_id() function. In the case of a CUDA worker, this device identifier is the logical device identifier exposed by CUDA (used by the function `cudaGetDevice()` for instance). The device identifier of a CPU worker is the logical identifier of the core on which the worker was bound; this identifier is either provided by the OS or by the library `hwloc` in case it is available.

29.7.5.15 enum starpu_worker_archtype starpu_worker_get_type (int *id*)

Return the type of processing unit associated to the worker `id`. The worker identifier is a value returned by the function starpu_worker_get_id()). The returned value indicates the architecture of the worker: STARPU_CPU_W-ORKER for a CPU core, STARPU_CUDA_WORKER for a CUDA device, and STARPU_OPENCL_WORKER for a OpenCL device. The value returned for an invalid identifier is unspecified.

29.7.5.16 void starpu_worker_get_name (int *id,* char * *dst,* size_t *maxlen*)

Allow to get the name of the worker `id`. StarPU associates a unique human readable string to each processing unit. This function copies at most the `maxlen` first bytes of the unique string associated to the worker `id` into the `dst` buffer. The caller is responsible for ensuring that `dst` is a valid pointer to a buffer of `maxlen` bytes at least. Calling this function on an invalid identifier results in an unspecified behaviour.

29.7.5.17 void starpu_worker_display_names (FILE * *output,* enum starpu_worker_archtype *type*)

Display on `output` the list (if any) of all the workers of the given `type`.

29.7.5.18   unsigned starpu_worker_get_memory_node (unsigned *workerid*)

Return the identifier of the memory node associated to the worker identified by `workerid`.

29.7.5.19   enum starpu_node_kind starpu_node_get_kind (unsigned *node*)

Return the type of `node` as defined by `starpu_node_kind`. For example, when defining a new data interface, this function should be used in the allocation function to determine on which device the memory needs to be allocated.

29.7.5.20   char ∗ starpu_worker_get_type_as_string (enum starpu_worker_archtype *type*)

Return worker `type` as a string.

29.7.5.21   int starpu_worker_sched_op_pending (void)

Return `!0` if current worker has a scheduling operation in progress, and `0` otherwise.

29.7.5.22   void starpu_worker_relax_on (void)

Allow other threads and workers to temporarily observe the current worker state, even though it is performing a scheduling operation. Must be called by a worker before performing a potentially blocking call such as acquiring a mutex other than its own sched_mutex. This function increases `state_relax_refcnt` from the current worker. No more than `UINT_MAX-1` nested relax_on calls should performed on the same worker. This function is automatically called by `starpu_worker_lock` to relax the caller worker state while attempting to lock the targer worker.

29.7.5.23   void starpu_worker_relax_off (void)

Must be called after a potentially blocking call is complete, to restore the relax state in place before the corresponding relax_on. Decreases `state_relax_refcnt`. Calls to `starpu_worker_relax_on` and `starpu_worker_relax_off` must be well parenthesized. This function is automatically called by `starpu_worker_unlock` after the target worker has been unlocked.

29.7.5.24   int starpu_worker_get_relax_state (void)

Returns `!0` if the current worker `state_relax_refcnt!=0` and `0` otherwise.

29.7.5.25   void starpu_worker_lock (int *workerid*)

Acquire the sched mutex of `workerid`. If the caller is a worker, distinct from `workerid`, the caller worker automatically enter relax state while acquiring the target worker lock.

29.7.5.26   int starpu_worker_trylock (int *workerid*)

Attempt to acquire the sched mutex of `workerid`. Returns `0` if successful, `!0` if `workerid` sched mutex is held or the corresponding worker is not in relaxed stated. If the caller is a worker, distinct from `workerid`, the caller worker automatically enter relax state if successfully acquiring the target worker lock.

29.7.5.27   void starpu_worker_unlock (int *workerid*)

Release the previously acquired sched mutex of `workerid`. Restore the relaxed state of the caller worker if needed.

29.7.5.28 void starpu_worker_lock_self (void)

Acquire the current worker sched mutex.

29.7.5.29 void starpu_worker_unlock_self (void)

Release the current worker sched mutex.

29.7.5.30 int starpu_wake_worker_relax (int *workerid*)

Wake up `workerid` while temporarily entering the current worker relaxed state if needed during the waiting process. Returns 1 if `workerid` has been woken up or its state_keep_awake flag has been set to 1, and 0 otherwise (if `workerid` was not in the STATE_SLEEPING or in the STATE_SCHEDULING).

29.8 Data Management

This section describes the data management facilities provided by StarPU. We show how to use existing data interfaces in Data Interfaces, but developers can design their own data interfaces if required.

Typedefs

- typedef struct _starpu_data_state ∗ starpu_data_handle_t
- typedef struct starpu_arbiter ∗ starpu_arbiter_t

Enumerations

- enum starpu_data_access_mode {
  STARPU_NONE, STARPU_R, STARPU_W, STARPU_RW,
  STARPU_SCRATCH, STARPU_REDUX, STARPU_COMMUTE, STARPU_SSEND,
  STARPU_LOCALITY, STARPU_ACCESS_MODE_MAX }

Basic Data Management API

Data management is done at a high-level in StarPU: rather than accessing a mere list of contiguous buffers, the tasks may manipulate data that are described by a high-level construct which we call data interface.

An example of data interface is the "vector" interface which describes a contiguous data array on a spefic memory node. This interface is a simple structure containing the number of elements in the array, the size of the elements, and the address of the array in the appropriate address space (this address may be invalid if there is no valid copy of the array in the memory node). More informations on the data interfaces provided by StarPU are given in Data Interfaces.

When a piece of data managed by StarPU is used by a task, the task implementation is given a pointer to an interface describing a valid copy of the data that is accessible from the current processing unit.

Every worker is associated to a memory node which is a logical abstraction of the address space from which the processing unit gets its data. For instance, the memory node associated to the different CPU workers represents main memory (RAM), the memory node associated to a GPU is DRAM embedded on the device. Every memory node is identified by a logical index which is accessible from the function starpu_worker_get_memory_node(). When registering a piece of data to StarPU, the specified memory node indicates where the piece of data initially resides (we also call this memory node the home node of a piece of data).

- void starpu_data_register (starpu_data_handle_t ∗handleptr, int home_node, void ∗data_interface, struct starpu_data_interface_ops ∗ops)

- void starpu_data_ptr_register (starpu_data_handle_t handle, unsigned node)
- void starpu_data_register_same (starpu_data_handle_t *handledst, starpu_data_handle_t handlesrc)
- void starpu_data_unregister (starpu_data_handle_t handle)
- void starpu_data_unregister_no_coherency (starpu_data_handle_t handle)
- void starpu_data_unregister_submit (starpu_data_handle_t handle)
- void starpu_data_invalidate (starpu_data_handle_t handle)
- void starpu_data_invalidate_submit (starpu_data_handle_t handle)
- void starpu_data_set_wt_mask (starpu_data_handle_t handle, uint32_t wt_mask)
- void starpu_data_set_name (starpu_data_handle_t handle, const char *name)
- void starpu_data_set_coordinates_array (starpu_data_handle_t handle, int dimensions, int dims[])
- void starpu_data_set_coordinates (starpu_data_handle_t handle, unsigned dimensions,...)
- int starpu_data_fetch_on_node (starpu_data_handle_t handle, unsigned node, unsigned async)
- int starpu_data_prefetch_on_node (starpu_data_handle_t handle, unsigned node, unsigned async)
- int starpu_data_idle_prefetch_on_node (starpu_data_handle_t handle, unsigned node, unsigned async)
- void starpu_data_wont_use (starpu_data_handle_t handle)
- starpu_data_handle_t starpu_data_lookup (const void *ptr)
- int starpu_data_request_allocation (starpu_data_handle_t handle, unsigned node)
- void starpu_data_query_status (starpu_data_handle_t handle, int memory_node, int *is_allocated, int *is_-valid, int *is_requested)
- void starpu_data_advise_as_important (starpu_data_handle_t handle, unsigned is_important)
- void starpu_data_set_reduction_methods (starpu_data_handle_t handle, struct starpu_codelet *redux_cl, struct starpu_codelet *init_cl)
- struct starpu_data_interface_ops * starpu_data_get_interface_ops (starpu_data_handle_t handle)
- void starpu_data_set_user_data (starpu_data_handle_t handle, void *user_data)
- void * starpu_data_get_user_data (starpu_data_handle_t handle)

Access registered data from the application

- #define STARPU_ACQUIRE_NO_NODE
- #define STARPU_ACQUIRE_NO_NODE_LOCK_ALL
- #define STARPU_DATA_ACQUIRE_CB(handle, mode, code)
- int starpu_data_acquire (starpu_data_handle_t handle, enum starpu_data_access_mode mode)
- int starpu_data_acquire_cb (starpu_data_handle_t handle, enum starpu_data_access_mode mode, void(*callback)(void *), void *arg)
- int starpu_data_acquire_cb_sequential_consistency (starpu_data_handle_t handle, enum starpu_data_-access_mode mode, void(*callback)(void *), void *arg, int sequential_consistency)
- int starpu_data_acquire_try (starpu_data_handle_t handle, enum starpu_data_access_mode mode)
- int starpu_data_acquire_on_node (starpu_data_handle_t handle, int node, enum starpu_data_access_mode mode)
- int starpu_data_acquire_on_node_cb (starpu_data_handle_t handle, int node, enum starpu_data_access_-mode mode, void(*callback)(void *), void *arg)
- int starpu_data_acquire_on_node_cb_sequential_consistency (starpu_data_handle_t handle, int node, enum starpu_data_access_mode mode, void(*callback)(void *), void *arg, int sequential_consistency)
- int starpu_data_acquire_on_node_cb_sequential_consistency_sync_jobids (starpu_data_handle_t handle, int node, enum starpu_data_access_mode mode, void(*callback)(void *), void *arg, int sequential_-consistency, long *pre_sync_jobid, long *post_sync_jobid)
- int starpu_data_acquire_on_node_try (starpu_data_handle_t handle, int node, enum starpu_data_access_-mode mode)
- void starpu_data_release (starpu_data_handle_t handle)
- void starpu_data_release_on_node (starpu_data_handle_t handle, int node)
- starpu_arbiter_t starpu_arbiter_create (void) STARPU_ATTRIBUTE_MALLOC
- void starpu_data_assign_arbiter (starpu_data_handle_t handle, starpu_arbiter_t arbiter)
- void starpu_arbiter_destroy (starpu_arbiter_t arbiter)

29.8.1 Detailed Description

This section describes the data management facilities provided by StarPU. We show how to use existing data interfaces in Data Interfaces, but developers can design their own data interfaces if required.

29.8.2 Macro Definition Documentation

29.8.2.1 #define STARPU_ACQUIRE_NO_NODE

This macro can be used to acquire data, but not require it to be available on a given node, only enforce R/W dependencies. This can for instance be used to wait for tasks which produce the data, but without requesting a fetch to the main memory.

29.8.2.2 #define STARPU_ACQUIRE_NO_NODE_LOCK_ALL

This is the same as STARPU_ACQUIRE_NO_NODE, but will lock the data on all nodes, preventing them from being evicted for instance. This is mostly useful inside starpu only.

29.8.2.3 #define STARPU_DATA_ACQUIRE_CB(*handle, mode, code*)

STARPU_DATA_ACQUIRE_CB() is the same as starpu_data_acquire_cb(), except that the code to be executed in a callback is directly provided as a macro parameter, and the data `handle` is automatically released after it. This permits to easily execute code which depends on the value of some registered data. This is non-blocking too and may be called from task callbacks.

29.8.3 Typedef Documentation

29.8.3.1 starpu_data_handle_t

StarPU uses starpu_data_handle_t as an opaque handle to manage a piece of data. Once a piece of data has been registered to StarPU, it is associated to a starpu_data_handle_t which keeps track of the state of the piece of data over the entire machine, so that we can maintain data consistency and locate data replicates for instance.

29.8.3.2 starpu_arbiter_t

This is an arbiter, which implements an advanced but centralized management of concurrent data accesses, see Concurrent Data Accesses for the details.

29.8.4 Enumeration Type Documentation

29.8.4.1 enum starpu_data_access_mode

This datatype describes a data access mode.

Enumerator:

STARPU_NONE TODO

STARPU_R read-only mode.

STARPU_W write-only mode.

STARPU_RW read-write mode. This is equivalent to STARPU_R|STARPU_W

STARPU_SCRATCH A temporary buffer is allocated for the task, but StarPU does not enforce data consistency—i.e. each device has its own buffer, independently from each other (even for CPUs), and no data transfer is ever performed. This is useful for temporary variables to avoid allocating/freeing buffers inside each task. Currently, no behavior is defined concerning the relation with the STARPU_R and STARPU_W modes and the value provided at registration — i.e., the value of the scratch buffer is undefined at entry of the codelet function. It is being considered for future extensions at least to define the initial value. For now, data to be used in STARPU_SCRATCH mode should be registered with node -1 and a NULL pointer, since the value of the provided buffer is simply ignored for now.

STARPU_REDUX todo

STARPU_COMMUTE STARPU_COMMUTE can be passed along STARPU_W or STARPU_RW to express that StarPU can let tasks commute, which is useful e.g. when bringing a contribution into some data, which can be done in any order (but still require sequential consistency against reads or non-commutative writes).

STARPU_SSEND used in starpu_mpi_insert_task() to specify the data has to be sent using a synchronous and non-blocking mode (see starpu_mpi_issend())

STARPU_LOCALITY used to tell the scheduler which data is the most important for the task, and should thus be used to try to group tasks on the same core or cache, etc. For now only the ws and lws schedulers take this flag into account, and only when rebuild with USE_LOCALITY flag defined in the src/sched_-policies/work_stealing_policy.c source code.

STARPU_ACCESS_MODE_MAX todo

29.8.5 Function Documentation

29.8.5.1 void starpu_data_register (starpu_data_handle_t * handleptr, int home_node, void * data_interface, struct starpu_data_interface_ops * ops)

Register a piece of data into the handle located at the `handleptr` address. The `data_interface` buffer contains the initial description of the data in the `home_node`. The `ops` argument is a pointer to a structure describing the different methods used to manipulate this type of interface. See starpu_data_interface_ops for more details on this structure. If `home_node` is -1, StarPU will automatically allocate the memory when it is used for the first time in write-only mode. Once such data handle has been automatically allocated, it is possible to access it using any access mode. Note that StarPU supplies a set of predefined types of interface (e.g. vector or matrix) which can be registered by the means of helper functions (e.g. starpu_vector_data_register() or starpu_matrix_-data_register()).

29.8.5.2 void starpu_data_ptr_register (starpu_data_handle_t handle, unsigned node)

Register that a buffer for `handle` on `node` will be set. This is typically used by starpu_*_ptr_register helpers before setting the interface pointers for this node, to tell the core that that is now allocated.

29.8.5.3 void starpu_data_register_same (starpu_data_handle_t * handledst, starpu_data_handle_t handlesrc)

Register a new piece of data into the handle `handledst` with the same interface as the handle `handlesrc`.

29.8.5.4 void starpu_data_unregister (starpu_data_handle_t handle)

Unregister a data `handle` from StarPU. If the data was automatically allocated by StarPU because the home node was -1, all automatically allocated buffers are freed. Otherwise, a valid copy of the data is put back into the home node in the buffer that was initially registered. Using a data handle that has been unregistered from StarPU results in an undefined behaviour. In case we do not need to update the value of the data in the home node, we can use the function starpu_data_unregister_no_coherency() instead.

29.8.5.5 void starpu_data_unregister_no_coherency (**starpu_data_handle_t** *handle*)

This is the same as starpu_data_unregister(), except that StarPU does not put back a valid copy into the home node, in the buffer that was initially registered.

29.8.5.6 void starpu_data_unregister_submit (**starpu_data_handle_t** *handle*)

Destroy the data `handle` once it is no longer needed by any submitted task. No coherency is assumed.

29.8.5.7 void starpu_data_invalidate (**starpu_data_handle_t** *handle*)

Destroy all replicates of the data `handle` immediately. After data invalidation, the first access to `handle` must be performed in STARPU_W mode. Accessing an invalidated data in STARPU_R mode results in undefined behaviour.

29.8.5.8 void starpu_data_invalidate_submit (**starpu_data_handle_t** *handle*)

Submit invalidation of the data `handle` after completion of previously submitted tasks.

29.8.5.9 void starpu_data_set_wt_mask (**starpu_data_handle_t** *handle,* uint32_t *wt_mask*)

Set the write-through mask of the data `handle` (and its children), i.e. a bitmask of nodes where the data should be always replicated after modification. It also prevents the data from being evicted from these nodes when memory gets scarse. When the data is modified, it is automatically transfered into those memory nodes. For instance a `1<<0` write-through mask means that the CUDA workers will commit their changes in main memory (node 0).

29.8.5.10 void starpu_data_set_name (**starpu_data_handle_t** *handle,* const char ∗ *name*)

Set the name of the data, to be shown in various profiling tools.

29.8.5.11 void starpu_data_set_coordinates_array (**starpu_data_handle_t** *handle,* int *dimensions,* int *dims[]*)

Set the coordinates of the data, to be shown in various profiling tools. `dimensions` is the size of the `dims` array This can be for instance the tile coordinates within a big matrix.

29.8.5.12 void starpu_data_set_coordinates (**starpu_data_handle_t** *handle,* unsigned *dimensions,* ...)

Set the coordinates of the data, to be shown in various profiling tools. `dimensions` is the number of subsequent `int` parameters. This can be for instance the tile coordinates within a big matrix.

29.8.5.13 int starpu_data_fetch_on_node (**starpu_data_handle_t** *handle,* unsigned *node,* unsigned *async*)

Issue a fetch request for the data `handle` to `node`, i.e. requests that the data be replicated to the given node as soon as possible, so that it is available there for tasks. If `async` is 0, the call will block until the transfer is achieved, else the call will return immediately, after having just queued the request. In the latter case, the request will asynchronously wait for the completion of any task writing on the data.

29.8.5.14 int starpu_data_prefetch_on_node (**starpu_data_handle_t** *handle,* unsigned *node,* unsigned *async*)

Issue a prefetch request for the data `handle` to `node`, i.e. requests that the data be replicated to `node` when there is room for it, so that it is available there for tasks. If `async` is 0, the call will block until the transfer is achieved, else the call will return immediately, after having just queued the request. In the latter case, the request will asynchronously wait for the completion of any task writing on the data.

29.8.5.15 int starpu_data_idle_prefetch_on_node (starpu_data_handle_t *handle,* **unsigned** *node,* **unsigned** *async* **)**

Issue an idle prefetch request for the data `handle` to `node`, i.e. requests that the data be replicated to `node`, so that it is available there for tasks, but only when the bus is really idle. If `async` is 0, the call will block until the transfer is achieved, else the call will return immediately, after having just queued the request. In the latter case, the request will asynchronously wait for the completion of any task writing on the data.

29.8.5.16 void starpu_data_wont_use (starpu_data_handle_t *handle* **)**

Advise StarPU that `handle` will not be used in the close future, and is thus a good candidate for eviction from GPUs. StarPU will thus write its value back to its home node when the bus is idle, and select this data in priority for eviction when memory gets low.

29.8.5.17 starpu_data_handle_t starpu_data_lookup (const void $*$ *ptr* **)**

Return the handle corresponding to the data pointed to by the `ptr` host pointer.

29.8.5.18 int starpu_data_request_allocation (starpu_data_handle_t *handle,* **unsigned** *node* **)**

Explicitly ask StarPU to allocate room for a piece of data on the specified memory `node`.

29.8.5.19 void starpu_data_query_status (starpu_data_handle_t *handle,* **int** *memory_node,* **int** $*$ *is_allocated,* **int** $*$ *is_valid,* **int** $*$ *is_requested* **)**

Query the status of `handle` on the specified `memory_node`.

29.8.5.20 void starpu_data_advise_as_important (starpu_data_handle_t *handle,* **unsigned** *is_important* **)**

Specify that the data `handle` can be discarded without impacting the application.

29.8.5.21 void starpu_data_set_reduction_methods (starpu_data_handle_t *handle,* **struct starpu_codelet** $*$ *redux_cl,* **struct starpu_codelet** $*$ *init_cl* **)**

Set the codelets to be used for `handle` when it is accessed in the mode STARPU_REDUX. Per-worker buffers will be initialized with the codelet `init_cl`, and reduction between per-worker buffers will be done with the codelet `redux_cl`.

29.8.5.22 struct starpu_data_interface_ops $*$ starpu_data_get_interface_ops (**starpu_data_handle_t** *handle* **)**
[read]

todo

29.8.5.23 void starpu_data_set_user_data (starpu_data_handle_t *handle,* **void** $*$ *user_data* **)**

Sset the field `user_data` for the `handle` to `user_data` . It can then be retrieved with starpu_data_get_user-_data(). `user_data` can be any application-defined value, for instance a pointer to an object-oriented container for the data.

29.8.5.24 void ∗ starpu_data_get_user_data (**starpu_data_handle_t** *handle*)

This retrieves the field `user_data` previously set for the `handle`.

29.8.5.25 int starpu_data_acquire (**starpu_data_handle_t** *handle,* enum **starpu_data_access_mode** *mode*)

The application must call this function prior to accessing registered data from main memory outside tasks. Star-PU ensures that the application will get an up-to-date copy of `handle` in main memory located where the data was originally registered, and that all concurrent accesses (e.g. from tasks) will be consistent with the access mode specified with `mode`. starpu_data_release() must be called once the application no longer needs to access the piece of data. Note that implicit data dependencies are also enforced by starpu_data_acquire(), i.e. starpu_data_acquire() will wait for all tasks scheduled to work on the data, unless they have been disabled explicitly by calling starpu_data_set_default_sequential_consistency_flag() or starpu_data_set_sequential_consistency_flag(). starpu_data_acquire() is a blocking call, so that it cannot be called from tasks or from their callbacks (in that case, starpu_data_acquire() returns −EDEADLK). Upon successful completion, this function returns 0.

29.8.5.26 int starpu_data_acquire_cb (**starpu_data_handle_t** *handle,* enum **starpu_data_access_mode** *mode,*
void(∗)(void ∗) *callback,* void ∗ *arg*)

Asynchronous equivalent of starpu_data_acquire(). When the data specified in `handle` is available in the access `mode`, the `callback` function is executed. The application may access the requested data during the execution of `callback`. The `callback` function must call starpu_data_release() once the application no longer needs to access the piece of data. Note that implicit data dependencies are also enforced by starpu_data_acquire_cb() in case they are not disabled. Contrary to starpu_data_acquire(), this function is non-blocking and may be called from task callbacks. Upon successful completion, this function returns 0.

29.8.5.27 int starpu_data_acquire_cb_sequential_consistency (**starpu_data_handle_t** *handle,* enum
starpu_data_access_mode *mode,* void(∗)(void ∗) *callback,* void ∗ *arg,* int *sequential_consistency*)

Equivalent of starpu_data_acquire_cb() with the possibility of enabling or disabling data dependencies. When the data specified in `handle` is available in the access `mode`, the `callback` function is executed. The application may access the requested data during the execution of this `callback`. The `callback` function must call starpu_data_release() once the application no longer needs to access the piece of data. Note that implicit data dependencies are also enforced by starpu_data_acquire_cb_sequential_consistency() in case they are not disabled specifically for the given `handle` or by the parameter `sequential_consistency`. Similarly to starpu_data_-acquire_cb(), this function is non-blocking and may be called from task callbacks. Upon successful completion, this function returns 0.

29.8.5.28 int starpu_data_acquire_try (**starpu_data_handle_t** *handle,* enum **starpu_data_access_mode** *mode*)

The application can call this function instead of starpu_data_acquire() so as to acquire the data like starpu_data_-acquire(), but only if all previously-submitted tasks have completed, in which case starpu_data_acquire_try() returns 0. StarPU will have ensured that the application will get an up-to-date copy of `handle` in main memory located where the data was originally registered. starpu_data_release() must be called once the application no longer needs to access the piece of data.

If not all previously-submitted tasks have completed, starpu_data_acquire_try returns -EAGAIN, and starpu_data_-release() must not be called.

29.8.5.29 int starpu_data_acquire_on_node (**starpu_data_handle_t** *handle,* int *node,* enum
starpu_data_access_mode *mode*)

This is the same as starpu_data_acquire(), except that the data will be available on the given memory node instead of main memory. STARPU_ACQUIRE_NO_NODE and STARPU_ACQUIRE_NO_NODE_LOCK_ALL can be used instead of an explicit node number.

29.8.5.30 int starpu_data_acquire_on_node_cb (**starpu_data_handle_t** *handle,* int *node,* enum **starpu_data_access_mode** *mode,* void(*)(void *) *callback,* void * *arg*)

This is the same as starpu_data_acquire_cb(), except that the data will be available on the given memory node instead of main memory. STARPU_ACQUIRE_NO_NODE and STARPU_ACQUIRE_NO_NODE_LOCK_ALL can be used instead of an explicit node number.

29.8.5.31 int starpu_data_acquire_on_node_cb_sequential_consistency (**starpu_data_handle_t** *handle,* int *node,* enum **starpu_data_access_mode** *mode,* void(*)(void *) *callback,* void * *arg,* int *sequential_consistency*)

This is the same as starpu_data_acquire_cb_sequential_consistency(), except that the data will be available on the given memory node instead of main memory. STARPU_ACQUIRE_NO_NODE and STARPU_ACQUIRE_NO_N-ODE_LOCK_ALL can be used instead of an explicit node number.

29.8.5.32 int starpu_data_acquire_on_node_cb_sequential_consistency_sync_jobids (**starpu_data_handle_t** *handle,* int *node,* enum **starpu_data_access_mode** *mode,* void(*)(void *) *callback,* void * *arg,* int *sequential_consistency,* long * *pre_sync_jobid,* long * *post_sync_jobid*)

This is the same as starpu_data_acquire_on_node_cb_sequential_consistency(), except that the *pre_sync_jobid* and *post_sync_jobid* parameters can be used to retrieve the jobid of the synchronization tasks. *pre_sync_jobid* happens just before the acquisition, and *post_sync_jobid* happens just after the release.

29.8.5.33 int starpu_data_acquire_on_node_try (**starpu_data_handle_t** *handle,* int *node,* enum **starpu_data_access_mode** *mode*)

This is the same as starpu_data_acquire_try(), except that the data will be available on the given memory node instead of main memory. STARPU_ACQUIRE_NO_NODE and STARPU_ACQUIRE_NO_NODE_LOCK_ALL can be used instead of an explicit node number.

29.8.5.34 void starpu_data_release (**starpu_data_handle_t** *handle*)

Release the piece of data acquired by the application either by starpu_data_acquire() or by starpu_data_acquire_-cb().

29.8.5.35 void starpu_data_release_on_node (**starpu_data_handle_t** *handle,* int *node*)

This is the same as starpu_data_release(), except that the data will be available on the given memory `node` instead of main memory. The `node` parameter must be exactly the same as the corresponding `starpu_data-_acquire_on_node*` call.

29.8.5.36 **starpu_arbiter_t** starpu_arbiter_create (void)

Create a data access arbiter, see Concurrent Data Accesses for the details

29.8.5.37 void starpu_data_assign_arbiter (**starpu_data_handle_t** *handle,* **starpu_arbiter_t** *arbiter*)

Make access to `handle` managed by `arbiter`

29.8.5.38 void starpu_arbiter_destroy (**starpu_arbiter_t** *arbiter*)

Destroy the `arbiter` . This must only be called after all data assigned to it have been unregistered.

29.9 Data Interfaces

Data Structures

- struct starpu_data_interface_ops
- struct starpu_data_copy_methods
- struct starpu_variable_interface
- struct starpu_vector_interface
- struct starpu_matrix_interface
- struct starpu_block_interface
- struct starpu_bcsr_interface
- struct starpu_csr_interface
- struct starpu_coo_interface

Enumerations

- enum starpu_data_interface_id {
  STARPU_UNKNOWN_INTERFACE_ID, STARPU_MATRIX_INTERFACE_ID, STARPU_BLOCK_INTERF-
  ACE_ID, STARPU_VECTOR_INTERFACE_ID,
  STARPU_CSR_INTERFACE_ID, STARPU_BCSR_INTERFACE_ID, STARPU_VARIABLE_INTERFACE_I-
  D, STARPU_VOID_INTERFACE_ID,
  STARPU_MULTIFORMAT_INTERFACE_ID, STARPU_COO_INTERFACE_ID, STARPU_MAX_INTERFA-
  CE_ID }

Registering Data

There are several ways to register a memory region so that it can be managed by StarPU. The functions below allow the registration of vectors, 2D matrices, 3D matrices as well as BCSR and CSR sparse matrices.

- void starpu_void_data_register (starpu_data_handle_t *handle)
- void starpu_variable_data_register (starpu_data_handle_t *handle, int home_node, uintptr_t ptr, size_t size)
- void starpu_variable_ptr_register (starpu_data_handle_t handle, unsigned node, uintptr_t ptr, uintptr_t dev_-handle, size_t offset)
- void starpu_vector_data_register (starpu_data_handle_t *handle, int home_node, uintptr_t ptr, uint32_t nx, size_t elemsize)
- void starpu_vector_ptr_register (starpu_data_handle_t handle, unsigned node, uintptr_t ptr, uintptr_t dev_-handle, size_t offset)
- void starpu_matrix_data_register (starpu_data_handle_t *handle, int home_node, uintptr_t ptr, uint32_t ld, uint32_t nx, uint32_t ny, size_t elemsize)
- void starpu_matrix_ptr_register (starpu_data_handle_t handle, unsigned node, uintptr_t ptr, uintptr_t dev_-handle, size_t offset, uint32_t ld)
- void starpu_block_data_register (starpu_data_handle_t *handle, int home_node, uintptr_t ptr, uint32_t ldy, uint32_t ldz, uint32_t nx, uint32_t ny, uint32_t nz, size_t elemsize)
- void starpu_block_ptr_register (starpu_data_handle_t handle, unsigned node, uintptr_t ptr, uintptr_t dev_-handle, size_t offset, uint32_t ldy, uint32_t ldz)
- void starpu_bcsr_data_register (starpu_data_handle_t *handle, int home_node, uint32_t nnz, uint32_t nrow, uintptr_t nzval, uint32_t *colind, uint32_t *rowptr, uint32_t firstentry, uint32_t r, uint32_t c, size_t elemsize)
- void starpu_csr_data_register (starpu_data_handle_t *handle, int home_node, uint32_t nnz, uint32_t nrow, uintptr_t nzval, uint32_t *colind, uint32_t *rowptr, uint32_t firstentry, size_t elemsize)
- void starpu_coo_data_register (starpu_data_handle_t *handleptr, int home_node, uint32_t nx, uint32_t ny, uint32_t n_values, uint32_t *columns, uint32_t *rows, uintptr_t values, size_t elemsize)
- void * starpu_data_get_interface_on_node (starpu_data_handle_t handle, unsigned memory_node)

Accessing Data Interfaces

Each data interface is provided with a set of field access functions. The ones using a `void *` parameter aimed to be used in codelet implementations (see for example the code in Vector Scaling Using StarPU's API).

- void * starpu_data_handle_to_pointer (starpu_data_handle_t handle, unsigned node)
- void * starpu_data_get_local_ptr (starpu_data_handle_t handle)
- enum starpu_data_interface_id starpu_data_get_interface_id (starpu_data_handle_t handle)
- size_t starpu_data_get_size (starpu_data_handle_t handle)
- int starpu_data_pack (starpu_data_handle_t handle, void **ptr, starpu_ssize_t *count)
- int starpu_data_unpack (starpu_data_handle_t handle, void *ptr, size_t count)

Accessing Variable Data Interfaces

- #define STARPU_VARIABLE_GET_PTR(interface)
- #define STARPU_VARIABLE_GET_ELEMSIZE(interface)
- #define STARPU_VARIABLE_GET_DEV_HANDLE(interface)
- #define STARPU_VARIABLE_GET_OFFSET(interface)
- size_t starpu_variable_get_elemsize (starpu_data_handle_t handle)
- uintptr_t starpu_variable_get_local_ptr (starpu_data_handle_t handle)

Accessing Vector Data Interfaces

- #define STARPU_VECTOR_GET_PTR(interface)
- #define STARPU_VECTOR_GET_DEV_HANDLE(interface)
- #define STARPU_VECTOR_GET_OFFSET(interface)
- #define STARPU_VECTOR_GET_NX(interface)
- #define STARPU_VECTOR_GET_ELEMSIZE(interface)
- #define STARPU_VECTOR_GET_SLICE_BASE(interface)
- uint32_t starpu_vector_get_nx (starpu_data_handle_t handle)
- size_t starpu_vector_get_elemsize (starpu_data_handle_t handle)
- uintptr_t starpu_vector_get_local_ptr (starpu_data_handle_t handle)

Accessing Matrix Data Interfaces

- #define STARPU_MATRIX_GET_PTR(interface)
- #define STARPU_MATRIX_GET_DEV_HANDLE(interface)
- #define STARPU_MATRIX_GET_OFFSET(interface)
- #define STARPU_MATRIX_GET_NX(interface)
- #define STARPU_MATRIX_GET_NY(interface)
- #define STARPU_MATRIX_GET_LD(interface)
- #define STARPU_MATRIX_GET_ELEMSIZE(interface)
- uint32_t starpu_matrix_get_nx (starpu_data_handle_t handle)
- uint32_t starpu_matrix_get_ny (starpu_data_handle_t handle)
- uint32_t starpu_matrix_get_local_ld (starpu_data_handle_t handle)
- uintptr_t starpu_matrix_get_local_ptr (starpu_data_handle_t handle)
- size_t starpu_matrix_get_elemsize (starpu_data_handle_t handle)

Accessing Block Data Interfaces

- #define STARPU_BLOCK_GET_PTR(interface)
- #define STARPU_BLOCK_GET_DEV_HANDLE(interface)
- #define STARPU_BLOCK_GET_OFFSET(interface)
- #define STARPU_BLOCK_GET_NX(interface)
- #define STARPU_BLOCK_GET_NY(interface)
- #define STARPU_BLOCK_GET_NZ(interface)
- #define STARPU_BLOCK_GET_LDY(interface)
- #define STARPU_BLOCK_GET_LDZ(interface)
- #define STARPU_BLOCK_GET_ELEMSIZE(interface)
- uint32_t starpu_block_get_nx (starpu_data_handle_t handle)
- uint32_t starpu_block_get_ny (starpu_data_handle_t handle)
- uint32_t starpu_block_get_nz (starpu_data_handle_t handle)
- uint32_t starpu_block_get_local_ldy (starpu_data_handle_t handle)
- uint32_t starpu_block_get_local_ldz (starpu_data_handle_t handle)
- uintptr_t starpu_block_get_local_ptr (starpu_data_handle_t handle)
- size_t starpu_block_get_elemsize (starpu_data_handle_t handle)

Accessing BCSR Data Interfaces

- #define STARPU_BCSR_GET_NNZ(interface)
- #define STARPU_BCSR_GET_NZVAL(interface)
- #define STARPU_BCSR_GET_NZVAL_DEV_HANDLE(interface)
- #define STARPU_BCSR_GET_COLIND(interface)
- #define STARPU_BCSR_GET_COLIND_DEV_HANDLE(interface)
- #define STARPU_BCSR_GET_ROWPTR(interface)
- #define STARPU_BCSR_GET_ROWPTR_DEV_HANDLE(interface)
- #define STARPU_BCSR_GET_OFFSET
- uint32_t starpu_bcsr_get_nnz (starpu_data_handle_t handle)
- uint32_t starpu_bcsr_get_nrow (starpu_data_handle_t handle)
- uint32_t starpu_bcsr_get_firstentry (starpu_data_handle_t handle)
- uintptr_t starpu_bcsr_get_local_nzval (starpu_data_handle_t handle)
- uint32_t * starpu_bcsr_get_local_colind (starpu_data_handle_t handle)
- uint32_t * starpu_bcsr_get_local_rowptr (starpu_data_handle_t handle)
- uint32_t starpu_bcsr_get_r (starpu_data_handle_t handle)
- uint32_t starpu_bcsr_get_c (starpu_data_handle_t handle)
- size_t starpu_bcsr_get_elemsize (starpu_data_handle_t handle)

Accessing CSR Data Interfaces

- #define STARPU_CSR_GET_NNZ(interface)
- #define STARPU_CSR_GET_NROW(interface)
- #define STARPU_CSR_GET_NZVAL(interface)
- #define STARPU_CSR_GET_NZVAL_DEV_HANDLE(interface)
- #define STARPU_CSR_GET_COLIND(interface)
- #define STARPU_CSR_GET_COLIND_DEV_HANDLE(interface)
- #define STARPU_CSR_GET_ROWPTR(interface)
- #define STARPU_CSR_GET_ROWPTR_DEV_HANDLE(interface)
- #define STARPU_CSR_GET_OFFSET
- #define STARPU_CSR_GET_FIRSTENTRY(interface)
- #define STARPU_CSR_GET_ELEMSIZE(interface)
- uint32_t starpu_csr_get_nnz (starpu_data_handle_t handle)
- uint32_t starpu_csr_get_nrow (starpu_data_handle_t handle)

- uint32_t starpu_csr_get_firstentry (starpu_data_handle_t handle)
- uintptr_t starpu_csr_get_local_nzval (starpu_data_handle_t handle)
- uint32_t * starpu_csr_get_local_colind (starpu_data_handle_t handle)
- uint32_t * starpu_csr_get_local_rowptr (starpu_data_handle_t handle)
- size_t starpu_csr_get_elemsize (starpu_data_handle_t handle)

Accessing COO Data Interfaces

- #define STARPU_COO_GET_COLUMNS(interface)
- #define STARPU_COO_GET_COLUMNS_DEV_HANDLE(interface)
- #define STARPU_COO_GET_ROWS(interface)
- #define STARPU_COO_GET_ROWS_DEV_HANDLE(interface)
- #define STARPU_COO_GET_VALUES(interface)
- #define STARPU_COO_GET_VALUES_DEV_HANDLE(interface)
- #define STARPU_COO_GET_OFFSET
- #define STARPU_COO_GET_NX(interface)
- #define STARPU_COO_GET_NY(interface)
- #define STARPU_COO_GET_NVALUES(interface)
- #define STARPU_COO_GET_ELEMSIZE(interface)

Defining Interface

Applications can provide their own interface as shown in Defining A New Data Interface.

- uintptr_t starpu_malloc_on_node_flags (unsigned dst_node, size_t size, int flags)
- void starpu_free_on_node_flags (unsigned dst_node, uintptr_t addr, size_t size, int flags)
- uintptr_t starpu_malloc_on_node (unsigned dst_node, size_t size)
- void starpu_free_on_node (unsigned dst_node, uintptr_t addr, size_t size)
- void starpu_malloc_on_node_set_default_flags (unsigned node, int flags)
- int starpu_interface_copy (uintptr_t src, size_t src_offset, unsigned src_node, uintptr_t dst, size_t dst_offset, unsigned dst_node, size_t size, void *async_data)
- uint32_t starpu_hash_crc32c_be_n (const void *input, size_t n, uint32_t inputcrc)
- uint32_t starpu_hash_crc32c_be (uint32_t input, uint32_t inputcrc)
- uint32_t starpu_hash_crc32c_string (const char *str, uint32_t inputcrc)
- int starpu_data_interface_get_next_id (void)

29.9.1   Detailed Description

29.9.2   Data Structure Documentation

29.9.2.1   struct starpu_data_interface_ops

Per-interface data transfer methods.

Data Fields

- void(* register_data_handle)(starpu_data_handle_t handle, unsigned home_node, void *data_interface)
- starpu_ssize_t(* allocate_data_on_node)(void *data_interface, unsigned node)
- void(* free_data_on_node)(void *data_interface, unsigned node)
- struct starpu_data_copy_methods * copy_methods
- void *(* handle_to_pointer)(starpu_data_handle_t handle, unsigned node)
- size_t(* get_size)(starpu_data_handle_t handle)

- uint32_t(∗ footprint)(starpu_data_handle_t handle)
- int(∗ compare)(void ∗data_interface_a, void ∗data_interface_b)
- void(∗ display)(starpu_data_handle_t handle, FILE ∗f)
- starpu_ssize_t(∗ describe)(void ∗data_interface, char ∗buf, size_t size)
- enum starpu_data_interface_id interfaceid
- size_t interface_size
- char is_multiformat
- char dontcache
- struct
  starpu_multiformat_data_interface_ops ∗(∗ get_mf_ops)(void ∗data_interface)
- int(∗ pack_data)(starpu_data_handle_t handle, unsigned node, void ∗∗ptr, starpu_ssize_t ∗count)
- int(∗ unpack_data)(starpu_data_handle_t handle, unsigned node, void ∗ptr, size_t count)

29.9.2.1.1 Field Documentation

29.9.2.1.1.1 void(∗ starpu_data_interface_ops::register_data_handle)(**starpu_data_handle_t** handle, unsigned home_node, void ∗data_interface)

Register an existing interface into a data handle.

29.9.2.1.1.2 starpu_ssize_t(∗ starpu_data_interface_ops::allocate_data_on_node)(void ∗data_interface, unsigned node)

Allocate data for the interface on a given node.

29.9.2.1.1.3 void(∗ starpu_data_interface_ops::free_data_on_node)(void ∗data_interface, unsigned node)

Free data of the interface on a given node.

29.9.2.1.1.4 const struct **starpu_data_copy_methods** ∗ starpu_data_interface_ops::copy_methods

ram/cuda/opencl synchronous and asynchronous transfer methods.

29.9.2.1.1.5 void ∗(∗ starpu_data_interface_ops::handle_to_pointer)(**starpu_data_handle_t** handle, unsigned node)

Return the current pointer (if any) for the handle on the given node.

29.9.2.1.1.6 size_t(∗ starpu_data_interface_ops::get_size)(**starpu_data_handle_t** handle)

Return an estimation of the size of data, for performance models.

29.9.2.1.1.7 uint32_t(∗ starpu_data_interface_ops::footprint)(**starpu_data_handle_t** handle)

Return a 32bit footprint which characterizes the data size.

29.9.2.1.1.8 int(∗ starpu_data_interface_ops::compare)(void ∗data_interface_a, void ∗data_interface_b)

Compare the data size of two interfaces.

29.9.2.1.1.9 void(∗ starpu_data_interface_ops::display)(**starpu_data_handle_t** handle, FILE ∗f)

Dump the sizes of a handle to a file.

29.9.2.1.1.10 starpu_ssize_t(∗ starpu_data_interface_ops::describe)(void ∗data_interface, char ∗buf, size_t size)

Describe the data into a string.

29.9.2.1.1.11 enum **starpu_data_interface_id** starpu_data_interface_ops::interfaceid

An identifier that is unique to each interface.

29.9.2.1.1.12   size_t starpu_data_interface_ops::interface_size

The size of the interface data descriptor.

29.9.2.1.1.13   char starpu_data_interface_ops::is_multiformat

todo

29.9.2.1.1.14   char starpu_data_interface_ops::dontcache

If set to non-zero, StarPU will never try to reuse an allocated buffer for a different handle. This can be notably useful for application-defined interfaces which have a dynamic size, and for which it thus does not make sense to reuse the buffer since will probably not have the proper size.

29.9.2.1.1.15   struct **starpu_multiformat_data_interface_ops** *(* starpu_data_interface_ops::get_mf_ops)(void *data_interface) `[read]`

todo

29.9.2.1.1.16   int(* starpu_data_interface_ops::pack_data)(**starpu_data_handle_t** handle, unsigned node, void **ptr, starpu_ssize_t *count)

Pack the data handle into a contiguous buffer at the address allocated with `starpu_malloc_flags(ptr, size, 0)` (and thus returned in `ptr`) and set the size of the newly created buffer in `count`. If `ptr` is NULL, the function should not copy the data in the buffer but just set count to the size of the buffer which would have been allocated. The special value -1 indicates the size is yet unknown.

29.9.2.1.1.17   int(* starpu_data_interface_ops::unpack_data)(**starpu_data_handle_t** handle, unsigned node, void *ptr, size_t count)

Unpack the data handle from the contiguous buffer at the address `ptr` of size `count`

29.9.2.2   struct starpu_data_copy_methods

Defines the per-interface methods. If the starpu_data_copy_methods::any_to_any method is provided, it will be used by default if no specific method is provided. It can still be useful to provide more specific method in case of e.g. available particular CUDA or OpenCL support.

Data Fields

- int(* can_copy)(void *src_interface, unsigned src_node, void *dst_interface, unsigned dst_node, unsigned handling_node)
- int(* ram_to_ram)(void *src_interface, unsigned src_node, void *dst_interface, unsigned dst_node)
- int(* ram_to_cuda)(void *src_interface, unsigned src_node, void *dst_interface, unsigned dst_node)
- int(* ram_to_opencl)(void *src_interface, unsigned src_node, void *dst_interface, unsigned dst_node)
- int(* ram_to_mic)(void *src_interface, unsigned src_node, void *dst_interface, unsigned dst_node)
- int(* cuda_to_ram)(void *src_interface, unsigned src_node, void *dst_interface, unsigned dst_node)
- int(* cuda_to_cuda)(void *src_interface, unsigned src_node, void *dst_interface, unsigned dst_node)
- int(* cuda_to_opencl)(void *src_interface, unsigned src_node, void *dst_interface, unsigned dst_node)
- int(* opencl_to_ram)(void *src_interface, unsigned src_node, void *dst_interface, unsigned dst_node)
- int(* opencl_to_cuda)(void *src_interface, unsigned src_node, void *dst_interface, unsigned dst_node)
- int(* opencl_to_opencl)(void *src_interface, unsigned src_node, void *dst_interface, unsigned dst_node)
- int(* mic_to_ram)(void *src_interface, unsigned srd_node, void *dst_interface, unsigned dst_node)
- int(* scc_src_to_sink)(void *src_interface, unsigned src_node, void *dst_interface, unsigned dst_node)
- int(* scc_sink_to_src)(void *src_interface, unsigned src_node, void *dst_interface, unsigned dst_node)
- int(* scc_sink_to_sink)(void *src_interface, unsigned src_node, void *dst_interface, unsigned dst_node)
- int(* ram_to_mpi_ms)(void *src_interface, unsigned src_node, void *dst_interface, unsigned dst_node)

- int(∗ mpi_ms_to_ram)(void ∗src_interface, unsigned src_node, void ∗dst_interface, unsigned dst_node)
- int(∗ mpi_ms_to_mpi_ms)(void ∗src_interface, unsigned src_node, void ∗dst_interface, unsigned dst_node)
- int(∗ ram_to_cuda_async)(void ∗src_interface, unsigned src_node, void ∗dst_interface, unsigned dst_node, starpu_cudaStream_t stream)
- int(∗ cuda_to_ram_async)(void ∗src_interface, unsigned src_node, void ∗dst_interface, unsigned dst_node, starpu_cudaStream_t stream)
- int(∗ cuda_to_cuda_async)(void ∗src_interface, unsigned src_node, void ∗dst_interface, unsigned dst_node, starpu_cudaStream_t stream)
- int(∗ ram_to_opencl_async)(void ∗src_interface, unsigned src_node, void ∗dst_interface, unsigned dst_node, cl_event ∗event)
- int(∗ opencl_to_ram_async)(void ∗src_interface, unsigned src_node, void ∗dst_interface, unsigned dst_node, cl_event ∗event)
- int(∗ opencl_to_opencl_async)(void ∗src_interface, unsigned src_node, void ∗dst_interface, unsigned dst_node, cl_event ∗event)
- int(∗ ram_to_mpi_ms_async)(void ∗src_interface, unsigned src_node, void ∗dst_interface, unsigned dst_node, void ∗event)
- int(∗ mpi_ms_to_ram_async)(void ∗src_interface, unsigned src_node, void ∗dst_interface, unsigned dst_node, void ∗event)
- int(∗ mpi_ms_to_mpi_ms_async)(void ∗src_interface, unsigned src_node, void ∗dst_interface, unsigned dst_node, void ∗event)
- int(∗ ram_to_mic_async)(void ∗src_interface, unsigned src_node, void ∗dst_interface, unsigned dst_node)
- int(∗ mic_to_ram_async)(void ∗src_interface, unsigned srd_node, void ∗dst_interface, unsigned dst_node)
- int(∗ any_to_any)(void ∗src_interface, unsigned src_node, void ∗dst_interface, unsigned dst_node, void ∗async_data)

29.9.2.2.1 Field Documentation

29.9.2.2.1.1 int(∗ starpu_data_copy_methods::can_copy)(void ∗src_interface, unsigned src_node, void ∗dst_interface, unsigned dst_node, unsigned handling_node)

If defined, allows the interface to declare whether it supports transferring from `src_interface` on node `src_node` to `dst_interface` on node `dst_node`, run from node `handling_node`. If not defined, it is assumed that the interface supports all transfers.

29.9.2.2.1.2 int(∗ starpu_data_copy_methods::ram_to_ram)(void ∗src_interface, unsigned src_node, void ∗dst_interface, unsigned dst_node)

Define how to copy data from the `src_interface` interface on the `src_node` CPU node to the `dst_interface` interface on the `dst_node` CPU node. Return 0 on success.

29.9.2.2.1.3 int(∗ starpu_data_copy_methods::ram_to_cuda)(void ∗src_interface, unsigned src_node, void ∗dst_interface, unsigned dst_node)

Define how to copy data from the `src_interface` interface on the `src_node` CPU node to the `dst_interface` interface on the `dst_node` CUDA node. Return 0 on success.

29.9.2.2.1.4 int(∗ starpu_data_copy_methods::ram_to_opencl)(void ∗src_interface, unsigned src_node, void ∗dst_interface, unsigned dst_node)

Define how to copy data from the `src_interface` interface on the `src_node` CPU node to the `dst_interface` interface on the `dst_node` OpenCL node. Return 0 on success.

29.9.2.2.1.5 int(∗ starpu_data_copy_methods::ram_to_mic)(void ∗src_interface, unsigned src_node, void ∗dst_interface, unsigned dst_node)

Define how to copy data from the `src_interface` interface on the `src_node` CPU node to the `dst_interface` interface on the `dst_node` MIC node. Return 0 on success.

29.9.2.2.1.6 int(∗ starpu_data_copy_methods::cuda_to_ram)(void ∗src_interface, unsigned src_node, void ∗dst_interface, unsigned dst_node)

Define how to copy data from the `src_interface` interface on the `src_node` CUDA node to the `dst_-interface` interface on the `dst_node` CPU node. Return 0 on success.

29.9.2.2.1.7 int(∗ starpu_data_copy_methods::cuda_to_cuda)(void ∗src_interface, unsigned src_node, void ∗dst_interface, unsigned dst_node)

Define how to copy data from the `src_interface` interface on the `src_node` CUDA node to the `dst_-interface` interface on the `dst_node` CUDA node. Return 0 on success.

29.9.2.2.1.8 int(∗ starpu_data_copy_methods::cuda_to_opencl)(void ∗src_interface, unsigned src_node, void ∗dst_interface, unsigned dst_node)

Define how to copy data from the `src_interface` interface on the `src_node` CUDA node to the `dst_-interface` interface on the `dst_node` OpenCL node. Return 0 on success.

29.9.2.2.1.9 int(∗ starpu_data_copy_methods::opencl_to_ram)(void ∗src_interface, unsigned src_node, void ∗dst_interface, unsigned dst_node)

Define how to copy data from the `src_interface` interface on the `src_node` OpenCL node to the `dst_-interface` interface on the `dst_node` CPU node. Return 0 on success.

29.9.2.2.1.10 int(∗ starpu_data_copy_methods::opencl_to_cuda)(void ∗src_interface, unsigned src_node, void ∗dst_interface, unsigned dst_node)

Define how to copy data from the `src_interface` interface on the `src_node` OpenCL node to the `dst_-interface` interface on the `dst_node` CUDA node. Return 0 on success.

29.9.2.2.1.11 int(∗ starpu_data_copy_methods::opencl_to_opencl)(void ∗src_interface, unsigned src_node, void ∗dst_interface, unsigned dst_node)

Define how to copy data from the `src_interface` interface on the `src_node` OpenCL node to the `dst_-interface` interface on the `dst_node` OpenCL node. Return 0 on success.

29.9.2.2.1.12 int(∗ starpu_data_copy_methods::mic_to_ram)(void ∗src_interface, unsigned src_node, void ∗dst_interface, unsigned dst_node)

Define how to copy data from the `src_interface` interface on the `src_node` MIC node to the `dst_-interface` interface on the `dst_node` CPU node. Return 0 on success.

29.9.2.2.1.13 int(∗ starpu_data_copy_methods::scc_src_to_sink)(void ∗src_interface, unsigned src_node, void ∗dst_interface, unsigned dst_node)

Define how to copy data from the `src_interface` interface on the `src_node` node to the `dst_interface` interface on the `dst_node` node. Must return 0 if the transfer was actually completed completely synchronously, or −EAGAIN if at least some transfers are still ongoing and should be awaited for by the core.

29.9.2.2.1.14 int(∗ starpu_data_copy_methods::scc_sink_to_src)(void ∗src_interface, unsigned src_node, void ∗dst_interface, unsigned dst_node)

Define how to copy data from the `src_interface` interface on the `src_node` node to the `dst_interface` interface on the `dst_node` node. Must return 0 if the transfer was actually completed completely synchronously, or −EAGAIN if at least some transfers are still ongoing and should be awaited for by the core.

29.9.2.2.1.15 int(∗ starpu_data_copy_methods::scc_sink_to_sink)(void ∗src_interface, unsigned src_node, void ∗dst_interface, unsigned dst_node)

Define how to copy data from the `src_interface` interface on the `src_node` node to the `dst_interface` interface on the `dst_node` node. Must return 0 if the transfer was actually completed completely synchronously, or −EAGAIN if at least some transfers are still ongoing and should be awaited for by the core.

29.9.2.2.1.16 int(∗ starpu_data_copy_methods::ram_to_mpi_ms)(void ∗src_interface, unsigned src_node, void ∗dst_interface, unsigned dst_node)

Define how to copy data from the `src_interface` interface on the `src_node` CPU node to the `dst_-interface` interface on the `dst_node` MPI Slave node. Return 0 on success.

29.9.2.2.1.17 int(∗ starpu_data_copy_methods::mpi_ms_to_ram)(void ∗src_interface, unsigned src_node, void ∗dst_interface, unsigned dst_node)

Define how to copy data from the `src_interface` interface on the `src_node` MPI Slave node to the `dst_-interface` interface on the `dst_node` CPU node. Return 0 on success.

29.9.2.2.1.18 int(∗ starpu_data_copy_methods::mpi_ms_to_mpi_ms)(void ∗src_interface, unsigned src_node, void ∗dst_interface, unsigned dst_node)

Define how to copy data from the `src_interface` interface on the `src_node` MPI Slave node to the `dst_-interface` interface on the `dst_node` MPI Slave node. Return 0 on success.

29.9.2.2.1.19 int(∗ starpu_data_copy_methods::ram_to_cuda_async)(void ∗src_interface, unsigned src_node, void ∗dst_interface, unsigned dst_node, cudaStream_t stream)

Define how to copy data from the `src_interface` interface on the `src_node` CPU node to the `dst_-interface` interface on the `dst_node` CUDA node, using the given stream. Must return 0 if the transfer was actually completed completely synchronously, or −EAGAIN if at least some transfers are still ongoing and should be awaited for by the core.

29.9.2.2.1.20 int(∗ starpu_data_copy_methods::cuda_to_ram_async)(void ∗src_interface, unsigned src_node, void ∗dst_interface, unsigned dst_node, cudaStream_t stream)

Define how to copy data from the `src_interface` interface on the `src_node` CUDA node to the `dst_-interface` interface on the `dst_node` CPU node, using the given stream. Must return 0 if the transfer was actually completed completely synchronously, or −EAGAIN if at least some transfers are still ongoing and should be awaited for by the core.

29.9.2.2.1.21 int(∗ starpu_data_copy_methods::cuda_to_cuda_async)(void ∗src_interface, unsigned src_node, void ∗dst_interface, unsigned dst_node, cudaStream_t stream)

Define how to copy data from the `src_interface` interface on the `src_node` CUDA node to the `dst_-interface` interface on the `dst_node` CUDA node, using the given stream. Must return 0 if the transfer was actually completed completely synchronously, or −EAGAIN if at least some transfers are still ongoing and should be awaited for by the core.

29.9.2.2.1.22 int(∗ starpu_data_copy_methods::ram_to_opencl_async)(void ∗src_interface, unsigned src_node, void ∗dst_interface, unsigned dst_node, cl_event ∗event)

Define how to copy data from the `src_interface` interface on the `src_node` CPU node to the `dst_-interface` interface on the `dst_node` OpenCL node, by recording in `event`, a pointer to a `cl_event`, the event of the last submitted transfer. Must return 0 if the transfer was actually completed completely synchronously, or −EAGAIN if at least some transfers are still ongoing and should be awaited for by the core.

29.9.2.2.1.23 int(∗ starpu_data_copy_methods::opencl_to_ram_async)(void ∗src_interface, unsigned src_node, void ∗dst_interface, unsigned dst_node, cl_event ∗event)

Define how to copy data from the `src_interface` interface on the `src_node` OpenCL node to the `dst_-interface` interface on the `dst_node` CPU node, by recording in `event`, a pointer to a `cl_event`, the event of the last submitted transfer. Must return 0 if the transfer was actually completed completely synchronously, or −EAGAIN if at least some transfers are still ongoing and should be awaited for by the core.

29.9.2.2.1.24 int(∗ starpu_data_copy_methods::opencl_to_opencl_async)(void ∗src_interface, unsigned src_node, void ∗dst_interface, unsigned dst_node, cl_event ∗event)

Define how to copy data from the `src_interface` interface on the `src_node` OpenCL node to the `dst_-interface` interface on the `dst_node` OpenCL node, by recording in `event`, a pointer to a `cl_event`, the event of the last submitted transfer. Must return 0 if the transfer was actually completed completely synchronously, or `-EAGAIN` if at least some transfers are still ongoing and should be awaited for by the core.

29.9.2.2.1.25 int(∗ starpu_data_copy_methods::ram_to_mpi_ms_async)(void ∗src_interface, unsigned src_node, void ∗dst_interface, unsigned dst_node, void ∗event)

Define how to copy data from the `src_interface` interface on the `src_node` CPU node to the `dst_-interface` interface on the `dst_node` MPI Slave node, with the given even. Must return 0 if the transfer was actually completed completely synchronously, or `-EAGAIN` if at least some transfers are still ongoing and should be awaited for by the core.

29.9.2.2.1.26 int(∗ starpu_data_copy_methods::mpi_ms_to_ram_async)(void ∗src_interface, unsigned src_node, void ∗dst_interface, unsigned dst_node, void ∗event)

Define how to copy data from the `src_interface` interface on the `src_node` MPI Slave node to the `dst_interface` interface on the `dst_node` CPU node, with the given event. Must return 0 if the transfer was actually completed completely synchronously, or `-EAGAIN` if at least some transfers are still ongoing and should be awaited for by the core.

29.9.2.2.1.27 int(∗ starpu_data_copy_methods::mpi_ms_to_mpi_ms_async)(void ∗src_interface, unsigned src_node, void ∗dst_interface, unsigned dst_node, void ∗event)

Define how to copy data from the `src_interface` interface on the `src_node` MPI Slave node to the `dst_-interface` interface on the `dst_node` MPI Slave node, using the given stream. Must return 0 if the transfer was actually completed completely synchronously, or `-EAGAIN` if at least some transfers are still ongoing and should be awaited for by the core.

29.9.2.2.1.28 int(∗ starpu_data_copy_methods::ram_to_mic_async)(void ∗src_intreface, unsigned src_node, void ∗dst_interface, unsigned dst_node)

Define how to copy data from the `src_interface` interface on the `src_node` CPU node to the `dst_-interface` interface on the `dst_node` MIC node. Must return 0 if the transfer was actually completed completely synchronously, or `-EAGAIN` if at least some transfers are still ongoing and should be awaited for by the core.

29.9.2.2.1.29 int(∗ starpu_data_copy_methods::mic_to_ram_async)(void ∗src_intreface, unsigned src_node, void ∗dst_interface, unsigned dst_node)

Define how to copy data from the `src_interface` interface on the `src_node` MIC node to the `dst_-interface` interface on the `dst_node` CPU node. Must return 0 if the transfer was actually completed completely synchronously, or `-EAGAIN` if at least some transfers are still ongoing and should be awaited for by the core.

29.9.2.2.1.30 int(∗ starpu_data_copy_methods::any_to_any)(void ∗src_interface, unsigned src_node, void ∗dst_interface, unsigned dst_node, void ∗async_data)

Define how to copy data from the `src_interface` interface on the `src_node` node to the `dst_interface` interface on the `dst_node` node. This is meant to be implemented through the starpu_interface_copy() helper, to which async_data should be passed as such, and will be used to manage asynchronicity. This must return `-EAG-AIN` if any of the starpu_interface_copy() calls has returned `-EAGAIN` (i.e. at least some transfer is still ongoing), and return 0 otherwise.

29.9.2.3 struct starpu_variable_interface

Variable interface for a single data (not a vector, a matrix, a list, ...)

Data Fields

enum starpu_data_-interface_id	id	Identifier of the interface
uintptr_t	ptr	local pointer of the variable
uintptr_t	dev_handle	device handle of the variable.
size_t	offset	offset in the variable
size_t	elemsize	size of the variable

29.9.2.4 struct starpu_vector_interface

Vector interface

Data Fields

enum starpu_data_-interface_id	id	Identifier of the interface
uintptr_t	ptr	local pointer of the vector
uintptr_t	dev_handle	device handle of the vector.
size_t	offset	offset in the vector
uint32_t	nx	number of elements on the x-axis of the vector
size_t	elemsize	size of the elements of the vector
uint32_t	slice_base	vector slice base, used by the StarPU OpenMP runtime support

29.9.2.5 struct starpu_matrix_interface

Matrix interface for dense matrices

Data Fields

enum starpu_data_-interface_id	id	Identifier of the interface
uintptr_t	ptr	local pointer of the matrix
uintptr_t	dev_handle	device handle of the matrix.
size_t	offset	offset in the matrix
uint32_t	nx	number of elements on the x-axis of the matrix
uint32_t	ny	number of elements on the y-axis of the matrix
uint32_t	ld	number of elements between each row of the matrix. Maybe be equal to starpu_matrix_interface::nx when there is no padding.
size_t	elemsize	size of the elements of the matrix

29.9.2.6 struct starpu_block_interface

Block interface for 3D dense blocks

Data Fields

enum starpu_data_-interface_id	id	identifier of the interface
uintptr_t	ptr	local pointer of the block
uintptr_t	dev_handle	device handle of the block.
size_t	offset	offset in the block.
uint32_t	nx	number of elements on the x-axis of the block.
uint32_t	ny	number of elements on the y-axis of the block.
uint32_t	nz	number of elements on the z-axis of the block.
uint32_t	ldy	number of elements between two lines
uint32_t	ldz	number of elements between two planes
size_t	elemsize	size of the elements of the block.

29.9.2.7 struct starpu_bcsr_interface

BCSR interface for sparse matrices (blocked compressed sparse row representation)

Data Fields

enum starpu_data_-interface_id	id	Identifier of the interface
uint32_t	nnz	number of non-zero BLOCKS
uint32_t	nrow	number of rows (in terms of BLOCKS)
uintptr_t	nzval	non-zero values
uint32_t *	colind	position of non-zero entried on the row
uint32_t *	rowptr	index (in nzval) of the first entry of the row
uint32_t	firstentry	k for k-based indexing (0 or 1 usually). Also useful when partitionning the matrix.
uint32_t	r	size of the blocks
uint32_t	c	size of the blocks
size_t	elemsize	size of the elements of the matrix

29.9.2.8 struct starpu_csr_interface

CSR interface for sparse matrices (compressed sparse row representation)

Data Fields

enum starpu_data_-interface_id	id	Identifier of the interface
uint32_t	nnz	number of non-zero entries
uint32_t	nrow	number of rows
uintptr_t	nzval	non-zero values
uint32_t *	colind	position of non-zero entries on the row
uint32_t *	rowptr	index (in nzval) of the first entry of the row
uint32_t	firstentry	k for k-based indexing (0 or 1 usually). also useful when partitionning the matrix.
size_t	elemsize	size of the elements of the matrix

29.9.2.9   struct starpu_coo_interface

29.9.2.9   struct starpu_coo_interface

COO Matrices

Data Fields

enum starpu_data_-interface_id	id	identifier of the interface
uint32_t *	columns	column array of the matrix
uint32_t *	rows	row array of the matrix
uintptr_t	values	values of the matrix
uint32_t	nx	number of elements on the x-axis of the matrix
uint32_t	ny	number of elements on the y-axis of the matrix
uint32_t	n_values	number of values registered in the matrix
size_t	elemsize	size of the elements of the matrix

29.9.3   Macro Definition Documentation

29.9.3.1   #define STARPU_VARIABLE_GET_PTR(*interface*)

Return a pointer to the variable designated by `interface`.

29.9.3.2   #define STARPU_VARIABLE_GET_ELEMSIZE(*interface*)

Return the size of the variable designated by `interface`.

29.9.3.3   #define STARPU_VARIABLE_GET_DEV_HANDLE(*interface*)

Return a device handle for the variable designated by `interface`, to be used with OpenCL. The offset documented below has to be used in addition to this.

29.9.3.4   #define STARPU_VARIABLE_GET_OFFSET(*interface*)

Return the offset in the variable designated by `interface`, to be used with the device handle.

29.9.3.5   #define STARPU_VECTOR_GET_PTR(*interface*)

Return a pointer to the array designated by `interface`, valid on CPUs and CUDA only. For OpenCL, the device handle and offset need to be used instead.

29.9.3.6   #define STARPU_VECTOR_GET_DEV_HANDLE(*interface*)

Return a device handle for the array designated by `interface`, to be used with OpenCL. the offset documented below has to be used in addition to this.

29.9.3.7   #define STARPU_VECTOR_GET_OFFSET(*interface*)

Return the offset in the array designated by `interface`, to be used with the device handle.

29.9.3.8   #define STARPU_VECTOR_GET_NX(*interface*)

Return the number of elements registered into the array designated by `interface`.

29.9.3.9   #define STARPU_VECTOR_GET_ELEMSIZE(*interface*)

Return the size of each element of the array designated by `interface`.

29.9.3.10   #define STARPU_VECTOR_GET_SLICE_BASE(*interface*)

Return the OpenMP slice base annotation of each element of the array designated by `interface`.

See Also

   starpu_omp_vector_annotate

29.9.3.11   #define STARPU_MATRIX_GET_PTR(*interface*)

Return a pointer to the matrix designated by `interface`, valid on CPUs and CUDA devices only. For OpenCL devices, the device handle and offset need to be used instead.

29.9.3.12   #define STARPU_MATRIX_GET_DEV_HANDLE(*interface*)

Return a device handle for the matrix designated by `interface`, to be used with OpenCL. The offset documented below has to be used in addition to this.

29.9.3.13   #define STARPU_MATRIX_GET_OFFSET(*interface*)

Return the offset in the matrix designated by `interface`, to be used with the device handle.

29.9.3.14   #define STARPU_MATRIX_GET_NX(*interface*)

Return the number of elements on the x-axis of the matrix designated by `interface`.

29.9.3.15   #define STARPU_MATRIX_GET_NY(*interface*)

Return the number of elements on the y-axis of the matrix designated by `interface`.

29.9.3.16   #define STARPU_MATRIX_GET_LD(*interface*)

Return the number of elements between each row of the matrix designated by `interface`. May be equal to nx when there is no padding.

29.9.3.17   #define STARPU_MATRIX_GET_ELEMSIZE(*interface*)

Return the size of the elements registered into the matrix designated by `interface`.

29.9.3.18   #define STARPU_BLOCK_GET_PTR(*interface*)

Return a pointer to the block designated by `interface`.

29.9.3.19   #define STARPU_BLOCK_GET_DEV_HANDLE(*interface*)

Return a device handle for the block designated by `interface`, to be used on OpenCL. The offset document below has to be used in addition to this.

29.9.3.20   #define STARPU_BLOCK_GET_OFFSET(*interface*)

Return the offset in the block designated by `interface`, to be used with the device handle.

29.9.3.21   #define STARPU_BLOCK_GET_NX(*interface*)

Return the number of elements on the x-axis of the block designated by `interface`.

29.9.3.22   #define STARPU_BLOCK_GET_NY(*interface*)

Return the number of elements on the y-axis of the block designated by `interface`.

29.9.3.23   #define STARPU_BLOCK_GET_NZ(*interface*)

Return the number of elements on the z-axis of the block designated by `interface`.

29.9.3.24   #define STARPU_BLOCK_GET_LDY(*interface*)

Return the number of elements between each row of the block designated by `interface`. May be equal to nx when there is no padding.

29.9.3.25   #define STARPU_BLOCK_GET_LDZ(*interface*)

Return the number of elements between each z plane of the block designated by `interface`. May be equal to nx∗ny when there is no padding.

29.9.3.26   #define STARPU_BLOCK_GET_ELEMSIZE(*interface*)

Return the size of the elements of the block designated by `interface`.

29.9.3.27   #define STARPU_BCSR_GET_NNZ(*interface*)

Return the number of non-zero values in the matrix designated by `interface`.

29.9.3.28   #define STARPU_BCSR_GET_NZVAL(*interface*)

Return a pointer to the non-zero values of the matrix designated by `interface`.

29.9.3.29   #define STARPU_BCSR_GET_NZVAL_DEV_HANDLE(*interface*)

Return a device handle for the array of non-zero values in the matrix designated by `interface`. The offset documented below has to be used in addition to this.

29.9.3.30   #define STARPU_BCSR_GET_COLIND(*interface*)

Return a pointer to the column index of the matrix designated by `interface`.

29.9.3.31   #define STARPU_BCSR_GET_COLIND_DEV_HANDLE(*interface*)

Return a device handle for the column index of the matrix designated by `interface`. The offset documented below has to be used in addition to this.

29.9.3.32   #define STARPU_BCSR_GET_ROWPTR(*interface*)

Return a pointer to the row pointer array of the matrix designated by `interface`.

29.9.3.33   #define STARPU_BCSR_GET_ROWPTR_DEV_HANDLE(*interface*)

Return a device handle for the row pointer array of the matrix designated by `interface`. The offset documented below has to be used in addition to this.

29.9.3.34   #define STARPU_BCSR_GET_OFFSET

Return the offset in the arrays (coling, rowptr, nzval) of the matrix designated by `interface`, to be used with the device handles.

29.9.3.35   #define STARPU_CSR_GET_NNZ(*interface*)

Return the number of non-zero values in the matrix designated by `interface`.

29.9.3.36   #define STARPU_CSR_GET_NROW(*interface*)

Return the size of the row pointer array of the matrix designated by `interface`.

29.9.3.37   #define STARPU_CSR_GET_NZVAL(*interface*)

Return a pointer to the non-zero values of the matrix designated by `interface`.

29.9.3.38   #define STARPU_CSR_GET_NZVAL_DEV_HANDLE(*interface*)

Return a device handle for the array of non-zero values in the matrix designated by `interface`. The offset documented below has to be used in addition to this.

29.9.3.39   #define STARPU_CSR_GET_COLIND(*interface*)

Return a pointer to the column index of the matrix designated by `interface`.

29.9.3.40   #define STARPU_CSR_GET_COLIND_DEV_HANDLE(*interface*)

Return a device handle for the column index of the matrix designated by `interface`. The offset documented below has to be used in addition to this.

29.9.3.41 #define STARPU_CSR_GET_ROWPTR(*interface*)

Return a pointer to the row pointer array of the matrix designated by `interface`.

29.9.3.42 #define STARPU_CSR_GET_ROWPTR_DEV_HANDLE(*interface*)

Return a device handle for the row pointer array of the matrix designated by `interface`. The offset documented below has to be used in addition to this.

29.9.3.43 #define STARPU_CSR_GET_OFFSET

Return the offset in the arrays (colind, rowptr, nzval) of the matrix designated by `interface`, to be used with the device handles.

29.9.3.44 #define STARPU_CSR_GET_FIRSTENTRY(*interface*)

Return the index at which all arrays (the column indexes, the row pointers...) of the `interface` start.

29.9.3.45 #define STARPU_CSR_GET_ELEMSIZE(*interface*)

Return the size of the elements registered into the matrix designated by `interface`.

29.9.3.46 #define STARPU_COO_GET_COLUMNS(*interface*)

Return a pointer to the column array of the matrix designated by `interface`.

29.9.3.47 #define STARPU_COO_GET_COLUMNS_DEV_HANDLE(*interface*)

Return a device handle for the column array of the matrix designated by `interface`, to be used with OpenCL. The offset documented below has to be used in addition to this.

29.9.3.48 #define STARPU_COO_GET_ROWS(*interface*)

Return a pointer to the rows array of the matrix designated by `interface`.

29.9.3.49 #define STARPU_COO_GET_ROWS_DEV_HANDLE(*interface*)

Return a device handle for the row array of the matrix designated by `interface`, to be used on OpenCL. The offset documented below has to be used in addition to this.

29.9.3.50 #define STARPU_COO_GET_VALUES(*interface*)

Return a pointer to the values array of the matrix designated by `interface`.

29.9.3.51 #define STARPU_COO_GET_VALUES_DEV_HANDLE(*interface*)

Return a device handle for the value array of the matrix designated by `interface`, to be used on OpenCL. The offset documented below has to be used in addition to this.

29.9.3.52   #define STARPU_COO_GET_OFFSET

Return the offset in the arrays of the COO matrix designated by `interface`.

29.9.3.53   #define STARPU_COO_GET_NX(*interface*)

Return the number of elements on the x-axis of the matrix designated by `interface`.

29.9.3.54   #define STARPU_COO_GET_NY(*interface*)

Return the number of elements on the y-axis of the matrix designated by `interface`.

29.9.3.55   #define STARPU_COO_GET_NVALUES(*interface*)

Return the number of values registered in the matrix designated by `interface`.

29.9.3.56   #define STARPU_COO_GET_ELEMSIZE(*interface*)

Return the size of the elements registered into the matrix designated by `interface`.

29.9.4   Enumeration Type Documentation

29.9.4.1   enum starpu_data_interface_id

Identifier for all predefined StarPU data interfaces

Enumerator:

    STARPU_UNKNOWN_INTERFACE_ID   Unknown interface

    STARPU_MATRIX_INTERFACE_ID   Identifier for the matrix data interface

    STARPU_BLOCK_INTERFACE_ID   Identifier for block data interface

    STARPU_VECTOR_INTERFACE_ID   Identifier for the vector data interface

    STARPU_CSR_INTERFACE_ID   Identifier for the csr data interface

    STARPU_BCSR_INTERFACE_ID   Identifier for the bcsr data interface

    STARPU_VARIABLE_INTERFACE_ID   Identifier for the variable data interface

    STARPU_VOID_INTERFACE_ID   Identifier for the void data interface

    STARPU_MULTIFORMAT_INTERFACE_ID   Identifier for the multiformat data interface

    STARPU_COO_INTERFACE_ID   Identifier for the coo data interface

    STARPU_MAX_INTERFACE_ID   Maximum number of data interfaces

29.9.5   Function Documentation

29.9.5.1   void starpu_void_data_register (**starpu_data_handle_t** ∗ *handle*)

Register a void interface. There is no data really associated to that interface, but it may be used as a synchronization mechanism. It also permits to express an abstract piece of data that is managed by the application internally: this makes it possible to forbid the concurrent execution of different tasks accessing the same `void` data in read-write concurrently.

29.9.5.2 void starpu_variable_data_register (starpu_data_handle_t * *handle*, int *home_node*, uintptr_t *ptr*, size_t *size*)

Register the `size` byte element pointed to by `ptr`, which is typically a scalar, and initialize `handle` to represent this data item.

Here an example of how to use the function.

```
float var = 42.0;
starpu_data_handle_t var_handle;
starpu_variable_data_register(&var_handle,
    STARPU_MAIN_RAM, (uintptr_t)&var, sizeof(var));
```

29.9.5.3 void starpu_variable_ptr_register (**starpu_data_handle_t** *handle*, unsigned *node*, uintptr_t *ptr*, uintptr_t *dev_handle*, size_t *offset*)

Register into the `handle` that to store data on node `node` it should use the buffer located at `ptr`, or device handle `dev_handle` and offset `offset` (for OpenCL, notably)

29.9.5.4 void starpu_vector_data_register (**starpu_data_handle_t** * *handle*, int *home_node*, uintptr_t *ptr*, uint32_t *nx*, size_t *elemsize*)

Register the `nx` `elemsize-byte` elements pointed to by `ptr` and initialize `handle` to represent it.

Here an example of how to use the function.

```
float vector[NX];
starpu_data_handle_t vector_handle;
starpu_vector_data_register(&vector_handle,
    STARPU_MAIN_RAM, (uintptr_t)vector, NX, sizeof(vector[0]));
```

29.9.5.5 void starpu_vector_ptr_register (**starpu_data_handle_t** *handle*, unsigned *node*, uintptr_t *ptr*, uintptr_t *dev_handle*, size_t *offset*)

Register into the `handle` that to store data on node `node` it should use the buffer located at `ptr`, or device handle `dev_handle` and offset `offset` (for OpenCL, notably)

29.9.5.6 void starpu_matrix_data_register (**starpu_data_handle_t** * *handle*, int *home_node*, uintptr_t *ptr*, uint32_t *ld*, uint32_t *nx*, uint32_t *ny*, size_t *elemsize*)

Register the `nx` x `ny` 2D matrix of `elemsize-byte` elements pointed by `ptr` and initialize `handle` to represent it. `ld` specifies the number of elements between rows. a value greater than `nx` adds padding, which can be useful for alignment purposes.

Here an example of how to use the function.

```
float *matrix;
starpu_data_handle_t matrix_handle;
matrix = (float*)malloc(width * height * sizeof(float));
starpu_matrix_data_register(&matrix_handle,
    STARPU_MAIN_RAM, (uintptr_t)matrix, width, width, height, sizeof
    (float));
```

29.9.5.7 void starpu_matrix_ptr_register (**starpu_data_handle_t** *handle*, unsigned *node*, uintptr_t *ptr*, uintptr_t *dev_handle*, size_t *offset*, uint32_t *ld*)

Register into the `handle` that to store data on node `node` it should use the buffer located at `ptr`, or device handle `dev_handle` and offset `offset` (for OpenCL, notably), with `ld` elements between rows.

29.9.5.8 void starpu_block_data_register (**starpu_data_handle_t** * *handle*, int *home_node*, uintptr_t *ptr*, uint32_t *ldy*, uint32_t *ldz*, uint32_t *nx*, uint32_t *ny*, uint32_t *nz*, size_t *elemsize*)

Register the `nx` x `ny` x `nz` 3D matrix of `elemsize` byte elements pointed by `ptr` and initialize `handle` to represent it. Again, `ldy` and `ldz` specify the number of elements between rows and between z planes.

Here an example of how to use the function.

```
float *block;
starpu_data_handle_t block_handle;
block = (float*)malloc(nx*ny*nz*sizeof(float));
starpu_block_data_register(&block_handle,
    STARPU_MAIN_RAM, (uintptr_t)block, nx, nx*ny, nx, ny, nz, sizeof
    (float));
```

29.9.5.9 void starpu_block_ptr_register (**starpu_data_handle_t** *handle*, unsigned *node*, uintptr_t *ptr*, uintptr_t *dev_handle*, size_t *offset*, uint32_t *ldy*, uint32_t *ldz*)

Register into the `handle` that to store data on node `node` it should use the buffer located at `ptr`, or device handle `dev_handle` and offset `offset` (for OpenCL, notably), with `ldy` elements between rows and `ldz` elements between z planes.

29.9.5.10 void starpu_bcsr_data_register (**starpu_data_handle_t** * *handle*, int *home_node*, uint32_t *nnz*, uint32_t *nrow*, uintptr_t *nzval*, uint32_t * *colind*, uint32_t * *rowptr*, uint32_t *firstentry*, uint32_t *r*, uint32_t *c*, size_t *elemsize*)

This variant of starpu_data_register() uses the BCSR (Blocked Compressed Sparse Row Representation) sparse matrix interface. Register the sparse matrix made of `nnz` non-zero blocks of elements of size `elemsize` stored in `nzval` and initializes `handle` to represent it. Blocks have size $r * c$. `nrow` is the number of rows (in terms of blocks), `colind`[i] is the block-column index for block i in `nzval`, `rowptr`[i] is the block-index (in `nzval`) of the first block of row i. `firstentry` is the index of the first entry of the given arrays (usually 0 or 1).

29.9.5.11 void starpu_csr_data_register (**starpu_data_handle_t** * *handle*, int *home_node*, uint32_t *nnz*, uint32_t *nrow*, uintptr_t *nzval*, uint32_t * *colind*, uint32_t * *rowptr*, uint32_t *firstentry*, size_t *elemsize*)

This variant of starpu_data_register() uses the CSR (Compressed Sparse Row Representation) sparse matrix interface. TODO

29.9.5.12 void starpu_coo_data_register (**starpu_data_handle_t** * *handleptr*, int *home_node*, uint32_t *nx*, uint32_t *ny*, uint32_t *n_values*, uint32_t * *columns*, uint32_t * *rows*, uintptr_t *values*, size_t *elemsize*)

Register the `nx` x `ny` 2D matrix given in the COO format, using the `columns`, `rows`, `values` arrays, which must have `n_values` elements of size `elemsize`. Initialize `handleptr`.

29.9.5.13 void * starpu_data_get_interface_on_node (**starpu_data_handle_t** *handle*, unsigned *memory_node*)

Return the interface associated with `handle` on `memory_node`.

29.9.5.14 void * starpu_data_handle_to_pointer (**starpu_data_handle_t** *handle*, unsigned *node*)

Return the pointer associated with `handle` on node `node` or `NULL` if handle's interface does not support this operation or data for this `handle` is not allocated on that `node`.

29.9.5.15   void ∗ starpu_data_get_local_ptr (**starpu_data_handle_t** *handle*)

Return the local pointer associated with `handle` or `NULL` if `handle`'s interface does not have any data allocated locally.

29.9.5.16   enum **starpu_data_interface_id** starpu_data_get_interface_id (**starpu_data_handle_t** *handle*)

Return the unique identifier of the interface associated with the given `handle`.

29.9.5.17   size_t starpu_data_get_size (**starpu_data_handle_t** *handle*)

Return the size of the data associated with `handle`.

29.9.5.18   int starpu_data_pack (**starpu_data_handle_t** *handle,* void ∗∗ *ptr,* starpu_ssize_t ∗ *count*)

Execute the packing operation of the interface of the data registered at `handle` (see starpu_data_interface_ops). This packing operation must allocate a buffer large enough at `ptr` and copy into the newly allocated buffer the data associated to `handle`. `count` will be set to the size of the allocated buffer. If `ptr` is `NULL`, the function should not copy the data in the buffer but just set `count` to the size of the buffer which would have been allocated. The special value -1 indicates the size is yet unknown.

29.9.5.19   int starpu_data_unpack (**starpu_data_handle_t** *handle,* void ∗ *ptr,* size_t *count*)

Unpack in handle the data located at `ptr` of size `count` as described by the interface of the data. The interface registered at `handle` must define a unpacking operation (see starpu_data_interface_ops). The memory at the address `ptr` is freed after calling the data unpacking operation.

29.9.5.20   size_t starpu_variable_get_elemsize (**starpu_data_handle_t** *handle*)

Return the size of the variable designated by `handle`.

29.9.5.21   uintptr_t starpu_variable_get_local_ptr (**starpu_data_handle_t** *handle*)

Return a pointer to the variable designated by `handle`.

29.9.5.22   uint32_t starpu_vector_get_nx (**starpu_data_handle_t** *handle*)

Return the number of elements registered into the array designated by `handle`.

29.9.5.23   size_t starpu_vector_get_elemsize (**starpu_data_handle_t** *handle*)

Return the size of each element of the array designated by `handle`.

29.9.5.24   uintptr_t starpu_vector_get_local_ptr (**starpu_data_handle_t** *handle*)

Return the local pointer associated with `handle`.

29.9.5.25   uint32_t starpu_matrix_get_nx (**starpu_data_handle_t** *handle*)

Return the number of elements on the x-axis of the matrix designated by `handle`.

29.9.5.26 uint32_t starpu_matrix_get_ny (starpu_data_handle_t *handle* **)**

Return the number of elements on the y-axis of the matrix designated by `handle`.

29.9.5.27 uint32_t starpu_matrix_get_local_ld (starpu_data_handle_t *handle* **)**

Return the number of elements between each row of the matrix designated by `handle`. Maybe be equal to nx when there is no padding.

29.9.5.28 uintptr_t starpu_matrix_get_local_ptr (starpu_data_handle_t *handle* **)**

Return the local pointer associated with `handle`.

29.9.5.29 size_t starpu_matrix_get_elemsize (starpu_data_handle_t *handle* **)**

Return the size of the elements registered into the matrix designated by `handle`.

29.9.5.30 uint32_t starpu_block_get_nx (starpu_data_handle_t *handle* **)**

Return the number of elements on the x-axis of the block designated by `handle`.

29.9.5.31 uint32_t starpu_block_get_ny (starpu_data_handle_t *handle* **)**

Return the number of elements on the y-axis of the block designated by `handle`.

29.9.5.32 uint32_t starpu_block_get_nz (starpu_data_handle_t *handle* **)**

Return the number of elements on the z-axis of the block designated by `handle`.

29.9.5.33 uint32_t starpu_block_get_local_ldy (starpu_data_handle_t *handle* **)**

Return the number of elements between each row of the block designated by `handle`, in the format of the current memory node.

29.9.5.34 uint32_t starpu_block_get_local_ldz (starpu_data_handle_t *handle* **)**

Return the number of elements between each z plane of the block designated by `handle`, in the format of the current memory node.

29.9.5.35 uintptr_t starpu_block_get_local_ptr (starpu_data_handle_t *handle* **)**

Return the local pointer associated with `handle`.

29.9.5.36 size_t starpu_block_get_elemsize (starpu_data_handle_t *handle* **)**

Return the size of the elements of the block designated by `handle`.

29.9.5.37 uint32_t starpu_bcsr_get_nnz (starpu_data_handle_t *handle* **)**

Return the number of non-zero elements in the matrix designated by `handle`.

29.9.5.38 uint32_t starpu_bcsr_get_nrow (**starpu_data_handle_t** *handle*)

Return the number of rows (in terms of blocks of size r∗c) in the matrix designated by `handle`.

29.9.5.39 uint32_t starpu_bcsr_get_firstentry (**starpu_data_handle_t** *handle*)

Return the index at which all arrays (the column indexes, the row pointers...) of the matrix desginated by `handle`.

29.9.5.40 uintptr_t starpu_bcsr_get_local_nzval (**starpu_data_handle_t** *handle*)

Return a pointer to the non-zero values of the matrix designated by `handle`.

29.9.5.41 uint32_t ∗ starpu_bcsr_get_local_colind (**starpu_data_handle_t** *handle*)

Return a pointer to the column index, which holds the positions of the non-zero entries in the matrix designated by `handle`.

29.9.5.42 uint32_t ∗ starpu_bcsr_get_local_rowptr (**starpu_data_handle_t** *handle*)

Return the row pointer array of the matrix designated by `handle`.

29.9.5.43 uint32_t starpu_bcsr_get_r (**starpu_data_handle_t** *handle*)

Return the number of rows in a block.

29.9.5.44 uint32_t starpu_bcsr_get_c (**starpu_data_handle_t** *handle*)

Return the number of columns in a block.

29.9.5.45 size_t starpu_bcsr_get_elemsize (**starpu_data_handle_t** *handle*)

Return the size of the elements in the matrix designated by `handle`.

29.9.5.46 uint32_t starpu_csr_get_nnz (**starpu_data_handle_t** *handle*)

Return the number of non-zero values in the matrix designated by `handle`.

29.9.5.47 uint32_t starpu_csr_get_nrow (**starpu_data_handle_t** *handle*)

Return the size of the row pointer array of the matrix designated by `handle`.

29.9.5.48 uint32_t starpu_csr_get_firstentry (**starpu_data_handle_t** *handle*)

Return the index at which all arrays (the column indexes, the row pointers...) of the matrix designated by `handle`.

29.9.5.49 uintptr_t starpu_csr_get_local_nzval (**starpu_data_handle_t** *handle*)

Return a local pointer to the non-zero values of the matrix designated by `handle`.

29.9.5.50 uint32_t ∗ starpu_csr_get_local_colind (starpu_data_handle_t *handle* **)**

Return a local pointer to the column index of the matrix designated by `handle`.

29.9.5.51 uint32_t ∗ starpu_csr_get_local_rowptr (starpu_data_handle_t *handle* **)**

Return a local pointer to the row pointer array of the matrix designated by `handle`.

29.9.5.52 size_t starpu_csr_get_elemsize (starpu_data_handle_t *handle* **)**

Return the size of the elements registered into the matrix designated by `handle`.

29.9.5.53 uintptr_t starpu_malloc_on_node_flags (unsigned *dst_node,* **size_t** *size,* **int** *flags* **)**

Allocate `size` bytes on node `dst_node` with the given allocation `flags`. This returns 0 if allocation failed, the allocation method should then return `-ENOMEM` as allocated size. Deallocation must be done with starpu_free_on-_node().

29.9.5.54 void starpu_free_on_node_flags (unsigned *dst_node,* **uintptr_t** *addr,* **size_t** *size,* **int** *flags* **)**

Free `addr` of `size` bytes on node `dst_node` which was previously allocated with starpu_malloc_on_node() with the given allocation `flags`.

29.9.5.55 uintptr_t starpu_malloc_on_node (unsigned *dst_node,* **size_t** *size* **)**

Allocate `size` bytes on node `dst_node` with the default allocation flags. This returns 0 if allocation failed, the allocation method should then return `-ENOMEM` as allocated size. Deallocation must be done with starpu_free_on-_node().

29.9.5.56 void starpu_free_on_node (unsigned *dst_node,* **uintptr_t** *addr,* **size_t** *size* **)**

Free `addr` of `size` bytes on node `dst_node` which was previously allocated with starpu_malloc_on_node().

29.9.5.57 void starpu_malloc_on_node_set_default_flags (unsigned *node,* **int** *flags* **)**

Define the default flags for allocations performed by starpu_malloc_on_node() and starpu_free_on_node(). The default is STARPU_MALLOC_PINNED | STARPU_MALLOC_COUNT.

29.9.5.58 int starpu_interface_copy (uintptr_t *src,* **size_t** *src_offset,* **unsigned** *src_node,* **uintptr_t** *dst,* **size_t** *dst_offset,* **unsigned** *dst_node,* **size_t** *size,* **void** ∗ *async_data* **)**

Copy `size` bytes from byte offset `src_offset` of `src` on `src_node` to byte offset `dst_offset` of `dst` on `dst_node`. This is to be used in the starpu_data_copy_methods::any_to_any copy method, which is provided with `async_data` to be passed to starpu_interface_copy(). this returns `-EAGAIN` if the transfer is still ongoing, or 0 if the transfer is already completed.

29.9.5.59 uint32_t starpu_hash_crc32c_be_n (const void ∗ *input,* **size_t** *n,* **uint32_t** *inputcrc* **)**

Compute the CRC of a byte buffer seeded by the `inputcrc` *current state*. The return value should be considered as the new *current state* for future CRC computation. This is used for computing data size footprint.

29.9.5.60   uint32_t starpu_hash_crc32c_be (uint32_t *input,* uint32_t *inputcrc*)

Compute the CRC of a 32bit number seeded by the `inputcrc` *current state.* The return value should be considered as the new *current state* for future CRC computation. This is used for computing data size footprint.

29.9.5.61   uint32_t starpu_hash_crc32c_string (const char ∗ *str,* uint32_t *inputcrc*)

Compute the CRC of a string seeded by the `inputcrc` *current state.* The return value should be considered as the new *current state* for future CRC computation. This is used for computing data size footprint.

29.9.5.62   int starpu_data_interface_get_next_id (void)

Return the next available id for a newly created data interface (Defining A New Data Interface).

29.10   Data Partition

Data Structures

- struct starpu_data_filter

Basic API

- void starpu_data_partition (starpu_data_handle_t initial_handle, struct starpu_data_filter ∗f)
- void starpu_data_unpartition (starpu_data_handle_t root_data, unsigned gathering_node)
- int starpu_data_get_nb_children (starpu_data_handle_t handle)
- starpu_data_handle_t starpu_data_get_child (starpu_data_handle_t handle, unsigned i)
- starpu_data_handle_t starpu_data_get_sub_data (starpu_data_handle_t root_data, unsigned depth,...)
- starpu_data_handle_t starpu_data_vget_sub_data (starpu_data_handle_t root_data, unsigned depth, va_list pa)
- void starpu_data_map_filters (starpu_data_handle_t root_data, unsigned nfilters,...)
- void starpu_data_vmap_filters (starpu_data_handle_t root_data, unsigned nfilters, va_list pa)

Asynchronous API

- void starpu_data_partition_plan (starpu_data_handle_t initial_handle, struct starpu_data_filter ∗f, starpu_data_handle_t ∗children)
- void starpu_data_partition_submit (starpu_data_handle_t initial_handle, unsigned nparts, starpu_data_handle_t ∗children)
- void starpu_data_partition_readonly_submit (starpu_data_handle_t initial_handle, unsigned nparts, starpu_data_handle_t ∗children)
- void starpu_data_partition_readwrite_upgrade_submit (starpu_data_handle_t initial_handle, unsigned nparts, starpu_data_handle_t ∗children)
- void starpu_data_unpartition_submit (starpu_data_handle_t initial_handle, unsigned nparts, starpu_data_handle_t ∗children, int gathering_node)
- void starpu_data_unpartition_readonly_submit (starpu_data_handle_t initial_handle, unsigned nparts, starpu_data_handle_t ∗children, int gathering_node)
- void starpu_data_partition_clean (starpu_data_handle_t root_data, unsigned nparts, starpu_data_handle_t ∗children)

Predefined Vector Filter Functions

This section gives a partial list of the predefined partitioning functions for vector data. Examples on how to use them are shown in Partitioning Data. The complete list can be found in the file `starpu_data_filters.h`.

- void starpu_vector_filter_block (void *father_interface, void *child_interface, struct starpu_data_filter *f, unsigned id, unsigned nparts)
- void starpu_vector_filter_block_shadow (void *father_interface, void *child_interface, struct starpu_data_filter *f, unsigned id, unsigned nparts)
- void starpu_vector_filter_list (void *father_interface, void *child_interface, struct starpu_data_filter *f, unsigned id, unsigned nparts)
- void starpu_vector_filter_divide_in_2 (void *father_interface, void *child_interface, struct starpu_data_filter *f, unsigned id, unsigned nparts)

Predefined Matrix Filter Functions

This section gives a partial list of the predefined partitioning functions for matrix data. Examples on how to use them are shown in Partitioning Data. The complete list can be found in the file `starpu_data_filters.h`.

- void starpu_matrix_filter_block (void *father_interface, void *child_interface, struct starpu_data_filter *f, unsigned id, unsigned nparts)
- void starpu_matrix_filter_block_shadow (void *father_interface, void *child_interface, struct starpu_data_filter *f, unsigned id, unsigned nparts)
- void starpu_matrix_filter_vertical_block (void *father_interface, void *child_interface, struct starpu_data_filter *f, unsigned id, unsigned nparts)
- void starpu_matrix_filter_vertical_block_shadow (void *father_interface, void *child_interface, struct starpu_data_filter *f, unsigned id, unsigned nparts)

Predefined Block Filter Functions

This section gives a partial list of the predefined partitioning functions for block data. Examples on how to use them are shown in Partitioning Data. The complete list can be found in the file `starpu_data_filters.h`. A usage example is available in examples/filters/shadow3d.c

- void starpu_block_filter_block (void *father_interface, void *child_interface, struct starpu_data_filter *f, unsigned id, unsigned nparts)
- void starpu_block_filter_block_shadow (void *father_interface, void *child_interface, struct starpu_data_filter *f, unsigned id, unsigned nparts)
- void starpu_block_filter_vertical_block (void *father_interface, void *child_interface, struct starpu_data_filter *f, unsigned id, unsigned nparts)
- void starpu_block_filter_vertical_block_shadow (void *father_interface, void *child_interface, struct starpu_data_filter *f, unsigned id, unsigned nparts)
- void starpu_block_filter_depth_block (void *father_interface, void *child_interface, struct starpu_data_filter *f, unsigned id, unsigned nparts)
- void starpu_block_filter_depth_block_shadow (void *father_interface, void *child_interface, struct starpu_data_filter *f, unsigned id, unsigned nparts)

Predefined BCSR Filter Functions

This section gives a partial list of the predefined partitioning functions for BCSR data. Examples on how to use them are shown in Partitioning Data. The complete list can be found in the file `starpu_data_filters.h`.

- void starpu_bcsr_filter_canonical_block (void *father_interface, void *child_interface, struct starpu_data_filter *f, unsigned id, unsigned nparts)
- void starpu_csr_filter_vertical_block (void *father_interface, void *child_interface, struct starpu_data_filter *f, unsigned id, unsigned nparts)

29.10.1 Detailed Description

29.10.2 Data Structure Documentation

29.10.2.1 struct starpu_data_filter

The filter structure describes a data partitioning operation, to be given to the starpu_data_partition() function.

Data Fields

- void(* filter_func)(void *father_interface, void *child_interface, struct starpu_data_filter *, unsigned id, unsigned nparts)
- unsigned nchildren
- unsigned(* get_nchildren)(struct starpu_data_filter *, starpu_data_handle_t initial_handle)
- struct
  starpu_data_interface_ops *(* get_child_ops)(struct starpu_data_filter *, unsigned id)
- unsigned filter_arg
- void * filter_arg_ptr

29.10.2.1.1 Field Documentation

29.10.2.1.1.1 void(* starpu_data_filter::filter_func)(void *father_interface, void *child_interface, struct **starpu_data_filter** *, unsigned id, unsigned nparts)

Fill the `child_interface` structure with interface information for the `id` -th child of the parent `father_-interface` (among `nparts`).

29.10.2.1.1.2 unsigned starpu_data_filter::nchildren

Number of parts to partition the data into.

29.10.2.1.1.3 unsigned(* starpu_data_filter::get_nchildren)(struct **starpu_data_filter** *, **starpu_data_handle_t** initial_handle)

Return the number of children. This can be used instead of starpu_data_filter::nchildren when the number of children depends on the actual data (e.g. the number of blocks in a sparse matrix).

29.10.2.1.1.4 struct **starpu_data_interface_ops** *(* starpu_data_filter::get_child_ops)(struct **starpu_data_filter** *, unsigned id) [read]

In case the resulting children use a different data interface, this function returns which interface is used by child number `id`.

29.10.2.1.1.5 unsigned starpu_data_filter::filter_arg

Allow to define an additional parameter for the filter function.

29.10.2.1.1.6 void * starpu_data_filter::filter_arg_ptr

Allow to define an additional pointer parameter for the filter function, such as the sizes of the different parts.

29.10.3 Function Documentation

29.10.3.1 void starpu_data_partition (**starpu_data_handle_t** *initial_handle,* struct **starpu_data_filter** * f)

Request the partitioning of `initial_handle` into several subdata according to the filter `f`.

Here an example of how to use the function.

```
struct starpu_data_filter f =
{
        .filter_func = starpu_matrix_filter_block
    ,
        .nchildren = nslicesx
};
starpu_data_partition(A_handle, &f);
```

29.10.3.2 void starpu_data_unpartition (starpu_data_handle_t *root_data,* **unsigned** *gathering_node* **)**

Unapply the filter which has been applied to `root_data`, thus unpartitioning the data. The pieces of data are collected back into one big piece in the `gathering_node` (usually STARPU_MAIN_RAM). Tasks working on the partitioned data must be already finished when calling starpu_data_unpartition().

Here an example of how to use the function.

```
starpu_data_unpartition(A_handle, STARPU_MAIN_RAM
        );
```

29.10.3.3 int starpu_data_get_nb_children (starpu_data_handle_t *handle* **)**

Return the number of children `handle` has been partitioned into.

29.10.3.4 starpu_data_handle_t starpu_data_get_child (starpu_data_handle_t *handle,* **unsigned** *i* **)**

Return the `i` -th child of the given `handle`, which must have been partitionned beforehand.

29.10.3.5 starpu_data_handle_t starpu_data_get_sub_data (starpu_data_handle_t *root_data,* **unsigned** *depth,* **...)**

After partitioning a StarPU data by applying a filter, starpu_data_get_sub_data() can be used to get handles for each of the data portions. `root_data` is the parent data that was partitioned. `depth` is the number of filters to traverse (in case several filters have been applied, to e.g. partition in row blocks, and then in column blocks), and the subsequent parameters are the indexes. The function returns a handle to the subdata.

Here an example of how to use the function.

```
h = starpu_data_get_sub_data(A_handle, 1, taskx);
```

29.10.3.6 starpu_data_handle_t starpu_data_vget_sub_data (starpu_data_handle_t *root_data,* **unsigned** *depth,* **va_list** *pa* **)**

This function is similar to starpu_data_get_sub_data() but uses a va_list for the parameter list.

29.10.3.7 void starpu_data_map_filters (starpu_data_handle_t *root_data,* **unsigned** *nfilters,* **...)**

Apply `nfilters` filters to the handle designated by `root_handle` recursively. `nfilters` pointers to variables of the type starpu_data_filter should be given.

29.10.3.8 void starpu_data_vmap_filters (starpu_data_handle_t *root_data,* **unsigned** *nfilters,* **va_list** *pa* **)**

Apply `nfilters` filters to the handle designated by `root_handle` recursively. It uses a va_list of pointers to variables of the type starpu_data_filter.

29.10.3.9 void starpu_data_partition_plan (starpu_data_handle_t *initial_handle,* struct **starpu_data_filter** ∗ *f,* **starpu_data_handle_t** ∗ *children*)

Plan to partition `initial_handle` into several subdata according to the filter `f`. The handles are returned into the `children` array, which has to be the same size as the number of parts described in `f`. These handles are not immediately usable, starpu_data_partition_submit() has to be called to submit the actual partitioning.

Here is an example of how to use the function:

```
starpu_data_handle_t children[nslicesx];
struct starpu_data_filter f =
{
        .filter_func = starpu_matrix_filter_block
    ,
        .nchildren = nslicesx
};
starpu_data_partition_plan(A_handle, &f, children);
```

29.10.3.10 void starpu_data_partition_submit (**starpu_data_handle_t** *initial_handle,* unsigned *nparts,* **starpu_data_handle_t** ∗ *children*)

Submit the actual partitioning of `initial_handle` into the `nparts children` handles. This call is asynchronous, it only submits that the partitioning should be done, so that the `children` handles can now be used to submit tasks, and `initial_handle` can not be used to submit tasks any more (to guarantee coherency).

For instance,

```
starpu_data_partition_submit(A_handle, nslicesx,
    children);
```

29.10.3.11 void starpu_data_partition_readonly_submit (**starpu_data_handle_t** *initial_handle,* unsigned *nparts,* **starpu_data_handle_t** ∗ *children*)

This is the same as starpu_data_partition_submit(), but it does not invalidate `initial_handle`. This allows to continue using it, but the application has to be careful not to write to `initial_handle` or `children` handles, only read from them, since the coherency is otherwise not guaranteed. This thus allows to submit various tasks which concurrently read from various partitions of the data.

When the application wants to write to `initial_handle` again, it should call starpu_data_unpartition_submit(), which will properly add dependencies between the reads on the `children` and the writes to be submitted.

If instead the application wants to write to `children` handles, it should call starpu_data_partition_readwrite_-upgrade_submit(), which will correctly add dependencies between the reads on the `initial_handle` and the writes to be submitted.

29.10.3.12 void starpu_data_partition_readwrite_upgrade_submit (**starpu_data_handle_t** *initial_handle,* unsigned *nparts,* **starpu_data_handle_t** ∗ *children*)

This assumes that a partitioning of `initial_handle` has already been submited in readonly mode through starpu_data_partition_readonly_submit(), and will upgrade that partitioning into read-write mode for the `children`, by invalidating `initial_handle`, and adding the necessary dependencies.

29.10.3.13 void starpu_data_unpartition_submit (**starpu_data_handle_t** *initial_handle,* unsigned *nparts,* **starpu_data_handle_t** ∗ *children,* int *gathering_node*)

This assumes that `initial_handle` is partitioned into `children`, and submits an unpartitionning of it, i.-e. submitting a gathering of the pieces on the requested `gathering_node` memory node, and submitting an invalidation of the children.

`gathering_node` can be set to -1 to let the runtime decide which memory node should be used to gather the pieces.

29.10.3.14 void starpu_data_unpartition_readonly_submit (**starpu_data_handle_t** *initial_handle*, unsigned *nparts*, **starpu_data_handle_t** * *children*, int *gathering_node*)

This assumes that `initial_handle` is partitioned into `children`, and submits just a readonly unpartitionning of it, i.e. submitting a gathering of the pieces on the requested `gathering_node` memory node. It does not invalidate the children. This brings `initial_handle` and `children` handles to the same state as obtained with starpu_data_partition_readonly_submit().

`gathering_node` can be set to -1 to let the runtime decide which memory node should be used to gather the pieces.

29.10.3.15 void starpu_data_partition_clean (**starpu_data_handle_t** *root_data*, unsigned *nparts*, **starpu_data_handle_t** * *children*)

This should be used to clear the partition planning established between `root_data` and `children` with starpu-_data_partition_plan(). This will notably submit an unregister all the `children`, which can thus not be used any more afterwards.

29.10.3.16 void starpu_vector_filter_block (void * *father_interface*, void * *child_interface*, struct **starpu_data_filter** * *f*, unsigned *id*, unsigned *nparts*)

Return in `child_interface` the id th element of the vector represented by `father_interface` once partitioned in `nparts` chunks of equal size.

29.10.3.17 void starpu_vector_filter_block_shadow (void * *father_interface*, void * *child_interface*, struct **starpu_data_filter** * *f*, unsigned *id*, unsigned *nparts*)

Return in `child_interface` the id th element of the vector represented by `father_interface` once partitioned in nparts chunks of equal size with a shadow border `filter_arg_ptr`, thus getting a vector of size `(n-2*shadow)/nparts+2*shadow`. The `filter_arg_ptr` field of f must be the shadow size casted into `void*`.

IMPORTANT: This can only be used for read-only access, as no coherency is enforced for the shadowed parts. An usage example is available in examples/filters/shadow.c

29.10.3.18 void starpu_vector_filter_list (void * *father_interface*, void * *child_interface*, struct **starpu_data_filter** * *f*, unsigned *id*, unsigned *nparts*)

Return in `child_interface` the id th element of the vector represented by `father_interface` once partitioned into `nparts` chunks according to the `filter_arg_ptr` field of f. The `filter_arg_ptr` field must point to an array of `nparts` uint32_t elements, each of which specifies the number of elements in each chunk of the partition.

29.10.3.19 void starpu_vector_filter_divide_in_2 (void * *father_interface*, void * *child_interface*, struct **starpu_data_filter** * *f*, unsigned *id*, unsigned *nparts*)

Return in `child_interface` the id th element of the vector represented by `father_interface` once partitioned in 2 chunks of equal size, ignoring nparts. Thus, `id` must be 0 or 1.

29.10.3.20 void starpu_matrix_filter_block (void * *father_interface*, void * *child_interface*, struct **starpu_data_filter** * *f*, unsigned *id*, unsigned *nparts*)

Partition a dense Matrix along the x dimension, thus getting (x/`nparts` ,y) matrices. If `nparts` does not divide x, the last submatrix contains the remainder.

29.10.3.21 void starpu_matrix_filter_block_shadow (void * *father_interface*, void * *child_interface*, struct **starpu_data_filter** * *f*, unsigned *id*, unsigned *nparts*)

Partition a dense Matrix along the x dimension, with a shadow border `filter_arg_ptr`, thus getting ((x-2*shadow)/nparts +2*shadow,y) matrices. If `nparts` does not divide x-2*shadow, the last submatrix contains the remainder.

IMPORTANT: This can only be used for read-only access, as no coherency is enforced for the shadowed parts. A usage example is available in examples/filters/shadow2d.c

29.10.3.22 void starpu_matrix_filter_vertical_block (void * *father_interface*, void * *child_interface*, struct **starpu_data_filter** * *f*, unsigned *id*, unsigned *nparts*)

Partition a dense Matrix along the y dimension, thus getting (x,y/`nparts`) matrices. If `nparts` does not divide y, the last submatrix contains the remainder.

29.10.3.23 void starpu_matrix_filter_vertical_block_shadow (void * *father_interface*, void * *child_interface*, struct **starpu_data_filter** * *f*, unsigned *id*, unsigned *nparts*)

Partition a dense Matrix along the y dimension, with a shadow border `filter_arg_ptr`, thus getting (x,(y-2*shadow)/nparts +2*shadow) matrices. If `nparts` does not divide y-2*shadow, the last submatrix contains the remainder.

IMPORTANT: This can only be used for read-only access, as no coherency is enforced for the shadowed parts. A usage example is available in examples/filters/shadow2d.c

29.10.3.24 void starpu_block_filter_block (void * *father_interface*, void * *child_interface*, struct **starpu_data_filter** * *f*, unsigned *id*, unsigned *nparts*)

Partition a block along the X dimension, thus getting (x/`nparts`,y,z) 3D matrices. If `nparts` does not divide x, the last submatrix contains the remainder.

29.10.3.25 void starpu_block_filter_block_shadow (void * *father_interface*, void * *child_interface*, struct **starpu_data_filter** * *f*, unsigned *id*, unsigned *nparts*)

Partition a block along the X dimension, with a shadow border `filter_arg_ptr`, thus getting ((x-2*shadow)/nparts +2*shadow,y,z) blocks. If `nparts` does not divide x, the last submatrix contains the remainder.

IMPORTANT: This can only be used for read-only access, as no coherency is enforced for the shadowed parts.

29.10.3.26 void starpu_block_filter_vertical_block (void * *father_interface*, void * *child_interface*, struct **starpu_data_filter** * *f*, unsigned *id*, unsigned *nparts*)

Partition a block along the Y dimension, thus getting (x,y/`nparts`,z) blocks. If `nparts` does not divide y, the last submatrix contains the remainder.

29.10.3.27 void starpu_block_filter_vertical_block_shadow (void * *father_interface*, void * *child_interface*, struct **starpu_data_filter** * *f*, unsigned *id*, unsigned *nparts*)

Partition a block along the Y dimension, with a shadow border `filter_arg_ptr`, thus getting (x,(y-2*shadow)/nparts +2*shadow,z) 3D matrices. If `nparts` does not divide y, the last submatrix contains the remainder.

IMPORTANT: This can only be used for read-only access, as no coherency is enforced for the shadowed parts.

29.10.3.28 void starpu_block_filter_depth_block (void * *father_interface,* void * *child_interface,* struct **starpu_data_filter** * f, unsigned *id,* unsigned *nparts*)

Partition a block along the Z dimension, thus getting (x,y,z/npart s) blocks. If nparts does not divide z, the last submatrix contains the remainder.

29.10.3.29 void starpu_block_filter_depth_block_shadow (void * *father_interface,* void * *child_interface,* struct **starpu_data_filter** * f, unsigned *id,* unsigned *nparts*)

Partition a block along the Z dimension, with a shadow border filter_arg_ptr, thus getting (x,y,(z-2*shadow)/nparts +2*shadow) blocks. If nparts does not divide z, the last submatrix contains the remainder.

IMPORTANT: This can only be used for read-only access, as no coherency is enforced for the shadowed parts.

29.10.3.30 void starpu_bcsr_filter_canonical_block (void * *father_interface,* void * *child_interface,* struct **starpu_data_filter** * f, unsigned *id,* unsigned *nparts*)

Partition a block-sparse matrix into dense matrices.

29.10.3.31 void starpu_csr_filter_vertical_block (void * *father_interface,* void * *child_interface,* struct **starpu_data_filter** * f, unsigned *id,* unsigned *nparts*)

Partition a block-sparse matrix into vertical block-sparse matrices.

29.11   Out Of Core

Data Structures

- struct starpu_disk_ops

Macros

- #define STARPU_DISK_SIZE_MIN

Functions

- int starpu_disk_register (struct starpu_disk_ops *func, void *parameter, starpu_ssize_t size)
- void * starpu_disk_open (unsigned node, void *pos, size_t size)
- void starpu_disk_close (unsigned node, void *obj, size_t size)

Variables

- int starpu_disk_swap_node
- struct starpu_disk_ops starpu_disk_stdio_ops
- struct starpu_disk_ops starpu_disk_unistd_ops
- struct starpu_disk_ops starpu_disk_unistd_o_direct_ops
- struct starpu_disk_ops starpu_disk_leveldb_ops

29.11.1 Detailed Description

29.11.2 Data Structure Documentation

29.11.2.1 struct starpu_disk_ops

This is a set of functions to manipulate datas on disk.

Data Fields

- void *(* plug)(void *parameter, starpu_ssize_t size)
- void(* unplug)(void *base)
- int(* bandwidth)(unsigned node)
- void *(* alloc)(void *base, size_t size)
- void(* free)(void *base, void *obj, size_t size)
- void *(* open)(void *base, void *pos, size_t size)
- void(* close)(void *base, void *obj, size_t size)
- int(* read)(void *base, void *obj, void *buf, off_t offset, size_t size)
- int(* write)(void *base, void *obj, const void *buf, off_t offset, size_t size)
- int(* full_read)(void *base, void *obj, void **ptr, size_t *size)
- int(* full_write)(void *base, void *obj, void *ptr, size_t size)
- void *(* async_write)(void *base, void *obj, void *buf, off_t offset, size_t size)
- void *(* async_read)(void *base, void *obj, void *buf, off_t offset, size_t size)
- void *(* async_full_read)(void *base, void *obj, void **ptr, size_t *size)
- void *(* async_full_write)(void *base, void *obj, void *ptr, size_t size)
- void *(* copy)(void *base_src, void *obj_src, off_t offset_src, void *base_dst, void *obj_dst, off_t offset_dst, size_t size)
- void(* wait_request)(void *async_channel)
- int(* test_request)(void *async_channel)
- void(* free_request)(void *async_channel)

29.11.2.1.1 Field Documentation

29.11.2.1.1.1 void *(* starpu_disk_ops::plug)(void *parameters, size_t size)

Connect a disk memory at location `parameter` with size `size`, and return a base as void*, which will be passed by StarPU to all other methods.

29.11.2.1.1.2 void(* starpu_disk_ops::unplug)(void *base)

Disconnect a disk memory `base`.

29.11.2.1.1.3 int(* starpu_disk_ops::bandwidth)(unsigned node)

Measure the bandwidth and the latency for the disk `node` and save it. Returns 1 if it could measure it.

29.11.2.1.1.4 void *(* starpu_disk_ops::alloc)(void *base, size_t size)

Create a new location for datas of size `size`. This returns an opaque object pointer.

29.11.2.1.1.5 void(* starpu_disk_ops::free)(void *base, void *obj, size_t size)

Free a data `obj` previously allocated with `alloc`.

29.11.2.1.1.6 void *(* starpu_disk_ops::open)(void *base, void *pos, size_t size)

Open an existing location of datas, at a specific position `pos` dependent on the backend.

29.11.2.1.1.7 void(* starpu_disk_ops::close)(void *base, void *obj, size_t size)

Close, without deleting it, a location of datas `obj`.

29.11.2.1.1.8 int(* starpu_disk_ops::read)(void *base, void *obj, void *buf, off_t offset, size_t size)

Read `size` bytes of data from `obj` in `base`, at offset `offset`, and put into `buf`. Returns the actual number of read bytes.

29.11.2.1.1.9 int(* starpu_disk_ops::write)(void *base, void *obj, const void *buf, off_t offset, size_t size)

Write `size` bytes of data to `obj` in `base`, at offset `offset`, from `buf`. Returns 0 on success.

29.11.2.1.1.10 int(* starpu_disk_ops::full_read)(void *base, void *obj, void **ptr, size_t *size)

Read all data from `obj` of `base`, from offset 0. Returns it in an allocated buffer `ptr`, of size `size`

29.11.2.1.1.11 int(* starpu_disk_ops::full_write)(void *base, void *obj, void *ptr, size_t size)

Write data in `ptr` to `obj` of `base`, from offset 0, and truncate `obj` to `size`, so that a `full_read` will get it.

29.11.2.1.1.12 void *(* starpu_disk_ops::async_write)(void *base, void *obj, const void *buf, off_t offset, size_t size)

Asynchronously write `size` bytes of data to `obj` in `base`, at offset `offset`, from `buf`. Returns a void* pointer that StarPU will pass to `*_request` methods for testing for the completion.

29.11.2.1.1.13 void *(* starpu_disk_ops::async_read)(void *base, void *obj, void *buf, off_t offset, size_t size)

Asynchronously read `size` bytes of data from `obj` in `base`, at offset `offset`, and put into `buf`. Returns a void* pointer that StarPU will pass to `*_request` methods for testing for the completion.

29.11.2.1.1.14 void *(* starpu_disk_ops::async_full_read)(void *base, void *obj, void **ptr, size_t *size)

Read all data from `obj` of `base`, from offset 0. Returns it in an allocated buffer `ptr`, of size `size`

29.11.2.1.1.15 void *(* starpu_disk_ops::async_full_write)(void *base, void *obj, void *ptr, size_t size)

Write data in `ptr` to `obj` of `base`, from offset 0, and truncate `obj` to `size`, so that a `full_read` will get it.

29.11.2.1.1.16 void *(* starpu_disk_ops::copy)(void *base_src, void *obj_src, off_t offset_src, void *base_dst, void *obj_dst, off_t offset_dst, size_t size)

Copy from offset `offset_src` of disk object `obj_src` in `base_src` to offset `offset_dst` of disk object `obj_dst` in `base_dst`. Returns a void* pointer that StarPU will pass to `*_request` methods for testing for the completion.

29.11.2.1.1.17 void(* starpu_disk_ops::wait_request)(void *async_channel)

Wait for completion of request `async_channel` returned by a previous asynchronous read, write or copy.

29.11.2.1.1.18 void(* starpu_disk_ops::test_request)(void *async_channel)

Test for completion of request `async_channel` returned by a previous asynchronous read, write or copy. Returns 1 on completion, 0 otherwise.

29.11.2.1.1.19 void(* starpu_disk_ops::free_request)(void *async_channel)

Free the request allocated by a previous asynchronous read, write or copy.

29.11.3 Macro Definition Documentation

29.11.3.1 #define STARPU_DISK_SIZE_MIN

Minimum size of a registered disk. The size of a disk is the last parameter of the function starpu_disk_register().

29.11.4 Function Documentation

29.11.4.1 int starpu_disk_register (struct **starpu_disk_ops** * *func*, void * *parameter*, starpu_ssize_t *size*)

Register a disk memory node with a set of functions to manipulate datas. The `plug` member of `func` will be passed `parameter`, and return a `base` which will be passed to all `func` methods.

SUCCESS: return the disk node.

FAIL: return an error code.

`size` must be at least STARPU_DISK_SIZE_MIN bytes ! `size` being negative means infinite size.

29.11.4.2 void * starpu_disk_open (unsigned *node*, void * *pos*, size_t *size*)

Open an existing file memory in a disk node. `size` is the size of the file. `pos` is the specific position dependent on the backend, given to the `open` method of the disk operations. This returns an opaque object pointer.

29.11.4.3 void starpu_disk_close (unsigned *node*, void * *obj*, size_t *size*)

Close an existing data opened with starpu_disk_open().

29.11.5 Variable Documentation

29.11.5.1 starpu_disk_swap_node

This contains the node number of the disk swap, if set up through the STARPU_DISK_SWAP variable.

29.11.5.2 starpu_disk_stdio_ops

This set uses the stdio library (fwrite, fread...) to read/write on disk.

Warning: It creates one file per allocation !

It doesn't support asynchronous transfers.

29.11.5.3 starpu_disk_unistd_ops

This set uses the unistd library (write, read...) to read/write on disk.

Warning: It creates one file per allocation !

29.11.5.4 starpu_disk_unistd_o_direct_ops

This set uses the unistd library (write, read...) to read/write on disk with the O_DIRECT flag.

Warning: It creates one file per allocation !

Only available on Linux systems.

29.11.5.5   starpu_disk_leveldb_ops

This set uses the leveldb created by Google

More information at https://code.google.com/p/leveldb/

It doesn't support asynchronous transfers.

29.12   Multiformat Data Interface

Data Structures

- struct starpu_multiformat_data_interface_ops
- struct starpu_multiformat_interface

Macros

- #define STARPU_MULTIFORMAT_GET_CPU_PTR(interface)
- #define STARPU_MULTIFORMAT_GET_CUDA_PTR(interface)
- #define STARPU_MULTIFORMAT_GET_OPENCL_PTR(interface)
- #define STARPU_MULTIFORMAT_GET_MIC_PTR(interface)
- #define STARPU_MULTIFORMAT_GET_NX(interface)

Functions

- void starpu_multiformat_data_register (starpu_data_handle_t *handle, int home_node, void *ptr, uint32_t nobjects, struct starpu_multiformat_data_interface_ops *format_ops)

29.12.1   Detailed Description

29.12.2   Data Structure Documentation

29.12.2.1   struct starpu_multiformat_data_interface_ops

The different fields are:

Data Fields

size_t	cpu_elemsize	the size of each element on CPUs
size_t	opencl_elemsize	the size of each element on OpenCL devices
struct starpu_codelet *	cpu_to_opencl_-cl	pointer to a codelet which converts from CPU to OpenCL
struct starpu_codelet *	opencl_to_cpu_-cl	pointer to a codelet which converts from OpenCL to CPU
size_t	cuda_elemsize	the size of each element on CUDA devices
struct starpu_codelet *	cpu_to_cuda_cl	pointer to a codelet which converts from CPU to CUDA
struct starpu_codelet *	cuda_to_cpu_cl	pointer to a codelet which converts from CUDA to CPU
size_t	mic_elemsize	the size of each element on MIC devices
struct starpu_codelet *	cpu_to_mic_cl	pointer to a codelet which converts from CPU to MIC
struct starpu_codelet *	mic_to_cpu_cl	pointer to a codelet which converts from MIC to CPU

29.12.2.2   struct starpu_multiformat_interface

todo

Data Fields

enum starpu_data_- interface_id	id	todo
void ∗	cpu_ptr	todo
void ∗	cuda_ptr	todo
void ∗	opencl_ptr	todo
void ∗	mic_ptr	todo
uint32_t	nx	todo
struct starpu_- multiformat_- data_interface_- ops ∗	ops	todo

29.12.3   Macro Definition Documentation

29.12.3.1   #define STARPU_MULTIFORMAT_GET_CPU_PTR(*interface*)

Return the local pointer to the data with CPU format.

29.12.3.2   #define STARPU_MULTIFORMAT_GET_CUDA_PTR(*interface*)

Return the local pointer to the data with CUDA format.

29.12.3.3   #define STARPU_MULTIFORMAT_GET_OPENCL_PTR(*interface*)

Return the local pointer to the data with OpenCL format.

29.12.3.4   #define STARPU_MULTIFORMAT_GET_MIC_PTR(*interface*)

Return the local pointer to the data with MIC format.

29.12.3.5   #define STARPU_MULTIFORMAT_GET_NX(*interface*)

Return the number of elements in the data.

29.12.4   Function Documentation

29.12.4.1   void starpu_multiformat_data_register (**starpu_data_handle_t** ∗ *handle*, int *home_node*, void ∗ *ptr*, uint32_t *nobjects*, struct **starpu_multiformat_data_interface_ops** ∗ *format_ops*)

Register a piece of data that can be represented in different ways, depending upon the processing unit that manipulates it. It allows the programmer, for instance, to use an array of structures when working on a CPU, and a structure of arrays when working on a GPU. `nobjects` is the number of elements in the data. `format_ops` describes the format.

29.13   Codelet And Tasks

This section describes the interface to manipulate codelets and tasks.

Data Structures

- struct starpu_codelet
- struct starpu_data_descr
- struct starpu task

Macros

- #define STARPU_NOWHERE
- #define STARPU_CPU
- #define STARPU_CUDA
- #define STARPU_OPENCL
- #define STARPU_MIC
- #define STARPU_MPI_MS
- #define STARPU_SCC
- #define STARPU_MAIN_RAM
- #define STARPU_MULTIPLE_CPU_IMPLEMENTATIONS
- #define STARPU_MULTIPLE_CUDA_IMPLEMENTATIONS
- #define STARPU_MULTIPLE_OPENCL_IMPLEMENTATIONS
- #define STARPU_NMAXBUFS
- #define STARPU_VARIABLE_NBUFFERS
- #define STARPU_CUDA_ASYNC
- #define STARPU_OPENCL_ASYNC
- #define STARPU_CODELET_SIMGRID_EXECUTE
- #define STARPU_CODELET_SIMGRID_EXECUTE_AND_INJECT
- #define STARPU_TASK_INITIALIZER
- #define STARPU_TASK_GET_NBUFFERS(task)
- #define STARPU_TASK_GET_HANDLE(task, i)
- #define STARPU_TASK_SET_HANDLE(task, handle, i)
- #define STARPU_CODELET_GET_MODE(codelet, i)
- #define STARPU_CODELET_SET_MODE(codelet, mode, i)
- #define STARPU_TASK_GET_MODE(task, i)
- #define STARPU_TASK_SET_MODE(task, mode, i)

Typedefs

- typedef void($*$ starpu_cpu_func_t)(void $**$, void $*$)
- typedef void($*$ starpu_cuda_func_t)(void $**$, void $*$)
- typedef void($*$ starpu_opencl_func_t)(void $**$, void $*$)
- typedef starpu_mic_kernel_t($*$ starpu_mic_func_t)(void)
- typedef starpu_mpi_ms_kernel_t($*$ starpu_mpi_ms_func_t)(void)
- typedef starpu_scc_kernel_t($*$ starpu_scc_func_t)(void)
- typedef void($*$ starpu_mic_kernel_t)(void $**$, void $*$)
- typedef void($*$ starpu_mpi_ms_kernel_t)(void $**$, void $*$)
- typedef void($*$ starpu_scc_kernel_t)(void $**$, void $*$)

Enumerations

- enum starpu_codelet_type { STARPU_SEQ, STARPU_SPMD, STARPU_FORKJOIN }
- enum starpu_task_status {
  STARPU_TASK_INVALID, **STARPU_TASK_INVALID**, STARPU_TASK_BLOCKED, STARPU_TASK_RE-
  ADY,
  STARPU_TASK_RUNNING, STARPU_TASK_FINISHED, STARPU_TASK_BLOCKED_ON_TAG, STARP-
  U_TASK_BLOCKED_ON_TASK,
  STARPU_TASK_BLOCKED_ON_DATA, STARPU_TASK_STOPPED }

Functions

- void starpu_codelet_init (struct starpu_codelet ∗cl)
- void starpu_task_init (struct starpu_task ∗task)
- struct starpu_task ∗ starpu_task_create (void) STARPU_ATTRIBUTE_MALLOC
- struct starpu_task ∗ starpu_task_dup (struct starpu_task ∗task)
- void starpu_task_clean (struct starpu_task ∗task)
- void starpu_task_destroy (struct starpu_task ∗task)
- int starpu_task_wait (struct starpu_task ∗task) STARPU_WARN_UNUSED_RESULT
- int starpu_task_wait_array (struct starpu_task ∗∗tasks, unsigned nb_tasks) STARPU_WARN_UNUSED_R-
  ESULT
- int starpu_task_submit (struct starpu_task ∗task) STARPU_WARN_UNUSED_RESULT
- int starpu_task_submit_to_ctx (struct starpu_task ∗task, unsigned sched_ctx_id)
- int starpu_task_wait_for_all (void)
- int starpu_task_wait_for_all_in_ctx (unsigned sched_ctx_id)
- int starpu_task_wait_for_n_submitted (unsigned n)
- int starpu_task_wait_for_n_submitted_in_ctx (unsigned sched_ctx_id, unsigned n)
- int starpu_task_nready (void)
- int starpu_task_nsubmitted (void)
- struct starpu_task ∗ starpu_task_get_current (void)
- const char ∗ starpu_task_get_name (struct starpu_task ∗task)
- const char ∗ starpu_task_get_model_name (struct starpu_task ∗task)
- void starpu_codelet_display_stats (struct starpu_codelet ∗cl)
- int starpu_task_wait_for_no_ready (void)
- void starpu_task_set_implementation (struct starpu_task ∗task, unsigned impl)
- unsigned starpu_task_get_implementation (struct starpu_task ∗task)
- void starpu_iteration_push (unsigned long iteration)
- void starpu_iteration_pop (void)
- void starpu_create_sync_task (starpu_tag_t sync_tag, unsigned ndeps, starpu_tag_t ∗deps, void(∗callback)(void
  ∗), void ∗callback_arg)

29.13.1 Detailed Description

This section describes the interface to manipulate codelets and tasks.

29.13.2 Data Structure Documentation

29.13.2.1 struct starpu_codelet

The codelet structure describes a kernel that is possibly implemented on various targets. For compatibility, make sure to initialize the whole structure to zero, either by using explicit memset, or the function starpu_codelet_init(), or by letting the compiler implicitly do it in e.g. static storage case.

Data Fields

- uint32_t where
- int(* can_execute)(unsigned workerid, struct starpu_task *task, unsigned nimpl)
- enum starpu_codelet_type type
- int max_parallelism
- starpu_cpu_func_t cpu_func
- starpu_cuda_func_t cuda_func
- starpu_opencl_func_t opencl_func
- starpu_cpu_func_t cpu_funcs [STARPU_MAXIMPLEMENTATIONS]
- starpu_cuda_func_t cuda_funcs [STARPU_MAXIMPLEMENTATIONS]
- char cuda_flags [STARPU_MAXIMPLEMENTATIONS]
- starpu_opencl_func_t opencl_funcs [STARPU_MAXIMPLEMENTATIONS]
- char opencl_flags [STARPU_MAXIMPLEMENTATIONS]
- starpu_mic_func_t mic_funcs [STARPU_MAXIMPLEMENTATIONS]
- starpu_mpi_ms_func_t mpi_ms_funcs [STARPU_MAXIMPLEMENTATIONS]
- starpu_scc_func_t scc_funcs [STARPU_MAXIMPLEMENTATIONS]
- const char * cpu_funcs_name [STARPU_MAXIMPLEMENTATIONS]
- int nbuffers
- enum starpu_data_access_mode modes [STARPU_NMAXBUFS]
- enum starpu_data_access_mode * dyn_modes
- unsigned specific_nodes
- int nodes [STARPU_NMAXBUFS]
- int * dyn_nodes
- struct starpu_perfmodel * model
- struct starpu_perfmodel * energy_model
- unsigned long per_worker_stats [STARPU_NMAXWORKERS]
- const char * name
- int flags

29.13.2.1.1 Field Documentation

29.13.2.1.1.1 uint32_t starpu_codelet::where

Optional field to indicate which types of processing units are able to execute the codelet. The different values STAR-PU_CPU, STARPU_CUDA, STARPU_OPENCL can be combined to specify on which types of processing units the codelet can be executed. STARPU_CPU|STARPU_CUDA for instance indicates that the codelet is implemented for both CPU cores and CUDA devices while STARPU_OPENCL indicates that it is only available on OpenCL devices. If the field is unset, its value will be automatically set based on the availability of the XXX_funcs fields defined below. It can also be set to STARPU_NOWHERE to specify that no computation has to be actually done.

29.13.2.1.1.2 int(* starpu_codelet::can_execute)(unsigned workerid, struct **starpu_task** *task, unsigned nimpl)

Define a function which should return 1 if the worker designated by `workerid` can execute the `nimpl` -th implementation of `task`, 0 otherwise.

29.13.2.1.1.3 enum **starpu_codelet_type** starpu_codelet::type

Optional field to specify the type of the codelet. The default is STARPU_SEQ, i.e. usual sequential implementation. Other values (STARPU_SPMD or STARPU_FORKJOIN declare that a parallel implementation is also available. See Parallel Tasks for details.

29.13.2.1.1.4 int starpu_codelet::max_parallelism

Optional field. If a parallel implementation is available, this denotes the maximum combined worker size that StarPU will use to execute parallel tasks for this codelet.

29.13.2.1.1.5 starpu_cpu_func_t starpu_codelet::cpu_func

Deprecated Optional field which has been made deprecated. One should use instead the field starpu_codelet-
::cpu_funcs.

29.13.2.1.1.6 starpu_cuda_func_t starpu_codelet::cuda_func

Deprecated Optional field which has been made deprecated. One should use instead the starpu_codelet::cuda_-
funcs field.

29.13.2.1.1.7 starpu_opencl_func_t starpu_codelet::opencl_func

Deprecated Optional field which has been made deprecated. One should use instead the starpu_codelet::opencl-
_funcs field.

29.13.2.1.1.8 starpu_cpu_func_t starpu_codelet::cpu_funcs[STARPU_MAXIMPLEMENTATIONS]

Optional array of function pointers to the CPU implementations of the codelet. The functions prototype must be:

```
void cpu_func(void *buffers[], void *cl_arg)
```

The first argument being the array of data managed by the data management library, and the second argument is
a pointer to the argument passed from the field starpu_task::cl_arg. If the field starpu_codelet::where is set, then
the field starpu_codelet::cpu_funcs is ignored if STARPU_CPU does not appear in the field starpu_codelet::where,
it must be non-NULL otherwise.

29.13.2.1.1.9 starpu_cuda_func_t starpu_codelet::cuda_funcs[STARPU_MAXIMPLEMENTATIONS]

Optional array of function pointers to the CUDA implementations of the codelet. The functions must be host-
functions written in the CUDA runtime API. Their prototype must be:

```
void cuda_func(void *buffers[], void *cl_arg)
```

If the field starpu_codelet::where is set, then the field starpu_codelet::cuda_funcs is ignored if STARPU_CUDA
does not appear in the field starpu_codelet::where, it must be non-NULL otherwise.

29.13.2.1.1.10 char starpu_codelet::cuda_flags[STARPU_MAXIMPLEMENTATIONS]

Optional array of flags for CUDA execution. They specify some semantic details about CUDA kernel execution,
such as asynchronous execution.

29.13.2.1.1.11 starpu_opencl_func_t starpu_codelet::opencl_funcs[STARPU_MAXIMPLEMENTATIONS]

Optional array of function pointers to the OpenCL implementations of the codelet. The functions prototype must be:

```
void opencl_func(void *buffers[], void *cl_arg)
```

If the field starpu_codelet::where field is set, then the field starpu_codelet::opencl_funcs is ignored if STARPU_O-
PENCL does not appear in the field starpu_codelet::where, it must be non-NULL otherwise.

29.13.2.1.1.12 char starpu_codelet::opencl_flags[STARPU_MAXIMPLEMENTATIONS]

Optional array of flags for OpenCL execution. They specify some semantic details about OpenCL kernel execution,
such as asynchronous execution.

29.13.2.1.1.13 starpu_mic_func_t starpu_codelet::mic_funcs[STARPU_MAXIMPLEMENTATIONS]

Optional array of function pointers to a function which returns the MIC implementation of the codelet. The functions
prototype must be:

```
starpu_mic_kernel_t mic_func(struct starpu_codelet
    *cl, unsigned nimpl)
```

If the field starpu_codelet::where is set, then the field starpu_codelet::mic_funcs is ignored if STARPU_MIC does not appear in the field starpu_codelet::where. It can be NULL if starpu_codelet::cpu_funcs_name is non-NULL, in which case StarPU will simply make a symbol lookup to get the implementation.

29.13.2.1.1.14   **starpu_mpi_ms_func_t** starpu_codelet::mpi_ms_funcs[**STARPU_MAXIMPLEMENTATIONS**]

Optional array of function pointers to a function which returns the MPI Master Slave implementation of the codelet. The functions prototype must be:

```
starpu_mpi_ms_kernel_t mpi_ms_func(struct starpu_codelet
    *cl, unsigned nimpl)
```

If the field starpu_codelet::where is set, then the field starpu_codelet::mpi_ms_funcs is ignored if STARPU_MP-I_MS does not appear in the field starpu_codelet::where. It can be NULL if starpu_codelet::cpu_funcs_name is non-NULL, in which case StarPU will simply make a symbol lookup to get the implementation.

29.13.2.1.1.15   **starpu_scc_func_t** starpu_codelet::scc_funcs[**STARPU_MAXIMPLEMENTATIONS**]

Optional array of function pointers to a function which returns the SCC implementation of the codelet. The functions prototype must be:

```
starpu_scc_kernel_t scc_func(struct starpu_codelet
    *cl, unsigned nimpl)
```

If the field starpu_codelet::where is set, then the field starpu_codelet::scc_funcs is ignored if STARPU_SCC does not appear in the field starpu_codelet::where. It can be NULL if starpu_codelet::cpu_funcs_name is non-NULL, in which case StarPU will simply make a symbol lookup to get the implementation.

29.13.2.1.1.16   char ∗ starpu_codelet::cpu_funcs_name[**STARPU_MAXIMPLEMENTATIONS**]

Optional array of strings which provide the name of the CPU functions referenced in the array starpu_codelet::cpu_funcs. This can be used when running on MIC devices or the SCC platform, for StarPU to simply look up the MIC function implementation through its name.

29.13.2.1.1.17   int starpu_codelet::nbuffers

Specify the number of arguments taken by the codelet. These arguments are managed by the DSM and are accessed from the void *buffers[] array. The constant argument passed with the field starpu_task::cl_arg is not counted in this number. This value should not be above STARPU_NMAXBUFS. It may be set to STARPU_VAR-IABLE_NBUFFERS to specify that the number of buffers and their access modes will be set in starpu_task::nbuffers and starpu_task::modes or starpu_task::dyn_modes, which thus permits to define codelets with a varying number of data.

29.13.2.1.1.18   enum **starpu_data_access_mode** starpu_codelet::modes[**STARPU_NMAXBUFS**]

Is an array of starpu_data_access_mode. It describes the required access modes to the data neeeded by the codelet (e.g. STARPU_RW). The number of entries in this array must be specified in the field starpu_codelet-::nbuffers, and should not exceed STARPU_NMAXBUFS. If unsufficient, this value can be set with the configure option --enable-maxbuffers.

29.13.2.1.1.19   enum **starpu_data_access_mode** ∗ starpu_codelet::dyn_modes

Is an array of starpu_data_access_mode. It describes the required access modes to the data needed by the codelet (e.g. STARPU_RW). The number of entries in this array must be specified in the field starpu_codelet::nbuffers. This field should be used for codelets having a number of datas greater than STARPU_NMAXBUFS (see Setting Many Data Handles For a Task). When defining a codelet, one should either define this field or the field starpu_codelet-::modes defined above.

29.13.2.1.1.20 unsigned starpu_codelet::specific_nodes

Default value is 0. If this flag is set, StarPU will not systematically send all data to the memory node where the task will be executing, it will read the starpu_codelet::nodes or starpu_codelet::dyn_nodes array to determine, for each data, whether to send it on the memory node where the task will be executing (-1), or on a specific node (!= -1).

29.13.2.1.1.21 int starpu_codelet::nodes[STARPU_NMAXBUFS]

Optional field. When starpu_codelet::specific_nodes is 1, this specifies the memory nodes where each data should be sent to for task execution. The number of entries in this array is starpu_codelet::nbuffers, and should not exceed STARPU_NMAXBUFS.

29.13.2.1.1.22 int * starpu_codelet::dyn_nodes

Optional field. When starpu_codelet::specific_nodes is 1, this specifies the memory nodes where each data should be sent to for task execution. The number of entries in this array is starpu_codelet::nbuffers. This field should be used for codelets having a number of datas greater than STARPU_NMAXBUFS (see Setting Many Data Handles For a Task). When defining a codelet, one should either define this field or the field starpu_codelet::nodes defined above.

29.13.2.1.1.23 struct **starpu_perfmodel** * starpu_codelet::model

Optional pointer to the task duration performance model associated to this codelet. This optional field is ignored when set to NULL or when its field starpu_perfmodel::symbol is not set.

29.13.2.1.1.24 struct **starpu_perfmodel** * starpu_codelet::energy_model

Optional pointer to the task energy consumption performance model associated to this codelet. This optional field is ignored when set to NULL or when its field starpu_perfmodel::symbol is not set. In the case of parallel codelets, this has to account for all processing units involved in the parallel execution.

29.13.2.1.1.25 unsigned long starpu_codelet::per_worker_stats[STARPU_NMAXWORKERS]

Optional array for statistics collected at runtime: this is filled by StarPU and should not be accessed directly, but for example by calling the function starpu_codelet_display_stats() (See starpu_codelet_display_stats() for details).

29.13.2.1.1.26 const char * starpu_codelet::name

Optional name of the codelet. This can be useful for debugging purposes.

29.13.2.1.1.27 const char * starpu_codelet::flags

Various flags for the codelet.

29.13.2.2 struct starpu_data_descr

This type is used to describe a data handle along with an access mode.

Data Fields

starpu_data_-handle_t	handle	describes a data
enum starpu_data_-access_mode	mode	describes its access mode

29.13.2.3   struct starpu_task

The structure describes a task that can be offloaded on the various processing units managed by StarPU. It instantiates a codelet. It can either be allocated dynamically with the function starpu_task_create(), or declared statically. In the latter case, the programmer has to zero the structure starpu_task and to fill the different fields properly. The indicated default values correspond to the configuration of a task allocated with starpu_task_create().

Data Fields

- const char * name
- struct starpu_codelet * cl
- int32_t where
- int nbuffers
- starpu_data_handle_t * dyn_handles
- void ** dyn_interfaces
- enum starpu_data_access_mode * dyn_modes
- starpu_data_handle_t handles [STARPU_NMAXBUFS]
- void * interfaces [STARPU_NMAXBUFS]
- enum starpu_data_access_mode modes [STARPU_NMAXBUFS]
- void * cl_arg
- size_t cl_arg_size
- void(* callback_func)(void *)
- void * callback_arg
- void(* prologue_callback_func)(void *)
- void * prologue_callback_arg
- void(* prologue_callback_pop_func)(void *)
- void * prologue_callback_pop_arg
- starpu_tag_t tag_id
- unsigned cl_arg_free:1
- unsigned callback_arg_free:1
- unsigned prologue_callback_arg_free:1
- unsigned prologue_callback_pop_arg_free:1
- unsigned use_tag:1
- unsigned sequential_consistency:1
- unsigned synchronous:1
- unsigned execute_on_a_specific_worker:1
- unsigned detach:1
- unsigned destroy:1
- unsigned regenerate:1
- unsigned scheduled:1
- unsigned int mf_skip:1
- unsigned workerid
- unsigned workerorder
- int priority
- enum starpu_task_status status
- int magic
- unsigned sched_ctx
- int hypervisor_tag
- unsigned possibly_parallel
- starpu_task_bundle_t bundle
- struct starpu_profiling_task_info * profiling_info
- double flops
- double predicted
- double predicted_transfer

- double predicted_start
- struct starpu_task ∗ prev
- struct starpu_task ∗ next
- void ∗ starpu_private
- unsigned prefetched
- struct starpu_omp_task ∗ omp_task

29.13.2.3.1 Field Documentation

29.13.2.3.1.1 const char ∗ starpu_task::name

Optional name of the task. This can be useful for debugging purposes.

29.13.2.3.1.2 struct starpu_codelet ∗ starpu_task::cl

Is a pointer to the corresponding structure starpu_codelet. This describes where the kernel should be executed, and supplies the appropriate implementations. When set to NULL, no code is executed during the tasks, such empty tasks can be useful for synchronization purposes. This field has been made deprecated. One should use instead the field starpu_task::handles to specify the data handles accessed by the task. The access modes are now defined in the field starpu_codelet::modes.

29.13.2.3.1.3 uint32_t starpu_task::where

When set, specifies where the task is allowed to be executed. When unset, it takes the value of starpu_codelet-::where.

29.13.2.3.1.4 int starpu_task::nbuffers

Specifies the number of buffers. This is only used when starpu_codelet::nbuffers is STARPU_VARIABLE_NBUFF-ERS.

29.13.2.3.1.5 starpu_data_handle_t ∗ starpu_task::dyn_handles

Is an array of starpu_data_handle_t. It specifies the handles to the different pieces of data accessed by the task. The number of entries in this array must be specified in the field starpu_codelet::nbuffers. This field should be used for tasks having a number of datas greater than STARPU_NMAXBUFS (see Setting Many Data Handles For a Task). When defining a task, one should either define this field or the field starpu_task::handles defined above.

29.13.2.3.1.6 void ∗∗ starpu_task::dyn_interfaces

The actual data pointers to the memory node where execution will happen, managed by the DSM. Is used when the field starpu_task::dyn_handles is defined.

29.13.2.3.1.7 enum starpu_data_access_mode ∗ starpu_task::dyn_modes

Is used only when starpu_codelet::nbuffers is STARPU_VARIABLE_NBUFFERS. It is an array of starpu_data_-access_mode. It describes the required access modes to the data needed by the codelet (e.g. STARPU_RW). The number of entries in this array must be specified in the field starpu_codelet::nbuffers. This field should be used for codelets having a number of datas greater than STARPU_NMAXBUFS (see Setting Many Data Handles For a Task). When defining a codelet, one should either define this field or the field starpu_task::modes defined above.

29.13.2.3.1.8 starpu_data_handle_t starpu_task::handles[STARPU_NMAXBUFS]

Is an array of starpu_data_handle_t. It specifies the handles to the different pieces of data accessed by the task. The number of entries in this array must be specified in the field starpu_codelet::nbuffers, and should not exceed STARPU_NMAXBUFS. If unsufficient, this value can be set with the configure option --enable-maxbuffers.

29.13.2.3.1.9 void ∗ starpu_task::interfaces[STARPU_NMAXBUFS]

The actual data pointers to the memory node where execution will happen, managed by the DSM.

29.13.2.3.1.10 enum starpu_data_access_mode starpu_task::modes[STARPU_NMAXBUFS]

Is used only when starpu_codelet::nbuffers is STARPU_VARIABLE_NBUFFERS. It is an array of starpu_data_-access_mode. It describes the required access modes to the data neeeded by the codelet (e.g. STARPU_RW). The number of entries in this array must be specified in the field starpu_task::nbuffers, and should not exceed STARPU_NMAXBUFS. If unsufficient, this value can be set with the configure option --enable-maxbuffers.

29.13.2.3.1.11 void * starpu_task::cl_arg

Optional pointer which is passed to the codelet through the second argument of the codelet implementation (e.g. starpu_codelet::cpu_func or starpu_codelet::cuda_func). The default value is NULL. starpu_codelet_pack_args() and starpu_codelet_unpack_args() are helpers that can can be used to respectively pack and unpack data into and from it, but the application can manage it any way, the only requirement is that the size of the data must be set in starpu_task::cl_arg_size .

29.13.2.3.1.12 size_t starpu_task::cl_arg_size

Optional field. For some specific drivers, the pointer starpu_task::cl_arg cannot not be directly given to the driver function. A buffer of size starpu_task::cl_arg_size needs to be allocated on the driver. This buffer is then filled with the starpu_task::cl_arg_size bytes starting at address starpu_task::cl_arg. In this case, the argument given to the codelet is therefore not the starpu_task::cl_arg pointer, but the address of the buffer in local store (LS) instead. This field is ignored for CPU, CUDA and OpenCL codelets, where the starpu_task::cl_arg pointer is given as such.

29.13.2.3.1.13 void(* starpu_task::callback_func)(void *)

Optional field, the default value is NULL. This is a function pointer of prototype void (*f)(void *) which specifies a possible callback. If this pointer is non-NULL, the callback function is executed on the host after the execution of the task. Tasks which depend on it might already be executing. The callback is passed the value contained in the starpu_task::callback_arg field. No callback is executed if the field is set to NULL.

29.13.2.3.1.14 void * starpu_task::callback_arg

Optional field, the default value is NULL. This is the pointer passed to the callback function. This field is ignored if the field starpu_task::callback_func is set to NULL.

29.13.2.3.1.15 void(* starpu_task::prologue_callback_func)(void *)

Optional field, the default value is NULL. This is a function pointer of prototype void (*f)(void *) which specifies a possible callback. If this pointer is non-NULL, the callback function is executed on the host when the task becomes ready for execution, before getting scheduled. The callback is passed the value contained in the starpu_task::prologue_callback_arg field. No callback is executed if the field is set to NULL.

29.13.2.3.1.16 void * starpu_task::prologue_callback_arg

Optional field, the default value is NULL. This is the pointer passed to the prologue callback function. This field is ignored if the field starpu_task::prologue_callback_func is set to NULL.

29.13.2.3.1.17 void(* starpu_task::prologue_callback_pop_func)(void *)

todo

29.13.2.3.1.18 void * starpu_task::prologue_callback_pop_arg

todo

29.13.2.3.1.19 starpu_tag_t starpu_task::tag_id

This optional field contains the tag associated to the task if the field starpu_task::use_tag is set, it is ignored otherwise.

29.13.2.3.1.20   unsigned starpu_task::cl_arg_free

Optional field. In case starpu_task::cl_arg was allocated by the application through `malloc()`, setting starpu_-task::cl_arg_free to 1 makes StarPU automatically call `free(cl_arg)` when destroying the task. This saves the user from defining a callback just for that. This is mostly useful when targetting MIC or SCC, where the codelet does not execute in the same memory space as the main thread.

29.13.2.3.1.21   unsigned starpu_task::callback_arg_free

Optional field. In case starpu_task::callback_arg was allocated by the application through `malloc()`, setting starpu_task::callback_arg_free to 1 makes StarPU automatically call `free(callback_arg)` when destroying the task.

29.13.2.3.1.22   unsigned starpu_task::prologue_callback_arg_free

Optional field. In case starpu_task::prologue_callback_arg was allocated by the application through `malloc()`, setting starpu_task::prologue_callback_arg_free to 1 makes StarPU automatically call `free(prologue_-callback_arg)` when destroying the task.

29.13.2.3.1.23   unsigned starpu_task::prologue_callback_pop_arg_free

todo

29.13.2.3.1.24   unsigned starpu_task::use_tag

Optional field, the default value is 0. If set, this flag indicates that the task should be associated with the tag contained in the starpu_task::tag_id field. Tag allow the application to synchronize with the task and to express task dependencies easily.

29.13.2.3.1.25   unsigned starpu_task::sequential_consistency

If this flag is set (which is the default), sequential consistency is enforced for the data parameters of this task for which sequential consistency is enabled. Clearing this flag permits to disable sequential consistency for this task, even if data have it enabled.

29.13.2.3.1.26   unsigned starpu_task::synchronous

If this flag is set, the function starpu_task_submit() is blocking and returns only when the task has been executed (or if no worker is able to process the task). Otherwise, starpu_task_submit() returns immediately.

29.13.2.3.1.27   unsigned starpu_task::execute_on_a_specific_worker

Default value is 0. If this flag is set, StarPU will bypass the scheduler and directly affect this task to the worker specified by the field starpu_task::workerid.

29.13.2.3.1.28   unsigned starpu_task::detach

Optional field, default value is 1. If this flag is set, it is not possible to synchronize with the task by the means of starpu_task_wait() later on. Internal data structures are only guaranteed to be freed once starpu_task_wait() is called if the flag is not set.

29.13.2.3.1.29   unsigned starpu_task::destroy

Optional value. Default value is 0 for starpu_task_init(), and 1 for starpu_task_create(). If this flag is set, the task structure will automatically be freed, either after the execution of the callback if the task is detached, or during starpu_task_wait() otherwise. If this flag is not set, dynamically allocated data structures will not be freed until starpu_task_destroy() is called explicitly. Setting this flag for a statically allocated task structure will result in undefined behaviour. The flag is set to 1 when the task is created by calling starpu_task_create(). Note that starpu_task_wait_for_all() will not free any task.

29.13.2.3.1.30   unsigned starpu_task::regenerate

Optional field. If this flag is set, the task will be re-submitted to StarPU once it has been executed. This flag must not be set if the flag starpu_task::destroy is set. This flag must be set before making another task depend on this one.

29.13.2.3.1.31   unsigned starpu_task::scheduled

Whether the scheduler has pushed the task on some queue

29.13.2.3.1.32   unsigned int starpu_task::mf_skip

This is only used for tasks that use multiformat handle. This should only be used by StarPU.

29.13.2.3.1.33   unsigned starpu_task::workerid

Optional field. If the field starpu_task::execute_on_a_specific_worker is set, this field indicates the identifier of the worker that should process this task (as returned by starpu_worker_get_id()). This field is ignored if the field starpu_task::execute_on_a_specific_worker is set to 0.

29.13.2.3.1.34   unsigned starpu_task::workerorder

Optional field. If the field starpu_task::execute_on_a_specific_worker is set, this field indicates the per-worker consecutive order in which tasks should be executed on the worker. Tasks will be executed in consecutive starpu_-task::workerorder values, thus ignoring the availability order or task priority. See Static Scheduling for more details. This field is ignored if the field starpu_task::execute_on_a_specific_worker is set to 0.

29.13.2.3.1.35   int starpu_task::priority

Optional field, the default value is STARPU_DEFAULT_PRIO. This field indicates a level of priority for the task. This is an integer value that must be set between the return values of the function starpu_sched_get_min_priority() for the least important tasks, and that of the function starpu_sched_get_max_priority() for the most important tasks (included). The STARPU_MIN_PRIO and STARPU_MAX_PRIO macros are provided for convenience and respectively returns the value of starpu_sched_get_min_priority() and starpu_sched_get_max_priority(). Default priority is STARPU_DEFAULT_PRIO, which is always defined as 0 in order to allow static task initialization. Scheduling strategies that take priorities into account can use this parameter to take better scheduling decisions, but the scheduling policy may also ignore it.

29.13.2.3.1.36   enum **starpu_task_status** starpu_task::status

Optional field. Current state of the task.

29.13.2.3.1.37   int starpu_task::magic

This field is set when initializing a task. The function starpu_task_submit() will fail if the field does not have the right value. This will hence avoid submitting tasks which have not been properly initialised.

29.13.2.3.1.38   unsigned starpu_task::sched_ctx

Scheduling context.

29.13.2.3.1.39   int starpu_task::hypervisor_tag

Helps the hypervisor monitor the execution of this task.

29.13.2.3.1.40   unsigned starpu_task::possibly_parallel

todo

29.13.2.3.1.41   starpu_task_bundle_t starpu_task::bundle

Optional field. The bundle that includes this task. If no bundle is used, this should be `NULL`.

29.13.2.3.1.42   struct starpu_profiling_task_info ∗ starpu_task::profiling_info

Optional field. Profiling information for the task.

29.13.2.3.1.43   double starpu_task::flops

This can be set to the number of floating points operations that the task will have to achieve. This is useful for easily getting GFlops curves from the tool `starpu_perfmodel_plot`, and for the hypervisor load balancing.

29.13.2.3.1.44   double starpu_task::predicted

Output field. Predicted duration of the task. This field is only set if the scheduling strategy uses performance models.

29.13.2.3.1.45   double starpu_task::predicted_transfer

Optional field. Predicted data transfer duration for the task in microseconds. This field is only valid if the scheduling strategy uses performance models.

29.13.2.3.1.46   double starpu_task::predicted_start

todo

29.13.2.3.1.47   struct starpu_task ∗ starpu_task::prev

A pointer to the previous task. This should only be used by StarPU.

29.13.2.3.1.48   struct starpu_task ∗ starpu_task::next

A pointer to the next task. This should only be used by StarPU.

29.13.2.3.1.49   void ∗ starpu_task::starpu_private

This is private to StarPU, do not modify. If the task is allocated by hand (without starpu_task_create()), this field should be set to `NULL`.

29.13.2.3.1.50   unsigned starpu_task::prefetched

todo

29.13.2.3.1.51   struct starpu_omp_task ∗ starpu_task::omp_task

todo

29.13.3   Macro Definition Documentation

29.13.3.1   #define STARPU_NOWHERE

This macro is used when setting the field starpu_codelet::where to specify that the codelet has no computation part, and thus does not need to be scheduled, and data does not need to be actually loaded. This is thus essentially used for synchronization tasks.

29.13.3.2 #define STARPU_CPU

This macro is used when setting the field starpu_codelet::where (or starpu_task::where) to specify the codelet (or the task) may be executed on a CPU processing unit.

29.13.3.3 #define STARPU_CUDA

This macro is used when setting the field starpu_codelet::where (or starpu_task::where) to specify the codelet (or the task) may be executed on a CUDA processing unit.

29.13.3.4 #define STARPU_OPENCL

This macro is used when setting the field starpu_codelet::where (or starpu_task::where) to specify the codelet (or the task) may be executed on a OpenCL processing unit.

29.13.3.5 #define STARPU_MIC

This macro is used when setting the field starpu_codelet::where (or starpu_task::where) to specify the codelet (or the task) may be executed on a MIC processing unit.

29.13.3.6 #define STARPU_MPI_MS

This macro is used when setting the field starpu_codelet::where (or starpu_task::where) to specify the codelet (or the task) may be executed on a MPI Slave processing unit.

29.13.3.7 #define STARPU_SCC

This macro is used when setting the field starpu_codelet::where (or starpu_task::where) to specify the codelet (or the task) may be executed on an SCC processing unit.

29.13.3.8 #define STARPU_MAIN_RAM

This macro is used when the RAM memory node is specified.

29.13.3.9 #define STARPU_MULTIPLE_CPU_IMPLEMENTATIONS

Deprecated Setting the field starpu_codelet::cpu_func with this macro indicates the codelet will have several implementations. The use of this macro is deprecated. One should always only define the field starpu_-codelet::cpu_funcs.

29.13.3.10 #define STARPU_MULTIPLE_CUDA_IMPLEMENTATIONS

Deprecated Setting the field starpu_codelet::cuda_func with this macro indicates the codelet will have several implementations. The use of this macro is deprecated. One should always only define the field starpu_codelet::cuda_funcs.

29.13.3.11 #define STARPU_MULTIPLE_OPENCL_IMPLEMENTATIONS

Deprecated Setting the field starpu_codelet::opencl_func with this macro indicates the codelet will have several implementations. The use of this macro is deprecated. One should always only define the field starpu_codelet::opencl_funcs.

29.13.3.12 #define STARPU_NMAXBUFS

Defines the maximum number of buffers that tasks will be able to take as parameters. The default value is 8, it can be changed by using the configure option --enable-maxbuffers.

29.13.3.13 #define STARPU_VARIABLE_NBUFFERS

Value to set in starpu_codelet::nbuffers to specify that the codelet can accept a variable number of buffers, specified in starpu_task::nbuffers.

29.13.3.14 #define STARPU_CUDA_ASYNC

Value to be set in starpu_codelet::cuda_flags to allow asynchronous CUDA kernel execution.

29.13.3.15 #define STARPU_OPENCL_ASYNC

Value to be set in starpu_codelet::opencl_flags to allow asynchronous OpenCL kernel execution.

29.13.3.16 #define STARPU_CODELET_SIMGRID_EXECUTE

Value to be set in starpu_codelet::flags to execute the codelet functions even in simgrid mode.

29.13.3.17 #define STARPU_CODELET_SIMGRID_EXECUTE_AND_INJECT

Value to be set in starpu_codelet::flags to execute the codelet functions even in simgrid mode, and later inject the measured timing inside the simulation.

29.13.3.18 #define STARPU_TASK_INITIALIZER

It is possible to initialize statically allocated tasks with this value. This is equivalent to initializing a structure starpu_task with the function starpu_task_init().

29.13.3.19 #define STARPU_TASK_GET_NBUFFERS(*task*)

Return the number of buffers for task, i.e. starpu_codelet::nbuffers, or starpu_task::nbuffers if the former is STARPU_VARIABLE_NBUFFERS.

29.13.3.20 #define STARPU_TASK_GET_HANDLE(*task, i*)

Return the i -th data handle of task. If task is defined with a static or dynamic number of handles, will either return the i -th element of the field starpu_task::handles or the i -th element of the field starpu_task::dyn_handles (see Setting Many Data Handles For a Task)

29.13.3.21 #define STARPU_TASK_SET_HANDLE(*task, handle, i*)

Set the i -th data handle of `task` with `handle`. If `task` is defined with a static or dynamic number of handles, will either set the i -th element of the field starpu_task::handles or the i -th element of the field starpu_task::dyn_-handles (see Setting Many Data Handles For a Task)

29.13.3.22 #define STARPU_CODELET_GET_MODE(*codelet, i*)

Return the access mode of the i -th data handle of `codelet`. If `codelet` is defined with a static or dynamic number of handles, will either return the i -th element of the field starpu_codelet::modes or the i -th element of the field starpu_codelet::dyn_modes (see Setting Many Data Handles For a Task)

29.13.3.23 #define STARPU_CODELET_SET_MODE(*codelet, mode, i*)

Set the access mode of the i -th data handle of `codelet`. If `codelet` is defined with a static or dynamic number of handles, will either set the i -th element of the field starpu_codelet::modes or the i -th element of the field starpu_codelet::dyn_modes (see Setting Many Data Handles For a Task)

29.13.3.24 #define STARPU_TASK_GET_MODE(*task, i*)

Return the access mode of the i -th data handle of `task`. If `task` is defined with a static or dynamic number of handles, will either return the i -th element of the field starpu_task::modes or the i -th element of the field starpu_task::dyn_modes (see Setting Many Data Handles For a Task)

29.13.3.25 #define STARPU_TASK_SET_MODE(*task, mode, i*)

Set the access mode of the i -th data handle of `task`. If `task` is defined with a static or dynamic number of handles, will either set the i -th element of the field starpu_task::modes or the i -th element of the field starpu_-task::dyn_modes (see Setting Many Data Handles For a Task)

29.13.4 Typedef Documentation

29.13.4.1 starpu_cpu_func_t

CPU implementation of a codelet.

29.13.4.2 starpu_cuda_func_t

CUDA implementation of a codelet.

29.13.4.3 starpu_opencl_func_t

OpenCL implementation of a codelet.

29.13.4.4 starpu_mic_func_t

MIC implementation of a codelet.

29.13.4.5 starpu_mpi_ms_func_t

MPI Master Slave implementation of a codelet.

29.13.4.6 starpu_scc_func_t

SCC implementation of a codelet.

29.13.4.7 starpu_mic_kernel_t

MIC kernel for a codelet

29.13.4.8 starpu_mpi_ms_kernel_t

MPI Master Slave kernel for a codelet

29.13.4.9 starpu_scc_kernel_t

SCC kernel for a codelet

29.13.5 Enumeration Type Documentation

29.13.5.1 enum starpu_codelet_type

Describes the type of parallel task. See Parallel Tasks for details.

Enumerator:

STARPU_SEQ (default) for classical sequential tasks.

STARPU_SPMD for a parallel task whose threads are handled by StarPU, the code has to use starpu_combined_worker_get_size() and starpu_combined_worker_get_rank() to distribute the work.

STARPU_FORKJOIN for a parallel task whose threads are started by the codelet function, which has to use starpu_combined_worker_get_size() to determine how many threads should be started.

29.13.5.2 enum starpu_task_status

Task status

Enumerator:

STARPU_TASK_BLOCKED The task has just been submitted, and its dependencies has not been checked yet.

STARPU_TASK_READY The task is ready for execution.

STARPU_TASK_RUNNING The task is running on some worker.

STARPU_TASK_FINISHED The task is finished executing.

STARPU_TASK_BLOCKED_ON_TAG The task is waiting for a tag.

STARPU_TASK_BLOCKED_ON_TASK The task is waiting for a task.

STARPU_TASK_BLOCKED_ON_DATA The task is waiting for some data.

STARPU_TASK_STOPPED The task is stopped.

29.13.6 Function Documentation

29.13.6.1 void starpu_codelet_init (struct starpu_codelet * cl)

Initialize `cl` with default values. Codelets should preferably be initialized statically as shown in Defining A Codelet. However such a initialisation is not always possible, e.g. when using C++.

29.13.6.2   void starpu_task_init (struct starpu_task ∗ *task*)

Initialize `task` with default values. This function is implicitly called by starpu_task_create(). By default, tasks initialized with starpu_task_init() must be deinitialized explicitly with starpu_task_clean(). Tasks can also be initialized statically, using STARPU_TASK_INITIALIZER.

29.13.6.3   struct starpu_task ∗ starpu_task_create (void)   [read]

Allocate a task structure and initialize it with default values. Tasks allocated dynamically with starpu_task_create() are automatically freed when the task is terminated. This means that the task pointer can not be used any more once the task is submitted, since it can be executed at any time (unless dependencies make it wait) and thus freed at any time. If the field starpu_task::destroy is explicitly unset, the resources used by the task have to be freed by calling starpu_task_destroy().

29.13.6.4   struct starpu_task ∗ starpu_task_dup (struct starpu_task ∗ *task*)   [read]

Allocate a task structure which is the exact duplicate of `task`.

29.13.6.5   void starpu_task_clean (struct starpu_task ∗ *task*)

Release all the structures automatically allocated to execute `task`, but not the task structure itself and values set by the user remain unchanged. It is thus useful for statically allocated tasks for instance. It is also useful when users want to execute the same operation several times with as least overhead as possible. It is called automatically by starpu_task_destroy(). It has to be called only after explicitly waiting for the task or after starpu_shutdown() (waiting for the callback is not enough, since StarPU still manipulates the task after calling the callback).

29.13.6.6   void starpu_task_destroy (struct starpu_task ∗ *task*)

Free the resource allocated during starpu_task_create() and associated with `task`. This function is called automatically after the execution of a task when the field starpu_task::destroy is set, which is the default for tasks created by starpu_task_create(). Calling this function on a statically allocated task results in an undefined behaviour.

29.13.6.7   int starpu_task_wait (struct starpu_task ∗ *task*)

Block until `task` has been executed. It is not possible to synchronize with a task more than once. It is not possible to wait for synchronous or detached tasks. Upon successful completion, this function returns 0. Otherwise, -EINVAL indicates that the specified task was either synchronous or detached.

29.13.6.8   int starpu_task_wait_array (struct starpu_task ∗∗ *tasks,* unsigned *nb_tasks*)

Allow to wait for an array of tasks. Upon successful completion, this function returns 0. Otherwise, -EINVAL indicates that one of the tasks was either synchronous or detached.

29.13.6.9   int starpu_task_submit (struct starpu_task ∗ *task*)

Submit `task` to StarPU. Calling this function does not mean that the task will be executed immediately as there can be data or task (tag) dependencies that are not fulfilled yet: StarPU will take care of scheduling this task with respect to such dependencies. This function returns immediately if the field starpu_task::synchronous is set to 0, and block until the termination of the task otherwise. It is also possible to synchronize the application with asynchronous tasks by the means of tags, using the function starpu_tag_wait() function for instance. In case of success, this function returns 0, a return value of -ENODEV means that there is no worker able to process this task (e.g. there is no GPU available and this task is only implemented for CUDA devices). starpu_task_submit() can be called from anywhere, including codelet functions and callbacks, provided that the field starpu_task::synchronous is set to 0.

29.13.6.10 int starpu_task_submit_to_ctx (struct **starpu_task** ∗ *task,* unsigned *sched_ctx_id*)

Submit task to the context sched_ctx_id. By default, starpu_task_submit() submits the task to a global context that is created automatically by StarPU.

29.13.6.11 int starpu_task_wait_for_all (void)

Block until all the tasks that were submitted (to the current context or the global one if there is no current context) are terminated. It does not destroy these tasks.

29.13.6.12 int starpu_task_wait_for_all_in_ctx (unsigned *sched_ctx_id*)

Wait until all the tasks that were already submitted to the context sched_ctx_id have been terminated.

29.13.6.13 int starpu_task_wait_for_n_submitted (unsigned *n*)

Block until there are n submitted tasks left (to the current context or the global one if there is no current context) to be executed. It does not destroy these tasks.

29.13.6.14 int starpu_task_wait_for_n_submitted_in_ctx (unsigned *sched_ctx_id,* unsigned *n*)

Wait until there are n tasks submitted left to be executed that were already submitted to the context sched_ctx_id.

29.13.6.15 int starpu_task_nready (void)

TODO

Return the number of submitted tasks which are ready for execution are already executing. It thus does not include tasks waiting for dependencies.

29.13.6.16 int starpu_task_nsubmitted (void)

Return the number of submitted tasks which have not completed yet.

29.13.6.17 struct **starpu_task** ∗ starpu_task_get_current (void) [read]

Return the task currently executed by the worker, or NULL if it is called either from a thread that is not a task or simply because there is no task being executed at the moment.

29.13.6.18 const char ∗ starpu_task_get_name (struct **starpu_task** ∗ *task*)

Return the name of task, i.e. either its starpu_task::name field, or the name of the corresponding performance model.

29.13.6.19 const char ∗ starpu_task_get_model_name (struct **starpu_task** ∗ *task*)

Return the name of the performance model of task.

29.13.6.20   void starpu_codelet_display_stats (struct **starpu_codelet** ∗ *cl*)

Output on `stderr` some statistics on the codelet `cl`.

29.13.6.21   int starpu_task_wait_for_no_ready (void)

Wait until there is no more ready task.

29.13.6.22   void starpu_task_set_implementation (struct **starpu_task** ∗ *task*, unsigned *impl*)

This function should be called by schedulers to specify the codelet implementation to be executed when executing `task`.

29.13.6.23   unsigned starpu_task_get_implementation (struct **starpu_task** ∗ *task*)

Return the codelet implementation to be executed when executing `task`.

29.13.6.24   void starpu_iteration_push (unsigned long *iteration*)

Sets the iteration number for all the tasks to be submitted after this call. This is typically called at the beginning of a task submission loop. This number will then show up in tracing tools. A corresponding starpu_iteration_pop() call must be made to match the call to starpu_iteration_push(), at the end of the same task submission loop, typically.

Nested calls to starpu_iteration_push and starpu_iteration_pop are allowed, to describe a loop nest for instance, provided that they match properly.

29.13.6.25   void starpu_iteration_pop (void)

Drops the iteration number for submitted tasks. This must match a previous call to starpu_iteration_push(), and is typically called at the end of a task submission loop.

29.13.6.26   void starpu_create_sync_task (starpu_tag_t *sync_tag*, unsigned *ndeps*, starpu_tag_t ∗ *deps*, void(∗)(void ∗) *callback*, void ∗ *callback_arg*)

Create (and submit) an empty task that unlocks a tag once all its dependencies are fulfilled.

29.14   Task Insert Utility

Macros

- #define STARPU_VALUE
- #define STARPU_CL_ARGS
- #define STARPU_CALLBACK
- #define STARPU_CALLBACK_WITH_ARG
- #define STARPU_CALLBACK_ARG
- #define STARPU_PRIORITY
- #define STARPU_DATA_ARRAY
- #define STARPU_DATA_MODE_ARRAY
- #define STARPU_EXECUTE_ON_WORKER
- #define STARPU_WORKER_ORDER
- #define STARPU_TAG

- #define STARPU_TAG_ONLY
- #define STARPU_NAME
- #define STARPU_FLOPS
- #define STARPU_SCHED_CTX

Functions

- int starpu_insert_task (struct starpu_codelet ∗cl,...)
- int starpu_task_insert (struct starpu_codelet ∗cl,...)
- void starpu_codelet_pack_args (void ∗∗arg_buffer, size_t ∗arg_buffer_size,...)
- void starpu_codelet_unpack_args (void ∗cl_arg,...)
- void starpu_codelet_unpack_args_and_copyleft (void ∗cl_arg, void ∗buffer, size_t buffer_size,...)
- struct starpu_task ∗ starpu_task_build (struct starpu_codelet ∗cl,...)

29.14.1 Detailed Description

29.14.2 Macro Definition Documentation

29.14.2.1 #define STARPU_VALUE

Used when calling starpu_task_insert(), must be followed by a pointer to a constant value and the size of the constant

29.14.2.2 #define STARPU_CL_ARGS

Used when calling starpu_task_insert(), must be followed by a memory buffer containing the arguments to be given to the task, and by the size of the arguments. The memory buffer should be the result of a previous call to starpu_-codelet_pack_args(), and will be freed (i.e. starpu_task::cl_arg_free will be set to 1)

29.14.2.3 #define STARPU_CALLBACK

Used when calling starpu_task_insert(), must be followed by a pointer to a callback function

29.14.2.4 #define STARPU_CALLBACK_WITH_ARG

Used when calling starpu_task_insert(), must be followed by two pointers: one to a callback function, and the other to be given as an argument to the callback function; this is equivalent to using both STARPU_CALLBACK and STARPU_CALLBACK_WITH_ARG.

29.14.2.5 #define STARPU_CALLBACK_ARG

Used when calling starpu_task_insert(), must be followed by a pointer to be given as an argument to the callback function

29.14.2.6 #define STARPU_PRIORITY

Used when calling starpu_task_insert(), must be followed by a integer defining a priority level

29.14.2.7 #define STARPU_DATA_ARRAY

TODO

29.14.2.8 #define STARPU_DATA_MODE_ARRAY

TODO

29.14.2.9 #define STARPU_EXECUTE_ON_WORKER

Used when calling starpu_task_insert(), must be followed by an integer value specifying the worker on which to execute the task (as specified by starpu_task::execute_on_a_specific_worker)

29.14.2.10 #define STARPU_WORKER_ORDER

used when calling starpu_task_insert(), must be followed by an integer value specifying the worker order in which to execute the tasks (as specified by starpu_task::workerorder)

29.14.2.11 #define STARPU_TAG

Used when calling starpu_task_insert(), must be followed by a tag.

29.14.2.12 #define STARPU_TAG_ONLY

Used when calling starpu_task_insert(), must be followed by a tag stored in starpu_task::tag_id. Leave starpu_-task::use_tag as 0.

29.14.2.13 #define STARPU_NAME

Used when calling starpu_task_insert(), must be followed by a char * stored in starpu_task::name.

29.14.2.14 #define STARPU_FLOPS

Used when calling starpu_task_insert(), must be followed by an amount of floating point operations, as a double. Users **MUST** explicitly cast into double, otherwise parameter passing will not work.

29.14.2.15 #define STARPU_SCHED_CTX

Used when calling starpu_task_insert(), must be followed by the id of the scheduling context to which to submit the task to.

29.14.3 Function Documentation

29.14.3.1 int starpu_insert_task (struct **starpu_codelet** * cl, ...)

Similar to starpu_task_insert(). Kept to avoid breaking old codes.

29.14.3.2 int starpu_task_insert (struct **starpu_codelet** * cl, ...)

Create and submit a task corresponding to cl with the following given arguments. The argument list must be zero-terminated.

The arguments following the codelet can be of the following types:

- STARPU_R, STARPU_W, STARPU_RW, STARPU_SCRATCH, STARPU_REDUX an access mode followed by a data handle;

- STARPU_DATA_ARRAY followed by an array of data handles and its number of elements;

- STARPU_DATA_MODE_ARRAY followed by an array of struct starpu_data_descr, i.e data handles with their associated access modes, and its number of elements;

- STARPU_EXECUTE_ON_WORKER, STARPU_WORKER_ORDER followed by an integer value specifying the worker on which to execute the task (as specified by starpu_task::execute_on_a_specific_worker)

- the specific values STARPU_VALUE, STARPU_CALLBACK, STARPU_CALLBACK_ARG, STARPU_CALL-BACK_WITH_ARG, STARPU_PRIORITY, STARPU_TAG, STARPU_TAG_ONLY, STARPU_FLOPS, STA-RPU_SCHED_CTX, STARPU_CL_ARGS followed by the appropriated objects as defined elsewhere.

When using STARPU_DATA_ARRAY, the access mode of the data handles is not defined, it will be taken from the codelet starpu_codelet::modes or starpu_codelet::dyn_modes field. One should use STARPU_DATA_MODE_AR-RAY to define the data handles along with the access modes.

Parameters to be passed to the codelet implementation are defined through the type STARPU_VALUE. The function starpu_codelet_unpack_args() must be called within the codelet implementation to retrieve them.

29.14.3.3   void starpu_codelet_pack_args (void ∗∗ arg_buffer, size_t ∗ arg_buffer_size, ...)

Pack arguments of type STARPU_VALUE into a buffer which can be given to a codelet and later unpacked with the function starpu_codelet_unpack_args().

29.14.3.4   void starpu_codelet_unpack_args (void ∗ cl_arg, ...)

Retrieve the arguments of type STARPU_VALUE associated to a task automatically created using the function starpu_task_insert(). If any parameter's value is 0, unpacking will stop there and ignore the remaining parameters.

29.14.3.5   void starpu_codelet_unpack_args_and_copyleft (void ∗ cl_arg, void ∗ buffer, size_t buffer_size, ...)

Similar to starpu_codelet_unpack_args(), but if any parameter is 0, copy the part of `cl_arg` that has not been read in `buffer` which can then be used in a later call to one of the unpack functions.

29.14.3.6   struct starpu_task ∗ starpu_task_build (struct starpu_codelet ∗ cl, ...)   [read]

Create a task corresponding to `cl` with the following arguments. The argument list must be zero-terminated. The arguments following the codelet are the same as the ones for the function starpu_task_insert(). If some arguments of type STARPU_VALUE are given, the parameter starpu_task::cl_arg_free will be set to 1.

29.15   Explicit Dependencies

Typedefs

- typedef uint64_t starpu_tag_t

Functions

- void starpu_task_declare_deps_array (struct starpu_task ∗task, unsigned ndeps, struct starpu_task ∗task_-array[])
- int starpu_task_get_task_succs (struct starpu_task ∗task, unsigned ndeps, struct starpu_task ∗task_array[])
- int starpu_task_get_task_scheduled_succs (struct starpu_task ∗task, unsigned ndeps, struct starpu_task ∗task_array[])
- void starpu_tag_declare_deps (starpu_tag_t id, unsigned ndeps,...)

- void starpu_tag_declare_deps_array (starpu_tag_t id, unsigned ndeps, starpu_tag_t *array)
- int starpu_tag_wait (starpu_tag_t id)
- int starpu_tag_wait_array (unsigned ntags, starpu_tag_t *id)
- void starpu_tag_restart (starpu_tag_t id)
- void starpu_tag_remove (starpu_tag_t id)
- void starpu_tag_notify_from_apps (starpu_tag_t id)

29.15.1 Detailed Description

29.15.2 Typedef Documentation

29.15.2.1 starpu_tag_t

Define a task logical identifer. It is possible to associate a task with a unique *tag* chosen by the application, and to express dependencies between tasks by the means of those tags. To do so, fill the field starpu_task::tag_id with a tag number (can be arbitrary) and set the field starpu_task::use_tag to 1. If starpu_tag_declare_deps() is called with this tag number, the task will not be started until the tasks which holds the declared dependency tags are completed.

29.15.3 Function Documentation

29.15.3.1 void starpu_task_declare_deps_array (struct **starpu_task** * *task,* unsigned *ndeps,* struct **starpu_task** * *task_array[]*)

Declare task dependencies between a `task` and an array of tasks of length `ndeps`. This function must be called prior to the submission of the task, but it may called after the submission or the execution of the tasks in the array, provided the tasks are still valid (i.e. they were not automatically destroyed). Calling this function on a task that was already submitted or with an entry of `task_array` that is no longer a valid task results in an undefined behaviour. If `ndeps` is 0, no dependency is added. It is possible to call starpu_task_declare_deps_array() several times on the same task, in this case, the dependencies are added. It is possible to have redundancy in the task dependencies.

29.15.3.2 int starpu_task_get_task_succs (struct **starpu_task** * *task,* unsigned *ndeps,* struct **starpu_task** * *task_array[]*)

Fill `task_array` with the list of tasks which are direct children of `task`. `ndeps` is the size of `task_array`. This function returns the number of direct children. `task_array` can be set to `NULL` if `ndeps` is 0, which allows to compute the number of children before allocating an array to store them. This function can only be called if `task` has not completed yet, otherwise the results are undefined. The result may also be outdated if some additional dependency has been added in the meanwhile.

29.15.3.3 int starpu_task_get_task_scheduled_succs (struct **starpu_task** * *task,* unsigned *ndeps,* struct **starpu_task** * *task_array[]*)

Behave like starpu_task_get_task_succs(), except that it only reports tasks which will go through the scheduler, thus avoiding tasks with not codelet, or with explicit placement.

29.15.3.4 void starpu_tag_declare_deps (**starpu_tag_t** *id,* unsigned *ndeps,* ...)

Specify the dependencies of the task identified by tag `id`. The first argument specifies the tag which is configured, the second argument gives the number of tag(s) on which `id` depends. The following arguments are the tags which have to be terminated to unlock the task. This function must be called before the associated task is submitted to StarPU with starpu_task_submit().

WARNING! Use with caution. Because of the variable arity of starpu_tag_declare_deps(), note that the last arguments must be of type starpu_tag_t : constant values typically need to be explicitly casted. Otherwise, due to integer sizes and argument passing on the stack, the C compiler might consider the tag `0x200000003` instead of `0x2` and `0x3` when calling `starpu_tag_declare_deps(0x1, 2, 0x2, 0x3)`. Using the starpu_tag_-declare_deps_array() function avoids this hazard.

```
/*  Tag 0x1 depends on tags 0x32 and 0x52 */
starpu_tag_declare_deps((starpu_tag_t)0x1, 2
     , (starpu_tag_t)0x32, (starpu_tag_t)0x52);
```

29.15.3.5 void starpu_tag_declare_deps (starpu_tag_t *id,* unsigned *ndeps,* starpu_tag_t ∗ *array*)

Similar to starpu_tag_declare_deps(), except that its does not take a variable number of arguments but an `array` of tags of size `ndeps`.

```
/*  Tag 0x1 depends on tags 0x32 and 0x52 */
starpu_tag_t tag_array[2] = {0x32, 0x52};
starpu_tag_declare_deps_array((starpu_tag_t
     )0x1, 2, tag_array);
```

29.15.3.6 int starpu_tag_wait (starpu_tag_t *id*)

Block until the task associated to tag `id` has been executed. This is a blocking call which must therefore not be called within tasks or callbacks, but only from the application directly. It is possible to synchronize with the same tag multiple times, as long as the starpu_tag_remove() function is not called. Note that it is still possible to synchronize with a tag associated to a task for which the strucuture starpu_task was freed (e.g. if the field starpu_task::destroy was enabled).

29.15.3.7 int starpu_tag_wait_array (unsigned *ntags,* starpu_tag_t ∗ *id*)

Similar to starpu_tag_wait() except that it blocks until all the `ntags` tags contained in the array `id` are terminated.

29.15.3.8 void starpu_tag_restart (starpu_tag_t *id*)

Clear the *already notified* status of a tag which is not associated with a task. Before that, calling starpu_tag_notify_-from_apps() again will not notify the successors. After that, the next call to starpu_tag_notify_from_apps() will notify the successors.

29.15.3.9 void starpu_tag_remove (starpu_tag_t *id*)

Release the resources associated to tag `id`. It can be called once the corresponding task has been executed and when there is no other tag that depend on this tag anymore.

29.15.3.10 void starpu_tag_notify_from_apps (starpu_tag_t *id*)

Explicitly unlock tag `id`. It may be useful in the case of applications which execute part of their computation outside StarPU tasks (e.g. third-party libraries). It is also provided as a convenient tool for the programmer, for instance to entirely construct the task DAG before actually giving StarPU the opportunity to execute the tasks. When called several times on the same tag, notification will be done only on first call, thus implementing "OR" dependencies, until the tag is restarted using starpu_tag_restart().

29.16 Implicit Data Dependencies

In this section, we describe how StarPU makes it possible to insert implicit task dependencies in order to enforce sequential data consistency. When this data consistency is enabled on a specific data handle, any data access will appear as sequentially consistent from the application. For instance, if the application submits two tasks that access the same piece of data in read-only mode, and then a third task that access it in write mode, dependencies will be added between the two first tasks and the third one. Implicit data dependencies are also inserted in the case of data accesses from the application.

Functions

- void starpu_data_set_default_sequential_consistency_flag (unsigned flag)
- unsigned starpu_data_get_default_sequential_consistency_flag (void)
- void starpu_data_set_sequential_consistency_flag (starpu_data_handle_t handle, unsigned flag)
- unsigned starpu_data_get_sequential_consistency_flag (starpu_data_handle_t handle)

29.16.1 Detailed Description

In this section, we describe how StarPU makes it possible to insert implicit task dependencies in order to enforce sequential data consistency. When this data consistency is enabled on a specific data handle, any data access will appear as sequentially consistent from the application. For instance, if the application submits two tasks that access the same piece of data in read-only mode, and then a third task that access it in write mode, dependencies will be added between the two first tasks and the third one. Implicit data dependencies are also inserted in the case of data accesses from the application.

29.16.2 Function Documentation

29.16.2.1 void starpu_data_set_default_sequential_consistency_flag (unsigned *flag*)

Set the default sequential consistency flag. If a non-zero value is passed, a sequential data consistency will be enforced for all handles registered after this function call, otherwise it is disabled. By default, StarPU enables sequential data consistency. It is also possible to select the data consistency mode of a specific data handle with the function starpu_data_set_sequential_consistency_flag().

29.16.2.2 unsigned starpu_data_get_default_sequential_consistency_flag (void)

Return the default sequential consistency flag

29.16.2.3 void starpu_data_set_sequential_consistency_flag (**starpu_data_handle_t** *handle,* unsigned *flag*)

Set the data consistency mode associated to a data handle. The consistency mode set using this function has the priority over the default mode which can be set with starpu_data_set_default_sequential_consistency_flag().

29.16.2.4 unsigned starpu_data_get_sequential_consistency_flag (**starpu_data_handle_t** *handle*)

Get the data consistency mode associated to the data handle `handle`

29.17 Performance Model

Data Structures

- struct starpu_perfmodel_device
- struct starpu_perfmodel_arch
- struct starpu_perfmodel
- struct starpu_perfmodel_regression_model

- struct starpu_perfmodel_per_arch
- struct starpu_perfmodel_history_list
- struct starpu_perfmodel_history_entry

Enumerations

- enum starpu_perfmodel_type {
  STARPU_PERFMODEL_INVALID, STARPU_PER_ARCH, STARPU_COMMON, STARPU_HISTORY_BA-
  SED,
  STARPU_REGRESSION_BASED, STARPU_NL_REGRESSION_BASED, STARPU_MULTIPLE_REGRE-
  SSION_BASED }

Functions

- void starpu_perfmodel_init (struct starpu_perfmodel *model)
- void starpu_perfmodel_free_sampling_directories (void)
- int starpu_perfmodel_load_file (const char *filename, struct starpu_perfmodel *model)
- int starpu_perfmodel_load_symbol (const char *symbol, struct starpu_perfmodel *model)
- int starpu_perfmodel_unload_model (struct starpu_perfmodel *model)
- void starpu_perfmodel_debugfilepath (struct starpu_perfmodel *model, struct starpu_perfmodel_arch *arch, char *path, size_t maxlen, unsigned nimpl)
- char * starpu_perfmodel_get_archtype_name (enum starpu_worker_archtype archtype)
- void starpu_perfmodel_get_arch_name (struct starpu_perfmodel_arch *arch, char *archname, size_t maxlen, unsigned nimpl)
- struct starpu_perfmodel_arch * starpu_worker_get_perf_archtype (int workerid, unsigned sched_ctx_id)
- int starpu_perfmodel_list (FILE *output)
- void starpu_perfmodel_directory (FILE *output)
- void starpu_perfmodel_print (struct starpu_perfmodel *model, struct starpu_perfmodel_arch *arch, unsigned nimpl, char *parameter, uint32_t *footprint, FILE *output)
- int starpu_perfmodel_print_all (struct starpu_perfmodel *model, char *arch, char *parameter, uint32_-t *footprint, FILE *output)
- int starpu_perfmodel_print_estimations (struct starpu_perfmodel *model, uint32_t footprint, FILE *output)
- void starpu_bus_print_bandwidth (FILE *f)
- void starpu_bus_print_affinity (FILE *f)
- void starpu_bus_print_filenames (FILE *f)
- void starpu_perfmodel_update_history (struct starpu_perfmodel *model, struct starpu_task *task, struct starpu_perfmodel_arch *arch, unsigned cpuid, unsigned nimpl, double measured)
- double starpu_transfer_bandwidth (unsigned src_node, unsigned dst_node)
- double starpu_transfer_latency (unsigned src_node, unsigned dst_node)
- double starpu_transfer_predict (unsigned src_node, unsigned dst_node, size_t size)
- double starpu_perfmodel_history_based_expected_perf (struct starpu_perfmodel *model, struct starpu_-perfmodel_arch *arch, uint32_t footprint)

29.17.1 Detailed Description

29.17.2 Data Structure Documentation

29.17.2.1 struct starpu_perfmodel_device

todo

Data Fields

enum starpu_-worker_archtype	type	type of the device
int	devid	identifier of the precise device
int	ncores	

29.17.2.2   struct starpu_perfmodel_arch

todo

Data Fields

int	ndevices	number of the devices for the given arch
struct starpu_- perfmodel_- device ∗	devices	list of the devices for the given arch

29.17.2.3   struct starpu_perfmodel

Contain all information about a performance model. At least the type and symbol fields have to be filled when defining a performance model for a codelet. For compatibility, make sure to initialize the whole structure to zero, either by using explicit memset, or by letting the compiler implicitly do it in e.g. static storage case. If not provided, other fields have to be zero.

Data Fields

- enum starpu_perfmodel_type type
- double(∗ cost_function)(struct starpu_task ∗, unsigned nimpl)
- double(∗ arch_cost_function)(struct starpu_task ∗, struct starpu_perfmodel_arch ∗arch, unsigned nimpl)
- size_t(∗ size_base)(struct starpu_task ∗, unsigned nimpl)
- uint32_t(∗ footprint)(struct starpu_task ∗)
- const char ∗ symbol
- unsigned is_loaded
- unsigned benchmarking
- unsigned is_init
- void(∗ parameters)(struct starpu_task ∗task, double ∗parameters)
- const char ∗∗ parameters_names
- unsigned nparameters
- unsigned ∗∗ combinations
- unsigned ncombinations
- starpu_perfmodel_state_t state

29.17.2.3.1   Field Documentation

29.17.2.3.1.1   enum **starpu_perfmodel_type** starpu_perfmodel::type

type of performance model

- STARPU_HISTORY_BASED, STARPU_REGRESSION_BASED, STARPU_NL_REGRESSION_BASED: No other fields needs to be provided, this is purely history-based.

- STARPU_MULTIPLE_REGRESSION_BASED: Need to provide fields starpu_perfmodel::nparameters (number of different parameters), starpu_perfmodel::ncombinations (number of parameters combinations-tuples) and table starpu_perfmodel::combinations which defines exponents of the equation. Function cl_perf_func also needs to define how to extract parameters from the task.

- STARPU_PER_ARCH: either field starpu_perfmodel::arch_cost_function has to be filled with a function that returns the cost in micro-seconds on the arch given as parameter, or field starpu_perfmodel::per_arch has to be filled with functions which return the cost in micro-seconds.

- STARPU_COMMON: field starpu_perfmodel::cost_function has to be filled with a function that returns the cost in micro-seconds on a CPU, timing on other archs will be determined by multiplying by an arch-specific factor.

29.17.2.3.1.2 double(∗ starpu_perfmodel::cost_function)(struct starpu_task ∗, unsigned nimpl)

Used by STARPU_COMMON. Take a task and implementation number, and must return a task duration estimation in micro-seconds.

29.17.2.3.1.3 double(∗ starpu_perfmodel::arch_cost_function)(struct starpu_task ∗, struct starpu_perfmodel_arch ∗arch, unsigned nimpl)

Used by STARPU_COMMON. Take a task, an arch and implementation number, and must return a task duration estimation in micro-seconds on that arch.

29.17.2.3.1.4 size_t(∗ starpu_perfmodel::size_base)(struct starpu_task ∗, unsigned nimpl)

Used by STARPU_HISTORY_BASED, STARPU_REGRESSION_BASED and STARPU_NL_REGRESSION_BASED. If not NULL, take a task and implementation number, and return the size to be used as index to distinguish histories and as a base for regressions.

29.17.2.3.1.5 uint32_t(∗ starpu_perfmodel::footprint)(struct starpu_task ∗)

Used by STARPU_HISTORY_BASED. If not NULL, take a task and return the footprint to be used as index to distinguish histories. The default is to use the starpu_task_data_footprint() function.

29.17.2.3.1.6 const char ∗ starpu_perfmodel::symbol

symbol name for the performance model, which will be used as file name to store the model. It must be set otherwise the model will be ignored.

29.17.2.3.1.7 unsigned starpu_perfmodel::is_loaded

Whether the performance model is already loaded from the disk.

29.17.2.3.1.8 unsigned starpu_perfmodel::benchmarking

todo

29.17.2.3.1.9 unsigned starpu_perfmodel::is_init

todo

29.17.2.3.1.10 void(∗ starpu_perfmodel::parameters)(struct starpu_task ∗task, double ∗parameters)

todo

29.17.2.3.1.11 const char ∗∗ starpu_perfmodel::parameters_names

Names of parameters used for multiple linear regression models (M, N, K)

29.17.2.3.1.12 unsigned starpu_perfmodel::nparameters

Number of parameters used for multiple linear regression models

29.17.2.3.1.13 unsigned ∗∗ starpu_perfmodel::combinations

Table of combinations of parameters (and the exponents) used for multiple linear regression models

29.17.2.3.1.14 unsigned starpu_perfmodel::ncombinations

Number of combination of parameters used for multiple linear regression models

29.17.2.3.1.15 starpu_perfmodel_state_t starpu_perfmodel::state

todo

29.17.2.4   struct starpu_perfmodel_regression_model

todo

Data Fields

double	sumlny	sum of ln(measured)
double	sumlnx	sum of ln(size)
double	sumlnx2	sum of ln(size)^2
unsigned long	minx	minimum size
unsigned long	maxx	maximum size
double	sumlnxlny	sum of ln(size)*ln(measured)
double	alpha	estimated = alpha $*$ size $^\wedge$ beta
double	beta	estimated = alpha $*$ size $^\wedge$ beta
unsigned	valid	whether the linear regression model is valid (i.e. enough measures)
double	a	estimated = a size $^\wedge$b + c
double	b	estimated = a size $^\wedge$b + c
double	c	estimated = a size $^\wedge$b + c
unsigned	nl_valid	whether the non-linear regression model is valid (i.e. enough measures)
unsigned	nsample	number of sample values for non-linear regression
double $*$	coeff	list of computed coefficients for multiple linear regression model
unsigned	ncoeff	number of coefficients for multiple linear regression model
unsigned	multi_valid	whether the multiple linear regression model is valid

29.17.2.5   struct starpu_perfmodel_per_arch

contains information about the performance model of a given arch.

Data Fields

starpu_-perfmodel_per_-arch_cost_-function	cost_function	Used by STARPU_PER_ARCH, must point to functions which take a task, the target arch and implementation number (as mere conveniency, since the array is already indexed by these), and must return a task duration estimation in micro-seconds.
starpu_-perfmodel_per_-arch_size_base	size_base	Same as in structure starpu_perfmodel, but per-arch, in case it depends on the architecture-specific implementation.
struct starpu_-perfmodel_-history_table $*$	history	The history of performance measurements.
struct starpu_-perfmodel_-history_list $*$	list	Used by STARPU_HISTORY_BASED, STARPU_NL_REGRESSION_B-ASED and STARPU_MULTIPLE_REGRESSION_BASED, records all execution history measures.
struct starpu_-perfmodel_-regression_-model	regression	Used by STARPU_REGRESSION_BASED, STARPU_NL_REGRESS-ION_BASED and STARPU_MULTIPLE_REGRESSION_BASED, contains the estimated factors of the regression.
char	debug_path	

29.17.2.6 struct starpu_perfmodel_history_list

todo

Data Fields

struct starpu_-perfmodel_-history_list *	next	todo
struct starpu_-perfmodel_-history_entry *	entry	todo

29.17.2.7 struct starpu_perfmodel_history_entry

todo

Data Fields

double	mean	mean_n = 1/n sum
double	deviation	n dev_n = sum2 - 1/n (sum)^2
double	sum	sum of samples (in µs)
double	sum2	sum of samples^2
unsigned	nsample	number of samples
unsigned	nerror	
uint32_t	footprint	data footprint
size_t	size	in bytes
double	flops	Provided by the application
double	duration	
starpu_tag_t	tag	
double *	parameters	

29.17.3 Enumeration Type Documentation

29.17.3.1 enum starpu_perfmodel_type

TODO

Enumerator:

STARPU_PERFMODEL_INVALID todo

STARPU_PER_ARCH Application-provided per-arch cost model function

STARPU_COMMON Application-provided common cost model function, with per-arch factor

STARPU_HISTORY_BASED Automatic history-based cost model

STARPU_REGRESSION_BASED Automatic linear regression-based cost model (alpha * size $^\wedge$ beta)

STARPU_NL_REGRESSION_BASED Automatic non-linear regression-based cost model (a * size $^\wedge$ b + c)

STARPU_MULTIPLE_REGRESSION_BASED Automatic multiple linear regression-based cost model. Application provides parameters, their combinations and exponents.

29.17.4 Function Documentation

29.17.4.1 void starpu_perfmodel_init (struct starpu_perfmodel ∗ _model_)

todo

29.17.4.2 void starpu_perfmodel_free_sampling_directories (void)

Free internal memory used for sampling directory management. It should only be called by an application which is not calling starpu_shutdown() as this function already calls it. See for example `tools/starpu_perfmodel_-display.c`.

29.17.4.3 int starpu_perfmodel_load_file (const char ∗ _filename_, struct starpu_perfmodel ∗ _model_)

Load the performance model found in the file named `filename`. `model` has to be completely zero, and will be filled with the information stored in the given file.

29.17.4.4 int starpu_perfmodel_load_symbol (const char ∗ _symbol_, struct starpu_perfmodel ∗ _model_)

Load a given performance model. `model` has to be completely zero, and will be filled with the information stored in `$STARPU_HOME/.starpu`. The function is intended to be used by external tools that want to read the performance model files.

29.17.4.5 int starpu_perfmodel_unload_model (struct starpu_perfmodel ∗ _model_)

Unload `model` which has been previously loaded through the function starpu_perfmodel_load_symbol()

29.17.4.6 void starpu_perfmodel_debugfilepath (struct starpu_perfmodel ∗ _model_, struct starpu_perfmodel_arch ∗ _arch_, char ∗ _path_, size_t _maxlen_, unsigned _nimpl_)

Return the path to the debugging information for the performance model.

29.17.4.7 char ∗ starpu_perfmodel_get_archtype_name (enum starpu_worker_archtype _archtype_)

todo

29.17.4.8 void starpu_perfmodel_get_arch_name (struct starpu_perfmodel_arch ∗ _arch_, char ∗ _archname_, size_t _maxlen_, unsigned _nimpl_)

Return the architecture name for `arch`

29.17.4.9 struct starpu_perfmodel_arch ∗ starpu_worker_get_perf_archtype (int _workerid_, unsigned _sched_ctx_id_)
          `[read]`

Return the architecture type of the worker `workerid`.

29.17.4.10 int starpu_perfmodel_list (FILE ∗ _output_)

Print a list of all performance models on `output`

29.17.4.11 void starpu_perfmodel_directory (FILE ∗ _output_)

Print the directory name storing performance models on `output`

29.17.4.12 void starpu_perfmodel_print (struct **starpu_perfmodel** ∗ *model,* struct **starpu_perfmodel_arch** ∗ *arch,* unsigned *nimpl,* char ∗ *parameter,* uint32_t ∗ *footprint,* FILE ∗ *output*)

todo

29.17.4.13 int starpu_perfmodel_print_all (struct **starpu_perfmodel** ∗ *model,* char ∗ *arch,* char ∗ *parameter,* uint32_t ∗ *footprint,* FILE ∗ *output*)

todo

29.17.4.14 int starpu_perfmodel_print_estimations (struct **starpu_perfmodel** ∗ *model,* uint32_t *footprint,* FILE ∗ *output*)

todo

29.17.4.15 void starpu_bus_print_bandwidth (FILE ∗ *f*)

Print a matrix of bus bandwidths on f.

29.17.4.16 void starpu_bus_print_affinity (FILE ∗ *f*)

Print the affinity devices on f.

29.17.4.17 void starpu_bus_print_filenames (FILE ∗ *f*)

Print on f the name of the files containing the matrix of bus bandwidths, the affinity devices and the latency.

29.17.4.18 void starpu_perfmodel_update_history (struct **starpu_perfmodel** ∗ *model,* struct **starpu_task** ∗ *task,* struct **starpu_perfmodel_arch** ∗ *arch,* unsigned *cpuid,* unsigned *nimpl,* double *measured*)

Feed the performance model model with an explicit measurement measured (in µs), in addition to measurements done by StarPU itself. This can be useful when the application already has an existing set of measurements done in good conditions, that StarPU could benefit from instead of doing on-line measurements. An example of use can be seen in Performance Model Example.

29.17.4.19 double starpu_transfer_bandwidth (unsigned *src_node,* unsigned *dst_node*)

Return the bandwidth of data transfer between two memory nodes

29.17.4.20 double starpu_transfer_latency (unsigned *src_node,* unsigned *dst_node*)

Return the latency of data transfer between two memory nodes

29.17.4.21 double starpu_transfer_predict (unsigned *src_node,* unsigned *dst_node,* size_t *size*)

Return the estimated time to transfer a given size between two memory nodes.

29.17.4.22 double starpu_perfmodel_history_based_expected_perf (struct **starpu_perfmodel** ∗ *model,* struct **starpu_perfmodel_arch** ∗ *arch,* uint32_t *footprint*)

Return the estimated time of a task with the given model and the given footprint.

29.18 Profiling

Data Structures

- struct starpu_profiling_task_info
- struct starpu_profiling_worker_info
- struct starpu_profiling_bus_info

Macros

- #define STARPU_PROFILING_DISABLE
- #define STARPU_PROFILING_ENABLE

Functions

- int starpu_profiling_status_set (int status)
- int starpu_profiling_status_get (void)
- void starpu_profiling_init (void)
- void starpu_profiling_set_id (int new_id)
- int starpu_profiling_worker_get_info (int workerid, struct starpu_profiling_worker_info *worker_info)
- int starpu_bus_get_profiling_info (int busid, struct starpu_profiling_bus_info *bus_info)
- int starpu_bus_get_count (void)
- int starpu_bus_get_id (int src, int dst)
- int starpu_bus_get_src (int busid)
- int starpu_bus_get_dst (int busid)
- double starpu_timing_timespec_delay_us (struct timespec *start, struct timespec *end)
- double starpu_timing_timespec_to_us (struct timespec *ts)
- void starpu_profiling_bus_helper_display_summary (void)
- void starpu_profiling_worker_helper_display_summary (void)
- void starpu_data_display_memory_stats ()

29.18.1 Detailed Description

29.18.2 Data Structure Documentation

29.18.2.1 struct starpu_profiling_task_info

This structure contains information about the execution of a task. It is accessible from the field starpu_task::profiling_info if profiling was enabled.

Data Fields

struct timespec	submit_time	Date of task submission (relative to the initialization of StarPU).
struct timespec	push_start_time	Time when the task was submitted to the scheduler.
struct timespec	push_end_time	Time when the scheduler finished with the task submission.
struct timespec	pop_start_time	Time when the scheduler started to be requested for a task, and eventually gave that task.
struct timespec	pop_end_time	Time when the scheduler finished providing the task for execution.
struct timespec	acquire_data_-start_time	Time when the worker started fetching input data.
struct timespec	acquire_data_-end_time	Time when the worker finished fetching input data.
struct timespec	start_time	Date of task execution beginning (relative to the initialization of StarPU).
struct timespec	end_time	Date of task execution termination (relative to the initialization of StarPU).

struct timespec	release_data_-start_time	Time when the worker started releasing data.
struct timespec	release_data_-end_time	Time when the worker finished releasing data.
struct timespec	callback_start_-time	Time when the worker started the application callback for the task.
struct timespec	callback_end_-time	Time when the worker finished the application callback for the task.
int	workerid	Identifier of the worker which has executed the task.
uint64_t	used_cycles	Number of cycles used by the task, only available in the MoviSim
uint64_t	stall_cycles	Number of cycles stalled within the task, only available in the MoviSim
double	energy_-consumed	Energy consumed by the task, only available in the MoviSim

29.18.2.2 struct starpu_profiling_worker_info

This structure contains the profiling information associated to a worker. The timing is provided since the previous call to starpu_profiling_worker_get_info()

Data Fields

struct timespec	start_time	Starting date for the reported profiling measurements.
struct timespec	total_time	Duration of the profiling measurement interval.
struct timespec	executing_time	Time spent by the worker to execute tasks during the profiling measurement interval.
struct timespec	sleeping_time	Time spent idling by the worker during the profiling measurement interval.
int	executed_tasks	Number of tasks executed by the worker during the profiling measurement interval.
uint64_t	used_cycles	Number of cycles used by the worker, only available in the MoviSim
uint64_t	stall_cycles	Number of cycles stalled within the worker, only available in the MoviSim
double	energy_-consumed	Energy consumed by the worker, only available in the MoviSim
double	flops	

29.18.2.3 struct starpu_profiling_bus_info

todo

Data Fields

struct timespec	start_time	Time of bus profiling startup.
struct timespec	total_time	Total time of bus profiling.
int long long	transferred_-bytes	Number of bytes transferred during profiling.
int	transfer_count	Number of transfers during profiling.

29.18.3 Macro Definition Documentation

29.18.3.1 STARPU_PROFILING_DISABLE

Used when calling the function starpu_profiling_status_set() to disable profiling.

29.18.3.2 STARPU_PROFILING_ENABLE

Used when calling the function starpu_profiling_status_set() to enable profiling.

29.18.4 Function Documentation

29.18.4.1 int starpu_profiling_status_set (int *status*)

Set the profiling status. Profiling is activated by passing STARPU_PROFILING_ENABLE in `status`. Passing STARPU_PROFILING_DISABLE disables profiling. Calling this function resets all profiling measurements. When profiling is enabled, the field starpu_task::profiling_info points to a valid structure starpu_profiling_task_info containing information about the execution of the task. Negative return values indicate an error, otherwise the previous status is returned.

29.18.4.2 int starpu_profiling_status_get (void)

Return the current profiling status or a negative value in case there was an error.

29.18.4.3 void starpu_profiling_init (void)

Reset performance counters and enable profiling if the environment variable STARPU_PROFILING is set to a positive value.

29.18.4.4 void starpu_profiling_set_id (int *new_id*)

Set the ID used for profiling trace filename. HAS to be called before starpu_init().

29.18.4.5 int starpu_profiling_worker_get_info (int *workerid,* struct **starpu_profiling_worker_info** * *worker_info*)

Get the profiling info associated to the worker identified by `workerid`, and reset the profiling measurements. If the argument `worker_info` is `NULL`, only reset the counters associated to worker `workerid`. Upon successful completion, this function returns 0. Otherwise, a negative value is returned.

29.18.4.6 int starpu_bus_get_profiling_info (int *busid,* struct **starpu_profiling_bus_info** * *bus_info*)

todo

29.18.4.7 int starpu_bus_get_count (void)

Return the number of buses in the machine

29.18.4.8 int starpu_bus_get_id (int *src,* int *dst*)

Return the identifier of the bus between src and dst

29.18.4.9 int starpu_bus_get_src (int *busid*)

Return the source point of bus busid

29.18.4.10 int starpu_bus_get_dst (int *busid*)

Return the destination point of bus `busid`

29.18.4.11 double starpu_timing_timespec_delay_us (struct timespec ∗ *start,* struct timespec ∗ *end*)

Return the time elapsed between `start` and `end` in microseconds.

29.18.4.12 double starpu_timing_timespec_to_us (struct timespec ∗ *ts*)

Convert the given timespec `ts` into microseconds

29.18.4.13 void starpu_profiling_bus_helper_display_summary (void)

Display statistics about the bus on `stderr`. if the environment variable STARPU_BUS_STATS is defined. The function is called automatically by starpu_shutdown().

29.18.4.14 void starpu_profiling_worker_helper_display_summary (void)

Displays statistic about the workers on `stderr` if the environment variable STARPU_WORKER_STATS is defined. The function is called automatically by starpu_shutdown().

29.18.4.15 void starpu_data_display_memory_stats ( )

Display statistics about the current data handles registered within StarPU. StarPU must have been configured with the configure option --enable-memory-stats (see Memory Feedback).

29.19   Theoretical Lower Bound on Execution Time

Compute theoretical upper computation efficiency bound corresponding to some actual execution.

Functions

- void starpu_bound_start (int deps, int prio)
- void starpu_bound_stop (void)
- void starpu_bound_print_dot (FILE ∗output)
- void starpu_bound_compute (double ∗res, double ∗integer_res, int integer)
- void starpu_bound_print_lp (FILE ∗output)
- void starpu_bound_print_mps (FILE ∗output)
- void starpu_bound_print (FILE ∗output, int integer)

29.19.1   Detailed Description

Compute theoretical upper computation efficiency bound corresponding to some actual execution.

29.19.2 Function Documentation

29.19.2.1 void starpu_bound_start (int *deps,* int *prio*)

Start recording tasks (resets stats). `deps` tells whether dependencies should be recorded too (this is quite expensive)

29.19.2.2 void starpu_bound_stop (void)

Stop recording tasks

29.19.2.3 void starpu_bound_print_dot (FILE * *output*)

Emit the DAG that was recorded on `output`.

29.19.2.4 void starpu_bound_compute (double * *res,* double * *integer_res,* int *integer*)

Get theoretical upper bound (in ms) (needs glpk support detected by configure script). It returns 0 if some performance models are not calibrated.

29.19.2.5 void starpu_bound_print_lp (FILE * *output*)

Emit the Linear Programming system on `output` for the recorded tasks, in the lp format

29.19.2.6 void starpu_bound_print_mps (FILE * *output*)

Emit the Linear Programming system on `output` for the recorded tasks, in the mps format

29.19.2.7 void starpu_bound_print (FILE * *output,* int *integer*)

Emit on `output` the statistics of actual execution vs theoretical upper bound. `integer` permits to choose between integer solving (which takes a long time but is correct), and relaxed solving (which provides an approximate solution).

29.20 CUDA Extensions

Macros

- #define STARPU_USE_CUDA
- #define STARPU_MAXCUDADEVS
- #define STARPU_CUDA_REPORT_ERROR(status)
- #define STARPU_CUBLAS_REPORT_ERROR(status)

Functions

- cudaStream_t starpu_cuda_get_local_stream (void)
- struct cudaDeviceProp * starpu_cuda_get_device_properties (unsigned workerid)
- void starpu_cuda_report_error (const char *func, const char *file, int line, cudaError_t status)
- int starpu_cuda_copy_async_sync (void *src_ptr, unsigned src_node, void *dst_ptr, unsigned dst_node, size_t ssize, cudaStream_t stream, enum cudaMemcpyKind kind)

- void starpu_cuda_set_device (unsigned devid)
- void starpu_cublas_init (void)
- void starpu_cublas_set_stream (void)
- void starpu_cublas_shutdown (void)
- void starpu_cublas_report_error (const char ∗func, const char ∗file, int line, int status)

29.20.1 Detailed Description

29.20.2 Macro Definition Documentation

29.20.2.1 #define STARPU_USE_CUDA

This macro is defined when StarPU has been installed with CUDA support. It should be used in your code to detect the availability of CUDA as shown in Full source code for the 'Scaling a Vector' example.

29.20.2.2 #define STARPU_MAXCUDADEVS

This macro defines the maximum number of CUDA devices that are supported by StarPU.

29.20.2.3 #define STARPU_CUDA_REPORT_ERROR(*status*)

Calls starpu_cuda_report_error(), passing the current function, file and line position.

29.20.2.4 #define STARPU_CUBLAS_REPORT_ERROR(*status*)

Calls starpu_cublas_report_error(), passing the current function, file and line position.

29.20.3 Function Documentation

29.20.3.1 cudaStream_t starpu_cuda_get_local_stream (void)

Return the current worker's CUDA stream. StarPU provides a stream for every CUDA device controlled by StarPU. This function is only provided for convenience so that programmers can easily use asynchronous operations within codelets without having to create a stream by hand. Note that the application is not forced to use the stream provided by starpu_cuda_get_local_stream() and may also create its own streams. Synchronizing with cuda-ThreadSynchronize() is allowed, but will reduce the likelihood of having all transfers overlapped.

29.20.3.2 const struct cudaDeviceProp ∗ starpu_cuda_get_device_properties (unsigned *workerid*) [read]

Return a pointer to device properties for worker workerid (assumed to be a CUDA worker).

29.20.3.3 void starpu_cuda_report_error (const char ∗ *func*, const char ∗ *file*, int *line*, cudaError_t *status*)

Report a CUDA error.

29.20.3.4 int starpu_cuda_copy_async_sync (void ∗ *src_ptr*, unsigned *src_node*, void ∗ *dst_ptr*, unsigned *dst_node*, size_t *ssize*, cudaStream_t *stream*, enum cudaMemcpyKind *kind*)

Copy ssize bytes from the pointer src_ptr on src_node to the pointer dst_ptr on dst_node. The function first tries to copy the data asynchronous (unless stream is NULL). If the asynchronous copy fails or if stream is NULL, it copies the data synchronously. The function returns -EAGAIN if the asynchronous launch was successfull. It returns 0 if the synchronous copy was successful, or fails otherwise.

29.20.3.5   void starpu_cuda_set_device (unsigned *devid*)

Calls `cudaSetDevice(devid)` or `cudaGLSetGLDevice(devid)`, according to whether `devid` is among the field starpu_conf::cuda_opengl_interoperability.

29.20.3.6   void starpu_cublas_init (void)

This function initializes CUBLAS on every CUDA device. The CUBLAS library must be initialized prior to any CUB-LAS call. Calling starpu_cublas_init() will initialize CUBLAS on every CUDA device controlled by StarPU. This call blocks until CUBLAS has been properly initialized on every device.

29.20.3.7   void starpu_cublas_set_stream (void)

This function sets the proper CUBLAS stream for CUBLAS v1. This must be called from the CUDA codelet before calling CUBLAS v1 kernels, so that they are queued on the proper CUDA stream. When using one thread per CUDA worker, this function does not do anything since the CUBLAS stream does not change, and is set once by starpu_cublas_init().

29.20.3.8   void starpu_cublas_shutdown (void)

This function synchronously deinitializes the CUBLAS library on every CUDA device.

29.20.3.9   void starpu_cublas_report_error (const char * *func,* const char * *file,* int *line,* int *status*)

Report a cublas error.

29.21   OpenCL Extensions

Data Structures

- struct starpu_opencl_program

Macros

- #define STARPU_USE_OPENCL
- #define STARPU_MAXOPENCLDEVS
- #define STARPU_OPENCL_DATADIR

Writing OpenCL kernels

- void starpu_opencl_get_context (int devid, cl_context *context)
- void starpu_opencl_get_device (int devid, cl_device_id *device)
- void starpu_opencl_get_queue (int devid, cl_command_queue *queue)
- void starpu_opencl_get_current_context (cl_context *context)
- void starpu_opencl_get_current_queue (cl_command_queue *queue)
- int starpu_opencl_set_kernel_args (cl_int *err, cl_kernel *kernel,...)

Compiling OpenCL kernels

Source codes for OpenCL kernels can be stored in a file or in a string. StarPU provides functions to build the program executable for each available OpenCL device as a cl_program object. This program executable can then be loaded within a specific queue as explained in the next section. These are only helpers, Applications can also fill a starpu_opencl_program array by hand for more advanced use (e.g. different programs on the different OpenCL devices, for relocation purpose for instance).

- int starpu_opencl_load_opencl_from_file (const char *source_file_name, struct starpu_opencl_program *opencl_programs, const char *build_options)
- int starpu_opencl_load_opencl_from_string (const char *opencl_program_source, struct starpu_opencl_program *opencl_programs, const char *build_options)
- int starpu_opencl_unload_opencl (struct starpu_opencl_program *opencl_programs)
- void starpu_opencl_load_program_source (const char *source_file_name, char *located_file_name, char *located_dir_name, char *opencl_program_source)
- void starpu_opencl_load_program_source_malloc (const char *source_file_name, char **located_file_name, char **located_dir_name, char **opencl_program_source)
- int starpu_opencl_compile_opencl_from_file (const char *source_file_name, const char *build_options)
- int starpu_opencl_compile_opencl_from_string (const char *opencl_program_source, const char *file_name, const char *build_options)
- int starpu_opencl_load_binary_opencl (const char *kernel_id, struct starpu_opencl_program *opencl_programs)

Loading OpenCL kernels

- int starpu_opencl_load_kernel (cl_kernel *kernel, cl_command_queue *queue, struct starpu_opencl_program *opencl_programs, const char *kernel_name, int devid)
- int starpu_opencl_release_kernel (cl_kernel kernel)

OpenCL statistics

- int starpu_opencl_collect_stats (cl_event event)

OpenCL utilities

- #define STARPU_OPENCL_DISPLAY_ERROR(status)
- #define STARPU_OPENCL_REPORT_ERROR(status)
- #define STARPU_OPENCL_REPORT_ERROR_WITH_MSG(msg, status)
- const char * starpu_opencl_error_string (cl_int status)
- void starpu_opencl_display_error (const char *func, const char *file, int line, const char *msg, cl_int status)
- static __starpu_inline void starpu_opencl_report_error (const char *func, const char *file, int line, const char *msg, cl_int status)
- cl_int starpu_opencl_allocate_memory (int devid, cl_mem *addr, size_t size, cl_mem_flags flags)
- cl_int starpu_opencl_copy_ram_to_opencl (void *ptr, unsigned src_node, cl_mem buffer, unsigned dst_node, size_t size, size_t offset, cl_event *event, int *ret)
- cl_int starpu_opencl_copy_opencl_to_ram (cl_mem buffer, unsigned src_node, void *ptr, unsigned dst_node, size_t size, size_t offset, cl_event *event, int *ret)
- cl_int starpu_opencl_copy_opencl_to_opencl (cl_mem src, unsigned src_node, size_t src_offset, cl_mem dst, unsigned dst_node, size_t dst_offset, size_t size, cl_event *event, int *ret)
- cl_int starpu_opencl_copy_async_sync (uintptr_t src, size_t src_offset, unsigned src_node, uintptr_t dst, size_t dst_offset, unsigned dst_node, size_t size, cl_event *event)

29.21.1   Detailed Description

29.21.2   Data Structure Documentation

29.21.2.1   struct starpu_opencl_program

Store the OpenCL programs as compiled for the different OpenCL devices.

Data Fields

cl_program	programs	Store each program for each OpenCL device.

29.21.3   Macro Definition Documentation

29.21.3.1   #define STARPU_USE_OPENCL

Defined when StarPU has been installed with OpenCL support. It should be used in your code to detect the availability of OpenCL as shown in Full source code for the 'Scaling a Vector' example.

29.21.3.2   #define STARPU_MAXOPENCLDEVS

Define the maximum number of OpenCL devices that are supported by StarPU.

29.21.3.3   #define STARPU_OPENCL_DATADIR

Define the directory in which the OpenCL codelets of the applications provided with StarPU have been installed.

29.21.3.4   #define STARPU_OPENCL_DISPLAY_ERROR(*status*)

Call the function starpu_opencl_display_error() with the error `status`, the current function name, current file and line number, and a empty message.

29.21.3.5   #define STARPU_OPENCL_REPORT_ERROR(*status*)

Call the function starpu_opencl_report_error() with the error `status`, the current function name, current file and line number, and a empty message.

29.21.3.6   #define STARPU_OPENCL_REPORT_ERROR_WITH_MSG(*msg, status*)

Call the function starpu_opencl_report_error() with `msg` and `status`, the current function name, current file and line number.

29.21.4   Function Documentation

29.21.4.1   void starpu_opencl_get_context (int *devid*, cl_context * *context*)

Return the OpenCL context of the device designated by `devid` in `context`.

29.21.4.2   void starpu_opencl_get_device (int *devid*, cl_device_id * *device*)

Return the cl_device_id corresponding to `devid` in `device`.

29.21.4.3 void starpu_opencl_get_queue (int *devid,* cl_command_queue * *queue*)

Return the command queue of the device designated by `devid` into `queue`.

29.21.4.4 void starpu_opencl_get_current_context (cl_context * *context*)

Return the context of the current worker.

29.21.4.5 void starpu_opencl_get_current_queue (cl_command_queue * *queue*)

Return the computation kernel command queue of the current worker.

29.21.4.6 int starpu_opencl_set_kernel_args (cl_int * *err,* cl_kernel * *kernel,* ...)

Set the arguments of a given kernel. The list of arguments must be given as (`size_t size_of_the_-`
`argument, cl_mem * pointer_to_the_argument`). The last argument must be 0. Return the number
of arguments that were successfully set. In case of failure, return the id of the argument that could not be set and
`err` is set to the error returned by OpenCL. Otherwise, return the number of arguments that were set.

Here an example:

```
int n;
cl_int err;
cl_kernel kernel;
n = starpu_opencl_set_kernel_args(&err, 2, &kernel
     ,
                               sizeof(foo), &foo,
                               sizeof(bar), &bar,
                               0);
if (n != 2)
   fprintf(stderr, "Error : %d\n", err);
```

29.21.4.7 int starpu_opencl_load_opencl_from_file (const char * *source_file_name,* struct **starpu_opencl_program** *
opencl_programs, const char * *build_options*)

Compile an OpenCL source code stored in a file.

29.21.4.8 int starpu_opencl_load_opencl_from_string (const char * *opencl_program_source,* struct
starpu_opencl_program * *opencl_programs,* const char * *build_options*)

Compile an OpenCL source code stored in a string.

29.21.4.9 int starpu_opencl_unload_opencl (struct **starpu_opencl_program** * *opencl_programs*)

Unload an OpenCL compiled code.

29.21.4.10 void starpu_opencl_load_program_source (const char * *source_file_name,* char * *located_file_name,* char *
located_dir_name, char * *opencl_program_source*)

Store the contents of the file `source_file_name` in the buffer `opencl_program_source`. The file
`source_file_name` can be located in the current directory, or in the directory specified by the environment
variable STARPU_OPENCL_PROGRAM_DIR, or in the directory `share/starpu/opencl` of the installation
directory of StarPU, or in the source directory of StarPU. When the file is found, `located_file_name` is the
full name of the file as it has been located on the system, `located_dir_name` the directory where it has been
located. Otherwise, they are both set to the empty string.

29.21.4.11 void starpu_opencl_load_program_source_malloc (const char * *source_file_name,* char ** *located_file_name,* char ** *located_dir_name,* char ** *opencl_program_source*)

Similar to function starpu_opencl_load_program_source() but allocate the buffers `located_file_name`, `located_dir_name` and `opencl_program_source`.

29.21.4.12 int starpu_opencl_compile_opencl_from_file (const char * *source_file_name,* const char * *build_options*)

Compile the OpenCL kernel stored in the file `source_file_name` with the given options `build_options` and store the result in the directory `$STARPU_HOME/.starpu/opencl` with the same filename as `source_file_name`. The compilation is done for every OpenCL device, and the filename is suffixed with the vendor id and the device id of the OpenCL device.

29.21.4.13 int starpu_opencl_compile_opencl_from_string (const char * *opencl_program_source,* const char * *file_name,* const char * *build_options*)

Compile the OpenCL kernel in the string `opencl_program_source` with the given options `build_options` and store the result in the directory `$STARPU_HOME/.starpu/opencl` with the filename `file_name`. The compilation is done for every OpenCL device, and the filename is suffixed with the vendor id and the device id of the OpenCL device.

29.21.4.14 int starpu_opencl_load_binary_opencl (const char * *kernel_id,* struct **starpu_opencl_program** * *opencl_programs*)

Compile the binary OpenCL kernel identified with `kernel_id`. For every OpenCL device, the binary Open-CL kernel will be loaded from the file `$STARPU_HOME/.starpu/opencl/<kernel_id>.<device_-type>.vendor_id_<vendor_id>_device_id_<device_id>`.

29.21.4.15 int starpu_opencl_load_kernel (cl_kernel * *kernel,* cl_command_queue * *queue,* struct **starpu_opencl_program** * *opencl_programs,* const char * *kernel_name,* int *devid*)

Create a kernel `kernel` for device `devid`, on its computation command queue returned in `queue`, using program `opencl_programs` and name `kernel_name`.

29.21.4.16 int starpu_opencl_release_kernel (cl_kernel *kernel*)

Release the given `kernel`, to be called after kernel execution.

29.21.4.17 int starpu_opencl_collect_stats (cl_event *event*)

Collect statistics on a kernel execution. After termination of the kernels, the OpenCL codelet should call this function with the event returned by `clEnqueueNDRangeKernel()`, to let StarPU collect statistics about the kernel execution (used cycles, consumed energy).

29.21.4.18 const char * starpu_opencl_error_string (cl_int *status*)

Return the error message in English corresponding to `status`, an OpenCL error code.

29.21.4.19 void starpu_opencl_display_error (const char * *func,* const char * *file,* int *line,* const char * *msg,* cl_int *status*)

Given a valid error status, print the corresponding error message on `stdout`, along with the function name `func`, the filename `file`, the line number `line` and the message `msg`.

29.21.4.20 void starpu_opencl_report_error (const char ∗ *func,* const char ∗ *file,* int *line,* const char ∗ *msg,* cl_int *status*) [static]

Call the function starpu_opencl_display_error() and abort.

29.21.4.21 cl_int starpu_opencl_allocate_memory (int *devid,* cl_mem ∗ *addr,* size_t *size,* cl_mem_flags *flags*)

Allocate `size` bytes of memory, stored in `addr`. `flags` must be a valid combination of `cl_mem_flags` values.

29.21.4.22 cl_int starpu_opencl_copy_ram_to_opencl (void ∗ *ptr,* unsigned *src_node,* cl_mem *buffer,* unsigned *dst_node,* size_t *size,* size_t *offset,* cl_event ∗ *event,* int ∗ *ret*)

Copy `size` bytes from the given `ptr` on RAM `src_node` to the given `buffer` on OpenCL `dst_node`. `offset` is the offset, in bytes, in `buffer`. if `event` is `NULL`, the copy is synchronous, i.e the queue is synchronised before returning. If not `NULL`, `event` can be used after the call to wait for this particular copy to complete. This function returns `CL_SUCCESS` if the copy was successful, or a valid OpenCL error code otherwise. The integer pointed to by `ret` is set to `-EAGAIN` if the asynchronous launch was successful, or to 0 if `event` was `NULL`.

29.21.4.23 cl_int starpu_opencl_copy_opencl_to_ram (cl_mem *buffer,* unsigned *src_node,* void ∗ *ptr,* unsigned *dst_node,* size_t *size,* size_t *offset,* cl_event ∗ *event,* int ∗ *ret*)

Copy `size` bytes asynchronously from the given `buffer` on OpenCL `src_node` to the given `ptr` on RAM `dst_node`. `offset` is the offset, in bytes, in `buffer`. if `event` is `NULL`, the copy is synchronous, i.e the queue is synchronised before returning. If not `NULL`, `event` can be used after the call to wait for this particular copy to complete. This function returns `CL_SUCCESS` if the copy was successful, or a valid OpenCL error code otherwise. The integer pointed to by `ret` is set to `-EAGAIN` if the asynchronous launch was successful, or to 0 if `event` was `NULL`.

29.21.4.24 cl_int starpu_opencl_copy_opencl_to_opencl (cl_mem *src,* unsigned *src_node,* size_t *src_offset,* cl_mem *dst,* unsigned *dst_node,* size_t *dst_offset,* size_t *size,* cl_event ∗ *event,* int ∗ *ret*)

Copy `size` bytes asynchronously from byte offset `src_offset` of `src` on OpenCL `src_node` to byte offset `dst_offset` of `dst` on OpenCL `dst_node`. if `event` is `NULL`, the copy is synchronous, i.e. the queue is synchronised before returning. If not `NULL`, `event` can be used after the call to wait for this particular copy to complete. This function returns `CL_SUCCESS` if the copy was successful, or a valid OpenCL error code otherwise. The integer pointed to by `ret` is set to `-EAGAIN` if the asynchronous launch was successful, or to 0 if `event` was `NULL`.

29.21.4.25 cl_int starpu_opencl_copy_async_sync (uintptr_t *src,* size_t *src_offset,* unsigned *src_node,* uintptr_t *dst,* size_t *dst_offset,* unsigned *dst_node,* size_t *size,* cl_event ∗ *event*)

Copy `size` bytes from byte offset `src_offset` of `src` on `src_node` to byte offset `dst_offset` of `dst` on `dst_node`. if `event` is `NULL`, the copy is synchronous, i.e. the queue is synchronised before returning. If not `NULL`, `event` can be used after the call to wait for this particular copy to complete. The function returns `-EAGAIN` if the asynchronous launch was successfull. It returns 0 if the synchronous copy was successful, or fails otherwise.

29.22 OpenMP Runtime Support

This section describes the interface provided for implementing OpenMP runtimes on top of StarPU.

Data Structures

- struct starpu_omp_lock_t
- struct starpu_omp_nest_lock_t
- struct starpu_omp_parallel_region_attr
- struct starpu_omp_task_region_attr

Enumerations

- enum starpu_omp_sched_value {
  starpu_omp_sched_undefined, starpu_omp_sched_static, starpu_omp_sched_dynamic, starpu_omp_-
  sched_guided,
  starpu_omp_sched_auto, starpu_omp_sched_runtime }
- enum starpu_omp_proc_bind_value {
  starpu_omp_proc_bind_undefined, starpu_omp_proc_bind_false, starpu_omp_proc_bind_true, starpu_omp-
  _proc_bind_master,
  starpu_omp_proc_bind_close, starpu_omp_proc_bind_spread }

Initialisation

- #define STARPU_OPENMP
- int starpu_omp_init (void) __STARPU_OMP_NOTHROW
- void starpu_omp_shutdown (void) __STARPU_OMP_NOTHROW

Parallel

- void starpu_omp_parallel_region (const struct starpu_omp_parallel_region_attr *attr) __STARPU_OMP_N-
  OTHROW
- void starpu_omp_master (void(*f)(void *arg), void *arg) __STARPU_OMP_NOTHROW
- int starpu_omp_master_inline (void) __STARPU_OMP_NOTHROW

Synchronization

- void starpu_omp_barrier (void) __STARPU_OMP_NOTHROW
- void starpu_omp_critical (void(*f)(void *arg), void *arg, const char *name) __STARPU_OMP_NOTHROW
- void starpu_omp_critical_inline_begin (const char *name) __STARPU_OMP_NOTHROW
- void starpu_omp_critical_inline_end (const char *name) __STARPU_OMP_NOTHROW

Worksharing

- void starpu_omp_single (void(*f)(void *arg), void *arg, int nowait) __STARPU_OMP_NOTHROW
- int starpu_omp_single_inline (void) __STARPU_OMP_NOTHROW
- void starpu_omp_single_copyprivate (void(*f)(void *arg, void *data, unsigned long long data_size), void *arg,
  void *data, unsigned long long data_size) __STARPU_OMP_NOTHROW
- void * starpu_omp_single_copyprivate_inline_begin (void *data) __STARPU_OMP_NOTHROW
- void starpu_omp_single_copyprivate_inline_end (void) __STARPU_OMP_NOTHROW
- void starpu_omp_for (void(*f)(unsigned long long _first_i, unsigned long long _nb_i, void *arg), void *arg,
  unsigned long long nb_iterations, unsigned long long chunk, int schedule, int ordered, int nowait) __STARP-
  U_OMP_NOTHROW
- int starpu_omp_for_inline_first (unsigned long long nb_iterations, unsigned long long chunk, int schedule, int
  ordered, unsigned long long *_first_i, unsigned long long *_nb_i) __STARPU_OMP_NOTHROW
- int starpu_omp_for_inline_next (unsigned long long nb_iterations, unsigned long long chunk, int schedule, int
  ordered, unsigned long long *_first_i, unsigned long long *_nb_i) __STARPU_OMP_NOTHROW

- void starpu_omp_for_alt (void(∗f)(unsigned long long _begin_i, unsigned long long _end_i, void ∗arg), void ∗arg, unsigned long long nb_iterations, unsigned long long chunk, int schedule, int ordered, int nowait) __S-TARPU_OMP_NOTHROW
- int starpu_omp_for_inline_first_alt (unsigned long long nb_iterations, unsigned long long chunk, int schedule, int ordered, unsigned long long ∗_begin_i, unsigned long long ∗_end_i) __STARPU_OMP_NOTHROW
- int starpu_omp_for_inline_next_alt (unsigned long long nb_iterations, unsigned long long chunk, int schedule, int ordered, unsigned long long ∗_begin_i, unsigned long long ∗_end_i) __STARPU_OMP_NOTHROW
- void starpu_omp_ordered (void(∗f)(void ∗arg), void ∗arg) __STARPU_OMP_NOTHROW
- void starpu_omp_ordered_inline_begin (void) __STARPU_OMP_NOTHROW
- void starpu_omp_ordered_inline_end (void) __STARPU_OMP_NOTHROW
- void starpu_omp_sections (unsigned long long nb_sections, void(∗∗section_f)(void ∗arg), void ∗∗section_arg, int nowait) __STARPU_OMP_NOTHROW
- void starpu_omp_sections_combined (unsigned long long nb_sections, void(∗section_f)(unsigned long long section_num, void ∗arg), void ∗section_arg, int nowait) __STARPU_OMP_NOTHROW

Task

- void starpu_omp_task_region (const struct starpu_omp_task_region_attr ∗attr) __STARPU_OMP_NOTHR-OW
- void starpu_omp_taskwait (void) __STARPU_OMP_NOTHROW
- void starpu_omp_taskgroup (void(∗f)(void ∗arg), void ∗arg) __STARPU_OMP_NOTHROW
- void starpu_omp_taskgroup_inline_begin (void) __STARPU_OMP_NOTHROW
- void starpu_omp_taskgroup_inline_end (void) __STARPU_OMP_NOTHROW

API

- void starpu_omp_set_num_threads (int threads) __STARPU_OMP_NOTHROW
- int starpu_omp_get_num_threads () __STARPU_OMP_NOTHROW
- int starpu_omp_get_thread_num () __STARPU_OMP_NOTHROW
- int starpu_omp_get_max_threads () __STARPU_OMP_NOTHROW
- int starpu_omp_get_num_procs (void) __STARPU_OMP_NOTHROW
- int starpu_omp_in_parallel (void) __STARPU_OMP_NOTHROW
- void starpu_omp_set_dynamic (int dynamic_threads) __STARPU_OMP_NOTHROW
- int starpu_omp_get_dynamic (void) __STARPU_OMP_NOTHROW
- void starpu_omp_set_nested (int nested) __STARPU_OMP_NOTHROW
- int starpu_omp_get_nested (void) __STARPU_OMP_NOTHROW
- int starpu_omp_get_cancellation (void) __STARPU_OMP_NOTHROW
- void starpu_omp_set_schedule (enum starpu_omp_sched_value kind, int modifier) __STARPU_OMP_NOT-HROW
- void starpu_omp_get_schedule (enum starpu_omp_sched_value ∗kind, int ∗modifier) __STARPU_OMP_N-OTHROW
- int starpu_omp_get_thread_limit (void) __STARPU_OMP_NOTHROW
- void starpu_omp_set_max_active_levels (int max_levels) __STARPU_OMP_NOTHROW
- int starpu_omp_get_max_active_levels (void) __STARPU_OMP_NOTHROW
- int starpu_omp_get_level (void) __STARPU_OMP_NOTHROW
- int starpu_omp_get_ancestor_thread_num (int level) __STARPU_OMP_NOTHROW
- int starpu_omp_get_team_size (int level) __STARPU_OMP_NOTHROW
- int starpu_omp_get_active_level (void) __STARPU_OMP_NOTHROW
- int starpu_omp_in_final (void) __STARPU_OMP_NOTHROW
- enum starpu_omp_proc_bind_value starpu_omp_get_proc_bind (void) __STARPU_OMP_NOTHROW
- void starpu_omp_set_default_device (int device_num) __STARPU_OMP_NOTHROW
- int starpu_omp_get_default_device (void) __STARPU_OMP_NOTHROW
- int starpu_omp_get_num_devices (void) __STARPU_OMP_NOTHROW
- int starpu_omp_get_num_teams (void) __STARPU_OMP_NOTHROW

- int starpu_omp_get_team_num (void) __STARPU_OMP_NOTHROW
- int starpu_omp_is_initial_device (void) __STARPU_OMP_NOTHROW
- int starpu_omp_get_max_task_priority (void) __STARPU_OMP_NOTHROW
- void starpu_omp_init_lock (starpu_omp_lock_t *lock) __STARPU_OMP_NOTHROW
- void starpu_omp_destroy_lock (starpu_omp_lock_t *lock) __STARPU_OMP_NOTHROW
- void starpu_omp_set_lock (starpu_omp_lock_t *lock) __STARPU_OMP_NOTHROW
- void starpu_omp_unset_lock (starpu_omp_lock_t *lock) __STARPU_OMP_NOTHROW
- int starpu_omp_test_lock (starpu_omp_lock_t *lock) __STARPU_OMP_NOTHROW
- void starpu_omp_init_nest_lock (starpu_omp_nest_lock_t *lock) __STARPU_OMP_NOTHROW
- void starpu_omp_destroy_nest_lock (starpu_omp_nest_lock_t *lock) __STARPU_OMP_NOTHROW
- void starpu_omp_set_nest_lock (starpu_omp_nest_lock_t *lock) __STARPU_OMP_NOTHROW
- void starpu_omp_unset_nest_lock (starpu_omp_nest_lock_t *lock) __STARPU_OMP_NOTHROW
- int starpu_omp_test_nest_lock (starpu_omp_nest_lock_t *lock) __STARPU_OMP_NOTHROW
- void starpu_omp_atomic_fallback_inline_begin (void) __STARPU_OMP_NOTHROW
- void starpu_omp_atomic_fallback_inline_end (void) __STARPU_OMP_NOTHROW
- double starpu_omp_get_wtime (void) __STARPU_OMP_NOTHROW
- double starpu_omp_get_wtick (void) __STARPU_OMP_NOTHROW
- void starpu_omp_vector_annotate (starpu_data_handle_t handle, uint32_t slice_base) __STARPU_OMP_- NOTHROW

29.22.1 Detailed Description

This section describes the interface provided for implementing OpenMP runtimes on top of StarPU.

29.22.2 Data Structure Documentation

29.22.2.1 struct starpu_omp_lock_t

Opaque Simple Lock object (Simple Locks) for inter-task synchronization operations.

See Also

> starpu_omp_init_lock()
> starpu_omp_destroy_lock()
> starpu_omp_set_lock()
> starpu_omp_unset_lock()
> starpu_omp_test_lock()

Data Fields

void *	internal	Is an opaque pointer for internal use.

29.22.2.2 struct starpu_omp_nest_lock_t

Opaque Nestable Lock object (Nestable Locks) for inter-task synchronization operations.

See Also

> starpu_omp_init_nest_lock()
> starpu_omp_destroy_nest_lock()
> starpu_omp_set_nest_lock()
> starpu_omp_unset_nest_lock()
> starpu_omp_test_nest_lock()

Data Fields

void *	internal	Is an opaque pointer for internal use.

29.22.2.3 struct starpu_omp_parallel_region_attr

Set of attributes used for creating a new parallel region.

See Also

starpu_omp_parallel_region()

Data Fields

struct starpu_codelet	cl	Is a starpu_codelet (Codelet And Tasks) to use for the parallel region implicit tasks. The codelet must provide a CPU implementation function.
starpu_data_-handle_t *	handles	Is an array of zero or more starpu_data_handle_t data handle to be passed to the parallel region implicit tasks.
void *	cl_arg	Is an optional pointer to an inline argument to be passed to the region implicit tasks.
size_t	cl_arg_size	Is the size of the optional inline argument to be passed to the region implicit tasks, or 0 if unused.
unsigned	cl_arg_free	Is a boolean indicating whether the optional inline argument should be automatically freed (true), or not (false).
int	if_clause	Is a boolean indicating whether the **if** clause of the corresponding `pragma omp parallel` is true or false.
int	num_threads	Is an integer indicating the requested number of threads in the team of the newly created parallel region, or 0 to let the runtime choose the number of threads alone. This attribute may be ignored by the runtime system if the requested number of threads is higher than the number of threads that the runtime can create.

29.22.2.4 struct starpu_omp_task_region_attr

Set of attributes used for creating a new task region.

See Also

starpu_omp_task_region()

Data Fields

struct starpu_codelet	cl	Is a starpu_codelet (Codelet And Tasks) to use for the task region explicit task. The codelet must provide a CPU implementation function or an accelerator implementation for offloaded target regions.
starpu_data_-handle_t *	handles	Is an array of zero or more starpu_data_handle_t data handle to be passed to the task region explicit tasks.
void *	cl_arg	Is an optional pointer to an inline argument to be passed to the region implicit tasks.
size_t	cl_arg_size	Is the size of the optional inline argument to be passed to the region implicit tasks, or 0 if unused.
unsigned	cl_arg_free	Is a boolean indicating whether the optional inline argument should be automatically freed (true), or not (false).
int	priority	

int	if_clause	Is a boolean indicating whether the **if** clause of the corresponding `pragma omp task` is true or false.
int	final_clause	Is a boolean indicating whether the **final** clause of the corresponding `pragma omp task` is true or false.
int	untied_clause	Is a boolean indicating whether the **untied** clause of the corresponding `pragma omp task` is true or false.
int	mergeable_-clause	Is a boolean indicating whether the **mergeable** clause of the corresponding `pragma omp task` is true or false.

29.22.3 Macro Definition Documentation

29.22.3.1 #define STARPU_OPENMP

This macro is defined when StarPU has been installed with OpenMP Runtime support. It should be used in your code to detect the availability of the runtime support for OpenMP.

29.22.4 Enumeration Type Documentation

29.22.4.1 enum starpu_omp_sched_value

Set of constants for selecting the for loop iteration scheduling algorithm (Parallel For) as defined by the OpenMP specification.

Enumerator:

starpu_omp_sched_undefined Undefined iteration scheduling algorithm.

starpu_omp_sched_static **Static** iteration scheduling algorithm.

starpu_omp_sched_dynamic **Dynamic** iteration scheduling algorithm.

starpu_omp_sched_guided **Guided** iteration scheduling algorithm.

starpu_omp_sched_auto **Automatically** choosen iteration scheduling algorithm.

starpu_omp_sched_runtime Choice of iteration scheduling algorithm deferred at **runtime**.

> See Also
>
> > starpu_omp_for()
> > starpu_omp_for_inline_first()
> > starpu_omp_for_inline_next()
> > starpu_omp_for_alt()
> > starpu_omp_for_inline_first_alt()
> > starpu_omp_for_inline_next_alt()

29.22.4.2 enum starpu_omp_proc_bind_value

Set of constants for selecting the processor binding method, as defined in the OpenMP specification.

Enumerator:

starpu_omp_proc_bind_undefined Undefined processor binding method.

starpu_omp_proc_bind_false Team threads may be moved between places at any time.

starpu_omp_proc_bind_true Team threads may not be moved between places.

starpu_omp_proc_bind_master Assign every thread in the team to the same place as the **master** thread.

starpu_omp_proc_bind_close Assign every thread in the team to a place **close** to the parent thread.

starpu_omp_proc_bind_spread Assign team threads as a sparse distribution over the selected places.

See Also

starpu_omp_get_proc_bind()

29.22.5 Function Documentation

29.22.5.1 int starpu_omp_init (void)

Initializes StarPU and its OpenMP Runtime support.

29.22.5.2 void starpu_omp_shutdown (void)

Shutdown StarPU and its OpenMP Runtime support.

29.22.5.3 void starpu_omp_parallel_region (const struct **starpu_omp_parallel_region_attr** ∗ *attr*)

Generates and launch an OpenMP parallel region and return after its completion. `attr` specifies the attributes for the generated parallel region. If this function is called from inside another, generating, parallel region, the generated parallel region is nested within the generating parallel region.

This function can be used to implement `#pragma omp parallel`.

29.22.5.4 void starpu_omp_master (void(∗)(void ∗arg) *f,* void ∗ *arg*)

Executes a function only on the master thread of the OpenMP parallel region it is called from. When called from a thread that is not the master of the parallel region it is called from, this function does nothing. `f` is the function to be called. `arg` is an argument passed to function `f`.

This function can be used to implement `#pragma omp master`.

29.22.5.5 int starpu_omp_master_inline (void)

Determines whether the calling thread is the master of the OpenMP parallel region it is called from or not.

This function can be used to implement `#pragma omp master` without code outlining.

Returns

! 0 if called by the region's master thread.
0 if not called by the region's master thread.

29.22.5.6 void starpu_omp_barrier (void)

Waits until each participating thread of the innermost OpenMP parallel region has reached the barrier and each explicit OpenMP task bound to this region has completed its execution.

This function can be used to implement `#pragma omp barrier`.

29.22.5.7 void starpu_omp_critical (void(∗)(void ∗arg) *f,* void ∗ *arg,* const char ∗ *name*)

Waits until no other thread is executing within the context of the selected critical section, then proceeds to the exclusive execution of a function within the critical section. `f` is the function to be executed in the critical section. `arg` is an argument passed to function `f`. name is the name of the selected critical section. If `name == NULL`, the selected critical section is the unique anonymous critical section.

This function can be used to implement `#pragma omp critical`.

29.22.5.8   void starpu_omp_critical_inline_begin (const char ∗ *name*)

Waits until execution can proceed exclusively within the context of the selected critical section. `name` is the name of the selected critical section. If `name == NULL`, the selected critical section is the unique anonymous critical section.

This function together with starpu_omp_critical_inline_end can be used to implement `#pragma omp critical` without code outlining.

29.22.5.9   void starpu_omp_critical_inline_end (const char ∗ *name*)

Ends the exclusive execution within the context of the selected critical section. `name` is the name of the selected critical section. If `name==NULL`, the selected critical section is the unique anonymous critical section.

This function together with starpu_omp_critical_inline_begin can be used to implement `#pragma omp critical` without code outlining.

29.22.5.10   void starpu_omp_single (void(∗)(void ∗arg) *f,* void ∗ *arg,* int *nowait*)

Ensures that a single participating thread of the innermost OpenMP parallel region executes a function. `f` is the function to be executed by a single thread. `arg` is an argument passed to function `f`. `nowait` is a flag indicating whether an implicit barrier is requested after the single section (`nowait==0`) or not (`nowait==!0`).

This function can be used to implement `#pragma omp single`.

29.22.5.11   int starpu_omp_single_inline (void)

Decides whether the current thread is elected to run the following single section among the participating threads of the innermost OpenMP parallel region.

This function can be used to implement `#pragma omp single` without code outlining.

Returns

     `!0` if the calling thread has won the election.
     `0` if the calling thread has lost the election.

29.22.5.12   void starpu_omp_single_copyprivate (void(∗)(void ∗arg, void ∗data, unsigned long long data_size) *f,* void ∗ *arg,* void ∗ *data,* unsigned long long *data_size*)

This function executes `f` on a single task of the current parallel region task, and then broadcast the contents of the memory block pointed by the copyprivate pointer `data` and of size `data_size` to the corresponding `data` pointed memory blocks of all the other participating region tasks. This function can be used to implement `#pragma omp single` with a copyprivate clause.

See Also

     starpu_omp_single_copyprivate_inline
     starpu_omp_single_copyprivate_inline_begin
     starpu_omp_single_copyprivate_inline_end

29.22.5.13   void ∗ starpu_omp_single_copyprivate_inline_begin (void ∗ *data*)

This function elects one task among the tasks of the current parallel region task to execute the following single section, and then broadcast the copyprivate pointer `data` to all the other participating region tasks. This function can be used to implement `#pragma omp single` with a copyprivate clause without code outlining.

See Also

starpu_omp_single_copyprivate_inline
starpu_omp_single_copyprivate_inline_end

29.22.5.14   void starpu_omp_single_copyprivate_inline_end (void)

This function completes the execution of a single section and returns the broadcasted copyprivate pointer for tasks that lost the election and `NULL` for the task that won the election. This function can be used to implement `#pragma omp single` with a copyprivate clause without code outlining.

Returns

the copyprivate pointer for tasks that lost the election and therefore did not execute the code of the single section.
`NULL` for the task that won the election and executed the code of the single section.

See Also

starpu_omp_single_copyprivate_inline
starpu_omp_single_copyprivate_inline_begin

29.22.5.15   void starpu_omp_for (void(*)(unsigned long long _first_i, unsigned long long _nb_i, void *arg) *f*, void * *arg*, unsigned long long *nb_iterations*, unsigned long long *chunk*, int *schedule*, int *ordered*, int *nowait*)

Executes a parallel loop together with the other threads participating to the innermost parallel region. `f` is the function to be executed iteratively. `arg` is an argument passed to function `f`. `nb_iterations` is the number of iterations to be performed by the parallel loop. `chunk` is the number of consecutive iterations that should be affected to the same thread when scheduling the loop workshares, it follows the semantics of the `modifier` argument in OpenMP `#pragma omp for` specification. `schedule` is the scheduling mode according to the OpenMP specification. `ordered` is a flag indicating whether the loop region may contain an ordered section (`ordered==!0`) or not (`ordered==0`). `nowait` is a flag indicating whether an implicit barrier is requested after the for section (`nowait==0`) or not (`nowait==!0`).

The function `f` will be called with arguments `_first_i`, the first iteration to perform, `_nb_i`, the number of consecutive iterations to perform before returning, `arg`, the free `arg` argument.

This function can be used to implement `#pragma omp for`.

29.22.5.16   int starpu_omp_for_inline_first (unsigned long long *nb_iterations*, unsigned long long *chunk*, int *schedule*, int *ordered*, unsigned long long * *_first_i*, unsigned long long * *_nb_i*)

Decides whether the current thread should start to execute a parallel loop section. See starpu_omp_for for the argument description.

This function together with starpu_omp_for_inline_next can be used to implement `#pragma omp for` without code outlining.

Returns

`!0` if the calling thread participates to the loop region and should execute a first chunk of iterations. In that case, `*_first_i` will be set to the first iteration of the chunk to perform and `*_nb_i` will be set to the number of iterations of the chunk to perform.
`0` if the calling thread does not participate to the loop region because all the available iterations have been affected to the other threads of the parallel region.

See Also

starpu_omp_for

29.22.5.17 int starpu_omp_for_inline_next (unsigned long long *nb_iterations,* unsigned long long *chunk,* int *schedule,* int *ordered,* unsigned long long * *_first_i,* unsigned long long * *_nb_i*)

Decides whether the current thread should continue to execute a parallel loop section. See starpu_omp_for for the argument description.

This function together with starpu_omp_for_inline_first can be used to implement `#pragma omp for` without code outlining.

Returns

!0 if the calling thread should execute a next chunk of iterations. In that case, `*_first_i` will be set to the first iteration of the chunk to perform and `*_nb_i` will be set to the number of iterations of the chunk to perform. 0 if the calling thread does not participate anymore to the loop region because all the available iterations have been affected to the other threads of the parallel region.

See Also

starpu_omp_for

29.22.5.18 void starpu_omp_for_alt (void(*)(unsigned long long _begin_i, unsigned long long _end_i, void *arg) *f,* void * *arg,* unsigned long long *nb_iterations,* unsigned long long *chunk,* int *schedule,* int *ordered,* int *nowait*)

Alternative implementation of a parallel loop. This function differs from starpu_omp_for in the expected arguments of the loop function `f`.

The function `f` will be called with arguments `_begin_i`, the first iteration to perform, `_end_i`, the first iteration not to perform before returning, `arg`, the free `arg` argument.

This function can be used to implement `#pragma omp for`.

See Also

starpu_omp_for

29.22.5.19 int starpu_omp_for_inline_first_alt (unsigned long long *nb_iterations,* unsigned long long *chunk,* int *schedule,* int *ordered,* unsigned long long * *_begin_i,* unsigned long long * *_end_i*)

Inline version of the alternative implementation of a parallel loop.

This function together with starpu_omp_for_inline_next_alt can be used to implement `#pragma omp for` without code outlining.

See Also

starpu_omp_for
starpu_omp_for_alt
starpu_omp_for_inline_first

29.22.5.20 int starpu_omp_for_inline_next_alt (unsigned long long *nb_iterations,* unsigned long long *chunk,* int *schedule,* int *ordered,* unsigned long long * *_begin_i,* unsigned long long * *_end_i*)

Inline version of the alternative implementation of a parallel loop.

This function together with starpu_omp_for_inline_first_alt can be used to implement `#pragma omp for` without code outlining.

See Also

> starpu_omp_for
> starpu_omp_for_alt
> starpu_omp_for_inline_next

29.22.5.21 void starpu_omp_ordered (void(∗)(void ∗arg) *f,* void ∗ *arg*)

Ensures that a function is sequentially executed once for each iteration in order within a parallel loop, by the thread that own the iteration. `f` is the function to be executed by the thread that own the current iteration. `arg` is an argument passed to function `f`.

This function can be used to implement `#pragma omp ordered`.

29.22.5.22 void starpu_omp_ordered_inline_begin (void)

Waits until all the iterations of a parallel loop below the iteration owned by the current thread have been executed.

This function together with starpu_omp_ordered_inline_end can be used to implement `#pragma omp ordered` without code code outlining.

29.22.5.23 void starpu_omp_ordered_inline_end (void)

Notifies that the ordered section for the current iteration has been completed.

This function together with starpu_omp_ordered_inline_begin can be used to implement `#pragma omp ordered` without code code outlining.

29.22.5.24 void starpu_omp_sections (unsigned long long *nb_sections,* void(∗∗)(void ∗arg) *section_f,* void ∗∗ *section_arg,* int *nowait*)

Ensures that each function of a given array of functions is executed by one and only one thread. `nb_sections` is the number of functions in the array `section_f`. `section_f` is the array of functions to be executed as sections. `section_arg` is an array of arguments to be passed to the corresponding function. `nowait` is a flag indicating whether an implicit barrier is requested after the execution of all the sections (`nowait==0`) or not (`nowait==!0`).

This function can be used to implement `#pragma omp sections` and `#pragma omp section`.

29.22.5.25 void starpu_omp_sections_combined (unsigned long long *nb_sections,* void(∗)(unsigned long long section_num, void ∗arg) *section_f,* void ∗ *section_arg,* int *nowait*)

Alternative implementation of sections. This function differs from starpu_omp_sections in that all the sections are combined within a single function in this version. `section_f` is the function implementing the combined sections.

The function `section_f` will be called with arguments `section_num`, the section number to be executed, `arg`, the entry of `section_arg` corresponding to this section.

This function can be used to implement `#pragma omp sections` and `#pragma omp section`.

See Also

> starpu_omp_sections

29.22.5.26   void starpu_omp_task_region (const struct starpu_omp_task_region_attr * *attr*)

Generates an explicit child task. The execution of the generated task is asynchronous with respect to the calling code unless specified otherwise. `attr` specifies the attributes for the generated task region.

This function can be used to implement `#pragma omp task`.

29.22.5.27   void starpu_omp_taskwait (void)

Waits for the completion of the tasks generated by the current task. This function does not wait for the descendants of the tasks generated by the current task.

This function can be used to implement `#pragma omp taskwait`.

29.22.5.28   void starpu_omp_taskgroup (void(*)(void *arg) *f,* void * *arg*)

Launches a function and wait for the completion of every descendant task generated during the execution of the function.

This function can be used to implement `#pragma omp taskgroup`.

See Also

   starpu_omp_taskgroup_inline_begin
   starpu_omp_taskgroup_inline_end

29.22.5.29   void starpu_omp_taskgroup_inline_begin (void)

Launches a function and gets ready to wait for the completion of every descendant task generated during the dynamic scope of the taskgroup.

This function can be used to implement `#pragma omp taskgroup` without code outlining.

See Also

   starpu_omp_taskgroup
   starpu_omp_taskgroup_inline_end

29.22.5.30   void starpu_omp_taskgroup_inline_end (void)

Waits for the completion of every descendant task generated during the dynamic scope of the taskgroup.

This function can be used to implement `#pragma omp taskgroup` without code outlining.

See Also

   starpu_omp_taskgroup
   starpu_omp_taskgroup_inline_begin

29.22.5.31   void starpu_omp_set_num_threads (int *threads*)

This function sets ICVS nthreads_var for the parallel regions to be created with the current region.

Note: The StarPU OpenMP runtime support currently ignores this setting for nested parallel regions.

See Also

starpu_omp_get_num_threads
starpu_omp_get_thread_num
starpu_omp_get_max_threads
starpu_omp_get_num_procs

29.22.5.32 int starpu_omp_get_num_threads ( )

This function returns the number of threads of the current region.

Returns

the number of threads of the current region.

See Also

starpu_omp_set_num_threads
starpu_omp_get_thread_num
starpu_omp_get_max_threads
starpu_omp_get_num_procs

29.22.5.33 int starpu_omp_get_thread_num ( )

This function returns the rank of the current thread among the threads of the current region.

Returns

the rank of the current thread in the current region.

See Also

starpu_omp_set_num_threads
starpu_omp_get_num_threads
starpu_omp_get_max_threads
starpu_omp_get_num_procs

29.22.5.34 int starpu_omp_get_max_threads ( )

This function returns the maximum number of threads that can be used to create a region from the current region.

Returns

the maximum number of threads that can be used to create a region from the current region.

See Also

starpu_omp_set_num_threads
starpu_omp_get_num_threads
starpu_omp_get_thread_num
starpu_omp_get_num_procs

29.22.5.35 int starpu_omp_get_num_procs (void)

This function returns the number of StarPU CPU workers.

Returns

    the number of StarPU CPU workers.

See Also

    starpu_omp_set_num_threads
    starpu_omp_get_num_threads
    starpu_omp_get_thread_num
    starpu_omp_get_max_threads

29.22.5.36 int starpu_omp_in_parallel (void)

This function returns whether it is called from the scope of a parallel region or not.

Returns

    ! 0 if called from a parallel region scope.
    0 otherwise.

29.22.5.37 void starpu_omp_set_dynamic (int *dynamic_threads*)

This function enables (1) or disables (0) dynamically adjusting the number of parallel threads.

Note: The StarPU OpenMP runtime support currently ignores the argument of this function.

See Also

    starpu_omp_get_dynamic

29.22.5.38 int starpu_omp_get_dynamic (void)

This function returns the state of dynamic thread number adjustment.

Returns

    ! 0 if dynamic thread number adjustment is enabled.
    0 otherwise.

See Also

    starpu_omp_set_dynamic

29.22.5.39 void starpu_omp_set_nested (int *nested*)

This function enables (1) or disables (0) nested parallel regions.

Note: The StarPU OpenMP runtime support currently ignores the argument of this function.

See Also

> starpu_omp_get_nested
> starpu_omp_get_max_active_levels
> starpu_omp_set_max_active_levels
> starpu_omp_get_level
> starpu_omp_get_active_level

29.22.5.40   int starpu_omp_get_nested (void)

This function returns whether nested parallel sections are enabled or not.

Returns

> ! 0 if nested parallel sections are enabled.
> 0 otherwise.

See Also

> starpu_omp_set_nested
> starpu_omp_get_max_active_levels
> starpu_omp_set_max_active_levels
> starpu_omp_get_level
> starpu_omp_get_active_level

29.22.5.41   int starpu_omp_get_cancellation (void)

This function returns the state of the cancel ICVS var.

29.22.5.42   void starpu_omp_set_schedule (enum starpu_omp_sched_value *kind,* int *modifier* **)**

This function sets the default scheduling kind for upcoming loops within the current parallel section. `kind` is the scheduler kind, `modifier` complements the scheduler kind with informations such as the chunk size, in accordance with the OpenMP specification.

See Also

> starpu_omp_get_schedule

29.22.5.43   void starpu_omp_get_schedule (enum starpu_omp_sched_value $*$ *kind,* int $*$ *modifier* **)**

This function returns the current selected default loop scheduler.

Returns

> the kind and the modifier of the current default loop scheduler.

See Also

> starpu_omp_set_schedule

29.22.5.44 int starpu_omp_get_thread_limit (void)

This function returns the number of StarPU CPU workers.

Returns

the number of StarPU CPU workers.

29.22.5.45 void starpu_omp_set_max_active_levels (int *max_levels*)

This function sets the maximum number of allowed active parallel section levels.

Note: The StarPU OpenMP runtime support currently ignores the argument of this function and assume `max_-levels` equals 1 instead.

See Also

starpu_omp_set_nested
starpu_omp_get_nested
starpu_omp_get_max_active_levels
starpu_omp_get_level
starpu_omp_get_active_level

29.22.5.46 int starpu_omp_get_max_active_levels (void)

This function returns the current maximum number of allowed active parallel section levels

Returns

the current maximum number of allowed active parallel section levels.

See Also

starpu_omp_set_nested
starpu_omp_get_nested
starpu_omp_set_max_active_levels
starpu_omp_get_level
starpu_omp_get_active_level

29.22.5.47 int starpu_omp_get_level (void)

This function returns the nesting level of the current parallel section.

Returns

the nesting level of the current parallel section.

See Also

starpu_omp_set_nested
starpu_omp_get_nested
starpu_omp_get_max_active_levels
starpu_omp_set_max_active_levels
starpu_omp_get_active_level

29.22.5.48   int starpu_omp_get_ancestor_thread_num (int *level*)

This function returns the number of the ancestor of the current parallel section.

Returns

the number of the ancestor of the current parallel section.

29.22.5.49   int starpu_omp_get_team_size (int *level*)

This function returns the size of the team of the current parallel section.

Returns

the size of the team of the current parallel section.

29.22.5.50   int starpu_omp_get_active_level (void)

This function returns the nestinglevel of the current innermost active parallel section.

Returns

the nestinglevel of the current innermost active parallel section.

See Also

starpu_omp_set_nested
starpu_omp_get_nested
starpu_omp_get_max_active_levels
starpu_omp_set_max_active_levels
starpu_omp_get_level

29.22.5.51   int starpu_omp_in_final (void)

This function checks whether the current task is final or not.

Returns

! 0 if called from a final task.
0 otherwise.

29.22.5.52   enum starpu_omp_proc_bind_value starpu_omp_get_proc_bind (void)

This function returns the proc_bind setting of the current parallel region.

Returns

the proc_bind setting of the current parallel region.

29.22.5.53 void starpu_omp_set_default_device (int *device_num*)

This function sets the number of the device to use as default.

Note: The StarPU OpenMP runtime support currently ignores the argument of this function.

See Also

> starpu_omp_get_default_device
> starpu_omp_is_initial_device

29.22.5.54 int starpu_omp_get_default_device (void)

This function returns the number of the device used as default.

Returns

> the number of the device used as default.

See Also

> starpu_omp_set_default_device
> starpu_omp_is_initial_device

29.22.5.55 int starpu_omp_get_num_devices (void)

This function returns the number of the devices.

Returns

> the number of the devices.

29.22.5.56 int starpu_omp_get_num_teams (void)

This function returns the number of teams in the current teams region.

Returns

> the number of teams in the current teams region.

See Also

> starpu_omp_get_num_teams

29.22.5.57 int starpu_omp_get_team_num (void)

This function returns the team number of the calling thread.

Returns

> the team number of the calling thread.

See Also

> starpu_omp_get_num_teams

29.22.5.58   int starpu_omp_is_initial_device (void)

This function checks whether the current device is the initial device or not.

29.22.5.59   int starpu_omp_get_max_task_priority (void)

The omp_get_max_task_priority routine returns the maximum value that can be specified in the priority clause.

Returns

> ! 0 if called from the host device.
> 0 otherwise.

See Also

> starpu_omp_set_default_device
> starpu_omp_get_default_device

29.22.5.60   void starpu_omp_init_lock (starpu_omp_lock_t ∗ lock)

This function initializes an opaque lock object.

See Also

> starpu_omp_destroy_lock
> starpu_omp_set_lock
> starpu_omp_unset_lock
> starpu_omp_test_lock

29.22.5.61   void starpu_omp_destroy_lock (starpu_omp_lock_t ∗ lock)

This function destroys an opaque lock object.

See Also

> starpu_omp_init_lock
> starpu_omp_set_lock
> starpu_omp_unset_lock
> starpu_omp_test_lock

29.22.5.62   void starpu_omp_set_lock (starpu_omp_lock_t ∗ lock)

This function locks an opaque lock object. If the lock is already locked, the function will block until it succeeds in exclusively acquiring the lock.

See Also

> starpu_omp_init_lock
> starpu_omp_destroy_lock
> starpu_omp_unset_lock
> starpu_omp_test_lock

29.22.5.63   void starpu_omp_unset_lock (**starpu_omp_lock_t** ∗ *lock*)

This function unlocks a previously locked lock object. The behaviour of this function is unspecified if it is called on an unlocked lock object.

See Also

>   starpu_omp_init_lock
>   starpu_omp_destroy_lock
>   starpu_omp_set_lock
>   starpu_omp_test_lock

29.22.5.64   int starpu_omp_test_lock (**starpu_omp_lock_t** ∗ *lock*)

This function unblockingly attempts to lock a lock object and returns whether it succeeded or not.

Returns

>   ! 0 if the function succeeded in acquiring the lock.
>   0 if the lock was already locked.

See Also

>   starpu_omp_init_lock
>   starpu_omp_destroy_lock
>   starpu_omp_set_lock
>   starpu_omp_unset_lock

29.22.5.65   void starpu_omp_init_nest_lock (**starpu_omp_nest_lock_t** ∗ *lock*)

This function initializes an opaque lock object supporting nested locking operations.

See Also

>   starpu_omp_destroy_nest_lock
>   starpu_omp_set_nest_lock
>   starpu_omp_unset_nest_lock
>   starpu_omp_test_nest_lock

29.22.5.66   void starpu_omp_destroy_nest_lock (**starpu_omp_nest_lock_t** ∗ *lock*)

This function destroys an opaque lock object supporting nested locking operations.

See Also

>   starpu_omp_init_nest_lock
>   starpu_omp_set_nest_lock
>   starpu_omp_unset_nest_lock
>   starpu_omp_test_nest_lock

29.22.5.67   void starpu_omp_set_nest_lock (**starpu_omp_nest_lock_t** * *lock*)

This function locks an opaque lock object supporting nested locking operations. If the lock is already locked by another task, the function will block until it succeeds in exclusively acquiring the lock. If the lock is already taken by the current task, the function will increase the nested locking level of the lock object.

See Also

> starpu_omp_init_nest_lock
> starpu_omp_destroy_nest_lock
> starpu_omp_unset_nest_lock
> starpu_omp_test_nest_lock

29.22.5.68   void starpu_omp_unset_nest_lock (**starpu_omp_nest_lock_t** * *lock*)

This function unlocks a previously locked lock object supporting nested locking operations. If the lock has been locked multiple times in nested fashion, the nested locking level is decreased and the lock remains locked. Otherwise, if the lock has only been locked once, it becomes unlocked. The behaviour of this function is unspecified if it is called on an unlocked lock object. The behaviour of this function is unspecified if it is called from a different task than the one that locked the lock object.

See Also

> starpu_omp_init_nest_lock
> starpu_omp_destroy_nest_lock
> starpu_omp_set_nest_lock
> starpu_omp_test_nest_lock

29.22.5.69   int starpu_omp_test_nest_lock (**starpu_omp_nest_lock_t** * *lock*)

This function unblocking attempts to lock an opaque lock object supporting nested locking operations and returns whether it succeeded or not. If the lock is already locked by another task, the function will return without having acquired the lock. If the lock is already taken by the current task, the function will increase the nested locking level of the lock object.

Returns

> ! 0 if the function succeeded in acquiring the lock.
> 0 if the lock was already locked.

See Also

> starpu_omp_init_nest_lock
> starpu_omp_destroy_nest_lock
> starpu_omp_set_nest_lock
> starpu_omp_unset_nest_lock

29.22.5.70   void starpu_omp_atomic_fallback_inline_begin (void)

This function implements the entry point of a fallback global atomic region. It blocks until it succeeds in acquiring exclusive access to the global atomic region.

See Also

> starpu_omp_atomic_fallback_inline_end

29.22.5.71   void starpu_omp_atomic_fallback_inline_end (void)

This function implements the exit point of a fallback global atomic region. It release the exclusive access to the global atomic region.

See Also

    starpu_omp_atomic_fallback_inline_begin

29.22.5.72   double starpu_omp_get_wtime (void)

This function returns the elapsed wallclock time in seconds.

Returns

    the elapsed wallclock time in seconds.

See Also

    starpu_omp_get_wtick

29.22.5.73   double starpu_omp_get_wtick (void)

This function returns the precision of the time used by `starpu_omp_get_wtime`.

Returns

    the precision of the time used by `starpu_omp_get_wtime`.

See Also

    starpu_omp_get_wtime

29.22.5.74   void starpu_omp_vector_annotate (**starpu_data_handle_t** *handle,* uint32_t *slice_base*)

This function enables setting additional vector metadata needed by the OpenMP Runtime Support.

`handle` is vector data handle. `slice_base` is the base of an array slice, expressed in number of vector elements from the array base.

See Also

    STARPU_VECTOR_GET_SLICE_BASE

29.23   MIC Extensions

Macros

  • #define STARPU_USE_MIC
  • #define STARPU_MAXMICDEVS

Typedefs

  • typedef void * starpu_mic_func_symbol_t

Functions

- int starpu_mic_register_kernel (starpu_mic_func_symbol_t ∗symbol, const char ∗func_name)
- starpu_mic_kernel_t starpu_mic_get_kernel (starpu_mic_func_symbol_t symbol)

29.23.1 Detailed Description

29.23.2 Macro Definition Documentation

29.23.2.1 #define STARPU_USE_MIC

Defined when StarPU has been installed with MIC support. It should be used in your code to detect the availability of MIC.

29.23.2.2 #define STARPU_MAXMICDEVS

Define the maximum number of MIC devices that are supported by StarPU.

29.23.3 Typedef Documentation

29.23.3.1 starpu_mic_func_symbol_t

Type for MIC function symbols

29.23.4 Function Documentation

29.23.4.1 int starpu_mic_register_kernel (starpu_mic_func_symbol_t ∗ symbol, const char ∗ func_name)

Initiate a lookup on each MIC device to find the address of the function named `func_name`, store it in the global array kernels and return the index in the array through `symbol`.

29.23.4.2 starpu_mic_kernel_t starpu_mic_get_kernel (starpu_mic_func_symbol_t symbol)

If successfull, return the pointer to the function defined by `symbol` on the device linked to the called device. This can for instance be used in a starpu_mic_func_t implementation.

29.24 SCC Extensions

Macros

- #define STARPU_USE_SCC
- #define STARPU_MAXSCCDEVS

Typedefs

- typedef void ∗ starpu_scc_func_symbol_t

Functions

- int starpu_scc_register_kernel (starpu_scc_func_symbol_t ∗symbol, const char ∗func_name)
- starpu_scc_kernel_t starpu_scc_get_kernel (starpu_scc_func_symbol_t symbol)

29.24.1   Detailed Description

29.24.2   Macro Definition Documentation

29.24.2.1   #define STARPU_USE_SCC

Defined when StarPU has been installed with SCC support. It should be used in your code to detect the availability of SCC.

29.24.2.2   #define STARPU_MAXSCCDEVS

Define the maximum number of SCC devices that are supported by StarPU.

29.24.3   Typedef Documentation

29.24.3.1   starpu_scc_func_symbol_t

Type for SCC function symbols

29.24.4   Function Documentation

29.24.4.1   int starpu_scc_register_kernel (**starpu_scc_func_symbol_t** * *symbol,* const char * *func_name*)

Initiate a lookup on each SCC device to find the adress of the function named `func_name`, store them in the global array kernels and return the index in the array through `symbol`.

29.24.4.2   **starpu_scc_kernel_t** starpu_scc_get_kernel (**starpu_scc_func_symbol_t** *symbol*)

If success, return the pointer to the function defined by `symbol` on the device linked to the called device. This can for instance be used in a starpu_scc_func_symbol_t implementation.

29.25   Miscellaneous Helpers

Functions

- int starpu_data_cpy (starpu_data_handle_t dst_handle, starpu_data_handle_t src_handle, int asynchronous, void(*callback_func)(void *), void *callback_arg)
- void starpu_execute_on_each_worker (void(*func)(void *), void *arg, uint32_t where)
- void starpu_execute_on_each_worker_ex (void(*func)(void *), void *arg, uint32_t where, const char *name)
- void starpu_execute_on_specific_workers (void(*func)(void *), void *arg, unsigned num_workers, unsigned *workers, const char *name)
- double starpu_timing_now (void)

29.25.1   Detailed Description

29.25.2   Function Documentation

29.25.2.1   int starpu_data_cpy (**starpu_data_handle_t** *dst_handle,* **starpu_data_handle_t** *src_handle,* int *asynchronous,* void(*)(void *) *callback_func,* void * *callback_arg*)

Copy the content of `src_handle` into `dst_handle`. The parameter `asynchronous` indicates whether the function should block or not. In the case of an asynchronous call, it is possible to synchronize with the termination of this operation either by the means of implicit dependencies (if enabled) or by calling starpu_task_wait_for_all(). If `callback_func` is not `NULL`, this callback function is executed after the handle has been copied, and it is given the pointer `callback_arg` as argument.

29.25.2.2 void starpu_execute_on_each_worker (void(∗)(void ∗) *func,* void ∗ *arg,* uint32_t *where*)

Execute the given function `func` on a subset of workers. When calling this method, the offloaded function `func` is executed by every StarPU worker that are eligible to execute the function. The argument `arg` is passed to the offloaded function. The argument `where` specifies on which types of processing units the function should be executed. Similarly to the field starpu_codelet::where, it is possible to specify that the function should be executed on every CUDA device and every CPU by passing STARPU_CPU|STARPU_CUDA. This function blocks until `func` has been executed on every appropriate processing units, and thus may not be called from a callback function for instance.

29.25.2.3 void starpu_execute_on_each_worker_ex (void(∗)(void ∗) *func,* void ∗ *arg,* uint32_t *where,* const char ∗ *name*)

Same as starpu_execute_on_each_worker(), except that the task name is specified in the argument `name`.

29.25.2.4 void starpu_execute_on_specific_workers (void(∗)(void ∗) *func,* void ∗ *arg,* unsigned *num_workers,* unsigned ∗ *workers,* const char ∗ *name*)

Call `func(arg)` on every worker in the `workers` array. `num_workers` indicates the number of workers in this array. This function is synchronous, but the different workers may execute the function in parallel.

29.25.2.5 double starpu_timing_now (void)

Return the current date in micro-seconds.

29.26 FxT Support

Data Structures

- struct starpu_fxt_codelet_event
- struct starpu_fxt_options

Functions

- void starpu_fxt_options_init (struct starpu_fxt_options ∗options)
- void starpu_fxt_generate_trace (struct starpu_fxt_options ∗options)
- void starpu_fxt_start_profiling (void)
- void starpu_fxt_stop_profiling (void)
- void starpu_fxt_autostart_profiling (int autostart)
- void starpu_fxt_write_data_trace (char ∗filename_in)
- void starpu_fxt_trace_user_event (unsigned long code)
- void starpu_fxt_trace_user_event_string (const char ∗s)

29.26.1 Detailed Description

29.26.2 Data Structure Documentation

29.26.2.1 struct starpu_fxt_codelet_event

todo

Data Fields

char	symbol	name of the codelet
int	workerid	todo
char	perfmodel_-archname	todo
uint32_t	hash	todo
size_t	size	todo
float	time	todo

29.26.2.2 struct starpu_fxt_options

todo

Data Fields

unsigned	per_task_colour	todo
unsigned	no_events	
unsigned	no_counter	todo
unsigned	no_bus	
unsigned	no_flops	
unsigned	ninputfiles	todo
unsigned	no_smooth	
char *	filenames	todo
char *	out_paje_path	todo
char *	distrib_time_-path	todo
char *	activity_path	todo
char *	dag_path	todo
char *	tasks_path	
char *	data_path	
char *	anim_path	
char *	states_path	
char *	file_prefix	In case we are going to gather multiple traces (e.g in the case of MPI processes), we may need to prefix the name of the containers.
uint64_t	file_offset	In case we are going to gather multiple traces (e.g in the case of MPI processes), we may need to prefix the name of the containers.
int	file_rank	In case we are going to gather multiple traces (e.g in the case of MPI processes), we may need to prefix the name of the containers.
char	worker_names	Output parameters
struct starpu_-perfmodel_arch	worker_-archtypes	Output parameters
int	nworkers	Output parameters
struct starpu_fxt-_codelet_event **	dumped_-codelets	In case we want to dump the list of codelets to an external tool
long	dumped_-codelets_count	In case we want to dump the list of codelets to an external tool

29.26.3 Function Documentation

29.26.3.1 void starpu_fxt_options_init (struct starpu_fxt_options ∗ *options*)

todo

29.26.3.2 void starpu_fxt_generate_trace (struct starpu_fxt_options ∗ *options*)

todo

29.26.3.3 void starpu_fxt_start_profiling (void)

Start recording the trace. The trace is by default started from starpu_init() call, but can be paused by using starpu_fxt_stop_profiling(), in which case starpu_fxt_start_profiling() should be called to resume recording events.

29.26.3.4 void starpu_fxt_stop_profiling (void)

Stop recording the trace. The trace is by default stopped when calling starpu_shutdown(). starpu_fxt_stop_profiling() can however be used to stop it earlier. starpu_fxt_start_profiling() can then be called to start recording it again, etc.

29.26.3.5 void starpu_fxt_autostart_profiling (int *autostart*)

Determine whether profiling should be started by starpu_init(), or only when starpu_fxt_start_profiling() is called. autostart should be 1 to do so, or 0 to prevent it.

29.26.3.6 void starpu_fxt_write_data_trace (char ∗ *filename_in*)

todo

29.26.3.7 void starpu_fxt_trace_user_event (unsigned long *code*)

Add an event in the execution trace if FxT is enabled.

29.26.3.8 void starpu_fxt_trace_user_event_string (const char ∗ *s*)

Add a string event in the execution trace if FxT is enabled.

29.27 FFT Support

Functions

- void ∗ starpufft_malloc (size_t n)
- void starpufft_free (void ∗p)
- starpufft_plan starpufft_plan_dft_1d (int n, int sign, unsigned flags)
- starpufft_plan starpufft_plan_dft_2d (int n, int m, int sign, unsigned flags)
- struct starpu_task ∗ starpufft_start (starpufft_plan p, void ∗in, void ∗out)
- struct starpu_task ∗ starpufft_start_handle (starpufft_plan p, starpu_data_handle_t in, starpu_data_handle_t out)
- int starpufft_execute (starpufft_plan p, void ∗in, void ∗out)
- int starpufft_execute_handle (starpufft_plan p, starpu_data_handle_t in, starpu_data_handle_t out)
- void starpufft_cleanup (starpufft_plan p)
- void starpufft_destroy_plan (starpufft_plan p)

29.27.1 Detailed Description

29.27.2 Function Documentation

29.27.2.1 void * starpufft_malloc (size_t *n*)

Allocate memory for `n` bytes. This is preferred over `malloc()`, since it allocates pinned memory, which allows overlapped transfers.

29.27.2.2 void * starpufft_free (void * *p*)

Release memory previously allocated.

29.27.2.3 struct starpufft_plan * starpufft_plan_dft_1d (int *n,* int *sign,* unsigned *flags*)

Initialize a plan for 1D FFT of size n. `sign` can be STARPUFFT_FORWARD or STARPUFFT_INVERSE. `flags` must be 0.

29.27.2.4 struct starpufft_plan * starpufft_plan_dft_2d (int *n,* int *m,* int *sign,* unsigned *flags*)

Initialize a plan for 2D FFT of size (n, m). `sign` can be STARPUFFT_FORWARD or STARPUFFT_INVERSE. flags must be 0.

29.27.2.5 struct **starpu_task** * starpufft_start (starpufft_plan *p,* void * *in,* void * *out*)   [read]

Start an FFT previously planned as `p`, using `in` and `out` as input and output. This only submits the task and does not wait for it. The application should call starpufft_cleanup() to unregister the

29.27.2.6 struct **starpu_task** * starpufft_start_handle (starpufft_plan *p,* **starpu_data_handle_t** *in,* **starpu_data_handle_t** *out*)   [read]

Start an FFT previously planned as `p`, using data handles `in` and `out` as input and output (assumed to be vectors of elements of the expected types). This only submits the task and does not wait for it.

29.27.2.7 void starpufft_execute (starpufft_plan *p,* void * *in,* void * *out*)

Execute an FFT previously planned as `p`, using `in` and `out` as input and output. This submits and waits for the task.

29.27.2.8 void starpufft_execute_handle (starpufft_plan *p,* **starpu_data_handle_t** *in,* **starpu_data_handle_t** *out*)

Execute an FFT previously planned as `p`, using data handles `in` and `out` as input and output (assumed to be vectors of elements of the expected types). This submits and waits for the task.

29.27.2.9 void starpufft_cleanup (starpufft_plan *p*)

Release data for plan `p`, in the starpufft_start() case.

29.27.2.10 void starpufft_destroy_plan (starpufft_plan *p*)

Destroy plan `p`, i.e. release all CPU (fftw) and GPU (cufft) resources.

29.28 MPI Support

Initialisation

- #define STARPU_USE_MPI
- int starpu_mpi_init_comm (int *argc, char ***argv, int initialize_mpi, MPI_Comm comm)
- int starpu_mpi_init (int *argc, char ***argv, int initialize_mpi)
- int starpu_mpi_initialize (void)
- int starpu_mpi_initialize_extended (int *rank, int *world_size)
- int starpu_mpi_shutdown (void)
- void starpu_mpi_comm_amounts_retrieve (size_t *comm_amounts)
- int starpu_mpi_comm_size (MPI_Comm comm, int *size)
- int starpu_mpi_comm_rank (MPI_Comm comm, int *rank)
- int starpu_mpi_world_rank (void)
- int starpu_mpi_world_size (void)

Communication

- int starpu_mpi_send (starpu_data_handle_t data_handle, int dest, int mpi_tag, MPI_Comm comm)
- int starpu_mpi_recv (starpu_data_handle_t data_handle, int source, int mpi_tag, MPI_Comm comm, MPI_-Status *status)
- int starpu_mpi_isend (starpu_data_handle_t data_handle, starpu_mpi_req *req, int dest, int mpi_tag, MPI_-Comm comm)
- int starpu_mpi_irecv (starpu_data_handle_t data_handle, starpu_mpi_req *req, int source, int mpi_tag, MPI-_Comm comm)
- int starpu_mpi_isend_detached (starpu_data_handle_t data_handle, int dest, int mpi_tag, MPI_Comm comm, void(*callback)(void *), void *arg)
- int starpu_mpi_irecv_detached (starpu_data_handle_t data_handle, int source, int mpi_tag, MPI_Comm comm, void(*callback)(void *), void *arg)
- int starpu_mpi_irecv_detached_sequential_consistency (starpu_data_handle_t data_handle, int source, int mpi_tag, MPI_Comm comm, void(*callback)(void *), void *arg, int sequential_consistency)
- int starpu_mpi_issend (starpu_data_handle_t data_handle, starpu_mpi_req *req, int dest, int mpi_tag, MPI-_Comm comm)
- int starpu_mpi_issend_detached (starpu_data_handle_t data_handle, int dest, int mpi_tag, MPI_Comm comm, void(*callback)(void *), void *arg)
- int starpu_mpi_wait (starpu_mpi_req *req, MPI_Status *status)
- int starpu_mpi_test (starpu_mpi_req *req, int *flag, MPI_Status *status)
- int starpu_mpi_barrier (MPI_Comm comm)
- int starpu_mpi_wait_for_all (MPI_Comm comm)
- int starpu_mpi_isend_detached_unlock_tag (starpu_data_handle_t data_handle, int dest, int mpi_tag, MPI_-Comm comm, starpu_tag_t tag)
- int starpu_mpi_irecv_detached_unlock_tag (starpu_data_handle_t data_handle, int source, int mpi_tag, MP-I_Comm comm, starpu_tag_t tag)
- int starpu_mpi_isend_array_detached_unlock_tag (unsigned array_size, starpu_data_handle_t *data_-handle, int *dest, int *mpi_tag, MPI_Comm *comm, starpu_tag_t tag)
- int starpu_mpi_irecv_array_detached_unlock_tag (unsigned array_size, starpu_data_handle_t *data_-handle, int *source, int *mpi_tag, MPI_Comm *comm, starpu_tag_t tag)
- int starpu_mpi_get_communication_tag (void)
- void starpu_mpi_set_communication_tag (int tag)
- int starpu_mpi_datatype_register (starpu_data_handle_t handle, starpu_mpi_datatype_allocate_func_t allocate_datatype_func, starpu_mpi_datatype_free_func_t free_datatype_func)
- int starpu_mpi_datatype_unregister (starpu_data_handle_t handle)

Communication Cache

- int starpu_mpi_cache_is_enabled ()
- int starpu_mpi_cache_set (int enabled)
- void starpu_mpi_cache_flush (MPI_Comm comm, starpu_data_handle_t data_handle)
- void starpu_mpi_cache_flush_all_data (MPI_Comm comm)
- int starpu_mpi_cached_receive (starpu_data_handle_t data_handle)
- int starpu_mpi_cached_send (starpu_data_handle_t data_handle, int dest)

MPI Insert Task

- #define starpu_mpi_data_register(data_handle, tag, rank)
- #define starpu_data_set_tag
- #define starpu_mpi_data_set_rank(handle, rank)
- #define starpu_data_set_rank
- #define starpu_data_get_rank
- #define starpu_data_get_tag
- #define STARPU_EXECUTE_ON_NODE
- #define STARPU_EXECUTE_ON_DATA
- #define STARPU_NODE_SELECTION_POLICY
- void starpu_mpi_data_register_comm (starpu_data_handle_t data_handle, int tag, int rank, MPI_Comm comm)
- void starpu_mpi_data_set_tag (starpu_data_handle_t handle, int tag)
- void starpu_mpi_data_set_rank_comm (starpu_data_handle_t handle, int rank, MPI_Comm comm)
- int starpu_mpi_data_get_rank (starpu_data_handle_t handle)
- int starpu_mpi_data_get_tag (starpu_data_handle_t handle)
- void starpu_mpi_data_migrate (MPI_Comm comm, starpu_data_handle_t handle, int new_rank)
- int starpu_mpi_insert_task (MPI_Comm comm, struct starpu_codelet *codelet,...)
- int starpu_mpi_task_insert (MPI_Comm comm, struct starpu_codelet *codelet,...)
- struct starpu_task * starpu_mpi_task_build (MPI_Comm comm, struct starpu_codelet *codelet,...)
- int starpu_mpi_task_post_build (MPI_Comm comm, struct starpu_codelet *codelet,...)
- void starpu_mpi_get_data_on_node (MPI_Comm comm, starpu_data_handle_t data_handle, int node)
- void starpu_mpi_get_data_on_node_detached (MPI_Comm comm, starpu_data_handle_t data_handle, int node, void(*callback)(void *), void *arg)

Node Selection Policy

- #define STARPU_MPI_NODE_SELECTION_CURRENT_POLICY
- #define STARPU_MPI_NODE_SELECTION_MOST_R_DATA
- int starpu_mpi_node_selection_get_current_policy ()
- int starpu_mpi_node_selection_set_current_policy (int policy)
- int starpu_mpi_node_selection_register_policy (starpu_mpi_select_node_policy_func_t policy_func)
- int starpu_mpi_node_selection_unregister_policy (int policy)

Collective Operations

- void starpu_mpi_redux_data (MPI_Comm comm, starpu_data_handle_t data_handle)
- int starpu_mpi_scatter_detached (starpu_data_handle_t *data_handles, int count, int root, MPI_Comm comm, void(*scallback)(void *), void *sarg, void(*rcallback)(void *), void *rarg)
- int starpu_mpi_gather_detached (starpu_data_handle_t *data_handles, int count, int root, MPI_Comm comm, void(*scallback)(void *), void *sarg, void(*rcallback)(void *), void *rarg)

MPI Master Slave

- #define STARPU_USE_MPI_MASTER_SLAVE

29.28.1 Detailed Description

29.28.2 Macro Definition Documentation

29.28.2.1 #define STARPU_USE_MPI

Defined when StarPU has been installed with MPI support. It should be used in your code to detect the availability of MPI.

29.28.2.2 #define starpu_mpi_data_register(*data_handle*, *tag*, *rank*)

Register to MPI a StarPU data handle with the given tag, rank and the MPI communicator `MPI_COMM_WORLD`. It also automatically clears the MPI communication cache when unregistering the data.

29.28.2.3 #define starpu_data_set_tag

Symbol kept for backward compatibility. Calling function starpu_mpi_data_set_tag()

29.28.2.4 #define starpu_mpi_data_set_rank(*handle*, *rank*)

Register to MPI a StarPU data handle with the given rank and the MPI communicator `MPI_COMM_WORLD`. No tag will be defined. It also automatically clears the MPI communication cache when unregistering the data. Symbol kept for backward compatibility. Calling function starpu_mpi_data_set_rank()

29.28.2.5 #define starpu_data_set_rank

Register to MPI a StarPU data handle with the given rank and the MPI communicator `MPI_COMM_WORLD`. No tag will be defined. It also automatically clears the MPI communication cache when unregistering the data. Symbol kept for backward compatibility. Calling function starpu_mpi_data_set_rank()

29.28.2.6 #define starpu_data_get_rank

Return the rank of the given data. Symbol kept for backward compatibility. Calling function starpu_mpi_data_get_-rank()

29.28.2.7 #define starpu_data_get_tag

Return the tag of the given data. Symbol kept for backward compatibility. Calling function starpu_mpi_data_get_-tag()

29.28.2.8 #define STARPU_EXECUTE_ON_NODE

Used when calling starpu_mpi_task_insert(), must be followed by a integer value which specified the node on which to execute the codelet.

29.28.2.9 #define STARPU_EXECUTE_ON_DATA

Used when calling starpu_mpi_task_insert(), must be followed by a data handle to specify that the node owning the given data will execute the codelet.

29.28.2.10 #define STARPU_NODE_SELECTION_POLICY

Used when calling starpu_mpi_task_insert(), must be followed by a identifier to a node selection policy. This is needed when several nodes own data in STARPU_W mode.

29.28.2.11 #define STARPU_MPI_NODE_SELECTION_CURRENT_POLICY

todo

29.28.2.12 #define STARPU_MPI_NODE_SELECTION_MOST_R_DATA

todo

29.28.2.13 #define STARPU_USE_MPI_MASTER_SLAVE

Defined when StarPU has been installed with MPI Master Slave support. It should be used in your code to detect the availability of MPI Master Slave.

29.28.3 Function Documentation

29.28.3.1 int starpu_mpi_init_comm (int * argc, char * argv, int initialize_mpi, MPI_Comm comm)**

Initialize the starpumpi library with the given communicator comm. initialize_mpi indicates if MPI should be initialized or not by StarPU. If the value is not 0, MPI will be initialized by calling MPI_Init_Thread(argc, argv, MPI_THREAD_SERIALIZED, ...). starpu_init() must be called before starpu_mpi_init_comm().

29.28.3.2 int starpu_mpi_init (int * argc, char * argv, int initialize_mpi)**

Call starpu_mpi_init_comm() with the MPI communicator MPI_COMM_WORLD.

29.28.3.3 int starpu_mpi_initialize (void)

Deprecated This function has been made deprecated. One should use instead the function starpu_mpi_init(). This function does not call MPI_Init(), it should be called beforehand.

29.28.3.4 int starpu_mpi_initialize_extended (int * rank, int * world_size)

Deprecated This function has been made deprecated. One should use instead the function starpu_mpi_init(). MPI will be initialized by starpumpi by calling MPI_Init_Thread(argc, argv, MPI_THREAD_-SERIALIZED, ...).

29.28.3.5 int starpu_mpi_shutdown (void)

Clean the starpumpi library. This must be called between calling starpu_mpi functions and starpu_shutdown(). MPI_Finalize() will be called if StarPU-MPI has been initialized by starpu_mpi_init().

29.28.3.6 void starpu_mpi_comm_amounts_retrieve (size_t * *comm_amounts*)

Retrieve the current amount of communications from the current node in the array `comm_amounts` which must have a size greater or equal to the world size. Communications statistics must be enabled (see STARPU_COMM-_STATS).

29.28.3.7 int starpu_mpi_comm_size (MPI_Comm *comm,* int * *size*)

Return in `size` the size of the communicator `comm`

29.28.3.8 int starpu_mpi_comm_rank (MPI_Comm *comm,* int * *rank*)

Return in `rank` the rank of the calling process in the communicator `comm`

29.28.3.9 int starpu_mpi_world_rank (void)

Return the rank of the calling process in the communicator `MPI_COMM_WORLD`

29.28.3.10 int starpu_mpi_world_size (void)

Return the size of the communicator `MPI_COMM_WORLD`

29.28.3.11 int starpu_mpi_send (**starpu_data_handle_t** *data_handle,* int *dest,* int *mpi_tag,* MPI_Comm *comm*)

Perform a standard-mode, blocking send of `data_handle` to the node `dest` using the message tag `mpi_tag` within the communicator `comm`.

29.28.3.12 int starpu_mpi_recv (**starpu_data_handle_t** *data_handle,* int *source,* int *mpi_tag,* MPI_Comm *comm,* MPI_Status * *status*)

Perform a standard-mode, blocking receive in `data_handle` from the node `source` using the message tag `mpi_tag` within the communicator `comm`.

29.28.3.13 int starpu_mpi_isend (**starpu_data_handle_t** *data_handle,* starpu_mpi_req * *req,* int *dest,* int *mpi_tag,* MPI_Comm *comm*)

Post a standard-mode, non blocking send of `data_handle` to the node `dest` using the message tag `mpi_tag` within the communicator `comm`. After the call, the pointer to the request `req` can be used to test or to wait for the completion of the communication.

29.28.3.14 int starpu_mpi_irecv (**starpu_data_handle_t** *data_handle,* starpu_mpi_req * *req,* int *source,* int *mpi_tag,* MPI_Comm *comm*)

Post a nonblocking receive in `data_handle` from the node `source` using the message tag `mpi_tag` within the communicator `comm`. After the call, the pointer to the request `req` can be used to test or to wait for the completion of the communication.

29.28.3.15 int starpu_mpi_isend_detached (**starpu_data_handle_t** *data_handle,* int *dest,* int *mpi_tag,* MPI_Comm *comm,* void(*)(void *) *callback,* void * *arg*)

Post a standard-mode, non blocking send of `data_handle` to the node `dest` using the message tag `mpi_tag` within the communicator `comm`. On completion, the `callback` function is called with the argument `arg`. Similarly to the pthread detached functionality, when a detached communication completes, its resources are automatically released back to the system, there is no need to test or to wait for the completion of the request.

29.28.3.16   int starpu_mpi_irecv_detached (**starpu_data_handle_t** *data_handle,* int *source,* int *mpi_tag,* MPI_Comm *comm,* void(∗)(void ∗) *callback,* void ∗ *arg*)

Post a nonblocking receive in `data_handle` from the node `source` using the message tag `mpi_tag` within the communicator `comm`. On completion, the `callback` function is called with the argument `arg`. Similarly to the pthread detached functionality, when a detached communication completes, its resources are automatically released back to the system, there is no need to test or to wait for the completion of the request.

29.28.3.17   int starpu_mpi_irecv_detached_sequential_consistency (**starpu_data_handle_t** *data_handle,* int *source,* int *mpi_tag,* MPI_Comm *comm,* void(∗)(void ∗) *callback,* void ∗ *arg,* int *sequential_consistency*)

Post a nonblocking receive in `data_handle` from the node `source` using the message tag `mpi_tag` within the communicator `comm`. On completion, the `callback` function is called with the argument `arg`. The parameter `sequential_consistency` allows to enable or disable the sequential consistency for `data` handle (sequential consistency will be enabled or disabled based on the value of the parameter `sequential_consistency` and the value of the sequential consistency defined for `data_handle`). Similarly to the pthread detached functionality, when a detached communication completes, its resources are automatically released back to the system, there is no need to test or to wait for the completion of the request.

29.28.3.18   int starpu_mpi_issend (**starpu_data_handle_t** *data_handle,* starpu_mpi_req ∗ *req,* int *dest,* int *mpi_tag,* MPI_Comm *comm*)

Perform a synchronous-mode, non-blocking send of `data_handle` to the node `dest` using the message tag `mpi_tag` within the communicator `comm`.

29.28.3.19   int starpu_mpi_issend_detached (**starpu_data_handle_t** *data_handle,* int *dest,* int *mpi_tag,* MPI_Comm *comm,* void(∗)(void ∗) *callback,* void ∗ *arg*)

Perform a synchronous-mode, non-blocking send of `data_handle` to the node `dest` using the message tag `mpi_tag` within the communicator `comm`. On completion, the `callback` function is called with the argument `arg`. Similarly to the pthread detached functionality, when a detached communication completes, its resources are automatically released back to the system, there is no need to test or to wait for the completion of the request.

29.28.3.20   int starpu_mpi_wait (starpu_mpi_req ∗ *req,* MPI_Status ∗ *status*)

Return when the operation identified by request `req` is complete.

29.28.3.21   int starpu_mpi_test (starpu_mpi_req ∗ *req,* int ∗ *flag,* MPI_Status ∗ *status*)

If the operation identified by `req` is complete, set `flag` to 1. The `status` object is set to contain information on the completed operation.

29.28.3.22   int starpu_mpi_barrier (MPI_Comm *comm*)

Block the caller until all group members of the communicator `comm` have called it.

29.28.3.23   int starpu_mpi_wait_for_all (MPI_Comm *comm*)

Wait until all StarPU tasks and communications for the given communicator are completed.

29.28.3.24 int starpu_mpi_isend_detached_unlock_tag (**starpu_data_handle_t** *data_handle*, int *dest*, int *mpi_tag*, MPI_Comm *comm*, **starpu_tag_t** *tag*)

Post a standard-mode, non blocking send of `data_handle` to the node `dest` using the message tag `mpi_tag` within the communicator `comm`. On completion, `tag` is unlocked.

29.28.3.25 int starpu_mpi_irecv_detached_unlock_tag (**starpu_data_handle_t** *data_handle*, int *source*, int *mpi_tag*, MPI_Comm *comm*, **starpu_tag_t** *tag*)

Post a nonblocking receive in `data_handle` from the node `source` using the message tag `mpi_tag` within the communicator `comm`. On completion, `tag` is unlocked.

29.28.3.26 int starpu_mpi_isend_array_detached_unlock_tag (unsigned *array_size*, **starpu_data_handle_t** ∗ *data_handle*, int ∗ *dest*, int ∗ *mpi_tag*, MPI_Comm ∗ *comm*, **starpu_tag_t** *tag*)

Post `array_size` standard-mode, non blocking send. Each post sends the n-th data of the array `data_handle` to the n-th node of the array `dest` using the n-th message tag of the array `mpi_tag` within the n-th communicator of the array `comm`. On completion of the all the requests, `tag` is unlocked.

29.28.3.27 int starpu_mpi_irecv_array_detached_unlock_tag (unsigned *array_size*, **starpu_data_handle_t** ∗ *data_handle*, int ∗ *source*, int ∗ *mpi_tag*, MPI_Comm ∗ *comm*, **starpu_tag_t** *tag*)

Post `array_size` nonblocking receive. Each post receives in the n-th data of the array `data_handle` from the n-th node of the array `source` using the n-th message tag of the array `mpi_tag` within the n-th communicator of the array `comm`. On completion of the all the requests, `tag` is unlocked.

29.28.3.28 int starpu_mpi_get_communication_tag (void)

todo

29.28.3.29 void starpu_mpi_set_communication_tag (int *tag*)

todo

29.28.3.30 int starpu_mpi_datatype_register (**starpu_data_handle_t** *handle*, starpu_mpi_datatype_allocate_func_t *allocate_datatype_func*, starpu_mpi_datatype_free_func_t *free_datatype_func*)

Register functions to create and free a MPI datatype for the given handle. It is important that the function is called before any communication can take place for a data with the given handle. See Exchanging User Defined Data Interface for an example.

29.28.3.31 int starpu_mpi_datatype_unregister (**starpu_data_handle_t** *handle*)

Unregister the MPI datatype functions stored for the interface of the given handle.

29.28.3.32 int starpu_mpi_cache_is_enabled ( )

Return 1 if the communication cache is enabled, 0 otherwise

29.28.3.33 int starpu_mpi_cache_set (int *enabled*)

If `enabled` is 1, enable the communication cache. Otherwise, clean the cache if it was enabled and disable it.

29.28.3.34 void starpu_mpi_cache_flush (MPI_Comm *comm,* **starpu_data_handle_t *data_handle*)**

Clear the send and receive communication cache for the data `data_handle` and invalidate the value. The function has to be called at the same point of task graph submission by all the MPI nodes on which the handle was registered. The function does nothing if the cache mechanism is disabled (see STARPU_MPI_CACHE).

29.28.3.35 void starpu_mpi_cache_flush_all_data (MPI_Comm *comm*)

Clear the send and receive communication cache for all data and invalidate their values. The function has to be called at the same point of task graph submission by all the MPI nodes. The function does nothing if the cache mechanism is disabled (see STARPU_MPI_CACHE).

29.28.3.36 int starpu_mpi_cached_receive (starpu_data_handle_t *data_handle*)**

Test whether `data_handle` is cached for reception, i.e. the value was previously received from the owner node, and not flushed since then.

29.28.3.37 int starpu_mpi_cached_send (starpu_data_handle_t *data_handle,* int *dest*)**

Test whether `data_handle` is cached for emission to node `dest` , i.e. the value was previously sent to `dest`, and not flushed since then.

29.28.3.38 void starpu_mpi_data_register_comm (starpu_data_handle_t *data_handle,* int *tag,* int *rank,* MPI_Comm *comm*)**

Register to MPI a StarPU data handle with the given tag, rank and MPI communicator. It also automatically clears the MPI communication cache when unregistering the data.

29.28.3.39 void starpu_mpi_data_set_tag (starpu_data_handle_t *handle,* int *tag*)**

Register to MPI a StarPU data handle with the given tag. No rank will be defined. It also automatically clears the MPI communication cache when unregistering the data.

29.28.3.40 void starpu_mpi_data_set_rank_comm (starpu_data_handle_t *handle,* int *rank,* MPI_Comm *comm*)**

Register to MPI a StarPU data handle with the given rank and given communicator. No tag will be defined. It also automatically clears the MPI communication cache when unregistering the data.

29.28.3.41 int starpu_mpi_data_get_rank (starpu_data_handle_t *handle*)**

Return the rank of the given data.

29.28.3.42 int starpu_mpi_data_get_tag (starpu_data_handle_t *handle*)**

Return the tag of the given data.

29.28.3.43 void starpu_mpi_data_migrate (MPI_Comm *comm,* **starpu_data_handle_t *handle,* int *new_rank*)**

Migrate the data onto the `new_rank` MPI node. This means both transferring the data to node `new_rank` if it hasn't been transferred already, and setting the home node of the data to the new node. Further data transfers triggered by starpu_mpi_task_insert() will be done from that new node. This function thus needs to be called on all nodes which have registered the data. This also flushes the cache for this data to avoid incoherencies.

29.28.3.44 int starpu_mpi_insert_task (MPI_Comm *comm,* struct **starpu_codelet ∗ *codelet, ...*)**

Call starpu_mpi_task_insert(). Symbol kept for backward compatibility.

29.28.3.45 int starpu_mpi_task_insert (MPI_Comm *comm,* struct **starpu_codelet ∗ *codelet, ...*)**

Create and submit a task corresponding to codelet with the following arguments. The argument list must be zero-terminated.

The arguments following the codelet are the same types as for the function starpu_task_insert(). Access modes for data can also be set with STARPU_SSEND to specify the data has to be sent using a synchronous and non-blocking mode (see starpu_mpi_issend()). The extra argument STARPU_EXECUTE_ON_NODE followed by an integer allows to specify the MPI node to execute the codelet. It is also possible to specify that the node owning a specific data will execute the codelet, by using STARPU_EXECUTE_ON_DATA followed by a data handle.

The internal algorithm is as follows:

1. Find out which MPI node is going to execute the codelet.

    - If there is only one node owning data in STARPU_W mode, it will be selected;
    - If there is several nodes owning data in STARPU_W mode, a node will be selected according to a given node selection policy (see STARPU_NODE_SELECTION_POLICY or starpu_mpi_node_selection_set_current_policy())
    - The argument STARPU_EXECUTE_ON_NODE followed by an integer can be used to specify the node;
    - The argument STARPU_EXECUTE_ON_DATA followed by a data handle can be used to specify that the node owing the given data will execute the codelet.

2. Send and receive data as requested. Nodes owning data which need to be read by the task are sending them to the MPI node which will execute it. The latter receives them.

3. Execute the codelet. This is done by the MPI node selected in the 1st step of the algorithm.

4. If several MPI nodes own data to be written to, send written data back to their owners.

The algorithm also includes a communication cache mechanism that allows not to send data twice to the same MPI node, unless the data has been modified. The cache can be disabled (see STARPU_MPI_CACHE).

29.28.3.46 struct starpu_task ∗ starpu_mpi_task_build (MPI_Comm *comm,* struct starpu_codelet ∗ *codelet, ...*)
    [read]

Create a task corresponding to codelet with the following given arguments. The argument list must be zero-terminated. The function performs the first two steps of the function starpu_mpi_task_insert(). Only the MPI node selected in the first step of the algorithm will return a valid task structure which can then be submitted, others will return NULL. The function starpu_mpi_task_post_build() MUST be called after that on all nodes, and after the submission of the task on the node which creates it, with the SAME list of arguments.

29.28.3.47 int starpu_mpi_task_post_build (MPI_Comm *comm,* struct **starpu_codelet ∗ *codelet, ...*)**

MUST be called after a call to starpu_mpi_task_build(), with the SAME list of arguments. Perform the fourth – last – step of the algorithm described in starpu_mpi_task_insert().

29.28.3.48 void starpu_mpi_get_data_on_node (MPI_Comm *comm,* **starpu_data_handle_t *data_handle,* int *node*)**

Transfer data data_handle to MPI node node, sending it from its owner if needed. At least the target node and the owner have to call the function.

29.28.3.49 void starpu_mpi_get_data_on_node_detached (MPI_Comm *comm*, **starpu_data_handle_t** *data_handle*, int *node*, void(∗)(void ∗) *callback*, void ∗ *arg*)

Transfer data `data_handle` to MPI node `node`, sending it from its owner if needed. At least the target node and the owner have to call the function. On reception, the `callback` function is called with the argument `arg`.

29.28.3.50 int starpu_mpi_node_selection_get_current_policy ( )

Return the current policy used to select the node which will execute the codelet

29.28.3.51 int starpu_mpi_node_selection_set_current_policy (int *policy*)

Set the current policy used to select the node which will execute the codelet. The policy STARPU_MPI_NODE_- SELECTION_MOST_R_DATA selects the node having the most data in STARPU_R mode so as to minimize the amount of data to be transfered.

29.28.3.52 int starpu_mpi_node_selection_register_policy (starpu_mpi_select_node_policy_func_t *policy_func*)

Register a new policy which can then be used when there is several nodes owning data in STARPU_W mode. Here an example of function defining a node selection policy. The codelet will be executed on the node owing the first data with a size bigger than 1M, or on the node 0 if no data fits the given size.

```
int my_node_selection_policy(int me, int nb_nodes, struct starpu_data_descr
      *descr, int nb_data)
{
      // me is the current MPI rank
      // nb_nodes is the number of MPI nodes
      // descr is the description of the data specified when calling
      starpu_mpi_task_insert
      // nb_data is the number of data in descr
      int i;
      for (i= 0 ; i<nb_data ; i++)
      {
            starpu_data_handle_t data = descr[i].handle
      ;
            enum starpu_data_access_mode mode =
      descr[i].mode;
            if (mode & STARPU_R)
            {
                  int rank = starpu_data_get_rank(
      data);
                  size_t size = starpu_data_get_size(
      data);
                  if (size > 1024*1024) return rank;
            }
      }
      return 0;
}
```

29.28.3.53 int starpu_mpi_node_selection_unregister_policy (int *policy*)

Unregister a previously registered policy.

29.28.3.54 void starpu_mpi_redux_data (MPI_Comm *comm*, **starpu_data_handle_t** *data_handle*)

Perform a reduction on the given data `handle`. All nodes send the data to its owner node which will perform a reduction.

29.28.3.55   int starpu_mpi_scatter_detached (**starpu_data_handle_t** ∗ *data_handles,* int *count,* int *root,* MPI_Comm *comm,*
void(∗)(void ∗) *scallback,* void ∗ *sarg,* void(∗)(void ∗) *rcallback,* void ∗ *rarg*)

Scatter data among processes of the communicator based on the ownership of the data. For each data of the array
`data_handles`, the process `root` sends the data to the process owning this data. Processes receiving data
must have valid data handles to receive them. On completion of the collective communication, the `scallback`
function is called with the argument `sarg` on the process `root`, the `rcallback` function is called with the
argument `rarg` on any other process.

29.28.3.56   int starpu_mpi_gather_detached (**starpu_data_handle_t** ∗ *data_handles,* int *count,* int *root,* MPI_Comm *comm,*
void(∗)(void ∗) *scallback,* void ∗ *sarg,* void(∗)(void ∗) *rcallback,* void ∗ *rarg*)

Gather data from the different processes of the communicator onto the process `root`. Each process owning data
handle in the array `data_handles` will send them to the process `root`. The process `root` must have valid data
handles to receive the data. On completion of the collective communication, the `rcallback` function is called
with the argument `rarg` on the process root, the `scallback` function is called with the argument `sarg` on any
other process.

29.29   Task Bundles

Typedefs

- typedef struct
  _starpu_task_bundle ∗ starpu_task_bundle_t

Functions

- void starpu_task_bundle_create (starpu_task_bundle_t ∗bundle)
- int starpu_task_bundle_insert (starpu_task_bundle_t bundle, struct starpu_task ∗task)
- int starpu_task_bundle_remove (starpu_task_bundle_t bundle, struct starpu_task ∗task)
- void starpu_task_bundle_close (starpu_task_bundle_t bundle)
- double starpu_task_bundle_expected_length (starpu_task_bundle_t bundle, struct starpu_perfmodel_arch
  ∗arch, unsigned nimpl)
- double starpu_task_bundle_expected_energy (starpu_task_bundle_t bundle, struct starpu_perfmodel_arch
  ∗arch, unsigned nimpl)
- double starpu_task_bundle_expected_data_transfer_time (starpu_task_bundle_t bundle, unsigned memory-
  _node)

29.29.1   Detailed Description

29.29.2   Typedef Documentation

29.29.2.1   starpu_task_bundle_t

Opaque structure describing a list of tasks that should be scheduled on the same worker whenever it's possible. It
must be considered as a hint given to the scheduler as there is no guarantee that they will be executed on the same
worker.

29.29.3   Function Documentation

29.29.3.1 void starpu_task_bundle_create (**starpu_task_bundle_t** * *bundle*)

Factory function creating and initializing `bundle`, when the call returns, memory needed is allocated and `bundle` is ready to use.

29.29.3.2 int starpu_task_bundle_insert (**starpu_task_bundle_t** *bundle,* struct **starpu_task** * *task*)

Insert `task` in `bundle`. Until `task` is removed from `bundle` its expected length and data transfer time will be considered along those of the other tasks of bundle. This function must not be called if `bundle` is already closed and/or `task` is already submitted. On success, it returns 0. There are two cases of error : if `bundle` is already closed it returns `-EPERM`, if `task` was already submitted it returns `-EINVAL`.

29.29.3.3 int starpu_task_bundle_remove (**starpu_task_bundle_t** *bundle,* struct **starpu_task** * *task*)

Remove `task` from `bundle`. Of course `task` must have been previously inserted in `bundle`. This function must not be called if `bundle` is already closed and/or `task` is already submitted. Doing so would result in undefined behaviour. On success, it returns 0. If `bundle` is already closed it returns `-ENOENT`.

29.29.3.4 void starpu_task_bundle_close (**starpu_task_bundle_t** *bundle*)

Inform the runtime that the user will not modify `bundle` anymore, it means no more inserting or removing task. Thus the runtime can destroy it when possible.

29.29.3.5 double starpu_task_bundle_expected_length (**starpu_task_bundle_t** *bundle,* struct **starpu_perfmodel_arch** * *arch,* unsigned *nimpl*)

Return the expected duration of `bundle` in micro-seconds.

29.29.3.6 double starpu_task_bundle_expected_energy (**starpu_task_bundle_t** *bundle,* struct **starpu_perfmodel_arch** * *arch,* unsigned *nimpl*)

Return the expected energy consumption of `bundle` in J.

29.29.3.7 double starpu_task_bundle_expected_data_transfer_time (**starpu_task_bundle_t** *bundle,* unsigned *memory_node*)

Return the time (in micro-seconds) expected to transfer all data used within `bundle`.

29.30 Task Lists

Data Structures

- struct starpu_task_list

Functions

- STARPU_TASK_LIST_INLINE void starpu_task_list_init (struct starpu_task_list *list)
- STARPU_TASK_LIST_INLINE void starpu_task_list_push_front (struct starpu_task_list *list, struct starpu_-task *task)
- STARPU_TASK_LIST_INLINE void starpu_task_list_push_back (struct starpu_task_list *list, struct starpu_-task *task)

- STARPU_TASK_LIST_INLINE struct
  starpu_task * starpu_task_list_front (const struct starpu_task_list *list)
- STARPU_TASK_LIST_INLINE struct
  starpu_task * starpu_task_list_back (const struct starpu_task_list *list)
- STARPU_TASK_LIST_INLINE int starpu_task_list_empty (const struct starpu_task_list *list)
- STARPU_TASK_LIST_INLINE void starpu_task_list_erase (struct starpu_task_list *list, struct starpu_task *task)
- STARPU_TASK_LIST_INLINE struct
  starpu_task * starpu_task_list_pop_front (struct starpu_task_list *list)
- STARPU_TASK_LIST_INLINE struct
  starpu_task * starpu_task_list_pop_back (struct starpu_task_list *list)
- STARPU_TASK_LIST_INLINE struct
  starpu_task * starpu_task_list_begin (const struct starpu_task_list *list)
- STARPU_TASK_LIST_INLINE struct
  starpu_task * starpu_task_list_next (const struct starpu_task *task)
- STARPU_TASK_LIST_INLINE int starpu_task_list_ismember (const struct starpu_task_list *list, const struct starpu_task *look)

29.30.1 Detailed Description

29.30.2 Data Structure Documentation

29.30.2.1 struct starpu_task_list

Stores a double-chained list of tasks

Data Fields

struct starpu_task *	head	head of the list
struct starpu_task *	tail	tail of the list

29.30.3 Function Documentation

29.30.3.1 void starpu_task_list_init (struct **starpu_task_list** * *list*)

Initialize a list structure

29.30.3.2 void starpu_task_list_push_front (struct **starpu_task_list** * *list,* struct **starpu_task** * *task*)

Push `task` at the front of `list`

29.30.3.3 void starpu_task_list_push_back (struct **starpu_task_list** * *list,* struct **starpu_task** * *task*)

Push `task` at the back of `list`

29.30.3.4 struct **starpu_task** * starpu_task_list_front (const struct **starpu_task_list** * *list*) [read]

Get the front of `list` (without removing it)

29.30.3.5　struct starpu_task * starpu_task_list_back (const struct starpu_task_list * *list*)　[read]

Get the back of `list` (without removing it)

29.30.3.6　int starpu_task_list_empty (const struct starpu_task_list * *list*)

Test if `list` is empty

29.30.3.7　void starpu_task_list_erase (struct starpu_task_list * *list*, struct starpu_task * *task*)

Remove `task` from `list`

29.30.3.8　struct starpu_task * starpu_task_list_pop_front (struct starpu_task_list * *list*)　[read]

Remove the element at the front of `list`

29.30.3.9　struct starpu_task * starpu_task_list_pop_back (struct starpu_task_list * *list*)　[read]

Remove the element at the back of `list`

29.30.3.10　struct starpu_task * starpu_task_list_begin (const struct starpu_task_list * *list*)　[read]

Get the first task of `list`.

29.30.3.11　struct starpu_task * starpu_task_list_next (const struct starpu_task * *task*)　[read]

Get the next task of `list`. This is not erase-safe.

29.30.3.12　int starpu_task_list_ismember (const struct starpu_task_list * *list*, const struct starpu_task * *look*)

Test whether the given task `look` is contained in the `list`.

29.31　Parallel Tasks

Functions

- int starpu_combined_worker_get_size (void)
- int starpu_combined_worker_get_rank (void)
- unsigned starpu_combined_worker_get_count (void)
- int starpu_combined_worker_get_id (void)
- int starpu_combined_worker_assign_workerid (int nworkers, int workerid_array[])
- int starpu_combined_worker_get_description (int workerid, int *worker_size, int **combined_workerid)
- int starpu_combined_worker_can_execute_task (unsigned workerid, struct starpu_task *task, unsigned nimpl)
- void starpu_parallel_task_barrier_init (struct starpu_task *task, int workerid)
- void starpu_parallel_task_barrier_init_n (struct starpu_task *task, int worker_size)

29.31.1 Detailed Description

29.31.2 Function Documentation

29.31.2.1 int starpu_combined_worker_get_size (void)

Return the size of the current combined worker, i.e. the total number of cpus running the same task in the case of STARPU_SPMD parallel tasks, or the total number of threads that the task is allowed to start in the case of STARPU_FORKJOIN parallel tasks.

29.31.2.2 int starpu_combined_worker_get_rank (void)

Return the rank of the current thread within the combined worker. Can only be used in STARPU_FORKJOIN parallel tasks, to know which part of the task to work on.

29.31.2.3 unsigned starpu_combined_worker_get_count (void)

Return the number of different combined workers.

29.31.2.4 int starpu_combined_worker_get_id (void)

Return the identifier of the current combined worker.

29.31.2.5 int starpu_combined_worker_assign_workerid (int *nworkers,* int *workerid_array[]*)

Register a new combined worker and get its identifier

29.31.2.6 int starpu_combined_worker_get_description (int *workerid,* int * *worker_size,* int ** *combined_workerid*)

Get the description of a combined worker

29.31.2.7 int starpu_combined_worker_can_execute_task (unsigned *workerid,* struct **starpu_task** * *task,* unsigned *nimpl*)

Variant of starpu_worker_can_execute_task() compatible with combined workers

29.31.2.8 void starpu_parallel_task_barrier_init (struct **starpu_task** * *task,* int *workerid*)

Initialise the barrier for the parallel task, and dispatch the task between the different workers of the given combined worker.

29.31.2.9 void starpu_parallel_task_barrier_init_n (struct **starpu_task** * *task,* int *worker_size*)

Initialise the barrier for the parallel task, to be pushed to `worker_size` workers (without having to explicit a given combined worker).

29.32 Running Drivers

Data Structures

- struct starpu_driver

- union starpu_driver.id

Functions

- int starpu_driver_run (struct starpu_driver *d)
- int starpu_driver_init (struct starpu_driver *d)
- int starpu_driver_run_once (struct starpu_driver *d)
- int starpu_driver_deinit (struct starpu_driver *d)
- void starpu_drivers_request_termination (void)

29.32.1 Detailed Description

29.32.2 Data Structure Documentation

29.32.2.1 struct starpu_driver

structure for a driver

Data Fields

enum starpu_-worker_archtype	type	Type of the driver. Only STARPU_CPU_WORKER, STARPU_CUDA_W-ORKER and STARPU_OPENCL_WORKER are currently supported.
union starpu_driver	id	Identifier of the driver.

29.32.2.2 union starpu_driver.id

Data Fields

unsigned	cpu_id	
unsigned	cuda_id	
cl_device_id	opencl_id	

29.32.3 Function Documentation

29.32.3.1 int starpu_driver_run (struct **starpu_driver** * *d*)

Initialize the given driver, run it until it receives a request to terminate, deinitialize it and return 0 on success. Return $-EINVAL$ if starpu_driver::type is not a valid StarPU device type (STARPU_CPU_WORKER, STARPU_CUDA_-WORKER or STARPU_OPENCL_WORKER).

This is the same as using the following functions: calling starpu_driver_init(), then calling starpu_driver_run_once() in a loop, and finally starpu_driver_deinit().

29.32.3.2 int starpu_driver_init (struct **starpu_driver** * *d*)

Initialize the given driver. Return 0 on success, $-EINVAL$ if starpu_driver::type is not a valid starpu_worker_-archtype.

29.32.3.3 int starpu_driver_run_once (struct **starpu_driver** * *d*)

Run the driver once, then return 0 on success, $-EINVAL$ if starpu_driver::type is not a valid starpu_worker_-archtype.

29.32.3.4   int starpu_driver_deinit (struct **starpu_driver** ∗ *d*)

Deinitialize the given driver. Return 0 on success, −EINVAL if starpu_driver::type is not a valid starpu_worker_-archtype.

29.32.3.5   void starpu_drivers_request_termination (void)

Notify all running drivers that they should terminate.

29.33   Expert Mode

Functions

- void starpu_wake_all_blocked_workers (void)
- int starpu_progression_hook_register (unsigned(∗func)(void ∗arg), void ∗arg)
- void starpu_progression_hook_deregister (int hook_id)

29.33.1   Detailed Description

29.33.2   Function Documentation

29.33.2.1   void starpu_wake_all_blocked_workers (void)

Wake all the workers, so they can inspect data requests and task submissions again.

29.33.2.2   int starpu_progression_hook_register (unsigned(∗)(void ∗arg) *func,* void ∗ *arg*)

Register a progression hook, to be called when workers are idle.

29.33.2.3   void starpu_progression_hook_deregister (int *hook_id*)

Unregister a given progression hook.

29.34   StarPU-Top Interface

Data Structures

- struct starpu_top_data
- struct starpu_top_param

Enumerations

- enum starpu_top_data_type { STARPU_TOP_DATA_BOOLEAN, STARPU_TOP_DATA_INTEGER, STAR-PU_TOP_DATA_FLOAT }
- enum starpu_top_param_type { STARPU_TOP_PARAM_BOOLEAN, STARPU_TOP_PARAM_INTEGER, STARPU_TOP_PARAM_FLOAT, STARPU_TOP_PARAM_ENUM }
- enum starpu_top_message_type {
  TOP_TYPE_GO, TOP_TYPE_SET, TOP_TYPE_CONTINUE, TOP_TYPE_ENABLE,
  TOP_TYPE_DISABLE, TOP_TYPE_DEBUG, TOP_TYPE_UNKNOW }

Functions to call before the initialisation

- struct starpu_top_data * starpu_top_add_data_boolean (const char *data_name, int active)
- struct starpu_top_data * starpu_top_add_data_integer (const char *data_name, int minimum_value, int maximum_value, int active)
- struct starpu_top_data * starpu_top_add_data_float (const char *data_name, double minimum_value, double maximum_value, int active)
- struct starpu_top_param * starpu_top_register_parameter_boolean (const char *param_name, int *parameter_field, void(*callback)(struct starpu_top_param *))
- struct starpu_top_param * starpu_top_register_parameter_float (const char *param_name, double *parameter_field, double minimum_value, double maximum_value, void(*callback)(struct starpu_top_param *))
- struct starpu_top_param * starpu_top_register_parameter_integer (const char *param_name, int *parameter_field, int minimum_value, int maximum_value, void(*callback)(struct starpu_top_param *))
- struct starpu_top_param * starpu_top_register_parameter_enum (const char *param_name, int *parameter_field, char **values, int nb_values, void(*callback)(struct starpu_top_param *))

Initialisation

- void starpu_top_init_and_wait (const char *server_name)

To call after initialisation

- void starpu_top_update_parameter (const struct starpu_top_param *param)
- void starpu_top_update_data_boolean (const struct starpu_top_data *data, int value)
- void starpu_top_update_data_integer (const struct starpu_top_data *data, int value)
- void starpu_top_update_data_float (const struct starpu_top_data *data, double value)
- void starpu_top_task_prevision (struct starpu_task *task, int devid, unsigned long long start, unsigned long long end)
- void starpu_top_debug_log (const char *message)
- void starpu_top_debug_lock (const char *message)

29.34.1 Detailed Description

29.34.2 Data Structure Documentation

29.34.2.1 struct starpu_top_data

todo

Data Fields

unsigned int	id	todo
const char *	name	todo
int	int_min_value	todo
int	int_max_value	todo
double	double_min_-value	todo
double	double_max_-value	todo
int	active	todo
enum starpu_-top_data_type	type	todo
struct starpu_top_data *	next	todo

29.34.2.2   struct starpu_top_param

todo

Data Fields

- unsigned int id
- const char ∗ name
- enum starpu_top_param_type type
- void ∗ value
- char ∗∗ enum_values
- int nb_values
- void(∗ callback)(struct starpu_top_param ∗)
- int int_min_value
- int int_max_value
- double double_min_value
- double double_max_value
- struct starpu_top_param ∗ next

29.34.2.2.1   Field Documentation

29.34.2.2.1.1   unsigned int starpu_top_param::id

todo

29.34.2.2.1.2   const char ∗ starpu_top_param::name

todo

29.34.2.2.1.3   enum **starpu_top_param_type** starpu_top_param::type

todo

29.34.2.2.1.4   void ∗ starpu_top_param::value

todo

29.34.2.2.1.5   char ∗∗ starpu_top_param::enum_values

only for enum type can be NULL

29.34.2.2.1.6   int starpu_top_param::nb_values

todo

29.34.2.2.1.7   void(∗ starpu_top_param::callback)(struct **starpu_top_param** ∗)

todo

29.34.2.2.1.8   int starpu_top_param::int_min_value

only for integer type

29.34.2.2.1.9   int starpu_top_param::int_max_value

todo

29.34.2.2.1.10   double starpu_top_param::double_min_value

only for double type

29.34.2.2.1.11 double starpu_top_param::double_max_value

todo

29.34.2.2.1.12 struct starpu_top_param * starpu_top_param::next

todo

29.34.3 Enumeration Type Documentation

29.34.3.1 enum starpu_top_data_type

StarPU-Top Data type

Enumerator:

> **STARPU_TOP_DATA_BOOLEAN** todo
>
> **STARPU_TOP_DATA_INTEGER** todo
>
> **STARPU_TOP_DATA_FLOAT** todo

29.34.3.2 enum starpu_top_param_type

StarPU-Top Parameter type

Enumerator:

> **STARPU_TOP_PARAM_BOOLEAN** todo
>
> **STARPU_TOP_PARAM_INTEGER** todo
>
> **STARPU_TOP_PARAM_FLOAT** todo
>
> **STARPU_TOP_PARAM_ENUM** todo

29.34.3.3 enum starpu_top_message_type

StarPU-Top Message type

Enumerator:

> **TOP_TYPE_GO** todo
>
> **TOP_TYPE_SET** todo
>
> **TOP_TYPE_CONTINUE** todo
>
> **TOP_TYPE_ENABLE** todo
>
> **TOP_TYPE_DISABLE** todo
>
> **TOP_TYPE_DEBUG** todo
>
> **TOP_TYPE_UNKNOW** todo

29.34.4 Function Documentation

29.34.4.1 struct starpu_top_data * starpu_top_add_data_boolean (const char * *data_name,* int *active*) `[read]`

Register a data named `data_name` of type boolean. If `active` is 0, the value will NOT be displayed to users. Any other value will make the value displayed.

29.34.4.2 struct **starpu_top_data** ∗ starpu_top_add_data_integer (const char ∗ *data_name,* int *minimum_value,* int *maximum_value,* int *active*) [read]

Register a data named `data_name` of type integer. `minimum_value` and `maximum_value` will be used to define the scale in the UI. If `active` is 0, the value will NOT be displayed to users. Any other value will make the value displayed.

29.34.4.3 struct **starpu_top_data** ∗ starpu_top_add_data_float (const char ∗ *data_name,* double *minimum_value,* double *maximum_value,* int *active*) [read]

Register a data named `data_name` of type float. `minimum_value` and `maximum_value` will be used to define the scale in the UI. If `active` is 0, the value will NOT be displayed to users. Any other value will make the value displayed.

29.34.4.4 struct **starpu_top_param** ∗ starpu_top_register_parameter_boolean (const char ∗ *param_name,* int ∗ *parameter_field,* void(∗)(struct **starpu_top_param** ∗) *callback*) [read]

Register a parameter named `parameter_name`, of type boolean. If not `NULL`, the `callback` function will be called when the parameter is modified by the UI.

29.34.4.5 struct **starpu_top_param** ∗ starpu_top_register_parameter_float (const char ∗ *param_name,* double ∗ *parameter_field,* double *minimum_value,* double *maximum_value,* void(∗)(struct **starpu_top_param** ∗) *callback*) [read]

Register a parameter named `param_name`, of type integer. `minimum_value` and `maximum_value` will be used to prevent users from setting incorrect value. If not `NULL`, the `callback` function will be called when the parameter is modified by the UI.

29.34.4.6 struct **starpu_top_param** ∗ starpu_top_register_parameter_integer (const char ∗ *param_name,* int ∗ *parameter_field,* int *minimum_value,* int *maximum_value,* void(∗)(struct **starpu_top_param** ∗) *callback*) [read]

Register a parameter named `param_name`, of type float. `minimum_value` and `maximum_value` will be used to prevent users from setting incorrect value. If not `NULL`, the `callback` function will be called when the parameter is modified by the UI.

29.34.4.7 struct **starpu_top_param** ∗ starpu_top_register_parameter_enum (const char ∗ *param_name,* int ∗ *parameter_field,* char ∗∗ *values,* int *nb_values,* void(∗)(struct **starpu_top_param** ∗) *callback*) [read]

Register a parameter named `param_name`, of type enum. `values` and `nb_values` will be used to prevent users from setting incorrect value. If not `NULL`, the `callback` function will be called when the parameter is modified by the UI.

29.34.4.8 void starpu_top_init_and_wait (const char ∗ *server_name*)

Must be called when all parameters and data have been registered AND initialised (for parameters). It will wait for a TOP to connect, send initialisation sentences, and wait for the GO message.

29.34.4.9 void starpu_top_update_parameter (const struct **starpu_top_param** ∗ *param*)

Should be called after every modification of a parameter from something other than starpu_top. It notices the UI that the configuration has changed.

29.34.4.10   void starpu_top_update_data_boolean (const struct **starpu_top_data** * *data*, int *value*)

Update the boolean value of `data` to `value` the UI.

29.34.4.11   void starpu_top_update_data_integer (const struct **starpu_top_data** * *data*, int *value*)

Update the integer value of `data` to `value` the UI.

29.34.4.12   void starpu_top_update_data_float (const struct **starpu_top_data** * *data*, double *value*)

Update the float value of `data` to `value` the UI.

29.34.4.13   void starpu_top_task_prevision (struct **starpu_task** * *task*, int *devid*, unsigned long long *start*, unsigned long long *end*)

Notift the UI that `task` is planned to run from `start` to `end`, on computation-core.

29.34.4.14   void starpu_top_debug_log (const char * *message*)

When running in debug mode, display `message` in the UI.

29.34.4.15   void starpu_top_debug_lock (const char * *message*)

When running in debug mode, send `message` to the UI and wait for a continue message to return. The lock (which creates a stop-point) should be called only by the main thread. Calling it from more than one thread is not supported.

29.35   Scheduling Contexts

StarPU permits on one hand grouping workers in combined workers in order to execute a parallel task and on the other hand grouping tasks in bundles that will be executed by a single specified worker. In contrast when we group workers in scheduling contexts we submit starpu tasks to them and we schedule them with the policy assigned to the context. Scheduling contexts can be created, deleted and modified dynamically.

Data Structures

- struct starpu_sched_ctx_performance_counters

Scheduling Contexts Basic API

- #define STARPU_SCHED_CTX_POLICY_NAME
- #define STARPU_SCHED_CTX_POLICY_STRUCT
- #define STARPU_SCHED_CTX_POLICY_MIN_PRIO
- #define STARPU_SCHED_CTX_POLICY_MAX_PRIO
- #define STARPU_SCHED_CTX_AWAKE_WORKERS
- #define STARPU_SCHED_CTX_POLICY_INIT
- #define STARPU_SCHED_CTX_USER_DATA
- #define STARPU_SCHED_CTX_SUB_CTXS
- #define STARPU_SCHED_CTX_CUDA_NSMS
- unsigned starpu_sched_ctx_create (int *workerids_ctx, int nworkers_ctx, const char *sched_ctx_name,...)

- unsigned starpu_sched_ctx_create_inside_interval (const char *policy_name, const char *sched_ctx_name, int min_ncpus, int max_ncpus, int min_ngpus, int max_ngpus, unsigned allow_overlap)
- void starpu_sched_ctx_register_close_callback (unsigned sched_ctx_id, void(*close_callback)(unsigned sched_ctx_id, void *args), void *args)
- void starpu_sched_ctx_add_workers (int *workerids_ctx, unsigned nworkers_ctx, unsigned sched_ctx_id)
- void starpu_sched_ctx_remove_workers (int *workerids_ctx, unsigned nworkers_ctx, unsigned sched_ctx_-id)
- void starpu_sched_ctx_display_workers (unsigned sched_ctx_id, FILE *f)
- void starpu_sched_ctx_delete (unsigned sched_ctx_id)
- void starpu_sched_ctx_set_inheritor (unsigned sched_ctx_id, unsigned inheritor)
- void starpu_sched_ctx_set_context (unsigned *sched_ctx_id)
- unsigned starpu_sched_ctx_get_context (void)
- void starpu_sched_ctx_stop_task_submission (void)
- void starpu_sched_ctx_finished_submit (unsigned sched_ctx_id)
- unsigned starpu_sched_ctx_get_workers_list (unsigned sched_ctx_id, int **workerids)
- unsigned starpu_sched_ctx_get_workers_list_raw (unsigned sched_ctx_id, int **workerids)
- unsigned starpu_sched_ctx_get_nworkers (unsigned sched_ctx_id)
- unsigned starpu_sched_ctx_get_nshared_workers (unsigned sched_ctx_id, unsigned sched_ctx_id2)
- unsigned starpu_sched_ctx_contains_worker (int workerid, unsigned sched_ctx_id)
- unsigned starpu_sched_ctx_worker_get_id (unsigned sched_ctx_id)
- unsigned starpu_sched_ctx_overlapping_ctxs_on_worker (int workerid)

Scheduling Context Priorities

- #define STARPU_MIN_PRIO
- #define STARPU_MAX_PRIO
- #define STARPU_DEFAULT_PRIO
- int starpu_sched_ctx_set_min_priority (unsigned sched_ctx_id, int min_prio)
- int starpu_sched_ctx_set_max_priority (unsigned sched_ctx_id, int max_prio)
- int starpu_sched_ctx_get_min_priority (unsigned sched_ctx_id)
- int starpu_sched_ctx_get_max_priority (unsigned sched_ctx_id)
- int starpu_sched_ctx_min_priority_is_set (unsigned sched_ctx_id)
- int starpu_sched_ctx_max_priority_is_set (unsigned sched_ctx_id)
- void * starpu_sched_ctx_get_user_data (unsigned sched_ctx_id)

Scheduling Context Worker Collection

- struct starpu_worker_collection * starpu_sched_ctx_create_worker_collection (unsigned sched_ctx_id, enum starpu_worker_collection_type type) STARPU_ATTRIBUTE_MALLOC
- void starpu_sched_ctx_delete_worker_collection (unsigned sched_ctx_id)
- struct starpu_worker_collection * starpu_sched_ctx_get_worker_collection (unsigned sched_ctx_id)

Scheduling Context Link with Hypervisor

- void starpu_sched_ctx_set_perf_counters (unsigned sched_ctx_id, void *perf_counters)
- void starpu_sched_ctx_call_pushed_task_cb (int workerid, unsigned sched_ctx_id)
- void starpu_sched_ctx_notify_hypervisor_exists (void)
- unsigned starpu_sched_ctx_check_if_hypervisor_exists (void)
- void starpu_sched_ctx_set_policy_data (unsigned sched_ctx_id, void *policy_data)
- void * starpu_sched_ctx_get_policy_data (unsigned sched_ctx_id)
- void * starpu_sched_ctx_exec_parallel_code (void *(*func)(void *), void *param, unsigned sched_ctx_id)
- int starpu_sched_ctx_get_nready_tasks (unsigned sched_ctx_id)
- double starpu_sched_ctx_get_nready_flops (unsigned sched_ctx_id)

29.35.1 Detailed Description

StarPU permits on one hand grouping workers in combined workers in order to execute a parallel task and on the other hand grouping tasks in bundles that will be executed by a single specified worker. In contrast when we group workers in scheduling contexts we submit starpu tasks to them and we schedule them with the policy assigned to the context. Scheduling contexts can be created, deleted and modified dynamically.

29.35.2 Data Structure Documentation

29.35.2.1 struct starpu_sched_ctx_performance_counters

Performance counters used by the starpu to indicate the hypervisor how the application and the resources are executing.

Data Fields

- void(∗ notify_idle_cycle)(unsigned sched_ctx_id, int worker, double idle_time)
- void(∗ notify_poped_task)(unsigned sched_ctx_id, int worker)
- void(∗ notify_pushed_task)(unsigned sched_ctx_id, int worker)
- void(∗ notify_post_exec_task)(struct starpu_task ∗task, size_t data_size, uint32_t footprint, int hypervisor_-tag, double flops)
- void(∗ notify_submitted_job)(struct starpu_task ∗task, uint32_t footprint, size_t data_size)
- void(∗ **notify_empty_ctx**)(unsigned sched_ctx_id, struct starpu_task ∗task)
- void(∗ notify_delete_context)(unsigned sched_ctx)

29.35.2.1.1 Field Documentation

29.35.2.1.1.1 void(∗ starpu_sched_ctx_performance_counters::notify_idle_cycle)(unsigned sched_ctx_id, int worker, double idle_time)

Inform the hypervisor for how long a worker has been idle in the specified context

29.35.2.1.1.2 void(∗ starpu_sched_ctx_performance_counters::notify_poped_task)(unsigned sched_ctx_id, int worker)

Inform the hypervisor that a task executing a specified number of instructions has been poped from the worker

29.35.2.1.1.3 void(∗ starpu_sched_ctx_performance_counters::notify_pushed_task)(unsigned sched_ctx_id, int worker)

Notify the hypervisor that a task has been scheduled on the queue of the worker corresponding to the specified context

29.35.2.1.1.4 void(∗ starpu_sched_ctx_performance_counters::notify_post_exec_task)(struct **starpu_task** ∗task, size_t data_size, uint32_t footprint, int hypervisor_tag, double flops)

Notify the hypervisor that a task has just been executed

29.35.2.1.1.5 void(∗ starpu_sched_ctx_performance_counters::notify_submitted_job)(struct **starpu_task** ∗task, uint32_t footprint, size_t data_size)

Notify the hypervisor that a task has just been submitted

29.35.2.1.1.6 void(∗ starpu_sched_ctx_performance_counters::notify_delete_context)(unsigned sched_ctx)

Notify the hypervisor that the context was deleted

29.35.3 Macro Definition Documentation

29.35.3.1   #define STARPU_SCHED_CTX_POLICY_NAME

Used when calling starpu_sched_ctx_create() to specify a name for a scheduling policy

29.35.3.2   #define STARPU_SCHED_CTX_POLICY_STRUCT

Used when calling starpu_sched_ctx_create() to specify a pointer to a scheduling policy

29.35.3.3   #define STARPU_SCHED_CTX_POLICY_MIN_PRIO

Used when calling starpu_sched_ctx_create() to specify a minimum scheduler priority value.

29.35.3.4   #define STARPU_SCHED_CTX_POLICY_MAX_PRIO

Used when calling starpu_sched_ctx_create() to specify a maximum scheduler priority value.

29.35.3.5   #define STARPU_SCHED_CTX_AWAKE_WORKERS

Used when calling starpu_sched_ctx_create() to specify a pointer to a scheduling policy

29.35.3.6   #define STARPU_SCHED_CTX_POLICY_INIT

Used when calling starpu_sched_ctx_create() to specify a function pointer allowing to initialize the scheduling policy.

29.35.3.7   #define STARPU_SCHED_CTX_USER_DATA

Used when calling starpu_sched_ctx_create() to specify a pointer to some user data related to the context being created.

29.35.3.8   #define STARPU_SCHED_CTX_SUB_CTXS

Used when calling starpu_sched_ctx_create() to specify a list of sub contextes of the current context.

29.35.3.9   #define STARPU_SCHED_CTX_CUDA_NSMS

Used when calling starpu_sched_ctx_create() in order to create a context on the NVIDIA GPU to specify the number of SMs the context should have

29.35.3.10   #define STARPU_MIN_PRIO

Provided for legacy reasons.

29.35.3.11   #define STARPU_MAX_PRIO

Provided for legacy reasons.

29.35.3.12   #define STARPU_DEFAULT_PRIO

By convention, the default priority level should be 0 so that we can statically allocate tasks with a default priority.

29.35.4   Function Documentation

29.35.4.1   unsigned starpu_sched_ctx_create (int * *workerids_ctx*, int *nworkers_ctx*, const char * *sched_ctx_name*, ...)

Create a scheduling context with the given parameters (see below) and assigns the workers in `workerids_ctx` to execute the tasks submitted to it. The return value represents the identifier of the context that has just been created. It will be further used to indicate the context the tasks will be submitted to. The return value should be at most STARPU_NMAX_SCHED_CTXS.

The arguments following the name of the scheduling context can be of the following types:

- STARPU_SCHED_CTX_POLICY_NAME, followed by the name of a predefined scheduling policy. Use an empty string to create the context with the default scheduling policy.

- STARPU_SCHED_CTX_POLICY_STRUCT, followed by a pointer to a custom scheduling policy (struct starpu_sched_policy *)

- STARPU_SCHED_CTX_POLICY_MIN_PRIO, followed by a integer representing the minimum priority value to be defined for the scheduling policy.

- STARPU_SCHED_CTX_POLICY_MAX_PRIO, followed by a integer representing the maximum priority value to be defined for the scheduling policy.

- STARPU_SCHED_CTX_POLICY_INIT, followed by a function pointer (ie. void init_sched(void)) allowing to initialize the scheduling policy.

- STARPU_SCHED_CTX_USER_DATA, followed by a pointer to a custom user data structure, to be retrieved by starpu_sched_ctx_get_user_data().

29.35.4.2   unsigned starpu_sched_ctx_create_inside_interval (const char * *policy_name*, const char * *sched_ctx_name*, int *min_ncpus*, int *max_ncpus*, int *min_ngpus*, int *max_ngpus*, unsigned *allow_overlap*)

Create a context indicating an approximate interval of resources

29.35.4.3   void starpu_sched_ctx_register_close_callback (unsigned *sched_ctx_id*, void(*)(unsigned sched_ctx_id, void *args) *close_callback*, void * *args*)

Execute the callback whenever the last task of the context finished executing, it is called with the parameters `sched_ctx` and any other parameter needed by the application (packed in `args`)

29.35.4.4   void starpu_sched_ctx_add_workers (int * *workerids_ctx*, unsigned *nworkers_ctx*, unsigned *sched_ctx_id*)

Add dynamically the workers in `workerids_ctx` to the context `sched_ctx_id`. The last argument cannot be greater than STARPU_NMAX_SCHED_CTXS.

29.35.4.5   void starpu_sched_ctx_remove_workers (int * *workerids_ctx*, unsigned *nworkers_ctx*, unsigned *sched_ctx_id*)

Remove the workers in `workerids_ctx` from the context `sched_ctx_id`. The last argument cannot be greater than STARPU_NMAX_SCHED_CTXS.

29.35.4.6   void starpu_sched_ctx_display_workers (unsigned *sched_ctx_id*, FILE * *f*)

Print on the file `f` the worker names belonging to the context `sched_ctx_id`

29.35.4.7 void starpu_sched_ctx_delete (unsigned *sched_ctx_id*)

Delete scheduling context `sched_ctx_id` and transfer remaining workers to the inheritor scheduling context.

29.35.4.8 void starpu_sched_ctx_set_inheritor (unsigned *sched_ctx_id,* unsigned *inheritor*)

Indicate which context whill inherit the resources of this context when he will be deleted.

29.35.4.9 void starpu_sched_ctx_set_context (unsigned ∗ *sched_ctx_id*)

Set the scheduling context the subsequent tasks will be submitted to

29.35.4.10 unsigned starpu_sched_ctx_get_context (void)

Return the scheduling context the tasks are currently submitted to, or STARPU_NMAX_SCHED_CTXS if no default context has been defined by calling the function starpu_sched_ctx_set_context().

29.35.4.11 void starpu_sched_ctx_stop_task_submission (void)

Stop submitting tasks from the empty context list until the next time the context has time to check the empty context list

29.35.4.12 void starpu_sched_ctx_finished_submit (unsigned *sched_ctx_id*)

Indicate starpu that the application finished submitting to this context in order to move the workers to the inheritor as soon as possible.

29.35.4.13 unsigned starpu_sched_ctx_get_workers_list (unsigned *sched_ctx_id,* int ∗∗ *workerids*)

Return the list of workers in the array `workerids`, the returned value is the number of workers. The user should free the `workerids` table after finishing using it (it is allocated inside the function with the proper size)

29.35.4.14 unsigned starpu_sched_ctx_get_workers_list_raw (unsigned *sched_ctx_id,* int ∗∗ *workerids*)

Return the list of workers in the array `workerids`, the returned value is the number of workers. This list is provided in raw order, i.e. not sorted by tree or list order, and the user should not free the `workerids` table. This function is thus much less costly than starpu_sched_ctx_get_workers_list.

29.35.4.15 unsigned starpu_sched_ctx_get_nworkers (unsigned *sched_ctx_id*)

Return the number of workers managed by the specified contexts (Usually needed to verify if it manages any workers or if it should be blocked)

29.35.4.16 unsigned starpu_sched_ctx_get_nshared_workers (unsigned *sched_ctx_id,* unsigned *sched_ctx_id2*)

Return the number of workers shared by two contexts.

29.35.4.17 unsigned starpu_sched_ctx_contains_worker (int *workerid,* unsigned *sched_ctx_id*)

Return 1 if the worker belongs to the context and 0 otherwise

29.35.4.18   unsigned starpu_sched_ctx_worker_get_id (unsigned *sched_ctx_id*)

Return the workerid if the worker belongs to the context and -1 otherwise. If the thread calling this function is not a worker the function returns -1 as it calls the function starpu_worker_get_id().

29.35.4.19   unsigned starpu_sched_ctx_overlapping_ctxs_on_worker (int *workerid*)

Check if a worker is shared between several contexts

29.35.4.20   int starpu_sched_ctx_set_min_priority (unsigned *sched_ctx_id*, int *min_prio*)

Define the minimum task priority level supported by the scheduling policy of the given scheduler context. The default minimum priority level is the same as the default priority level which is 0 by convention. The application may access that value by calling the function starpu_sched_ctx_get_min_priority(). This function should only be called from the initialization method of the scheduling policy, and should not be used directly from the application.

29.35.4.21   int starpu_sched_ctx_set_max_priority (unsigned *sched_ctx_id*, int *max_prio*)

Define the maximum priority level supported by the scheduling policy of the given scheduler context. The default maximum priority level is 1. The application may access that value by calling the starpu_sched_ctx_get_max_priority function. This function should only be called from the initialization method of the scheduling policy, and should not be used directly from the application.

29.35.4.22   int starpu_sched_ctx_get_min_priority (unsigned *sched_ctx_id*)

Return the current minimum priority level supported by the scheduling policy of the given scheduler context.

29.35.4.23   int starpu_sched_ctx_get_max_priority (unsigned *sched_ctx_id*)

Return the current maximum priority level supported by the scheduling policy of the given scheduler context.

29.35.4.24   int starpu_sched_ctx_min_priority_is_set (unsigned *sched_ctx_id*)

todo

29.35.4.25   int starpu_sched_ctx_max_priority_is_set (unsigned *sched_ctx_id*)

todo

29.35.4.26   void * starpu_sched_ctx_get_user_data (unsigned *sched_ctx_id*)

Return the user data pointer associated to the scheduling context.

29.35.4.27   struct **starpu_worker_collection** * starpu_sched_ctx_create_worker_collection (unsigned *sched_ctx_id*, enum **starpu_worker_collection_type** *type*)   [read]

Create a worker collection of the type indicated by the last parameter for the context specified through the first parameter.

29.35.4.28 void starpu_sched_ctx_delete_worker_collection (unsigned *sched_ctx_id*)

Delete the worker collection of the specified scheduling context

29.35.4.29 struct **starpu_worker_collection** ∗ starpu_sched_ctx_get_worker_collection (unsigned *sched_ctx_id*) [read]

Return the worker collection managed by the indicated context

29.35.4.30 void starpu_sched_ctx_set_perf_counters (unsigned *sched_ctx_id,* void ∗ *perf_counters*)

Indicate to starpu the pointer to the performance counter

29.35.4.31 void starpu_sched_ctx_call_pushed_task_cb (int *workerid,* unsigned *sched_ctx_id*)

Callback that lets the scheduling policy tell the hypervisor that a task was pushed on a worker

29.35.4.32 void starpu_sched_ctx_notify_hypervisor_exists (void)

Allow the hypervisor to let starpu know he's initialised

29.35.4.33 unsigned starpu_sched_ctx_check_if_hypervisor_exists (void)

Ask starpu if he is informed if the hypervisor is initialised

29.35.4.34 void starpu_sched_ctx_set_policy_data (unsigned *sched_ctx_id,* void ∗ *policy_data*)

Allocate the scheduling policy data (private information of the scheduler like queues, variables, additional condition variables) the context

29.35.4.35 void ∗ starpu_sched_ctx_get_policy_data (unsigned *sched_ctx_id*)

Return the scheduling policy data (private information of the scheduler) of the contexts previously assigned to.

29.35.4.36 void ∗ starpu_sched_ctx_exec_parallel_code (void ∗(∗)(void ∗) *func,* void ∗ *param,* unsigned *sched_ctx_id*)

Execute any parallel code on the workers of the sched_ctx (workers are blocked)

29.35.4.37 int starpu_sched_ctx_get_nready_tasks (unsigned *sched_ctx_id*)

todo

29.35.4.38 double starpu_sched_ctx_get_nready_flops (unsigned *sched_ctx_id*)

todo

29.36 Scheduling Policy

TODO. While StarPU comes with a variety of scheduling policies (see Task Scheduling Policies), it may sometimes be desirable to implement custom policies to address specific problems. The API described below allows users to write their own scheduling policy.

Data Structures

- struct starpu_sched_policy

Macros

- #define STARPU_MAXIMPLEMENTATIONS

Functions

- struct starpu_sched_policy ** starpu_sched_get_predefined_policies ()
- void starpu_worker_get_sched_condition (int workerid, starpu_pthread_mutex_t **sched_mutex, starpu_-pthread_cond_t **sched_cond)
- int starpu_sched_set_min_priority (int min_prio)
- int starpu_sched_set_max_priority (int max_prio)
- int starpu_sched_get_min_priority (void)
- int starpu_sched_get_max_priority (void)
- int starpu_push_local_task (int workerid, struct starpu_task *task, int back)
- int starpu_push_task_end (struct starpu_task *task)
- int starpu_worker_can_execute_task (unsigned workerid, struct starpu_task *task, unsigned nimpl)
- int starpu_worker_can_execute_task_impl (unsigned workerid, struct starpu_task *task, unsigned *impl_-mask)
- int starpu_worker_can_execute_task_first_impl (unsigned workerid, struct starpu_task *task, unsigned *nimpl)
- uint32_t starpu_task_footprint (struct starpu_perfmodel *model, struct starpu_task *task, struct starpu_-perfmodel_arch *arch, unsigned nimpl)
- uint32_t starpu_task_data_footprint (struct starpu_task *task)
- double starpu_task_expected_length (struct starpu_task *task, struct starpu_perfmodel_arch *arch, un-signed nimpl)
- double starpu_worker_get_relative_speedup (struct starpu_perfmodel_arch *perf_arch)
- double starpu_task_expected_data_transfer_time (unsigned memory_node, struct starpu_task *task)
- double starpu_data_expected_transfer_time (starpu_data_handle_t handle, unsigned memory_node, enum starpu_data_access_mode mode)
- double starpu_task_expected_energy (struct starpu_task *task, struct starpu_perfmodel_arch *arch, un-signed nimpl)
- double starpu_task_expected_conversion_time (struct starpu_task *task, struct starpu_perfmodel_arch *arch, unsigned nimpl)
- int starpu_get_prefetch_flag (void)
- int starpu_prefetch_task_input_on_node (struct starpu_task *task, unsigned node)
- int starpu_idle_prefetch_task_input_on_node (struct starpu_task *task, unsigned node)
- void starpu_sched_ctx_worker_shares_tasks_lists (int workerid, int sched_ctx_id)

Scheduling Contexts Basic API

- #define STARPU_NMAX_SCHED_CTXS

29.36.1 Detailed Description

TODO. While StarPU comes with a variety of scheduling policies (see Task Scheduling Policies), it may sometimes be desirable to implement custom policies to address specific problems. The API described below allows users to write their own scheduling policy.

29.36.2 Data Structure Documentation

29.36.2.1 struct starpu_sched_policy

Contain all the methods that implement a scheduling policy. An application may specify which scheduling strategy in the field starpu_conf::sched_policy passed to the function starpu_init().

For each task going through the scheduler, the following methods get called in the given order:

- starpu_sched_policy::submit_hook when the task is submitted

- starpu_sched_policy::push_task when the task becomes ready. The scheduler is here **given** the task

- starpu_sched_policy::pop_task when the worker is idle. The scheduler here **gives** back the task to the core

- starpu_sched_policy::pre_exec_hook right before the worker actually starts the task computation (after transferring any missing data).

- starpu_sched_policy::post_exec_hook right after the worker actually completes the task computation.

For each task not going through the scheduler (because starpu_task::execute_on_a_specific_worker was set), these get called:

- starpu_sched_policy::submit_hook when the task is submitted

- starpu_sched_policy::push_task_notify when the task becomes ready. This is just a notification, the scheduler does not have to do anything about the task.

- starpu_sched_policy::pre_exec_hook right before the worker actually starts the task computation (after transferring any missing data).

- starpu_sched_policy::post_exec_hook right after the worker actually completes the task computation.

Data Fields

- void(* init_sched)(unsigned sched_ctx_id)
- void(* deinit_sched)(unsigned sched_ctx_id)
- int(* push_task)(struct starpu_task *)
- double(* **simulate_push_task**)(struct starpu_task *)
- void(* push_task_notify)(struct starpu_task *, int workerid, int perf_workerid, unsigned sched_ctx_id)
- struct starpu_task *(* pop_task)(unsigned sched_ctx_id)
- struct starpu_task *(* pop_every_task)(unsigned sched_ctx_id)
- void(* submit_hook)(struct starpu_task *task)
- void(* pre_exec_hook)(struct starpu_task *, unsigned sched_ctx_id)
- void(* post_exec_hook)(struct starpu_task *, unsigned sched_ctx_id)
- void(* do_schedule)(unsigned sched_ctx_id)
- void(* add_workers)(unsigned sched_ctx_id, int *workerids, unsigned nworkers)
- void(* remove_workers)(unsigned sched_ctx_id, int *workerids, unsigned nworkers)
- const char * policy_name
- const char * policy_description
- enum starpu_worker_collection_type **worker_type**

29.36.2.1.1   Field Documentation

29.36.2.1.1.1   void(∗ starpu_sched_policy::init_sched)(unsigned sched_ctx_id)

Initialize the scheduling policy, called before any other method.

29.36.2.1.1.2   void(∗ starpu_sched_policy::deinit_sched)(unsigned sched_ctx_id)

Cleanup the scheduling policy, called before any other method.

29.36.2.1.1.3   int(∗ starpu_sched_policy::push_task)(struct **starpu_task** ∗)

Insert a task into the scheduler, called when the task becomes ready for execution.

29.36.2.1.1.4   void(∗ starpu_sched_policy::push_task_notify)(struct **starpu_task** ∗, int workerid, int perf_workerid, unsigned sched_ctx_id)

Notify the scheduler that a task was pushed on a given worker. This method is called when a task that was explicitly assigned to a worker becomes ready and is about to be executed by the worker. This method therefore permits to keep the state of the scheduler coherent even when StarPU bypasses the scheduling strategy.

29.36.2.1.1.5   struct **starpu_task** ∗(∗ starpu_sched_policy::pop_task)(unsigned sched_ctx_id)   [read]

Get a task from the scheduler. If this method returns NULL, the worker will start sleeping. If later on some task are pushed for this worker, starpu_wake_worker() must be called to wake the worker so it can call the pop_task() method again.

The mutex associated to the worker is already taken when this method is called. This method may release it (e.g. for scalability reasons when doing work stealing), but it must acquire it again before taking the decision whether to return a task or NULL, so the atomicity of deciding to return NULL and making the worker actually sleep is preserved. Otherwise in simgrid or blocking driver mode the worker might start sleeping while a task has just been pushed for it.

If this method is defined as NULL, the worker will only execute tasks from its local queue. In this case, the push_task method should use the starpu_push_local_task method to assign tasks to the different workers.

29.36.2.1.1.6   struct **starpu_task** ∗(∗ starpu_sched_policy::pop_every_task)(unsigned sched_ctx_id)   [read]

Remove all available tasks from the scheduler (tasks are chained by the means of the field starpu_task::prev and starpu_task::next). The mutex associated to the worker is already taken when this method is called. This is currently not used and can be discarded.

29.36.2.1.1.7   void(∗ starpu_sched_policy::submit_hook)(struct **starpu_task** ∗)

Optional field. This method is called when a task is submitted.

29.36.2.1.1.8   void(∗ starpu_sched_policy::pre_exec_hook)(struct **starpu_task** ∗)

Optional field. This method is called every time a task is starting.

29.36.2.1.1.9   void(∗ starpu_sched_policy::post_exec_hook)(struct **starpu_task** ∗)

Optional field. This method is called every time a task has been executed.

29.36.2.1.1.10   void(∗ starpu_sched_policy::do_schedule)(unsigned sched_ctx_id)

Optional field. This method is called when it is a good time to start scheduling tasks. This is notably called when the application calls starpu_task_wait_for_all or starpu_do_schedule explicitly.

29.36.2.1.1.11   void(∗ starpu_sched_policy::add_workers)(unsigned sched_ctx_id, int ∗workerids, unsigned nworkers)

Initialize scheduling structures corresponding to each worker used by the policy.

29.36.2.1.1.12 void(∗ starpu_sched_policy::remove_workers)(unsigned sched_ctx_id, int ∗workerids, unsigned nworkers)

Deinitialize scheduling structures corresponding to each worker used by the policy.

29.36.2.1.1.13 const char ∗ starpu_sched_policy::policy_name

Optional field. Name of the policy.

29.36.2.1.1.14 const char ∗ starpu_sched_policy::policy_description

Optional field. Human readable description of the policy.

29.36.3 Macro Definition Documentation

29.36.3.1 #define STARPU_NMAX_SCHED_CTXS

Define the maximum number of scheduling contexts managed by StarPU. The default value can be modified at configure by using the option --enable-max-sched-ctxs.

29.36.3.2 #define STARPU_MAXIMPLEMENTATIONS

Define the maximum number of implementations per architecture. The default value can be modified at configure by using the option --enable-maximplementations.

29.36.4 Function Documentation

29.36.4.1 struct starpu_sched_policy ∗∗ starpu_sched_get_predefined_policies ( ) [read]

Return an NULL-terminated array of all the predefined scheduling policies.

29.36.4.2 void starpu_worker_get_sched_condition (int *workerid,* starpu_pthread_mutex_t ∗∗ *sched_mutex,* starpu_pthread_cond_t ∗∗ *sched_cond*)

When there is no available task for a worker, StarPU blocks this worker on a condition variable. This function specifies which condition variable (and the associated mutex) should be used to block (and to wake up) a worker. Note that multiple workers may use the same condition variable. For instance, in the case of a scheduling strategy with a single task queue, the same condition variable would be used to block and wake up all workers.

29.36.4.3 int starpu_sched_set_min_priority (int *min_prio*)

TODO: check if this is correct Define the minimum task priority level supported by the scheduling policy. The default minimum priority level is the same as the default priority level which is 0 by convention. The application may access that value by calling the function starpu_sched_get_min_priority(). This function should only be called from the initialization method of the scheduling policy, and should not be used directly from the application.

29.36.4.4 int starpu_sched_set_max_priority (int *max_prio*)

TODO: check if this is correct Define the maximum priority level supported by the scheduling policy. The default maximum priority level is 1. The application may access that value by calling the function starpu_sched_get_max_priority(). This function should only be called from the initialization method of the scheduling policy, and should not be used directly from the application.

29.36.4.5 int starpu_sched_get_min_priority (void)

TODO: check if this is correct Return the current minimum priority level supported by the scheduling policy

29.36.4.6 int starpu_sched_get_max_priority (void)

TODO: check if this is correct Return the current maximum priority level supported by the scheduling policy

29.36.4.7 int starpu_push_local_task (int *workerid*, struct **starpu_task** * *task*, int *back*)

The scheduling policy may put tasks directly into a worker's local queue so that it is not always necessary to create its own queue when the local queue is sufficient. If `back` is not 0, `task` is put at the back of the queue where the worker will pop tasks first. Setting `back` to 0 therefore ensures a FIFO ordering.

29.36.4.8 int starpu_push_task_end (struct **starpu_task** * *task*)

Must be called by a scheduler to notify that the given task has just been pushed.

29.36.4.9 int starpu_worker_can_execute_task (unsigned *workerid*, struct **starpu_task** * *task*, unsigned *nimpl*)

Check if the worker specified by workerid can execute the codelet. Schedulers need to call it before assigning a task to a worker, otherwise the task may fail to execute.

29.36.4.10 int starpu_worker_can_execute_task_impl (unsigned *workerid*, struct **starpu_task** * *task*, unsigned * *impl_mask*)

Check if the worker specified by workerid can execute the codelet and returns which implementation numbers can be used. Schedulers need to call it before assigning a task to a worker, otherwise the task may fail to execute. This should be preferred rather than calling starpu_worker_can_execute_task for each and every implementation. It can also be used with `impl_mask` `==` `NULL` to check for at least one implementation without determining which.

29.36.4.11 int starpu_worker_can_execute_task_first_impl (unsigned *workerid*, struct **starpu_task** * *task*, unsigned * *nimpl*)

Check if the worker specified by workerid can execute the codelet and returns the first implementation which can be used. Schedulers need to call it before assigning a task to a worker, otherwise the task may fail to execute. This should be preferred rather than calling starpu_worker_can_execute_task for each and every implementation. It can also be used with `impl_mask` `==` `NULL` to check for at least one implementation without determining which.

29.36.4.12 uint32_t starpu_task_footprint (struct **starpu_perfmodel** * *model*, struct **starpu_task** * *task*, struct **starpu_perfmodel_arch** * *arch*, unsigned *nimpl*)

Return the footprint for a given task, taking into account user-provided perfmodel footprint or size_base functions.

29.36.4.13 uint32_t starpu_task_data_footprint (struct **starpu_task** * *task*)

Return the raw footprint for the data of a given task (without taking into account user-provided functions).

29.36.4.14 double starpu_task_expected_length (struct **starpu_task** * *task*, struct **starpu_perfmodel_arch** * *arch*, unsigned *nimpl*)

Return expected task duration in micro-seconds.

29.36.4.15   double starpu_worker_get_relative_speedup (struct **starpu_perfmodel_arch** ∗ *perf_arch*)

Return an estimated speedup factor relative to CPU speed

29.36.4.16   double starpu_task_expected_data_transfer_time (unsigned *memory_node,* struct **starpu_task** ∗ *task*)

Return expected data transfer time in micro-seconds.

29.36.4.17   double starpu_data_expected_transfer_time (**starpu_data_handle_t** *handle,* unsigned *memory_node,* enum **starpu_data_access_mode** *mode*)

Predict the transfer time (in micro-seconds) to move `handle` to a memory node

29.36.4.18   double starpu_task_expected_energy (struct **starpu_task** ∗ *task,* struct **starpu_perfmodel_arch** ∗ *arch,* unsigned *nimpl*)

Return expected energy consumption in J

29.36.4.19   double starpu_task_expected_conversion_time (struct **starpu_task** ∗ *task,* struct **starpu_perfmodel_arch** ∗ *arch,* unsigned *nimpl*)

Return expected conversion time in ms (multiformat interface only)

29.36.4.20   int starpu_get_prefetch_flag (void)

Whether STARPU_PREFETCH was set

29.36.4.21   int starpu_prefetch_task_input_on_node (struct **starpu_task** ∗ *task,* unsigned *node*)

Prefetch data for a given task on a given node

29.36.4.22   int starpu_idle_prefetch_task_input_on_node (struct **starpu_task** ∗ *task,* unsigned *node*)

Prefetch data for a given task on a given node when the bus is idle

29.36.4.23   void starpu_sched_ctx_worker_shares_tasks_lists (int *workerid,* int *sched_ctx_id*)

The scheduling policies indicates if the worker may pop tasks from the list of other workers or if there is a central list with task for all the workers

29.37   Tree

This section describes the tree facilities provided by StarPU.

Data Structures

- struct starpu_tree

Functions

- void starpu_tree_reset_visited (struct starpu_tree *tree, char *visited)
- void starpu_tree_insert (struct starpu_tree *tree, int id, int level, int is_pu, int arity, struct starpu_tree *father)
- struct starpu_tree * starpu_tree_get (struct starpu_tree *tree, int id)
- struct starpu_tree * starpu_tree_get_neighbour (struct starpu_tree *tree, struct starpu_tree *node, char *visited, char *present)
- void starpu_tree_free (struct starpu_tree *tree)

29.37.1 Detailed Description

This section describes the tree facilities provided by StarPU.

29.37.2 Data Structure Documentation

29.37.2.1 struct starpu_tree

Data Fields

struct starpu_tree *	nodes	todo
struct starpu_tree *	father	todo
int	arity	todo
int	id	todo
int	level	todo
int	is_pu	todo

29.37.3 Function Documentation

29.37.3.1 void starpu_tree_reset_visited (struct **starpu_tree** * *tree*, char * *visited*)

todo

29.37.3.2 void starpu_tree_insert (struct **starpu_tree** * *tree*, int *id*, int *level*, int *is_pu*, int *arity*, struct **starpu_tree** * *father*)

todo

29.37.3.3 struct **starpu_tree** * starpu_tree_get (struct **starpu_tree** * *tree*, int *id*) [read]

todo

29.37.3.4 struct **starpu_tree** * starpu_tree_get_neighbour (struct **starpu_tree** * *tree*, struct **starpu_tree** * *node*, char * *visited*, char * *present*) [read]

todo

29.37.3.5 void starpu_tree_free (struct **starpu_tree** * *tree*)

todo

29.38 Scheduling Context Hypervisor - Regular usage

Macros

- #define SC_HYPERVISOR_MAX_IDLE
- #define SC_HYPERVISOR_PRIORITY
- #define SC_HYPERVISOR_MIN_WORKERS
- #define SC_HYPERVISOR_MAX_WORKERS
- #define SC_HYPERVISOR_GRANULARITY
- #define SC_HYPERVISOR_FIXED_WORKERS
- #define SC_HYPERVISOR_MIN_TASKS
- #define SC_HYPERVISOR_NEW_WORKERS_MAX_IDLE
- #define SC_HYPERVISOR_TIME_TO_APPLY
- #define SC_HYPERVISOR_ISPEED_W_SAMPLE
- #define SC_HYPERVISOR_ISPEED_CTX_SAMPLE
- #define SC_HYPERVISOR_NULL

Functions

- void * sc_hypervisor_init (struct sc_hypervisor_policy *policy)
- void sc_hypervisor_shutdown (void)
- void sc_hypervisor_register_ctx (unsigned sched_ctx, double total_flops)
- void sc_hypervisor_unregister_ctx (unsigned sched_ctx)
- void sc_hypervisor_resize_ctxs (unsigned *sched_ctxs, int nsched_ctxs, int *workers, int nworkers)
- void sc_hypervisor_stop_resize (unsigned sched_ctx)
- void sc_hypervisor_start_resize (unsigned sched_ctx)
- const char * sc_hypervisor_get_policy ()
- void sc_hypervisor_add_workers_to_sched_ctx (int *workers_to_add, unsigned nworkers_to_add, unsigned sched_ctx)
- void sc_hypervisor_remove_workers_from_sched_ctx (int *workers_to_remove, unsigned nworkers_to_-remove, unsigned sched_ctx, unsigned now)
- void sc_hypervisor_move_workers (unsigned sender_sched_ctx, unsigned receiver_sched_ctx, int *workers-_to_move, unsigned nworkers_to_move, unsigned now)
- void sc_hypervisor_size_ctxs (unsigned *sched_ctxs, int nsched_ctxs, int *workers, int nworkers)
- void sc_hypervisor_set_type_of_task (struct starpu_codelet *cl, unsigned sched_ctx, uint32_t footprint, size-_t data_size)
- void sc_hypervisor_update_diff_total_flops (unsigned sched_ctx, double diff_total_flops)
- void sc_hypervisor_update_diff_elapsed_flops (unsigned sched_ctx, double diff_task_flops)
- void sc_hypervisor_ctl (unsigned sched_ctx,...)

29.38.1 Detailed Description

29.38.2 Macro Definition Documentation

29.38.2.1 #define SC_HYPERVISOR_MAX_IDLE

This macro is used when calling sc_hypervisor_ctl() and must be followed by 3 arguments: an array of int for the workerids to apply the condition, an int to indicate the size of the array, and a double value indicating the maximum idle time allowed for a worker before the resizing process should be triggered

29.38.2.2 #define SC_HYPERVISOR_PRIORITY

This macro is used when calling sc_hypervisor_ctl() and must be followed by 3 arguments: an array of int for the workerids to apply the condition, an int to indicate the size of the array, and an int value indicating the priority of the workers previously mentioned. The workers with the smallest priority are moved the first.

29.38.2.3 #define SC_HYPERVISOR_MIN_WORKERS

This macro is used when calling sc_hypervisor_ctl() and must be followed by 1 argument(int) indicating the minimum number of workers a context should have, underneath this limit the context cannot execute.

29.38.2.4 #define SC_HYPERVISOR_MAX_WORKERS

This macro is used when calling sc_hypervisor_ctl() and must be followed by 1 argument(int) indicating the maximum number of workers a context should have, above this limit the context would not be able to scale

29.38.2.5 #define SC_HYPERVISOR_GRANULARITY

This macro is used when calling sc_hypervisor_ctl() and must be followed by 1 argument(int) indicating the granularity of the resizing process (the number of workers should be moved from the context once it is resized) This parameter is ignore for the Gflops rate based strategy (see Resizing Strategies), the number of workers that have to be moved is calculated by the strategy.

29.38.2.6 #define SC_HYPERVISOR_FIXED_WORKERS

This macro is used when calling sc_hypervisor_ctl() and must be followed by 2 arguments: an array of int for the workerids to apply the condition and an int to indicate the size of the array. These workers are not allowed to be moved from the context.

29.38.2.7 #define SC_HYPERVISOR_MIN_TASKS

This macro is used when calling sc_hypervisor_ctl() and must be followed by 1 argument (int) that indicated the minimum number of tasks that have to be executed before the context could be resized. This parameter is ignored for the Application Driven strategy (see Resizing Strategies) where the user indicates exactly when the resize should be done.

29.38.2.8 #define SC_HYPERVISOR_NEW_WORKERS_MAX_IDLE

This macro is used when calling sc_hypervisor_ctl() and must be followed by 1 argument, a double value indicating the maximum idle time allowed for workers that have just been moved from other contexts in the current context.

29.38.2.9 #define SC_HYPERVISOR_TIME_TO_APPLY

This macro is used when calling sc_hypervisor_ctl() and must be followed by 1 argument (int) indicating the tag an executed task should have such that this configuration should be taken into account.

29.38.2.10 #define SC_HYPERVISOR_ISPEED_W_SAMPLE

This macro is used when calling sc_hypervisor_ctl() and must be followed by 1 argument, a double, that indicates the number of flops needed to be executed before computing the speed of a worker

29.38.2.11 #define SC_HYPERVISOR_ISPEED_CTX_SAMPLE

This macro is used when calling sc_hypervisor_ctl() and must be followed by 1 argument, a double, that indicates the number of flops needed to be executed before computing the speed of a context

29.38.2.12   #define SC_HYPERVISOR_NULL

This macro is used when calling sc_hypervisor_ctl() and must be followed by 1 arguments

29.38.3   Function Documentation

29.38.3.1   void * sc_hypervisor_init (struct **sc_hypervisor_policy** * *policy*)

There is a single hypervisor that is in charge of resizing contexts and the resizing strategy is chosen at the initialization of the hypervisor. A single resize can be done at a time.

The Scheduling Context Hypervisor Plugin provides a series of performance counters to StarPU. By incrementing them, StarPU can help the hypervisor in the resizing decision making process.

This function initializes the hypervisor to use the strategy provided as parameter and creates the performance counters (see starpu_sched_ctx_performance_counters). These performance counters represent actually some callbacks that will be used by the contexts to notify the information needed by the hypervisor.

Note: The Hypervisor is actually a worker that takes this role once certain conditions trigger the resizing process (there is no additional thread assigned to the hypervisor).

29.38.3.2   void sc_hypervisor_shutdown (void)

The hypervisor and all information concerning it is cleaned. There is no synchronization between this function and starpu_shutdown(). Thus, this should be called after starpu_shutdown(), because the performance counters will still need allocated callback functions.

29.38.3.3   void sc_hypervisor_register_ctx (unsigned *sched_ctx,* double *total_flops*)

Scheduling Contexts that have to be resized by the hypervisor must be first registered to the hypervisor. This function registers the context to the hypervisor, and indicate the number of flops the context will execute (used for Gflops rate based strategy or any other custom strategy needing it, for the others we can pass 0.0)

29.38.3.4   void sc_hypervisor_unregister_ctx (unsigned *sched_ctx*)

Whenever we want to exclude contexts from the resizing process we have to unregister them from the hypervisor.

29.38.3.5   void sc_hypervisor_resize_ctxs (unsigned * *sched_ctxs,* int *nsched_ctxs,* int * *workers,* int *nworkers*)

Requires reconsidering the distribution of ressources over the indicated scheduling contexts

29.38.3.6   void sc_hypervisor_stop_resize (unsigned *sched_ctx*)

The user can totally forbid the resizing of a certain context or can then change his mind and allow it (in this case the resizing is managed by the hypervisor, that can forbid it or allow it)

29.38.3.7   void sc_hypervisor_start_resize (unsigned *sched_ctx*)

Allow resizing of a context. The user can then provide information to the hypervisor concerning the conditions of resizing.

29.38.3.8   char * sc_hypervisor_get_policy ( )

Returns the name of the resizing policy the hypervisor uses

29.38.3.9   void sc_hypervisor_add_workers_to_sched_ctx (int * *workers_to_add*, unsigned *nworkers_to_add*, unsigned *sched_ctx*)

Ask the hypervisor to add workers to a sched_ctx

29.38.3.10   void sc_hypervisor_remove_workers_from_sched_ctx (int * *workers_to_remove*, unsigned *nworkers_to_remove*, unsigned *sched_ctx*, unsigned *now*)

Ask the hypervisor to remove workers from a sched_ctx

29.38.3.11   void sc_hypervisor_move_workers (unsigned *sender_sched_ctx*, unsigned *receiver_sched_ctx*, int * *workers_to_move*, unsigned *nworkers_to_move*, unsigned *now*)

Moves workers from one context to another

29.38.3.12   void sc_hypervisor_size_ctxs (unsigned * *sched_ctxs*, int *nsched_ctxs*, int * *workers*, int *nworkers*)

Ask the hypervisor to chose a distribution of workers in the required contexts

29.38.3.13   void sc_hypervisor_set_type_of_task (struct **starpu_codelet** * *cl*, unsigned *sched_ctx*, uint32_t *footprint*, size_t *data_size*)

Indicate the types of tasks a context will execute in order to better decide the sizing of ctxs

29.38.3.14   void sc_hypervisor_update_diff_total_flops (unsigned *sched_ctx*, double *diff_total_flops*)

Change dynamically the total number of flops of a context, move the deadline of the finishing time of the context

29.38.3.15   void sc_hypervisor_update_diff_elapsed_flops (unsigned *sched_ctx*, double *diff_task_flops*)

Change dynamically the number of the elapsed flops in a context, modify the past in order to better compute the speed

29.38.3.16   void sc_hypervisor_ctl (unsigned *sched_ctx*, ...)

Inputs conditions to the context sched_ctx with the following arguments. The argument list must be zero-terminated.

29.39   Scheduling Context Hypervisor - Building a new resizing policy

Data Structures

- struct sc_hypervisor_policy
- struct sc_hypervisor_policy_config
- struct sc_hypervisor_wrapper
- struct sc_hypervisor_resize_ack
- struct sc_hypervisor_policy_task_pool

Macros

- #define STARPU_HYPERVISOR_TAG

Functions

- void sc_hypervisor_post_resize_request (unsigned sched_ctx, int task_tag)
- unsigned sc_hypervisor_get_size_req (unsigned ∗∗sched_ctxs, int ∗nsched_ctxs, int ∗∗workers, int ∗nworkers)
- void sc_hypervisor_save_size_req (unsigned ∗sched_ctxs, int nsched_ctxs, int ∗workers, int nworkers)
- void sc_hypervisor_free_size_req (void)
- unsigned sc_hypervisor_can_resize (unsigned sched_ctx)
- struct sc_hypervisor_policy_config ∗ sc_hypervisor_get_config (unsigned sched_ctx)
- void sc_hypervisor_set_config (unsigned sched_ctx, void ∗config)
- unsigned ∗ sc_hypervisor_get_sched_ctxs ()
- int sc_hypervisor_get_nsched_ctxs ()
- struct sc_hypervisor_wrapper ∗ sc_hypervisor_get_wrapper (unsigned sched_ctx)
- double sc_hypervisor_get_elapsed_flops_per_sched_ctx (struct sc_hypervisor_wrapper ∗sc_w)

29.39.1 Detailed Description

29.39.2 Data Structure Documentation

29.39.2.1 struct sc_hypervisor_policy

This structure contains all the methods that implement a hypervisor resizing policy.

Data Fields

- const char ∗ name
- unsigned custom
- void(∗ size_ctxs)(unsigned ∗sched_ctxs, int nsched_ctxs, int ∗workers, int nworkers)
- void(∗ resize_ctxs)(unsigned ∗sched_ctxs, int nsched_ctxs, int ∗workers, int nworkers)
- void(∗ handle_idle_cycle)(unsigned sched_ctx, int worker)
- void(∗ handle_pushed_task)(unsigned sched_ctx, int worker)
- void(∗ handle_poped_task)(unsigned sched_ctx, int worker, struct starpu_task ∗task, uint32_t footprint)
- void(∗ handle_idle_end)(unsigned sched_ctx, int worker)
- void(∗ handle_post_exec_hook)(unsigned sched_ctx, int task_tag)
- void(∗ handle_submitted_job)(struct starpu_codelet ∗cl, unsigned sched_ctx, uint32_t footprint, size_t data_size)
- void(∗ end_ctx)(unsigned sched_ctx)
- void(∗ **start_ctx**)(unsigned sched_ctx)
- void(∗ **init_worker**)(int workerid, unsigned sched_ctx)

29.39.2.1.1 Field Documentation

29.39.2.1.1.1 sc_hypervisor_policy::name

Indicates the name of the policy, if there is not a custom policy, the policy corresponding to this name will be used by the hypervisor

29.39.2.1.1.2 sc_hypervisor_policy::custom

Indicates whether the policy is custom or not

29.39.2.1.1.3 sc_hypervisor_policy::size_ctxs

Distribute workers to contexts even at the beginning of the program

29.39.2.1.1.4 sc_hypervisor_policy::resize_ctxs

Require explicit resizing

29.39.2.1.1.5 sc_hypervisor_policy::handle_idle_cycle

It is called whenever the indicated worker executes another idle cycle in sched_ctx

29.39.2.1.1.6 sc_hypervisor_policy::handle_pushed_task

It is called whenever a task is pushed on the worker's queue corresponding to the context sched_ctx

29.39.2.1.1.7 sc_hypervisor_policy::handle_poped_task

It is called whenever a task is poped from the worker's queue corresponding to the context sched_ctx

The hypervisor takes a decision when another task was poped from this worker in this ctx

29.39.2.1.1.8 sc_hypervisor_policy::handle_idle_end

It is called whenever a task is executed on the indicated worker and context after a long period of idle time

29.39.2.1.1.9 sc_hypervisor_policy::handle_post_exec_hook

It is called whenever a tag task has just been executed. The table of resize requests is provided as well as the tag

29.39.2.1.1.10 sc_hypervisor_policy::handle_submitted_job

The hypervisor takes a decision when a job was submitted in this ctx

29.39.2.1.1.11 sc_hypervisor_policy::end_ctx

The hypervisor takes a decision when a certain ctx was deleted

29.39.2.2 struct sc_hypervisor_policy_config

This structure contains all configuration information of a context. It contains configuration information for each context, which can be used to construct new resize strategies.

Data Fields

int	min_nworkers	Indicates the minimum number of workers needed by the context
int	max_nworkers	Indicates the maximum number of workers needed by the context
int	granularity	Indicates the workers granularity of the context
int	priority	Indicates the priority of each worker in the context
double	max_idle	Indicates the maximum idle time accepted before a resize is triggered
double	min_working	Indicates that underneath this limit the priority of the worker is reduced
int	fixed_workers	Indicates which workers can be moved and which ones are fixed
double	new_workers_-max_idle	Indicates the maximum idle time accepted before a resize is triggered for the workers that just arrived in the new context
double	ispeed_w_-sample	Indicates the sample used to compute the instant speed per worker
double	ispeed_ctx_-sample	Indicates the sample used to compute the instant speed per ctxs
double	time_sample	todo

29.39.2.3 struct sc_hypervisor_wrapper

This structure is a wrapper of the contexts available in StarPU and contains all information about a context obtained by incrementing the performance counters.

Data Fields

unsigned	sched_ctx	The context wrapped
struct sc_hypervisor_- policy_config *	config	The corresponding resize configuration
double	start_time_w	
double	current_idle_- time	The idle time counter of each worker of the context
double	idle_time	The time the workers were idle from the last resize
double	idle_start_time	The moment when the workers started being idle
double	exec_time	
double	exec_start_time	
int	worker_to_be_- removed	The list of workers that will leave this contexts (lazy resizing process)
int	pushed_tasks	The number of pushed tasks of each worker of the context
int	poped_tasks	The number of poped tasks of each worker of the context
double	total_flops	The total number of flops to execute by the context
double	total_elapsed_- flops	The number of flops executed by each workers of the context
double	elapsed_flops	The number of flops executed by each worker of the context from last resize
size_t	elapsed_data	The quantity of data (in bytes) used to execute tasks on each worker in this ctx
int	elapsed_tasks	The nr of tasks executed on each worker in this ctx
double	ref_speed	The average speed of the workers (type of workers) when they belonged to this context 0 - cuda 1 - cpu
double	submitted_flops	The number of flops submitted to this ctx
double	remaining_flops	The number of flops that still have to be executed by the workers in the context
double	start_time	The time when he started executed
double	real_start_time	The first time a task was pushed to this context
double	hyp_react_start- _time	
struct sc_hypervisor_- resize_ack	resize_ack	The structure confirming the last resize finished and a new one can be done
starpu_pthread- _mutex_t	mutex	The mutex needed to synchronize the acknowledgment of the workers into the receiver context
unsigned	total_flops_- available	A boolean indicating if the hypervisor can use the flops corresponding to the entire execution of the context
unsigned	to_be_sized	
unsigned	compute_idle	
unsigned	compute_partial- _idle	
unsigned	consider_max	

29.39.2.4 struct sc_hypervisor_resize_ack

This structures checks if the workers moved to another context are actually taken into account in that context.

Data Fields

int	receiver_sched-_ctx	The context receiving the new workers
int *	moved_workers	The workers moved to the receiver context
int	nmoved_workers	The number of workers moved
int *	acked_workers	If the value corresponding to a worker is 1, this one is taken into account in the new context if 0 not yet

29.39.2.5 struct sc_hypervisor_policy_task_pool

task wrapper linked list

Data Fields

struct starpu_codelet *	cl	Which codelet has been executed
uint32_t	footprint	Task footprint key
unsigned	sched_ctx_id	Context the task belongs to
unsigned long	n	Number of tasks of this kind
size_t	data_size	The quantity of data(in bytes) needed by the task to execute
struct sc_hypervisor_-policy_task_pool *	next	Other task kinds

29.39.3 Macro Definition Documentation

29.39.3.1 #define STARPU_HYPERVISOR_TAG

todo

29.39.4 Function Documentation

29.39.4.1 void sc_hypervisor_post_resize_request (unsigned *sched_ctx*, int *task_tag*)

Requires resizing the context `sched_ctx` whenever a task tagged with the id `task_tag` finished executing

29.39.4.2 unsigned sc_hypervisor_get_size_req (unsigned ** *sched_ctxs*, int * *nsched_ctxs*, int ** *workers*, int * *nworkers*)

Check if there are pending demands of resizing

29.39.4.3 void sc_hypervisor_save_size_req (unsigned * *sched_ctxs*, int *nsched_ctxs*, int * *workers*, int *nworkers*)

Save a demand of resizing

29.39.4.4 void sc_hypervisor_free_size_req (void)

Clear the list of pending demands of resizing

29.39.4.5 unsigned sc_hypervisor_can_resize (unsigned *sched_ctx*)

Check out if a context can be resized

29.39.4.6 struct **sc_hypervisor_policy_config** * sc_hypervisor_get_config (unsigned *sched_ctx*) [read]

Returns the configuration structure of a context

29.39.4.7 void sc_hypervisor_set_config (unsigned *sched_ctx,* void * *config*)

Set a certain configuration to a contexts

29.39.4.8 unsigned * sc_hypervisor_get_sched_ctxs ( )

Gets the contexts managed by the hypervisor

29.39.4.9 int sc_hypervisor_get_nsched_ctxs ( )

Gets the number of contexts managed by the hypervisor

29.39.4.10 struct **sc_hypervisor_wrapper** * sc_hypervisor_get_wrapper (unsigned *sched_ctx*) [read]

Returns the wrapper corresponding the context sched_ctx

29.39.4.11 double sc_hypervisor_get_elapsed_flops_per_sched_ctx (struct **sc_hypervisor_wrapper** * *sc_w*)

Returns the flops of a context elapsed from the last resize

29.40 Modularized Scheduler Interface

Data Structures

- struct starpu_sched_component
- struct starpu_sched_tree
- struct starpu_sched_component_fifo_data
- struct starpu_sched_component_prio_data
- struct starpu_sched_component_mct_data
- struct starpu_sched_component_perfmodel_select_data
- struct starpu_sched_component_composed_recipe
- struct starpu_sched_component_specs

Macros

- #define STARPU_SCHED_COMPONENT_IS_HOMOGENEOUS(component)
- #define STARPU_SCHED_COMPONENT_IS_SINGLE_MEMORY_NODE(component)

Enumerations

- enum starpu_sched_component_properties { STARPU_SCHED_COMPONENT_HOMOGENEOUS, STAR-PU_SCHED_COMPONENT_SINGLE_MEMORY_NODE }

Scheduling Tree API

- struct starpu_sched_tree * starpu_sched_tree_create (unsigned sched_ctx_id) STARPU_ATTRIBUTE_MA-LLOC
- void starpu_sched_tree_destroy (struct starpu_sched_tree *tree)
- void starpu_sched_tree_update_workers (struct starpu_sched_tree *t)
- void starpu_sched_tree_update_workers_in_ctx (struct starpu_sched_tree *t)
- int starpu_sched_tree_push_task (struct starpu_task *task)
- struct starpu_task * starpu_sched_tree_pop_task (unsigned sched_ctx)
- void starpu_sched_tree_add_workers (unsigned sched_ctx_id, int *workerids, unsigned nworkers)
- void starpu_sched_tree_remove_workers (unsigned sched_ctx_id, int *workerids, unsigned nworkers)
- void starpu_sched_component_connect (struct starpu_sched_component *parent, struct starpu_sched_-component *child)

Generic Scheduling Component API

- struct starpu_sched_component * starpu_sched_component_create (struct starpu_sched_tree *tree, const char *name) STARPU_ATTRIBUTE_MALLOC
- void starpu_sched_component_destroy (struct starpu_sched_component *component)
- void starpu_sched_component_destroy_rec (struct starpu_sched_component *component)
- int starpu_sched_component_can_execute_task (struct starpu_sched_component *component, struct starpu_task *task)
- int STARPU_WARN_UNUSED_RESULT starpu_sched_component_execute_preds (struct starpu_sched_-component *component, struct starpu_task *task, double *length)
- double starpu_sched_component_transfer_length (struct starpu_sched_component *component, struct starpu_task *task)

Worker Component API

- struct starpu_sched_component * starpu_sched_component_worker_get (unsigned sched_ctx, int workerid)
- int starpu_sched_component_worker_get_workerid (struct starpu_sched_component *worker_component)
- int starpu_sched_component_is_worker (struct starpu_sched_component *component)
- int starpu_sched_component_is_simple_worker (struct starpu_sched_component *component)
- int starpu_sched_component_is_combined_worker (struct starpu_sched_component *component)
- void starpu_sched_component_worker_pre_exec_hook (struct starpu_task *task, unsigned sched_ctx_id)
- void starpu_sched_component_worker_post_exec_hook (struct starpu_task *task, unsigned sched_ctx_id)

Flow-control Fifo Component API

- double starpu_sched_component_estimated_load (struct starpu_sched_component *component)
- double starpu_sched_component_estimated_end_min (struct starpu_sched_component *component)
- double starpu_sched_component_estimated_end_average (struct starpu_sched_component *component)
- struct starpu_sched_component * starpu_sched_component_fifo_create (struct starpu_sched_tree *tree, struct starpu_sched_component_fifo_data *fifo_data) STARPU_ATTRIBUTE_MALLOC
- int starpu_sched_component_is_fifo (struct starpu_sched_component *component)

Flow-control Prio Component API

- struct starpu_sched_component * starpu_sched_component_prio_create (struct starpu_sched_tree *tree, struct starpu_sched_component_prio_data *prio_data) STARPU_ATTRIBUTE_MALLOC
- int starpu_sched_component_is_prio (struct starpu_sched_component *component)

Resource-mapping Work-Stealing Component API

- int starpu_sched_tree_work_stealing_push_task (struct starpu_task *task)
- int starpu_sched_component_is_work_stealing (struct starpu_sched_component *component)

Resource-mapping Random Component API

- int starpu_sched_component_is_random (struct starpu_sched_component *)

Resource-mapping Eager Component API

- int starpu_sched_component_is_eager (struct starpu_sched_component *)

Resource-mapping Eager-Calibration Component API

- int starpu_sched_component_is_eager_calibration (struct starpu_sched_component *)

Resource-mapping MCT Component API

- struct starpu_sched_component * starpu_sched_component_mct_create (struct starpu_sched_tree *tree, struct starpu_sched_component_mct_data *mct_data) STARPU_ATTRIBUTE_MALLOC
- int starpu_sched_component_is_mct (struct starpu_sched_component *component)

Resource-mapping Heft Component API

- struct starpu_sched_component * starpu_sched_component_heft_create (struct starpu_sched_tree *tree, struct starpu_sched_component_mct_data *mct_data) STARPU_ATTRIBUTE_MALLOC
- int starpu_sched_component_is_heft (struct starpu_sched_component *component)

Special-purpose Perfmodel_Select Component API

- struct starpu_sched_component * starpu_sched_component_perfmodel_select_create (struct starpu_sched_tree *tree, struct starpu_sched_component_perfmodel_select_data *perfmodel_select_data) STARPU_ATTRIBUTE_MALLOC
- int starpu_sched_component_is_perfmodel_select (struct starpu_sched_component *component)

Recipe Component API

- struct starpu_sched_component_composed_recipe * starpu_sched_component_composed_recipe_create (void) STARPU_ATTRIBUTE_MALLOC
- struct starpu_sched_component_composed_recipe * starpu_sched_component_composed_recipe_create_singleton (struct starpu_sched_component *(*create_component)(struct starpu_sched_tree *tree, void *arg), void *arg) STARPU_ATTRIBUTE_MALLOC
- void starpu_sched_component_composed_recipe_add (struct starpu_sched_component_composed_recipe *recipe, struct starpu_sched_component *(*create_component)(struct starpu_sched_tree *tree, void *arg), void *arg)
- void starpu_sched_component_composed_recipe_destroy (struct starpu_sched_component_composed_recipe *)
- struct starpu_sched_component * starpu_sched_component_composed_component_create (struct starpu_sched_tree *tree, struct starpu_sched_component_composed_recipe *recipe) STARPU_ATTRIBUTE_MALLOC

- struct starpu_sched_tree * starpu_sched_component_make_scheduler (unsigned sched_ctx_id, struct starpu_sched_component_specs s)
- int starpu_sched_component_push_task (struct starpu_sched_component *from, struct starpu_sched_-component *to, struct starpu_task *task)
- struct starpu_task * starpu_sched_component_pull_task (struct starpu_sched_component *from, struct starpu_sched_component *to)

29.40.1   Detailed Description

29.40.2   Data Structure Documentation

29.40.2.1   struct starpu_sched_component

This structure represent a scheduler module. A scheduler is a tree-like structure of them, some parts of scheduler can be shared by several contexes to perform some local optimisations, so, for all components, a list of parent is defined by `sched_ctx_id`. They embed there specialised method in a pseudo object-style, so calls are like `component->push_task(component,task)`

Data Fields

- struct starpu_sched_tree * tree
- struct starpu_bitmap * workers
- struct starpu_bitmap * workers_in_ctx
- void * data
- char * **name**
- int nchildren
- struct starpu_sched_component ** children
- int nparents
- struct starpu_sched_component ** parents
- void(* add_child)(struct starpu_sched_component *component, struct starpu_sched_component *child)
- void(* remove_child)(struct starpu_sched_component *component, struct starpu_sched_component *child)
- void(* add_parent)(struct starpu_sched_component *component, struct starpu_sched_component *parent)
- void(* remove_parent)(struct starpu_sched_component *component, struct starpu_sched_component *parent)
- int(* push_task)(struct starpu_sched_component *, struct starpu_task *)
- struct starpu_task *(* pull_task)(struct starpu_sched_component *)
- int(* can_push)(struct starpu_sched_component *component)
- void(* can_pull)(struct starpu_sched_component *component)
- double(* estimated_load)(struct starpu_sched_component *component)
- double(* estimated_end)(struct starpu_sched_component *component)
- void(* deinit_data)(struct starpu_sched_component *component)
- void(* notify_change_workers)(struct starpu_sched_component *component)
- int properties
- hwloc_obj_t obj

29.40.2.1.1   Field Documentation

29.40.2.1.1.1   struct **starpu_sched_tree** * starpu_sched_component::tree

The tree containing the component

29.40.2.1.1.2   struct **starpu_bitmap** * starpu_sched_component::workers

this member contain the set of underlying workers

29.40.2.1.1.3 starpu_sched_component::workers_in_ctx

this member contain the subset of starpu_sched_component::workers that is currently available in the context The push method should take this member into account. this member is set with : component->workers UNION tree->workers UNION component->child[i]->workers_in_ctx iff exist x such as component->children[i]->parents[x] == component

29.40.2.1.1.4 void * starpu_sched_component::data

private data

29.40.2.1.1.5 int starpu_sched_component::nchildren

the number of compoments's children

29.40.2.1.1.6 struct **starpu_sched_component** ** starpu_sched_component::children

the vector of component's children

29.40.2.1.1.7 int starpu_sched_component::nparents

the numbers of component's parents

29.40.2.1.1.8 struct **starpu_sched_component** ** starpu_sched_component::parents

the vector of component's parents

29.40.2.1.1.9 void(* starpu_sched_component::add_child)(struct **starpu_sched_component** *component, struct **starpu_sched_component** *child)

add a child to component

29.40.2.1.1.10 void(* starpu_sched_component::remove_child)(struct **starpu_sched_component** *component, struct **starpu_sched_component** *child)

remove a child from component

29.40.2.1.1.11 void(* starpu_sched_component::add_parent)(struct **starpu_sched_component** *component, struct **starpu_sched_component** *parent)

todo

29.40.2.1.1.12 void(* starpu_sched_component::remove_parent)(struct **starpu_sched_component** *component, struct **starpu_sched_component** *parent)

todo

29.40.2.1.1.13 int(* starpu_sched_component::push_task)(struct **starpu_sched_component** *, struct **starpu_task** *)

push a task in the scheduler module. this function is called to push a task on component subtree, this can either perform a recursive call on a child or store the task in the component, then it will be returned by a further pull_task call. the caller must ensure that component is able to execute task. This method must either return 0 if it the task was properly stored or passed over to a child component, or return a value different from 0 if the task could not be consumed (e.g. the queue is full).

29.40.2.1.1.14 struct **starpu_task** *(* starpu_sched_component::pull_task)(struct **starpu_sched_component** *)
        [read]

pop a task from the scheduler module. this function is called by workers to get a task from their parents. this function should first return a locally stored task or perform a recursive call on the parents. the task returned by this function is executable by the caller

29.40.2.1.1.15 int(∗ starpu_sched_component::can_push)(struct starpu_sched_component ∗component)

This function is called by a component which implements a queue, allowing it to signify to its parents that an empty slot is available in its queue. The basic implementation of this function is a recursive call to its parents, the user has to specify a personally-made function to catch those calls.

29.40.2.1.1.16 void(∗ starpu_sched_component::can_pull)(struct starpu_sched_component ∗component)

This function allow a component to wake up a worker. It is currently called by component which implements a queue, to signify to its children that a task have been pushed in its local queue, and is available to be popped by a worker, for example. The basic implementation of this function is a recursive call to its children, until at least one worker have been woken up.

29.40.2.1.1.17 double(∗ starpu_sched_component::estimated_load)(struct starpu_sched_component ∗component)

is an heuristic to compute load of scheduler module. Basically the number of tasks divided by the sum of relatives speedup of workers available in context. estimated_load(component) = sum(estimated_load(component_children)) + nb_local_tasks / average(relative_speedup(underlying_worker))

29.40.2.1.1.18 starpu_sched_component::estimated_end

return the time when a worker will enter in starvation. This function is relevant only if the task->predicted member has been set.

29.40.2.1.1.19 void(∗ starpu_sched_component::deinit_data)(struct starpu_sched_component ∗component)

called by starpu_sched_component_destroy. Should free data allocated during creation

29.40.2.1.1.20 void(∗ starpu_sched_component::notify_change_workers)(struct starpu_sched_component ∗component)

this function is called for each component when workers are added or removed from a context

29.40.2.1.1.21 int starpu_sched_component::properties

todo

29.40.2.1.1.22 hwloc_obj_t starpu_sched_component::obj

the hwloc object associated to scheduler module. points to the part of topology that is binded to this component, eg: a numa node for a ws component that would balance load between underlying sockets

29.40.2.2 struct starpu_sched_tree

The actual scheduler

Data Fields

struct starpu_sched_component ∗	root	this is the entry module of the scheduler
struct starpu_bitmap ∗	workers	this is the set of workers available in this context, this value is used to mask workers in modules
unsigned	sched_ctx_id	the context id of the scheduler
starpu_pthread_mutex_t	lock	this lock is used to protect the scheduler, it is taken in read mode pushing a task and in write mode for adding or removing workers

29.40.2.3 struct starpu_sched_component_fifo_data

Data Fields

unsigned	ntasks_threshold	todo
double	exp_len_-threshold	todo

29.40.2.4 struct starpu_sched_component_prio_data

Data Fields

unsigned	ntasks_threshold	todo
double	exp_len_-threshold	todo

29.40.2.5 struct starpu_sched_component_mct_data

Data Fields

double	alpha	todo
double	beta	todo
double	_gamma	todo
double	idle_power	todo

29.40.2.6 struct starpu_sched_component_perfmodel_select_data

Data Fields

struct starpu_sched_-component *	calibrator_-component	todo
struct starpu_sched_-component *	no_perfmodel_-component	todo
struct starpu_sched_-component *	perfmodel_-component	todo

29.40.2.7 struct starpu_sched_component_composed_recipe

parameters for starpu_sched_component_composed_component_create

29.40.2.8 struct starpu_sched_component_specs

Define how build a scheduler according to topology. Each level (except for hwloc_machine_composed_sched_-component) can be NULL, then the level is just skipped. Bugs everywhere, do not rely on.

Data Fields

- struct starpu_sched_component_composed_recipe * **hwloc_machine_composed_sched_component**

- struct
  starpu_sched_component_composed_recipe ∗ **hwloc_component_composed_sched_component**
- struct
  starpu_sched_component_composed_recipe ∗ **hwloc_socket_composed_sched_component**
- struct
  starpu_sched_component_composed_recipe ∗ **hwloc_cache_composed_sched_component**
- struct
  starpu_sched_component_composed_recipe ∗(∗ **worker_composed_sched_component**)(enum starpu_-
  worker_archtype archtype)
- int **mix_heterogeneous_workers**

29.40.3 Macro Definition Documentation

29.40.3.1 #define STARPU_SCHED_COMPONENT_IS_HOMOGENEOUS(*component*)

indicate if component is homogeneous

29.40.3.2 #define STARPU_SCHED_COMPONENT_IS_SINGLE_MEMORY_NODE(*component*)

indicate if all workers have the same memory component

29.40.4 Enumeration Type Documentation

29.40.4.1 enum **starpu_sched_component_properties**

flags for starpu_sched_component::properties

Enumerator:

STARPU_SCHED_COMPONENT_HOMOGENEOUS indicate that all workers have the same starpu_worker-
_archtype

STARPU_SCHED_COMPONENT_SINGLE_MEMORY_NODE indicate that all workers have the same memory component

29.40.5 Function Documentation

29.40.5.1 struct **starpu_sched_tree** ∗ starpu_sched_tree_create (unsigned *sched_ctx_id*) [read]

create a empty initialized starpu_sched_tree

29.40.5.2 void starpu_sched_tree_destroy (struct **starpu_sched_tree** ∗ *tree*)

destroy tree and free all non shared component in it.

29.40.5.3 void starpu_sched_tree_update_workers (struct **starpu_sched_tree** ∗ *t*)

recursively set all starpu_sched_component::workers, do not take into account shared parts (except workers).

29.40.5.4 void starpu_sched_tree_update_workers_in_ctx (struct **starpu_sched_tree** ∗ *t*)

recursively set all starpu_sched_component::workers_in_ctx, do not take into account shared parts (except workers)

29.40.5.5   int starpu_sched_tree_push_task (struct **starpu_task** * *task*)

compatibility with starpu_sched_policy interface

29.40.5.6   struct **starpu_task** * starpu_sched_tree_pop_task (unsigned *sched_ctx*)   [read]

compatibility with starpu_sched_policy interface

29.40.5.7   void starpu_sched_tree_add_workers (unsigned *sched_ctx_id*, int * *workerids*, unsigned *nworkers*)

compatibility with starpu_sched_policy interface

29.40.5.8   void starpu_sched_tree_remove_workers (unsigned *sched_ctx_id*, int * *workerids*, unsigned *nworkers*)

compatibility with starpu_sched_policy interface

29.40.5.9   void starpu_sched_component_connect (struct **starpu_sched_component** * *parent,* struct **starpu_sched_component** * *child*)

Attaches component `child` to parent `parent`. Some component may accept only one child, others accept several (e.g. MCT)

29.40.5.10   struct **starpu_sched_component** * starpu_sched_component_create (struct **starpu_sched_tree** * *tree,* const char * *name*)   [read]

allocate and initialize component field with defaults values : .pop_task make recursive call on father .estimated_load compute relative speedup and tasks in sub tree .estimated_end return the average of recursive call on children .add_child is starpu_sched_component_add_child .remove_child is starpu_sched_component_remove_child .notify_change_workers does nothing .deinit_data does nothing

29.40.5.11   void starpu_sched_component_destroy (struct **starpu_sched_component** * *component*)

free data allocated by starpu_sched_component_create and call component->deinit_data(component) set to `NULL` the member starpu_sched_component::fathers[sched_ctx_id] of all child if its equal to `component`

29.40.5.12   void starpu_sched_component_destroy_rec (struct **starpu_sched_component** * *component*)

recursively destroy non shared parts of a `component` 's tree

29.40.5.13   int starpu_sched_component_can_execute_task (struct **starpu_sched_component** * *component,* struct **starpu_task** * *task*)

return true iff `component` can execute `task`, this function take into account the workers available in the scheduling context

29.40.5.14   int starpu_sched_component_execute_preds (struct **starpu_sched_component** * *component,* struct **starpu_task** * *task,* double * *length*)

return a non `NULL` value if `component` can execute `task`. write the execution prediction length for the best implementation of the best worker available and write this at `length` address. this result is more relevant if starpu_sched_component::is_homogeneous is non `NULL`. if a worker need to be calibrated for an implementation, nan is set to `length`.

29.40.5.15 double starpu_sched_component_transfer_length (struct **starpu_sched_component** * *component,* struct **starpu_task** * *task*)

return the average time to transfer `task` data to underlying `component` workers.

29.40.5.16 struct **starpu_sched_component** * starpu_sched_component_worker_get (unsigned *sched_ctx,* int *workerid*) `[read]`

return the struct starpu_sched_component corresponding to `workerid`. Undefined if `workerid` is not a valid workerid

29.40.5.17 int starpu_sched_component_worker_get_workerid (struct **starpu_sched_component** * *worker_component*)

return the workerid of `worker_component`, undefined if starpu_sched_component_is_worker(worker_-component) == 0

29.40.5.18 int starpu_sched_component_is_worker (struct **starpu_sched_component** * *component*)

return true iff `component` is a worker component

29.40.5.19 int starpu_sched_component_is_simple_worker (struct **starpu_sched_component** * *component*)

return true iff `component` is a simple worker component

29.40.5.20 int starpu_sched_component_is_combined_worker (struct **starpu_sched_component** * *component*)

return true iff `component` is a combined worker component

29.40.5.21 void starpu_sched_component_worker_pre_exec_hook (struct **starpu_task** * *task,* unsigned *sched_ctx_id*)

compatibility with starpu_sched_policy interface update predictions for workers

29.40.5.22 void starpu_sched_component_worker_post_exec_hook (struct **starpu_task** * *task,* unsigned *sched_ctx_id*)

compatibility with starpu_sched_policy interface

29.40.5.23 double starpu_sched_component_estimated_load (struct **starpu_sched_component** * *component*)

default function for the estimated_load component method, just sums up the loads of the children of the component.

29.40.5.24 double starpu_sched_component_estimated_end_min (struct **starpu_sched_component** * *component*)

function that can be used for the estimated_end component method, which just computes the minimum completion time of the children.

29.40.5.25 double starpu_sched_component_estimated_end_average (struct **starpu_sched_component** * *component*)

default function for the estimated_end component method, which just computes the average completion time of the children.

29.40.5.26   struct **starpu_sched_component** * starpu_sched_component_fifo_create (struct **starpu_sched_tree** * *tree,* struct **starpu_sched_component_fifo_data** * *fifo_data*)   [read]

Return a struct starpu_sched_component with a fifo. A stable sort is performed according to tasks priorities. A push-_task call on this component does not perform recursive calls, underlying components will have to call pop_task to get it. starpu_sched_component::estimated_end function compute the estimated length by dividing the sequential length by the number of underlying workers. Do not take into account tasks that are currently executed.

29.40.5.27   int starpu_sched_component_is_fifo (struct **starpu_sched_component** * *component*)

return true iff component is a fifo component

29.40.5.28   struct **starpu_sched_component** * starpu_sched_component_prio_create (struct **starpu_sched_tree** * *tree,* struct **starpu_sched_component_prio_data** * *prio_data*)   [read]

todo

29.40.5.29   int starpu_sched_component_is_prio (struct **starpu_sched_component** * *component*)

todo

29.40.5.30   int starpu_sched_tree_work_stealing_push_task (struct **starpu_task** * *task*)

undefined if there is no work stealing component in the scheduler. If any, task is pushed in a default way if the caller is the application, and in the caller's fifo if its a worker.

29.40.5.31   int starpu_sched_component_is_work_stealing (struct **starpu_sched_component** * *component*)

return true iff component is a work stealing component

29.40.5.32   int starpu_sched_component_is_random (struct **starpu_sched_component** *)

return true iff component is a random component

29.40.5.33   int starpu_sched_component_is_eager (struct **starpu_sched_component** *)

todo

29.40.5.34   int starpu_sched_component_is_eager_calibration (struct **starpu_sched_component** *)

todo

29.40.5.35   struct **starpu_sched_component** * starpu_sched_component_mct_create (struct **starpu_sched_tree** * *tree,* struct **starpu_sched_component_mct_data** * *mct_data*)   [read]

create a component with mct_data paremeters. the mct component doesnt do anything but pushing tasks on no_-perf_model_component and calibrating_component

29.40.5.36   int starpu_sched_component_is_mct (struct **starpu_sched_component** * *component*)

todo

29.40.5.37   struct **starpu_sched_component** * starpu_sched_component_heft_create (struct **starpu_sched_tree** * *tree*, struct **starpu_sched_component_mct_data** * *mct_data*) [read]

this component perform a heft scheduling

29.40.5.38   int starpu_sched_component_is_heft (struct **starpu_sched_component** * *component*)

return true iff component is a heft component

29.40.5.39   struct **starpu_sched_component** * starpu_sched_component_perfmodel_select_create (struct **starpu_sched_tree** * *tree*, struct **starpu_sched_component_perfmodel_select_data** * *perfmodel_select_data*) [read]

todo

29.40.5.40   int starpu_sched_component_is_perfmodel_select (struct **starpu_sched_component** * *component*)

todo

29.40.5.41   struct **starpu_sched_component_composed_recipe** * starpu_sched_component_composed_recipe_create (void) [read]

return an empty recipe for a composed component, it should not be used without modification

29.40.5.42   struct **starpu_sched_component_composed_recipe** * starpu_sched_component_composed_recipe_create_singleton (struct **starpu_sched_component** *(*)(struct **starpu_sched_tree** *tree, void *arg) *create_component*, void * *arg*) [read]

return a recipe to build a composed component with a create_component

29.40.5.43   void starpu_sched_component_composed_recipe_add (struct **starpu_sched_component_composed_recipe** * *recipe*, struct **starpu_sched_component** *(*)(struct **starpu_sched_tree** *tree, void *arg) *create_component*, void * *arg*)

add create_component under all previous components in recipe

29.40.5.44   void starpu_sched_component_composed_recipe_destroy (struct **starpu_sched_component_composed_recipe** *)

destroy composed_sched_component, this should be done after starpu_sched_component_composed_component_create was called

29.40.5.45   struct **starpu_sched_component** * starpu_sched_component_composed_component_create (struct **starpu_sched_tree** * *tree*, struct **starpu_sched_component_composed_recipe** * *recipe*) [read]

create a component that behave as all component of recipe where linked. Except that you cant use starpu_sched_component_is_foo function if recipe contain a single create_foo arg_foo pair, create_foo(arg_foo) is returned instead of a composed component

29.40.5.46   struct **starpu_sched_tree** ∗ starpu_sched_component_make_scheduler (unsigned *sched_ctx_id,* struct **starpu_sched_component_specs** *s*)   [read]

this function build a scheduler for `sched_ctx_id` according to s and the hwloc topology of the machine.

29.40.5.47   int starpu_sched_component_push_task (struct **starpu_sched_component** ∗ *from,* struct **starpu_sched_component** ∗ *to,* struct **starpu_task** ∗ *task*)

Push a task to a component. This is a helper for `component->push_task(component, task)` plus tracing.

29.40.5.48   struct **starpu_task** ∗ starpu_sched_component_pull_task (struct **starpu_sched_component** ∗ *from,* struct **starpu_sched_component** ∗ *to*)   [read]

Pull a task from a component. This is a helper for `component->pull_task(component)` plus tracing.

29.41   Clustering Machine

Macros

- #define STARPU_CLUSTER_AWAKE_WORKERS

29.41.1   Detailed Description

29.41.2   Macro Definition Documentation

29.41.2.1   #define STARPU_CLUSTER_AWAKE_WORKERS

TODO

Chapter 30

File Index

30.1 File List

Here is a list of all documented files with brief descriptions:

Chapter 31

File Documentation

31.1 starpu.h File Reference

```
#include <stdlib.h>
#include <stdint.h>
#include <starpu_config.h>
#include <starpu_opencl.h>
#include <starpu_thread.h>
#include <starpu_thread_util.h>
#include <starpu_util.h>
#include <starpu_data.h>
#include <starpu_disk.h>
#include <starpu_data_interfaces.h>
#include <starpu_data_filters.h>
#include <starpu_stdlib.h>
#include <starpu_perfmodel.h>
#include <starpu_worker.h>
#include <starpu_task.h>
#include <starpu_task_list.h>
#include <starpu_task_util.h>
#include <starpu_sched_ctx.h>
#include <starpu_expert.h>
#include <starpu_rand.h>
#include <starpu_cuda.h>
#include <starpu_cublas.h>
#include <starpu_cusparse.h>
#include <starpu_bound.h>
#include <starpu_hash.h>
#include <starpu_profiling.h>
#include <starpu_top.h>
#include <starpu_fxt.h>
#include <starpu_driver.h>
#include <starpu_tree.h>
#include <starpu_openmp.h>
#include <starpu_simgrid_wrap.h>
#include <starpu_bitmap.h>
#include <starpu_clusters_util.h>
#include "starpu_deprecated_api.h"
```

Data Structures

- struct starpu_conf

Functions

- int starpu_conf_init (struct starpu_conf *conf)
- int starpu_init (struct starpu_conf *conf) STARPU_WARN_UNUSED_RESULT
- int starpu_initialize (struct starpu_conf *user_conf, int *argc, char ***argv)
- void starpu_pause (void)
- void starpu_resume (void)
- void starpu_shutdown (void)
- void starpu_topology_print (FILE *f)
- int starpu_asynchronous_copy_disabled (void)
- int starpu_asynchronous_cuda_copy_disabled (void)
- int starpu_asynchronous_opencl_copy_disabled (void)
- int starpu_asynchronous_mic_copy_disabled (void)
- int starpu_asynchronous_mpi_ms_copy_disabled (void)
- void **starpu_display_stats** ()
- void starpu_get_version (int *major, int *minor, int *release)

31.1.1 Detailed Description

31.2 starpu_bitmap.h File Reference

Functions

- struct starpu_bitmap * starpu_bitmap_create (void) STARPU_ATTRIBUTE_MALLOC
- void starpu_bitmap_destroy (struct starpu_bitmap *b)
- void starpu_bitmap_set (struct starpu_bitmap *b, int e)
- void starpu_bitmap_unset (struct starpu_bitmap *b, int e)
- void starpu_bitmap_unset_all (struct starpu_bitmap *b)
- int starpu_bitmap_get (struct starpu_bitmap *b, int e)
- void starpu_bitmap_unset_and (struct starpu_bitmap *a, struct starpu_bitmap *b, struct starpu_bitmap *c)
- void starpu_bitmap_or (struct starpu_bitmap *a, struct starpu_bitmap *b)
- int starpu_bitmap_and_get (struct starpu_bitmap *b1, struct starpu_bitmap *b2, int e)
- int starpu_bitmap_cardinal (struct starpu_bitmap *b)
- int starpu_bitmap_first (struct starpu_bitmap *b)
- int starpu_bitmap_last (struct starpu_bitmap *b)
- int starpu_bitmap_next (struct starpu_bitmap *b, int e)
- int starpu_bitmap_has_next (struct starpu_bitmap *b, int e)

31.2.1 Detailed Description

31.3 starpu_bound.h File Reference

```
#include <stdio.h>
```

Functions

- void starpu_bound_start (int deps, int prio)
- void starpu_bound_stop (void)
- void starpu_bound_print_dot (FILE *output)
- void starpu_bound_compute (double *res, double *integer_res, int integer)
- void starpu_bound_print_lp (FILE *output)
- void starpu_bound_print_mps (FILE *output)
- void starpu_bound_print (FILE *output, int integer)

31.3.1 Detailed Description

31.4 starpu_clusters_util.h File Reference

```
#include <hwloc.h>
```

Data Structures

- struct starpu_cluster_machine

Macros

- #define **STARPU_CLUSTER_MIN_NB**
- #define **STARPU_CLUSTER_MAX_NB**
- #define **STARPU_CLUSTER_NB**
- #define **STARPU_CLUSTER_POLICY_NAME**
- #define **STARPU_CLUSTER_POLICY_STRUCT**
- #define **STARPU_CLUSTER_KEEP_HOMOGENEOUS**
- #define **STARPU_CLUSTER_PREFERE_MIN**
- #define **STARPU_CLUSTER_CREATE_FUNC**
- #define **STARPU_CLUSTER_CREATE_FUNC_ARG**
- #define **STARPU_CLUSTER_TYPE**
- #define STARPU_CLUSTER_AWAKE_WORKERS
- #define **STARPU_CLUSTER_PARTITION_ONE**
- #define **STARPU_CLUSTER_NEW**
- #define **STARPU_CLUSTER_NCORES**
- #define **starpu_intel_openmp_mkl_prologue**

Typedefs

- typedef struct
  _starpu_cluster_group_list **starpu_cluster_group_list_t**
- typedef struct
  starpu_cluster_machine **starpu_clusters**

Enumerations

- enum **starpu_cluster_types** { **OPENMP**, **INTEL_OPENMP_MKL** }

Functions

- struct starpu_cluster_machine * **starpu_cluster_machine** (hwloc_obj_type_t cluster_level,...)
- int **starpu_uncluster_machine** (struct starpu_cluster_machine *clusters)
- int **starpu_cluster_print** (struct starpu_cluster_machine *clusters)
- void **starpu_openmp_prologue** (void *)

31.4.1 Detailed Description

31.4.2 Data Structure Documentation

31.4.2.1 struct starpu_cluster_machine

Data Fields

unsigned	id	
hwloc_topology- _t	topology	
unsigned	nclusters	
unsigned	ngroups	
starpu_cluster_- group_list_t *	groups	
struct _starpu_cluster- _parameters *	params	

31.5 starpu_config.h File Reference

```
#include <sys/types.h>
```

Macros

- #define STARPU_MAJOR_VERSION
- #define STARPU_MINOR_VERSION
- #define STARPU_RELEASE_VERSION
- #define **STARPU_USE_CPU**
- #define STARPU_USE_CUDA
- #define STARPU_USE_OPENCL
- #define STARPU_USE_MIC
- #define STARPU_USE_SCC
- #define **STARPU_SIMGRID**
- #define **STARPU_SIMGRID_HAVE_XBT_BARRIER_INIT**
- #define **STARPU_HAVE_SIMGRID_MSG_H**
- #define **STARPU_HAVE_XBT_SYNCHRO_H**
- #define **STARPU_NON_BLOCKING_DRIVERS**
- #define **STARPU_HAVE_ICC**
- #define **STARPU_ATLAS**
- #define **STARPU_GOTO**
- #define **STARPU_MKL**
- #define **STARPU_SYSTEM_BLAS**
- #define **STARPU_BUILD_DIR**

- #define STARPU_OPENCL_DATADIR
- #define **STARPU_HAVE_MAGMA**
- #define **STARPU_OPENGL_RENDER**
- #define **STARPU_USE_GTK**
- #define **STARPU_HAVE_X11**
- #define **STARPU_HAVE_POSIX_MEMALIGN**
- #define **STARPU_HAVE_MEMALIGN**
- #define **STARPU_HAVE_MALLOC_H**
- #define **STARPU_HAVE_SYNC_BOOL_COMPARE_AND_SWAP**
- #define **STARPU_HAVE_SYNC_VAL_COMPARE_AND_SWAP**
- #define **STARPU_HAVE_SYNC_FETCH_AND_ADD**
- #define **STARPU_HAVE_SYNC_FETCH_AND_OR**
- #define **STARPU_HAVE_SYNC_LOCK_TEST_AND_SET**
- #define **STARPU_HAVE_SYNC_SYNCHRONIZE**
- #define **STARPU_MODEL_DEBUG**
- #define **STARPU_NO_ASSERT**
- #define **STARPU_DEBUG**
- #define **STARPU_HAVE_FFTW**
- #define **STARPU_HAVE_FFTWF**
- #define **STARPU_HAVE_FFTWL**
- #define **STARPU_HAVE_CURAND**
- #define STARPU_MAXNODES
- #define STARPU_NMAXBUFS
- #define STARPU_MAXCPUS
- #define STARPU_MAXCUDADEVS
- #define STARPU_MAXOPENCLDEVS
- #define STARPU_MAXMICDEVS
- #define STARPU_MAXSCCDEVS
- #define STARPU_NMAXWORKERS
- #define STARPU_MAXIMPLEMENTATIONS
- #define **STARPU_MAXMPKERNELS**
- #define **STARPU_USE_SC_HYPERVISOR**
- #define **STARPU_SC_HYPERVISOR_DEBUG**
- #define **STARPU_HAVE_GLPK_H**
- #define **STARPU_HAVE_LIBNUMA**
- #define **STARPU_HAVE_WINDOWS**
- #define **STARPU_LINUX_SYS**
- #define **STARPU_HAVE_SETENV**
- #define **STARPU_HAVE_UNSETENV**
- #define **STARPU_HAVE_UNISTD_H**
- #define **STARPU_FXT_LOCK_TRACES**
- #define **__starpu_func__**
- #define **__starpu_inline**
- #define **STARPU_QUICK_CHECK**
- #define **STARPU_USE_DRAND48**
- #define **STARPU_USE_ERAND48_R**
- #define **STARPU_HAVE_NEARBYINTF**
- #define **STARPU_HAVE_RINTF**
- #define **STARPU_USE_TOP**
- #define **STARPU_HAVE_HWLOC**
- #define **STARPU_HAVE_PTHREAD_SPIN_LOCK**
- #define **STARPU_HAVE_PTHREAD_BARRIER**
- #define **STARPU_HAVE_PTHREAD_SETNAME_NP**
- #define **STARPU_HAVE_STRUCT_TIMESPEC**
- #define **STARPU_HAVE_HELGRIND_H**

- #define **HAVE_MPI_COMM_F2C**
- #define **STARPU_HAVE_DARWIN**
- #define **STARPU_HAVE_CXX11**
- #define **STARPU_HAVE_STRERROR_R**
- #define **STARPU_HAVE_STATEMENT_EXPRESSIONS**

MPI Master Slave

- #define STARPU_USE_MPI_MASTER_SLAVE

Initialisation

- #define STARPU_OPENMP

Initialisation

- #define STARPU_USE_MPI

Scheduling Contexts Basic API

- #define STARPU_NMAX_SCHED_CTXS

Typedefs

- typedef ssize_t **starpu_ssize_t**

31.5.1   Detailed Description

31.6   starpu_cublas.h File Reference

Functions

- void starpu_cublas_init (void)
- void starpu_cublas_set_stream (void)
- void starpu_cublas_shutdown (void)

31.6.1   Detailed Description

31.7   starpu_cuda.h File Reference

```
#include <starpu_config.h>
#include <cuda.h>
#include <cuda_runtime.h>
#include <cuda_runtime_api.h>
```

Macros

- #define STARPU_CUBLAS_REPORT_ERROR(status)
- #define STARPU_CUDA_REPORT_ERROR(status)

Functions

- void starpu_cublas_report_error (const char ∗func, const char ∗file, int line, int status)
- void starpu_cuda_report_error (const char ∗func, const char ∗file, int line, cudaError_t status)
- cudaStream_t starpu_cuda_get_local_stream (void)
- struct cudaDeviceProp ∗ starpu_cuda_get_device_properties (unsigned workerid)
- int starpu_cuda_copy_async_sync (void ∗src_ptr, unsigned src_node, void ∗dst_ptr, unsigned dst_node, size_t ssize, cudaStream_t stream, enum cudaMemcpyKind kind)
- void starpu_cuda_set_device (unsigned devid)

31.7.1 Detailed Description

31.8 starpu_data.h File Reference

```
#include <starpu.h>
```

Data Structures

- struct starpu_data_descr

Macros

- #define starpu_data_malloc_pinned_if_possible
- #define starpu_data_free_pinned_if_possible
- #define STARPU_MAIN_RAM

Typedefs

- typedef struct _starpu_data_state ∗ starpu_data_handle_t
- typedef struct starpu_arbiter ∗ starpu_arbiter_t

Enumerations

- enum starpu_data_access_mode {
  STARPU_NONE, STARPU_R, STARPU_W, STARPU_RW,
  STARPU_SCRATCH, STARPU_REDUX, STARPU_COMMUTE, STARPU_SSEND,
  STARPU_LOCALITY, STARPU_ACCESS_MODE_MAX }
- enum starpu_node_kind {
  STARPU_UNUSED, STARPU_CPU_RAM, STARPU_CUDA_RAM, STARPU_OPENCL_RAM,
  STARPU_DISK_RAM, STARPU_MIC_RAM, STARPU_SCC_RAM, STARPU_SCC_SHM,
  STARPU_MPI_MS_RAM }

Functions

- void starpu_data_display_memory_stats ()
- int **starpu_data_prefetch_on_node_prio** (starpu_data_handle_t handle, unsigned node, unsigned async, int prio)
- int **starpu_data_idle_prefetch_on_node_prio** (starpu_data_handle_t handle, unsigned node, unsigned async, int prio)
- unsigned starpu_worker_get_memory_node (unsigned workerid)
- unsigned **starpu_memory_nodes_get_count** (void)

- enum starpu_node_kind starpu_node_get_kind (unsigned node)
- void starpu_data_set_sequential_consistency_flag (starpu_data_handle_t handle, unsigned flag)
- unsigned starpu_data_get_sequential_consistency_flag (starpu_data_handle_t handle)
- unsigned starpu_data_get_default_sequential_consistency_flag (void)
- void starpu_data_set_default_sequential_consistency_flag (unsigned flag)
- unsigned **starpu_data_test_if_allocated_on_node** (starpu_data_handle_t handle, unsigned memory_-node)
- void **starpu_memchunk_tidy** (unsigned memory_node)
- int starpu_data_cpy (starpu_data_handle_t dst_handle, starpu_data_handle_t src_handle, int asynchronous, void(∗callback_func)(void ∗), void ∗callback_arg)

Basic Data Management API

Data management is done at a high-level in StarPU: rather than accessing a mere list of contiguous buffers, the tasks may manipulate data that are described by a high-level construct which we call data interface.

An example of data interface is the "vector" interface which describes a contiguous data array on a spefic memory node. This interface is a simple structure containing the number of elements in the array, the size of the elements, and the address of the array in the appropriate address space (this address may be invalid if there is no valid copy of the array in the memory node). More informations on the data interfaces provided by StarPU are given in Data Interfaces.

When a piece of data managed by StarPU is used by a task, the task implementation is given a pointer to an interface describing a valid copy of the data that is accessible from the current processing unit.

Every worker is associated to a memory node which is a logical abstraction of the address space from which the processing unit gets its data. For instance, the memory node associated to the different CPU workers represents main memory (RAM), the memory node associated to a GPU is DRAM embedded on the device. Every memory node is identified by a logical index which is accessible from the function starpu_worker_get_memory_node(). When registering a piece of data to StarPU, the specified memory node indicates where the piece of data initially resides (we also call this memory node the home node of a piece of data).

- void starpu_data_set_name (starpu_data_handle_t handle, const char ∗name)
- void starpu_data_set_coordinates_array (starpu_data_handle_t handle, int dimensions, int dims[])
- void starpu_data_set_coordinates (starpu_data_handle_t handle, unsigned dimensions,...)
- void starpu_data_unregister (starpu_data_handle_t handle)
- void starpu_data_unregister_no_coherency (starpu_data_handle_t handle)
- void starpu_data_unregister_submit (starpu_data_handle_t handle)
- void starpu_data_invalidate (starpu_data_handle_t handle)
- void starpu_data_invalidate_submit (starpu_data_handle_t handle)
- void starpu_data_advise_as_important (starpu_data_handle_t handle, unsigned is_important)
- int starpu_data_request_allocation (starpu_data_handle_t handle, unsigned node)
- int starpu_data_fetch_on_node (starpu_data_handle_t handle, unsigned node, unsigned async)
- int starpu_data_prefetch_on_node (starpu_data_handle_t handle, unsigned node, unsigned async)
- int starpu_data_idle_prefetch_on_node (starpu_data_handle_t handle, unsigned node, unsigned async)
- void starpu_data_wont_use (starpu_data_handle_t handle)
- void starpu_data_set_wt_mask (starpu_data_handle_t handle, uint32_t wt_mask)
- void starpu_data_query_status (starpu_data_handle_t handle, int memory_node, int ∗is_allocated, int ∗is_-_valid, int ∗is_requested)
- void starpu_data_set_reduction_methods (starpu_data_handle_t handle, struct starpu_codelet ∗redux_cl, struct starpu_codelet ∗init_cl)
- struct starpu_data_interface_ops ∗ starpu_data_get_interface_ops (starpu_data_handle_t handle)
- void starpu_data_set_user_data (starpu_data_handle_t handle, void ∗user_data)
- void ∗ starpu_data_get_user_data (starpu_data_handle_t handle)

Access registered data from the application

- #define STARPU_ACQUIRE_NO_NODE
- #define STARPU_ACQUIRE_NO_NODE_LOCK_ALL
- #define STARPU_DATA_ACQUIRE_CB(handle, mode, code)
- int starpu_data_acquire (starpu_data_handle_t handle, enum starpu_data_access_mode mode)

- int starpu_data_acquire_on_node (starpu_data_handle_t handle, int node, enum starpu_data_access_mode mode)
- int starpu_data_acquire_cb (starpu_data_handle_t handle, enum starpu_data_access_mode mode, void(∗callback)(void ∗), void ∗arg)
- int starpu_data_acquire_on_node_cb (starpu_data_handle_t handle, int node, enum starpu_data_access_- mode mode, void(∗callback)(void ∗), void ∗arg)
- int starpu_data_acquire_cb_sequential_consistency (starpu_data_handle_t handle, enum starpu_data_- access_mode mode, void(∗callback)(void ∗), void ∗arg, int sequential_consistency)
- int starpu_data_acquire_on_node_cb_sequential_consistency (starpu_data_handle_t handle, int node, enum starpu_data_access_mode mode, void(∗callback)(void ∗), void ∗arg, int sequential_consistency)
- int starpu_data_acquire_on_node_cb_sequential_consistency_sync_jobids (starpu_data_handle_t han- dle, int node, enum starpu_data_access_mode mode, void(∗callback)(void ∗), void ∗arg, int sequential_- consistency, long ∗pre_sync_jobid, long ∗post_sync_jobid)
- int starpu_data_acquire_try (starpu_data_handle_t handle, enum starpu_data_access_mode mode)
- int starpu_data_acquire_on_node_try (starpu_data_handle_t handle, int node, enum starpu_data_access_- mode mode)
- void starpu_data_release (starpu_data_handle_t handle)
- void starpu_data_release_on_node (starpu_data_handle_t handle, int node)
- starpu_arbiter_t starpu_arbiter_create (void) STARPU_ATTRIBUTE_MALLOC
- void starpu_data_assign_arbiter (starpu_data_handle_t handle, starpu_arbiter_t arbiter)
- void starpu_arbiter_destroy (starpu_arbiter_t arbiter)

31.8.1   Detailed Description

31.9   starpu_data_filters.h File Reference

```
#include <starpu.h>
#include <stdarg.h>
```

Data Structures

- struct starpu_data_filter

Functions

Basic API

- void starpu_data_partition (starpu_data_handle_t initial_handle, struct starpu_data_filter ∗f)
- void starpu_data_unpartition (starpu_data_handle_t root_data, unsigned gathering_node)
- int starpu_data_get_nb_children (starpu_data_handle_t handle)
- starpu_data_handle_t starpu_data_get_child (starpu_data_handle_t handle, unsigned i)
- starpu_data_handle_t starpu_data_get_sub_data (starpu_data_handle_t root_data, unsigned depth,...)
- starpu_data_handle_t starpu_data_vget_sub_data (starpu_data_handle_t root_data, unsigned depth, va_- list pa)
- void starpu_data_map_filters (starpu_data_handle_t root_data, unsigned nfilters,...)
- void starpu_data_vmap_filters (starpu_data_handle_t root_data, unsigned nfilters, va_list pa)

Asynchronous API

- void starpu_data_partition_plan (starpu_data_handle_t initial_handle, struct starpu_data_filter ∗f, starpu- _data_handle_t ∗children)
- void starpu_data_partition_submit (starpu_data_handle_t initial_handle, unsigned nparts, starpu_data_- handle_t ∗children)

- void starpu_data_partition_readonly_submit (starpu_data_handle_t initial_handle, unsigned nparts, starpu_data_handle_t *children)
- void starpu_data_partition_readwrite_upgrade_submit (starpu_data_handle_t initial_handle, unsigned nparts, starpu_data_handle_t *children)
- void starpu_data_unpartition_submit (starpu_data_handle_t initial_handle, unsigned nparts, starpu_data_handle_t *children, int gathering_node)
- void starpu_data_unpartition_readonly_submit (starpu_data_handle_t initial_handle, unsigned nparts, starpu_data_handle_t *children, int gathering_node)
- void starpu_data_partition_clean (starpu_data_handle_t root_data, unsigned nparts, starpu_data_handle_t *children)

Predefined BCSR Filter Functions

This section gives a partial list of the predefined partitioning functions for BCSR data. Examples on how to use them are shown in Partitioning Data. The complete list can be found in the file starpu_data_filters.h.

- void starpu_bcsr_filter_canonical_block (void *father_interface, void *child_interface, struct starpu_data_filter *f, unsigned id, unsigned nparts)
- void starpu_csr_filter_vertical_block (void *father_interface, void *child_interface, struct starpu_data_filter *f, unsigned id, unsigned nparts)

Predefined Matrix Filter Functions

This section gives a partial list of the predefined partitioning functions for matrix data. Examples on how to use them are shown in Partitioning Data. The complete list can be found in the file starpu_data_filters.h.

- void starpu_matrix_filter_block (void *father_interface, void *child_interface, struct starpu_data_filter *f, unsigned id, unsigned nparts)
- void starpu_matrix_filter_block_shadow (void *father_interface, void *child_interface, struct starpu_data_filter *f, unsigned id, unsigned nparts)
- void starpu_matrix_filter_vertical_block (void *father_interface, void *child_interface, struct starpu_data_filter *f, unsigned id, unsigned nparts)
- void starpu_matrix_filter_vertical_block_shadow (void *father_interface, void *child_interface, struct starpu_data_filter *f, unsigned id, unsigned nparts)

Predefined Vector Filter Functions

This section gives a partial list of the predefined partitioning functions for vector data. Examples on how to use them are shown in Partitioning Data. The complete list can be found in the file starpu_data_filters.h.

- void starpu_vector_filter_block (void *father_interface, void *child_interface, struct starpu_data_filter *f, unsigned id, unsigned nparts)
- void starpu_vector_filter_block_shadow (void *father_interface, void *child_interface, struct starpu_data_filter *f, unsigned id, unsigned nparts)
- void starpu_vector_filter_list (void *father_interface, void *child_interface, struct starpu_data_filter *f, unsigned id, unsigned nparts)
- void starpu_vector_filter_divide_in_2 (void *father_interface, void *child_interface, struct starpu_data_filter *f, unsigned id, unsigned nparts)

Predefined Block Filter Functions

This section gives a partial list of the predefined partitioning functions for block data. Examples on how to use them are shown in Partitioning Data. The complete list can be found in the file starpu_data_filters.h. *A usage example is available in examples/filters/shadow3d.c*

- void starpu_block_filter_block (void *father_interface, void *child_interface, struct starpu_data_filter *f, unsigned id, unsigned nparts)
- void starpu_block_filter_block_shadow (void *father_interface, void *child_interface, struct starpu_data_filter *f, unsigned id, unsigned nparts)
- void starpu_block_filter_vertical_block (void *father_interface, void *child_interface, struct starpu_data_filter *f, unsigned id, unsigned nparts)
- void starpu_block_filter_vertical_block_shadow (void *father_interface, void *child_interface, struct starpu_data_filter *f, unsigned id, unsigned nparts)

- void starpu_block_filter_depth_block (void *father_interface, void *child_interface, struct starpu_data_filter *f, unsigned id, unsigned nparts)
- void starpu_block_filter_depth_block_shadow (void *father_interface, void *child_interface, struct starpu_data_filter *f, unsigned id, unsigned nparts)

31.9.1 Detailed Description

31.10 starpu_data_interfaces.h File Reference

```
#include <starpu.h>
#include <cuda_runtime.h>
```

Data Structures

- struct starpu_data_copy_methods
- struct starpu_data_interface_ops
- struct starpu_matrix_interface
- struct starpu_coo_interface
- struct starpu_block_interface
- struct starpu_vector_interface
- struct starpu_variable_interface
- struct starpu_csr_interface
- struct starpu_bcsr_interface
- struct starpu_multiformat_data_interface_ops
- struct starpu_multiformat_interface

Macros

- #define STARPU_MULTIFORMAT_GET_CPU_PTR(interface)
- #define STARPU_MULTIFORMAT_GET_CUDA_PTR(interface)
- #define STARPU_MULTIFORMAT_GET_OPENCL_PTR(interface)
- #define STARPU_MULTIFORMAT_GET_MIC_PTR(interface)
- #define STARPU_MULTIFORMAT_GET_NX(interface)

Accessing COO Data Interfaces

- #define STARPU_COO_GET_COLUMNS(interface)
- #define STARPU_COO_GET_COLUMNS_DEV_HANDLE(interface)
- #define STARPU_COO_GET_ROWS(interface)
- #define STARPU_COO_GET_ROWS_DEV_HANDLE(interface)
- #define STARPU_COO_GET_VALUES(interface)
- #define STARPU_COO_GET_VALUES_DEV_HANDLE(interface)
- #define STARPU_COO_GET_OFFSET
- #define STARPU_COO_GET_NX(interface)
- #define STARPU_COO_GET_NY(interface)
- #define STARPU_COO_GET_NVALUES(interface)
- #define STARPU_COO_GET_ELEMSIZE(interface)

Typedefs

- typedef cudaStream_t **starpu_cudaStream_t**

Enumerations

- enum starpu_data_interface_id {
  STARPU_UNKNOWN_INTERFACE_ID, STARPU_MATRIX_INTERFACE_ID, STARPU_BLOCK_INTERF-
  ACE_ID, STARPU_VECTOR_INTERFACE_ID,
  STARPU_CSR_INTERFACE_ID, STARPU_BCSR_INTERFACE_ID, STARPU_VARIABLE_INTERFACE_I-
  D, STARPU_VOID_INTERFACE_ID,
  STARPU_MULTIFORMAT_INTERFACE_ID, STARPU_COO_INTERFACE_ID, STARPU_MAX_INTERFA-
  CE_ID }

Functions

- void starpu_multiformat_data_register (starpu_data_handle_t *handle, int home_node, void *ptr, uint32_t
  nobjects, struct starpu_multiformat_data_interface_ops *format_ops)

Defining Interface

Applications can provide their own interface as shown in Defining A New Data Interface.

- int starpu_interface_copy (uintptr_t src, size_t src_offset, unsigned src_node, uintptr_t dst, size_t dst_-
  offset, unsigned dst_node, size_t size, void *async_data)
- uintptr_t starpu_malloc_on_node_flags (unsigned dst_node, size_t size, int flags)
- uintptr_t starpu_malloc_on_node (unsigned dst_node, size_t size)
- void starpu_free_on_node_flags (unsigned dst_node, uintptr_t addr, size_t size, int flags)
- void starpu_free_on_node (unsigned dst_node, uintptr_t addr, size_t size)
- void starpu_malloc_on_node_set_default_flags (unsigned node, int flags)
- int starpu_data_interface_get_next_id (void)

Basic Data Management API

Data management is done at a high-level in StarPU: rather than accessing a mere list of contiguous buffers, the tasks may manipulate data that are described by a high-level construct which we call data interface.

An example of data interface is the "vector" interface which describes a contiguous data array on a spefic memory node. This interface is a simple structure containing the number of elements in the array, the size of the elements, and the address of the array in the appropriate address space (this address may be invalid if there is no valid copy of the array in the memory node). More informations on the data interfaces provided by StarPU are given in Data Interfaces.

When a piece of data managed by StarPU is used by a task, the task implementation is given a pointer to an interface describing a valid copy of the data that is accessible from the current processing unit.

Every worker is associated to a memory node which is a logical abstraction of the address space from which the processing unit gets its data. For instance, the memory node associated to the different CPU workers represents main memory (RAM), the memory node associated to a GPU is DRAM embedded on the device. Every memory node is identified by a logical index which is accessible from the function starpu_worker_get_memory_node(). When registering a piece of data to StarPU, the specified memory node indicates where the piece of data initially resides (we also call this memory node the home node of a piece of data).

- void starpu_data_register (starpu_data_handle_t *handleptr, int home_node, void *data_interface, struct
  starpu_data_interface_ops *ops)
- void starpu_data_ptr_register (starpu_data_handle_t handle, unsigned node)
- void starpu_data_register_same (starpu_data_handle_t *handledst, starpu_data_handle_t handlesrc)
- starpu_data_handle_t starpu_data_lookup (const void *ptr)

Accessing Data Interfaces

Each data interface is provided with a set of field access functions. The ones using a void * *parameter aimed to be used in codelet implementations (see for example the code in Vector Scaling Using StarPU's API).*

- void * starpu_data_handle_to_pointer (starpu_data_handle_t handle, unsigned node)
- void * starpu_data_get_local_ptr (starpu_data_handle_t handle)
- enum starpu_data_interface_id starpu_data_get_interface_id (starpu_data_handle_t handle)

- int starpu_data_pack (starpu_data_handle_t handle, void **ptr, starpu_ssize_t *count)
- int starpu_data_unpack (starpu_data_handle_t handle, void *ptr, size_t count)
- size_t starpu_data_get_size (starpu_data_handle_t handle)

Registering Data

There are several ways to register a memory region so that it can be managed by StarPU. The functions below allow the registration of vectors, 2D matrices, 3D matrices as well as BCSR and CSR sparse matrices.

- void * starpu_data_get_interface_on_node (starpu_data_handle_t handle, unsigned memory_node)
- void starpu_matrix_data_register (starpu_data_handle_t *handle, int home_node, uintptr_t ptr, uint32_t ld, uint32_t nx, uint32_t ny, size_t elemsize)
- void starpu_matrix_ptr_register (starpu_data_handle_t handle, unsigned node, uintptr_t ptr, uintptr_t dev-_handle, size_t offset, uint32_t ld)
- void starpu_coo_data_register (starpu_data_handle_t *handleptr, int home_node, uint32_t nx, uint32_t ny, uint32_t n_values, uint32_t *columns, uint32_t *rows, uintptr_t values, size_t elemsize)
- void starpu_block_data_register (starpu_data_handle_t *handle, int home_node, uintptr_t ptr, uint32_t ldy, uint32_t ldz, uint32_t nx, uint32_t ny, uint32_t nz, size_t elemsize)
- void starpu_block_ptr_register (starpu_data_handle_t handle, unsigned node, uintptr_t ptr, uintptr_t dev-_handle, size_t offset, uint32_t ldy, uint32_t ldz)
- void starpu_vector_data_register (starpu_data_handle_t *handle, int home_node, uintptr_t ptr, uint32_t nx, size_t elemsize)
- void starpu_vector_ptr_register (starpu_data_handle_t handle, unsigned node, uintptr_t ptr, uintptr_t dev-_handle, size_t offset)
- void starpu_variable_data_register (starpu_data_handle_t *handle, int home_node, uintptr_t ptr, size_t size)
- void starpu_variable_ptr_register (starpu_data_handle_t handle, unsigned node, uintptr_t ptr, uintptr_t dev_handle, size_t offset)
- void starpu_void_data_register (starpu_data_handle_t *handle)
- void starpu_csr_data_register (starpu_data_handle_t *handle, int home_node, uint32_t nnz, uint32_-t nrow, uintptr_t nzval, uint32_t *colind, uint32_t *rowptr, uint32_t firstentry, size_t elemsize)
- void starpu_bcsr_data_register (starpu_data_handle_t *handle, int home_node, uint32_t nnz, uint32_-t nrow, uintptr_t nzval, uint32_t *colind, uint32_t *rowptr, uint32_t firstentry, uint32_t r, uint32_t c, size_t elemsize)

Variables

- struct starpu_data_interface_ops **starpu_interface_matrix_ops**
- struct starpu_data_interface_ops **starpu_interface_coo_ops**
- struct starpu_data_interface_ops **starpu_interface_block_ops**
- struct starpu_data_interface_ops **starpu_interface_vector_ops**
- struct starpu_data_interface_ops **starpu_interface_variable_ops**
- struct starpu_data_interface_ops **starpu_interface_void_ops**
- struct starpu_data_interface_ops **starpu_interface_csr_ops**
- struct starpu_data_interface_ops **starpu_interface_bcsr_ops**

Accessing Variable Data Interfaces

- #define STARPU_VARIABLE_GET_PTR(interface)
- #define STARPU_VARIABLE_GET_OFFSET(interface)
- #define STARPU_VARIABLE_GET_ELEMSIZE(interface)
- #define STARPU_VARIABLE_GET_DEV_HANDLE(interface)
- size_t starpu_variable_get_elemsize (starpu_data_handle_t handle)
- uintptr_t starpu_variable_get_local_ptr (starpu_data_handle_t handle)

Accessing Vector Data Interfaces

- #define STARPU_VECTOR_GET_PTR(interface)
- #define STARPU_VECTOR_GET_DEV_HANDLE(interface)
- #define STARPU_VECTOR_GET_OFFSET(interface)
- #define STARPU_VECTOR_GET_NX(interface)
- #define STARPU_VECTOR_GET_ELEMSIZE(interface)
- #define STARPU_VECTOR_GET_SLICE_BASE(interface)
- uint32_t starpu_vector_get_nx (starpu_data_handle_t handle)
- size_t starpu_vector_get_elemsize (starpu_data_handle_t handle)
- uintptr_t starpu_vector_get_local_ptr (starpu_data_handle_t handle)

Accessing Matrix Data Interfaces

- #define STARPU_MATRIX_GET_PTR(interface)
- #define STARPU_MATRIX_GET_DEV_HANDLE(interface)
- #define STARPU_MATRIX_GET_OFFSET(interface)
- #define STARPU_MATRIX_GET_NX(interface)
- #define STARPU_MATRIX_GET_NY(interface)
- #define STARPU_MATRIX_GET_LD(interface)
- #define STARPU_MATRIX_GET_ELEMSIZE(interface)
- uint32_t starpu_matrix_get_nx (starpu_data_handle_t handle)
- uint32_t starpu_matrix_get_ny (starpu_data_handle_t handle)
- uint32_t starpu_matrix_get_local_ld (starpu_data_handle_t handle)
- uintptr_t starpu_matrix_get_local_ptr (starpu_data_handle_t handle)
- size_t starpu_matrix_get_elemsize (starpu_data_handle_t handle)

Accessing Block Data Interfaces

- #define STARPU_BLOCK_GET_PTR(interface)
- #define STARPU_BLOCK_GET_DEV_HANDLE(interface)
- #define STARPU_BLOCK_GET_OFFSET(interface)
- #define STARPU_BLOCK_GET_NX(interface)
- #define STARPU_BLOCK_GET_NY(interface)
- #define STARPU_BLOCK_GET_NZ(interface)
- #define STARPU_BLOCK_GET_LDY(interface)
- #define STARPU_BLOCK_GET_LDZ(interface)
- #define STARPU_BLOCK_GET_ELEMSIZE(interface)
- uint32_t starpu_block_get_nx (starpu_data_handle_t handle)
- uint32_t starpu_block_get_ny (starpu_data_handle_t handle)
- uint32_t starpu_block_get_nz (starpu_data_handle_t handle)
- uint32_t starpu_block_get_local_ldy (starpu_data_handle_t handle)
- uint32_t starpu_block_get_local_ldz (starpu_data_handle_t handle)
- uintptr_t starpu_block_get_local_ptr (starpu_data_handle_t handle)
- size_t starpu_block_get_elemsize (starpu_data_handle_t handle)

Accessing BCSR Data Interfaces

- #define STARPU_BCSR_GET_NNZ(interface)
- #define STARPU_BCSR_GET_NZVAL(interface)
- #define STARPU_BCSR_GET_NZVAL_DEV_HANDLE(interface)
- #define STARPU_BCSR_GET_COLIND(interface)
- #define STARPU_BCSR_GET_COLIND_DEV_HANDLE(interface)
- #define STARPU_BCSR_GET_ROWPTR(interface)
- #define STARPU_BCSR_GET_ROWPTR_DEV_HANDLE(interface)
- #define STARPU_BCSR_GET_OFFSET
- uint32_t starpu_bcsr_get_nnz (starpu_data_handle_t handle)
- uint32_t starpu_bcsr_get_nrow (starpu_data_handle_t handle)
- uint32_t starpu_bcsr_get_firstentry (starpu_data_handle_t handle)
- uintptr_t starpu_bcsr_get_local_nzval (starpu_data_handle_t handle)
- uint32_t ∗ starpu_bcsr_get_local_colind (starpu_data_handle_t handle)
- uint32_t ∗ starpu_bcsr_get_local_rowptr (starpu_data_handle_t handle)
- uint32_t starpu_bcsr_get_r (starpu_data_handle_t handle)
- uint32_t starpu_bcsr_get_c (starpu_data_handle_t handle)
- size_t starpu_bcsr_get_elemsize (starpu_data_handle_t handle)

Accessing CSR Data Interfaces

- #define STARPU_CSR_GET_NNZ(interface)
- #define STARPU_CSR_GET_NROW(interface)
- #define STARPU_CSR_GET_NZVAL(interface)
- #define STARPU_CSR_GET_NZVAL_DEV_HANDLE(interface)
- #define STARPU_CSR_GET_COLIND(interface)
- #define STARPU_CSR_GET_COLIND_DEV_HANDLE(interface)
- #define STARPU_CSR_GET_ROWPTR(interface)
- #define STARPU_CSR_GET_ROWPTR_DEV_HANDLE(interface)
- #define STARPU_CSR_GET_OFFSET
- #define STARPU_CSR_GET_FIRSTENTRY(interface)
- #define STARPU_CSR_GET_ELEMSIZE(interface)
- uint32_t starpu_csr_get_nnz (starpu_data_handle_t handle)
- uint32_t starpu_csr_get_nrow (starpu_data_handle_t handle)
- uint32_t starpu_csr_get_firstentry (starpu_data_handle_t handle)
- uintptr_t starpu_csr_get_local_nzval (starpu_data_handle_t handle)
- uint32_t ∗ starpu_csr_get_local_colind (starpu_data_handle_t handle)
- uint32_t ∗ starpu_csr_get_local_rowptr (starpu_data_handle_t handle)
- size_t starpu_csr_get_elemsize (starpu_data_handle_t handle)

31.10.1 Detailed Description

31.11 starpu_deprecated_api.h File Reference

Macros

- #define **starpu_permodel_history_based_expected_perf**

31.11.1   Detailed Description

31.12   starpu_disk.h File Reference

```
#include <sys/types.h>
#include <starpu_config.h>
```

Data Structures

- struct starpu_disk_ops

Macros

- #define STARPU_DISK_SIZE_MIN

Functions

- void starpu_disk_close (unsigned node, void *obj, size_t size)
- void * starpu_disk_open (unsigned node, void *pos, size_t size)
- int starpu_disk_register (struct starpu_disk_ops *func, void *parameter, starpu_ssize_t size)

Variables

- struct starpu_disk_ops starpu_disk_stdio_ops
- struct starpu_disk_ops starpu_disk_unistd_ops
- struct starpu_disk_ops starpu_disk_unistd_o_direct_ops
- struct starpu_disk_ops starpu_disk_leveldb_ops
- int starpu_disk_swap_node

31.12.1   Detailed Description

31.13   starpu_driver.h File Reference

```
#include <starpu_config.h>
#include <starpu_opencl.h>
```

Data Structures

- struct starpu_driver
- union starpu_driver.id

Functions

- int starpu_driver_run (struct starpu_driver *d)
- void starpu_drivers_request_termination (void)
- int starpu_driver_init (struct starpu_driver *d)
- int starpu_driver_run_once (struct starpu_driver *d)
- int starpu_driver_deinit (struct starpu_driver *d)

31.13.1   Detailed Description

31.14   starpu_expert.h File Reference

```
#include <starpu.h>
```

Functions

- void starpu_wake_all_blocked_workers (void)
- int starpu_progression_hook_register (unsigned(*func)(void *arg), void *arg)
- void starpu_progression_hook_deregister (int hook_id)

31.14.1   Detailed Description

31.15   starpu_fxt.h File Reference

```
#include <starpu_perfmodel.h>
```

Data Structures

- struct starpu_fxt_codelet_event
- struct starpu_fxt_options

Macros

- #define **STARPU_FXT_MAX_FILES**

Functions

- void starpu_fxt_options_init (struct starpu_fxt_options *options)
- void starpu_fxt_generate_trace (struct starpu_fxt_options *options)
- void starpu_fxt_autostart_profiling (int autostart)
- void starpu_fxt_start_profiling (void)
- void starpu_fxt_stop_profiling (void)
- void starpu_fxt_write_data_trace (char *filename_in)
- void starpu_fxt_trace_user_event (unsigned long code)
- void starpu_fxt_trace_user_event_string (const char *s)

31.15.1   Detailed Description

31.16   starpu_hash.h File Reference

```
#include <stdint.h>
#include <stddef.h>
```

Functions

Defining Interface

Applications can provide their own interface as shown in Defining A New Data Interface.

- uint32_t starpu_hash_crc32c_be_n (const void *input, size_t n, uint32_t inputcrc)
- uint32_t starpu_hash_crc32c_be (uint32_t input, uint32_t inputcrc)
- uint32_t starpu_hash_crc32c_string (const char *str, uint32_t inputcrc)

31.16.1   Detailed Description

31.17   starpu_mic.h File Reference

```
#include <starpu_config.h>
```

Typedefs

- typedef void * starpu_mic_func_symbol_t

Functions

- int starpu_mic_register_kernel (starpu_mic_func_symbol_t *symbol, const char *func_name)
- starpu_mic_kernel_t starpu_mic_get_kernel (starpu_mic_func_symbol_t symbol)

31.17.1   Detailed Description

31.18   starpu_opencl.h File Reference

```
#include <starpu_config.h>
#include <CL/cl.h>
#include <assert.h>
```

Data Structures

- struct starpu_opencl_program

Functions

Writing OpenCL kernels

- void starpu_opencl_get_context (int devid, cl_context *context)
- void starpu_opencl_get_device (int devid, cl_device_id *device)
- void starpu_opencl_get_queue (int devid, cl_command_queue *queue)
- void starpu_opencl_get_current_context (cl_context *context)
- void starpu_opencl_get_current_queue (cl_command_queue *queue)
- int starpu_opencl_set_kernel_args (cl_int *err, cl_kernel *kernel,...)

Compiling OpenCL kernels

Source codes for OpenCL kernels can be stored in a file or in a string. StarPU provides functions to build the program executable for each available OpenCL device as a cl_program object. This program executable can then be loaded within a specific queue as explained in the next section. These are only helpers, Applications can also fill a starpu_opencl_program array by hand for more advanced use (e.g. different programs on the different OpenCL devices, for relocation purpose for instance).

- void starpu_opencl_load_program_source (const char *source_file_name, char *located_file_name, char *located_dir_name, char *opencl_program_source)
- void starpu_opencl_load_program_source_malloc (const char *source_file_name, char **located_file_-name, char **located_dir_name, char **opencl_program_source)
- int starpu_opencl_compile_opencl_from_file (const char *source_file_name, const char *build_options)
- int starpu_opencl_compile_opencl_from_string (const char *opencl_program_source, const char *file_-name, const char *build_options)
- int starpu_opencl_load_binary_opencl (const char *kernel_id, struct starpu_opencl_program *opencl_-programs)
- int starpu_opencl_load_opencl_from_file (const char *source_file_name, struct starpu_opencl_program *opencl_programs, const char *build_options)
- int starpu_opencl_load_opencl_from_string (const char *opencl_program_source, struct starpu_opencl_-program *opencl_programs, const char *build_options)
- int starpu_opencl_unload_opencl (struct starpu_opencl_program *opencl_programs)

Loading OpenCL kernels

- int starpu_opencl_load_kernel (cl_kernel *kernel, cl_command_queue *queue, struct starpu_opencl_-program *opencl_programs, const char *kernel_name, int devid)
- int starpu_opencl_release_kernel (cl_kernel kernel)

OpenCL statistics

- int starpu_opencl_collect_stats (cl_event event)

OpenCL utilities

- #define STARPU_OPENCL_DISPLAY_ERROR(status)
- #define STARPU_OPENCL_REPORT_ERROR(status)
- #define STARPU_OPENCL_REPORT_ERROR_WITH_MSG(msg, status)
- const char * starpu_opencl_error_string (cl_int status)
- void starpu_opencl_display_error (const char *func, const char *file, int line, const char *msg, cl_int status)
- static __starpu_inline void starpu_opencl_report_error (const char *func, const char *file, int line, const char *msg, cl_int status)
- cl_int starpu_opencl_allocate_memory (int devid, cl_mem *addr, size_t size, cl_mem_flags flags)
- cl_int starpu_opencl_copy_ram_to_opencl (void *ptr, unsigned src_node, cl_mem buffer, unsigned dst_node, size_t size, size_t offset, cl_event *event, int *ret)
- cl_int starpu_opencl_copy_opencl_to_ram (cl_mem buffer, unsigned src_node, void *ptr, unsigned dst_node, size_t size, size_t offset, cl_event *event, int *ret)
- cl_int starpu_opencl_copy_opencl_to_opencl (cl_mem src, unsigned src_node, size_t src_offset, cl_mem dst, unsigned dst_node, size_t dst_offset, size_t size, cl_event *event, int *ret)
- cl_int starpu_opencl_copy_async_sync (uintptr_t src, size_t src_offset, unsigned src_node, uintptr_t dst, size_t dst_offset, unsigned dst_node, size_t size, cl_event *event)

31.18.1 Detailed Description

31.19 starpu_openmp.h File Reference

```
#include <starpu_config.h>
```

Data Structures

- struct starpu_omp_lock_t
- struct starpu_omp_nest_lock_t
- struct starpu_omp_parallel_region_attr
- struct starpu_omp_task_region_attr

Macros

- #define **__STARPU_OMP_NOTHROW**

Enumerations

- enum starpu_omp_sched_value {
  starpu_omp_sched_undefined, starpu_omp_sched_static, starpu_omp_sched_dynamic, starpu_omp_-sched_guided,
  starpu_omp_sched_auto, starpu_omp_sched_runtime }
- enum starpu_omp_proc_bind_value {
  starpu_omp_proc_bind_undefined, starpu_omp_proc_bind_false, starpu_omp_proc_bind_true, starpu_omp-_proc_bind_master,
  starpu_omp_proc_bind_close, starpu_omp_proc_bind_spread }

Functions

- int **starpu_omp_get_num_places** (void) __STARPU_OMP_NOTHROW
- int **starpu_omp_get_place_num_procs** (int place_num) __STARPU_OMP_NOTHROW
- void **starpu_omp_get_place_proc_ids** (int place_num, int ∗ids) __STARPU_OMP_NOTHROW
- int **starpu_omp_get_place_num** (void) __STARPU_OMP_NOTHROW
- int **starpu_omp_get_partition_num_places** (void) __STARPU_OMP_NOTHROW
- void **starpu_omp_get_partition_place_nums** (int ∗place_nums) __STARPU_OMP_NOTHROW
- int **starpu_omp_get_initial_device** (void) __STARPU_OMP_NOTHROW
- struct starpu_arbiter ∗ **starpu_omp_get_default_arbiter** (void) __STARPU_OMP_NOTHROW

Initialisation

- int starpu_omp_init (void) __STARPU_OMP_NOTHROW
- void starpu_omp_shutdown (void) __STARPU_OMP_NOTHROW

Parallel

- void starpu_omp_parallel_region (const struct starpu_omp_parallel_region_attr ∗attr) __STARPU_OMP_-NOTHROW
- void starpu_omp_master (void(∗f)(void ∗arg), void ∗arg) __STARPU_OMP_NOTHROW
- int starpu_omp_master_inline (void) __STARPU_OMP_NOTHROW

Synchronization

- void starpu_omp_barrier (void) __STARPU_OMP_NOTHROW
- void starpu_omp_critical (void(∗f)(void ∗arg), void ∗arg, const char ∗name) __STARPU_OMP_NOTHROW
- void starpu_omp_critical_inline_begin (const char ∗name) __STARPU_OMP_NOTHROW
- void starpu_omp_critical_inline_end (const char ∗name) __STARPU_OMP_NOTHROW

Worksharing

- void starpu_omp_single (void(∗f)(void ∗arg), void ∗arg, int nowait) __STARPU_OMP_NOTHROW
- int starpu_omp_single_inline (void) __STARPU_OMP_NOTHROW

- void starpu_omp_single_copyprivate (void(∗f)(void ∗arg, void ∗data, unsigned long long data_size), void ∗arg, void ∗data, unsigned long long data_size) __STARPU_OMP_NOTHROW
- void ∗ starpu_omp_single_copyprivate_inline_begin (void ∗data) __STARPU_OMP_NOTHROW
- void starpu_omp_single_copyprivate_inline_end (void) __STARPU_OMP_NOTHROW
- void starpu_omp_for (void(∗f)(unsigned long long _first_i, unsigned long long _nb_i, void ∗arg), void ∗arg, unsigned long long nb_iterations, unsigned long long chunk, int schedule, int ordered, int nowait) __STA-RPU_OMP_NOTHROW
- int starpu_omp_for_inline_first (unsigned long long nb_iterations, unsigned long long chunk, int schedule, int ordered, unsigned long long ∗_first_i, unsigned long long ∗_nb_i) __STARPU_OMP_NOTHROW
- int starpu_omp_for_inline_next (unsigned long long nb_iterations, unsigned long long chunk, int schedule, int ordered, unsigned long long ∗_first_i, unsigned long long ∗_nb_i) __STARPU_OMP_NOTHROW
- void starpu_omp_for_alt (void(∗f)(unsigned long long _begin_i, unsigned long long _end_i, void ∗arg), void ∗arg, unsigned long long nb_iterations, unsigned long long chunk, int schedule, int ordered, int nowait) __STARPU_OMP_NOTHROW
- int starpu_omp_for_inline_first_alt (unsigned long long nb_iterations, unsigned long long chunk, int schedule, int ordered, unsigned long long ∗_begin_i, unsigned long long ∗_end_i) __STARPU_OMP_NOTHROW
- int starpu_omp_for_inline_next_alt (unsigned long long nb_iterations, unsigned long long chunk, int schedule, int ordered, unsigned long long ∗_begin_i, unsigned long long ∗_end_i) __STARPU_OMP_NOTHROW
- void starpu_omp_ordered_inline_begin (void) __STARPU_OMP_NOTHROW
- void starpu_omp_ordered_inline_end (void) __STARPU_OMP_NOTHROW
- void starpu_omp_ordered (void(∗f)(void ∗arg), void ∗arg) __STARPU_OMP_NOTHROW
- void starpu_omp_sections (unsigned long long nb_sections, void(∗∗section_f)(void ∗arg), void ∗∗section_arg, int nowait) __STARPU_OMP_NOTHROW
- void starpu_omp_sections_combined (unsigned long long nb_sections, void(∗section_f)(unsigned long long section_num, void ∗arg), void ∗section_arg, int nowait) __STARPU_OMP_NOTHROW

Task

- void starpu_omp_task_region (const struct starpu_omp_task_region_attr ∗attr) __STARPU_OMP_NOT-HROW
- void starpu_omp_taskwait (void) __STARPU_OMP_NOTHROW
- void starpu_omp_taskgroup (void(∗f)(void ∗arg), void ∗arg) __STARPU_OMP_NOTHROW
- void starpu_omp_taskgroup_inline_begin (void) __STARPU_OMP_NOTHROW
- void starpu_omp_taskgroup_inline_end (void) __STARPU_OMP_NOTHROW

API

- void starpu_omp_set_num_threads (int threads) __STARPU_OMP_NOTHROW
- int starpu_omp_get_num_threads () __STARPU_OMP_NOTHROW
- int starpu_omp_get_thread_num () __STARPU_OMP_NOTHROW
- int starpu_omp_get_max_threads () __STARPU_OMP_NOTHROW
- int starpu_omp_get_num_procs (void) __STARPU_OMP_NOTHROW
- int starpu_omp_in_parallel (void) __STARPU_OMP_NOTHROW
- void starpu_omp_set_dynamic (int dynamic_threads) __STARPU_OMP_NOTHROW
- int starpu_omp_get_dynamic (void) __STARPU_OMP_NOTHROW
- void starpu_omp_set_nested (int nested) __STARPU_OMP_NOTHROW
- int starpu_omp_get_nested (void) __STARPU_OMP_NOTHROW
- int starpu_omp_get_cancellation (void) __STARPU_OMP_NOTHROW
- void starpu_omp_set_schedule (enum starpu_omp_sched_value kind, int modifier) __STARPU_OMP_N-OTHROW
- void starpu_omp_get_schedule (enum starpu_omp_sched_value ∗kind, int ∗modifier) __STARPU_OMP-_NOTHROW
- int starpu_omp_get_thread_limit (void) __STARPU_OMP_NOTHROW
- void starpu_omp_set_max_active_levels (int max_levels) __STARPU_OMP_NOTHROW
- int starpu_omp_get_max_active_levels (void) __STARPU_OMP_NOTHROW
- int starpu_omp_get_level (void) __STARPU_OMP_NOTHROW
- int starpu_omp_get_ancestor_thread_num (int level) __STARPU_OMP_NOTHROW
- int starpu_omp_get_team_size (int level) __STARPU_OMP_NOTHROW
- int starpu_omp_get_active_level (void) __STARPU_OMP_NOTHROW
- int starpu_omp_in_final (void) __STARPU_OMP_NOTHROW

- enum starpu_omp_proc_bind_value starpu_omp_get_proc_bind (void) __STARPU_OMP_NOTHROW
- void starpu_omp_set_default_device (int device_num) __STARPU_OMP_NOTHROW
- int starpu_omp_get_default_device (void) __STARPU_OMP_NOTHROW
- int starpu_omp_get_num_devices (void) __STARPU_OMP_NOTHROW
- int starpu_omp_get_num_teams (void) __STARPU_OMP_NOTHROW
- int starpu_omp_get_team_num (void) __STARPU_OMP_NOTHROW
- int starpu_omp_is_initial_device (void) __STARPU_OMP_NOTHROW
- int starpu_omp_get_max_task_priority (void) __STARPU_OMP_NOTHROW
- void starpu_omp_init_lock (starpu_omp_lock_t *lock) __STARPU_OMP_NOTHROW
- void starpu_omp_destroy_lock (starpu_omp_lock_t *lock) __STARPU_OMP_NOTHROW
- void starpu_omp_set_lock (starpu_omp_lock_t *lock) __STARPU_OMP_NOTHROW
- void starpu_omp_unset_lock (starpu_omp_lock_t *lock) __STARPU_OMP_NOTHROW
- int starpu_omp_test_lock (starpu_omp_lock_t *lock) __STARPU_OMP_NOTHROW
- void starpu_omp_init_nest_lock (starpu_omp_nest_lock_t *lock) __STARPU_OMP_NOTHROW
- void starpu_omp_destroy_nest_lock (starpu_omp_nest_lock_t *lock) __STARPU_OMP_NOTHROW
- void starpu_omp_set_nest_lock (starpu_omp_nest_lock_t *lock) __STARPU_OMP_NOTHROW
- void starpu_omp_unset_nest_lock (starpu_omp_nest_lock_t *lock) __STARPU_OMP_NOTHROW
- int starpu_omp_test_nest_lock (starpu_omp_nest_lock_t *lock) __STARPU_OMP_NOTHROW
- void starpu_omp_atomic_fallback_inline_begin (void) __STARPU_OMP_NOTHROW
- void starpu_omp_atomic_fallback_inline_end (void) __STARPU_OMP_NOTHROW
- double starpu_omp_get_wtime (void) __STARPU_OMP_NOTHROW
- double starpu_omp_get_wtick (void) __STARPU_OMP_NOTHROW
- void starpu_omp_vector_annotate (starpu_data_handle_t handle, uint32_t slice_base) __STARPU_OMP-_NOTHROW

31.19.1 Detailed Description

31.20 starpu_perfmodel.h File Reference

```
#include <starpu.h>
#include <stdio.h>
#include <starpu_util.h>
#include <starpu_worker.h>
#include <starpu_task.h>
```

Data Structures

- struct starpu_perfmodel_device
- struct starpu_perfmodel_arch
- struct starpu_perfmodel_history_entry
- struct starpu_perfmodel_history_list
- struct starpu_perfmodel_regression_model
- struct starpu_perfmodel_per_arch
- struct starpu_perfmodel

Macros

- #define **STARPU_NARCH**
- #define **starpu_per_arch_perfmodel**

Typedefs

- typedef double(* **starpu_perfmodel_per_arch_cost_function**)(struct starpu_task *task, struct starpu_perfmodel_arch *arch, unsigned nimpl)
- typedef size_t(* **starpu_perfmodel_per_arch_size_base**)(struct starpu_task *task, struct starpu_perfmodel_arch *arch, unsigned nimpl)
- typedef struct _starpu_perfmodel_state * **starpu_perfmodel_state_t**

Enumerations

- enum starpu_perfmodel_type {
  STARPU_PERFMODEL_INVALID, STARPU_PER_ARCH, STARPU_COMMON, STARPU_HISTORY_BASED,
  STARPU_REGRESSION_BASED, STARPU_NL_REGRESSION_BASED, STARPU_MULTIPLE_REGRESSION_BASED }

Functions

- void starpu_perfmodel_init (struct starpu_perfmodel *model)
- int starpu_perfmodel_load_file (const char *filename, struct starpu_perfmodel *model)
- int starpu_perfmodel_load_symbol (const char *symbol, struct starpu_perfmodel *model)
- int starpu_perfmodel_unload_model (struct starpu_perfmodel *model)
- void **starpu_perfmodel_get_model_path** (const char *symbol, char *path, size_t maxlen)
- void starpu_perfmodel_free_sampling_directories (void)
- struct starpu_perfmodel_arch * starpu_worker_get_perf_archtype (int workerid, unsigned sched_ctx_id)
- int **starpu_perfmodel_get_narch_combs** ()
- int **starpu_perfmodel_arch_comb_add** (int ndevices, struct starpu_perfmodel_device *devices)
- int **starpu_perfmodel_arch_comb_get** (int ndevices, struct starpu_perfmodel_device *devices)
- struct starpu_perfmodel_per_arch * **starpu_perfmodel_get_model_per_arch** (struct starpu_perfmodel *model, struct starpu_perfmodel_arch *arch, unsigned impl)
- struct starpu_perfmodel_per_arch * **starpu_perfmodel_get_model_per_devices** (struct starpu_perfmodel *model, int impl,...)
- int **starpu_perfmodel_set_per_devices_cost_function** (struct starpu_perfmodel *model, int impl, starpu_perfmodel_per_arch_cost_function func,...)
- int **starpu_perfmodel_set_per_devices_size_base** (struct starpu_perfmodel *model, int impl, starpu_perfmodel_per_arch_size_base func,...)
- void starpu_perfmodel_debugfilepath (struct starpu_perfmodel *model, struct starpu_perfmodel_arch *arch, char *path, size_t maxlen, unsigned nimpl)
- char * starpu_perfmodel_get_archtype_name (enum starpu_worker_archtype archtype)
- void starpu_perfmodel_get_arch_name (struct starpu_perfmodel_arch *arch, char *archname, size_t maxlen, unsigned nimpl)
- double starpu_perfmodel_history_based_expected_perf (struct starpu_perfmodel *model, struct starpu_perfmodel_arch *arch, uint32_t footprint)
- int starpu_perfmodel_list (FILE *output)
- void starpu_perfmodel_print (struct starpu_perfmodel *model, struct starpu_perfmodel_arch *arch, unsigned nimpl, char *parameter, uint32_t *footprint, FILE *output)
- int starpu_perfmodel_print_all (struct starpu_perfmodel *model, char *arch, char *parameter, uint32_t *footprint, FILE *output)
- int starpu_perfmodel_print_estimations (struct starpu_perfmodel *model, uint32_t footprint, FILE *output)
- int **starpu_perfmodel_list_combs** (FILE *output, struct starpu_perfmodel *model)
- void starpu_perfmodel_update_history (struct starpu_perfmodel *model, struct starpu_task *task, struct starpu_perfmodel_arch *arch, unsigned cpuid, unsigned nimpl, double measured)
- void starpu_perfmodel_directory (FILE *output)
- void starpu_bus_print_bandwidth (FILE *f)

- void starpu_bus_print_affinity (FILE *f)
- void starpu_bus_print_filenames (FILE *f)
- double starpu_transfer_bandwidth (unsigned src_node, unsigned dst_node)
- double starpu_transfer_latency (unsigned src_node, unsigned dst_node)
- double starpu_transfer_predict (unsigned src_node, unsigned dst_node, size_t size)

31.20.1   Detailed Description

31.21   starpu_profiling.h File Reference

```
#include <starpu.h>
#include <errno.h>
#include <time.h>
#include <starpu_util.h>
```

Data Structures

- struct starpu_profiling_task_info
- struct starpu_profiling_worker_info
- struct starpu_profiling_bus_info

Macros

- #define STARPU_PROFILING_DISABLE
- #define STARPU_PROFILING_ENABLE
- #define **starpu_timespec_cmp**(a, b, CMP)

Functions

- void starpu_profiling_init (void)
- void starpu_profiling_set_id (int new_id)
- int starpu_profiling_status_set (int status)
- int starpu_profiling_status_get (void)
- int starpu_profiling_worker_get_info (int workerid, struct starpu_profiling_worker_info *worker_info)
- int starpu_bus_get_count (void)
- int starpu_bus_get_id (int src, int dst)
- int starpu_bus_get_src (int busid)
- int starpu_bus_get_dst (int busid)
- void **starpu_bus_set_direct** (int busid, int direct)
- int **starpu_bus_get_direct** (int busid)
- void **starpu_bus_set_ngpus** (int busid, int ngpus)
- int **starpu_bus_get_ngpus** (int busid)
- int starpu_bus_get_profiling_info (int busid, struct starpu_profiling_bus_info *bus_info)
- static __starpu_inline void **starpu_timespec_clear** (struct timespec *tsp)
- static __starpu_inline void **starpu_timespec_add** (struct timespec *a, struct timespec *b, struct timespec *result)
- static __starpu_inline void **starpu_timespec_accumulate** (struct timespec *result, struct timespec *a)
- static __starpu_inline void **starpu_timespec_sub** (const struct timespec *a, const struct timespec *b, struct timespec *result)
- double starpu_timing_timespec_delay_us (struct timespec *start, struct timespec *end)
- double starpu_timing_timespec_to_us (struct timespec *ts)
- void starpu_profiling_bus_helper_display_summary (void)
- void starpu_profiling_worker_helper_display_summary (void)

31.21.1   Detailed Description

31.22   starpu_rand.h File Reference

```
#include <stdlib.h>
#include <starpu_config.h>
```

Macros

- #define **starpu_seed**(seed)
- #define **starpu_srand48**(seed)
- #define **starpu_drand48**()
- #define **starpu_lrand48**()
- #define **starpu_erand48**(xsubi)
- #define **starpu_srand48_r**(seed, buffer)
- #define **starpu_erand48_r**(xsubi, buffer, result)

Typedefs

- typedef int **starpu_drand48_data**

31.22.1   Detailed Description

31.23   starpu_scc.h File Reference

```
#include <starpu_config.h>
```

Typedefs

- **typedef void** * starpu_scc_func_symbol_t

Functions

- int starpu_scc_register_kernel (starpu_scc_func_symbol_t *symbol, const char *func_name)
- starpu_scc_kernel_t starpu_scc_get_kernel (starpu_scc_func_symbol_t symbol)

31.23.1   Detailed Description

31.24   starpu_sched_ctx.h File Reference

```
#include <starpu.h>
```

Macros

- #define **STARPU_SCHED_CTX_HIERARCHY_LEVEL**
- #define **STARPU_SCHED_CTX_NESTED**

Functions

- unsigned **starpu_sched_ctx_get_inheritor** (unsigned sched_ctx_id)
- unsigned **starpu_sched_ctx_get_hierarchy_level** (unsigned sched_ctx_id)
- unsigned **starpu_sched_ctx_contains_type_of_worker** (enum starpu_worker_archtype arch, unsigned sched_ctx_id)
- unsigned **starpu_sched_ctx_get_ctx_for_task** (struct starpu_task *task)
- int starpu_sched_get_min_priority (void)
- int starpu_sched_get_max_priority (void)
- int starpu_sched_set_min_priority (int min_prio)
- int starpu_sched_set_max_priority (int max_prio)
- struct starpu_sched_policy * **starpu_sched_ctx_get_sched_policy** (unsigned sched_ctx_id)
- void **starpu_sched_ctx_list_task_counters_increment** (unsigned sched_ctx_id, int workerid)
- void **starpu_sched_ctx_list_task_counters_decrement** (unsigned sched_ctx_id, int workerid)
- void **starpu_sched_ctx_list_task_counters_reset** (unsigned sched_ctx_id, int workerid)
- void **starpu_sched_ctx_list_task_counters_increment_all_ctx_locked** (struct starpu_task *task, unsigned sched_ctx_id)
- void **starpu_sched_ctx_list_task_counters_decrement_all_ctx_locked** (struct starpu_task *task, unsigned sched_ctx_id)
- void **starpu_sched_ctx_list_task_counters_reset_all** (struct starpu_task *task, unsigned sched_ctx_id)
- void **starpu_sched_ctx_set_priority** (int *workers, int nworkers, unsigned sched_ctx_id, unsigned priority)
- unsigned **starpu_sched_ctx_get_priority** (int worker, unsigned sched_ctx_id)
- void **starpu_sched_ctx_get_available_cpuids** (unsigned sched_ctx_id, int **cpuids, int *ncpuids)
- void **starpu_sched_ctx_bind_current_thread_to_cpuid** (unsigned cpuid)
- int **starpu_sched_ctx_book_workers_for_task** (unsigned sched_ctx_id, int *workerids, int nworkers)
- void **starpu_sched_ctx_unbook_workers_for_task** (unsigned sched_ctx_id, int master)
- unsigned **starpu_sched_ctx_worker_is_master_for_child_ctx** (int workerid, unsigned sched_ctx_id)
- unsigned **starpu_sched_ctx_master_get_context** (int masterid)
- void **starpu_sched_ctx_revert_task_counters_ctx_locked** (unsigned sched_ctx_id, double flops)
- void **starpu_sched_ctx_move_task_to_ctx_locked** (struct starpu_task *task, unsigned sched_ctx, unsigned with_repush)
- int **starpu_sched_ctx_get_worker_rank** (unsigned sched_ctx_id)
- unsigned **starpu_sched_ctx_has_starpu_scheduler** (unsigned sched_ctx_id, unsigned *awake_workers)
- int **starpu_sched_ctx_get_stream_worker** (unsigned sub_ctx)
- int **starpu_sched_ctx_get_nsms** (unsigned sched_ctx)
- void **starpu_sched_ctx_get_sms_interval** (int stream_workerid, int *start, int *end)

Scheduling Context Worker Collection

- struct starpu_worker_collection * starpu_sched_ctx_create_worker_collection (unsigned sched_ctx_id, enum starpu_worker_collection_type type) STARPU_ATTRIBUTE_MALLOC
- void starpu_sched_ctx_delete_worker_collection (unsigned sched_ctx_id)
- struct starpu_worker_collection * starpu_sched_ctx_get_worker_collection (unsigned sched_ctx_id)

Scheduling Context Link with Hypervisor

- void starpu_sched_ctx_set_policy_data (unsigned sched_ctx_id, void *policy_data)
- void * starpu_sched_ctx_get_policy_data (unsigned sched_ctx_id)
- void * starpu_sched_ctx_exec_parallel_code (void *(*func)(void *), void *param, unsigned sched_ctx_id)
- int starpu_sched_ctx_get_nready_tasks (unsigned sched_ctx_id)
- double starpu_sched_ctx_get_nready_flops (unsigned sched_ctx_id)
- void starpu_sched_ctx_call_pushed_task_cb (int workerid, unsigned sched_ctx_id)

Variables

- void(*)(unsigned) **starpu_sched_ctx_get_sched_policy_init** (unsigned sched_ctx_id)

Scheduling Contexts Basic API

- #define STARPU_SCHED_CTX_POLICY_NAME
- #define STARPU_SCHED_CTX_POLICY_STRUCT
- #define STARPU_SCHED_CTX_POLICY_MIN_PRIO
- #define STARPU_SCHED_CTX_POLICY_MAX_PRIO
- #define STARPU_SCHED_CTX_AWAKE_WORKERS
- #define STARPU_SCHED_CTX_POLICY_INIT
- #define STARPU_SCHED_CTX_USER_DATA
- #define STARPU_SCHED_CTX_CUDA_NSMS
- #define STARPU_SCHED_CTX_SUB_CTXS
- unsigned starpu_sched_ctx_create (int *workerids_ctx, int nworkers_ctx, const char *sched_ctx_name,...)
- unsigned starpu_sched_ctx_create_inside_interval (const char *policy_name, const char *sched_ctx_name, int min_ncpus, int max_ncpus, int min_ngpus, int max_ngpus, unsigned allow_overlap)
- void starpu_sched_ctx_register_close_callback (unsigned sched_ctx_id, void(*close_callback)(unsigned sched_ctx_id, void *args), void *args)
- void starpu_sched_ctx_add_workers (int *workerids_ctx, unsigned nworkers_ctx, unsigned sched_ctx_id)
- void starpu_sched_ctx_remove_workers (int *workerids_ctx, unsigned nworkers_ctx, unsigned sched_ctx_-id)
- void starpu_sched_ctx_display_workers (unsigned sched_ctx_id, FILE *f)
- void starpu_sched_ctx_delete (unsigned sched_ctx_id)
- void starpu_sched_ctx_set_inheritor (unsigned sched_ctx_id, unsigned inheritor)
- void starpu_sched_ctx_set_context (unsigned *sched_ctx_id)
- unsigned starpu_sched_ctx_get_context (void)
- void starpu_sched_ctx_stop_task_submission (void)
- void starpu_sched_ctx_finished_submit (unsigned sched_ctx_id)
- unsigned starpu_sched_ctx_get_workers_list (unsigned sched_ctx_id, int **workerids)
- unsigned starpu_sched_ctx_get_workers_list_raw (unsigned sched_ctx_id, int **workerids)
- unsigned starpu_sched_ctx_get_nworkers (unsigned sched_ctx_id)
- unsigned starpu_sched_ctx_get_nshared_workers (unsigned sched_ctx_id, unsigned sched_ctx_id2)
- unsigned starpu_sched_ctx_contains_worker (int workerid, unsigned sched_ctx_id)
- unsigned starpu_sched_ctx_worker_get_id (unsigned sched_ctx_id)
- unsigned starpu_sched_ctx_overlapping_ctxs_on_worker (int workerid)

Scheduling Context Priorities

- #define STARPU_MIN_PRIO
- #define STARPU_MAX_PRIO
- #define STARPU_DEFAULT_PRIO
- int starpu_sched_ctx_get_min_priority (unsigned sched_ctx_id)
- int starpu_sched_ctx_get_max_priority (unsigned sched_ctx_id)
- int starpu_sched_ctx_set_min_priority (unsigned sched_ctx_id, int min_prio)
- int starpu_sched_ctx_set_max_priority (unsigned sched_ctx_id, int max_prio)
- int starpu_sched_ctx_min_priority_is_set (unsigned sched_ctx_id)
- int starpu_sched_ctx_max_priority_is_set (unsigned sched_ctx_id)
- void * starpu_sched_ctx_get_user_data (unsigned sched_ctx_id)

31.24.1 Detailed Description

31.25 starpu_sched_ctx_hypervisor.h File Reference

Data Structures

- struct starpu_sched_ctx_performance_counters

Functions

- void **starpu_sched_ctx_update_start_resizing_sample** (unsigned sched_ctx_id, double start_sample)

Scheduling Context Link with Hypervisor

- void starpu_sched_ctx_set_perf_counters (unsigned sched_ctx_id, void *perf_counters)
- void starpu_sched_ctx_notify_hypervisor_exists (void)
- unsigned starpu_sched_ctx_check_if_hypervisor_exists (void)

31.25.1 Detailed Description

31.26 starpu_scheduler.h File Reference

```
#include <starpu.h>
```

Data Structures

- struct starpu_sched_policy

Functions

- struct starpu_sched_policy ** starpu_sched_get_predefined_policies ()
- void starpu_worker_get_sched_condition (int workerid, starpu_pthread_mutex_t **sched_mutex, starpu_-pthread_cond_t **sched_cond)
- unsigned long **starpu_task_get_job_id** (struct starpu_task *task)
- int **starpu_wake_worker_no_relax** (int workerid)
- int **starpu_wake_worker_locked** (int workerid)
- int starpu_worker_can_execute_task (unsigned workerid, struct starpu_task *task, unsigned nimpl)
- int starpu_worker_can_execute_task_impl (unsigned workerid, struct starpu_task *task, unsigned *impl_-mask)
- int starpu_worker_can_execute_task_first_impl (unsigned workerid, struct starpu_task *task, unsigned *nimpl)
- int starpu_push_local_task (int workerid, struct starpu_task *task, int back)
- int starpu_push_task_end (struct starpu_task *task)
- int starpu_combined_worker_assign_workerid (int nworkers, int workerid_array[ ])
- int starpu_combined_worker_get_description (int workerid, int *worker_size, int **combined_workerid)
- int starpu_combined_worker_can_execute_task (unsigned workerid, struct starpu_task *task, unsigned nimpl)
- int starpu_get_prefetch_flag (void)
- int **starpu_prefetch_task_input_on_node_prio** (struct starpu_task *task, unsigned node, int prio)
- int starpu_prefetch_task_input_on_node (struct starpu_task *task, unsigned node)
- int **starpu_idle_prefetch_task_input_on_node_prio** (struct starpu_task *task, unsigned node, int prio)
- int starpu_idle_prefetch_task_input_on_node (struct starpu_task *task, unsigned node)
- uint32_t starpu_task_footprint (struct starpu_perfmodel *model, struct starpu_task *task, struct starpu_-perfmodel_arch *arch, unsigned nimpl)
- uint32_t starpu_task_data_footprint (struct starpu_task *task)
- double starpu_task_expected_length (struct starpu_task *task, struct starpu_perfmodel_arch *arch, un-signed nimpl)
- double starpu_worker_get_relative_speedup (struct starpu_perfmodel_arch *perf_arch)
- double starpu_task_expected_data_transfer_time (unsigned memory_node, struct starpu_task *task)
- double starpu_data_expected_transfer_time (starpu_data_handle_t handle, unsigned memory_node, enum starpu_data_access_mode mode)

- double starpu_task_expected_energy (struct starpu_task *task, struct starpu_perfmodel_arch *arch, unsigned nimpl)
- double starpu_task_expected_conversion_time (struct starpu_task *task, struct starpu_perfmodel_arch *arch, unsigned nimpl)
- double starpu_task_bundle_expected_length (starpu_task_bundle_t bundle, struct starpu_perfmodel_arch *arch, unsigned nimpl)
- double starpu_task_bundle_expected_data_transfer_time (starpu_task_bundle_t bundle, unsigned memory_node)
- double starpu_task_bundle_expected_energy (starpu_task_bundle_t bundle, struct starpu_perfmodel_arch *arch, unsigned nimpl)
- void starpu_sched_ctx_worker_shares_tasks_lists (int workerid, int sched_ctx_id)

31.26.1   Detailed Description

31.27   starpu_sink.h File Reference

Functions

- void **starpu_sink_common_worker** (int argc, char **argv)

31.27.1   Detailed Description

31.28   starpu_stdlib.h File Reference

```
#include <starpu.h>
```

Macros

- #define STARPU_MALLOC_PINNED
- #define STARPU_MALLOC_COUNT
- #define STARPU_MALLOC_NORECLAIM
- #define STARPU_MEMORY_WAIT
- #define STARPU_MEMORY_OVERFLOW
- #define STARPU_MALLOC_SIMULATION_FOLDED

Functions

- void starpu_malloc_set_align (size_t align)
- int starpu_malloc (void **A, size_t dim) STARPU_ATTRIBUTE_ALLOC_SIZE(2)
- int starpu_free (void *A)
- int starpu_malloc_flags (void **A, size_t dim, int flags) STARPU_ATTRIBUTE_ALLOC_SIZE(2)
- int starpu_free_flags (void *A, size_t dim, int flags)
- int starpu_memory_pin (void *addr, size_t size)
- int starpu_memory_unpin (void *addr, size_t size)
- starpu_ssize_t starpu_memory_get_total (unsigned node)
- starpu_ssize_t starpu_memory_get_available (unsigned node)
- starpu_ssize_t starpu_memory_get_total_all_nodes ()
- starpu_ssize_t starpu_memory_get_available_all_nodes ()
- void starpu_memory_wait_available (unsigned node, size_t size)
- int starpu_memory_allocate (unsigned node, size_t size, int flags)
- void starpu_memory_deallocate (unsigned node, size_t size)
- void starpu_sleep (float nb_sec)

31.28.1   Detailed Description

31.29   starpu_task.h File Reference

```
#include <starpu.h>
#include <starpu_data.h>
#include <starpu_util.h>
#include <starpu_task_bundle.h>
#include <errno.h>
#include <assert.h>
#include <cuda.h>
```

Data Structures

- struct starpu_codelet
- struct starpu_task

Macros

- #define STARPU_NOWHERE
- #define STARPU_CPU
- #define STARPU_CUDA
- #define STARPU_OPENCL
- #define STARPU_MIC
- #define STARPU_SCC
- #define STARPU_MPI_MS
- #define STARPU_CODELET_SIMGRID_EXECUTE
- #define STARPU_CODELET_SIMGRID_EXECUTE_AND_INJECT
- #define STARPU_CUDA_ASYNC
- #define STARPU_OPENCL_ASYNC
- #define STARPU_TASK_INVALID
- #define STARPU_MULTIPLE_CPU_IMPLEMENTATIONS
- #define STARPU_MULTIPLE_CUDA_IMPLEMENTATIONS
- #define STARPU_MULTIPLE_OPENCL_IMPLEMENTATIONS
- #define STARPU_VARIABLE_NBUFFERS
- #define STARPU_TASK_INITIALIZER
- #define STARPU_TASK_GET_NBUFFERS(task)
- #define STARPU_TASK_GET_HANDLE(task, i)
- #define **STARPU_TASK_GET_HANDLES**(task)
- #define STARPU_TASK_SET_HANDLE(task, handle, i)
- #define STARPU_CODELET_GET_MODE(codelet, i)
- #define STARPU_CODELET_SET_MODE(codelet, mode, i)
- #define STARPU_TASK_GET_MODE(task, i)
- #define STARPU_TASK_SET_MODE(task, mode, i)
- #define **STARPU_CODELET_GET_NODE**(codelet, i)
- #define **STARPU_CODELET_SET_NODE**(codelet, __node, i)

Typedefs

- typedef uint64_t starpu_tag_t
- typedef void(∗ starpu_cpu_func_t)(void ∗∗, void ∗)
- typedef void(∗ starpu_cuda_func_t)(void ∗∗, void ∗)
- typedef void(∗ starpu_opencl_func_t)(void ∗∗, void ∗)
- typedef void(∗ starpu_mic_kernel_t)(void ∗∗, void ∗)
- typedef void(∗ starpu_mpi_ms_kernel_t)(void ∗∗, void ∗)
- typedef void(∗ starpu_scc_kernel_t)(void ∗∗, void ∗)
- typedef starpu_mic_kernel_t(∗ starpu_mic_func_t)(void)
- typedef starpu_mpi_ms_kernel_t(∗ starpu_mpi_ms_func_t)(void)
- typedef starpu_scc_kernel_t(∗ starpu_scc_func_t)(void)

Enumerations

- enum starpu_codelet_type { STARPU_SEQ, STARPU_SPMD, STARPU_FORKJOIN }
- enum starpu_task_status {
  STARPU_TASK_INVALID, **STARPU_TASK_INVALID**, STARPU_TASK_BLOCKED, STARPU_TASK_READY,
  STARPU_TASK_RUNNING, STARPU_TASK_FINISHED, STARPU_TASK_BLOCKED_ON_TAG, STARPU_TASK_BLOCKED_ON_TASK,
  STARPU_TASK_BLOCKED_ON_DATA, STARPU_TASK_STOPPED }

Functions

- void starpu_tag_declare_deps (starpu_tag_t id, unsigned ndeps,...)
- void starpu_tag_declare_deps_array (starpu_tag_t id, unsigned ndeps, starpu_tag_t ∗array)
- void starpu_task_declare_deps_array (struct starpu_task ∗task, unsigned ndeps, struct starpu_task ∗task_array[])
- int starpu_task_get_task_succs (struct starpu_task ∗task, unsigned ndeps, struct starpu_task ∗task_array[])
- int starpu_task_get_task_scheduled_succs (struct starpu_task ∗task, unsigned ndeps, struct starpu_task ∗task_array[])
- int starpu_tag_wait (starpu_tag_t id)
- int starpu_tag_wait_array (unsigned ntags, starpu_tag_t ∗id)
- void starpu_tag_notify_from_apps (starpu_tag_t id)
- void starpu_tag_restart (starpu_tag_t id)
- void starpu_tag_remove (starpu_tag_t id)
- struct starpu_task ∗ **starpu_tag_get_task** (starpu_tag_t id)
- void starpu_task_init (struct starpu_task ∗task)
- void starpu_task_clean (struct starpu_task ∗task)
- struct starpu_task ∗ starpu_task_create (void) STARPU_ATTRIBUTE_MALLOC
- void starpu_task_destroy (struct starpu_task ∗task)
- int starpu_task_submit (struct starpu_task ∗task) STARPU_WARN_UNUSED_RESULT
- int starpu_task_submit_to_ctx (struct starpu_task ∗task, unsigned sched_ctx_id)
- int **starpu_task_finished** (struct starpu_task ∗task) STARPU_WARN_UNUSED_RESULT
- int starpu_task_wait (struct starpu_task ∗task) STARPU_WARN_UNUSED_RESULT
- int starpu_task_wait_array (struct starpu_task ∗∗tasks, unsigned nb_tasks) STARPU_WARN_UNUSED_RESULT
- int starpu_task_wait_for_all (void)
- int starpu_task_wait_for_n_submitted (unsigned n)
- int starpu_task_wait_for_all_in_ctx (unsigned sched_ctx_id)
- int starpu_task_wait_for_n_submitted_in_ctx (unsigned sched_ctx_id, unsigned n)
- int starpu_task_wait_for_no_ready (void)
- int starpu_task_nready (void)

- int starpu_task_nsubmitted (void)
- void starpu_iteration_push (unsigned long iteration)
- void starpu_iteration_pop (void)
- void **starpu_do_schedule** (void)
- void starpu_codelet_init (struct starpu_codelet ∗cl)
- void starpu_codelet_display_stats (struct starpu_codelet ∗cl)
- struct starpu_task ∗ starpu_task_get_current (void)
- const char ∗ starpu_task_get_model_name (struct starpu_task ∗task)
- const char ∗ starpu_task_get_name (struct starpu_task ∗task)
- void starpu_parallel_task_barrier_init (struct starpu_task ∗task, int workerid)
- void starpu_parallel_task_barrier_init_n (struct starpu_task ∗task, int worker_size)
- struct starpu_task ∗ starpu_task_dup (struct starpu_task ∗task)
- void starpu_task_set_implementation (struct starpu_task ∗task, unsigned impl)
- unsigned starpu_task_get_implementation (struct starpu_task ∗task)

31.29.1 Detailed Description

31.29.2 Macro Definition Documentation

31.29.2.1 starpu_task_status::STARPU_TASK_INVALID

The task has just been initialized.

31.30 starpu_task_bundle.h File Reference

Typedefs

- typedef struct
  _starpu_task_bundle ∗ starpu_task_bundle_t

Functions

- void starpu_task_bundle_create (starpu_task_bundle_t ∗bundle)
- int starpu_task_bundle_insert (starpu_task_bundle_t bundle, struct starpu_task ∗task)
- int starpu_task_bundle_remove (starpu_task_bundle_t bundle, struct starpu_task ∗task)
- void starpu_task_bundle_close (starpu_task_bundle_t bundle)

31.30.1 Detailed Description

31.31 starpu_task_list.h File Reference

```
#include <starpu_task.h>
#include <starpu_util.h>
```

Data Structures

- struct starpu_task_list

Macros

- #define **STARPU_TASK_LIST_INLINE**

Functions

- STARPU_TASK_LIST_INLINE void starpu_task_list_init (struct starpu_task_list *list)
- STARPU_TASK_LIST_INLINE void starpu_task_list_push_front (struct starpu_task_list *list, struct starpu_-task *task)
- STARPU_TASK_LIST_INLINE void starpu_task_list_push_back (struct starpu_task_list *list, struct starpu_-task *task)
- STARPU_TASK_LIST_INLINE struct
  starpu_task * starpu_task_list_front (const struct starpu_task_list *list)
- STARPU_TASK_LIST_INLINE struct
  starpu_task * starpu_task_list_back (const struct starpu_task_list *list)
- STARPU_TASK_LIST_INLINE int starpu_task_list_empty (const struct starpu_task_list *list)
- STARPU_TASK_LIST_INLINE void starpu_task_list_erase (struct starpu_task_list *list, struct starpu_task *task)
- STARPU_TASK_LIST_INLINE struct
  starpu_task * starpu_task_list_pop_front (struct starpu_task_list *list)
- STARPU_TASK_LIST_INLINE struct
  starpu_task * starpu_task_list_pop_back (struct starpu_task_list *list)
- STARPU_TASK_LIST_INLINE struct
  starpu_task * starpu_task_list_begin (const struct starpu_task_list *list)
- STARPU_TASK_LIST_INLINE struct
  starpu_task * **starpu_task_list_end** (const struct starpu_task_list *list STARPU_ATTRIBUTE_UNUSED)
- STARPU_TASK_LIST_INLINE struct
  starpu_task * starpu_task_list_next (const struct starpu_task *task)
- STARPU_TASK_LIST_INLINE int starpu_task_list_ismember (const struct starpu_task_list *list, const struct starpu_task *look)

31.31.1 Detailed Description

31.32 starpu_task_util.h File Reference

```
#include <stdio.h>
#include <stdlib.h>
#include <string.h>
#include <assert.h>
#include <starpu.h>
```

Macros

- #define **STARPU_MODE_SHIFT**
- #define STARPU_VALUE
- #define STARPU_CALLBACK
- #define STARPU_CALLBACK_WITH_ARG
- #define STARPU_CALLBACK_ARG
- #define STARPU_PRIORITY
- #define STARPU_DATA_ARRAY
- #define STARPU_DATA_MODE_ARRAY
- #define STARPU_TAG

- #define STARPU_HYPERVISOR_TAG
- #define STARPU_FLOPS
- #define STARPU_SCHED_CTX
- #define **STARPU_PROLOGUE_CALLBACK**
- #define **STARPU_PROLOGUE_CALLBACK_ARG**
- #define **STARPU_PROLOGUE_CALLBACK_POP**
- #define **STARPU_PROLOGUE_CALLBACK_POP_ARG**
- #define STARPU_EXECUTE_ON_WORKER
- #define **STARPU_EXECUTE_WHERE**
- #define STARPU_TAG_ONLY
- #define **STARPU_POSSIBLY_PARALLEL**
- #define STARPU_WORKER_ORDER
- #define STARPU_NAME
- #define STARPU_CL_ARGS
- #define **STARPU_SHIFTED_MODE_MAX**

MPI Insert Task

- #define STARPU_EXECUTE_ON_NODE
- #define STARPU_EXECUTE_ON_DATA
- #define STARPU_NODE_SELECTION_POLICY

Functions

- void starpu_create_sync_task (starpu_tag_t sync_tag, unsigned ndeps, starpu_tag_t *deps, void(*callback)(void *), void *callback_arg)
- struct starpu_task * starpu_task_build (struct starpu_codelet *cl,...)
- int starpu_task_insert (struct starpu_codelet *cl,...)
- int starpu_insert_task (struct starpu_codelet *cl,...)
- void starpu_codelet_unpack_args (void *cl_arg,...)
- void starpu_codelet_unpack_args_and_copyleft (void *cl_arg, void *buffer, size_t buffer_size,...)
- void starpu_codelet_pack_args (void **arg_buffer, size_t *arg_buffer_size,...)

31.32.1   Detailed Description

31.33   starpu_thread.h File Reference

```
#include <starpu_config.h>
#include <starpu_util.h>
#include <xbt/synchro_core.h>
#include <msg/msg.h>
#include <stdint.h>
```

Data Structures

- struct starpu_pthread_barrier_t
- struct starpu_pthread_spinlock_t
- struct starpu_pthread_wait_t
- struct starpu_pthread_queue_t

Macros

- #define **starpu_pthread_setname**(name)
- #define STARPU_PTHREAD_MUTEX_INITIALIZER
- #define STARPU_PTHREAD_COND_INITIALIZER
- #define **STARPU_PTHREAD_BARRIER_SERIAL_THREAD**

Typedefs

- typedef msg_process_t **starpu_pthread_t**
- typedef int **starpu_pthread_attr_t**
- typedef xbt_mutex_t **starpu_pthread_mutex_t**
- typedef int **starpu_pthread_mutexattr_t**
- typedef int **starpu_pthread_key_t**
- typedef xbt_cond_t **starpu_pthread_cond_t**
- typedef int **starpu_pthread_condattr_t**
- typedef xbt_mutex_t **starpu_pthread_rwlock_t**
- typedef int **starpu_pthread_rwlockattr_t**
- typedef int **starpu_pthread_barrierattr_t**
- typedef msg_sem_t **starpu_sem_t**

Functions

- int **starpu_pthread_equal** (starpu_pthread_t t1, starpu_pthread_t t2)
- starpu_pthread_t **starpu_pthread_self** (void)
- int **starpu_pthread_create_on** (char *name, starpu_pthread_t *thread, const starpu_pthread_attr_t *attr, void *(*start_routine)(void *), void *arg, msg_host_t host)
- int starpu_pthread_create (starpu_pthread_t *thread, const starpu_pthread_attr_t *attr, void *(*start_routine)(void *), void *arg)
- int starpu_pthread_join (starpu_pthread_t thread, void **retval)
- int starpu_pthread_exit (void *retval) STARPU_ATTRIBUTE_NORETURN
- int starpu_pthread_attr_init (starpu_pthread_attr_t *attr)
- int starpu_pthread_attr_destroy (starpu_pthread_attr_t *attr)
- int starpu_pthread_attr_setdetachstate (starpu_pthread_attr_t *attr, int detachstate)
- int starpu_pthread_mutex_init (starpu_pthread_mutex_t *mutex, const starpu_pthread_mutexattr_t *mutexattr)
- int starpu_pthread_mutex_destroy (starpu_pthread_mutex_t *mutex)
- int starpu_pthread_mutex_lock (starpu_pthread_mutex_t *mutex)
- int starpu_pthread_mutex_unlock (starpu_pthread_mutex_t *mutex)
- int starpu_pthread_mutex_trylock (starpu_pthread_mutex_t *mutex)
- int starpu_pthread_mutexattr_gettype (const starpu_pthread_mutexattr_t *attr, int *type)
- int starpu_pthread_mutexattr_settype (starpu_pthread_mutexattr_t *attr, int type)
- int starpu_pthread_mutexattr_destroy (starpu_pthread_mutexattr_t *attr)
- int starpu_pthread_mutexattr_init (starpu_pthread_mutexattr_t *attr)
- int **starpu_pthread_mutex_lock_sched** (starpu_pthread_mutex_t *mutex)
- int **starpu_pthread_mutex_unlock_sched** (starpu_pthread_mutex_t *mutex)
- int **starpu_pthread_mutex_trylock_sched** (starpu_pthread_mutex_t *mutex)
- void **starpu_pthread_mutex_check_sched** (starpu_pthread_mutex_t *mutex, char *file, int line)
- int starpu_pthread_key_create (starpu_pthread_key_t *key, void(*destr_function)(void *))
- int starpu_pthread_key_delete (starpu_pthread_key_t key)
- int starpu_pthread_setspecific (starpu_pthread_key_t key, const void *pointer)
- void * starpu_pthread_getspecific (starpu_pthread_key_t key)
- int starpu_pthread_cond_init (starpu_pthread_cond_t *cond, starpu_pthread_condattr_t *cond_attr)
- int starpu_pthread_cond_signal (starpu_pthread_cond_t *cond)

- int starpu_pthread_cond_broadcast (starpu_pthread_cond_t *cond)
- int starpu_pthread_cond_wait (starpu_pthread_cond_t *cond, starpu_pthread_mutex_t *mutex)
- int starpu_pthread_cond_timedwait (starpu_pthread_cond_t *cond, starpu_pthread_mutex_t *mutex, const struct timespec *abstime)
- int starpu_pthread_cond_destroy (starpu_pthread_cond_t *cond)
- int starpu_pthread_rwlock_init (starpu_pthread_rwlock_t *rwlock, const starpu_pthread_rwlockattr_t *attr)
- int starpu_pthread_rwlock_destroy (starpu_pthread_rwlock_t *rwlock)
- int starpu_pthread_rwlock_rdlock (starpu_pthread_rwlock_t *rwlock)
- int starpu_pthread_rwlock_tryrdlock (starpu_pthread_rwlock_t *rwlock)
- int starpu_pthread_rwlock_wrlock (starpu_pthread_rwlock_t *rwlock)
- int starpu_pthread_rwlock_trywrlock (starpu_pthread_rwlock_t *rwlock)
- int starpu_pthread_rwlock_unlock (starpu_pthread_rwlock_t *rwlock)
- int starpu_pthread_barrier_init (starpu_pthread_barrier_t *barrier, const starpu_pthread_barrierattr_t *attr, unsigned count)
- int starpu_pthread_barrier_destroy (starpu_pthread_barrier_t *barrier)
- int starpu_pthread_barrier_wait (starpu_pthread_barrier_t *barrier)
- int starpu_pthread_spin_init (starpu_pthread_spinlock_t *lock, int pshared)
- int starpu_pthread_spin_destroy (starpu_pthread_spinlock_t *lock)
- int starpu_pthread_spin_lock (starpu_pthread_spinlock_t *lock)
- int starpu_pthread_spin_trylock (starpu_pthread_spinlock_t *lock)
- int starpu_pthread_spin_unlock (starpu_pthread_spinlock_t *lock)
- int **starpu_pthread_queue_init** (starpu_pthread_queue_t *q)
- int **starpu_pthread_queue_signal** (starpu_pthread_queue_t *q)
- int **starpu_pthread_queue_broadcast** (starpu_pthread_queue_t *q)
- int **starpu_pthread_queue_destroy** (starpu_pthread_queue_t *q)
- int **starpu_pthread_wait_init** (starpu_pthread_wait_t *w)
- int **starpu_pthread_queue_register** (starpu_pthread_wait_t *w, starpu_pthread_queue_t *q)
- int **starpu_pthread_queue_unregister** (starpu_pthread_wait_t *w, starpu_pthread_queue_t *q)
- int **starpu_pthread_wait_reset** (starpu_pthread_wait_t *w)
- int **starpu_pthread_wait_wait** (starpu_pthread_wait_t *w)
- int **starpu_pthread_wait_destroy** (starpu_pthread_wait_t *w)
- int **starpu_sem_destroy** (starpu_sem_t *)
- int **starpu_sem_getvalue** (starpu_sem_t *, int *)
- int **starpu_sem_init** (starpu_sem_t *, int, unsigned)
- int **starpu_sem_post** (starpu_sem_t *)
- int **starpu_sem_trywait** (starpu_sem_t *)
- int **starpu_sem_wait** (starpu_sem_t *)

31.33.1 Detailed Description

31.33.2 Data Structure Documentation

31.33.2.1 struct starpu_pthread_barrier_t

Data Fields

starpu_pthread-_mutex_t	mutex	
starpu_pthread-_cond_t	cond	
starpu_pthread-_cond_t	cond_destroy	
unsigned	count	
unsigned	done	
unsigned	busy	

31.33.2.2 struct starpu_pthread_spinlock_t

Data Fields

int	taken	

31.33.2.3 struct starpu_pthread_wait_t

Data Fields

starpu_pthread-_mutex_t	mutex	
starpu_pthread-_cond_t	cond	
unsigned	block	

31.33.2.4 struct starpu_pthread_queue_t

Data Fields

starpu_pthread-_mutex_t	mutex	
starpu_pthread-_wait_t **	queue	
unsigned	allocqueue	
unsigned	nqueue	

31.34 starpu_thread_util.h File Reference

```
#include <starpu_util.h>
#include <starpu_thread.h>
#include <errno.h>
```

Macros

- #define STARPU_PTHREAD_CREATE_ON(name, thread, attr, routine, arg, where)
- #define STARPU_PTHREAD_CREATE(thread, attr, routine, arg)
- #define STARPU_PTHREAD_MUTEX_INIT(mutex, attr)
- #define STARPU_PTHREAD_MUTEX_DESTROY(mutex)
- #define **_STARPU_CHECK_NOT_SCHED_MUTEX**(mutex, file, line)
- #define STARPU_PTHREAD_MUTEX_LOCK(mutex)
- #define **STARPU_PTHREAD_MUTEX_LOCK_SCHED**(mutex)
- #define **STARPU_PTHREAD_MUTEX_TRYLOCK**(mutex)
- #define **STARPU_PTHREAD_MUTEX_TRYLOCK_SCHED**(mutex)
- #define STARPU_PTHREAD_MUTEX_UNLOCK(mutex)
- #define **STARPU_PTHREAD_MUTEX_UNLOCK_SCHED**(mutex)
- #define STARPU_PTHREAD_KEY_CREATE(key, destr)
- #define STARPU_PTHREAD_KEY_DELETE(key)
- #define STARPU_PTHREAD_SETSPECIFIC(key, ptr)
- #define STARPU_PTHREAD_GETSPECIFIC(key)
- #define STARPU_PTHREAD_RWLOCK_INIT(rwlock, attr)

- #define STARPU_PTHREAD_RWLOCK_RDLOCK(rwlock)
- #define **STARPU_PTHREAD_RWLOCK_TRYRDLOCK**(rwlock)
- #define STARPU_PTHREAD_RWLOCK_WRLOCK(rwlock)
- #define **STARPU_PTHREAD_RWLOCK_TRYWRLOCK**(rwlock)
- #define STARPU_PTHREAD_RWLOCK_UNLOCK(rwlock)
- #define STARPU_PTHREAD_RWLOCK_DESTROY(rwlock)
- #define STARPU_PTHREAD_COND_INIT(cond, attr)
- #define STARPU_PTHREAD_COND_DESTROY(cond)
- #define STARPU_PTHREAD_COND_SIGNAL(cond)
- #define STARPU_PTHREAD_COND_BROADCAST(cond)
- #define STARPU_PTHREAD_COND_WAIT(cond, mutex)
- #define STARPU_PTHREAD_BARRIER_INIT(barrier, attr, count)
- #define STARPU_PTHREAD_BARRIER_DESTROY(barrier)
- #define STARPU_PTHREAD_BARRIER_WAIT(barrier)

Functions

- static STARPU_INLINE int **_starpu_pthread_mutex_trylock** (starpu_pthread_mutex_t *mutex, char *file, int line)
- static STARPU_INLINE int **_starpu_pthread_mutex_trylock_sched** (starpu_pthread_mutex_t *mutex, char *file, int line)
- static STARPU_INLINE int **_starpu_pthread_rwlock_tryrdlock** (starpu_pthread_rwlock_t *rwlock, char *file, int line)
- static STARPU_INLINE int **_starpu_pthread_rwlock_trywrlock** (starpu_pthread_rwlock_t *rwlock, char *file, int line)

31.34.1   Detailed Description

31.35   starpu_top.h File Reference

```
#include <starpu.h>
#include <stdlib.h>
#include <time.h>
```

Data Structures

- struct starpu_top_data
- struct starpu_top_param

Enumerations

- enum starpu_top_data_type { STARPU_TOP_DATA_BOOLEAN, STARPU_TOP_DATA_INTEGER, STARPU_TOP_DATA_FLOAT }
- enum starpu_top_param_type { STARPU_TOP_PARAM_BOOLEAN, STARPU_TOP_PARAM_INTEGER, STARPU_TOP_PARAM_FLOAT, STARPU_TOP_PARAM_ENUM }
- enum starpu_top_message_type {
  TOP_TYPE_GO, TOP_TYPE_SET, TOP_TYPE_CONTINUE, TOP_TYPE_ENABLE,
  TOP_TYPE_DISABLE, TOP_TYPE_DEBUG, TOP_TYPE_UNKNOW }

Functions

Functions to call before the initialisation

- struct starpu_top_data * starpu_top_add_data_boolean (const char *data_name, int active)
- struct starpu_top_data * starpu_top_add_data_integer (const char *data_name, int minimum_value, int maximum_value, int active)
- struct starpu_top_data * starpu_top_add_data_float (const char *data_name, double minimum_value, double maximum_value, int active)
- struct starpu_top_param * starpu_top_register_parameter_boolean (const char *param_name, int *parameter_field, void(*callback)(struct starpu_top_param *))
- struct starpu_top_param * starpu_top_register_parameter_integer (const char *param_name, int *parameter_field, int minimum_value, int maximum_value, void(*callback)(struct starpu_top_param *))
- struct starpu_top_param * starpu_top_register_parameter_float (const char *param_name, double *parameter_field, double minimum_value, double maximum_value, void(*callback)(struct starpu_top__param *))
- struct starpu_top_param * starpu_top_register_parameter_enum (const char *param_name, int *parameter_field, char **values, int nb_values, void(*callback)(struct starpu_top_param *))

Initialisation

- void starpu_top_init_and_wait (const char *server_name)

To call after initialisation

- void starpu_top_update_parameter (const struct starpu_top_param *param)
- void starpu_top_update_data_boolean (const struct starpu_top_data *data, int value)
- void starpu_top_update_data_integer (const struct starpu_top_data *data, int value)
- void starpu_top_update_data_float (const struct starpu_top_data *data, double value)
- void starpu_top_task_prevision (struct starpu_task *task, int devid, unsigned long long start, unsigned long long end)
- void starpu_top_debug_log (const char *message)
- void starpu_top_debug_lock (const char *message)

31.35.1 Detailed Description

31.36 starpu_tree.h File Reference

Data Structures

- struct starpu_tree

Functions

- void starpu_tree_reset_visited (struct starpu_tree *tree, char *visited)
- void **starpu_tree_prepare_children** (unsigned arity, struct starpu_tree *father)
- void starpu_tree_insert (struct starpu_tree *tree, int id, int level, int is_pu, int arity, struct starpu_tree *father)
- struct starpu_tree * starpu_tree_get (struct starpu_tree *tree, int id)
- struct starpu_tree * starpu_tree_get_neighbour (struct starpu_tree *tree, struct starpu_tree *node, char *visited, char *present)
- void starpu_tree_free (struct starpu_tree *tree)

31.36.1 Detailed Description

31.37 starpu_util.h File Reference

```
#include <stdio.h>
#include <stdlib.h>
#include <stdint.h>
#include <string.h>
#include <assert.h>
#include <starpu_config.h>
#include <sys/time.h>
```

Macros

- #define STARPU_GNUC_PREREQ(maj, min)
- #define STARPU_UNLIKELY(expr)
- #define STARPU_LIKELY(expr)
- #define STARPU_ATTRIBUTE_UNUSED
- #define **STARPU_ATTRIBUTE_NORETURN**
- #define STARPU_ATTRIBUTE_INTERNAL
- #define STARPU_ATTRIBUTE_MALLOC
- #define STARPU_ATTRIBUTE_WARN_UNUSED_RESULT
- #define STARPU_ATTRIBUTE_PURE
- #define STARPU_ATTRIBUTE_ALIGNED(size)
- #define **STARPU_ATTRIBUTE_FORMAT**(type, string, first)
- #define **STARPU_INLINE**
- #define **STARPU_ATTRIBUTE_CALLOC_SIZE**(num, size)
- #define **STARPU_ATTRIBUTE_ALLOC_SIZE**(size)
- #define **endif**
- #define STARPU_WARN_UNUSED_RESULT
- #define STARPU_POISON_PTR
- #define STARPU_MIN(a, b)
- #define STARPU_MAX(a, b)
- #define **STARPU_BACKTRACE_LENGTH**
- #define **STARPU_DUMP_BACKTRACE**()
- #define **STARPU_SIMGRID_ASSERT**(x)
- #define STARPU_ASSERT(x)
- #define STARPU_ASSERT_MSG(x, msg,...)
- #define **STARPU_ASSERT_ACCESSIBLE**(ptr)
- #define **_starpu_abort**()
- #define STARPU_ABORT()
- #define STARPU_ABORT_MSG(msg,...)
- #define STARPU_CHECK_RETURN_VALUE(err, message,...)
- #define STARPU_CHECK_RETURN_VALUE_IS(err, value, message,...)
- #define **STARPU_ATOMIC_SOMETHING**(name, expr)
- #define **STARPU_ATOMIC_SOMETHINGL**(name, expr)
- #define STARPU_RMB()
- #define STARPU_WMB()

Functions

- char * **starpu_getenv** (const char *str)
- static __starpu_inline int starpu_get_env_number (const char *str)
- static __starpu_inline int **starpu_get_env_number_default** (const char *str, int defval)
- static __starpu_inline float **starpu_get_env_float_default** (const char *str, float defval)
- void starpu_execute_on_each_worker (void(*func)(void *), void *arg, uint32_t where)
- void starpu_execute_on_each_worker_ex (void(*func)(void *), void *arg, uint32_t where, const char *name)
- void starpu_execute_on_specific_workers (void(*func)(void *), void *arg, unsigned num_workers, unsigned *workers, const char *name)
- double starpu_timing_now (void)

Variables

- int **_starpu_silent**

31.37.1 Detailed Description

31.38 starpu_worker.h File Reference

```
#include <stdlib.h>
#include <starpu_config.h>
#include <starpu_thread.h>
#include <starpu_task.h>
```

Data Structures

- struct starpu_sched_ctx_iterator
- struct starpu_worker_collection

Macros

- #define starpu_worker_get_id_check()

Enumerations

- enum starpu_worker_archtype {
  STARPU_CPU_WORKER, STARPU_CUDA_WORKER, STARPU_OPENCL_WORKER, STARPU_MIC_-WORKER,
  STARPU_SCC_WORKER, STARPU_MPI_MS_WORKER, STARPU_ANY_WORKER }
- enum starpu_worker_collection_type { STARPU_WORKER_TREE, STARPU_WORKER_LIST }

Functions

- unsigned starpu_worker_get_count (void)
- unsigned starpu_combined_worker_get_count (void)
- unsigned **starpu_worker_is_combined_worker** (int id)
- unsigned starpu_cpu_worker_get_count (void)
- unsigned starpu_cuda_worker_get_count (void)
- unsigned starpu_opencl_worker_get_count (void)

- unsigned starpu_mic_worker_get_count (void)
- unsigned starpu_scc_worker_get_count (void)
- unsigned starpu_mpi_ms_worker_get_count (void)
- unsigned starpu_mic_device_get_count (void)
- int starpu_worker_get_id (void)
- unsigned **_starpu_worker_get_id_check** (const char *f, int l)
- int **starpu_worker_get_bindid** (int workerid)
- int starpu_combined_worker_get_id (void)
- int starpu_combined_worker_get_size (void)
- int starpu_combined_worker_get_rank (void)
- enum starpu_worker_archtype starpu_worker_get_type (int id)
- int starpu_worker_get_count_by_type (enum starpu_worker_archtype type)
- unsigned starpu_worker_get_ids_by_type (enum starpu_worker_archtype type, int *workerids, unsigned maxsize)
- int starpu_worker_get_by_type (enum starpu_worker_archtype type, int num)
- int starpu_worker_get_by_devid (enum starpu_worker_archtype type, int devid)
- void starpu_worker_get_name (int id, char *dst, size_t maxlen)
- void starpu_worker_display_names (FILE *output, enum starpu_worker_archtype type)
- int starpu_worker_get_devid (int id)
- int **starpu_worker_get_mp_nodeid** (int id)
- struct starpu_tree * **starpu_workers_get_tree** (void)
- unsigned **starpu_worker_get_sched_ctx_list** (int worker, unsigned **sched_ctx)
- unsigned **starpu_worker_is_blocked_in_parallel** (int workerid)
- unsigned **starpu_worker_is_slave_somewhere** (int workerid)
- char * starpu_worker_get_type_as_string (enum starpu_worker_archtype type)
- int **starpu_bindid_get_workerids** (int bindid, int **workerids)
- int **starpu_worker_get_devids** (enum starpu_worker_archtype type, int *devids, int num)
- int **starpu_worker_get_stream_workerids** (unsigned devid, int *workerids, enum starpu_worker_archtype type)
- unsigned **starpu_worker_get_sched_ctx_id_stream** (unsigned stream_workerid)
- int starpu_worker_sched_op_pending (void)
- void starpu_worker_relax_on (void)
- void starpu_worker_relax_off (void)
- int starpu_worker_get_relax_state (void)
- void starpu_worker_lock (int workerid)
- int starpu_worker_trylock (int workerid)
- void starpu_worker_unlock (int workerid)
- void starpu_worker_lock_self (void)
- void starpu_worker_unlock_self (void)
- int starpu_wake_worker_relax (int workerid)

Variables

- struct starpu_worker_collection **worker_list**
- struct starpu_worker_collection **worker_tree**

31.38.1   Detailed Description

31.39   starpu_mpi.h File Reference

```
#include <starpu.h>
#include <mpi.h>
```

Typedefs

- typedef void ∗ **starpu_mpi_req**
- typedef int(∗ **starpu_mpi_select_node_policy_func_t**)(int me, int nb_nodes, struct starpu_data_descr ∗descr, int nb_data)
- typedef void(∗ **starpu_mpi_datatype_allocate_func_t**)(starpu_data_handle_t, MPI_Datatype ∗)
- typedef void(∗ **starpu_mpi_datatype_free_func_t**)(MPI_Datatype ∗)

Functions

- int **starpu_mpi_pre_submit_hook_register** (void(∗f)(struct starpu_task ∗))
- int **starpu_mpi_pre_submit_hook_unregister** ()

Communication

- int starpu_mpi_isend (starpu_data_handle_t data_handle, starpu_mpi_req ∗req, int dest, int mpi_tag, M-PI_Comm comm)
- int starpu_mpi_irecv (starpu_data_handle_t data_handle, starpu_mpi_req ∗req, int source, int mpi_tag, MPI_Comm comm)
- int starpu_mpi_send (starpu_data_handle_t data_handle, int dest, int mpi_tag, MPI_Comm comm)
- int starpu_mpi_recv (starpu_data_handle_t data_handle, int source, int mpi_tag, MPI_Comm comm, MPI-_Status ∗status)
- int starpu_mpi_isend_detached (starpu_data_handle_t data_handle, int dest, int mpi_tag, MPI_Comm comm, void(∗callback)(void ∗), void ∗arg)
- int starpu_mpi_irecv_detached (starpu_data_handle_t data_handle, int source, int mpi_tag, MPI_Comm comm, void(∗callback)(void ∗), void ∗arg)
- int starpu_mpi_issend (starpu_data_handle_t data_handle, starpu_mpi_req ∗req, int dest, int mpi_tag, MPI_Comm comm)
- int starpu_mpi_issend_detached (starpu_data_handle_t data_handle, int dest, int mpi_tag, MPI_Comm comm, void(∗callback)(void ∗), void ∗arg)
- int starpu_mpi_wait (starpu_mpi_req ∗req, MPI_Status ∗status)
- int starpu_mpi_test (starpu_mpi_req ∗req, int ∗flag, MPI_Status ∗status)
- int starpu_mpi_barrier (MPI_Comm comm)
- int starpu_mpi_irecv_detached_sequential_consistency (starpu_data_handle_t data_handle, int source, int mpi_tag, MPI_Comm comm, void(∗callback)(void ∗), void ∗arg, int sequential_consistency)
- int starpu_mpi_isend_detached_unlock_tag (starpu_data_handle_t data_handle, int dest, int mpi_tag, M-PI_Comm comm, starpu_tag_t tag)
- int starpu_mpi_irecv_detached_unlock_tag (starpu_data_handle_t data_handle, int source, int mpi_tag, MPI_Comm comm, starpu_tag_t tag)
- int starpu_mpi_isend_array_detached_unlock_tag (unsigned array_size, starpu_data_handle_t ∗data_-handle, int ∗dest, int ∗mpi_tag, MPI_Comm ∗comm, starpu_tag_t tag)
- int starpu_mpi_irecv_array_detached_unlock_tag (unsigned array_size, starpu_data_handle_t ∗data_-handle, int ∗source, int ∗mpi_tag, MPI_Comm ∗comm, starpu_tag_t tag)
- int starpu_mpi_get_communication_tag (void)
- void starpu_mpi_set_communication_tag (int tag)
- int starpu_mpi_wait_for_all (MPI_Comm comm)
- int starpu_mpi_datatype_register (starpu_data_handle_t handle, starpu_mpi_datatype_allocate_func_-t allocate_datatype_func, starpu_mpi_datatype_free_func_t free_datatype_func)
- int starpu_mpi_datatype_unregister (starpu_data_handle_t handle)

Initialisation

- int starpu_mpi_init_comm (int ∗argc, char ∗∗∗argv, int initialize_mpi, MPI_Comm comm)
- int starpu_mpi_init (int ∗argc, char ∗∗∗argv, int initialize_mpi)
- int starpu_mpi_initialize (void)
- int starpu_mpi_initialize_extended (int ∗rank, int ∗world_size)
- int starpu_mpi_shutdown (void)
- void starpu_mpi_comm_amounts_retrieve (size_t ∗comm_amounts)
- int starpu_mpi_comm_size (MPI_Comm comm, int ∗size)
- int starpu_mpi_comm_rank (MPI_Comm comm, int ∗rank)

- int starpu_mpi_world_rank (void)
- int starpu_mpi_world_size (void)

Collective Operations

- void starpu_mpi_redux_data (MPI_Comm comm, starpu_data_handle_t data_handle)
- int starpu_mpi_scatter_detached (starpu_data_handle_t *data_handles, int count, int root, MPI_Comm comm, void(*scallback)(void *), void *sarg, void(*rcallback)(void *), void *rarg)
- int starpu_mpi_gather_detached (starpu_data_handle_t *data_handles, int count, int root, MPI_Comm comm, void(*scallback)(void *), void *sarg, void(*rcallback)(void *), void *rarg)

Communication Cache

- void starpu_mpi_cache_flush (MPI_Comm comm, starpu_data_handle_t data_handle)
- void starpu_mpi_cache_flush_all_data (MPI_Comm comm)
- int starpu_mpi_cached_receive (starpu_data_handle_t data_handle)
- int starpu_mpi_cached_send (starpu_data_handle_t data_handle, int dest)
- int starpu_mpi_cache_is_enabled ()
- int starpu_mpi_cache_set (int enabled)

MPI Insert Task

- #define starpu_mpi_data_register(data_handle, tag, rank)
- #define starpu_mpi_data_set_rank(handle, rank)
- #define starpu_data_set_rank
- #define starpu_data_set_tag
- #define starpu_data_get_rank
- #define starpu_data_get_tag
- struct starpu_task * starpu_mpi_task_build (MPI_Comm comm, struct starpu_codelet *codelet,...)
- int starpu_mpi_task_post_build (MPI_Comm comm, struct starpu_codelet *codelet,...)
- int starpu_mpi_task_insert (MPI_Comm comm, struct starpu_codelet *codelet,...)
- int starpu_mpi_insert_task (MPI_Comm comm, struct starpu_codelet *codelet,...)
- void starpu_mpi_get_data_on_node (MPI_Comm comm, starpu_data_handle_t data_handle, int node)
- void starpu_mpi_get_data_on_node_detached (MPI_Comm comm, starpu_data_handle_t data_handle, int node, void(*callback)(void *), void *arg)
- void starpu_mpi_data_register_comm (starpu_data_handle_t data_handle, int tag, int rank, MPI_Comm comm)
- void starpu_mpi_data_set_rank_comm (starpu_data_handle_t handle, int rank, MPI_Comm comm)
- void starpu_mpi_data_set_tag (starpu_data_handle_t handle, int tag)
- int starpu_mpi_data_get_rank (starpu_data_handle_t handle)
- int starpu_mpi_data_get_tag (starpu_data_handle_t handle)
- void starpu_mpi_data_migrate (MPI_Comm comm, starpu_data_handle_t handle, int new_rank)

Node Selection Policy

- #define STARPU_MPI_NODE_SELECTION_CURRENT_POLICY
- #define STARPU_MPI_NODE_SELECTION_MOST_R_DATA
- int starpu_mpi_node_selection_register_policy (starpu_mpi_select_node_policy_func_t policy_func)
- int starpu_mpi_node_selection_unregister_policy (int policy)
- int starpu_mpi_node_selection_get_current_policy ()
- int starpu_mpi_node_selection_set_current_policy (int policy)

31.39.1 Detailed Description

31.40 starpufft.h File Reference

Typedefs

- typedef double _Complex **starpufft_complex**
- typedef struct starpufft_plan * **starpufft_plan**
- typedef float _Complex **starpufftf_complex**
- typedef struct starpufftf_plan * **starpufftf_plan**
- typedef long double _Complex **starpufftl_complex**
- typedef struct starpufftl_plan * **starpufftl_plan**

Functions

- starpufft_plan starpufft_plan_dft_1d (int n, int sign, unsigned flags)
- starpufft_plan starpufft_plan_dft_2d (int n, int m, int sign, unsigned flags)
- starpufft_plan **starpufft_plan_dft_r2c_1d** (int n, unsigned flags)
- starpufft_plan **starpufft_plan_dft_c2r_1d** (int n, unsigned flags)
- void * starpufft_malloc (size_t n)
- void starpufft_free (void *p)
- int starpufft_execute (starpufft_plan p, void *in, void *out)
- struct starpu_task * starpufft_start (starpufft_plan p, void *in, void *out)
- int starpufft_execute_handle (starpufft_plan p, starpu_data_handle_t in, starpu_data_handle_t out)
- struct starpu_task * starpufft_start_handle (starpufft_plan p, starpu_data_handle_t in, starpu_data_handle_t out)
- void starpufft_cleanup (starpufft_plan p)
- void starpufft_destroy_plan (starpufft_plan p)
- void **starpufft_startstats** (void)
- void **starpufft_stopstats** (void)
- void **starpufft_showstats** (FILE *out)
- starpufftf_plan **starpufftf_plan_dft_1d** (int n, int sign, unsigned flags)
- starpufftf_plan **starpufftf_plan_dft_2d** (int n, int m, int sign, unsigned flags)
- starpufftf_plan **starpufftf_plan_dft_r2c_1d** (int n, unsigned flags)
- starpufftf_plan **starpufftf_plan_dft_c2r_1d** (int n, unsigned flags)
- void * **starpufftf_malloc** (size_t n)
- void **starpufftf_free** (void *p)
- int **starpufftf_execute** (starpufftf_plan p, void *in, void *out)
- struct starpu_task * **starpufftf_start** (starpufftf_plan p, void *in, void *out)
- int **starpufftf_execute_handle** (starpufftf_plan p, starpu_data_handle_t in, starpu_data_handle_t out)
- struct starpu_task * **starpufftf_start_handle** (starpufftf_plan p, starpu_data_handle_t in, starpu_data_handle_t out)
- void **starpufftf_cleanup** (starpufftf_plan p)
- void **starpufftf_destroy_plan** (starpufftf_plan p)
- void **starpufftf_startstats** (void)
- void **starpufftf_stopstats** (void)
- void **starpufftf_showstats** (FILE *out)
- starpufftl_plan **starpufftl_plan_dft_1d** (int n, int sign, unsigned flags)
- starpufftl_plan **starpufftl_plan_dft_2d** (int n, int m, int sign, unsigned flags)
- starpufftl_plan **starpufftl_plan_dft_r2c_1d** (int n, unsigned flags)
- starpufftl_plan **starpufftl_plan_dft_c2r_1d** (int n, unsigned flags)
- void * **starpufftl_malloc** (size_t n)
- void **starpufftl_free** (void *p)
- int **starpufftl_execute** (starpufftl_plan p, void *in, void *out)

- struct starpu_task * **starpufftl_start** (starpufftl_plan p, void *in, void *out)
- int **starpufftl_execute_handle** (starpufftl_plan p, starpu_data_handle_t in, starpu_data_handle_t out)
- struct starpu_task * **starpufftl_start_handle** (starpufftl_plan p, starpu_data_handle_t in, starpu_data_-
  handle_t out)
- void **starpufftl_cleanup** (starpufftl_plan p)
- void **starpufftl_destroy_plan** (starpufftl_plan p)
- void **starpufftl_startstats** (void)
- void **starpufftl_stopstats** (void)
- void **starpufftl_showstats** (FILE *out)

Variables

- int **starpufft_last_plan_number**

31.40.1   Detailed Description

31.41   sc_hypervisor.h File Reference

```
#include <starpu.h>
#include <starpu_sched_ctx_hypervisor.h>
#include <sc_hypervisor_config.h>
#include <sc_hypervisor_monitoring.h>
#include <math.h>
```

Data Structures

- struct sc_hypervisor_policy

Functions

- void * sc_hypervisor_init (struct sc_hypervisor_policy *policy)
- void sc_hypervisor_shutdown (void)
- void sc_hypervisor_register_ctx (unsigned sched_ctx, double total_flops)
- void sc_hypervisor_unregister_ctx (unsigned sched_ctx)
- void sc_hypervisor_post_resize_request (unsigned sched_ctx, int task_tag)
- void sc_hypervisor_resize_ctxs (unsigned *sched_ctxs, int nsched_ctxs, int *workers, int nworkers)
- void sc_hypervisor_stop_resize (unsigned sched_ctx)
- void sc_hypervisor_start_resize (unsigned sched_ctx)
- const char * sc_hypervisor_get_policy ()
- void sc_hypervisor_add_workers_to_sched_ctx (int *workers_to_add, unsigned nworkers_to_add, unsigned
  sched_ctx)
- void sc_hypervisor_remove_workers_from_sched_ctx (int *workers_to_remove, unsigned nworkers_to_-
  remove, unsigned sched_ctx, unsigned now)
- void sc_hypervisor_move_workers (unsigned sender_sched_ctx, unsigned receiver_sched_ctx, int *workers-
  _to_move, unsigned nworkers_to_move, unsigned now)
- void sc_hypervisor_size_ctxs (unsigned *sched_ctxs, int nsched_ctxs, int *workers, int nworkers)
- unsigned sc_hypervisor_get_size_req (unsigned **sched_ctxs, int *nsched_ctxs, int **workers, int
  *nworkers)
- void sc_hypervisor_save_size_req (unsigned *sched_ctxs, int nsched_ctxs, int *workers, int nworkers)
- void sc_hypervisor_free_size_req (void)
- unsigned sc_hypervisor_can_resize (unsigned sched_ctx)

- void sc_hypervisor_set_type_of_task (struct starpu_codelet *cl, unsigned sched_ctx, uint32_t footprint, size_t data_size)
- void sc_hypervisor_update_diff_total_flops (unsigned sched_ctx, double diff_total_flops)
- void sc_hypervisor_update_diff_elapsed_flops (unsigned sched_ctx, double diff_task_flops)
- void **sc_hypervisor_update_resize_interval** (unsigned *sched_ctxs, int nsched_ctxs, int max_nworkers)
- void **sc_hypervisor_get_ctxs_on_level** (unsigned **sched_ctxs, int *nsched_ctxs, unsigned hierarchy_level, unsigned father_sched_ctx_id)
- unsigned **sc_hypervisor_get_nhierarchy_levels** (void)
- void **sc_hypervisor_get_leaves** (unsigned *sched_ctxs, int nsched_ctxs, unsigned *leaves, int *nleaves)
- double **sc_hypervisor_get_nready_flops_of_all_sons_of_sched_ctx** (unsigned sched_ctx)
- void **sc_hypervisor_print_overhead** ()
- void **sc_hypervisor_init_worker** (int workerid, unsigned sched_ctx)

Variables

- starpu_pthread_mutex_t **act_hypervisor_mutex**

31.41.1 Detailed Description

31.42 sc_hypervisor_config.h File Reference

```
#include <sc_hypervisor.h>
```

Data Structures

- struct sc_hypervisor_policy_config

Macros

- #define SC_HYPERVISOR_MAX_IDLE
- #define **SC_HYPERVISOR_MIN_WORKING**
- #define SC_HYPERVISOR_PRIORITY
- #define SC_HYPERVISOR_MIN_WORKERS
- #define SC_HYPERVISOR_MAX_WORKERS
- #define SC_HYPERVISOR_GRANULARITY
- #define SC_HYPERVISOR_FIXED_WORKERS
- #define SC_HYPERVISOR_MIN_TASKS
- #define SC_HYPERVISOR_NEW_WORKERS_MAX_IDLE
- #define SC_HYPERVISOR_TIME_TO_APPLY
- #define SC_HYPERVISOR_NULL
- #define SC_HYPERVISOR_ISPEED_W_SAMPLE
- #define SC_HYPERVISOR_ISPEED_CTX_SAMPLE
- #define **SC_HYPERVISOR_TIME_SAMPLE**
- #define **MAX_IDLE_TIME**
- #define **MIN_WORKING_TIME**

Functions

- void sc_hypervisor_set_config (unsigned sched_ctx, void *config)
- struct
  sc_hypervisor_policy_config * sc_hypervisor_get_config (unsigned sched_ctx)
- void sc_hypervisor_ctl (unsigned sched_ctx,...)

31.42.1 Detailed Description

31.43 sc_hypervisor_lp.h File Reference

```
#include <sc_hypervisor.h>
#include <starpu_config.h>
```

Functions

- double **sc_hypervisor_lp_get_nworkers_per_ctx** (int nsched_ctxs, int ntypes_of_workers, double res[nsched_ctxs][ntypes_of_workers], int total_nw[ntypes_of_workers], struct types_of_workers *tw, unsigned *in_sched_ctxs)
- double **sc_hypervisor_lp_get_tmax** (int nw, int *workers)
- void **sc_hypervisor_lp_round_double_to_int** (int ns, int nw, double res[ns][nw], int res_rounded[ns][nw])
- void **sc_hypervisor_lp_redistribute_resources_in_ctxs** (int ns, int nw, int res_rounded[ns][nw], double res[ns][nw], unsigned *sched_ctxs, struct types_of_workers *tw)
- void **sc_hypervisor_lp_distribute_resources_in_ctxs** (unsigned *sched_ctxs, int ns, int nw, int res_rounded[ns][nw], double res[ns][nw], int *workers, int nworkers, struct types_of_workers *tw)
- void **sc_hypervisor_lp_distribute_floating_no_resources_in_ctxs** (unsigned *sched_ctxs, int ns, int nw, double res[ns][nw], int *workers, int nworkers, struct types_of_workers *tw)
- void **sc_hypervisor_lp_place_resources_in_ctx** (int ns, int nw, double w_in_s[ns][nw], unsigned *sched_ctxs, int *workers, unsigned do_size, struct types_of_workers *tw)
- void **sc_hypervisor_lp_share_remaining_resources** (int ns, unsigned *sched_ctxs, int nworkers, int *workers)
- double **sc_hypervisor_lp_find_tmax** (double t1, double t2)
- unsigned **sc_hypervisor_lp_execute_dichotomy** (int ns, int nw, double w_in_s[ns][nw], unsigned solve_lp_integer, void *specific_data, double tmin, double tmax, double smallest_tmax, double(*lp_estimated_distrib_func)(int ns, int nw, double draft_w_in_s[ns][nw], unsigned is_integer, double tmax, void *specifc_data))

31.43.1 Detailed Description

31.44 sc_hypervisor_monitoring.h File Reference

```
#include <sc_hypervisor.h>
```

Data Structures

- struct sc_hypervisor_resize_ack
- struct sc_hypervisor_wrapper

Functions

- struct sc_hypervisor_wrapper * sc_hypervisor_get_wrapper (unsigned sched_ctx)
- unsigned * sc_hypervisor_get_sched_ctxs ()
- int sc_hypervisor_get_nsched_ctxs ()
- int **sc_hypervisor_get_nworkers_ctx** (unsigned sched_ctx, enum starpu_worker_archtype arch)
- double sc_hypervisor_get_elapsed_flops_per_sched_ctx (struct sc_hypervisor_wrapper *sc_w)
- double **sc_hypervisor_get_total_elapsed_flops_per_sched_ctx** (struct sc_hypervisor_wrapper *sc_w)
- double **sc_hypervisorsc_hypervisor_get_speed_per_worker_type** (struct sc_hypervisor_wrapper *sc_w, enum starpu_worker_archtype arch)

- double **sc_hypervisor_get_speed** (struct sc_hypervisor_wrapper *sc_w, enum starpu_worker_archtype arch)

31.44.1 Detailed Description

31.45 sc_hypervisor_policy.h File Reference

```
#include <sc_hypervisor.h>
```

Data Structures

- struct types_of_workers
- struct sc_hypervisor_policy_task_pool

Macros

- #define **HYPERVISOR_REDIM_SAMPLE**
- #define **HYPERVISOR_START_REDIM_SAMPLE**
- #define **SC_NOTHING**
- #define **SC_IDLE**
- #define **SC_SPEED**

Functions

- void **sc_hypervisor_policy_add_task_to_pool** (struct starpu_codelet *cl, unsigned sched_ctx, uint32_t footprint, struct sc_hypervisor_policy_task_pool **task_pools, size_t data_size)
- void **sc_hypervisor_policy_remove_task_from_pool** (struct starpu_task *task, uint32_t footprint, struct sc_hypervisor_policy_task_pool **task_pools)
- struct sc_hypervisor_policy_task_pool * **sc_hypervisor_policy_clone_task_pool** (struct sc_hypervisor_policy_-task_pool *tp)
- void **sc_hypervisor_get_tasks_times** (int nw, int nt, double times[nw][nt], int *workers, unsigned size_ctxs, struct sc_hypervisor_policy_task_pool *task_pools)
- unsigned **sc_hypervisor_find_lowest_prio_sched_ctx** (unsigned req_sched_ctx, int nworkers_to_move)
- int * **sc_hypervisor_get_idlest_workers** (unsigned sched_ctx, int *nworkers, enum starpu_worker_-archtype arch)
- int * **sc_hypervisor_get_idlest_workers_in_list** (int *start, int *workers, int nall_workers, int *nworkers, enum starpu_worker_archtype arch)
- int **sc_hypervisor_get_movable_nworkers** (struct sc_hypervisor_policy_config *config, unsigned sched_-ctx, enum starpu_worker_archtype arch)
- int **sc_hypervisor_compute_nworkers_to_move** (unsigned req_sched_ctx)
- unsigned **sc_hypervisor_policy_resize** (unsigned sender_sched_ctx, unsigned receiver_sched_ctx, un-signed force_resize, unsigned now)
- unsigned **sc_hypervisor_policy_resize_to_unknown_receiver** (unsigned sender_sched_ctx, unsigned now)
- double **sc_hypervisor_get_ctx_speed** (struct sc_hypervisor_wrapper *sc_w)
- double **sc_hypervisor_get_slowest_ctx_exec_time** (void)
- double **sc_hypervisor_get_fastest_ctx_exec_time** (void)
- double **sc_hypervisor_get_speed_per_worker** (struct sc_hypervisor_wrapper *sc_w, unsigned worker)
- double **sc_hypervisor_get_speed_per_worker_type** (struct sc_hypervisor_wrapper *sc_w, enum starpu_-worker_archtype arch)

- double **sc_hypervisor_get_ref_speed_per_worker_type** (struct sc_hypervisor_wrapper *sc_w, enum starpu_worker_archtype arch)
- double **sc_hypervisor_get_avg_speed** (enum starpu_worker_archtype arch)
- void **sc_hypervisor_check_if_consider_max** (struct types_of_workers *tw)
- void **sc_hypervisor_group_workers_by_type** (struct types_of_workers *tw, int *total_nw)
- enum starpu_worker_archtype **sc_hypervisor_get_arch_for_index** (unsigned w, struct types_of_workers *tw)
- unsigned **sc_hypervisor_get_index_for_arch** (enum starpu_worker_archtype arch, struct types_of_workers *tw)
- unsigned **sc_hypervisor_criteria_fulfilled** (unsigned sched_ctx, int worker)
- unsigned **sc_hypervisor_check_Idle** (unsigned sched_ctx, int worker)
- unsigned **sc_hypervisor_check_speed_gap_btw_ctxs** (unsigned *sched_ctxs, int nsched_ctxs, int *workers, int nworkers)
- unsigned **sc_hypervisor_check_speed_gap_btw_ctxs_on_level** (int level, int *workers_in, int nworkers_in, unsigned father_sched_ctx_id, unsigned **sched_ctxs, int *nsched_ctxs)
- unsigned **sc_hypervisor_get_resize_criteria** ()
- struct types_of_workers * **sc_hypervisor_get_types_of_workers** (int *workers, unsigned nworkers)

31.45.1 Detailed Description

31.45.2 Data Structure Documentation

31.45.2.1 struct types_of_workers

Data Fields

unsigned	ncpus	
unsigned	ncuda	
unsigned	nw	

Chapter 32

Deprecated List

Global starpu_codelet::cpu_func

Optional field which has been made deprecated. One should use instead the field starpu_codelet::cpu_funcs.

Global starpu_codelet::cuda_func

Optional field which has been made deprecated. One should use instead the starpu_codelet::cuda_funcs field.

Global starpu_codelet::opencl_func

Optional field which has been made deprecated. One should use instead the starpu_codelet::opencl_funcs field.

Global starpu_data_free_pinned_if_possible

Equivalent to starpu_free(). This macro is provided to avoid breaking old codes.

Global starpu_data_malloc_pinned_if_possible

Equivalent to starpu_malloc(). This macro is provided to avoid breaking old codes.

Global starpu_mpi_initialize **(void)**

This function has been made deprecated. One should use instead the function starpu_mpi_init(). This function does not call `MPI_Init()`, it should be called beforehand.

Global starpu_mpi_initialize_extended **(int ∗rank, int ∗world_size)**

This function has been made deprecated. One should use instead the function starpu_mpi_init(). MPI will be initialized by starpumpi by calling `MPI_Init_Thread(argc, argv, MPI_THREAD_SERIALIZED, ...)`.

Global STARPU_MULTIPLE_CPU_IMPLEMENTATIONS

Setting the field starpu_codelet::cpu_func with this macro indicates the codelet will have several implementations. The use of this macro is deprecated. One should always only define the field starpu_codelet::cpu_funcs.

Global STARPU_MULTIPLE_CUDA_IMPLEMENTATIONS

Setting the field starpu_codelet::cuda_func with this macro indicates the codelet will have several implementations. The use of this macro is deprecated. One should always only define the field starpu_codelet::cuda_funcs.

Global STARPU_MULTIPLE_OPENCL_IMPLEMENTATIONS

Setting the field starpu_codelet::opencl_func with this macro indicates the codelet will have several implementations. The use of this macro is deprecated. One should always only define the field starpu_codelet::opencl_funcs.

Part VI

Appendix

Chapter 33

Full Source Code for the 'Scaling a Vector' Example

33.1 Main Application

```c
/*
 * This example demonstrates how to use StarPU to scale an array by a factor.
 * It shows how to manipulate data with StarPU's data management library.
 *  1- how to declare a piece of data to StarPU (starpu_vector_data_register)
 *  2- how to describe which data are accessed by a task (task->handles[0])
 *  3- how a kernel can manipulate the data (buffers[0].vector.ptr)
 */
#include <starpu.h>

#define    NX    2048

extern void scal_cpu_func(void *buffers[], void *_args);
extern void scal_sse_func(void *buffers[], void *_args);
extern void scal_cuda_func(void *buffers[], void *_args);
extern void scal_opencl_func(void *buffers[], void *_args);

static struct starpu_codelet cl =
{
    .where = STARPU_CPU | STARPU_CUDA | STARPU_OPENCL
        ,
    /* CPU implementation of the codelet */
    .cpu_funcs = { scal_cpu_func, scal_sse_func },
    .cpu_funcs_name = { "scal_cpu_func", "scal_sse_func" },
#ifdef STARPU_USE_CUDA
    /* CUDA implementation of the codelet */
    .cuda_funcs = { scal_cuda_func },
#endif
#ifdef STARPU_USE_OPENCL
    /* OpenCL implementation of the codelet */
    .opencl_funcs = { scal_opencl_func },
#endif
    .nbuffers = 1,
    .modes = { STARPU_RW }
};

#ifdef STARPU_USE_OPENCL
struct starpu_opencl_program programs;
#endif

int main(int argc, char **argv)
{
    /* We consider a vector of float that is initialized just as any of C
      * data */
    float vector[NX];
    unsigned i;
    for (i = 0; i < NX; i++)
        vector[i] = 1.0f;

    fprintf(stderr, "BEFORE: First element was %f\n", vector[0]);

    /* Initialize StarPU with default configuration */
    starpu_init(NULL);

#ifdef STARPU_USE_OPENCL
        starpu_opencl_load_opencl_from_file(
                "examples/basic_examples/vector_scal_opencl_kernel.cl", &
    programs, NULL);
#endif
```

```
    /* Tell StaPU to associate the "vector" vector with the "vector_handle"
     * identifier. When a task needs to access a piece of data, it should
     * refer to the handle that is associated to it.
     * In the case of the "vector" data interface:
     *  - the first argument of the registration method is a pointer to the
     *    handle that should describe the data
     *  - the second argument is the memory node where the data (ie. "vector")
     *    resides initially: STARPU_MAIN_RAM stands for an address in main
       memory, as
     *    opposed to an adress on a GPU for instance.
     *  - the third argument is the adress of the vector in RAM
     *  - the fourth argument is the number of elements in the vector
     *  - the fifth argument is the size of each element.
     */
    starpu_data_handle_t vector_handle;
    starpu_vector_data_register(&vector_handle,
      STARPU_MAIN_RAM, (uintptr_t)vector,
                                  NX, sizeof(vector[0]));

    float factor = 3.14;

    /* create a synchronous task: any call to starpu_task_submit will block
     * until it is terminated */
    struct starpu_task *task = starpu_task_create(
      );
    task->synchronous = 1;

    task->cl = &cl;

    /* the codelet manipulates one buffer in RW mode */
    task->handles[0] = vector_handle;

    /* an argument is passed to the codelet, beware that this is a
     * READ-ONLY buffer and that the codelet may be given a pointer to a
     * COPY of the argument */
    task->cl_arg = &factor;
    task->cl_arg_size = sizeof(factor);

    /* execute the task on any eligible computational ressource */
    starpu_task_submit(task);

    /* StarPU does not need to manipulate the array anymore so we can stop
     * monitoring it */
    starpu_data_unregister(vector_handle);

#ifdef STARPU_USE_OPENCL
    starpu_opencl_unload_opencl(&programs);
#endif

    /* terminate StarPU, no task can be submitted after */
    starpu_shutdown();

    fprintf(stderr, "AFTER First element is %f\n", vector[0]);

    return 0;
}
```

33.2   CPU Kernel

```
#include <starpu.h>
#include <xmmintrin.h>

/* This kernel takes a buffer and scales it by a constant factor */
void scal_cpu_func(void *buffers[], void *cl_arg)
{
    unsigned i;
    float *factor = cl_arg;

    /*
     * The "buffers" array matches the task->handles array: for instance
     * task->handles[0] is a handle that corresponds to a data with
     * vector "interface", so that the first entry of the array in the
     * codelet  is a pointer to a structure describing such a vector (ie.
     * struct starpu_vector_interface *). Here, we therefore manipulate
     * the buffers[0] element as a vector: nx gives the number of elements
     * in the array, ptr gives the location of the array (that was possibly
     * migrated/replicated), and elemsize gives the size of each elements.
     */
    struct starpu_vector_interface *vector = buffers[0];

    /* length of the vector */
    unsigned n = STARPU_VECTOR_GET_NX(vector);
```

```
        /* get a pointer to the local copy of the vector: note that we have to
         * cast it in (float *) since a vector could contain any type of
         * elements so that the .ptr field is actually a uintptr_t */
        float *val = (float *)STARPU_VECTOR_GET_PTR(vector);

        /* scale the vector */
        for (i = 0; i < n; i++)
            val[i] *= *factor;
}

void scal_sse_func(void *buffers[], void *cl_arg)
{
    float *vector = (float *) STARPU_VECTOR_GET_PTR(
      buffers[0]);
    unsigned int n = STARPU_VECTOR_GET_NX(buffers[0]);
    unsigned int n_iterations = n/4;

    __m128 *VECTOR = (__m128*) vector;
    __m128 FACTOR STARPU_ATTRIBUTE_ALIGNED(16);
    float factor = *(float *) cl_arg;
    FACTOR = _mm_set1_ps(factor);

    unsigned int i;
    for (i = 0; i < n_iterations; i++)
        VECTOR[i] = _mm_mul_ps(FACTOR, VECTOR[i]);

    unsigned int remainder = n%4;
    if (remainder != 0)
    {
        unsigned int start = 4 * n_iterations;
        for (i = start; i < start+remainder; ++i)
        {
            vector[i] = factor * vector[i];
        }
    }
}
```

33.3 CUDA Kernel

```
#include <starpu.h>

static __global__ void vector_mult_cuda(unsigned n, float *val,
                                        float factor)
{
        unsigned i = blockIdx.x*blockDim.x + threadIdx.x;
        if (i < n)
                val[i] *= factor;
}

extern "C" void scal_cuda_func(void *buffers[], void *_args)
{
        float *factor = (float *)_args;

        /* length of the vector */
        unsigned n = STARPU_VECTOR_GET_NX(buffers[0]);
        /* local copy of the vector pointer */
        float *val = (float *)STARPU_VECTOR_GET_PTR(
    buffers[0]);
        unsigned threads_per_block = 64;
        unsigned nblocks = (n + threads_per_block-1) / threads_per_block;

        vector_mult_cuda<<<nblocks,threads_per_block, 0,
    starpu_cuda_get_local_stream()>>>
                        (n, val, *factor);

        cudaStreamSynchronize(starpu_cuda_get_local_stream
    ());
}
```

33.4 OpenCL Kernel

33.4.1 Invoking the Kernel

```
#include <starpu.h>

extern struct starpu_opencl_program programs;
```

```
void scal_opencl_func(void *buffers[], void *_args)
{
    float *factor = _args;
    int id, devid, err;                 /* OpenCL specific code */
    cl_kernel kernel;                   /* OpenCL specific code */
    cl_command_queue queue;             /* OpenCL specific code */
    cl_event event;                     /* OpenCL specific code */

    /* length of the vector */
    unsigned n = STARPU_VECTOR_GET_NX(buffers[0]);
    /* OpenCL copy of the vector pointer */
    cl_mem val = (cl_mem)STARPU_VECTOR_GET_DEV_HANDLE
      (buffers[0]);

    {  /* OpenCL specific code */
        id = starpu_worker_get_id();
        devid = starpu_worker_get_devid(id);

        err = starpu_opencl_load_kernel(&kernel, &
    queue,
                                    &programs,
                                    "vector_mult_opencl", /* Name of the
     codelet */
                                    devid);
            (err != CL_SUCCESS) STARPU_OPENCL_REPORT_ERROR
        (err);

        err = clSetKernelArg(kernel, 0, sizeof(n), &n);
        err |= clSetKernelArg(kernel, 1, sizeof(val), &val);
        err |= clSetKernelArg(kernel, 2, sizeof(*factor), factor);
            (err) STARPU_OPENCL_REPORT_ERROR(err);
    }

    {  /* OpenCL specific code */
        size_t global=n;
        size_t local;
        size_t s;
        cl_device_id device;

        starpu_opencl_get_device(devid, &device);
        err = clGetKernelWorkGroupInfo (kernel, device,
    CL_KERNEL_WORK_GROUP_SIZE,
                                    sizeof(local), &local, &s);
            (err != CL_SUCCESS) STARPU_OPENCL_REPORT_ERROR
        (err);
            (local > global) local=global;

        err = clEnqueueNDRangeKernel(queue, kernel, 1, NULL, &global, &local, 0
      ,
                                    NULL, &event);
            (err != CL_SUCCESS) STARPU_OPENCL_REPORT_ERROR
        (err);
    }

    {  /* OpenCL specific code */
        clFinish(queue);
        starpu_opencl_collect_stats(event);
        clReleaseEvent(event);

        starpu_opencl_release_kernel(kernel);
    }
}
```

33.4.2   Source of the Kernel

```
__kernel void vector_mult_opencl(int nx, __global float* val, float factor)
{
        const int i = get_global_id(0);
        (i < nx)
        {
                val[i] *= factor;
        }
}
```

Chapter 34

GNU Free Documentation License

Version 1.3, 3 November 2008

1. PREAMBLE

The purpose of this License is to make a manual, textbook, or other functional and useful document *free* in the sense of freedom: to assure everyone the effective freedom to copy and redistribute it, with or without modifying it, either commercially or noncommercially. Secondarily, this License preserves for the author and publisher a way to get credit for their work, while not being considered responsible for modifications made by others.

This License is a kind of "copyleft", which means that derivative works of the document must themselves be free in the same sense. It complements the GNU General Public License, which is a copyleft license designed for free software.

We have designed this License in order to use it for manuals for free software, because free software needs free documentation: a free program should come with manuals providing the same freedoms that the software does. But this License is not limited to software manuals; it can be used for any textual work, regardless of subject matter or whether it is published as a printed book. We recommend this License principally for works whose purpose is instruction or reference.

2. APPLICABILITY AND DEFINITIONS

This License applies to any manual or other work, in any medium, that contains a notice placed by the copyright holder saying it can be distributed under the terms of this License. Such a notice grants a world-wide, royalty-free license, unlimited in duration, to use that work under the conditions stated herein. The "Document", below, refers to any such manual or work. Any member of the public is a licensee, and is addressed as "you". You accept the license if you copy, modify or distribute the work in a way requiring permission under copyright law.

A "Modified Version" of the Document means any work containing the Document or a portion of it, either copied verbatim, or with modifications and/or translated into another language.

A "Secondary Section" is a named appendix or a front-matter section of the Document that deals exclusively with the relationship of the publishers or authors of the Document to the Document's overall subject (or to related matters) and contains nothing that could fall directly within that overall subject. (Thus, if the Document is in part a textbook of mathematics, a Secondary Section may not explain any mathematics.) The relationship could be a matter of historical connection with the subject or with related matters, or of legal, commercial, philosophical, ethical or political position regarding them.

The "Invariant Sections" are certain Secondary Sections whose titles are designated, as being those of Invariant Sections, in the notice that says that the Document is released under this License. If a section does not fit the above definition of Secondary then it is not allowed to be designated as Invariant. The Document may contain zero Invariant Sections. If the Document does not identify any Invariant Sections then there are none.

The "Cover Texts" are certain short passages of text that are listed, as Front-Cover Texts or Back-Cover Texts, in the notice that says that the Document is released under this License. A Front-Cover Text may be at most 5 words, and a Back-Cover Text may be at most 25 words.

A "Transparent" copy of the Document means a machine-readable copy, represented in a format whose specification is available to the general public, that is suitable for revising the document straightforwardly with generic text editors or (for images composed of pixels) generic paint programs or (for drawings) some widely available drawing editor, and that is suitable for input to text formatters or for automatic translation to a variety of formats suitable for input to text formatters. A copy made in an otherwise Transparent file format whose markup, or absence of markup, has been arranged to thwart or discourage subsequent modification by readers is not Transparent. An image format is not Transparent if used for any substantial amount of text. A copy that is not "Transparent" is called "Opaque".

Examples of suitable formats for Transparent copies include plain ASCII without markup, Texinfo input format, LaTeX input format, SGML or XML using a publicly available DTD, and standard-conforming simple HTML, PostScript or PDF designed for human modification. Examples of transparent image formats include PNG, XCF and JPG. Opaque formats include proprietary formats that can be read and edited only by proprietary word processors, SGML or XML for which the DTD and/or processing tools are not generally available, and the machine-generated HTML, PostScript or PDF produced by some word processors for output purposes only.

The "Title Page" means, for a printed book, the title page itself, plus such following pages as are needed to hold, legibly, the material this License requires to appear in the title page. For works in formats which do not have any title page as such, "Title Page" means the text near the most prominent appearance of the work's title, preceding the beginning of the body of the text.

The "publisher" means any person or entity that distributes copies of the Document to the public.

A section "Entitled XYZ" means a named subunit of the Document whose title either is precisely XYZ or contains XYZ in parentheses following text that translates XYZ in another language. (Here XYZ stands for a specific section name mentioned below, such as "Acknowledgements", "Dedications", "Endorsements", or "History".) To "Preserve the Title" of such a section when you modify the Document means that it remains a section "Entitled XYZ" according to this definition.

The Document may include Warranty Disclaimers next to the notice which states that this License applies to the Document. These Warranty Disclaimers are considered to be included by reference in this License, but only as regards disclaiming warranties: any other implication that these Warranty Disclaimers may have is void and has no effect on the meaning of this License.

3. VERBATIM COPYING

You may copy and distribute the Document in any medium, either commercially or noncommercially, provided that this License, the copyright notices, and the license notice saying this License applies to the Document are reproduced in all copies, and that you add no other conditions whatsoever to those of this License. You may not use technical measures to obstruct or control the reading or further copying of the copies you make or distribute. However, you may accept compensation in exchange for copies. If you distribute a large enough number of copies you must also follow the conditions in section 3.

You may also lend copies, under the same conditions stated above, and you may publicly display copies.

4. COPYING IN QUANTITY

If you publish printed copies (or copies in media that commonly have printed covers) of the Document, numbering more than 100, and the Document's license notice requires Cover Texts, you must enclose the copies in covers that carry, clearly and legibly, all these Cover Texts: Front-Cover Texts on the front cover, and Back-Cover Texts on the back cover. Both covers must also clearly and legibly identify you as the publisher of these copies. The front cover must present the full title with all words of the title equally prominent and visible. You may add other material on the covers in addition. Copying with changes limited to the covers, as long as they preserve the title of the Document and satisfy these conditions, can be treated as verbatim copying in other respects.

If the required texts for either cover are too voluminous to fit legibly, you should put the first ones listed (as many as fit reasonably) on the actual cover, and continue the rest onto adjacent pages.

If you publish or distribute Opaque copies of the Document numbering more than 100, you must either include a machine-readable Transparent copy along with each Opaque copy, or state in or with each Opaque copy a computer-network location from which the general network-using public has access to download using public-standard network protocols a complete Transparent copy of the Document, free of added material. If you use the latter option, you must take reasonably prudent steps, when you begin distribution of Opaque copies in quantity, to ensure that this Transparent copy will remain thus accessible at the stated location until at least one year after the last time you distribute an Opaque copy (directly or through your agents or retailers) of that edition to the public.

It is requested, but not required, that you contact the authors of the Document well before redistributing any large number of copies, to give them a chance to provide you with an updated version of the Document.

5. MODIFICATIONS

You may copy and distribute a Modified Version of the Document under the conditions of sections 2 and 3 above, provided that you release the Modified Version under precisely this License, with the Modified Version filling the role of the Document, thus licensing distribution and modification of the Modified Version to whoever possesses a copy of it. In addition, you must do these things in the Modified Version:

(a) Use in the Title Page (and on the covers, if any) a title distinct from that of the Document, and from those of previous versions (which should, if there were any, be listed in the History section of the Document). You may use the same title as a previous version if the original publisher of that version gives permission.

(b) List on the Title Page, as authors, one or more persons or entities responsible for authorship of the modifications in the Modified Version, together with at least five of the principal authors of the Document (all of its principal authors, if it has fewer than five), unless they release you from this requirement.

(c) State on the Title page the name of the publisher of the Modified Version, as the publisher.

(d) Preserve all the copyright notices of the Document.

(e) Add an appropriate copyright notice for your modifications adjacent to the other copyright notices.

(f) Include, immediately after the copyright notices, a license notice giving the public permission to use the Modified Version under the terms of this License, in the form shown in the Addendum below.

(g) Preserve in that license notice the full lists of Invariant Sections and required Cover Texts given in the Document's license notice.

(h) Include an unaltered copy of this License.

(i) Preserve the section Entitled "History", Preserve its Title, and add to it an item stating at least the title, year, new authors, and publisher of the Modified Version as given on the Title Page. If there is no section Entitled "History" in the Document, create one stating the title, year, authors, and publisher of the Document as given on its Title Page, then add an item describing the Modified Version as stated in the previous sentence.

(j) Preserve the network location, if any, given in the Document for public access to a Transparent copy of the Document, and likewise the network locations given in the Document for previous versions it was based on. These may be placed in the "History" section. You may omit a network location for a work that was published at least four years before the Document itself, or if the original publisher of the version it refers to gives permission.

(k) For any section Entitled "Acknowledgements" or "Dedications", Preserve the Title of the section, and preserve in the section all the substance and tone of each of the contributor acknowledgements and/or dedications given therein.

(l) Preserve all the Invariant Sections of the Document, unaltered in their text and in their titles. Section numbers or the equivalent are not considered part of the section titles.

(m) Delete any section Entitled "Endorsements". Such a section may not be included in the Modified Version.

(n) Do not retitle any existing section to be Entitled "Endorsements" or to conflict in title with any Invariant Section.

(o) Preserve any Warranty Disclaimers.

If the Modified Version includes new front-matter sections or appendices that qualify as Secondary Sections and contain no material copied from the Document, you may at your option designate some or all of these sections as invariant. To do this, add their titles to the list of Invariant Sections in the Modified Version's license notice. These titles must be distinct from any other section titles.

You may add a section Entitled "Endorsements", provided it contains nothing but endorsements of your Modified Version by various parties—for example, statements of peer review or that the text has been approved by an organization as the authoritative definition of a standard.

You may add a passage of up to five words as a Front-Cover Text, and a passage of up to 25 words as a Back-Cover Text, to the end of the list of Cover Texts in the Modified Version. Only one passage of Front-Cover Text and one of Back-Cover Text may be added by (or through arrangements made by) any one entity. If the Document already includes a cover text for the same cover, previously added by you or by arrangement made by the same entity you are acting on behalf of, you may not add another; but you may replace the old one, on explicit permission from the previous publisher that added the old one.

The author(s) and publisher(s) of the Document do not by this License give permission to use their names for publicity for or to assert or imply endorsement of any Modified Version.

6. COMBINING DOCUMENTS

You may combine the Document with other documents released under this License, under the terms defined in section 4 above for modified versions, provided that you include in the combination all of the Invariant Sections of all of the original documents, unmodified, and list them all as Invariant Sections of your combined work in its license notice, and that you preserve all their Warranty Disclaimers.

The combined work need only contain one copy of this License, and multiple identical Invariant Sections may be replaced with a single copy. If there are multiple Invariant Sections with the same name but different contents, make the title of each such section unique by adding at the end of it, in parentheses, the name of the original author or publisher of that section if known, or else a unique number. Make the same adjustment to the section titles in the list of Invariant Sections in the license notice of the combined work.

In the combination, you must combine any sections Entitled "History" in the various original documents, forming one section Entitled "History"; likewise combine any sections Entitled "Acknowledgements", and any sections Entitled "Dedications". You must delete all sections Entitled "Endorsements."

7. COLLECTIONS OF DOCUMENTS

You may make a collection consisting of the Document and other documents released under this License, and replace the individual copies of this License in the various documents with a single copy that is included in the collection, provided that you follow the rules of this License for verbatim copying of each of the documents in all other respects.

You may extract a single document from such a collection, and distribute it individually under this License, provided you insert a copy of this License into the extracted document, and follow this License in all other respects regarding verbatim copying of that document.

8. AGGREGATION WITH INDEPENDENT WORKS

A compilation of the Document or its derivatives with other separate and independent documents or works, in or on a volume of a storage or distribution medium, is called an "aggregate" if the copyright resulting from the compilation is not used to limit the legal rights of the compilation's users beyond what the individual works permit. When the Document is included in an aggregate, this License does not apply to the other works in the aggregate which are not themselves derivative works of the Document.

If the Cover Text requirement of section 3 is applicable to these copies of the Document, then if the Document is less than one half of the entire aggregate, the Document's Cover Texts may be placed on covers that bracket the Document within the aggregate, or the electronic equivalent of covers if the Document is in electronic form. Otherwise they must appear on printed covers that bracket the whole aggregate.

9. TRANSLATION

Translation is considered a kind of modification, so you may distribute translations of the Document under the terms of section 4. Replacing Invariant Sections with translations requires special permission from their copyright holders, but you may include translations of some or all Invariant Sections in addition to the original versions of these Invariant Sections. You may include a translation of this License, and all the license notices in the Document, and any Warranty Disclaimers, provided that you also include the original English version of this License and the original versions of those notices and disclaimers. In case of a disagreement between the translation and the original version of this License or a notice or disclaimer, the original version will prevail.

If a section in the Document is Entitled "Acknowledgements", "Dedications", or "History", the requirement (section 4) to Preserve its Title (section 1) will typically require changing the actual title.

10. TERMINATION

You may not copy, modify, sublicense, or distribute the Document except as expressly provided under this License. Any attempt otherwise to copy, modify, sublicense, or distribute it is void, and will automatically terminate your rights under this License.

However, if you cease all violation of this License, then your license from a particular copyright holder is reinstated (a) provisionally, unless and until the copyright holder explicitly and finally terminates your license, and (b) permanently, if the copyright holder fails to notify you of the violation by some reasonable means prior to 60 days after the cessation.

Moreover, your license from a particular copyright holder is reinstated permanently if the copyright holder notifies you of the violation by some reasonable means, this is the first time you have received notice of violation of this License (for any work) from that copyright holder, and you cure the violation prior to 30 days after your receipt of the notice.

Termination of your rights under this section does not terminate the licenses of parties who have received copies or rights from you under this License. If your rights have been terminated and not permanently reinstated, receipt of a copy of some or all of the same material does not give you any rights to use it.

11. FUTURE REVISIONS OF THIS LICENSE

The Free Software Foundation may publish new, revised versions of the GNU Free Documentation License from time to time. Such new versions will be similar in spirit to the present version, but may differ in detail to address new problems or concerns. See http://www.gnu.org/copyleft/.

Each version of the License is given a distinguishing version number. If the Document specifies that a particular numbered version of this License "or any later version" applies to it, you have the option of following the terms and conditions either of that specified version or of any later version that has been published (not as a draft) by the Free Software Foundation. If the Document does not specify a version number of this License, you may choose any version ever published (not as a draft) by the Free Software Foundation. If the Document specifies that a proxy can decide which future versions of this License can be used, that proxy's public statement of acceptance of a version permanently authorizes you to choose that version for the Document.

12. RELICENSING

"Massive Multiauthor Collaboration Site" (or "MMC Site") means any World Wide Web server that publishes copyrightable works and also provides prominent facilities for anybody to edit those works. A public wiki that anybody can edit is an example of such a server. A "Massive Multiauthor Collaboration" (or "MMC") contained in the site means any set of copyrightable works thus published on the MMC site.

"CC-BY-SA" means the Creative Commons Attribution-Share Alike 3.0 license published by Creative Commons Corporation, a not-for-profit corporation with a principal place of business in San Francisco, California, as well as future copyleft versions of that license published by that same organization.

"Incorporate" means to publish or republish a Document, in whole or in part, as part of another Document.

An MMC is "eligible for relicensing" if it is licensed under this License, and if all works that were first published under this License somewhere other than this MMC, and subsequently incorporated in whole or in part into the MMC, (1) had no cover texts or invariant sections, and (2) were thus incorporated prior to November 1, 2008.

The operator of an MMC Site may republish an MMC contained in the site under CC-BY-SA on the same site at any time before August 1, 2009, provided the MMC is eligible for relicensing.

34.1 ADDENDUM: How to use this License for your documents

To use this License in a document you have written, include a copy of the License in the document and put the following copyright and license notices just after the title page:

Copyright (C) *year your name*. Permission is granted to copy, distribute and/or modify this document under the terms of the GNU Free Documentation License, Version 1.3 or any later version published by the Free Software Foundation; with no Invariant Sections, no Front-Cover Texts, and no Back-Cover Texts. A copy of the license is included in the section entitled "GNU Free Documentation License".

If you have Invariant Sections, Front-Cover Texts and Back-Cover Texts, replace the "with...Texts." line with this:

> with the Invariant Sections being *list their titles*, with the Front-Cover Texts being *list*, and with the Back-Cover Texts being *list*.

If you have Invariant Sections without Cover Texts, or some other combination of the three, merge those two alternatives to suit the situation.

If your document contains nontrivial examples of program code, we recommend releasing these examples in parallel under your choice of free software license, such as the GNU General Public License, to permit their use in free software.

Part VII

Index

Index

write

    starpu_disk_ops, 254

www.ingramcontent.com/pod-product-compliance
Lightning Source LLC
LaVergne TN
LVHW060132070326
832902LV00018B/2760